FOREWORD

The theme of the 1990 ASCE Water Resources Planning and Management Division Specialty Conference is "Optimizing The Resources for Water Management". The goal of this conference is to demonstrate innovative applications in optimizing the existing resources for Water Management. In addition, for the last decade much attention has been given to the deteriorating state of the nation's infrastructure. In recognition of this fact, the Water Resources Planning and Management Division also sponsored an Infrastructure Symposium in Conjunction with the 17th Annual Specialty Conference which was held at Fort Worth, TX, from April 17–20, 1990.

These proceedings contain all papers presented at the 58 conference sessions sponsored by different committee of the Water Resources Planning and Management Division, which were submitted to the Editors in time for their inclusion in this volume. The papers are in order of their presentation at the conference. Each of the papers has been accepted for publication by the Editors. All papers are eligible for discussion in the journal of the Water Resources Planning and Management Division, ASCE. All papers are eligible for ASCE awards.

Organizing and planning for the Conference have been the responsibility of the following individuals

    KYLE E. SCHILLING, General Chair
    REZA M. KHANBILVARDI, Conference Technical Program
    JOHN F. SCOTT, Symposium Technical Program

    WRP&M DIVISION EXECUTIVE COMMITTEE:
    DARELL D. ZIMBELMAN, Chair
    KYLE E. SCHILLING, Vice Chair
    MARSHALL S. GOULDING, Secretary
    WILLIAM E. COX
    MICHAEL A. PORTS
    JERRY R. ROGERS

    LOCAL ARRANGEMENTS COMMITTEE:
    C. DIANE PALMER, Chair
    ROXANNE L PILLAR, Co-Chair
    DAVID G. WYNN, Co-Chair
    JOHN W. BAIRD, Publicity
    J. KELLY CARTA, Program Design, Layout and Typesetting
    JANIS R. CULLUM, Hospitality and information
    SCOTT DYER, Transportation

THOMAS C. GOOCH, Technical Program
ROLAND S. JARY, Entertainment

DERRELL E. JOHNSON, Golf Tournament
SANFORD P. LAHUE, Student Activities
RONNIE M. LEMONS, Finance
ROBERT V. LOPEZ, Exhibits
BECCY RATLIFF, Guests' Activities
WM. BENNETT RATLIFF, Hotel Arrangements
R. DAVID RUBENKOENIG, Tennis Tournament
STEVEN C. VEAL, Technical Field Trips

The conference organizers extend their sincere appreciation to all authors and session chairmen for their contributions.

Reza M. Khanbilvardi
The City University of New York
New York, NY

OPTIMIZING THE RESOURCES FOR WATER MANAGEMENT

Proceedings of the 17th Annual National Conference

Sponsored by the Water Resources Planning and Management
Division of the American Society of Civil Engineers

Co-Sponsors:
American Water Resources Association
American Water Works Association
ASCE Urban Water Resources Research Council
Brazos River Authority
City of Arlington Water Utilities
City of Dallas Water Utilities
City of Fort Worth Water Department
Federal Emergency Management Agency, Region VI
International Water Resources Association
National Water Well Association
North Central Texas Council of Governments
North Texas Municipal Water District
Tarrant County Water Control and Improvement District
    Number One
Texas Water Commission
Texas Water Conservation Association
Texas Water Development Board
Trinity River Authority
U.S. Bureau of Reclamation, Austin
U.S. Environmental Protection Agency, Region VI
U.S. Geological Survey, Texas District
U.S. Soil Conservation Service

In cooperation with:
U.S. Army Corps of Engineers, Fort Worth District
U.S. Army Corps of Engineers, Southwestern Division

The Worthington Hotel, Forth Worth, Texas
April 17-21, 1990

Edited by Reza M. Khanbilvardi and Thomas C. Gooch

Published by the
American Society of Civil Engineers
345 East 47th Street
New York, New York 10017-2398

ABSTRACT

This proceedings, *Optimizing the Resources for Water Management*, contians papers presented at the 11th Annual National Conference that was sponsored by the ASCE Water Resources Planning and Management Division along with many other national and local organizations. The Conference was held on April 17-21, 1990 in Fort Worth, Texas. These papers examine social, environmental, economic, governmental, and inter-governmental concerns in water resources management. Areas related to fish, wildlife, surface water, groundwater, reservoirs, expert systems, geographic information systems, water allocation, hydraulics and hydrology in water resources are discussed within these various contexts. Engineers, scientists, and governmental officials who must make pragmatic decisions related to water resources will find this proceedings to be a useful tool.

The Society is not responsibile for any statements made or opinions expressed in its publications.

Authorization to photocopy material for internal or personal use under circumstances not falling within the fair use provisions of the Copyright Act is granted by ASCE to libraries and other users registered with the Copyright Clearance Center (CCC) Transactional Reporting Service, provided that the base fee of $1.00 per article plus $.15 per page is paid directly to CCC, 27 Congress Street, Salem, MA 01970. The identification for ASCE Books is 0-87262/88. $1 + .15. Requests for special permission or bulk copying should be addressed to Reprints/Permissions Department.

Copyright © 1990 by the American Society of Civil Engineers,
All Rights Reserved.
Library of Congress Catalog Card No. 90-451
ISBN 0-87262-756-X
Manufactured in the United States of America.

CONTENTS

Challenges and Opportunities in the '90s and Beyond, A U.S. Army Corps
of Engineer's Perspective
Patrick J. Kelley xvii

Session A1
DEMAND FORECASTING

An Analysis of the Impact of Weather Variation on Monthly Water Demand
Ken C. Hall and David Maidment 1
Water Utility Demand Forecasting Using Lotus 1-2-3 Spreadsheet
Jobaid Kabir 7
The Multi-WATFORE Method: A Water Demand Forecasting System
Vigil Adderly and David Maidment. 13
The Use of the IWR-Main Systems as a Planning Tool in Phoenix, Arizona
Jeff Dewitt 810

Session A2
TEXAS AND LOUISIANA WATER RESOURCES PROJECTS

Preliminary Report of the Feasibility of an Interbasin Water Transfer
Through Existing Canal Systems
John Rutledge and Ronnie M. Lemons 19
Sediment Management of the Red River Waterway Navigation Project
Phil Combs and W. H. Espey, Jr. 24
A Water Pricing Model for Lake Texana
Stuart R. Wilson and Ronald E. Anderson 28
Challenges Facing Reservoir Development: the Little Cypress Project
Bill Hilliard . . . . *

Session A3
COMPUTER APPLICATIONS IN WATER RESOURCES

Expert System for Budget Preparation and Optimal Operation of an
Interconnected Power Utility
J. Grahovac and S. Simonovic 34
Optimal Real-Time Operation of TE-CHI Reservoir
Jan-Tai Kuo, Nien-Sheng Hsu, Wen-Sen Chu, and Chain-Min Wu 39
Appropriate Cost Factors for System Reliability
Paul Jacobs and Ian Goulter 44
Estimating the Energy Rate Function for Hydropower Production Optimization
K. Reznicek and S. Simonovic 48

*Paper not available at time of printing.

Session A4
REGIONAL WATER SUPPLY AND WASTEWATER DEVELOPMENT

The Development of Lake Granbury SWATS Regional Electrodialysis Reversal
Demineralizer Treatment Plant
Rodger K. Noak and R. Anne Smith 52
Developing a Wastewater Plan for an Urbanizing Area: The Case of
Johnson County, Texas
Adrian Huckabee. 57
Financing Water Supply and Wastewater Facilities in Low Income Areas
G. E. "Sonny" Kretzschmar 62

Session A5
FEDERAL ACTIVITIES IN THE SOUTHWEST

The Spirit of Bandera: an Experiment in Interagency Team Building
Barry G. Rough 65
Army Science Board Study of Water Use on Western Millitary Installation
Jim Comiskey 71

Session A6
WATER QUALITY ISSUES

A Treavel Time Template for Water Body Field Surveys
Altaf A. Memon and Michael J. Haydon. 74
Wastewater Balance for Storage Pond at Land Treatment Site
Khamis A. Alomari and Steven G. Buchberger 80

Session B2
REALLOCATION AND MANAGEMENT OF EXISTING RESOURCES (I)

Using Corps of Engineers' Reservoirs for Water Supply
Cheryl P. Ulrich and Kenneth R. Sims 86
Managing Two Lakes with Significant Tailwater Fisheries
William P. Mathis 91
Simulation of Surface Water Allocation Systems
W. Brian Walls and Ralph Wurbs. 95

Session B3
GIS IN WATER RESOURCES: PAST, PRESENT, AND FUTURE

History of Geographic Information Systems, with Applications in
Water Resources Planning and Management
Richard M. Males 100
The Present of GIS
Dean Djokic, David Maidment, and Kenneth G. Laurence 106
GIS in Water Resources in the Year 2000
Walter M. Grayman 111

Session B4
WATER MANAGEMENT CHALLENGES AND SOLUTIONS

Ute Mountain Ute Indian Water Rights Settlement of 1988
Steven C. Harris 115

Administration of the Pacos River Compact between New Mexico and Texas
Neil S. Grigg... 120
Water Rights, Water Development, and Growth Issues in Goleta, California
Daniel Wendell.. 124
Water Basins in the Middle East
Philippe Zgheib.. 130

Session B5
WATER FOR THE SOUTHWEST: HISTORICAL PERSPECTIVES

Water Development Ideology: A New Status Quo
D. Clayton Brown...................................... 134
Water for Houston: The Wallievilie Case
Bonnie Pendergrass 138

Session B6
PERMITTING AND MANAGEMENT OF WATER RESOURCES PROJECTS

Environmental Permitting a Major Expressway Facility in Florida
Kenneth A. Carper...................................... 144
Weighting Factor for Transferable Discharge Permit Programs that Group
Several Pollutants
Barbara J. Lence...................................... 149
Sacramento's Proactive Program for Stormwater Permitting
Graig E. Crough, Donald M. Dodge, and Robert A. Witzgall .... *
Stormwater Management Planning for the Rush Creek Watershed,
Arlington Texas
Duke G. Altman, William H. Espey, David D. Gieber, and Jerome F. Ewen...... 153
Lake Zephyr Watershed Stormwater Management
Master Plan
Ellot Silverston, C. Lynn Miller, and Stephen R. Noe 158

Session C1
**URBAN WATER RESOURCES MANAGEMENT: A TECHNICAL PERSPECTIVE
ON THE TRINITY TIVER CORRIDOR**

Hydrology Review for Corps 404 Permit Process
Paul K. Rodman....................................... 164
Non-Point Source Runoff and Urban Water Management
Michael Collins, Mark Boyd, and Roger O. Dickey..................... 167
Impacts of EPA Storm Water Regulations on the Dallas-Fort Worth Metroplex
Brent Larsen and Wren Stenger............................. 171
Application of GIS to Storm Water Quality Monitoring
Steven J. Haness, John J. Warwick, and Roger O. Dickey 176

Session C2
REALLOCATION AND MANAGEMENT OF EXISTING RESOURCES (II)

Tucson, Arizona's 110-Year Water Resources Plan
Norm Brazelton and Karen Dotson............................ 180
A Methodology for Analyzing Alternative Reservoir sizing shortage and Operating criteria
George Oamek, Larry Schluntz, Loren Buttorff, and Eldon Johns 192

*Paper not available at time of printing.

Optimization of Water Resources Allocation using the MODSIM Model
L. Philip Graham, David M. Frick, Daniel L. Law, and Peter Binney 199

Session C3
APPLICATION OF REMOTE SENSING AND GEOGRAPHICAL INFORMATION SYSTEMS TO WATER RESOURCES

Application of Remote Sensing to Flood Forecasting
N. Kouwen, E. D. Soulis, A. Pietroniro, and R. A. Harrington 208
Use of Remote Sensing and GIS in the Economic Analysis of Flood Damage Reduction—Three Recent Case Histories
Peter H. Shaw 213
Applying a Simple Geographic Information System to Probable Maximum Flood Analysis in a Microcomputer Environment
Mark W. Killgore 219

Session C5
CONJUNCTIVE USE OF GROUNDWATER AND SURFACE WATER

Stochastic Optimization of Conjunctive Use in Pakistan
Christine A. Shoemaker and Carolyn J. Logan 222
Evaluation of Conjunctive Use and Drainage Reduction Strategies
Nigel W. T. Quinn 226
Cranes Roost Lake Level Management Project
Thomas R. Sears and Nicolase Andreyer 232

Session C6
WATER RESOURCES MANAGEMENT AS IT IMPACTS LAND USE DECISION MAKING (I)

Non-Point Source Pollution Control and Land Use
William Whipple 237
Land Use Considerations and the Siting of Water Facilities
Jeanne Munoz 242

Session D1
WATER DISTRIBUTION

Real-Time Optimized Control of a Water Distribution System
Bryan Coulbeck and Chun-Hou Orr 248
Telemetry Data Considerations in Water Systems
Chun-Hou Orr, Bryan Coulbeck, Masud Parkar, and Steven Tennant 252
METASITE Water Distribution System Analysis Software
Ed P. Odom 257
On Obtaining Best Compromise Solutions for Municipal Water Use
Ronald K. Williams and G. Padmanabhan 261

Session D2
MORRIS SHEPPARD DAM AND POSSUM KINGDOM RESERVOIR

The Impact of the Morris Sheppard Dam Experience on Buttress Dam Safety Evaluations
Jerry L. Foster 265
Morris Sheppard Dam: A Rational Approach to Stability Analysis
John A. Focht and Robert P. Ringholtz 277

Possum Kingdom: The Impact of Releases for Fish and Wildlife
Thomas C. Gooch 282

Session D3
APPLICATION OF EXPERT SYSTEMS IN WATER RESOURCES

Planning the Development of the OASIS Advisory System
Vinio Floris and Garry Goforth 288
The Center for Advanced Decision Support for Water and Environmental Systems
Kenneon M. Strzepek 816

Session D4
CLOSING THE GAP BETWEEN WATER RESOURCES SYSTEMS' EDUCATION AND PRACTICE

Closing the Gap Between Water Resources Systems' Education and Practice
Mohammad Karamouz 298

Session D5
ADVANCES IN MODELING

Application of the SWRRB Watershed Simulation Model to a Large Watershed
T. G. Gebhard, D. C. Wheelock, and F. J. Manka .... *
Minimizing the Risk of Unsuccessful Modeling Exercises
John J. Warwick 302
Beyond Basic Modeling
Daniel H. Leighton 308
Site Specific Hydrological Model for Permaculture Application
William Blatner and Reza M. Khanbilvardi 312

Session D6
WATER RESOURCES MANAGEMENT AS IT IMPACTS LAND USE DECISION MAKING (II)

Land-Water Management: Theory and Practice
Warren Viessman 321
Changing Land Use in the Platte and Arkansas Basins
Gary Lewis 326

Session E1
SYSTEM OPERATION OF RESERVOIRS

Optimizing Dallas' Multiple Reservoir Supply System
Robert M. McCarthy 332
Microcomputer Tools for the Management of a Multiple Reservoir Water Supply System
Charles L. Moore and Christopher C. Clarkson 338
Optimal Operation of Multiple Reservoir Systems
Oinghui Zhong and Kevin E. Lansey 342
Storage Reallocation Evaluation for Reservoir System
Patrick E. Carriere and Ralph Wurbs 347

*Paper not available at time of printing.

Session E2
FLOOD DAMAGE ANALYSIS AND REDUCTION

Economic Benefits of a Flood Warning System: The Ventura County, California Experience
  Dolores Taylor 353
Benefit/Cost Analysis of Stormwater Detention Systems
  Richard H. McCuen and Glenn E. Moglen. 360
Reliance on Structural Controls for Water Supply Protection in Urbanizing Watersheds
  John P. Hartigan, Thomas F. Quasebarth, Kelly Cave, and David A. Nailor 364
Considerations for Multiple-Use Stormwater Detention Facility
  David P. Smith and Barend W. Meiling 369

Session E3
WATER IN TEXAS

Fort Worth: Where the West Began with Water
  Roxanne L. Pillar 373
The Genesis of Surface Water for San Antonio
  William C. Allanach and Barbara A. Nickerson 377
The Dallas Floodway: Past and Present Successes in Flood Protection Benefits
  Nancy E. Begel and Gary M. Pettit. 381
Water Reuse in Las Colinas, Irving, Texas
  Mark R. Ernst and Stanford Lynch 387
Evaluation of Global Warming Impact on Soil Moisture and Water Runoff in Texas
  J. B. Valdes, G. R. North, and Tomothy Raines. 392

Session E4
CRITICAL GROUND WATER ISSUES

Groundwater Contamination from an Unlined, Poorly Capped Landfill
  Alejandro J. Gonzalez, Ching-Pi Wang, and Hideo Fujitta 396
The Market Value of Water in the Ogallele Aquifer as Implied by Recent Farm Sales
  L. Allen Torell, James D. Libbin, and Robert R. Lansford 402

Session E5
EMERGING TECHNOLOGIES

Contributions of Satellite Imagery to Water Resource Evaluations
  Aubie Oslin. 407
Old Ideas, New Applications: Expanding the State of the Practice
  Dean Randall and Daniel Sheer 413
Is There a Future for Vaccuum Sewers?
  Donald D. Gray 418
Combining Groundwater Simulation and Non Linear Optimization Models
  James G. Uber 424

Session E6
APPLICATIONS OF BAYESIAN DECISION THEORY AND
FUZZY SETS THEORY IN WATER RESOURCES SYSTEMS:
UNCERTAINTY VS. IMPRECISION

Fuzzy Sets in Civil Engineering: A Tutorial
  J. L. Chameau 430
Tutorial: Fuzzy Sets Theory in Water Resources Systems
  L. Duckstein, L. Bogardi, and A. Bardossy 434

Risk Management for Ground Water Contamination: A Fuzzy Set Approach
L. Bogardi, A. Bardossy, and L. Duckstein 442
Uncertainty and Imprecision in Water Resources Systems Operation: A Fuzzy
Set Approach
Mohammad Karamouz. 449
Bayesian Decision Principle for Flood Warnings
Roman Krzysztofowicz 454
Reservoir Operation by Fuzzy Goal Programming
G. V. Loganathan and D. Bhattacharya. 456

Session F1
RIVER BASIN MANAGEMENT

Use of an Index Stream to Make Instream Flow Decisions
Daniel R. Harvey and Peter F. Brooks 462
Estimating Lake Inflows for Storage by Linear Programming
Quentin W. Martin. 468

Session F2
WATER REALLOCATION IN RESERVOIRS

Reservoir Reevaluation in TVA
Jack L. Davis. 473
Water Reallocation on the Carson River
John W. Bird. . . . . *

Session F3
IS THERE A SAFE CONTAINMENT OF MUNICIPAL
AND HAZARDOUS WASTES

Comparison between the Field and Laboratory Measured Properties of a Clay Liner
A. S. Rogowski 476
Conductivity and Transet Time Estimates of a Soil Liner
Ivan G. Krapac, K. Cartwright, S. V. Panno, B. R. Hansel, K. H. Rehfeldt,
and B. L. Herzog. 820
Measuring Performance of Clay Containment Barriers
Walter E. Grube, Jr. 482
A Rational Basis for Determining Safety of Containment
David E. Daniel 489

Session G1
CRITICAL ISSUES IN WATER RESOURCES

Estimating the Earthquake Hazard of Municipal Water Systems
Howard Hwang and Otto J. Helweg 494
Effects and Risk Analysis for Time Variable Exposures
John Mancini and Peggy W. Glass 499
Water Measurement and Accounting of Lake Michigan Diversion
W. H. Espey, Jr. Harry H. Barnes, and D. Westfall 505
Waterway Navigation Study
Nelson Cordoba . . . . *
Measuring Benefits of Water Supply Projetcs
Farhad Farnam. 513

*Paper not available at time of printing.

Session G2
INTER-GOVERNMENTAL COOPERATION IN WATER RESOURCES PLANNING AND MANAGEMENT

Abilene, Texas Flood Control Study—Case History
  Weldon K. Scrivner 519
Conflict Resolution: Reallocation and Management of Lake Texoma Resources
  Philip A. Cline and Paul Westbrook 525
Contracting Provisions to Delay Capital Costs and Extended the Use of Available Water Supplies
  J. Tom Ray.. 529
Water Resources: Transfer of Development Rights
  James Legrotte 532

Session G3
CRITICAL SOCIAL AND ENVIRONMENTAL IMPACTS IN WATER MANAGEMENT (II)

Some Hydrological Impacts of Climate Changes for the Delaware River Basin
  Gary D. Trasker 541
Predicting Effects of Global Changes on Reservoir Water Quality and Fish Habitat
  Lisa H. Chang and Steve Railsback............................. 545
EPA's Environmental Monitoring and Assessment Program: Overview
  Dean Carpenter, Carolyn Hunsaker, and Jay Messer............... *
EPA's Environmental Monitoring and Assessment Program: Indicators and Sampling Design for Inland Waters
  Dean Carpenter, Carolyn Hunsaker, and Jay Messer............... *

Session G4
GROUNDWATER MODELING

Non-point Source Contamination of Aquifers
  John C. Tracy 551
Modeling Groundwater Flow in the San Joaquin Valley, California
  Alireza S. Taghavi, Nigel W. Quinn, and Lyle B. Everett 555
Groundwater Modeling of the Tustin/Irvine Basin
  Jennifer Goodel, Shih-Huang Chen, and Melih Ozbilgin 559

Session G5
GEOSTATISTICS IN WATER RESOURCES

Special Averging of Statistically Anisotropic Point Conductivities
  Jaime Gomze-Hernandez and Yoram Rubin 566
Design of Sampling Networks for Water Table Monitoring
  Donald E. Myers... 572
Analysis of Uncertainty in Groundwater Quality Monitoring Network Design
  Hugo A. Loaiciga 576

Session H1
STREAM FLOW HYDRAULICS AND HYDROLOGY

Advances in Hydraulic Stream Modeling Using HEC-2
  Degaldra Gurley 582

*Paper not available at time of printing.

Mongomery Point Lock and Dam Entrance to the McClellan-Kerr Arkansas River
Navigation System
  R. Chris Hicklin 588
Instream Habitat Considering Hydro-Peaking
  Robert T. Milhous 593

Session H3
GIS AND WATER RESOURCES

Application of GRASS Geographic Information System in a Sensitive Environment
of the Arkansas River Navigation System
  Manuel Barnes 599

Session H4
GROUNDWATER

Identification of Aquifer Parameters in Confined Groundwater Flow:
A Geostatistical Approach
  Mohamed M. Hantush and Miguel A. Marino 604
Optimization of a Groundwater Well Monitoring Network
  Fethi Ben Jemaa and Miguel A. Marino 610
Modeling Volatile Organic Transport with Vapor Sorption
  Teresa B. Culver, Christine A. Shoemaker, and Leonard W. Lion 615
Groundwater Quality Network Design
  Donald P. Walker and Miguel A. Marino. 621
An Economic Evaluation of Property Rights to Groundwater Resources in the
State of Texas
  Duane J. Rosa 625

Session H5
RESERVOIR MANAGEMENT

A Newsboy Approach to Real-Time Reservoir Operation Modeling
  Emmanuel V. Nzewi. 630
Applications of Probability Matrix Methods for Texas Reservoirs
  Samuel K. Vaugh 634
Marginal Cost Techniques for Reservoir Optimization
  Fred Pinkey, Frank Shorney, and Jeff Klein 640
A Comparison of Two Reservoir Projects and Associated Fisheries Impacts
  Barbara A. Schauer and Alan B. Cooper 648

Session H7
REUSE OF RECLAIMED WASTEWATER

Study of Direct Potable Reuse of reclaimed Wastewater: Preliminary Results of a
Five Year Study
  Adam W. Ollvieri, Don Eisenberg, R. E. Danielson, R. Rudnicki, and
  R. C. Cooper 653
Hueco Bolson Recharge Demonstration Project
  Bethany Barron and Randy Brock. 661

Session H8
TEXAS SIZED WATER PROBLEMS: A CLOSER LOOK

Conjunctive Management of the Edwards Aquifer and Connected Surface Streams
in South Central Texas
  John H. Specht. 666

Managing and Interuptable Water Supply
  Gene Richardson and Wes Birdbell 670
Corps of Engineers Drought Contingency Plans in Texas
  Arnold Escobar 675

Session I1
FLOOD CONTROL AND FLOODPLAIN MANAGEMENT

Benefits from Floodplain Management Activities in Relation to Operating
South Hoiston Dam
  Forest T. Crayford, Gregory W. Lowe, and Arland W. Whitlock 681
Causes and Possible Control Measures of Flood in Bangladesh
  Jobaid Kabir and Nadira Kabir 692
Review of the Design, Construction, and Operation of the Lake Carolyn Flood Control
Pump Station
  George E. Gay, Ernest Clement, and Sanford W. Lynch 686

Session I3
ADMINISTRATRION OF WATER RESOURCES

Government Cooperation in Water Resources Planning and Management
  John W. Brown and Neil W. Schild 698
Streamflow Prediction and Allocation Model for State Waters in Texas
  Richard E. Brown and Norman D. Johns 703
Watermaster Administration of State Waters in Texas
  Norman D. Johns and Richard E. Brown 708
Water for Texans Using the Water Development Fund
  Bobbie R. Ceitendon 712

Session I4
DROUGHT MANAGEMENT

The Comming Drought: Are You Ready?
  Michael D. Day 716
Drought Indication and Responses: A Model for the South Central Connecticut Regional
Water Authority Reservoir System
  Ronald J. Nault, David J. Wall, and Peter Gaewski : 720
Transferable Rations for Drought Management
  Robert V. Reed and Jay R. Lund 726

Session I6
WATER PROBLEMS IN THE SUBSURFACE ENVIRONMENT

Flownets by Computer Graphics
  Sarma Seemanapalli and Vijay P. Singh 731
A 2-D Model for Estimating Leachate Flow in Landfills
  Shabbir Ahmed, Reza M. Khanbilvardi, John Fillos, and Philip Gleason 738
Hydrologic Investigation Techniques in a Limestone Aquifer for Large-Scale
Tunnel Construction
  Andrew J. Turnbull .... *
Numerical Model Study of Groundwater Movement in an Aquifer of Bangladesh
  Shabbir Ahmed and Jahir Uddin Choudhury 759

*Paper not available at time of printing.

Analysis of Groundwater Quality: A Database Application for the Nassau County
New York Water Management Plan
  Laurense Van Der Tak and Mark Maimone .... *
Development of an Optimization Model For Goundwater Withdrawal
  Shabbir Ahmed and Reza M. Khanbilvardi......................... 768

Session I7
MANAGEMENT SPILLS

Why the Concern?
  Water A. Lyon.. *
Spills: The Human-Machine Interface, State of Our Knowledge
  Leo Weaver... 776
Human Error—A Major Cause of Spills
  Harold E. (Smoke) Price................................. 778
Oil Spill Impacts on Aquifers
  Otto J. Heleg, John Smith, and Howard Hwang...................... 784

Session I8
CONSIDERATIONS IN WATER SUPPLY PLANNING

Applicatiuon of Risk Management and Value Engineering Techniques to Evaluation
of Water Resources Projects with Special Emphasis on Geological Hazards
  David W. Eckhoff and Jeffrey R. Keaton 794
Application of a Water Budget for Instream Flows
  Terry J. Waddle 788
Optimization of Freshwater Inflow to Estuaries
  Yeou-Koung Tung, Yixing Bao, and Larry W. Mays 801
Key Environmental Development Issues
  Jeff Civins 806

Subject Index 831

Author Index 837

*Paper not available at time of printing.

Challenges and Opportunities in the '90s and Beyond

A U.S. Army Corps of Engineer's Perspective

Major General Patrick J. Kelly[1]

The U.S. Army Corps of Engineers has, for more than 200 years, provided the Nation with water resources projects and regulatory controls necessary for orderly economic, environmental and social well-being development, as well as military facilities and combat support for U.S. forces in the exercise of their defense missions. The successful conduct of these combined civil/military functions demanded an organizational expertise which now virtually touches on all areas of infrastructure. This expertise embodies every element of project development and implementation, i.e., planning, design, construction, operation and maintenance, and the overreaching imperative of sound project management.

As we enter this decade, on the threshold of the 21st Century, the Corps envisions broad applications of its experience and array of public works expertise. This not only applies to new and emerging challenges in water resources, but also to a wider spectrum of problems associated with needs for major environmental restoration and general infrastructure rehabilitation. These are problems of an enormous scale, the solutions of which will demand a coordinated national effort with innovative partnerships between all levels of government and the private sector. The Corps believes it can assist and be part of the problem solving network. A vision of what the challenges are, how these can be met and where the Corps might assist in the process is the subject of this paper.

One of the self-evident truths of man's existence is that water is essential for survival and to the sustenance of economic enterprises that contribute to social well-being. Among the important governmental functions

---

[1] Director of Civil Works, U.S. Army Corps of Engineers

exercised by the colonies and later by the states, and Federal Government related to the regulation of harbors, waterways and fisheries. State and private responsibility characterized water development through the early decades of the 19th century with Federal responsibility gradually increasing through the end of that period.

The 20th century ushered in a period of strong public support and demand for water projects to address the needs (flood control, navigation, irrigation and power) of a rapidly expanding national economy and population. With that, came an increasing Federal involvement in multi-purpose water planning for regional and national benefits brought about by such legislative landmarks as the 1902 Reclamation Act; 1917 Flood Control Act; 1920 Federal Power Act; 1933 TVA Act; and the 1936 Flood Control Act. Intense water resources development was undertaken during the economic depression of the 1930's characterized by dam construction programs that provided 5,000 dams between 1933 and 1944 and resulted in a doubling of the Nation's water storage capacity. A resurgence of dam construction followed, with more than 25,000 new dams built between 1945 and 1964. By the end of the 1960's however, major water resources project development became a matter of less importance and this coincided with a growing awareness of environmental impacts associated with water resources projects. The emerging national consciousness regarding environmental quality and the related issues of water quality led to the 1969 National Environmental Policy Act (NEPA) and the 1972 Clean Water Act. Major emphasis was placed on new wastewater treatment plant construction. Although there were no significant authorizations of major water resources projects from 1970 to 1986, an important milestone was reached in 1979 with the promulgation of the National Water Resource Council's "Principles and Standards" which have been modified to the present "Principle and Guidelines". These constitute the rigorous procedures applied to the investigations and formulations of Federally supported water resource projects.

The lull in Federal water projects authorizations after 1970 was broken by the 1986 Water Resources Development Act (WRDA '86). This act not only authorized a number of major water resources projects for construction by the Corps, but also significantly changed the roles and responsibilities of the Federal/non-Federal interests. Principal among these changes were: a) non-Federal cost sharing in feasibility studies; b) greater involvement in the planning and design process by local project sponsors; c) higher construction cost shares and increased operations/maintenance responsibilities for non-Federal sponsors; d) highly definitive Local Cooperation Agreements; and e) pro forma conditions for deauthorization of projects not funded for construction after set time periods following initial authorizations. In short, WRDA'86 required substantially increased non-Federal project involvement and continued non-Federal advocacy of a project, after initial authorization, in order to assure its fruition. Many of the provisions of WRDA '86, particularly the cost sharing provisions, will be directly applicable to rebuilding America's infrastructure.

In the foreseeable future, water resources expenditures will probably be dominated by environmental/water quality concerns. Therefore within this decade, the Corps does not expect substantial increases in real dollar terms, for its traditional flood control and navigation programs, though it can be assumed that high priority needs in those areas will be met. On the other hand, strong focus is coming to bear on the state of repair, rehabilitation and management of existing water resource infrastructure to meet changing needs. This situation not only applies to Federal water projects but to projects operated by other levels of government. In the setting of restrained new project construction, the Corps sees many difficult problems and challenges, but also, definite opportunities to serve the Nation's water resources needs. Some of these challenges and opportunities are discussed below as a means of illustration and emphasis.

First, within the broad area of current concerns regarding the quality of our environment, the Corps recognizes the need to gain the wherewithal and undertake an intensive program to restore damaged natural habitats and altered ecological functions in and adjoining Corps-managed water projects. Major inroads to these problems have been made in both riverine and estuarine systems. For example, the Corps has implemented extensive research and field applications in the creation of wetland habitats with dredged material. Second, rehabilitation of water resources infrastructure as well as all categories of infrastructure is a crucial challenge. The Corps is working to meet this challenge with on-going restoration activities and comprehensive research in improved maintenance and rehabilitation techniques. Complementing this effort, the Corps has entered into a partnership with the U.S. construction industry to research and develop better and more productive construction methodologies. All of the civil works and much of the military related research and development conducted by the Corps is accompanied by technology transfer activities in order to achieve broad public benefits. Third, the potential for major global climate change as a result of so-called "greenhouse-gas" emissions presents challenges for the world in many respects, including water resources. The Corps, along with other agencies of the Federal government, is actively involved in examining those facets of potential global warming pertaining to water resources impacts. Those activities relate not only to the domestic interest but also global concerns through participation in the Intergovernmental Panel on Climate Change under the auspices of the United Nations. Last on this list of illustrations is the Corps' dedication to the notion that improved resources management is the key to the solutions of many problems besetting the use and conservation of water resources. The Corps sees a continuing challenge to examine and improve the management of its projects in terms of efficiency and effectiveness. The lessons learned and successful techniques must be conveyed to the general water resources community. Examples of past successes now in use by others are the IWR-MAIN Water Demand Analysis model[2]; Inland Waterway Review Support Methodology, and Benefit/Cost and Risk Analysis techniques. A current National Drought Study is expected to result in significant water resources management information having immediate value and in the event of future global warming.

Beyond the singular issue of water resources development and its affects on the environment, the Corps perceives the general concerns and problems related to environment as constituting the primary engineering problems to be addressed in the 90's and beyond. This will not be a continuation of the debate between conservation and development that was witnessed in the 60's and 70's, but rather the forging of new partnerships focused on solving these monumental National problems. However, the Nation's public engineering assets are not always aligned well with major engineering needs. This is particularly true with the need to clean up accumulated hazardous and radiologic wastes. These are basically environmental engineering problems and the budgets for these programs represent some of the country's largest public works expenditures to date. Yet, most of the Nation's public engineering capacity has not been applied to these problems. The clean up of contaminated Department of Defense, Superfund and Department of Energy sites is a National imperative. The Corps has major capabilities in these areas and believes it could contribute dramatically without adding to the size of the Federal bureaucracy. This has already been demonstrated by the Corps in its environmental engineering efforts in the Defense Environmental Restoration Program and in assisting EPA in the conduct of the Superfund program. The Corps also has the opportunity and capability to make an important contribution to a new non-water infrastructure-related technology by means of a pilot program for a

---

[2]Developed by the US Army Corps of Engineers, Institute for Water Resources (IWR).

magnetic levitation (MAGLEV) transportation system. This cooperative pilot program will offer a new concept in transportation and likely result in the development of second generation MAGLEV technology. It may provide the U.S. with one of its best opportunities for economic expansion in the 21st Century, both as a powerful new mode of transportation and as a globally marketable industry with technological spin-offs to other U.S. industries.

Little has to be said to the engineering and public administration communities as regards the challenges posed by the deterioration of the Nation's basic infrastructure components. This condition was amply described in the report Fragile Foundations issued in 1988 by the National Council on Public Works Improvement. The Council's report concluded: "The Nation's infrastructure is barely adequate to fulfill current requirements and insufficient to meet the demands of future economic growth and development". In addition to increased investments for infrastructure, the Council identified other important needs including clarification of the respective roles of the various levels of government, improved performance of existing facilities, rational budgeting processes, incentives to insure adequate maintenance and adoption of new technologies, and use of low capital techniques for delivering services.

Activities that the Corps has initiated to address the needs of water resources infrastructure were previously discussed and some of these are directly applicable to other components of infrastructure. Indeed, the Corps interests extend to many areas of infrastructure. This is evidenced by its representation, through the Director of Civil Works, on ASCE's National Infrastructure Policy Committee. Within its own organization, the Corps has instituted an infrastructure action plan that involves water resources, energy, transportation, solid waste disposal and hazardous waste disposal. Much of this plan calls for building further on Corps partnerships with other agencies of government and improved technology transfer. The Civil Works Directorate recently established a Corps Infrastructure Task Force, made up of representatives of the major program elements of the Corps and field representatives. The Task Force will work to implement this infrastructure action plan as a Corps contribution to assist the Nation to address its many infrastructure problems. In a broader perspective on the question of infrastructure, the Corps sees a dire need for an integrated Federal policy or strategy to guide legislative actions in addressing the Nation's many infrastructure problems. Such a strategy, consonant with the needs identified by the National Council on Public Works Improvement, could be established through a collaborative, interagency, intergovernmental forum designed to formulate the governmental and private sector partnerships necessary for solving the ubiquitous problems of infrastructure. Specific issues that such a forum could address are:

- What the Federal role in infrastructure should be.

    - R&D, technology transfer
    - catalyst for other levels of government & private sector
    - cost sharing partners
    - program manager/director/integrator

- What specific actions the Federal agencies should undertake.

- What the constraints to the Federal roles are and how they are to be dealt with.

- What state and local government roles should be.

- What role the private sector should play.

- What the total value and benefits of infrastructure are (including economic, social, environmental, and national security benefits) and how these benefits can be used to prioritize both public and private investment.

- What new institutions and institutional changes are needed.

An Analysis of the Impact of Weather Variation on Monthly Water Demand

Ken C. Hall[1] and David R. Maidment[2]

Abstract

In many areas of the world, weather is the primary factor influencing short term variations in water demand. As existing supplies of water become overstressed, quantification of short term demand for water becomes more critical. A methodology is utilized to analyze and model the impact of weather variation on monthly long distance water deliveries in Southern California. Monthly water demand is viewed as a combination of four components; trend, seasonal cycle, autocorrelation, and climatic variations. The model utilized allows variation of model coefficients from month to month throughout the year. Twenty-five member agencies of the Metropolitan Water District of Southern California are analyzed as case studies, lending insight into the water demand process and the applicability of the model to water supply planning.

Introduction

The Metropolitan Water District of Southern California (MWD) must develop facilities and plan water deliveries based upon the expected demands of its twenty-seven member agencies. Each agency purchases from MWD the difference between the total water demanded by its population and the water supplies locally available. The amount of water demanded of MWD is influenced by many factors including population growth, changing sources of water demand (e.g. agricultural to urban), socio-political factors, water quality issues, and climatic variations.

Many variables have been utilized in models to account for the impact of climate on water use. Temperature and precipitation are two of the most common, and possibly the

---

(1) Assoc. Member, ASCE; Water Resources Engineer, CH2M HILL, 229 Peachtree St. NE, Suite 300, Atlanta, GA 30303.
(2) M.ASCE; Associate Professor, Department of Civil Engineering, The University of Texas at Austin. Austin, TX.

most effective, meteorological variables. Morgan and Smolen (1976) found these two variables most significant when compared with potential evapotranspiration minus precipitation and monthly binary seasonal variables in a cross sectional study for thirty-three cities in Southern California. Maidment and Parzen (1984) utilize precipitation, temperature and pan evaporation as climatic variables in a study of six Texas cities.

Recent studies have attempted to analyze water demand by defining components of the time series. Salas-LaCruz and Yevjevich (1972) develop a general time series model for monthly water use incorporating components of trend, periodic (seasonal cycles) and stochastic nature. Autoregressive effects are also captured in the model. Maidment and Parzen (1984) analyze monthly water use time series by detrending, deseasonalizing, autoregressive filtering, and multiple regression.

Franklin and Maidment (1986) utilized Maidment and Parzen's procedure to model weekly and monthly water use in Deerfield Beach, Florida. The rainfall component in the model is proposed as useful in risk analysis, since historic rainfall sequences may be used to develop water use scenarios.

In a study for the MWD, Maidment, Djokic, Hall and Saenz de Ormijana (1988) analyze annual and monthly time series of MWD water deliveries. The MWD annual demand model, which approximates trend, is the aggregation of annual models for each of twenty-five of the MWD's member agencies. Monthly demand models are designed to utilize the trend component of the annual model and incorporate seasonal cycles and impacts due to climatic deviations from mean monthly weather conditions.

Hall and Maidment (1989) proposed a methodology and model based on the development of a weather adjustment factor (WAF) for monthly MWD water demand. The WAF allows estimation of the influence of weather variation on MWD water deliveries. The methodology addresses quantification of variation due to seasonal cycles, and allows analysis of historical demands or creation of future demand projections.

This study incorporates four components of water demand, 1)trend, 2)seasonality, 3)autocorrelation, and 4) stochastic, into a methodology which lends insight to the influence of weather variation on water use or demand. In spite of the economic definition of demand, the terms "water demand" and "water use" will be used interchangeably and synonymously. The modelling effort focuses on the latter three components.

Analysis

As a result of the nature of the water demand process, particularly in arid climates, a strong seasonal cycle in water demand is observed. MWD water deliveries follow a similar pattern, merging the fluctuations in total demand and local supplies. A monthly MWD demand fraction, $C_s(m)$, may be defined as the average fraction of annual MWD water demand normally observed in month m. Determined from historical data, $C_s(m)$ provides an unbiased estimate of the fraction of annual MWD water delivered in each month.

Conceptually, the WAF may be described as the ratio of the observed MWD water demand to the MWD water demand expected under mean, or "normal", weather conditions. A monthly WAF may be defined as

$$F(m,y) = M(m,y) / M_n(m,y) \qquad (1)$$

where
- $F(m,y)$ is a monthly WAF
- $M(m,y)$ is the MWD water demand in month m of fiscal year y under observed or projected weather conditions
- $M_n(m,y)$ is the MWD water demand expected in month m of fiscal year y under normal weather conditions for month m.

Monthly MWD water demand may then be modelled as

$$\hat{M}(m,y) = [\hat{M}_n(y) * C_s(m)] * \hat{F}(m,y) \qquad (2)$$

where the "^" designates a modelled or fitted value.

In order to obtain a fitted series for monthly MWD water demand, a WAF statistical model and some annual normal weather demand model must be defined. A model for annual MWD normal weather demand, incorporating the aspects of both the total demand series and local supply series, was defined in a previous report to the MWD (Maidment et.al, 1988).

A general prospective WAF model is shown of the form

$$[1 - b_{f1}(m) B]*[F(m,y) - 1] = [b_t(m) + b_{t1}(m) B + b_{t2}(m) B^2]$$
$$*[T(m,y) - T_{mean}(m)]$$
$$+ [b_p(m) + b_{p1}(m) B + b_{p2}(m) B^2]$$
$$*[P(m,y) - P_{mean}(m)] \qquad (3)$$

where $b_t(m)$ is a coefficient of the T series varying with month m

$b_{t1}(m)$ is a coefficient of the lag 1 T series
$b_{t2}(m)$ is a coefficient of the lag 2 T series
$b_p(m)$ is a coefficient of the P series
$b_{p1}(m)$ is a coefficient of the lag 1 P series
$b_{p2}(m)$ is a coefficient of the lag 2 P series
$b_{f1}(m)$ is a coefficient of the lag 1 F series
B is the backward shift operator; such that $B*F(m,y) = F(m-1,y)$.

NOTE: T represents average maximum daily temperature (°F) and P represents monthly precipitation (inches).

Each coefficient is allowed to vary from month to month according to the Fourier relationship

$$b(m) = q + r*\cos(2pi*m/12) + s*\sin(2pi*m/12) \quad (4)$$

where q, r, and s are coefficients determined by regression.

This basic model was used to analyze data for the MWD service area, and all agencies (excluding San Fernando and San Marino). Forward stepwise least squares regression was used in each case to develop the WAF model and identify statistically significant variables.

Results

The MWD service area WAF model exhibits an $R^2adj.$ value of 0.65, implying that the model explains about 65% of the total variance of the WAF series. This figure is reasonable because the WAF series is developed from MWD water delivery data, rather than total water demand data. Since MWD water deliveries represent the difference between total water demand and local supplies, the WAF model must contend with all of the uncertainties in the local supply series as well as the total demand series. However, the MWD water demand projection created using equation (2) and the WAF model results in an $R^2adj.$ value of 0.89, with a good fit to the observed demand series.

WAF models were also fit for the individual local agencies, with varying degrees of success. For the five agencies with the greatest MWD water deliveries, the WAF models showed San Diego CWA with an $R^2adj.$ of 0.74, MWD of Orange County with an $R^2adj.$ of 0.47, West Basin MWD with an $R^2adj.$ of 0.60, Central Basin MWD with an $R^2adj.$ of 0.55, and Los Angeles with an $R^2adj.$ of 0.59.

Variables found significant in the largest number of agencies were the lag 1 WAF (25 agencies), temperature (20 agencies), precipitation (11 agencies), and lag 1 temperature (11 agencies). As might be expected, at the agency level some model results were good while others were poor. Results ranged from a high R^2adj. value of 0.89 in Fullerton, to a low R^2adj. value of 0.24 in Upper San Gabriel Valley MWD.

Several possible explanations exist for the variability in model results at the member agency level. First, the analysis is performed at a smaller demand scale, and thus irregularities in the data are not washed out as in the service area analysis. While the size of an irregularity in the analysis of an individual agency may make it significant, it is a relatively small portion of the aggregated analysis.

Second, some agencies' total demand processes may respond more strongly to the influence of weather than others due to differences in vegetation, traditional water use, etcetera. Third, local supplies may be so erratic, and so large in comparison with MWD deliveries, that weather influences on MWD deliveries are difficult to detect. Fourth, the local supply process may respond to weather in an opposing manner to the total supply process, damping the detectable weather induced variation.

Fifth, adequate normal weather annual demand projections are difficult to obtain for some agencies, and these projections are critical to the accuracy of the monthly analysis. Sixth, local supply data for some agencies is less reliable than for others.

Conclusions

Although factors such as legal adjudication, release management, water quality scares, and socio-economic changes are difficult or impossible to relate to water demand using the available data, weather effects are much more feasible to quantify. By focusing on weather effects, utilizing knowledge of seasonal trends in water demand and the structure of the physical demand system, much valuable information may be obtained. This information is best utilized in a form which is intuitively logical, adaptable to both analysis of past water demands and projection of future demands, and of a form which can incorporate normal weather demand projections from various statistical or econometric demand models.

References

Franklin, Sheryl L., and Maidment, David R., "An Evaluation of Weekly and Monthly Time Series Forecasts of Municipal Water Use", Water Resources Bulletin, AWRA, vol 22, no 4, August 1986.

Hall, Ken C. and Maidment, David R., "Development of a Weather Adjustment Factor for Monthly Water Demand Forecasting", Proceedings of the 16th Annual ASCE Water Resources Planning and Management Division Conference, Sacramento, CA, 1989.

Maidment, David R., Djokic, Dean, Hall, Ken C., and Saenz de Ormijana, Fidel A., "Water Demand Forecasting with Metrowatfore", Report prepared for the Metropolitan Water District of Southern California, by the Center for Research in Water Resources, The University of Texas at Austin, Austin, Texas, December 1988.

Maidment, David R., and Parzen, Emanuel, "Time Patterns of Water Use in Six Texas Cities", Journal of Water Resources Planning and Management, ASCE, vol 110, no 1, January 1984.

Morgan, W.D., and Smolen, J. C., "Climatic Indicators in the Estimation of Municipal Water Demand", Water Resources Bulletin, AWRA, vol 12, no 3, June 1976.

Salas-LaCruz, J.D., and Yevjevich, V., "Stochastic Structure of Water Use Time Series", Hydrology Paper No. 52, Colorado State University, Fort Collins, Colorado, 1972.

Units

1 inch = 2.54 centimeters
°C = $(5/9)(°F - 32°)$
Water demand $[M(m,y), M(y),$ etc.] may be expressed in any consistent system of units, since $C_s(m)$ and $F(m,y)$ are dimensionless. In this study, volume units of acre-feet were used.

Acknowledgement

This paper describes a portion of a study funded by the Metropolitan Water District of Southern California through a research grant to the Center for Research in Water Resources at The University of Texas at Austin.

WATER UTILITY DEMAND FORECASTING USING LOTUS 1-2-3 SPREADSHEET

Jobaid Kabir[1], M ASCE

ABSTRACT

Population allocation and demand forecasting are essential parts of any planning activity for the implementation of a regional water and wastewater development project. In this study, a technique has been developed using Lotus 1-2-3 spreadsheet for distributing projected populations to small sectors throughout the study area. This procedure divides the study area into grids of small subareas. These subareas are used as the basic units to identify and allocate the future distribution of population within the study area. Utilizing the graphics capabilities of Lotus 1-2-3, this spreadsheet develops maps of the study area with allocated population, water demands, and/or wastewater flows for each grid cell. It has been successfully used by the Lower Colorado River Authority in several feasibility studies of regional water and wastewater projects.

PROCEDURE

In this study, a Lotus 1-2-3 spreadsheet was developed for allocating projected populations to small sectors throughout the study area using a population allocation technique (1). The study area was divided into a grid of small subareas referred as cells. These cells

---

1. Engineer, LCRA, P.O.Box 220, Austin, Texas 78767

are used as the basic units to identify and allocate the future distribution of population within the study area. This spreadsheet computes an advantage rating for each grid square from the input data. Advantage rating is comprised of two parts: an attractiveness rating and an infrastructure rating.

The attractiveness rating is a measure of the desirability of a location as a place to live. Lotus 1-2-3 spreadsheet computes attractiveness rating for each grid square from various factors defined by the user. These user defined factors may include parameters which makes an area more of less desirable place to live.

The infrastructure rating is a measure of the expected availability of water and/or wastewater service for which the study is being conducted. Properties with access to existing and proposed water and wastewater systems would receive higher infrastructure rating compared to the properties which will continue to depend on-site wells and septic tanks.

This spreadsheet uses the populations allocated to grid cells for computing water and/or wastewater demands. Utilizing the graphics capabilities of Lotus 1-2-3 this spreadsheet develops maps of the study area with allocated population, water demands, and/or wastewater flows for each grid cell.

CASE STUDY

Lotus 1-2-3 spreadsheet developed for allocating projected population, water demands, and wastewater flows were used for several feasibility studies by the Lower Colorado River Authority (LCRA). These studies included regional water and wastewater systems for rural areas. Elgin Regional Wastewater Feasibility Study (2) was selected for this paper to discuss the features of the spreadsheet.

The study area is located at central Texas in Bastrop and Travis counties. This area is comprised of Wilbarger Creek watershed, Big Sandy Creek watershed, and a small area which drains directly to the Colorado River. Growth potentials of different locations, within the study area, varies widely due to their different levels of expected economic developments through the study period of 1987-2020. The study area was divided into cells of dimension

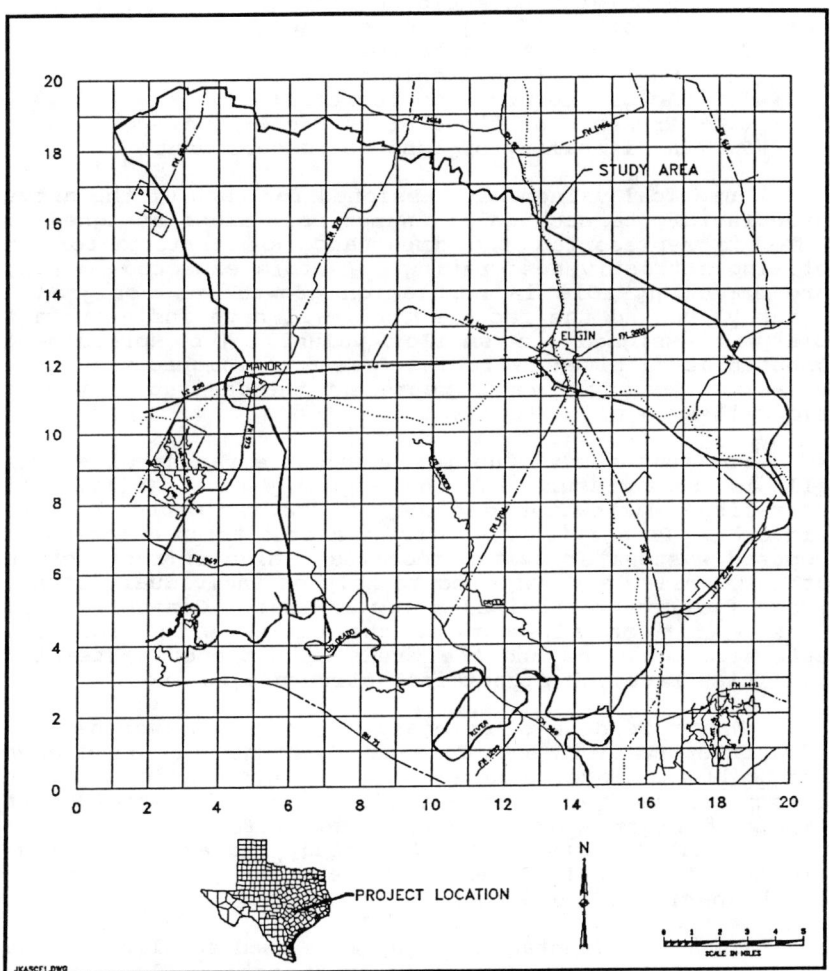

Figure 1 - Study Area With Grid Cells

1.33 mile square. Figure 1 shows the study area with the grid cells.

The study area was then objectively analyzed on the basis of several criteria that were expected to have significant influence on the population growth. These factors include the following:

1. Proximity to employment;
2. Presence of major development;
3. Proximity to major roads;
4. Quality of environment;
5. Access to urban communities;
6. Presence of flood prone areas; and
7. Availability of land for development.

Numerical values were assigned for each of the above seven factors to each cell. Numerical values assigned to a factor represented the importance of that factor in defining attractiveness rating. Factors expected to play more important role in population growth was assigned a higher value and the factors that will have insignificant role was assigned a smaller value. The spreadsheet computed attractiveness rating from the assigned values of the above seven factors to represent the desirability of a grid cell as a place to live.

For this study, the infrastructure rating of a grid cell is the measure of the expected availability of centralized wastewater service to the residents of that grid cell. Properties with direct access to an existing or proposed wastewater system received a high infrastructure ratings, while land required to rely on individual private sewage facilities received a low ratings. Generally, the areas within or adjacent to the cities with organized wastewater services and the areas of proposed wastewater facilities received higher infrastructure ratings.

The spreadsheet combined the attractiveness and infrastructure ratings to compute advantage rating for each grid cell. Since some of the factors making up the attractiveness rating change with time, the spreadsheet computed different attractiveness rating for each grid cell for designated years. For this study, advantage ratings were computed for 1987, and for every ten year increments for the period of 1990 to 2020.

Computed advantage ratings were used to allocate the total projected populations to each grid cells for the designated years. Figure 2 shows the allocated population for each grid cell within the study area for 2020. Population allocation for projections with different growth scenarios were obtained by simply changing the projected populations.

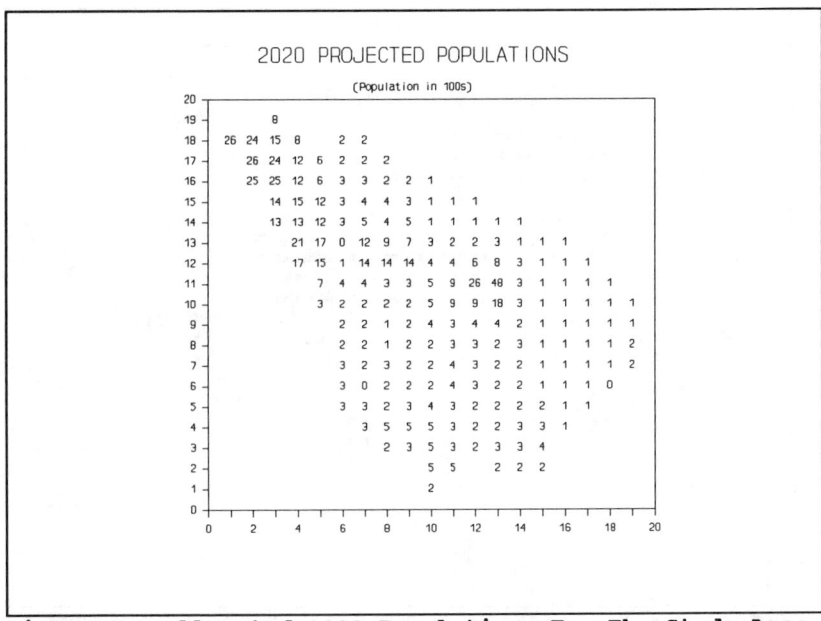

Figure 2 - Allocated 2020 Populations For The Study Area.

This spreadsheet was also used to compute projected wastewater demands for each grid cell for various levels of growth scenarios. An example of daily peak domestic wastewater flows for the study area in 2020 is shown in Figure 3. Daily peak domestic wastewater flows for the study area were computed by assuming an average per capita dry weather flow of 80 gallons per day with 2.0 peaking factor. Projected wastewater flows for grid cells are very useful for planning and preliminary design of collection, treatment, and disposal systems.

CONCLUSIONS

Lotus 1-2-3 spreadsheet can be used as an effective tool for population allocation and for demand forecasting for the implementation of a regional water and wastewater development projects. Allocated demands for small geographic areas (grid cell) are very useful for planning

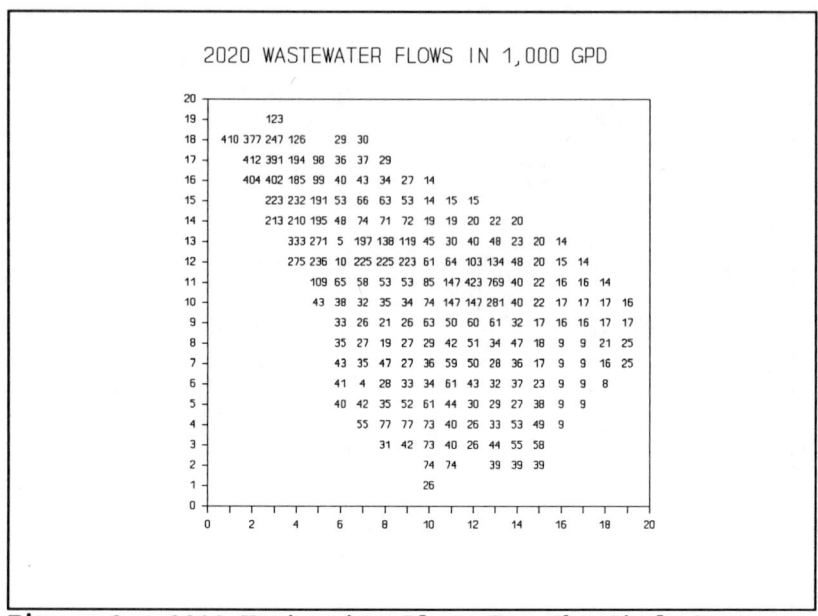

Figure 3 - 2020 Wastewater Flows For The Study Area.

and design of water and wastewater facilities.

These microcomputer based spreadsheet provide sufficient flexibility to the user to tailor them for each project to meet specific design needs. These spreadsheet are simple to use. This technique has been used by the Lower Colorado River Authority in several water and wastewater feasibility studies for population allocation and for demand forecasting. This spreadsheet can be used as an effective tool for conducting sensitivity analysis.

REFERENCES

1. Lower Colorado River Authority, "Bastrop Regional Wastewater Study, Maha Creek / Cedar Creek Extended Study Area", Appendix Volume 3, February 1988.

2. Lower Colorado River Authority, "Elgin Regional Wastewater Study", November 1988.

THE MULTI-WATFORE METHOD: A WATER DEMAND FORECASTING SYSTEM

By Virgil C. Adderley[1], David R. Maidment[2]

Abstract

Common to most applications of water demand forecasting is the need to understand the processes that drive water consumption, and the need to estimate the reliability of future forecasts. The multi-Watfore method, which combines the cascade model and a first order analysis of uncertainty, is a system of practical steps to develop models of water demand while generating confidence intervals to bracket the uncertainty of those forecasts. This paper describes the multi-Watfore method and its implementation in a study[3] performed for the Central Texas region along the Colorado River. Annual and monthly water demand models for the area's cities and counties are presented.

Methodology

The Cascade Model. The multi-Watfore method employs the cascade model originally presented by Maidment and Parzen (1981). The cascade model is a set of linear equations describing water demand in terms of annual trend, seasonality, autocorrelation, and weather effects. The equations are developed by a series of transformations, including regression, applied to water consumption, socio-economic and weather data.

The water demand, $W(m,y)$, for month 'm' during year 'y' is modeled as a long term memory component, $W_l(m,y)$, and a short term memory component $W_s(m,y)$:

---

[1]Water Resources Division, CH2M Hill Southeast, Inc., 7201 NW 11th Place, Gainesville, Florida, 32602
[2]Member; Associate Professor, Dept. of Civil Engineering, The University of Texas at Austin, Austin, Texas, 78712
[3]This project was funded by the Lower Colorado River Authority (LCRA) and managed by Camp, Dresser & McKee of Austin, Texas.

$$W(m,y) = W_1(m,y) + W_s(m,y) \qquad (1)$$

Annual trend, $W_a(y)$, and the monthly seasonal cycle, $C_s(m)$, make up the long term memory components of water demand:

$$W_1(m,y) = W_a(y) * C_s(m) \qquad (2)$$

The annual trend of water demand is modeled by regressing against socio-economic variables such as population, income, and water price. Annual precipitation can also be included to account for unusually wet or dry years.

The seasonal cycle of water demand is modeled by fitting a seasonal curve to the monthly values of the detrended water use. The seasonal curve can be described by a Fourier series or more simply, a set of twelve monthly ratios (average monthly water use to annual water use). The data series is deseasonalized by removing the fitted seasonal curve.

The model for short term memory, $W_s(m,y)$, consists of auto-correlation and weather effects:

$$W_s(m,y) = \sum_{i=1}^{p} \alpha_i * W_s(m-i,y) + \sum_{j=1}^{q} \beta_j * X_j(m,y) + \varepsilon(m,y) \qquad (3)$$

where p is the order of the autoregressive model (usually two) and q is the number of weather components (two in this study: precipitation and temperature).

Autocorrelation is the effect of the previous month(s) on the demand of the current month. It is removed from the detrended and deseasonalized monthly water demand by regression. This process is known as autoregressive filtering or "pre-whitening" the data.

The pre-whitened water use residuals are then regressed against pre-whitened monthly precipitation and mean maximum temperature. The residuals of this final transformation are examined for any remaining components which have not been completely removed. The final residuals, $\varepsilon(m,y)$, should be normally distributed.

<u>Simplified Models</u>. Where appropriate, simplified models of annual and monthly water demand can be applied. A popular technique for estimating annual demand is to use a constant consumption rate in gallons per capita day (GPCD). This model indicates that population alone is sufficient to estimate the annual water demand. It can be applied where the GPCD value is shown to be constant through time.

Monthly models can be simplified by applying a constant seasonal curve applied to the annual forecast. In coastal areas, the seasonal curve may be insignificant compared to the effects of weather and autocorrelation.

<u>Sources of Uncertainty</u>. In water demand models, expressed here as: $W = f(x) + \varepsilon$, there exists four sources of uncertainty:
1. The natural randomness of the process.
2. The model error due to the form of $f(x)$.
3. Parameters estimated for $f(x)$.
4. Errors in forecasting future values of x.

In modelling past water demand, the residuals (ε) incorporate the first three sources of uncertainty as measured from lack of fit. The independent variable (x) is assumed to have been measured without error and therefore has no uncertainty.

The uncertainty in future water demand forecasts is far more complex. As in the past, the natural variance of the process will provide some measure of uncertainty in forecasting. In addition, the form (linear, log, etc.) of our original model, $f(x)$, may no longer be appropriate 5 or 10 years later. Also, as more data becomes available in the future, it is likely that the values of the regression coefficients will change. Finally, our independent variables, as <u>estimated</u> future values of population, income and/or precipitation, carry their own measure of uncertainty. It is necessary to account for these unknowns when generating the confidence limits for future water demand forecasts.

<u>First Order Analysis of Uncertainty</u>. Given an estimated future value of the independent variable x', we can forecast the future water demand W as $W'=f(x')$. The deviation of W' from the actual value of W can be estimated using the first order terms of a Taylor series expansion of $f(x')$ about $x'=x$:

$$W = f(x') + \partial f/\partial x * (x-x')$$

where the derivative(s) of $\partial f/\partial x$ are evaluated at $x=x'$. Substituting and rearranging, we can express the forecast error as: $(W-W') = \partial f/\partial x * (x-x')$. Solving for the variance of this error yields:

$$S_{W'}^2 = (\partial f/\partial x)^2 * S_x^2 \qquad (4)$$

where $S_{W'}^2$ and S_x^2 are the variances of the water demand estimate, W, and the independent variable estimate, x.

For the purposes of illustrating the use of Equation (4), we assume a simple water demand model (annual or monthly):

$$W' = f(x_1) = a + b*x_1 \tag{5}$$

The uncertainty in the water demand forecast due to error in the independent variable, $S_{W_v}^2$, is found by applying (4):

$$S_{W_v}^2 = (\partial f/\partial x_1)^2 * S_{x_1}^2 = b^2 * S_{x_1}^2 \tag{6}$$

This requires that the variance, $S_{x_1}^2$ be determined while developing the future forecasts of the independent variables.

The uncertainty due to parameter error, $S_{W_p}^2$, is found by calculating the derivatives of (4) with respect to a and b:

$$S_{W_p}^2 = (\partial f/\partial a)^2 S_a^2 + (\partial f/\partial b)^2 S_b^2 + 2(\partial f/\partial a)(\partial f/\partial b) S_a S_b \rho_{a,b}$$

$$S_{W_p}^2 = S_a^2 + (x_1)^2 * S_b^2 + 2*(x_1)*S_a*S_b*\rho_{a,b} \tag{7}$$

where: S_a^2 = Variance of estimated constant 'a'
S_b^2 = Variance of estimated coefficient 'b'
$\rho_{a,b}$ = Correlation coefficient between 'a' & 'b'

The variance of the coefficients and their correlation are obtained from regression analysis.

The first two components of uncertainty, inherent and model error, are calculated from the variance of the residuals:

$$Var[\varepsilon] = E[(W - f(x))^2] = \sigma_W^2 \tag{8}$$

Combining the four components, the full uncertainty of the future water demand forecasts can be modelled as:

$$S_{W'}^2 = \sigma_W^2 + S_a^2 + x_1^2 S_b^2 + 2x_1 S_a S_b \rho_{a,b} + b^2 S_{x_1}^2 \tag{9}$$

    Inherent,   -- Error in the parameters --   Error in the
  model error   variable forecasts

For convenience in calculations, the above equation should be re-written in terms of the coefficients of variation.

<u>Simplified Analysis of Uncertainty</u>. The uncertainty of future forecasts can be estimated by a simplified method which assumes that the errors are multiplicative for all models as: $W(x) = f(x) * \varepsilon$, where $f(x)$ is the function used to estimate the future water demand $W(x)$. The assumption that the errors are multiplicative causes the estimated variance to increase proportionately with the mean of the forecast. Thus, the variance of future demand forecasts is:

$$S_{W'}^2 = (W' * C_v)^2$$

where W' is the forecasted water demand (annual or monthly), and C_v is the coefficient of variation for the multiplicative errors. The advantage of the simplified method is that the uncertainty due to parameter error and the future independent variables need not be calculated. Scenarios (high, medium or low growth, wet-weather, etc.) can be used to bracket the effects of uncertainty in the future independent variables.

Application of Methodology in Central Texas

The service area of the Lower Colorado River Authority (LCRA) in Central Texas extends along the Colorado River from San Saba County to the Gulf of Mexico. Water demand data for the 10 counties and cities of population 1,000 or more located within the LCRA service area was analyzed during this project. Annual and monthly water demand models were developed for both the cities and counties within the study region. The analysis of uncertainty was then applied to the five largest cities and counties with results given below.

<u>Annual Models for Cities</u>. Three models were developed to forecast annual water demand for the cities studied:

- Linear: $W(y) = a + bX_1 + cX_2 + dX_3 + eX_4 + \varepsilon$ (10)
- Log: $W(y) = a * X_1^b * X_2^c * X_3^d * X_4^e * \varepsilon$ (11)
- Regional: $W(y) = a * C_c * X_1^b * X_2^c * X_3^d * X_4^e * \varepsilon$ (12)

where: $W(y)$ = Annual water use X_3 = County income/capita
X_1 = Population X_4 = Annual precipitation
X_2 = Water price C_c = City coefficient

The linear and log models produced very similar results with R^2 values between 96% (Austin) to 62% (Bastrop). Population and income were generally the most significant variables.

The regional model was formed by combining the city data into one large set for analysis with a dummy variable added to represent each city. The fit of the regional model was not as good as the other two, but it provided insight into the behavior of the region's water demand and allowed interpolation for cities with missing data.

<u>Annual Models for Counties</u>. Development of the county demand models was driven by lack of data. Only five, discontinuous years of annual water demand was available. For this reason, the county data was combined and two models were developed:

- GPCD: Water Use = GPCD * County Population
- ALPHA: Water Use = ALPHA * Summed City Water Use

where GPCD is the consumption rate in gallons per capita day (132 gpcd for the region) and ALPHA is the ratio of the total county water use to the summed volume of water use for the major cities within the county (1.68 for the region). Because of the large differences in population between Travis County (major city is Austin) and the other counties, separate model coefficients were determined. Travis' GPCD consumption rate is 190 gpcd, and its ALPHA ratio is 1.13.

Monthly Demand Models. Water demand for month 'm' in year 'y' is modelled as: $W(m,y) = W_a(y) * C(m,y)$ where $W_a(y)$ is the annual water demand and $C(m,y)$ is the dimensionless monthly use from:

$$C(m,y) = C(m) + \sum_{i=1}^{p} \alpha_i * C(m-i,y) + \sum_{j=1}^{q} \beta_j * X_j(m,y) + \varepsilon(m,y) \qquad (13)$$

In this equation, $C(m)$ is the seasonal cycle, $C(m-i,y)$ is the past monthly values of water demand (lagged by p months), and $X_j(m,y)$ is the vector of q pre-whitened weather variables. The results from the analysis of monthly water demand showed that the components of annual demand and seasonal variation accounted for 85% of the model fit, while autocorrelation and weather effects accounted for only 15% of the model fit.

Results of Analysis of Uncertainty. The complete first order analysis of uncertainty was applied to a 10-year forecast for Austin's future annual water demand. The coefficient of variation for the 10-year forecast was 15%. The distribution of uncertainty within the forecast was as follows: Natural uncertainty and model error (7%), parameter error (31%), population forecast with 10% error (62% of total variance).

Conclusions

The multi-Watfore models were developed to provide short-term (about 10-years) water demand forecasts for cities and counties of a specific region with confidence limits to bracket the uncertainty of those forecasts. Because the project was designed for a water management agency, the methods developed were made to be practical and deal with realistic problems such as lack of complete data.

References

Maidment, D.R., and E. Parzen. Time Patterns of Water Use in Six Texas Cities., *ASCE Journal of Water Resources Planning and Management,* Vol 110, No.1, January, 1984, pp. 90-106.

Preliminary Report of the Feasibility of an
Interbasin Water Transfer Through Existing Canal Systems

Mr. John Lee Rutledge, P.E., Associate Member, ASCE[1]
Mr. Ronnie M. Lemons, P.E., Member, ASCE[2]

Abstract

A preliminary feasibility study of the interbasin transport of water from the Sabine River on the Texas Louisiana border to the San Jacinto River Basin, northeast of Houston, Texas, using existing canal systems has been completed. The transfer will involve the cooperation of three river authorities, as the water would actually cross both the Neches and Trinity River Basins on its way from the Sabine River to the San Jacinto. Depending on the alternative chosen, the transfer of water will consist of as much as 50 miles of existing canals and the construction of as much as 62 miles of new canals.

Technical considerations of the transfer and the estimated project costs are presented. The study reviewed the potential for transporting 75 million gallons per day (MGD), 100 MGD, 200 MGD and 300 MGD.

Introduction

In 1989, a reconnaissance study was performed to review the possibility of delivering water from the Sabine River to the San Jacinto River Authority service area using existing facilities wherever possible. The purpose of the study was to determine the general physical and financial feasibility of such a transfer using existing canal facilities and pump stations to minimize capital expenditures and delivery costs. The transfer would have to use or cross both the Neches and Trinity Rivers. Preliminary cost estimates were developed for delivery systems with capacities of 75, 100, 200, and 300 million
----
[1]Design Engineer, [2] Principal, Freese and Nichols, Inc. 811 Lamar St., Fort Worth, Texas 76102

gallons per day (MGD) under varying conditions. Two potential final destinations were considered. The Highlands Reservoir, a balancing reservoir owned by the San Jacinto River Authority and located northeast of the Town of Highlands, could be used with the 75 and 100 MGD systems. This destination was not considered for the 200 and 300 MGD systems, as it was felt that the demand potential does not exist in the area serviced by the Highlands Reservoir. Lake Houston, owned by the City of Houston, the was considered as a destination point for all four options.

Several existing canal systems were reviewed for their potential inclusion into the system. These canal systems included those belonging to the Sabine River Authority of Texas (SRA), the Lower Neches Valley Authority (LNVA), the Coastal Water Authority (CWA), the San Jacinto River Authority (SJRA), the American Rice Growers Association (Dayton Canal), and Boyt Realty (Devers Canal).

Existing Systems

Each of the existing systems was analyzed to determine any available flow capacity in their pumping systems and their canal systems. Their pumping volumes for the past 10 years were reviewed and averaged on a monthly basis. In all cases, the capacity of the pumping station controlled, as it was less than the capacity of the canal system. The available capacity of a pump station was defined as the maximum pumping capacity with one of the largest pumps available unused, minus the peak average monthly demand. Only existing pumping capacities were considered, though some of the pump stations involved do have room for additional pumps and a higher ultimate capacity.

Implicit in the definition of available capacity is the assumption that some flexibility in flow rates will be possible. This would mean that the appropriate water rights permits would be structured so that equal volumes of water would need to be dropped into and pumped out of the appropriate rivers over a period of time such as a month or a year, but that the individual flow rates in each portion of the system would not necessarily have to be equal at all times. The need to reduce the total design capacity of the system would control the potential differences in flow rates and prevent large discrepancies of flow rates at any given time. This setup would allow for occasional higher pumping rates in existing systems, that would otherwise reduce the available capacity, to be used as needed without hampering the delivery capabilities of the entire system. A thorough analysis of the operations scheme of the entire delivery system was beyond the scope of this study, but will be needed before final design begins.

Big Thicket National Preserve

Another element affecting the analysis was the existence of the Big Thicket National Preserve along the Neches River. Getting approval for any construction within the Preserve could be difficult and time consuming. Therefore, this study made an effort to avoid the Big Thicket entirely.

Study Components

The proposed canal system was broken into three components, separated by the major rivers. The first component consisted of a system to transport water from the Sabine River to the Neches River. This segment included portions of the existing SRA Canal System and a proposed new canal to the Neches River. The second component consisted of transporting water from the Neches River through the LNVA system to the Trinity River. This included the options of dropping the water into the Trinity River and of piping it underneath the river. In addition to the LNVA Canal system, the use of the Devers Canal was also considered. The third component consisted of transporting water from the Trinity River to the San Jacinto River Authority area. As described earlier, two final destinations were considered, the Highlands Reservoir and Lake Houston. For the 200 and 300 MGD options, only the Lake Houston alternative was considered.

Sabine River to Neches River Segment

The transport of water from the Sabine River to the Neches River will require the use of the existing SRA pump station on the Sabine River north of Orange, as well as the first 4-1/2 miles of the existing SRA canal. Beyond that point, the proposed route consists of 18.5 miles of new canal, an additional pump station, and two drop structures. This canal system will release water into the Neches River at the Community of Lakeview just upstream of the LNVA Lakeview Canal. Expansion of the SRA pump station would be necessary for the 200 MGD and 300 MGD capacity options only.

Neches River to Trinity River Segment

The proposed route for transporting water from the Neches River to the Trinity River consists of the use of the entire 5.5 mile length of the Lakeview Canal, 27 miles of the LNVA Neches Main Canal, including its two pump stations, and 23.3 miles of new canal, including an additional pump station and two drop structures.

An option reviewed within this study segment involved the use of an additional pump station and six miles of pipeline in order to pipe water underneath the Trinity River and to completely avoid the use of Trinity River water in the transport system. The pump station would be located at the site of the first proposed drop structure and the pipeline would carry water to a bluff on the west bank of the Trinity River. From this point, the water would be carried through new canals to Lake Houston or to the Highlands Reservoir.

The options of expanding the capacities of the existing Devers Canal was reviewed and found not to be economical. The use of the Devers system would require extensive reconstruction of the existing canal in order to reverse the flow to an east to west direction. It would also require that the existing customers of the Devers system be supplied by water pumped over from the Sabine and Neches Rivers. Due to these constraints, it was found to be more economical to completely bypass the Devers system with a new canal.

Trinity River to San Jacinto River Authority Segment

Two final destination points were reviewed for this segment. The first was the Highlands Reservoir for the 75 and 100 MGD options only. If water were taken out of the Trinity River, the CWA canal system would be used to transport it to a point just east of the Highlands Reservoir and a new pump station and 2,200 feet of pipeline would be used to transport the water from the CWA Canal to the Highlands Reservoir. If the option to pipe water underneath the Trinity River were used, then 16.5 miles of new canal from the Trinity River to the Highlands Reservoir would be needed.

The second final destination point considered was Lake Houston. For this option, a new canal from the Trinity River west to Lake Houston would be needed. If water were taken out of the Trinity River, a pump station at the river, another on the canal 13 miles later, and one drop structure at Lake Houston would be required. If water were piped underneath the Trinity River, the same canal system would be required, but only the second pump station and the drop structure would be needed.

The use of the Dayton Canal within the system to transport water from the Trinity River to Lake Houston was considered. However, this canal system has no available capacity in either the pump station or the canal, and it would not be economical to expand it for use in this system.

Summary of Costs

Delivery systems for four possible delivery rates, 75, 100, 200 and 300 MGD, were reviewed. The systems studied would transport water from the Sabine River either to the Highlands Reservoir or to Lake Houston. Each of these systems was studied with the option of using Trinity River water or piping water underneath the river.

Table 1 shows a final summary of the estimated cost of all the options considered. Included in these figures are estimates of the capital costs of construction, the cost of debt service for the initial capital investment, the operations and maintenance cost for each of the alternatives, and the estimated conveyance charges for transporting the water through existing systems. For these calculations, an interest rate of 9 percent was assumed with a payoff period of 30 years. The cost to the San Jacinto River Authority of the purchase of the raw Sabine River water is not included in these cost figures.

Table 1

	75 MGD	100 MGD	200 MGD	300 MGD
Sabine to Lake Houston:				
Pipe Under Trinity				
Capital Cost ($Million)	66.1	77.1	111.0	149.6
Unit Costs (¢/1000 gal)	35.6	31.4	23.5	21.3
Drop Into Trinity				
Capital Cost ($Million)	57.9	65.5	91.9	120.1
Unit Costs (¢/1000 gal)	32.4	28.2	21.3	19.1
Sabine to Highland Res.				
Pipe Under Trinity				
Capital Cost ($Million)	66.0	76.2	–	–
Unit Costs (¢/1000 gal)	35.0	30.7	–	–
Drop Into Trinity				
Capital Cost ($Million)	40.5	46.0	–	–
Unit Costs (¢/1000 gal)	27.9	24.9	–	–

Sediment Management Challenges of the
Red River Waterway Project

by

Phil Combs[1], M.ASCE
and
W.H. Espey, Jr.[2], M.ASCE

Introduction

In 1968 the 90th Congress passed public law 90-483 authorizing the construction of the Red River Waterway. This is one of the largest civil works projects with an estimated cost in excess of $1.3 billion. At the present time the Corps of Engineers (USCE) has the project well under construction. The project consists of channel stabilization and construction of navigation locks and dams to provide a 9 foot minimum depth for a distance of approximately 236 miles, from the confluence of the Red River at the Mississippi River upstream to Shreveport, Louisiana. This is being accomplished by channel realignment and/or stabilization to ensure a stable and efficient channel for the passage of flood flows and navigation traffic and by the construction of five locks and dams to provide minimum depths (9 feet).

At the present time two of the locks and dam (1 and 2) are completed and operating and providing navigable depths approximately 100 miles (Alexandria, Louisiana), while Lock and Dam 3 is under construction and Locks and Dams 4 and 5 are under detailed design (Figure 1). Lock and Dam 1 was completed in the Fall of 1984 and has operated for five years while Lock and Dam 2 was completed in the Fall of 1987.

---

[1]Chief Hydraulics Section, Vicksburg District, U.S. Army Corps of Engineers, Vicksburg, Mississippi.

[2]President, Espey, Huston & Associates, Inc., Austin, TX.

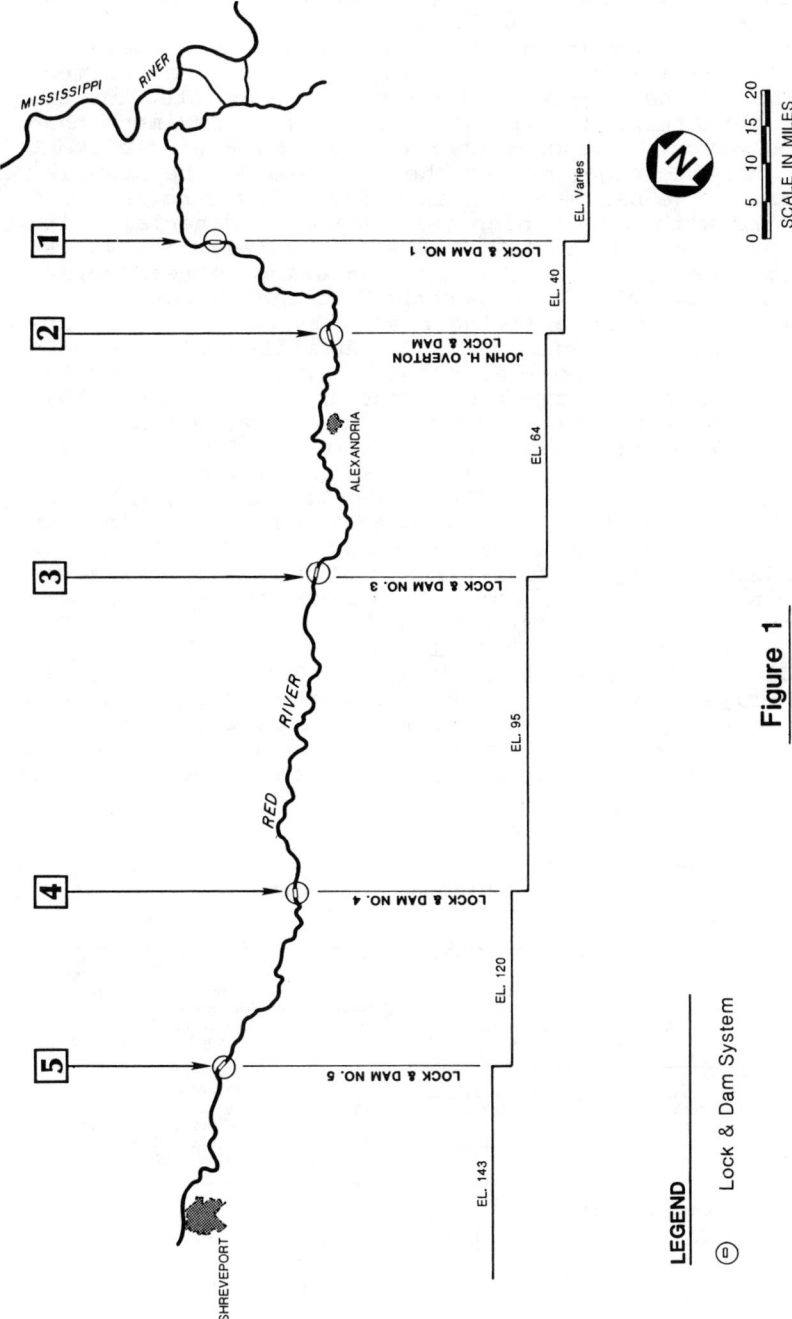

Figure 1
OVERALL PROJECT PLAN AND PROFILE

The Red River is ranked third in total annual sediment load; however, in terms of average annual suspended sediment yield (tons/mi^2) the Red River ranks number one of major rivers within the U.S. (Table 1). The Arkansas River had previously carried more sediment but due to the comprehensive project completed in the 1960's the Arkansas River now carries less sediment than the Red River. The character of the Red River sediment load makes it unique due to the fineness of the granular material. The bed material is principally fine and very fine sand with a very high percentage of material being silt and clay. The river is in a natural alluvial valley and is characterized by a meandering streamcourse, various oxbow lakes and abandoned stream channels. The Red River is in an evolving state trying to assume new channel configurations. The Red has frequently eroded new channels and created cut-off loops and deposited sediment in various overflow areas as it meanders within the alluvial floodplain. At present, a nearly continuous man-made levee protects both banks of the Red River from Bowie County, Texas, to a point downstream from Alexandria, Louisiana. The USCE has been conducting realignment and stabilization measures for approximately 30 years. The total drainage of the Red River is approximately 96,000 square miles of which approximately 50,000 square miles is controlled above the Denison Dam. Denison Dam is an effective sediment trap for the Red River. The Red River below Denison Dam is therefore in a sediment "starved" condition. The Red River is constantly shifting its banks and bank caving as much as 300 feet per year is not uncommon. It is estimated that bank caving results in a volume of material twice the annual sediment load being placed in the river system.

TABLE 1

COMPARATIVE SUSPENDED SEDIMENT LOADS FOR RIVERS IN USA

River	Station	Drainage Area (mi^2)	Average Flow (ft^3/sec)	Annual Suspended Sediment Load	Annual Suspended Sediment Yield (tons/mi^2)
Red	Alexandria, LA	67,333	31,000	37,000,000	550
Mississippi	Tarbert Lndg., MS	1,218,875	450,000	350,000,000	287
Arkansas*	Little Rock, AR	158,201	47,500	104,900,000	663
Ohio	Paducah, KY	203,000	174,000	58,800,000	290
Tennessee	Johnsonville, TN	38,520	64,500	18,400,000	478

*Data prior to USCE project (1960).

Since completion of Locks and Dams 1 and 2 several problems have surfaced that have required extensive evaluation and analysis to assure that the navigation project can coexist with the highly sediment laden river. After one year of operation of Lock and Dam 1 there were five areas of significant sediment problems which interfered with the operation of the lock. Physical model studies had been performed previously and the structures were constructed similar to the recommendations of the model studies. However, the size of the Red River sediments and the suspended load could not be adequately evaluated with the physical models. When the problems surfaced the USCE immediately utilized 2-D hydrodynamic numerical models which assisted in the analysis and description of the fine grained sediment load. Recommendations from these numerical model studies resulted in construction modifications upstream and downstream of Lock and Dam 1 which significantly reduced the sediment problem. The construction converted the sediment problem to a manageable maintenance item.

A problem surfaced at Lock and Dam 2 shortly after placing it in operation at the upstream miter gates. During high flows sediment began to accumulate against the upstream miter gates rendering them out of service. The USCE utilized a unique solution technique by installing hydraulic jets to sweep the sediments away and allow the gates to operate. Studies are underway to determine the need for and viability of installing similar systems at the remaining locks and dams.

Another technique for sediment management is the use of hinged-pool operations at Locks and Dams 3, 4 and 5. Lock and Dam 3 will be operated with a hinged pool and Locks and Dams 4 and 5 are being designed to accommodate such an operation. The hinged pool operation allows for the drawdown of the pool at the lock and dam to increase the slope through the pool which will provide for better sediment management of the pool areas as well as minimizing adverse impacts to real estate.

The sediment management is being approached in a systematic way to identify macroscopically the sediment sources and characteristics in order to develop a long-term management strategy. USCE is conducting geomorphic studies of the river systems to determine the nature of the channel, identify reaches which are degrading or aggrading and determine reasons for the channel behavior. The goal is to identify ways to reduce the overall sediment load within the navigation project to an acceptable level to allow the navigation project to coexist efficiently.

A WATER PRICING MODEL FOR LAKE TEXANA

Stuart R. Wilson,[1] Member, ASCE
Ronald E. Anderson,[2] Member, ASCE

Abstract

Faced with water sales and recreation revenues insufficient to service the project debt, the Lavaca-Navidad River Authority (L-NRA), operators of Lake Texana, decided upon a novel approach to the marketing of its surface water supply to municipal and industrial customers. Realizing that many potential water customers were: 1) satisfied with their current ground water supplies but facing the task of planning for future growth; and 2) concerned about the costs of investing in a surface water supply system, the L-NRA authorized the preparation of a computer-based water pricing model. The model would allow a potential surface water customer (or group of customers) to obtain a quick estimate of the cost of delivered water for a wide variety of supply scenarios.

Introduction

The Palmetto Bend Project (Lake Texana) was completed by the United States Bureau of Reclamation in 1985 for the primary purpose of providing municipal and industrial water supply to the central Gulf Coast area of Texas. The lake has a conservation storage capacity of 170,000 acre-feet and a firm yield of 75,000 acre-feet of water per year. Lake Texana is located on the Navidad River near the town of Edna, approximately 100 miles southwest of Houston.

Through a repayment contract with the Bureau of Reclamation, the project is jointly owned by the Texas

---
[1] Project Manager, HDR Engineering, Inc., 3000 South IH-35, Suite 400, Austin, Texas 78704
[2] Project Engineer, HDR Engineering, Inc., 3000 South IH-35, Suite 400, Austin, Texas 78704

Water Development Board (TWDB) and the L-NRA. The TWDB is responsible for 57.33% of the debt service while the L-NRA is responsible for 42.67%, as well as all project operation and maintenance. Out of the total project yield of 75,000 acre-feet per year, only 5,000 acre-feet per year had been committed as of 1987. Since L-NRA's income comes solely from water sales and recreational fees, plus a county ad-valorem tax to cover day-to-day operating expenses, it was important for the project owners to promote the sale of uncommitted water supplies from the lake.

The purpose of HDR's effort was to develop a user-friendly computer model which would allow a potential water customer to make quick, reconnaissance-level cost estimates for new water systems.

Model Description

The model requires the user to provide information about a proposed water system in the form of fill-in-the-blank type responses describing the system's size, configuration, and options. The model accounts for all the cost components of a water delivery project: intake facilities, pumping stations, transmission, storage, and treatment of water, as well as debt service for the Palmetto Bend Project expressed as the cost of raw water from the lake. Once the user has completed making the necessary inputs, the model calculates the estimated cost to construct the system and the annual costs for operating it. Capital and annual costs are then converted to a unit cost of water (i.e. dollars per thousand gallons). A summary is provided describing the physical characteristics of the system along with a complete cost breakdown.

Special features of the model include a routine to optimize pipeline sizing, user-specified intake type and location, and the ability to handle systems: 1) with constant, as well as varying, demands; 2) with branches to serve multiple customers; and, 3) to serve a customer who desires to tie into then existing pumping and pipeline system. The model is especially valuable in comparing different water supply alternatives on a cost basis as well as sizing a supply system based on budget constraints.

A generalized flow chart for the model is shown in Exhibit 1.

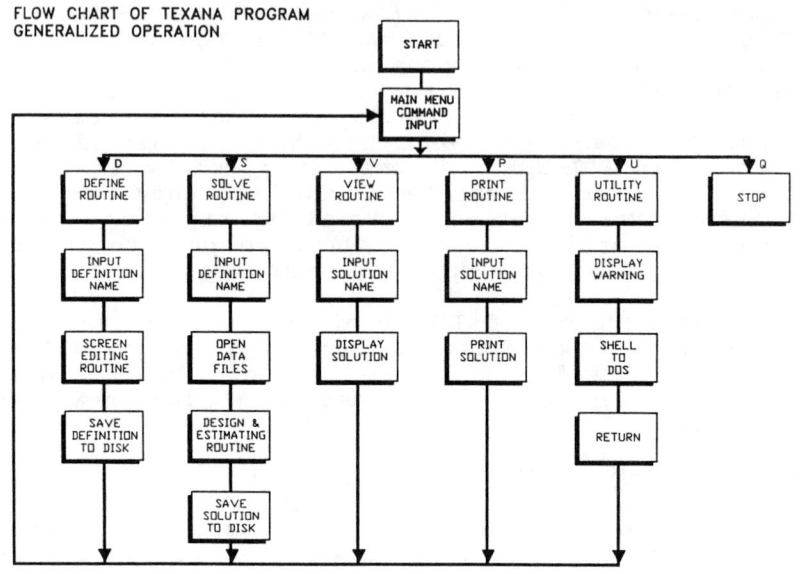

Exhibit 1

Using the Model

The model can be run on any IBM-compatible personal computer with a minimum of one floppy drive and 128K of memory. The user operates the program from a main menu which contains the following six commands: Define, Solve, View, Print, Utility, and Quit. In a typical application, the user will first define (i.e. set demands, select treatment and storage options, give pipeline length, etc.) the system using the Define command, then solve the system (i.e. calculate its costs) using the Solve command. The solution can then be examined on the screen using the View command or on a printout using the Print command. After examining the costs, the user may then choose to make changes to the water system using the Define command and repeat the above steps. The Utility command allows the user to temporarily access the operating system (i.e. DOS).

While in the Define mode, the user is asked to enter a wide variety of planning, engineering, and financial data. The planning data required includes projected population growth, demand growth (both average and max day), and planning period lengths.

Required engineering data consists of pipeline lengths, pipe roughness coefficients, pipe laying conditions, water elevations at source and termination, and storage and treatment requirements. Financial data includes electrical utility rates, loan period, interest rate, and ENR Construction Cost Index.

Cost Data Files

In order to develop reasonable estimates of the costs of proposed water delivery systems, the model makes use of a set of cost data files. These data files, or cost curves, were developed externally from the model and are based on previous HDR experience with intakes, pipelines, treatment plants, storage facilities, etc. supplemented by other cost references as appropriate. The cost curves are intended to be site-specific to Lake Texana.

In order to use the cost curves, the program identifies the independent variable appropriate for the particular curve and extracts the cost (i.e. dependent variable) associated with it, through an interpolation procedure if necessary. The independent variable may be user input (i.e. treatment capacity in mgd for treatment plant cost) or calculated from user inputs (i.e. diameter in inches for pipeline cost). The independent variable used for each cost curve is that variable deemed most influential in determining the cost of a particular system component.

Example Application

The following example will demonstrate some of the capabilities of the model:

Grover City, Texas is attempting to attract new industry and, if successful, anticipates water needs of 1.3 mgd in 1990 increasing to 2.9 mgd in 2010. In addition, its current ground water supply of 0.5 mgd is diminishing and expected to be depleted by 2010.

Exhibit 2 summarizes the inputs made by the city manager of Grover City to describe the necessary system. The exhibit also summarizes the physical aspects of the system and the estimated costs (output). For the case of Grover City, the model indicates that the project will have an initial construction cost of almost eight million dollars and that water costs will decrease from 3.68 $/1000 gallons in 1990 to $1.91/1000 gallons in 1999.

EXHIBIT 2

PRINTED INPUT

```
PROJECT DEFINITION: sample

PLANNING INPUT DATA:
  CUSTOMER NAME                                              Grover City, Texas
  INITIAL POPULATION                              [CAPITA]   10000
  INITIAL AVG ANNUAL WATER USAGE                  [MGD]      1.30
  INITIAL MAX DAY WATER USAGE                     [MGD]      2.60
  INITIAL SUPP. WATER AVAILABLE                   [MGD]      0.50
  PLANNING PERIOD                                 [YRS]      20
  FUTURE POPULATION                               [CAPITA]   22000
  FUTURE AVG ANNUAL WATER USAGE                   [MGD]      2.90
  FUTURE MAX DAY WATER USAGE                      [MGD]      5.70
  FUTURE SUPP. WATER AVAILABLE                    [MGD]      0
  PIPELINE DESIGN PERIOD                          [YRS]      30
  INTAKE DESIGN PERIOD                            [YRS]      20
  TREATMENT PLANT DESIGN PERIOD                   [YRS]      20
  YEAR OF START-UP                                           1990

ENGINEERING AND FINANCIAL INPUT DATA:
  INTAKE OPTION            (C, W, E, P, or N)                W
  PIPELINE LENGTH                                 [FT]       36960
  HAZEN-WILLIAMS COEFFICIENT                                 110
  PIPE SUBSURFACE          (1=soil to 3=rock)                1.0
  PIPE ENVIRONMENT         (1=rural to 3=urban)              1.1
  WATER ELEVATION AT SOURCE                                  45
  WATER ELEVATION AT TERMINATION                             175
  STORAGE TYPE             (G, B, E, or N)                   E
  STORAGE VOLUME                                  [MG]       1.0
  TREATMENT REQUIRED?      (Y or N)                          Y
  BRANCHED SEGMENT?        (Y or N)                          N
  ELECTRICAL ENERGY CHARGE                        [$/KWHR]   .014
  MONTHLY ELECTRICAL DEMAND CHARGE                [$/KW]     6.5
  ADDITIONAL LUMP SUM COST                        [$]        20000
  PERIOD OF LOAN                                  [YR]       20
  INTEREST RATE                                   [%]        8.4
  CURRENT ENR CONSTRUCTION COST INDEX                        4605.78
```

PRINTED RESULTS

```
                      PROJECT COST ESTIMATE
               FOR WATER SUPPLIED FROM LAKE TEXANA
                          version 1.3

ESTIMATE FOR Grover City, Texas                       09-07-1989

DESCRIPTION OF THE PROPOSED WATER SYSTEM
> Construct new intake at the west M & I outlet based on a
  design flow of 7.25 mgd with 358 ' TDH and 662 hp.
> The 36960 foot pipeline is sized for 5.7 MGD and will
  be constructed of 18 -inch, class  250 pipe.
> The maximum velocity is 4.9 fps and the design pressure is 154 psi.
> Treatment capacity of 3.9 MGD is required.
> Elevated storage capacity of 1 MG is required.
> Anticipated financing is at 8.4 % for 20 years.
> Costs per 1000 gals. may be inaccurate due to supplemental water.

INITIAL PROJECT COSTS
  Intake Facilities                           $850,000
  Pipeline Facilities                       $1,359,788
  Storage Facilities                          $876,000
  Treatment Facilities                      $3,220,000
  Engineering, Legal, & Financial           $1,576,447
  Additional Lump Sum Cost                     $20,000

  TOTAL PROJECT COST                        $7,902,236

WATER COST SCHEDULE BY CONSUMPTION

YEAR  PLANT    INTAKE   DEBT     RAW WATER  ANNUAL    WATER MGD  WATER COST
      O & M    O & M    SERVICE  COST       TOTAL     [MGD]      [$/1000 GAL]
----  -------  -------  -------- --------- ---------  --------- ----------
1990  $185000  $38569   $828965  $22354    $1074888   0.80      $3.681
1991  $192000  $38897   $828965  $28351    $1088213   0.90      $3.294
1992  $205000  $39513   $828965  $38648    $1112126   1.12      $2.722
1993  $212000  $39985   $828965  $50768    $1131713   1.22      $2.541
1994  $218000  $40365   $828965  $59735    $1147065   1.33      $2.372
1995  $225000  $41186   $828965  $78215    $1180366   1.53      $2.107
1996  $232000  $41596   $828965  $89233    $1198794   1.64      $2.003
1997  $239000  $42052   $828965  $101021   $1217038   1.75      $1.911

WATER COST SCHEDULE BY CAPITA

YEAR   FORECASTED POPULATION     WATER COST
         [CAPITA]                [$/CAPITA]
----   ---------------------     ----------
1990        10,000               $107.49
1991        10,600               $102.66
1992        11,400                $94.59
1993        12,400                $91.27
1994        13,000                $88.24
1995        14,200                $83.12
1996        14,800                $81.00
1997        15,400                $79.03
```

Summary and Conclusions

The Lake Texana Water Pricing Model has been a valuable tool for potential Lake Texana water customers as well as for the L-NRA staff. Its simplicity and user-friendly nature offer both potential customers and staff an opportunity to develop cost estimates in an expedient manner. There are two cautions which accompany the use of the model, however. The first is that the model is specific to Lake Texana and shouldn't be used at other sites without proper modification and documentation. The second is that the cost estimates provided by the model are reconnaissance-level only and do not take the place of a detailed estimate. As mentioned previously, the model's greatest values are in making economic comparisons between alternative projects and in rough-sizing a system to meet a particular capital and operation budget constraint.

Acknowledgement

The authors would like to express their appreciation to the staffs and board members of the Lavaca-Navidad River Authority and the Texas Water Development Board for their roles in making the development of this paper possible.

Appendix. References

Department of the Army, Corps of Engineers, Office of the Chief of Engineer, "Methodology for Area Wide Planning Studies (MAPS) Documentation", EM 1110-2-502, November 28, 1980.

HDR Engineering, Inc., "User's Manual - Lake Texana Water Pricing Model", May, 1988.

United States Department of the Interior, Bureau of Reclamation, "Palmetto Bend Project (Stage 1) Texas, Definite Plan Report", September, 1971.

Expert System for Budget Preparation and Optimal Operation of an Interconnected Power Utility

Jovan Grahovac[1] and Slobodan P. Simonovic[2]

Introduction

Manitoba Hydro operates a complex system of 13 reservoirs, 2 thermal and 13 hydro generating stations, and 9 interconnections to other neighbouring power utilities. The Energy Management and Maintenance Analysis computer program, known as EMMA, has been developed by the Information Systems Division and Energy Resources Section of Manitoba Hydro. EMMA optimizes planned operations of the system for a specified stream flow scenario and within a specified time horizon, conveniently divided into time steps. The program formulates release policy, electricity generation, imports, and exports, as well as maintenance schedule using linear programming. EMMA algorithm ensures meeting the loads while maximizing revenues and minimizing costs. The program's intrinsic complexity stems from the nature of modelling operation of virtually any interconnected power utility, the task that includes dealing simultaneously with three distinct subsystems: (1) hydraulic network of rivers, lakes and reservoirs; (2) electrical network of hydro and thermal generating stations and tielines to adjacent utilities; and (3) maintenance subsystem.

Linear programming problem formulated and solved by EMMA includes up to 23 different types of constraints that range from flow and mass continuity to maintenance crew availability. Obviously, in order to make a good use of EMMA, one has to develop good understanding of both the underlying physical system, and the basics of the systems approach used in optimization of its operation. Furthermore, EMMA requires massive input preparation, and produces number of reports, both of which can be very discouraging and frustrating for an inexperienced user. The scale, complexity, and impact of the system whose operation is optimized by EMMA raises a number of political, environmental and social issues. Dealing with and accounting for all of them in EMMA requires a lot of knowledge, experience, and intuitive reasoning that cannot be learned from books. All these aspects indicated that the use of EMMA may be well suited for development of an expert system that would try to capture and formulate as much as possible of the diverse expertise involved in it. Potential benefits

---

[1]Research Assistant, Dept. of Civ. Eng., Univ. of Manitoba, Winnipeg, Manitoba, Canada, R3T 2N2.
[2]Associate Professor, Dept. of Civ. Eng., Univ. of Manitoba, Winnipeg, Manitoba, Canada, R3T 2N2.

were seen in improving and facilitating expert's work, as well as making transfer of his knowledge to inexperienced colleagues easier and faster.

Expert System Prototyping

The development of the expert system to be discussed in this article is part of a broader joint research effort by the University of Manitoba and Manitoba Hydro. Previous work, reported by Barlishen (1989) and Nagy et al. (1989), on knowledge acquisition in water resources engineering and used EMMA as a case study, greatly contributed to this project. It established knowledge acquisition procedures that consisted of regular, tape recorded, weekly interviews with the expert from Manitoba Hydro. It also provided the expert with experience in formulating step-by-step procedures and organizing knowledge he uses in his work to forms that can be transferred into computer codes. After a number of interviews three different contexts in which EMMA can be used were recognized: (1) preparation of annual budget; (2) preparation of weekly schedules for releases, thermal and hydro power generation, and imports and exports of energy; and (3) long term planning that can include tasks like evaluation of benefits from installing additional capacities, or examining some particular operational condition that may occur in the system.

Extensive interviews with the expert revealed whole different sequences of EMMA runs that have to be performed within each of the contexts. All these runs are made with appropriate adjustments of input data and with focus on particular parts of EMMA output. At this point, it seemed natural to constrain the scope of the expert system, and try to trace back all the steps and rules used by the expert in budget preparation. This decision was brought according to the principle of incremental development of expert systems (Barlishen, 1989), which means beginning with a prototype and slowly and carefully expanding the knowledge base to deal with more complexity and involve more expertise.

The structure of the envisioned expert system for the full support in all the contexts of EMMA use is shown in Figure 1. It enables step-by-step introduction to linear programming and EMMA followed by comprehensive advice and guide-lines on what runs to perform, and what data to use. The option to actually create an input data set as a product of the expert system consultation is also included. More experienced users may seek just a particular advice from the knowledge base, and do not have to run the entire consultation. The parts that will deal with weekly scheduling and long term studies will conform to the structure established for the completed budgetary branch of the expert system.

Preparation of Annual Budget

As the work on the budgetary branch of the expert system progressed perception of the whole project as being exclusively focused on EMMA gradually evolved. It becomes apparent that the crucial point is what and why the expert does, and not EMMA itself. Once it was placed where it really belongs, among other tools used by the Reservoir and Energy Scheduling (RES) Engineer, EMMA became much easier to understand and run.

Formulation of basic steps necessary for budget preparation took four one-hour interviews with the expert:

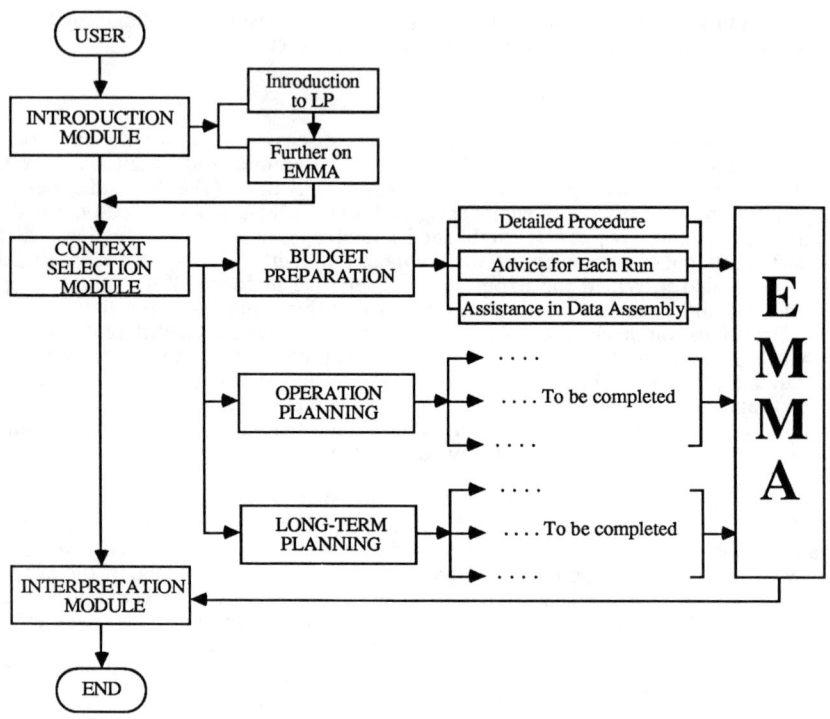

Figure 1. Structure of EMMA Expert System

Step (1): Firmness test should be performed in order to evaluate reserves that are necessary in order to ensure reliable supply of energy to the customers in case of a severe drought or outage in the system. This test is performed just once, and outside EMMA, for a specified time horizon, and its results are used thereafter in input for subsequent runs of the program.

Step (2): Severe Case with 5% probability low flows and early freeze-up dates causing lower production capability and higher demand of energy is run through EMMA. This formulates operating policy that will satisfy energy demand under unfavorable conditions and preserve necessary reserves determined in step 1.

Step (3): Expected Case with 50% probability flows and the likeliest freeze-up date is run through EMMA. Since more water is available, cheap hydro generation will be larger than in step 2.

Step (4): Severe Case is re-run iteratively, gradually increasing lower bounds on hydro generation in time steps in the immediate future. The idea is to get as close as possible to the expected case and use more hydro generation, while still being prepared for the severe case if it should occur. This way, the system will perform economically in the immediate future, and for later time steps, it has a small probability, equal to that of the occurrence of the severe case, of paying penalty in form of expensive thermal generation. For the likeliest sequence of flows however (expected case from step 3), it will continue to operate economically.

The procedure described above is used for optimization of the system operation in immediate future. Thus formulated policy also enters annual budget and its updates. Since budget has to account for the time horizon till the end of the fiscal year, which is usually far ahead, and since it should be based on the likeliest sequence of events, operation policy formulated in step 3 is used for later time in steps in its preparation.

Formulation of this basic procedure, enabled the construction of a simple prototype that gradually grew and became more detailed as the work on the expert system progressed. Coming up with a prototype sped up the development because it is sometimes easier for the expert to formulate rules by looking at, and criticizing what has already been entered to the computer.

Another important benefit of this method of work was that verification of the expert system began early in its development. The expert system is currently being expanded to cover the other two contexts, and the completed budgetary part is being tested by inexperienced users of EMMA. This will enable both final test for the budgetary part of the expert system and immediate incorporation of thus gained experience in other two parts.

The work on this expert system was carried out on the Apollo Domain Personal Workstations and using Rulemaster 2 as a rule-based expert system development tool. Modular structure and flexibility of Rulemaster 2 greatly facilitated creation of the prototype and its gradual growth. The only shortcoming of the tool is its poor graphic and screen control capability. Breaking long sequences of text with graphs and refreshing the appearance of the expert system with colours would make the transfer of information and knowledge to the user much more efficient and less tiring. The work on the project in the near future will continue using Rulemater 3, that is expected to be free from some minor bugs noticed in Rulemaster 2 and equipped with better graphical capabilities.

Successful Application of Expert Systems

Apparently, expert system development can start at the point when a need for a computer application that can assist in solving a problem by incorporating engineering knowledge and judgement, principles of systems analysis, experience, and intuition into the solution procedure (Barlishen et al., 1989) is recognized. This development is later, to some extent, a journey into the unknown. Neither experts nor knowledge engineers can have a completely clear vision of the final shape of the expert system at the very beginning of the project. It is through time consuming, sometimes frustrating and discouraging, process of knowledge acquisition and gradual growth of the prototype expert system that both sides slowly realize where real problems lie and where and what kind of expertise comes into play. Ending up with something slightly different from what was originally expected means that some misconceptions, either about expert systems or about the problem itself, have been rectified.

The developed expert system will likely provide the expert with new insights into his own expertise and serve him as a useful help later in his work. To a novice engineer, a successful expert system will provide a patient, consistent, non-judgemental assistance in gaining necessary expertise (Barlishen, 1989). The organization where this process takes place will benefit from the captured knowledge and its availability to more of its members in their everyday practice.

In the development of an expert system, the importance of permanent interaction between the expert, knowledge engineer, and the final user cannot be overstressed. Their joint effort and communication, interest, motivation, and persistence are the most important condition in the development of an expert system.

Acknowledgements

The authors would like to acknowledge the financial support from Manitoba Hydro, approved by the Research and Development Committee, as well as the contribution of Mr. A.D. Cormie.

References

Barlishen, K.D., "Knowledge Acquisition in Water Resources Engineering", Master's Thesis, Department of Civil Engineering, The University of Manitoba, 1989.

Barlishen, K.D., D.H. Burn and S.P. Simonovic, "Knowledge Acquisition for an Engineering Expert System", Proceedings of the 4th Canadian Seminar on Systems Theory for Civil Engineer, pp. 55-63, 1989.

Nagy, A., K.D. Barlishen, D.H. Burn, and S.P. Simonovic, "Toward an Expert System for Improving the Operations Planning in Manitoba Hydro", Proceedings of the 16th Annual ASCE Water Resources Planning and Management Conference, pp. 477-481, 1989.

OPTIMAL REAL-TIME OPERATION
OF TE-CHI RESERVOIR

Jan-Tai Kuo [†], Member, ASCE, Nien-Sheng Hsu [†], Wen-Sen Chu[†]
, Assoc. Member, ASCE, and Chian-Min Wu [‡]

Abstract

An optimization model for the 10-day operation of Te-Chi Reservoir in central Taiwan is developed. The inflow to the reservoir is forecasted by an ARX model with a Kalmam Filter updating routine. The optimization formulation is solved by a discrete differential dynamic programming routine. The optimization model results are shown to be more superior than the current operating rule. The entire optimization model and the streamflow forecasting scheme were run on an IBM-AT compatible personnal computer.

Introduction

Te-Chi Reservoir, the fourth largest reservoir in Taiwan, is located on the upstream of Ta-Chia River in central Taiwan (Fig.1). The reservoir has an effective storage volume of 1.83×10^8 m^3 and

---

[†] Respectively, Prof., Assoc. Prof., and Visiting Assoc. Prof., Dept. of Civil Engineering, National Taiwan University, Taipei, Taiwan, R.O.C.
[‡] Chief Engineer, Water Resources Planning Commission, Ministry of Economic Affairs, Taipei, Taiwan, R.O.C.

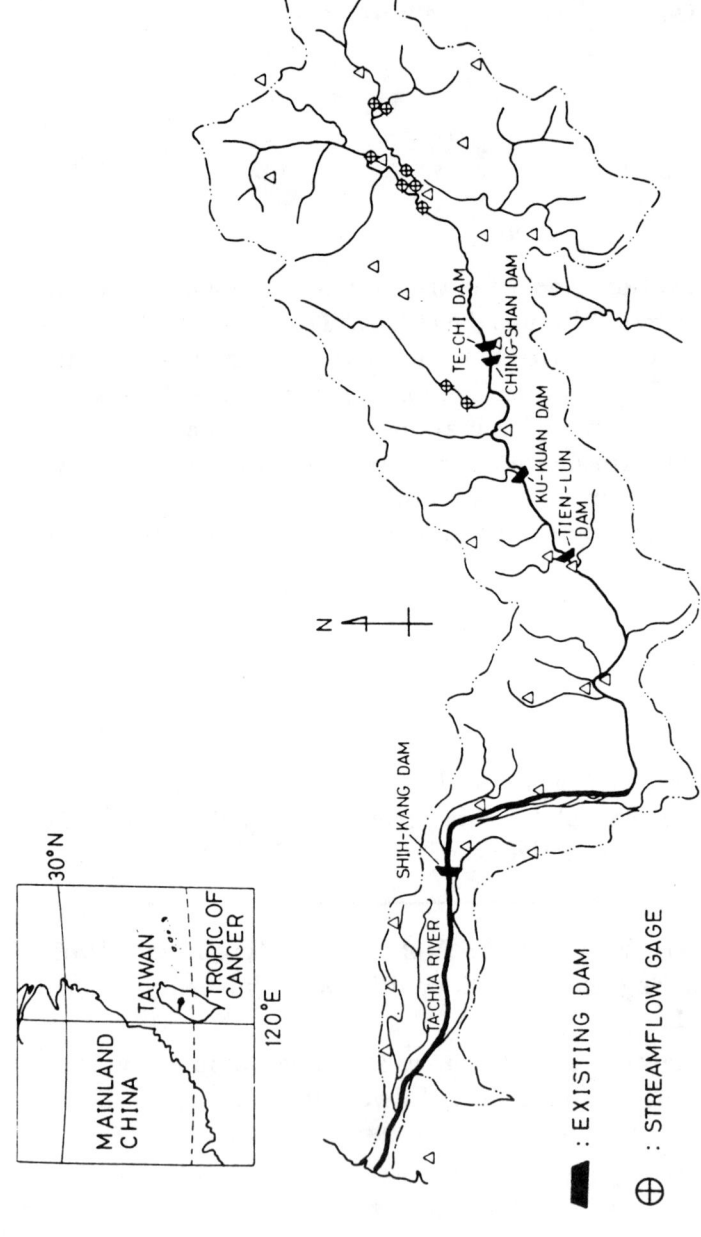

Fig. 1 Ta-Chia River Basin

a drainage area of 592 km². The major objectives of the reservoir are hydropower production, irrigation, and domestic water supply. Te-Chi and its three downstream reservoirs has a combined hydropower generating capacity of 865 Megawatts which is almost 6% of the total installed power capacity on Taiwan. Water released from Te-Chi is used for irrigation (mainly rice) and domestic water supply (Taichung County and City) from Shih-Kang Reservoir downstream. The growing demand on water and power in the region has rendered the allocation of the water resources in Ta-Chia River, especially during drought periods, a very difficult task in recent years.

Present operations of the reservoirs are based entirely on rule curves. At the beginning of each hydrologic year, a coordination meeting is called by the Water Resources Planning Commission. Based on the streamflow data prior to the meeting and historical data, a suitable operating policy is negotiated among all water users. Further monthly meetings are called to review the policy based on observed streamflow conditions.

The objective of this study is to develop a practical model for the optimal operation of the reservoirs in Ta-Chia River Basin. The period considered in the model is 10-day, the traditional reservoir operation period in Taiwan. The reservoir inflow in the model was to be given by a time series streamflow forecasting scheme and the model was to be executable on personal computers. Because Te-Chi is the only storage (and the largest) reservoir in the basin, the optimization model considers only Te-Chi Reservoir. The other three downstream regulating reservoirs are lumped together as release points. Incremental inflow downstream of Te-Chi Reservoir is considered.

Streamflow Forecast Scheme

Using similar methodologies from a previous study (*Kuo, et al., 1990*), an ARX(1,0) model was developed for forecasting 10-day streamflow to Te-Chi Reservoir. The model equation can be expressed as

$$q_t = aq_{t-1} + bp_t + \epsilon_t \tag{1}$$

where q_t and q_{t-1} are streamflows at time t and $t-1$ respectively, p_t is the forecasted precipitation (*given by Central Weather Bureau*) at time t, ϵ_t is a standard normally distributed random variable, and a and b are coefficients that can be determined from historical data.

The above ARX model is also equipped with a Kalman Filter routine to allow constant updating of the forecasted streamflow based on observed data. The forecast model has been satisfactorily tested and compared with observed streamflow record of 1987. Further study of the model's sensitivity to precipitation forecast has confirmed that forecasted streamflow is better with more accurate precipitation forecast.

Optimization Model and Applicaton Results

The objective function of the model is to minimize sum of the weighted differences between the targets (hydropower, water supply, and irrigation) and the releases (to be determined by the model). The objective function is subject to the contraints of flow continuity, penstock, water intake, release structures, and reservoir storage limitations. The optimization problem is solved by a discrete differential dynamic programming routine developed by the authors (*Kuo, et al., 1990*).

The preliminary application of the model has shown that the model is capable of improving the present operation of Te-Chi Reservoir by reducing the water shortage downstream while providing a more uniform power production schedule. The difference is due to the facts that the current rule curve operation is too conservative and the optimization model produces a more rational rule based on its better forecasted streamflow. Further improvements to the model, including the consideration of risk and reliability factors in its formulation, are underway.

Acknowledgement

The work upon which this presentation is based was supported by the Water Resources Planning Commission of the Republic of China. The continuing support of Chairman Hong-Hsi Hsu of the Commission is deeply appreciated. The streamflow forecast scheme and the dynamic programming routine are developed and applied by Youn-Jan Lin and Shian Wan respectively.

Reference

Kuo, J-T., Hsu, N-S., Chu, W-S., Wan, S. and Lin, Y-J., 1989. " Real-Time Operation of Tanshui River Reservoir ", paper to appear in the Journal of Water Resources Planning and Management, ASCE, 1990.

Appropriate Cost Factors for System Reliability

P. Jacobs[1] and I. Goulter[1], A.M. ASCE

Abstract

Reliability of networks, such as water distribution systems, must be assessed in terms of the possibility of failure of the system and the implications or costs of that failure. This paper examines the development of appropriate costs to be associated with various levels of failure of water distribution networks and water supply systems. A clear distinction is made between "hard", costs which are usually economic, and "soft" costs normally associated with the social implications of the failure. As the disruption caused by a system failure increases these, "soft" costs actually become hard and determine the response to the failure.

Introduction

The design of reliable networked systems is of interest in a number of fields including urban water supply, electrical distribution, and computer communications. A number of models have been proposed to aid in the design of such systems in the water supply field, e.g., Morgan and Goulter (1985), Su et al. (1987) and Lansey et al. (1989), and the systems supplying them, e.g., Hobbs and Biem (1988) and Biem and Hobbs (1988). These models generally use a cost function based on some combination of the cost to maintain and build and the cost to repair such systems. Reliability implications beyond the purely economic aspects are usually brought into the procedures only as constraints.

The advantages of the "constrained reliability" approach are that it is computationally more tractable and that the costs considered are the easily documentable "hard" costs. The main disadvantage of the method is that it does not adequately take into account the "soft" costs that arise when a system is not sufficiently reliable. The effects of insufficient reliability range from those effects which are a minor nuisance to extremely severe effects that can make a system unusable. The costs associated with these effects range from nil, in cases where a minor nuisance can be ignored or tolerated, to the scrapping or replacement of the system if reliability is sufficiently impaired.

The best way to describe these issues for water distribution systems is to detail specific examples. System failures are related in a qualitative manner to the cost base

---

[1]Dept. of Civ. Eng., Univ. of Manitoba, Winnipeg, Manitoba, Canada, R3T 2N2.

that should be used to judge whether the investment of resources is justified for their prevention. It is asserted, again in a qualitative manner, that as the disruption caused by a system failure increases in severity, frequency and duration, the "soft" costs can in fact become quite "hard" and may even exceed or overwhelm both the total capital and maintenance costs of a system. Four specific failures are proposed with both "hard" and "soft" costs identified for each case. These examples, in increasing levels of severity are:

1. A one time localized interruption of service caused by a pipe break. Duration less than 4 hours.

2. A series of intermittent failures caused by repeated breaks of a sector main. Duration of each break around 24 hours.

3. Failure of a main carrying approximately 1/2 of city inflow. Duration of outage 1 month.

4. Pollution of a major water supply well rendering it unusable for a number of years.

Discussion

The "hard" costs of Case I, representing an unrepeated, localized interruption of service of short duration caused by a pipe break, are:

i) loss of water (which was treated and transported with energy costs);
ii) cost of material to repair the pipe; and
iii) cost of labor to repair the pipe.

The "soft" costs in this case are:

i) inconvenience to the water utilities customers during the failure and repair; and
ii) system overhead labor spent explaining when service is to be restored.

It should be noted that in this case the event does not greatly disrupt the normal working of the water distribution system. This statement assumes of course that there is sufficient redundancy in the system to provide adequate fire service while the pipe is out of service. The "soft" costs amount to nuisance value for both utility customers and utility management, the cost of which is very difficult to estimate. The "hard" costs on the other hand are easily calculable and so predominate in this instance.

The case of a series of intermittent failures caused by repeated breaks of a sector main (Case II) is more serious with respect to system integrity and consumer service. The "hard" costs in this case are the three costs listed for Case I plus the cost of providing minimally adequate replacement water supplies.

The "soft" costs, however, are:

i) inconvenience to the water utilities customers;
ii) frequent disruption of traffic near the sector main breaks;
iii) increased risk of inadequate water pressure for fire fighting;
iv) loss of confidence by the water users in the system's reliability and safety;
v) system overhead labor spent dealing with the problem; and
vi) risk of contamination of water from ground water infiltration during periods of low water pressure.

In this case, the operation of the system is impaired to a much greater degree than in the first case. Because of the increased area affected by the breaks and their repetitive nature the "hard" costs have increased significantly. The "soft" costs, however, are no longer simply a nuisance to be ignored. They are a significant factor in the justification of any expenditures necessary to repair the situation, and should a major fire occur, would become "hard" costs very quickly.

Another point to note for this case is that it is very difficult to justify watermain replacement on a purely economic or "hard" basis. The cost of repairing a broken watermain (as long as it is not the primary water supply to a particular area), is, generally, far less than the cost of replacing the pipe. This situation holds for even repeated failures in relatively short lengths of pipe. In Gothenburg, Sweden, engineers working on watermain failure problems there have stated that it would take up to 8 or 9 breaks per kilometer of pipe per year before there was economic justification for replacing the pipe. However, the social pressure to have the pipe repaired, i.e., the "soft" costs, would necessitate replacing the pipe well before the breakage rate reached 8 or 9 breaks per kilometer per year (G. Swensson, personal communication).

For Case III, namely, a failure of a major watermain carrying 1/2 of city inflow for 1 month, the types of "hard" and "soft" costs are unchanged from the previous case. The major difference in this case is the extended period of inadequate pressure and flow that would result from this failure. There is a strong likelihood that adequate fire fighting capacity could not be maintained during the extended period of time when the main is inoperative. In effect, the cost of the main failing could be severe fire damage to a large part of the city with its "hard" economic costs plus the nonquantifiable cost associated with exposing the population to the much increased fire risk plus the political implication of such a situation. This "soft" cost could be greater than the value of the entire water supply system.

The final example of pollution of a major water supply well rendering it unusable for a number of years has only one "hard" cost associated with it, namely, the cost of obtaining a new usable water supply. In this case the "soft" cost of risk of waterborne disease is the major reason for changing the water supply. In fact the "soft" cost is the "hard" cost, part of which can be enumerated through assessment of the high legal costs and possible health care costs associated with this situation. The economic role of construction and repair costs is limited to a selection of the best option for replacement of the supply rather than a decision on whether to act at all.

Another general factor which should be considered in the relationship between "soft" and "hard" costs lies in the perception of the consumer as to the implications of a particular situation. Ziess (1989) asserts that society tends to weight losses from the status quo more heavily than the gains. In other words, the cost of loss of one unit of service is greater than the value of an increase of one unit of service. The loss is viewed far more critically. Consumers tend to favour preventative measures more than engineers despite possible higher economic cots. Hence the losses in service associated with the last three cases are likely to have considerably more "soft" costs than might be anticipated by technical managers. In fact "soft" costs start to dominate the decision process earlier.

Conclusions

This paper presents a number of examples of possible water supply and distribution failures. In a qualitative way it is shown that as the extent, duration and severity of a failure increases, the costs associated with building or repairing the system tend to increase only in direct proportion to the physical extent of the failure. On the other hand, costs which are less easily quantifiable such as consumer inconvenience or possible health and fire hazards, but which are the original justification for creating a reliable water supply system, can easily increase beyond the "hard" cost, and in some cases reaching the total value of the entire water supply system.

References

Biem, G. and Hobbs, B. (1988). "Analytical simulation of water system reliability, 2; A Markov chain approach and verification of the models", Water Resources Research, 24 (a), 1445-1458.

Hobbs, B. and Biem, G. (1988). "Analytical simulation of water system capacity reliability, 1; Modified frequency-duration analysis", Water Resources Research, 24(a), 1431-1444.

Lansey, K., Duan, N., Mays, L. and Tung, Y. (1989). "Water distribution system design under uncertainties", Journal of the Water Resources Planning and Management Division, ASCE, 115 (5), 630-657.

Morgan, D.R. and Goulter, I.C. (1985). "Optimal urban water distribution design", Water Resources Research, 21 (5), 642-652.

Su, Y., Mays, L., Duan, N. and Lansey, K. (1987). "Reliability based optimization model for water distribution systems", Journal of the Hydraulics Division, ASCE, 114 (12), 1539-1557.

Ziess, C. (1989). "Impact management priorities of waste facilities: Differences between host community residents' and technical decision makers' values", submitted to Journal of Environmental Sciences

Estimating the Energy Rate Function for Hydro Power Production Optimization

Karolj K. Reznicek[1] and Slobodan P. Simonovic[2]

Abstract

Operations planning at Manitoba Hydro is aided by using the Energy Management and Maintenance Analysis (EMMA) computer program. EMMA is a Linear Programming based model with the objective of maximizing system revenue and minimizing generation costs (Barritt-Flatt and Cormie, 1988). Due to the nonlinear character of the hydro production function an approximation has to be introduced in order to apply the LP problem formulation. EMMA approximates the hydro production function by assuming a constant head from one iteration to the other. At the University of Manitoba a Successive Linear Programming (SLP) approach is applied to solve the same optimization problem. SLP approximates the hydro production function by a first order Taylor series expansion around the chosen points of the solution space. The approach requires a smooth and differentiable analytic function for the energy rate function to be derived. The paper presents the direct application of the regression analysis to the measured data to derive the energy rate function. The approach is illustrated using the data for Kettle reservoir in Manitoba.

Introduction

Planning the operations of the Manitoba Integrated Generation System involves scheduling reservoir releases from 13 reservoirs for subsequent generation at 13 hydro generating stations and scheduling 2 thermal power station production. The operations planning at Manitoba Hydro is aided by the use of EMMA program. The basic purpose of the program is to determine the optimal releases from the reservoirs and to maximize the net revenue of the electric utility. The program optimizes the production, taking into account the interconnections of the system with the adjacent electric utilities by tielines. The surplus energy produced in the system can be exported, and the system demand can be satisfied from the import if needed.

Given the system configuration, load requirement, inflow and time structure EMMA formulates and iteratively resolves the linear problem. The LP problem is formulated to minimize costs of import energy, hydraulic and thermal generation, to maximize benefits from interruptible export sales and from the stored water for future

---

[1]Research Assistant, Dept. of Civ. Eng., Univ. of Manitoba, Winnipeg, Manitoba, Canada, R3T 2N2.
[2]Associate Professor, Dept. of Civ. Eng., Univ. of Manitoba, Winnipeg, Manitoba, Canada, R3T 2N2.

production, while satisfying the system load and contracted export requirements. The Energy Management by Successive Linear Programming (EMSLP) offers an alternative way to model the nonlinear hydro production function while keeping the same problem formulation of optimizing the production of the interconnected utility (Reznicek and Simonovic, 1989).

Description of the EMSLP Program and the Energy Rate Function

In the EMSLP program the nonlinear hydro energy production relationship is approximated by a first order Taylor series expansion around the estimated values of the solution space. The hydro energy relationship has the following form:

$$E = \text{gamma} \times Q \times H \times T \times e(Q, H) \tag{1}$$

The energy equation (1) can be written in the following form:

$$E = R \times ERF \tag{2}$$

where ERF stands for Energy Rate Function:

$$ERF = \text{gamma} \times H \times e. \tag{3}$$

ERF denotes the specific produced energy per unit volume released from the turbines of the power plant. R stands for release:

$$R = Q \times T \tag{4}$$

The ERF is a function of head H and discharge Q. However, since the head is a function of the reservoir stage and the tailwater level it can be described as the function of discharge Q, spill S and storage ST. Therefore the ERF can be described as:

$$ERF = ERF(ST, R, S) \tag{5}$$

Usually the plant is operated so that spill does not occur. Therefore the ERF relationship can be described for these cases as

$$ERF = ERF(ST, R) \tag{6}$$

This relationship is dependant on the specific characteristics of the power plant and the form of the function cannot be known in advance. However, the linear approximation procedure of first order Taylor series expansion requires an analytical function which has to be smooth and differentiable around the points of expansion. The shape of the ERF depends on the specific characteristics of the power plant and cannot be known in advance.

Two alternative ways are studied to derive the desired multivariate functional relationship. One of the alternatives is to directly relate the power plant measurements of power, discharge and reservoir storage to the value of the energy rate function by applying a regression fit. The other approach is to separately model the dependencies of the plant efficiency and tailwater on the storage, discharge and spill. The separately derived relationships are then combined into the energy rate function. The first approach has been presented in this paper.

The Integral Regression Analysis Approach

In this approach regression analysis is directly applied to the measured data. The stage-storage relationship of the reservoir is the only relationship which has to be known in advance. The latter is needed to include the storage variable in the analysis via the observed stage of the forebay. In this way the ERF is derived straightly from the observations taken at the power plant. The observations include the value of the power, discharge through the turbines, the value of the head and the tailwater level. Since a multivariate function has to be fit to the data a great number of observations are needed to obtain a reasonable accuracy of the estimated parameters of the model. The observations have to cover the full range of possible values of the head and discharge of the power plant.

The approach was practically applied to the measurements on the Kettle hydro power plant on the Nelson River in northern Manitoba (Manitoba Hydro, 1987). According to the preceding guidelines 360 observations were taken to cover the full range of the discharge from 5 to 170 KCFS (KCFS - 28.37 m^3) with increments of 5 KCFS and the reservoir operation range of 5 ft (ft - 0.305 m) with the increments of 0.5 ft. A second order polynomial fit was tried to be applied to the data. Two different schemes were attempted. They had the following form:

$$ERF = B_0 + B_1 \times ST + B_2 \times Q + B_{11} \times ST^2 + B_{12} \times ST \times Q + B_{22} \times Q \times Q \quad (7)$$

$$ERF = B_0 + B_1 \times ST^{-5} + B_2 \times Q + B_{11} \times ST^2 + B_{12} \times ST \times Q + B_{22} \times Q \times Q \quad (8)$$

Where B-s denote the coefficients of the model which have to be determined. The STEPWISE and RSQUARE procedures of SAS were used to evaluate the partial and full models of the above form. The full range of the input data did not show satisfactory results. The coefficient of multiple determination R^2 did not exceed the value of 0.55 for any of the models. The weakness of the fit could be anticipated from the shape of the ERF surface given in Figure 1. Due to the specific characteristics of the surface, which has a zig-zag shape for the low flow values, the application of a second order polynomial model could not give a satisfactory fit to the data. The oscillation of the energy rate function value for the small value of discharge is due to the change in the efficiency levels at which the turbines operate. These are specific situations where the total plant discharge is more than the capacity of one or two unit's capacity but the addition of another unit makes the average unit discharge much less than the optimal value. For example if the unit's optimal operation is 10 KCFS and the capacity is 13 KCFS, then for the situation of 15 KCFS total plant discharge, two units have to be activated with the 7.5 KCFS average discharge level. The operation of the plant under these circumstances is not energy efficient and therefore in practical situations this cannot occur. Therefore, eliminating these discharge values from the data set is not a deficiency of the approach. The data where the discharge ranges from 35 to 170 KCFS has the ERF surface which is substantially smoother than the original. Applying the same modelling scheme the results were substantially better. The R^2 values were almost equal to 0.9 which is substantially better than for the original data.

HYDRO POWER OPTIMIZATION 51

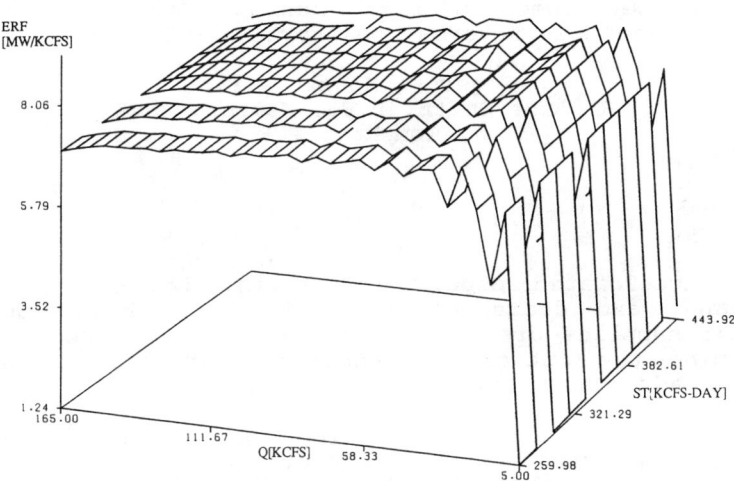

Figure 1. The energy rate function surface

Conclusions

Using the SLP approach in approximating the hydro production function by a first order Taylor series expansion requires a smooth and differentiable energy rate function. Application of the regression analysis has been shown to be one approach in deriving the analytical form of the energy rate function. This approach seems to be viable, but it needs a careful analysis of the range of the input data for which it can be applied. The work is in progress to derive the energy rate function by modelling separately the dependencies of the plant efficiency and tailwater on the storage, discharge and spill.

Acknowledgements

The financial support and cooperation of the experts from Manitoba Hydro is gratefully acknowledged.

References

Barritt-Flatt, P.E. and Cormie, A.D. (1988), "A Comprehensive Optimization Model for Hydro-Electric Reservoir Operations", Proceedings, Computerized Decision Support Systems for Water Managers, ASCE.

Manitoba Hydro (1987), Kettle Reservoir Operations Data Book, Manitoba Hydro Report.

Reznicek, K.K. and Simonovic, S.P. (1989), "An Improved Method for Hydropower Optimization", Water Resources Research, in print.

The Development of Lake Granbury SWATS Regional
Electrodialysis Reversal Demineralizer Treatment Plant

Roger K. Noack, P.E.[1]
R. Anne Smith, P.E., Member, ASCE[1]
J. Tom Ray, P.E.[2]

Abstract

Accelerated population growth, increasing water demand, and decreased availability of high quality water supplies are forcing communities to more closely examine the option of treating lower quality water using advanced treatment processes.

Due to high population growth and rapidly declining groundwater levels, the Brazos River Authority of Texas initiated a regional study to evaluate existing and potential surface water supply sources capable of meeting the needs of Johnson County, Texas. The study found that advanced treatment of abundant, but saline (brackish) water supplies stored in existing reservoirs was more economical than the development of new, higher quality, surface water sources.

This paper summarizes the planning, design, and proposed operation of the Lake Granbury Surface Water and Treatment System (SWATS) electrodialysis reversal (EDR) plant, which is presently the largest inland municipal demineralizer water treatment plant in Texas.

Introduction

Lake Granbury is a surface water impoundment on the Brazos River in Texas. Because the Salt Fork of the Brazos river discharges brackish water into the river upstream of Lake Granbury, raw water in the lake has a high dissolved solids content. The historic maximum total dissolved solids (TDS) has reached 2,200 mg/l and the chloride concentration has approached 1,000 mg/l.

---

[1]Project Manager, HDR Engineering, Inc., 3000 South IH 35, Suite 400, Austin, Texas 78704
[2]Planning Division Manager, Brazos River Authority, 4400 Cobbs Drive, Waco, Texas 76710

TREATMENT PLANT DEVELOPMENT

The current State of Texas standards for potable water are 1,000 mg/l for TDS and 300 mg/l for chlorides. Therefore, an advanced water treatment process is required to produce potable water. In order to determine the most effective treatment process, a water quality sampling and monitoring program was instituted on the lake for one year. In addition, baseline levels of all 83 contaminants proposed for regulation under the 1986 Safe Drinking Water Act Amendments were monitored. The level of each contaminant was considered during design of the treatment plant to ensure compliance with the regulations.

Based on the results of the sampling program, it was decided to design the plant so that when it is operating at full capacity, it can supply an acceptable potable water when the raw water contains 90% of the historical levels of TDS, chlorides and sulfates. If the water contains more than 90% of the historical levels of these constituents, which will rarely occur, it was decided to reduce the plant capacity. This is possible because the plant's customers also obtain a portion of their water supply from groundwater. The design criteria for the plant is shown below in Table 1.

Table 1

Lake Granbury EDR Plant - Design Criteria

Consti- tuent	Raw Water Historical Levels (mg/l)			90% values less than (mg/l)	Finish Water (mg/l)	State Maximum Allow- able (mg/l)
	Annual Avg	High	Low			
TDS	1430	2200	510	2020	950	1000
Chlorides	525	820	145	750	275	300
Sulfates	275	510	85	400	275	300

The advanced treatment process selected to treat the Lake Granbury raw water was electrodialysis reversal. This is an electrochemical separation process in which ions are transferred through membranes from a less to a more concentrated solution as a result of the flow of direct electric current (DC).

The more concentrated solution, noted above, becomes a waste stream from the EDR process. The most economical means of disposal of this concentrated solution is to discharge it directly back into Lake Granbury. A waste discharge permit was required by the Texas Water Commission for this discharge. Water quality impact studies were conducted which showed that the designated stream standards would not be violated by the discharge, and the local impacts to fish would not be adverse, as the discharge is into and remains within the hypolimnion of the reservoir where there is not enough dissolved oxygen to support fishlife. The permitted discharge limitations are shown in Table 2.

Table 2

Lake Granbury EDR Plant - Permitted Discharge			
	Discharge Limitations (mg/l)		
Constituent	Daily Average	Daily Maximum	Single Grab
Chlorides	9,900	14,200	25,500
Sulfates	4,700	5,000	5,700

Design

The Rules and Regulations of the Texas Department of Health require conventional treatment of a public water supplied from a surface water source. Also, conventional treatment was necessary in order to remove suspended solids to an acceptable level before treatment by the EDR process. See Figure 1 for the Flow Schematic of the Lake Granbury SWATS Water Treatment Plant.

The conventional treatment portion of the plant includes two stage rapid mix basin where aluminum sulfate (alum) is added for coagulation and sodium hydroxide (caustic) is added for pH adjustment. It also includes solids contact clarification using polymer as a flocculation aid, dual media filtration, and filtered water storage. Chloramination is added as a primary disinfectant at the Raw Water Pump Station, intermediate points in the plant, and as a secondary disinfectant before the water leaves the plant.

The system which pumps filtered water from the Filtered Water Storage Tank to the EDR units maintains the set feed pressure required for the operation of the EDR units. Before water reaches the EDR units, 10 micron cartridge filters remove any suspended particles that may have passed the dual media filters.

TREATMENT PLANT DEVELOPMENT

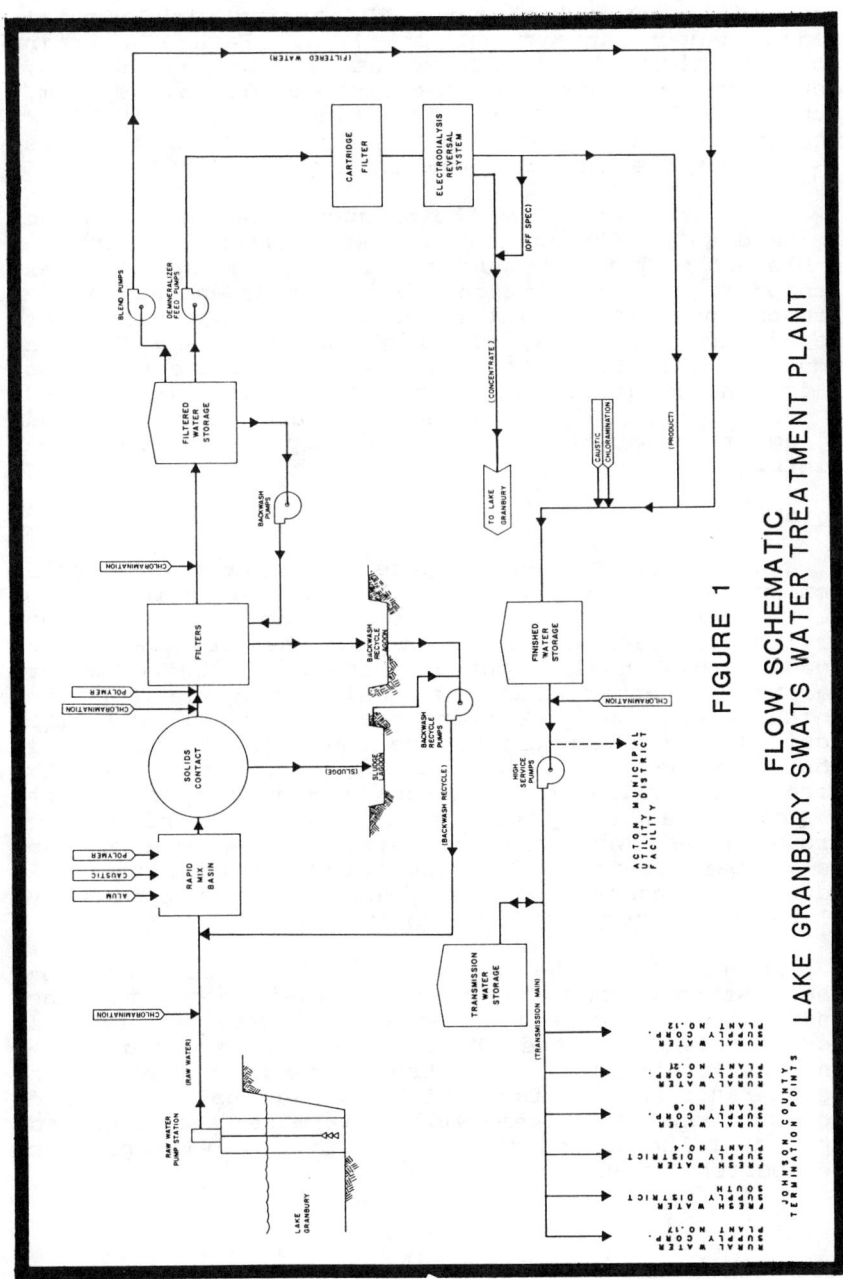

FIGURE 1
FLOW SCHEMATIC
LAKE GRANBURY SWATS WATER TREATMENT PLANT

The electrodialysis reversal demineralization system is comprised of three EDR trains with a total product water capacity of 3.5 MGD. Each EDR train includes eight lines of two-stage membrane stacks, rectifiers, a concentrate recycle and blowdown system, a chemical feed system for injecting a scale inhibiter into the concentrate recycle system, and clean-in-place systems for cleaning the membrane stacks.

From the EDR units, the product water flows to the Finished Water Storage Tank, where filtered water can be blended with the product water. The amount of water blended from each of these sources is dependent on the product and filtered water quality and the demands of the system. Finally, the High Service Pump Station pumps the finished water from storage at the plant to an in-line Transmission Storage Tank, which is located at the high point of the system, and to the ground storage tanks at the project participants' termination points.

Operation

The quality of the raw water to be treated at this facility will vary significantly, due to inflows into the reservoir. This will result in the need for varying degrees of treatment of the raw water to produce a high quality potable water. If the raw water quality is better than the design criteria for the finish water, only conventional treatment will be required. At other times, the raw water quality will require blending of the product water from the EDR process with filtered water from conventional treatment to produce an acceptable finish water. Under some circumstances, when the raw water quality exceeds the design parameters, only product water from the EDR system will comprise the finished water that will be delivered to the plant's customers.

To assist in the operation of this facility, on-line instrumentation has been provided to monitor the conductivity of the raw water, filtered water, and product water from the EDR process. In addition, on-line instrumentation and controls have been provided so the Operator can set the finished water quality desired and the control system will determine the required ratio of filtered and product water which will produce the desired finish water.

DEVELOPING A WASTEWATER PLAN FOR AN URBANIZING AREA
-THE CASE OF JOHNSON COUNTY, TEXAS

by

Adrian J. Huckabee, P.E. *

Johnson County, Texas, is located south of Ft. Worth, Texas, and is influenced by the entire Dallas-Ft. Worth Metroplex, which has a population of more than 3 million people. The rapid population growth of Johnson County in the 1980's and the resulting proliferation of substandard on-site wastewater disposal systems and package wastewater treatment plants has caused concern among the citizens of the County. Situations such as have occurred in one large subdivision in the northeast part of the county, where untreated wastewater has been found flowing in drainage ditches in residential areas, are indeed alarming. Also of concern is the projection (by many qualified sources) that the County's population will more than double in the next 20 to 30 years. In order to maintain an acceptable quality of life for its citizens, many leaders in Johnson County have joined forces with the State of Texas to develop a long-term plan for managing wastewater.

In 1988 the County, acting through the Commissioners Court, Johnson County Rural Water Supply Corporation (JCRWSC) and Johnson County Fresh Water Supply District No. 1 (JCFWSD), applied to the Texas Water Development Board (TWDB) to obtain a matching grant for the purpose of developing a plan to effectively correct existing problems and manage future needs in wastewater disposal on a county-wide basis. In early 1989 the grant was approved and work was initiated in May. The results of this planning effort are summarized in this paper.

Johnson County is located on the divide between the Trinity and Brazos Rivers. There are 12 major drainage basins within the County. Because of the terrain, regionalization of wastewater in the County becomes a management phenomenon rather than one characterized by a single (or even a few) collection system(s). Because of this, there are many separate service areas in the plan, even though they are all referred to as "regional." The approach in developing the systems was to focus on those service areas where centralized

*HDR Engineering Inc., Austin, TX

systems appear to be feasible, relative to other options for wastewater treatment and disposal.

BASIS AND APPROACH

The basis on which the centralized wastewater collection and treatment systems are defined for the target years 2020 and 1990 are the population projections and the use of drainage basin topography in determining the potential physical characteristics of the systems. From the population projections the projected wastewater flows can be determined. The reason for dividing these populations particularly in the rural areas can be seen in the following discussion when relating the potential developed systems to each drainage basin. In this study the term regional is not limited to any particular geographic boundary. For instance a regional facility might cross drainage basin divides.

Another basis for determining the economic feasibility of regional systems is the comparison of monthly costs with that of the typical amortization cost of an on-site disposal system at a residence. Assuming that a typical home mortgage is at a 10% interest rate and that the mortgage has a term of 30 years, the approximate monthly cost of a $5,000 on-site disposal system is $48 per month. Since economic feasibility deals with the allocation of resources among equally effective methods of problem solving, then this provides a comparison basis for determining what might be feasible in centralized systems. Therefore, in each of the evaluations we compared the monthly cost of the operation and maintenance and the capital amortization per connection to a typical house connection. Those systems which fell near the $48 per month cost or less where considered economically feasible and viable alternatives.

The approach to identifying regional systems was to first look at those feasible systems which could be in place by year 2020. Utilizing year 2020 as a planning target year we have an approximate 30-year planning horizon. Those systems in year 2020 which appear to have promising cost profiles will then be evaluated as to the feasibility for year 1990 development. After identifying systems potentially feasible by year 1990, the next step is determining the various phases of development between 1990 and year 2020 which will result in the ultimate development of the 2020 plan. For those systems which are not feasible in year 1990

URBANIZING AREA WASTEWATER PLAN   59

then an attempt will be made to identify the year
within the planning horizon in which the initial
development may occur and then identifying the path
which needs to be taken to reach regional development
by year 2020.

YEAR 2020 REGIONAL WASTEWATER SYSTEMS

The regional systems will not be developed "overnight."
Decisions will be made at each point of wastewater
service expansion and at each regulatory change to more
stringent effluent limitations which will either follow
a "regional" approach or will not. For this reason it
is important to evaluate the future conditions first.
If regional systems are not economically feasible using
future population densities, then they will almost
certainly not be for current conditions.

By year 2020 there will be significant economic
justification for the development of regional
wastewater collection and treatment systems. These
regional systems will be less costly than either on-
site disposal or individual municipal systems. The
average total monthly cost per connection (in current
dollars) for these systems ranges from $19 to $49. For
comparison, the average on-site system costs about $48
per month when amortized within a typical residential
mortgage (10%, 30 years).

YEAR 1990 REGIONAL WASTEWATER SYSTEMS

The areas needing centralized wastewater collection and
treatment systems in Johnson County in the year 1990
are largely in the rural areas. Therefore, it is not
surprising that the cost effectiveness of regional
systems is not as good for the year 1990 as the year
2020. Also the number of potential systems is less
than in the year 2020. The main reason for these
differences has to do with the population densities
that are in place currently versus those that will be
in place by year 2020 according to the population
projections.

Although the number of potential systems is limited in
the year 1990, there are several groups of subdivisions
in the rural areas outside of any existing municipal
jurisdiction that appear to have affordable costs for
new wastewater collection and treatment systems. As
many as 4,000 connections appear to be feasible at the
present time.

While several entities within the County have portions of the sum of the authorities needed, no one entity can function as a regional manager. The County has jurisdiction over subdivision regulations and the Texas Department of Health has transferred the on-site regulatory authority in the County to the County government. However, counties in Texas cannot create another political subdivision having wastewater service authority, as they can with water in the creation of W.C.I.D.'s. Home rule cities have complete authority in this area but as a matter of policy do not provide service outside their city limits. The JCFWSD also has the appropriate authority and can even contract with other entities to provide financing and management. However, again the JCFWSD is limited in direct service area by its statutory boundaries. The several rural water supply corporations in the County have no such authority in wastewater.

The only way to establish a single entity with all the authority and geographical coverage is to have one created by the State Legislature. Considering the political difficulty such an act would have, it was not the recommended institutional approach.

The County ultimately should have a wastewater management agency whose jurisdiction would be county-wide. The agency would assume the on-site disposal authority of the Commissioner's Court, have the authority to contract with other political subdivisions and non-profit homeowner's organizations in the County to provide them service and/or financing through revenue bonds, develop and operate facilities for proper collection and treatment of septage, and implement regional centralized wastewater facilities.

As an interim institutional approach, there are entities and mechanisms available to initiate the development of a regional wastewater management system. JCFWSD can contract with other entities, including cities, to provide watewater service for those entities. Examples of such entities are municipal utility districts (MUD), water control and improvement districts (WCID), water supply corporations (WSC), and non-profit homeowners organizations. Another option for the areas near municipalities which have centralized systems is for citizens in these areas to request annexation and thus acquire wastewater service through the city.

FINANCIAL

There are several mechanisms in Texas to finance public wastewater projects. However, it is clear that the initial projects which are located outside the boundaries of an existing wastewater authority cannot be financed through the bond market. There are too many limitations on the power to require connection to an existing system and to enforce payment by controlling the water meter to satisfy the bond market's security interest. Certainly, as the regional system grows and establishes a track record, future projects can be financed through the bond market.

The initial projects be financed with State of Texas Water Quality Enhancement Bonds. These bonds are available for this purpose and have terms and rates similar to those in the bond market. There will need to be a preliminary engineering report prepared to provide the evidence to the Texas Water Development Board (TWDB) that the following conditions exist for each project proposed:

    1. That sufficient numbers of residents in the service areas desire service and will contract for service.

    2. That the most cost-effective engineering plans are proposed for each service area.

    3. That the plans are part of a regional approach to wastewater management.

    4. That the proposed financing can be amortized by the service area over the life of the bonds.

Financing Water Supply and Wastewater
Facilities in Low Income Areas

G.E. "Sonny" Kretzschmar [1]

Abstract

The Texas Water Development Fund (the "Fund") was created by amendment to the Texas Constitution in 1957 as a reaction to the droughts of the 1950's. This amendment empowered the Texas Water Development Board (the "Board") to issue $200,000,000 in Water Development Bonds, general obligations of the State of Texas, to develop water storage projects and systems necessary for the wholesale distribution of water.

Subsequent amendments to the Texas Constitution have increased the amount of Water Development Bonds authorized and expanded the type of projects eligible for financing. Projects for wastewater and flood control are now acceptable for financing and have received appropriate bond authorization.

Another program, the State Participation Account, allows the Board to finance projects which anticipate growth, by initially purchasing a portion of the project and the borrower buying the state's portion in the future.

As cf August 31, 1989, the Board has available the following unissued bonding authority:

Water Supply   - $201,840,000

Wastewater   - $288,660,000

Flood Control   - $199,000,000

State Participation - $400,000,000

---

[1] Executive Administrator, Texas Water Development Board, P.O. Box 13231, Capitol Station, Austin, Texas 78711-3231.

WATER SUPPLY FINANCING

Financing programs are available to all eligible political subdivisions (municipalities, districts and authorities) as well as non-profit water supply corporations. Of the following three eligibility requirements, a borrower or the project must meet at least one:

1. Hardship - defined as the inability of the borrower to sell its own bonds on the commercial bond market at a reasonable interest rate.

2. Conversion of the water supply from ground to surface water.

3. Regional project - defined as a project that will provide service to two or more eligible borrowers or a project that will provide service to an area outside the borrower's boundaries.

The Board evidences its project financing through the purchase of the borrower's bonds; the transaction is called a loan. No state appropriated funds are provided and the borrower pays all debt service. The Board has closed on 739 projects for a total of approximately $843,000,000 without default on a single loan.

Since the Fund relies not on appropriated funds but on the ability of the borrower to repay a loan, it has been difficult for the Board to finance projects in low income areas, especially those that exist outside the boundaries of an eligible borrower.

In reaction to the growing health problems caused by the unsanitary conditions in these poorer areas of the state and the inability of the inhabitants of these areas to pay for the necessary water and wastewater facilities; the 71st Legislature of the State of Texas passed, in 1989, Senate Bill 2 ("SB2"). The intent of this legislation is to provide financial assistance to these economically distressed areas.

This bill provides up to $100,000,000 in Water Development Bonds for water and wastewater project financing to eligible borrowers. Eligible borrowers are political subdivisions within certain counties as defined by statute.

While the needed facilities could possibly be financed through both the commercial and private debt markets, the costs associated with these financing mechanisms would be prohibitive. Therefore, SB2 will authorize the Board to provide financial assistance, for which repayment is not required, of up to fifty percent of the principal and interest of the loan. However, in cases where the Texas Department of Health issues a finding that a public nuisance exists within the area to be served, then greater repayment of the debt may be financed by the state. At no time, though, may the amount paid by the state exceed seventy-five percent of the $100,000,000.

To determine the amount of the loan to be repaid, SB2 provided for a borrower's "ability to pay." This is defined by statute as "rates, fees and charges that the average customer to be served by the project will be able to pay based on a comparison of what other families of similar income who are similarly situated pay for comparable services." The state will agree to pay the area's proportionate share, based on "ability to pay," of the required project capital cost.

To stop proliferation of these areas, the county in which the applicant exists must approve model rules for development of subdivisions. These rules, which encompass water and wastewater service have been designed by a joint committee of the Board, the Texas Water Commission, the Texas Department of Health and the Texas Attorney General's Office.

There are still situations that have not been resolved that will determine the future timing of project financing. One crucial example is the lack of residential facilities, i.e. bathrooms. Another question to solve is that of determining which political subdivision will borrow these funds. Financing for these facilities must be solved prior to the Board's sale of bonds!

Obviously, there are still many questions to be answered. However, due to this growing health menace within our state, SB2 will make the first large scale attempt to address this situation.

"The Spirit of Bandera"
An Experiment in Inter-Agency Team-Building

Barry G. Rought[1]

ABSTRACT

An experiment to improve intergovernmental cooperation in water resources planning and management was initiated by the Southwestern Division, U.S. Army Corps of Engineers, in 1988 at Bandera, Texas. Four Federal agencies and Texas Parks and Wildlife Department came together in a team-building experience. These agencies initiated a 2-day team briefing session facilitated and led by a specialist in interpersonal relationships. The exercise facilitated professional cooperation leading to a better product and more productive use of tax dollars.

INTRODUCTION

Improvement in intergovernmental cooperation in water resources planning and management has been needed for many years. A step towards obtaining some fullfillment of this need began in late 1988 at Bandera, Texas.

A remote conference ranch near Bandera, Texas, was the site where field and regional level personnel from four Federal agencies and a state agency, who have historically clashed over National Environmental Protection Act (NEPA) and environmental issues, were brought together in a team-building experience. The U.S. Army Corps of Engineers, Fish and Wildlife Service, National Marine Fisheries Service, Environmental Protection Agency, and the Texas Parks and Wildlife Department, initiated this effort consisting of a 2-day session facilitated and led by a highly qualified specialist in interpersonal relationships.

----

[1]Chief, Planning Division, U.S. Army Corps of Engineers, 1114 Commerce Street, Dallas, Texas 75242-0216

The relational setting for the team-building was one of hostility concerning major water projects. The situation had become critical concerning very controversial environmental issues on several projects that had led to polarized positions of individual agency members. Other areas of major controversy were the maintenance of completed projects and administration of the regulatory program.

A proposed large navigation project, as well as several controversial regulatory permits, brought the confrontation to a boiling point and served to crystalize positions. The Division Commander of the Southwestern Division, U. S. Army Corps of Engineers and the Director, Fish and Wildlife Service Region VI, agreed to a team-building exercise to provide a mechanism for conflict resolution. The goal of the exercise would be to facilitate professional cooperation that would lead to a better product and more productive use of tax dollars.

THE SITUATION:

How to utilize the Nation's natural resources has for many years been an issue due to changing regional and national priorities and perspectives. In the early phases of the United States history, the Nation was concerned with developing its economy and infrastructure base. The Nation's natural resources were utilized to support those objectives. The Nation achieved a high state of infrastructure development near the turn of the century: The focus began to change to one of concern for the life expectancy and the natural beauty of the Nation's natural resources. Beginning in the 1960's through the present time, the environmental aspect of resources including the natural environment, the environment of man and the social well-being of our society has developed as areas of equal concern. Various agencies both at the state and Federal levels were formed to meet specific needs and with specific constituencies to support the programs that developed to meet those needs. The U.S. Army Corps of Engineers major focus was on Nation-building. The Corps had an internal environmental respect during those early years of development in Nation-building but the primary focus was on economic output and developmental aspects of the utilization of our natural resources such as waterways, flood control, and water supply. Other agencies were formed to focus on the environmental and natural resource tasks that the Corps of Engineers may have been involved in initially. The new agencies developed specific constituencies. Examples are: the Fish and Wildlife Service of the Department of Interior, who were tasked with the enhancement preservation and utilization of the wildlife of the Nation; the National Marine Fisheries agency who was tasked with the utilization of and preservation of the anadromas fisheries of the United States; the Environmental Protection Agency, with the task of solidifying and enforcing policy concerning the clean up of the environment of man to include air, water, and soil. Similar agencies at the state level in Texas are: the Texas Park and Wildlife Department with the task of preservation and enhancement of the utilization of wildlife resources of the state; and the General Land Office who has the responsibilities of overall coordination of the utilization of the lands and minerals of the state including environmental programs.

The U.S. Army Corps of Engineers, responding to Congressional and local requests to develop a navigation project, came into sharp confrontation with the aforementioned natural resource agencies. The Corps of Engineers views its mission and constituants as multifaceted, involving developers, economical and environmental social groups. The resource agencies have specific constituencies such as the National or Regional environmental organizations, or groups who are specifically interested in preservation or enhancement of one particular facet of natural resources. The proposed widening and deepening Houston/Galveston Ship Channel became a focus of the controversy that had developed over many years between the Corps of Engineers and these agencies. The Galveston District Corps of Engineers and the area offices of these agencies were the most involved. By the spring of 1988, the controversy and the verbal conflict had become so intense that it seemed that the conduct of business between the agencies was grinding to an impasse. The Southwestern Commander, General Lee, and the Fish and Wildlife Director, Mr. Michael Spear, discussed the situation and decided it was time for a working relationship to be developed between the agencies. They directed that a team-building session be accomplished by the end of the summer.

THE SESSION:

The Division Office of the Southwestern Division, U.S. Army Corps of Engineers, took the lead on locating a consultant to facilitate a team-building session, selection of a time and place to hold the session. The Division and the consultant prepared the agenda. The Training Office of the personnel support unit of the Fort Worth District became the Contracting Officer and logistics office for accomplishment of the team-building session. After some discussion, it became apparent that a neutral location, not in an agency office, should be picked for the team-building effort and that a period of 2 days would be required to obtain any meaningful results. Dr. Norma Barr, Barr & Barr Communication Consultants, was selected as the contractor for facilitating the session. It was agreed with her that a conference center ranch complex near Bandera, Texas, should be the site of the conference. The Mayan Ranch, including a conference center, a number of cabins and rooms that could be used to house the participants, and well-known for its pleasant atmosphere that facilitated good conferences was then selected.

The session began on Sunday afternoon with the arrival of all the parties including Brigadier General Lee and Director, Mr. Michael Spear, who set the tone of the session, then left allowing the participants to work for a day and one-half without their presence. Mr. Spear appointed Ken Russell, Ph.D., Deputy Assistant Regional Director of Fish and Wildlife Enhancement, and General Lee appointed Barry Rought, his Chief of Planning, to be nonparticipating observers and expeditors of the session. Sunday evening began with an icebreaker and a hearty meal, and then a 2-hour get acquainted work session.

Monday began with breakfast at 0700, then a morning session analyzing the personality traits as exhibited through the Myers-Briggs testing mechanism. A series of work groups utilizing nonspecific issues were utilized to allow the participants to see how different personality traits responded to different situations. The intent of the Monday effort, including the work groups, was to provide the individual members an appreciation of how others approached and resolved problems. Following dinner that evening, there was a 2-hour work session where the various individuals began expressing their concerns about other agencies in the group. The session generally exhibited a division of the resource agencies expressing their dissatisfaction with the Corps of Engineers employees, and the Corps of Engineers employees responding with their dissatisfaction of the resource agencies. There seemed to be a measured constraint throughout the group to try and state their problem without direct attacks on individuals. The previous evening and the Monday daytime activity that had already taken place were an important factor in gaining this restrain.

Tuesday morning the program resumed with 0700 breakfast. The morning activities were designed to take problems that had been developed the previous evening and rate them into logical work groupings. Work groups were then formed to discuss measures that could be taken to provide an atmosphere for problem resolution rather than confrontation and nonresolution. The groups developed a list of specific individual and agency commitments to improve future working relationships. These commitments were then prioritized for the entire group and a total commitment was reached on a list of goals and a plan for doing a better job of problem resolution. Mr. Spear and General Lee returned at 1 p.m. and were given a 1-hour briefing followed by an hour of interactive discussion with the participants concerning the plan and their commitment to its success. It was agreed that a follow-up session approximately a year later would be advantageous.

THE RESULTS:

The anticipated results were for slightly improved communications and some reduced conflict over problems concerning resource development in the future. The actual results far exceeded the anticipated. The individual participants involved began having regular meetings within a month of Bandera to try to understand each others methodologies and professional viewpoints. Letters of the agencies were being precoordinated to determine if the person receiving the letter would understand it and not be offended. The news media seemed to be receiving more information of a professional nature and less inflamatory rhetoric. One of the most outstanding examples of the improved cooperation of understanding was a cooperative action taken at the Aransas National Wildlife Refuge concerning a many-years-old problem. The issue was loss of Whooping Crane Habitat due to erosion along the Gulf Intercoastal Waterway as it passes through the Aransas Wildlife National Refuge. The long-term problem was a focal point of conflict between the Fish and Wildlife Service and the Army Corps of Engineers. Within a short time of the Bandera team-building experience, the two agencies met in the field, looked at opportunities to solve the problem in a cooperative manner. Based on that meeting they developed a landmark volunteer effort. Enlisting the aid of volunteers and private donations of funds and equipment as well as the employees and resources of the two agencies they used economical emergency methods to stabilize the shoreline over a short test reach. It is too early to say whether the emergency measures were a total success, but certainly the attitude exhibited and the splendid effort in the field to accomplish the emergency efforts including use of volunteers was an outstanding example of agency cooperation.

Conflict between the missions of developmental and environmental organizations has been a major problem that could increase as the Nation moves into the 21st century. Cooperation and understanding by all disciplines involved will be essential if we are to move forward effectively and efficiently in addressing the many Engineering problems associated with an expanding population. This paper presents one team-building experience and the role of the team-building consultant including her background and approach.

The utilization of team-building sessions such as Bandera appears to be one more tool that can be used to better serve the public.

CONSERVATION AND WATER SUPPLY PLANNING AT ARMY INSTALLATIONS

James Comiskey[1]

Water is essential for industrial processes, military operations, and domestic uses at Army installations. For installation commanders at many Western facilities, the availability of fresh water is becoming a critical factor in installation operation, expansion planning, and the stationing of future troops.

The purpose of this paper is to summarize the research being conducted by the U.S. Army Institute for Water Resources in providing technical assistance to the Installation Planning Division, Office of Assistant Chief of Engineers, Pentagon, Washington in the area of water supply planning and conservation for military installations. This research is being performed in response to recommendations contained in a report on the subject by the Army Science Board (ASB) ad hoc subcommittee entitled "Water Supply and Management on Army Installations in the Western United States".

Major recommendations of this ad hoc study report included: 1) adaption and implementation of a consistent policy towards state water rights; 2) improvement of installation planning process; and 3) development of improved water use management and conservation practices at Army installations.

Various ways to implement these ASB report recommendations were the principal elements of discussion at a conference held in Alexandria, Virginia in June 1989. At this conference, a consensus emerged about the research

---

[1]Community Planner, Policy Division, U.S. Army Corps of Engineers, Institute for Water Resources, Casey Bldg., Fort Belvoir, VA 22060-5586

required before many of the ASB recommendations could be implemented. In response to this consensus, the Institute for Water Resources is conducting studies that will result in the development of water planning tools for military installations. These include: 1) a survey of state administrative and procedural requirements for water supply planning; 2) planning manual; 3) forecasting and water conservation model; and 4) a legal primer on state water law.

In addition to summarizing relevant procedures for water supply withdrawal (permits, licenses, etc.), the survey of state administrative requirements will also provide a list of appropriate points of contact associated with water use and water supply in each of the 50 states. The survey will also cover such elements of water research planning as acquisition, administration, and loss of water rights; development of surface water sources; purchase of water from water utilities; ground water withdrawals; and drinking water quality.

The planning manual will provide step-by-step guidance for various types of studies and planning activities related to water use. Its format should provide easy access for use by installation planners and facility engineers. In addition to describing analytical and forecasting procedures, the manual will be capable of estimating the total and sectorial amounts of water use, evaluating the feasibility and effectiveness of water conservation programs and thereby demonstrating the adequacy of existing sources or justifying the acquisition of new sources, estimating the impact of mobilization on water use and supply, designing adequate drought management plans, and achieving cost savings in water and wastewater treatment through demand reduction.

While there are currently three models or algorithms for predicting water use at military installations, none of these can provide results similar, even at a macro level to models used in civilian communities. Part of this research effort will therefore include the development of a new forecasting tool tailored expressly for Army installations. Data for the model will be collected at five active Army posts. Verification of this model will be performed at Fort Hunter-Legett, California and White Sands Missile Range, New Mexico.

In order to provide installation commanders and post planning personnel with some useful information about perhaps one of the most controversial areas of water supply planning and conservation (water law), a survey of water law for all 50 states will be conducted. The result of this survey will form the basis of a legal primer on water use. This primer will be organized and written to serve as a practical guide for the water planner and should not provide any strictly legal analysis. Topics in the survey will include state water rights law (both riparian and appropriated), major state environmental laws affecting water withdrawal as well as important recent court decisions potentially impacting on future water supply development.

Assisting the U.S. Army Institute for Water Resources in the two-year research effort is an Advisory Committee providing overall study direction and guidance. This Committee consists of senior level Army planners and scientists with a wide range of expertise in the area of water supply and conservation.

A Travel Time Template for Water Body Field Surveys

Altaf A. Memon,[1] AM.ASCE and Michael J. Haydon[2]

Abstract

A LOTUS 1-2-3^{tm} spreadsheet application has been developed to help plan water body surveys. The template calculates travel times between sampling stations and outputs a time schedule for sampling at various stations along the stream from start to finish. This paper discusses the development and utility of this template and presents an example demonstrating its use.

Introduction

Water quality management agencies are increasingly using water quality models for screening, prioritization and analysis of water bodies in order to comply with federal requirements. Water body surveys are performed not only to collect stream data for water quality assessment but also for calibration and/or verification of water quality models.

This paper discusses a worksheet template which is designed as a management and planning tool that helps the water body survey team prepare a sampling schedule for a stream survey. The template requires a 80286 - based PC and uses LOTUS 1-2-3^{tm} spreadsheet. The calculations are performed in the template using stream velocity equations to develop travel times between various sampling stations.

This paper explains the purpose of water body surveys, theoretical basis of the template, features of the template and a demonstration example of the template usage.

----

[1] Project Manager, Buchart-Horn, Inc., P. O. Box M-55, York, PA 17405-7065

[2] Information Systems Coordinator, BWQM, PA. Dept. of Env. Resources, P. O. Box 2063, Harrisburg, PA 17120

Water Body Surveys

Federal requirements under the Clean Water Act Sections 305(b) and 304(1) necessitate for the water quality regulatory agencies to perform water body surveys in order to prioritize program actions. Therefore, these surveys are called Priority Water Body Surveys (PWBS). For example , Pennsylvania Department of Environmental Resources has developed a system, whereby, stream segments are ranked to perform TMDL/WLA Screenings and Water Quality Assessments. PWBS are then performed followed by detailed TMDL/WLA analysis and implementation actions (PADER 1987). Therefore, the primary purpose of the PWBS is the collection of physical, chemical and biological data on water bodies and discharges in accordance with established protocols. The results of the surveys are used to support a detailed water quality analysis for implementation decisions related to permitting, compliance, grants, standards, coordination, etc. (Memon; et.al 1988).

Travel Time Model

The Travel Time Template uses the following basic equations:

$$T = L / V \qquad (1)$$

$$V = aQ^{0.56} D^b S^c \qquad (2)$$

and a = 2.62; b = -0.22; c = 0.083 for D < 500 (3)
         1.64   -0.15   0.055 otherwise

where, T = Travel Time (Days),   Q = Stream Flow (cfs),
        D = Drainage Area (sq. mi.), S = Slope (ft/mi),
        V = Stream Velocity (mpd), L = Reach Length (mi).

The above Equation (2) or the velocity equation is contained in EPA guidance to the state water quality agencies for water quality modeling (PADER 1988).

Template Features

The Travel Time Program, Version 2.0 (TTP2.0) is a LOTUS 1-2-3^{tm} worksheet template. The system requirements for TTP2.0 include a legally installed copy of LOTUS 1-2-3^{tm}, Release 2.0 or higher, a 80286-based desktop or laptop portable personal computer with at least 512K of RAM, and a hard disk drive. A math coprocessor is recommended.

The template is used as a planning tool to help PWBS teams prepare their survey schedules. This program allows field crews to determine the survey schedule up to the day of the survey to compensate for changing stream flow conditions. Under normal conditions, dye studies would be conducted in the field to establish the travel times between discharges and stream reaches. This template can estimate them for the user by calculating the velocity in the stream reach with above described velocity equations. Appropriate changes in the velocity equations can be made for different geographic areas supported by statistical analysis.

The template handles up to 200 stations on a continuous stream segment. The template cannot handle branched stream systems in the same file. Instead the user must create a separate file for each stream. The data requirements for running the template are the cumulative drainage area (sq.mi.), river mile index, elevation, name of the discharge, and total stream flow (cfs). This stream flow is the observed or calculated stream flow at the Q7-10 design condition or can be the observed flow on the day the survey is being conducted. The calibration of stream flow and velocity are possible in the program based on the observations either from a reconnaissance survey or on the day of PWBS. This is handled by obtaining and inputing the measured velocity at several points along the survey. The template then determines a calibration factor (C-FACT) for each observed velocity measurement and uses this constant in the velocity equation for the appropriate reaches. Similarly, flow calculation is adjusted from observed flows. The purpose of survey, resources available and type of the computer available will determine the necessity of the reconnaissance survey and/or calibration.

Running The Template

Before running TTP2.0, the user must install the program on the hard disk drive. To run the TTP2.0, the user loads 1-2-3, changes the current data directory to **c:\time,** and retrieves the file **timecal2.wk1**. The template is completely menu driven using custom menus and prompts. The TTP2.0 main menu options are **Input, Execute, File, Print, Reset** and **Quit**. The **Input** menu option is used to input the data for a new or existing file. When the user selects **Input** a sub-menu appears containing the options **Reach-Data, Calibration-Data, Insert-Reach** and **Exit**. These options are used to enter particular pieces of data and are self explanatory. The **Insert-Reach** option is used to insert new reaches into a file, when you need to break the survey up into shorter reaches.

The **Execute** option is selected when the user wants to run the program. When the user selects **Execute** a sub-menu appears containing the options **Go, Date, Time, Workday** and **Exit**. The **Go** option is selected when the user is ready to run the program. The **Date** option is used to set or change the survey start date. The **Time** option is selected to change the survey start time from the default time of 7:00 am. The **Workday** option is used to change the current workday length from the default value of 11 hours.

The **File** option is used to load and save data files. The submenu under this option contains the options **Save, Load** and **Exit**.

The **Print** option is selected when the user wants to print and/or view the output report. Under the **Print** option is a submenu containing the options **Screen, Printer** and **Exit** which are used to view on screen or print the results. The **Printer** option may be used when its time to obtain the hard copy, usually when the survey is finalized.

The **Reset** option is used to reset TTP2.0. When the user selects **Reset,** the existing data is cleared and the template default values are reset. The program prompts the user to save the existing data before resetting to avoid any accidental loss.

The **Quit** option is selected whenever the user is ready to quit the template and leave the 1-2-3 environment.

If there is observed velocity or flow data for calibration, the user can **Calibrate** the template. To do this, the user answers the prompt: **Run Calibration?** **(Y/N)...:** which appears when the user selects **Execute** and **Go**. Calibrations are possible by inputing the flow and/or velocity data at an appropriate reach. The user can input these data by scrolling to the correct location on the worksheet. In absence of observed flows the velocity equation uses the Q7-10 values. Care should be exercised when using the template with real data.

Example

Figure 1 depicts a printout from a template run of a typical ten station example. Different sections of the printout portray data inputs and result outputs.

The input data is located in the upper portion of the output report, and the results are located in the middle and lower portions of the report. The clock times displayed begin from the survey start time which is entered by the user. The user can also override the default workday which is set at 11 hours.

When the template is executed the program calculates the travel times for Q7-10 and five multiples of Q7-10. The user can go to the nearest available USGS gaging station, determine the flow on the morning of the sample, then determine if the flow is between 1 to 5*Q7-10. If the flow is within the template range, then the sample times for that day can easily be interpolated from the template printout. The interpolation is not required if flow calibration is performed from observed flows. The template results are displayed as the clock time at each station, based upon initial conditions of the survey start time and the date, under each stream flow design condition. This is the time that a sample should be collected at that station.

Stream Survey Travel Time Program, VERSION 2.0 (c) 1987,1989 PA DER Bureau of Water Quality Management & Michael J. Haydon

Case Name	> Test Case	<	Analyst	> MJH, AAM	<	Time:	03:59 PM
Stream	> NoName Creek	<	County	> Anywhere USA	<	Date:	10-Sep-89
File Name	> DEMO.TT2						

Reach Data	INPUT DATA AREA		1	2	3	4	5	6	7	8	9	10
Input Data - TOTAL CUMULATIVE Drainage Area (mi^2)			10.00000	22.50000	35.50000	42.67000	51.30000	67.78000	70.98000	85.50000	90.00000	110.11000
Input Data - River Mile Index (RMI)			7.50000	5.00000	3.75000	3.30000	3.12000	2.60000	2.45000	1.75000	1.10000	0.00100
Input Data - Elevation (feet)			490.00000	440.00000	435.00000	410.00000	400.00000	395.00000	390.00000	360.00000	335.00000	300.00000
Input Data - Type (MAIN, TRIB, DISC)			N/A	Tributary	UNT 1	US Steel 001	US Steel 002	Tributary	East STP	Tributary	Southeast STP	US Steel 003
Input Data - TOTAL Stream Flow, Q cfs				3.16913	5.00018	6.01007	7.22561	9.54681	9.99753	12.04268	12.67650	15.50899
< CALCULATED REACH Length (feet)		>	0.00000	13200.00000	6600.00000	2376.00000	950.40000	2745.60000	792.00000	3696.00000	3432.00000	5802.72000
< CALCULATED SLOPE (ft/ft)		>	0.00000	0.00379	0.00076	0.01052	0.01052	0.00182	0.00631	0.00812	0.00728	0.00603
< CALCULATED Velocity (mi/day)		>	0.00000	5.48179	5.60072	3.60817	3.84136	3.65085	4.11167	4.47259	4.51058	4.75564

Stream Flows	SURVEY SCHEDULE INFORMATION		START DAY	2	3	4	5	6	7	8	9	10
		Survey Date >	11-Sep-89		12-Sep-89			13-Sep-89			14-Sep-89	
Q7-10		Time >	08:00 AM	06:56 PM	01:21 PM	04:20 PM	05:28 PM	11:25 AM	12:17 PM	04:03 PM	11:27 AM	05:00 PM
			11-Sep-89		12-Sep-89					13-Sep-89		
2 * Q7-10			08:00 AM	03:25 PM	11:37 AM	01:39 PM	02:25 PM	04:44 PM	05:20 PM	10:32 AM	12:53 PM	04:39 PM
			11-Sep-89			12-Sep-89						13-Sep-89
2.5 * Q7-10			08:00 AM	02:33 PM	05:45 PM	09:47 AM	10:27 AM	12:30 PM	01:02 PM	03:17 PM	05:21 PM	11:19 AM
			11-Sep-89				12-Sep-89					
3 * Q7-10			08:00 AM	01:54 PM	04:48 PM	06:25 PM	08:36 AM	10:27 AM	10:55 AM	12:57 PM	02:49 PM	05:49 PM
			11-Sep-89						12-Sep-89			
4 * Q7-10			08:00 AM	01:02 PM	03:30 PM	04:52 PM	05:23 PM	06:58 PM	08:24 AM	10:07 AM	11:43 AM	02:16 PM
			11-Sep-89							12-Sep-89		
5 * Q7-10			08:00 AM	12:26 PM	02:37 PM	03:50 PM	04:17 PM	05:40 PM	06:02 PM	09:31 AM	10:55 AM	01:10 PM

Flows	STREAM FLOW CALCULATIONS		1	2	3	4	5	6	7	8	9	10
2 * Q7-10			0.00000	6.33825	10.00035	12.02014	14.45121	19.09363	19.99507	24.08535	25.35300	31.01799
2.5 * Q7-10			0.00000	7.92281	12.50044	15.02517	18.06401	23.86703	24.99383	30.10669	31.69125	38.77248
3 * Q7-10			0.00000	9.50738	15.00053	18.03021	21.67682	28.64044	29.99260	36.12803	38.02950	46.52698
4 * Q7-10			0.00000	12.67650	20.00070	24.04028	28.90242	38.18725	39.99013	48.17070	50.70600	62.03597
5 * Q7-10			0.00000	15.84563	25.00088	30.05035	36.12803	47.73407	49.98767	60.21338	63.38250	77.54497
	CALIBRATION DATA AREA											
Calibration Factor			1.00000	1.69664	1.69664	0.82533	0.82533	0.82533	0.82533	0.82533	0.82533	0.82533
Calculated Velocity (fps)			0.00000	0.33500	0.34227	0.22050	0.23475	0.22311	0.25127	0.27332	0.27565	0.29062
Input Data - Observed Velocity (fps)		>	0.00000	0.33500	0.00000	0.22050	0.00000	0.00000	0.00000	0.00000	0.00000	0.00000
Input Data - Observed Stream Flow (cfs)		>	0.00000	0.00000	0.00000	0.00000	0.00000	0.00000	0.00000	0.00000	0.00000	0.00000

FIGURE 1 - TYPICAL INPUT - OUTPUT REPORT

The template also displays the survey start date above the very first station. The template determines how many stations can be sampled on each day and the number of days that the survey will take under these different flows. Each time a new day starts, the date is displayed above that station. The time displayed at that station is also the time the sample must be collected at that station on that date. The printout of the template shows the results in which how the times and dates are applied. Although not shown in Figure 1, if the travel time between two points exceeds the workday length, the message **OUT OF RANGE** is displayed. This means that the travel time through the reach exceeds the workday length. At this point the user inserts a new reach, breaks up the long reach into two shorter ones, and then re-runs the program until a valid time is computed. The user can also extend the workday length if the reach in question is just outside the range.

Conclusions

This template is used to help provide an estimate of travel times in a stream. It is not intended to replace the more detailed dye study. However, given the costs and time involved in dye studies, this template does provide a fairly good means of estimating where the sample stations are located and when the samples should be collected. The hardcopy printout is useful in the conduct of the survey. In another instance, a portable or lap top PC can be used to run the template while in the field and on the day of the survey. This makes the program useful to have when in the field.

References

"PADER Draft Guidance on Selection, Ranking, and TMDL/WLA Screening Priority Water Bodies." (1987). Pennsylvania Dept. of Environmental Resources, Bur. of Water Qual. Management, Harrisburg, Pennsylvania.

Memon, A. A.;et.al (1988). "Water Quality Assessment and Management System in Regulatory Environments," Proceeding of the 15th Annual ASCE Water Resources Conference, Norfolk, VA, June 1 - 3, 1988.

"PADER Water Quality Analysis Template Version 2.01 User Guide." (1988). Pennsylvania Department of Environmental Resources, Bur. of Water Qual. Management, Harrisburg, Pennsylvania.

Wastewater Balance for Storage Pond at Land Treatment Site

Khamis A. Al-Omari[1], A.M., ASCE and Steven G. Buchberger[2], A.M., ASCE

Abstract

Land application is an established method for treating municipal wastewater in the United States. Most land application operations include on-site facilities to store wastewater during periods when the effluent supply exceeds the allowable release to the treatment field. This paper presents a case study which demonstrates how a monthly wastewater balance at a storage pond can be used to measure the performance of an existing land treatment operation. The case study involves the Hancock Farm land application system near Lubbock, Texas where municipal wastewater has been used for nearly 10 years to irrigate approximately 1,150 hectares of cultivated land.

Introduction

Slow rate irrigation involves controlled application of wastewater to a vegetated land surface at a rate typically measured in centimeters per week. This paper examines the slow rate irrigation system used by the City of Lubbock, Texas to treat its municipal wastewater. Gray Farm (1,489 hectares) near Lubbock had been since the 1930's the primary disposal site for wastewater from the city. The Gray Farm, however, could not accommodate the increasing hydraulic flow which accompanied the city's growth. Groundwater mounded beneath Gray Farm and crops were over-irrigated. A program called "The Lubbock Land Treatment System Research and Demonstration Program" was developed in 1978 to address these problems. To reduce the hydraulic overloading of Gray Farm, the Lubbock land treatment system was expanded to include the Hancock Farm in November 1980 (George et al, 1986).

Using monthly estimates of municipal effluent inflows, hydraulic loading, precipitation, evaporation, and seepage, the wastewater levels in the Hancock Farm storage ponds are reconstructed for the 69 month period from April 1982 to December 1987. The resulting sequence of wastewater levels indicates that the Hancock Farm storage ponds experienced a three year period of severe overloading which, on several occasions, apparently led to forced wastewater spills from the ponds.

---

[1] Civil Engineer, Black & Veatch/Engineers-Architects, 600 Renaissance Center, Suite 1240, Detroit, Michigan 48243

[2] Assistant Professor, Department of Civil and Environmental Engineering, The University of Cincinnati, Cincinnati, Ohio 45221

Site Location, Layout, and Operation

Hancock Farm is located about 25 km southeast of Lubbock in the Southern High Plains region of northwestern Texas. The farm encompasses 1,478 hectares (ha) of which 1,153 ha are cultivated land. Irrigation by a sprinkler system covers 1,082 ha while 72 ha are irrigated with the ridge-and-furrow technique. Irrigation water comes from the City of Lubbock's Southeast Water Reclamation Plant (SeWRP). The treated wastewater effluent is conveyed to the Hancock Farm from a pumping station at SeWRP through a 25 km force main with a diameter of 0.69 m. At the northern boundary of Hancock Farm, the effluent is routed through three 0.38 m plastic pipelines to three separate reservoirs. The wastewater distribution system is designed to transport and accommodate 28,000 m^3/day (7.4 MGD).

The three reservoirs at the Hancock Farm are built on playa lakes. They are designed to account for high precipitation events and to provide necessary storage during periods of seeding, cultivation, and harvesting on the farm. A 3.5 month storage period is provided by the reservoirs to account for emergency conditions and zero-application months. An average of 0.6 m freeboard zone is provided for each reservoir. The combined capacity of the three reservoirs is 3.82×10^6 m^3 with an embankment height of 6.3 m. The bottom lining of the reservoirs is 0.6 m thick and constructed from compacted clay having an estimated permeability coefficient of 10^{-4} m/day. In this paper, combined pond areas and capacities are used in the analyses. The combined pond area is the collective surface area of all three reservoirs and is estimated to be 621,266 m^2 at a median depth of 3.15 m (Al-Omari and Buchberger, 1989).

Operation of the reservoirs is based on two chief criteria:

(1) The reservoirs should be empty by August 20 each year, the time at which it is advisable to stop irrigating; and
(2) The combined contents of the reservoirs should never exceed 3.5×10^6 m^3 (LCC Institute of Water Research, 1981).

Although the reservoir storage capacity accounted for a maximum inflow of 28,000 m^3/day (7.4 MGD) at a hydraulic loading rate of 1.16 m/year, it did not account for unusual precipitation events, the low application rate of wastewater by farmers, and the variation in wastewater supply from SeWRP. The wastewater inflow increased over the study period from 11,734 m^3/day (3.1 MGD) in January 1984 to 26,764 m^3/day (7.1 MGD) in March 1987. This hydraulic overburden at the Hancock Farm was the result of a substantial decrease in wastewater use by the Southwestern Public Service in 1986. While wastewater inflows increased, the hydraulic loading rate remained at 30-40 cm/year between 1983 and 1987. This can be attributed to occurrence of adequate precipitation for crop growth and reluctance on the part of farmers' to accept more wastewater for fear of damaging cash crops by over-irrigating.

The increasing wastewater inflow, high precipitation rate, and low hydraulic loading created emergency conditions that forced the operators of the Hancock Farm reservoirs to dispose of excess wastewater by discharging directly into the moats around the reservoirs. Despite these contingency measures, wastewater levels in the storage reservoirs were never lowered to the desired operating range due to hydraulic overloading of the Hancock Farm treatment system during the period 1985 through 1987 (Leftwich, 1988).

Data Collection and Screening

Monthly data on wastewater inflows, hydraulic loading, precipitation, evaporation, and seepage rates were obtained and used to compute monthly changes in storage and to reconstruct the storage levels in the combined ponds at the land application site. Sources and characteristics of these data are described below.

Wastewater Inflows: Wastewater inflows to the Hancock Farm were obtained from Leftwich (1988), George et al (1986), and from the City of Lubbock, Texas. The minimum inflow was 259,000 m^3 (41.7 cm) in September 1983 and the maximum inflow was 832,923 m^3 (134.0 cm) in March 1987. The average monthly inflow rate ranged from 305,542 m^3/month (49.2 cm/month) in 1982 to 636,694 m^3/month (102.5 cm/month) in 1987.

Hydraulic Loading Rate: The monthly hydraulic loading rates were obtained for each irrigated lot from Leftwich (1988). Average weighted monthly rates were computed in cm/month and were expressed in terms of the average combined pond area (Al-Omari and Buchberger, 1989). During the period of April 1982 to December 1987, the hydraulic loading rate ranged from 0.0 to 229.4 cm/month. The average hydraulic loading rate ranged between 19.5 cm/month in 1982 to 58.5 cm/month in 1985. Those rates were very low since the average wastewater inflow was 40.2 cm/month in 1982 and 101.3 cm/month in 1985.

Precipitation: The precipitation data for the Hancock Farm were obtained from the National Oceanic and Atmospheric Administration (NOAA, 1982-1987), Leftwich et al (1988), and Ramsey et al (1986). The maximum precipitation rate was 27.4 cm in October 1983 while the minimum rate was 0.05 cm in December 1985. The average monthly precipitation rate ranged from 5.49 cm/month in 1982 to 3.98 cm/month in 1987.

Evaporation: The evaporation data were obtained from NOAA (1982-1987) and from the LCC Institute of Water Research (1981). The minimum evaporation rate at the Hancock Farm occurs in January and the maximum occurs in June, July, or August of each year. The highest evaporation rate was 22.25 cm in June 1984 for the 1982-1985 period. The annual evaporation rate is relatively constant, averaging about 140 cm/year.

Seepage: Seepage rates from the combined pond were calculated using (equation 4.2) from Al-Omari and Buchberger (1989). The average seepage rate ranged between 0.7 cm/month in 1982 and 3.3 cm/month in 1986. The total amount of wastewater lost by seepage through the reservoir's lining is estimated to be 150 cm between 1982 and 1987.

Wastewater Balance

A monthly wastewater balance was performed by computing the water supply (wastewater inflow + precipitation) to the ponds and the demand (hydraulic loading + seepage + evaporation) from the ponds. Storage levels were computed on a monthly basis using equations (1) and (2)

$$S(t+1) = S(t) + [Q(t)/A] - Y(t). \qquad (1)$$

$$Y(t) = E(t) + G(t) - P(t) + \Theta R(t). \qquad (2)$$

where $Q(t)$ is the monthly volume of wastewater supply and $Y(t)$ is the monthly wastewater demand per unit pond area. $E(t)$, $G(t)$, $P(t)$ and $R(t)$ are the monthly rates of evaporation, seepage, precipitation and hydraulic loading, respectively. The term Θ represents the field to pond area ratio which in this case equals 18.5. $S(t)$ is the estimated monthly storage level with t = 1,2,3,...,69 months for the study period. The resulting sequence of pond storage levels is shown in Figure 1. At the upper boundary, equation (1) offers two possibilities:

(1) If $0 < S(t+1) < S_{max}$, then storage remains below the freeboard zone and the pond does not spill;

(2) If $S(t+1) > S_{max}$, then storage exceeds the freeboard zone and the pond is forced to make an emergency spill given by: Spill = $S(t+1) - S_{max}$

Further details regarding boundary constraints in wastewater balance computations are given in Buchberger and Maidment (1989). Allowing 60 cm for freeboard, the maximum permissible depth of storage in the ponds is 5.7 m.

The Hancock Farm reservoirs began operation in April 1982. Figure 1 shows that reservoir storage increased from an initially empty condition until January 1983 when large withdrawals drew the storage level down to its minimum in August 1983. Filling of the reservoirs resumed in September 1983 and continued until February 1984 when again storage decreased and reached a minimum of 71.3 cm in August 1984. From this point, wastewater levels increased dramatically in response to high supplies and low releases. The contents of the ponds soon reached their maximum allowable level and remained near the freeboard zone for much of the time in 1985, 1986, and 1987. During these years, forced spills of wastewater from the storage reservoirs were evidently quite common. Water balance calculations indicate that there were four forced spills in 1985, three in 1986, and eight in 1987. This postulated sequence of forced spills is plotted in Figure 2.

Summary and Conclusions

Storage ponds are important components of land treatment systems since they hold the wastewater flow during non-application and high precipitation periods. A wastewater balance for a storage pond can be used to evaluate the overall performance of an existing land treatment system. All hydrologic parameters must be specified, including the wastewater inflow, hydraulic loading, precipitation, evaporation, and seepage rates. In principle, storage levels reconstructed from such a wastewater balance represent the integrated effects of all factors influencing wastewater treatment and disposal at land application sites. Application of a monthly wastewater balance to data from the Hancock Farm near Lubbock Texas indicates:

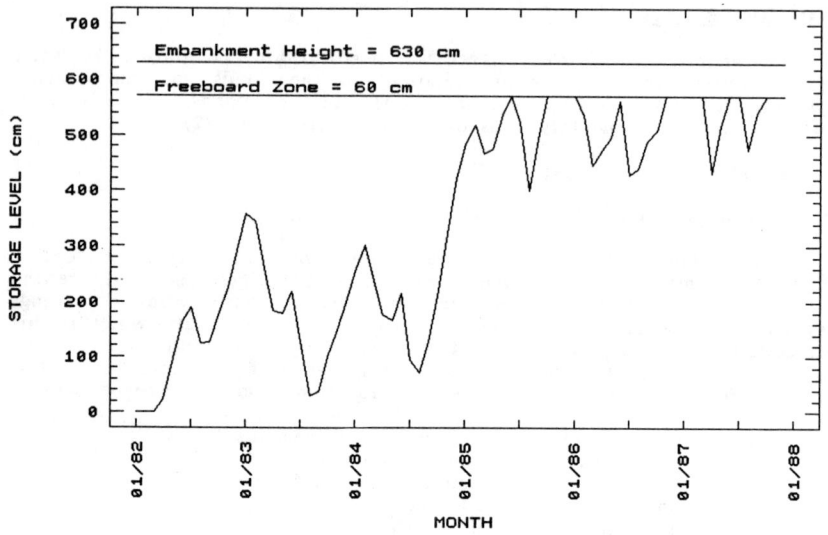

Figure 1. Monthly storage levels at Hancock Farm combined pond.

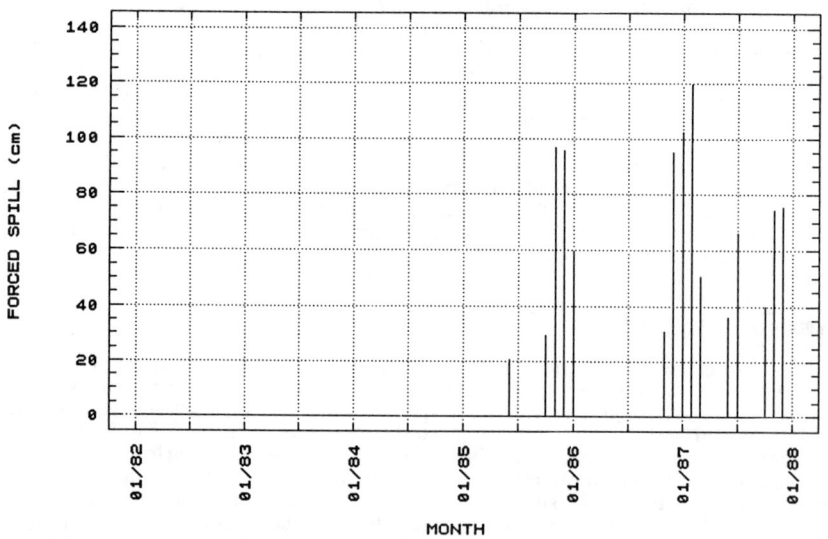

Figure 2. Monthly forced spills at Hancock Farm combined pond.

(1) Storage levels in the pond hit the upper boundary (5.7 m) several times during 1986 and 1987. Results show that storage was not appreciably depleted in 1986 and 1987, thus violating the first operation rule of emptying the reservoirs by August 20 of each year.

(2) The storage ponds were overloaded during 1985, 1986 and 1987. Results show that the first forced spill occurred in June 1985 and was followed by 14 more forced spills over the ensuing three years. These spills violate the second operation rule of maintaining wastewater storage below the 5.7 m level.

(3) The annual hydraulic loading rate (per average pond area) is very low (6.1 m/year) compared to the annual wastewater inflow to the Hancock Farm (9.84 m/year).

(4) The reservoir storage capacity at the Hancock Farm is not sufficient to accommodate the wastewater supply from SeWRP. Based on the current inflow of 6,813,000 m^3/year (5 MGD) with 12% variation (Leftwich, 1988), the storage capacity should be increased by about 17% to reasonably accommodate the volume of annual wastewater inflows.

References

Al-Omari, K. A., and Buchberger, S. G., "Design of Wastewater Ponds Based on Stochastic Storage Analysis", Technical Report CRWR 193, Department of Civil and Environmental Engineering, The University of Cincinnati, based on research initiated at Center for Research in Water Resources, The University of Texas at Austin, Austin, Texas, February 1989.

Buchberger, S.G., and D.R. Maidment (1989) "Design of Wastewater Storage Ponds at Land Treatment Sites. I: Parallels with Applied Reservoir Theory" and "II: Equilibrium Storage Performance Functions", ASCE Journal of Environmental Engineering, 115(4):689-724.

Department of Commerce, National Oceanic and Atmospheric Administration, Monthly Climatological Data for Texas, Washington, D.C., January 1982-December 1987.

George, D. B., Leftwich, B., and Klein, D. B., The Lubbock Land Treatment System Research and Demonstration Project: Volume 1. Demonstration/Hydrological Study. USEPA-600/2-86-027a (PB86-173598), Lubbock, Texas, 1986.

LCC Institute of Water Research, Lubbock Land Treatment System Research and Demonstration Project: Operation and Maintenance Manual, Engineering Enterprises, Inc., 1981.

Leftwich, B., Lubbock Land Treatment and Demonstration Project: 1984 to 1987 Report, LCC Institute of Water Research, Lubbock, Texas, 1988.

Ramsey, R. H., and Sweazy, R. M., Lubbock Land Treatment System Research and Demonstration Project: Volume 2. Percolate Investigation in the Root Zone, USEPA/600-2-86-027b (PB86-173606), Lubbock, Texas, 1986.

Using Corps of Engineers'
Reservoirs for
Water Supply

Ms. Cheryl P. Ulrich, P.E.[1] and Mr. Kenneth R. Sims[2]

Abstract.

This paper provides an historical overview of the Corps of Engineers (COE) authority in the water supply arena and discusses the methodologies and procedures used to reallocate storage in existing COE' reservoirs to water supply. Pertinent laws and current policy procedures are presented. A step-by-step outline is displayed for the water user that wishes to obtain water supply from an existing COE reservoir. The four storage reallocation pricing methodologies and reimbursement credit policy are also discussed.

Introduction.

The COE operates approximately 600 reservoirs including locks and dams which contain about 215 million acre-feet (af) of storage. Approximately 6 million af of storage is used for municipal and industrial (M&I) water supply. There is an additional 3.3 million af allocated for future M&I water supply and approximately 0.94 million af that is not under contract. Sixty-five percent of the storage not under contract is available in the Southwestern Division with the majority in the state of Oklahoma. Another 20 % is available in the Lower Mississippi Valley Division (U.S. COE, Institute for Water Resources, July 1988.)

---

[1] Civil Engineer, Corps of Engineers, Mobile District, P.O. Box 2288, Mobile, Alabama 36628.

[2] Wildlife Biologist, Corps of Engineers, Mobile District, P.O. Box 2288, Mobile, Alabama 36628.

This paper will provide an historical overview of the COE authority in the water supply arena, discuss the procedures and methodologies used to reallocate storage in existing COE reservoirs to water supply, and present the current position on hydropower credit.

Pertinent Laws.

Flood Control Act of 1944. - This act established a federal interest in water supply. It authorized the Secretary of the Army to dispose of excess (surplus) water from reservoirs for domestic, M&I, and agricultural use.

Water Supply Act of 1958. - This act provided that storage may be included in reservoirs for present and future water supply. The act authorizes the Secretary of the Army to modify existing projects for water supply as long as the modification does not "seriously affect the purposes for which the project was authorized" or "involve major structural or operational changes." This is the authority for storage reallocation.

Water Resources Development Act of 1974. - This act established authority for the Chief of Engineers to provide an emergency supply of safe drinking water for "drought distressed " communities. The Governor of the state must request assistance for the Chief of Engineers to use this act.

Water Resources Development Act of 1986. - This act amended the Water Supply Act of 1958 as follows: Eliminated the 10 year interest free period for future water supply; modifies the interest rate formula; limits repayments to 30 years; and requires operation, maintenance, and replacement costs to be reimbursed on an annual basis. The non-federal share is 100% for M&I water supply. However, on February 28, 1989, Congressman Hopkins from Kentucky introduced a bill HR 1155 which would change the M&I cost sharing amount from 100% non-federal to 35% non-federal.

Water Resources Development Act of 1988. - This act states that "before the Secretary may make changes in the operation of any reservoir which will result in or require a reallocation of storage space in such reservoir or will significantly affect any project purpose, the Secretary shall provide an opportunity for public review and comment."

Agency Regulations.

The COE policy on reallocation has emerged over the years in conformance with the pertinent laws and as experience has been gained. Current agency regulations indicate if the above criteria in the Water Supply Act of 1958 are not violated then "15 percent of total storage capacity allocated to all authorized project purposes or 50,000 af, whichever is less," may be allocated from storage authorized for other purposes to serve as storage for M&I water supply at the discretion of the Commander, USACE. The Secretary of the Army may approve reallocations greater than these limits, provided a decision is reached that the impacts are not significant. Reallocations determined to have significant impacts must be authorized by Congress.

In order to comply with the National Environmental Policy Act of 1969, environmental documentation must be prepared to accompany the proposed reallocation. If the impacts are not significant, an environmental assessment is prepared. If the impacts are significant, an environmental impact statement is prepared. The proper coordination of the environmental documents is also performed.

Procedure.

The following is a schematic of the process a local government would need to go through in order to obtain a water supply reallocation contract with the COE.

Locals Determine Future Water Supply Demands and Needs.
⇩
Send a Letter to the COE Requesting Water Supply Storage.
⇩
COE Prepare a Reallocation Report, Environmental Documentation and Draft Contract.
⇩
Public Coordination of Environmental Documentation.
⇩
Division Approval.
⇩
Washington Level Approval.
⇩
Negotiate Contract.
⇩
Execute Contract.

Pricing Methodology. -

COE policy states that the cost to the water user will normally be established as the highest of four methods: Benefits Foregone, Revenues Foregone, Replacement Cost and Updated Cost of Storage. Benefits foregone are estimated using a standard COE economic evaluation which evaluates the loss of power or flood control benefits. Revenues foregone are the reduction in revenues accruing to the Treasury, based on the existing repayment agreement as a result of the reduction in hydropower output. If the reallocated storage is being taken from the flood control pool, it may be appropriate to utilize the replacement cost of equivalent protection to adequately reflect monetary and nonmonetary costs. Similarly, if the reallocation storage is being taken from the conservation pool, and the measurable losses are to the production of power, the replacement cost of power is the cost the power marketing agency would incur to obtain power from an alternate source. The updated cost of storage is an updating of the joint-use construction cost using the COE Civil Works Construction Cost Index System (CCWIS) and Engineering News Record indices for items not covered by CCWIS. Land values are updated on a case-by-case basis by a qualified COE real estate appraiser. In addition to the cost of the highest method, the non-Federal sponsor is responsible for a portion of the annual joint use operation, maintenance and replacement costs. If the cost is based on the updated cost of storage menthod the non-Federal sponsor may choose to finance their proportionate share of the storage over thirty years or pay in cash the full amount less a 10% reduction.

A financial feasibility test is performed to verify that the reallocation of water from the existing reservoir is the most likely, least costly alternative that would provide an equivalent quality and quantity of water.

Credit to Power Marketing Agency.

Current policy requires that the power marketing agency receive a credit against their repayment obligation to reflect the fact that they are no longer responsible for repaying the cost of the reallocated storage. Over the long term, this credit will be equal to revenues foregone. However, the power marketing agency still has an obligation to deliver the power lost due to reallocation throughout the remainder of their current power marketing contract, to their customers. Therefore, the power marketing agency will be given credit equal to the cost of acquiring replacement power throughout the remainder of their current power marketing contract. The amount of credit to the power marketing agency will be documented in the annual Income Statement Report of the project.

Conclusion.

As the population in our country continues to grow, so does the demand on our water resources. Using COE' reservoirs for water supply should be investigated when looking at viable alternatives to meet future water supply needs. The procedure for obtaining storage space in a Federal reservoir is fairly simplistic and there is about 1 million af that is not currently under contract. Issues concerning the pricing of storage for the water users and the compensation of losses to the power beneficiaries will continue to be debated among the involved local, state, and Federal agencies. The COE objective will continue to be that of providing the most economically efficient use of reservoir storage at equitable costs and compensation (Goode, 1989). Perhaps the true value of water will not be obtained until the day arrives that we turn on the tap and no water flows. Or as Benjamin Franklin said "When the well's dry, we know the worth of water."

Appendix

U.S. Army Corps of Engineers, Institute for Water resources, "Opportunities for Reservoir Storage Reallocation, IWR Policy Study 88-PS-2," July 1989.

Goode, Joseph A., "Storage Reallocation in Hydropower Projects of North Georgia," 1989.

MANAGING TWO LAKES WITH SIGNIFICANT TAILWATER FISHERIES

William P. Mathis*

ABSTRACT

Norfork and Bull Shoals Dams on the White River in Arkansas were constructed in 1944 and 1951, respectively. The authorized purposes were for flood control, hydropower generation, and other beneficial purposes. Water supply has since been added to the list of purposes. While recreation, fish, and wildlife were not specifically authorized purposes, these uses have assumed a larger role as time has gone by. In addition to the very popular warm water fisheries in both lakes, a two-story fishery featuring rainbow trout in the colder, oxygenated layers of Bull Shoals Lake was developed by the Arkansas Game and Fish Commission. As a natural consequence of the cold water hydropower releases, the warm water fisheries in both the White River and the North Fork River were diminished. A nationally significant put-grow-and-take trout fishery has been developed to replace those fisheries. However, the development of the trout fishery has not occurred without problems. The generation schedule has not always been sufficient to maintain the trout fishery, particularly in the area of Sylamore, which is about 78 river miles downstream of Bull Shoals Dam and about 50 miles downstream of Norfork Dam.

Various schemes have been developed which, with modifications, have evolved into the present operation which is considered to be effective in maintaining the trout fishery (table 1). The management of the lakes is somewhat complicated by the presence of the trout fishery. These "conflicts" between the upstream and downstream fisheries and the solutions considered by the Little Rock District are the subject of this paper.

---

*Biologist, Little Rock District Corps of Engineers

BACKGROUND

Norfork and Bull Shoals Dams were constructed in the '40s and '50s, respectively. About 1948, the Arkansas Game and Fish Commission (AGFC) biologists, realizing that it was going to be difficult to maintain any kind of a native fishery in the Norfork tailwater, secured fingerling rainbow trout from the Neosho, Missouri, National Fish Hatchery, and a token stocking of less than 1,000 trout was made. The result was a rousing success. More trout were stocked, and when Bull Shoals Dam began to produce power in the middle '50s, the AGFC biologists were ready with a stocking program for that tailwater also. The AGFC biologists also moved invertebrate-rich vegetation from the Spring River of north Arkansas into these tailwaters where it became established and flourished. In 1957, the Norfork National Fish Hatchery was constructed, and the increasing numbers of trout produced there allowed the fish managers to extend the trout stocking downstream to Sylamore and Guion, a distance of about 91 miles from Bull Shoals Dam, and 50 from Norfork Dam. The extent (in miles) of this trout fishery had not been envisioned prior to construction. The Corps, Southwestern Power Administration, and the state and Federal fishery agencies then sought operational modifications which would susiain trout downstream to the vicinity of Sylamore. This effort culminated, in the early '70s in an operation which involved holding additional water in the flood control pool of the lakes which could be released through the turbines at a time and rate which would afford protection to the fishery. In the beginning, these releases were dependent on information furnished by fishery interests in the private sector. When it became evident that human error could not be eliminated, automatic, continuous recording satellite-connected temperature recorders were installed.

During the interim, management techniques for managing these large, multipurpose impoundments were being developed in Arkansas and elsewhere. Management, consisting of water level fluctuations had proven very successful on flood control lakes like Nimrod and Blue Mountain in west-central Arkansas. These techniques proved efficacious on the large lakes, but the lakes being larger than normal, and given the constraints of power generation, water level fluctuations were more difficult.

WHITE RIVER LAKES STUDY

A restudy of the lakes on the upper White River was begun in 1975. This study was to examine the present authorities and operational procedures with a view to improving recreation and fish and wildlife in both the lakes and their tailwaters, and for other purposes. Fisheries personnel in both Arkansas and Missouri proposed plans of water level fluctuations which would involve, roughly, high water levels in the spring followed by declining water levels into the following spring and summer. Benefits would accrue to the lake fishery in an improved spawn and survival of game fishes.

In evaluating these proposals, we determined that this type of operation was not compatible with congressionally mandated purposes such as hydroelectric power production and flood control. We felt also that this type of operation had the potential to completely wipe out the lucrative trout fisheries in the tailwaters due to a lack of water remaining for releases during the critical months of July, August, and September.

The fisheries interests in both states also made proposals for the improvement of the tailwater fisheries. Instream-flow studies were done on the White, Black, and Little Red Rivers. The desired flows were analyzed, and we found that flows of the requested magnitude were incompatible with project purposes and indeed were impossible to maintain in conjunction with the proposed water level operations on the lakes.

CONCLUSION

After evaluating the proposals for recreation and fish and wildlife, along with agriculture, municipal, industrial, and other purposes, the study concluded that we could increase the winter and early spring stages downstream at Newport without adverse impacts to the agricultural interests. This would enhance our ability to evacuate flood waters from the lakes in a more timely manner, providing benefits to the agricultural interests downstream while not interfering with fish and wildlife in the lakes. This mode of operation would be a step in the direction of returning the river flows to preproject conditions. We concluded that any move in that direction would provide more "nearly normal" conditions in the batture lands downstream in the important fishing and hunting areas of the lower basin, and thus restore productivity to that area.

We also felt that the addition of continuous-reading temperature recorders installed at advantageous places along the rivers would provide the luxury of monitoring water temperatures at any time, would remove the human error factor, and thus render the release regime previously devised more effective. When predicted rises in ambient air temperatures and rising water temperatures point to a potential problem, releases are made at a predetermined daily rate to counter the warming of the stream.

PRESENT AND FUTURE STUDIES

A study now underway is evaluating the effects of present operation procedures on recreational boating (including fishing) needs. If this study proves the need for additional releases to accommodate recreational navigation on the White River, and those releases are provided, there will be other benefits that will accrue. The added water to provide boat passages both upstream and downstream will also alleviate the existing situation where water temperatures in some reaches warm to near lethal limits during long (3-day) weekends of little or no generation. Benefits to the lake will accrue due to higher water levels in the spring with slightly lower stages late in the summer and fall.

TABLE 1
MINIMUM DAILY RELEASES
DOWNSTREAM FROM BULL SHOALS AND NORFORK DAMS

Forecast Max air temp for tomorrow	Norfork Dam	Bull Shoals Dam
90 or below	145 DSF*	250 DSF
91-95	218 "	375 "
96-104	290 "	500 "
105 & above	360 "	750 "

*Day-second-feet. The volume of water equal to 1 cubic foot per second for a 24-hour period.

The minimum Bull Shoals and Norfork combined 3-day running average release shall not be less than 2,000 DSF when the next days' forecast air temperature in the area is above 85 degrees F. as determined by the National Weather Service(NWS), Little Rock, Arkansas.

SIMULATION OF A SURFACE WATER ALLOCATION SYSTEM

W. Brian Walls, Associate Member ASCE[1]
Dr. Ralph A. Wurbs, Associate Member ASCE

ABSTRACT

This paper outlines the water rights system in Texas and a newly developed computer simulation program for modeling this system. In addition, an overview of a river basin simulation using the program is provided.

INTRODUCTION

Modeling and analysis of surface water rights is becoming an increasingly important aspect of water resources development and management in Texas. The state has recently implemented a permit system for allocating surface water between users. The amount of water available to particular users or management entities depends upon the impacts of senior rights in the river basin. Effective water management requires an understanding of institutional as well as hydrologic water availability.

WATER RIGHTS

Generally, legal rights to the use of streamflow are based on two alternative doctrines, riparian and prior appropriation. The basic concept of the riparian doctrine is that water rights are related to ownership of land adjacent to a stream. The prior appropriation doctrine is based on the concept, "first in time, first in right." In a prior appropriation system, priorities are established by the dates that users first appropriate water.

Texas Water Law. - Surface water law in Texas developed over several centuries (McNeeley and Lacewell 1977 and Templer 1981). Claims are presently recognized to water rights granted under Spanish, Mexican, Republic of Texas,

---

[1]Staff Engineer, Waste Management of North America, 1320 Greenway Drive Suite 900, Irving, TX 75038

United States, and State of Texas laws. Early water rights were granted based on various versions of the riparian doctrine. A prior appropriation system was later adopted and modified. The Water Rights Adjudication Act of 1967 converted the riparian water rights into appropriation rights. Texas now uses a modified prior appropriation system that requires a permit.

Water right permits grant use of a specified amount of water, at a specific location, for a specific purpose. Any person, public or private corporation or political subdivision of the state may acquire a permit to appropriate water.

With the exception of the water master operations in the lower Rio Grande Valley, there has been very little active management of water rights in Texas. Few situations have arisen in which junior water rights holders had to curtail diversions to protect senior water rights. The next severe drought will necessitate development of a detailed mechanism for policing water users and curtailing water use in accordance with water rights priorities.

WATER RIGHTS ANALYSIS MODEL

The Texas A&M University Water Rights Analysis Program (TAMUWRAP) is documented by Walls and Wurbs (1988). TAMUWRAP is a generalized computer model for simulating surface water management under a prior appropriation water rights system. The capabilities of a river basin to satisfy existing water rights and the amount of streamflow remaining for additional water rights applicants can be evaluated. A TAMUWRAP simulation typically will be based on assumptions of (1) a repetition of historical hydrology and (2) diversion of the full amount permitted as long as water is available. The model performs water accounting computations for each month of the simulation period. Output includes monthly diversions, diversion shortages, reservoir storage levels, streamflow depletions, and unappropriated streamflows.

System Components. - A stream/reservoir/rights system is represented in the model by the following components: (1) control points, (2) basin hydrology, (3) reservoirs, and (4) water rights.

Control points are specified to indicate the location of streamflow data and serve to locate reservoirs, and water rights. The basin hydrology consists of naturalized streamflows and reservoir evaporation rates at each control point for each month of the simulation period. A water right is represented by the following model input data: (1) control point location, (2) annual diversion amount,

(3) reservoir storage capacity, (4) priority number, (5) type of use, and (6) return flow factor. A single reservoir may be associated with several water rights with different combinations of priority dates, storage capacities and other variables.

Model Computations. - The water balance computations proceed by month and, within each month, by water right on a priority basis. An accounting is maintained of storage levels in each reservoir and streamflow available at each control point. TAMUWRAP computes streamflow depletions associated with each water right and unappropriated streamflows at each control point. A streamflow depletion represents the streamflow taken by a water right to meet the target water right diversion and to fill previously drawn-down reservoir capacity. Unappropriated streamflow represents water available after all streamflow depletions.

BRAZOS RIVER BASIN STUDY

TAMUWRAP and HEC-3 simulation analyses were a major component of the study of the hydrologic and institutional water availability in the Brazos River Basin documented by Wurbs, Bergman, Carriere, and Walls (1988).

Reservoir System. - The investigation focused on a system of 12 principal reservoirs. Numerous other reservoirs in the basin were considered from the perspective of their impacts on the 12 principal reservoirs. Significant diversions from the river occur at substantial distances below the dams and can be met by releases from various combinations of several reservoirs. Forty-six percent of the permitted diversions in the basin are below the reservoir system.

Water Rights. - About 1,040 individual citizens, private companies, cities, and public agencies hold permits to use the waters of the Brazos River and tributaries. The water rights include diversions totalling 84.9 m^3/S and storage capacities totalling 5,634 million m^3 in 598 reservoirs.

The water rights associated with the 12 reservoirs have different priority dates, and some reservoirs have several rights with different priorities. Each of the reservoirs are constrained by numerous senior water rights. Inflows must be passed through a reservoir to meet senior water rights at downstream locations.

Water Rights Analysis. - The results of a base simulation (run 1) and two alternative simulation runs are summarized in Table 1. Run 1 is based on applying priority dates specified by the water rights to both diversions and refilling reservoir capacity. Run 2 is identical to run 1 with the exception that all municipal rights with priority dates after May 17, 1931 are changed to reflect the Wagstaff Act. Run 3 is identical to run 1 except the priorities associated with refilling reservoir storage in the major reservoirs are made junior to all diversions.

TABLE 1. - Basin Summary of TAMUWRAP Simulation Results

Quantity (1)	1900-1984 Means (m^3/S)		
	Run 1 (2)	Run 2 (3)	Run 3 (4)
naturalized streamflow	221.7	221.7	221.7
permitted diversions	84.9	84.9	84.9
actual diversions	76.8	76.1	79.4
shortages	8.1	8.8	5.5
reservoir evaporation	20.7	21.1	20.7
return flows	14.0	13.4	14.0
unappropriated streamflow	138.7	138.5	136.1
storage change	0.6	0.6	0.6

Table 1 presents basin totals of pertinent quantities expressed as averages over the 85-year simulation period. The unappropriated streamflow represents flows into the Gulf of Mexico or water available for additional water right permit applicants. The sum of naturalized streamflows and return flows equals the sum of actual diversions, reservoir evaporation, unappropriated streamflow, and reservoir storage change.

CONCLUSIONS

During application of this general modeling approach in the case study, several key aspects of evaluating water availability were identified. These modeling considerations can be categorized as (1) basic hydrology and water use data, (2) reservoir system operations, and (3) policies and procedures for administering water rights.

Water rights permits in Texas are written for individual reservoirs, not multireservoir systems. Expanded consideration of multireservoir system operations in both the administration and modeling of water rights is a major area of needed additional work. Administration of a water rights system during drought conditions requires subjective judgments as well as quantitative criteria and, consequently, is difficult to precisely model. The priority allocation system is based on priority dates. However, a provision of the Texas Water Code, originally enacted as the Wagstaff Act, allows municipalities to appropriate water previously appropriated by other users. Under drought conditions, municipalities could be given priority over other senior nonmunicipal appropriators.

Reservoir operation in Texas is based on providing long-term storage as protection against infrequent, but severe, droughts. The right to store water is as important as the right to divert water. Protecting reservoir inflows is critical to achieving the purpose of the reservoir, which is to provide a dependable water supply. However, forcing junior appropriators to curtail diversions to maintain inflows to an almost full, or even an almost empty, reservoir is difficult.

Effective management and utilization of the water resource provided by a stream/reservoir system requires an understanding of the amount of water which can be supplied under various conditions. Water availability is subject to institutional as well as hydrologic constraints. The continually increasing demands on surface water resources and the recently implemented permit system, have made water rights an increasingly important aspect of water resources development and management. TAMUWRAP provides a broad range of water rights modeling and analysis capabilities to assist in meeting these development challenges.

APPENDIX I - REFERENCES

McNeely, J.G., and Lacewell, R.D. (1977). "Surface Water Management in Texas," Texas Agricultural Experiment Station, Texas A & M University, College Station, TX.

Walls, W.B., and Wurbs, R.A. (1988). "Water Rights Analysis Program (TAMUWRAP), Program Description and Users Manual," Technical Report 146, Texas Water Resources Institute, College Station, TX.

Wurbs, R.A., Bergman, C.E., Carriere, P.E., and Walls, W.B. (1988). "Hydrologic and Institutional Water Availability in the Brazos River Basin," Technical Report 144, Texas Water Resources Institute, College Station, TX.

History of Geographic Information Systems, with Applications
in Water Resources Planning and Management

Richard M. Males, M.ASCE1

Introduction

Geographic Information System (GIS) technology is an
increasingly popular approach to working on a variety of
natural resources problems of interest in the field of
water resources planning and management. Many of the
supporters of use of GIS technology believe it to be a
relatively new tool with little history or experience in
application in our field. In fact, GIS technology has been
used extensively in a variety of water resource-related
studies for at least fifteen years. The character of much
recent work is simply 're-invention of the wheel', as
researchers and workers proceed without attempting to
examine the literature and learn from prior experience.
The purpose of this paper is to provide some idea of the
threads that have led to the current GIS technology.

Background of GIS Technology

GIS technology includes, at minimum, the ability to enter,
display, edit, and manipulate computer-stored information
that has locational attributes. It differs from computer-
aided mapping or drafting technologies in that, in
addition, GIS technology provides the ability to perform
spatial analysis on this data, i.e. to examine the data
using concepts that are unique to locational data, such as
nearness, sequential location on a network, etc.
Frequently, GIS technology stores topological relationships
between spatial data elements to accomplish this end, where
mapping or drafting technologies may be restricted to
storage of geometry only. Finally, GIS technology may
include varying degrees of modeling capability, that is,
the ability to use the stored spatial data as the basis for
analytical or simulation modeling of phenomenona.

1RMM Technical Services, Inc., 3319 Eastside Avenue,
Cincinnati, OH 45208

GIS technology has evolved from a variety of sources, including computer mapping, surveying and photogrammetry, and planning (in particular certain schools of landscape architecture). Computerized map-making has been of interest to cartographers since the '60s. The goal was simply to make the production and modification of maps simpler. The growth of such technology has paralleled the rise of computer-aided drafting techniques in general. Both computer-aided drafting and mapping initially had as their goal the generation of paper products, i.e. maps or drafting sheets. Eventually, it was recognized that the data base that is required to generate the paper products can be used for other analyses, and a more 'model-oriented' approach was born, in which the data stored was seen as a model of the world, rather than as simply the set of coordinates necessary to draw the desired map. Distinctions were made between cartographic applications, in which the maps needed to be of publication quality, and planning and analysis applications, for which computer generated maps could make use of the only commonly available output device, the line printer. The SYMAP program (Robertson), developed at Harvard University's Laboratory for Computer Graphics and Spatial Analysis in 1963, provided a mechanism for generating various forms of maps on a line printer, and was widely used.

Another source for GIS technology was computerized photogrammetry and surveying. Again in the early '60s, the desire to manipulate spatial data in a computer led to such well-known civil engineering programs as COGO, developed at MIT for calculating surveying analyses on coordinate data. At the same time, the concept of the Digital Terrain Model (DTM) was developed, in which the computer would be used to store a digital data base representing the earth's surface. Early attempts were made to use DTM's for analysis and modeling - one project at MIT in 1964 involved attempting to develop optimal highway routings based on modeling of costs of alternative routes using DTM's. (This project was ultimately unsuccesful due to constraints inherent in the grid-based technology that was used to store the digital terrain model).

Much of GIS modeling technology, as it is used today, is largely an outgrowth of planning approaches that are based on the work of Ian McHarg, as articulated in his book "Design with Nature" (McHarg, 1969). McHarg, a landscape architect (and strong critic of civil engineers), popularized, in the late '60s, a methodology of planning called 'suitability analysis'. His manual methods involved overlaying a grid on the area to be studied, and comparing and combining values for different types of attributes in a grid cell, to determine the 'suitability' of each grid cell for various uses. When computerized, this became the basis

of the common 'overlay analysis' or 'weighting' of GIS
technology, which served as the basic 'modeling' technology
of GIS for many years.

Due to the two different GIS ancestors of cartography and
planning, the technologies in GIS were divided into the
'polygon-based' approaches derived from cartography, in
which detailed coordinates of the curving lines of maps are
stored, and the 'grid-based' approach of the planners. The
polygon approach provides good representation of mapped
information, but proved difficult to use in analysis. The
'grid-based' approaches derived from planning, and from
mapping programs based on the line printer such as SYMAP
(Robertson, 1967), which were constrained to grid-cell
oriented representation. The grid approach, based on a
matrix and thus easily handled by FORTRAN programming,
provided easy analysis capabilities of the overlay type,
but did not provide very good representations. In the
early and mid-70's, the arguments about the merits of the
two approaches were continual. Eventually, the problem was
'resolved' by the use of polygon-to-grid technology, in
which data is captured originally in polygon format, and
converted to a grid-based format for analysis
(Comprehensive Planning Organization, 1974).

In general, terrain and network data, both of prime
significance to water resources applications, were ignored.
Terrain data presented a significant problem for
incorporation into either the polygon or grid systems. The
innate variation in terrain means that selection of grid
size is critical, and it is essentially impossible to
select an appropriate grid size for an area that captures
fine-scale terrain variations in the steep areas without
storing vast quantities of redundant data in the flatter
areas. This became known as the 'variable grid resolution'
problem, and a variety of methods were tried to overcome
this, including the use of hierarchical grids (where sub-
grids were used in detail areas) and triangulated surfaces
(called TIN's, for Triangulated Irregular Networks)
(Peucker,1973; Grayman,1975; Gold, 1976). The hierarchical
grid method never proved workable in practice, but the TIN
has developed into a fundamental method of storing terrain
data in GIS.

By and large, the issue of handling terrain data was
considered to be a specialized field, not really in the
mainstream of GIS concern. Accordingly, few systems made
any attempt to adequately integrate terrain data with
'coverage' data such as soils, land use, etc. Network
data was usually considered to be the province of
transportation planning, and few applications were oriented
towards stream, water, or sewer networks. Modeling within
early GIS technology was, in general, restricted to

weighting, distance measures, and overlay analysis within
grid cells. There was little or no true simulation or
design modeling, even though such models were available
outside the world of GIS. Only recently has the general
GIS community given any attention to integrating GIS with
complex modeling capability.

Water Resources Applications of GIS Technology

For applications in water resources, GIS technology in
general must handle coverage data relating to land use,
land cover, geology, and soils. Network-oriented data
(streams, water distribution systems, sewer systems) and
terrain information are very significant. Frequently, subsurface information is of significance (e.g. for ground
water modeling).

In the field of water resources, the major spatial data
base was EPA's STORET water quality data base (initially
implemented by the US Public Health Service in 1964),
storing stream quality information that could be referenced
by location (primarily by river mile index). In the early
days of STORET development, the system was crude and
difficult to use, and spatial retrieval capability was
minimal, but the system has since been expanded and made
into a powerful tool with significant spatially-oriented
data retrieval and display capabilities.

EPA also maintains the Reach File, a data system initiated
in 1981-82, that is organized by hydrologic structure and
has significant spatial data retrieval and analysis
capabilities organized by hydrologic units. Stream
reaches within the system have been digitized, and a good
deal of data (discharger location, water supply intake
location, etc.) has been referenced to the reach. The
system maintains reach connectivity, allowing for routing-
type analyses, and planning-level modeling of flows, toxics
discharges, etc. The Reach File exists at various levels
of detail (it was originally based on 1:500,000 scale NOAA
maps), and will contain all of the streams represented on
USGS topo sheets (1:24000 scale).

The US Army Corps of Engineers has had a long involvement
with GIS technology, starting with sponsorship of research
on resource analysis methods (Harvard University Department
of Landscape Architecture, 1969). The Honey Hill study
using this methodology (1971) was followed by the Santa Ana
River Basin Study (1975) using grid-based methods for river
basin planning. Problems with the Santa Ana study led to
designation of the Hydrologic Engineering Center (HEC) of
the Corps as a center of expertise and development work for
GIS work within the Corps. HEC worked with grid-based
technology, and linked it to HEC models, in particular the

HEC-1 model, developing the HEC-SAM (Spatial Analysis Methodology). HEC-SAM methods were tested on a Corps Flood Plain Information Study (Phase I Oconee Basin Pilot Study, 1975), and were later widely used in a variety of Corps studies. The study and approach are notable for the combination of GIS and hydrologic modeling technology, in particular because the modeling was not simplified or subordinated to the GIS aspects of the study - rather, the GIS served as a database to 'feed' the models used. HEC has continued to utilize spatial analysis technology (preferring the term spatial analysis to GIS) and has produced a variety of computerized tools that make use of spatial data bases.

Studies of non-point source pollution, given great impetus by Public Law 92-500 in the early '70s, led to the development and use of a number of GIS systems. Most such systems used grid-based technologies and simple overlay analysis as the modeling component. More sophisticated systems were developed, however, to provide enhanced modeling capability. In particular, the ADAPT (Areal Design and Planning Tool) system was a TIN-based GIS, developed in 1972, with the primary objective of serving as a GIS-based modeling system for engineering design of wastewater systems and hydrologic analyses. The ADAPT system (Grayman, 1975, Males, 1980) used the triangulated irregular network technique of storing terrain, but also used each triangular element as a grid cell, for storing soil, land use, and land cover data. The edges of the triangles formed links of stream systems, or boundaries of polygons, providing an integrated network, cell, polygon, and digital terrain system that was later adopted as the basis of the statewide Planning and Engineering Management System of Ohio, maintained by the Ohio Environmental Protection Agency. The ADAPT system was notable for having variable resolution cells (i.e. triangle size could vary, depending upon the level of detail that needed to be captured), for the integration of terrain, network, and coverage data, and for the manual nature of database creation - the triangular data structure was developed as a true surface model, and the triangular plates were hand-developed based on examination of topo maps.

Summary

While this is an admittedly incomplete overview, it is clear that elements of computerized spatial analysis have been used in water resources since the mid '60s, and sophisticated and complex systems incorporating GIS and modeling technology were developed, tested, and applied to a wide variety of projects starting in the early '70s. The findings of the early developers, that GIS technology must support complex engineering modeling, and that it must provide representations of terrain and network information, as well as 2-dimensional information (soils, land cover, etc.), for it to be of use in water resources applications, are still valid today, and need not be re-discovered by those just entering the field.

References

Comprehensive Planning Organization, PIOS II Polygon to Grid Conversion, San Diego, 1974

Gold, C.M., "Triangular Element Data Structures", University of Alberta Computing Services, Users Applications Symposium Proceedings, Edmonton, 1976

Grayman, W., Males, R.M., et al, "Land-Based Modeling System for Water Quality Management Studies", Journal of the Hydraulics Division, ASCE, Vol 101, No. HY5, May, 1975

The Hydrologic Engineering Center, "Phase I Oconee Basin Pilot Study, Trail Creek Test", Corps of Engineers, September 1975

IWR Report 71-9, "Honey Hill: A Systems Analysis for Planning the Multiple Use of Controlled Water Areas", Corps of Engineers, October 1971

IWR Contract Report 75-3, "The Santa Ana Basin: An Example of the Use of Computer Graphics in Regional Plan Evaluation", Corps of Engineers, June 1975

Males, R.M., "ADAPT: The Use of Complex Models with a Geographic Data Base", Proceedings, Specialty Conference, The Planning and Engineering Interface with a Modernized Land Data System, ASCE, 1980.

McHarg, Ian, Design With Nature, Natural History Press, Garden City, New York 1969

Peucker, T.K., "Geographic Data Structures Report After Year One", Office of Naval Research Contract N00014-73-C-0109, Department of Geography, Simon Fraser University, Burnaby, B.C., 1973

Robertson, J.C., "The SYMAP program for Computer Mapping", The Cartographic Journal, Vol. 4, No. 2, pp 108-113, 1967

Steinitz et al, "A Comparative Study of Resource Analysis Methods", Department of Landscape Architecture Research Office, Graduate School of Design, Harvard University, July 1969

The present of GIS

Dean Djokic and David R. Maidment [1]

Abstract

A review of GIS as a spatial database is presented. CAD and relational database features of GIS are explained, as well as possible types of spatial database queries. Advanced GIS features provide the opportunity for integration of data management, design and analysis in a single environment.

Introduction

In recent years, with the rapid development of microcomputers and computer workstations, there has been a significant advance in technology for computer aided design and drafting (CAD) and geographic information systems (GIS), and their application in the engineering field. With the evolution of CAD and GIS packages, more and more advanced features can be found in both types of software. This paper explains the basic ideas behind GIS structure and describes how advanced GIS features provide ideal opportunity for integration of data management, design and analysis in a single environment.

GIS as a spatial database

There is a vast literature on GIS properties and they will not be discussed here in detail. In short, GIS can be viewed as a spatial database program ie., a combination of relational database and geographic (geometric) image. Each element in the geographic image can have a corresponding entry in the relational database that describes its attributes.

---

[1] Graduate research assistant and associated professor respectively, The University of Texas at Austin, Department of Civil Engineering, Austin, Tx 78712

A relational database is a rectangular table whose columns are categories of information and whose rows are data records. A subset of the columns, called the "key", contains the basic identifiers for each data record. The other columns are connected to those in the key through "relations", hence the name "relational database". For example, an inventory of pipes in city's sewer system has an identifier which specifies which pipe it is, and attributes such as material, diameter, pipe to which it connects downstream, types of inlet structures, etc. In this case, the identifier is located in the key column, and the other items are in the same row in different columns according to the type of information.

Special operations can be defined for merging two databases so that result will contain no duplicate entries - if data elements in two rows of the key are identical, one of them is eliminated. Also new records can be created by merging tables which are unique combinations of separate attributes in the original table. For example, if one table presents mapped soil information, and another land cover information, they can be combined to produce a larger number of soil-land cover combinations.

A geographic image is an electronic version of a map on which each element is represented as a point, a line or a polygon - a closed set of lines forming an object (eg. the outline of the area occupied by a particular soil type). Geographic (geometric) images like this can be created in any CAD package by digitizing paper maps, or built up from site surveys and design drawings. Each entity in a geographic image is stored in a data file and specified by a unique identifier, type of image (point, line or polygon), and geographic location (x,y,z coordinates).

A geographic information system combines the relational database and the graphic image by having a common identifier that is used between a row in the database and an entry in the image (Figure 1). This enables two types of queries : first, on graphical images and second, on database attributes. The queries on the graphic image, are of the form "show me all the pipes within this area", and the system will go to the relational database, search for all pipes with the correct x,y,z locations, determine their graphic identifiers, and highlight them on the screen. Likewise, one can query by the attributes in the database through the form "find (and display) all the pipes of diameter greater that 10 inches".

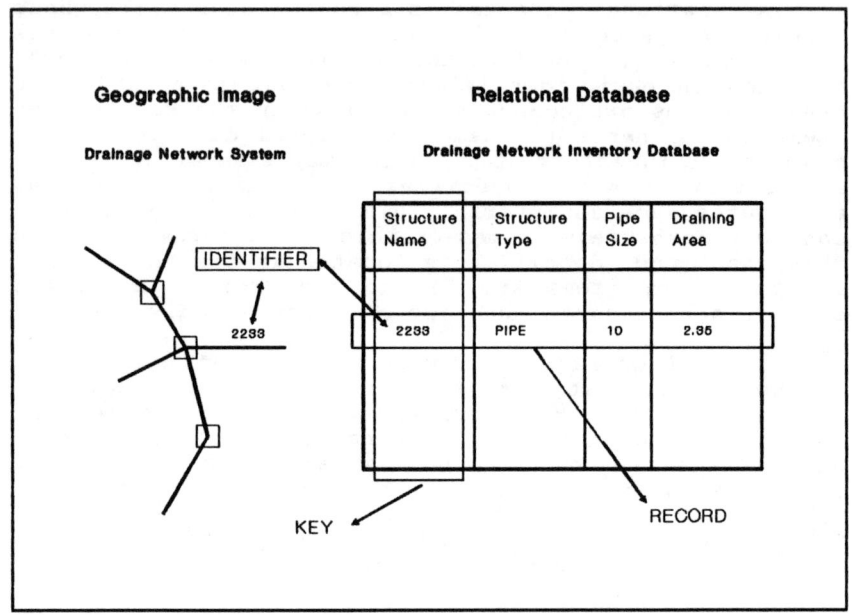

Figure 1. Geographic images and database records share a common identifier in a GIS

Advanced GIS packages can combine the two types of queries and also perform basic mathematical operations (such as "find the total length of the pipes within a given area that have diameter greater than 10 inches"). The query is both graphical (pipes within user-defined area) and through attributes (pipes of certain profile), and at the same time the summation of the resulting set of pipes is performed. Another advanced GIS feature is that the records in the database can also be formulas, thus allowing a much more flexible data structure and information manipulation than is possible with data tables alone.

GIS, CAD, database and expert systems

Early GIS programs did not have the precision and drafting capabilities of CAD programs, nor the full flexibility of database systems. Current trends in GIS development tend to diminish these differences. The new programs combine the precision of a CAD with the functionality and versatility of a database package.

In most cases, specialized CAD and database software still provides more functionality for a specialized application than GIS does, but the gap is narrowing with the inclusion of advanced database functions (eg. structured query language) and CAD capabilities (eg. coordinate geometry) in new and existing GIS packages.

Expert systems, or knowledge base systems, differ from GIS in that they are based around the logic of the search process and have less emphasis on data records and their manipulation. Expert systems are more suited to problems where the reasoning process is inherently very complicated and does not depend much on external data entry. Also expert systems do not have the graphical orientation to mapped information that GIS systems do.

GIS applications

Typical uses of GIS involve query and inventory of mapped information, probably in combinations of maps. For example : "calculate the area of each soil type in this watershed". This type of query involves interaction between the attributes of the relational database and their geographic location, and cannot be accomplished when the graphic image and the database are not electronically integrated.

Most of the current GIS applications are in the management area, such as facility, land and resource management, traffic planning, etc. It is mainly used as an information or planning tool for answering relatively simple questions by interrogating large amounts of spatially-oriented data.

A significant feature of modern GIS programs is the capability of integration and easy transition between the raster representation (eg. photographs or video images) and vector representation (eg. drawings) in a single environment. This makes remotely sensed data contained in aircraft or satellite images more useful for engineering computation.

GIS assessment

The chief advantage of GIS is that it takes information on maps and databases and makes better use of it by integrating it electronically rather than having separate tables of data and mapped representation of these data. The results can be represented graphically in color coded maps which enable a greater degree of human understanding of spatial relationships of information. In the engineering environment, the CAD features of GIS can be used to make a detailed layout of the facilities (and easily change it if necessary) while the database features add the information handling of spatial data that is needed for analysis.

The chief limitation of GIS is that it does not have much capacity at the moment for complex analysis of the type needed in engineering design. The new, openly structured GIS software enables the use of GIS features as a pre- and post-processor to engineering analysis, where the user develops the main calculation routine and uses GIS to prepare input data files and display the results of computations. With the increase in functionality, GIS is becoming a viable environment for integration of data management, design and analysis in engineering practice.

GIS IN WATER RESOURCES IN THE YEAR 2000

Walter M. Grayman, Member, ASCE[1]

Introduction

Geographic Information System (GIS) technology has been applied in the water resources area for the past two decades. And though some of the early applications in water resources were pioneering efforts in the overall GIS field, presently most GIS applications in the water resources field utilize technology developed by and for the general planning community. Frequently, this technology is not adequately robust to support the technical requirements of water resources applications such as hydrologic modeling, surface and groundwater interaction, etc.

In order to better define the requirements of water resources planning and management in the GIS area, this paper will present a look at what the GIS, as applied to water resources, may look like in the year 2000. The presentation will not be constrained by either the present GIS technology nor by technological problems for which solutions do not currently exist. Rather, this paper will present a description of what a water resources engineer would want from a GIS in order to support the kind of analyses and displays needed in the field of water resources. Such a system would be user friendly, have ready access to spatial data bases containing topographic, hydrographic, demographic, and land use information, and support a wide range of modeling, analysis and display capabilities.

Overview

The GIS in the year 2000 will have graduated from its present position as a means of generating pretty maps and performing simple analyses to a full role in the field of water resources planning, design and management. As a consequence of its capability of managing and using spatial

---

[1] Owner, W.M. Grayman Consulting Engineer, 730 Avon Fields Lane, Cincinnati, Ohio 45229

information it will have moved the hydrologic models and other analysis tools in the field of water resources from their present place as quasi spatially distributed tools to ones that fully appreciate and utilize the spatial information inherent in all water resources problems.

The primary change within the GIS field will be the integration of the GIS with other computer based tools to form a spatially based analysis and display system. Integration will include hardware-software integration, integration of GIS with models, and integration of the fields of CAD, AM-FM, DBMS, and computer cartography into a single spatially based entity promoting the needs of the water resources engineer.

The integrated GIS will be composed of several, tightly connected components which together will allow a virtually seamless system for manipulating spatial information. These components will include: the hardware system, the spatial data, the software for managing and manipulating the data, models for using the spatial information, and means for displaying the spatial data and results of the analysis. The characteristics and needs of each of these components are described below.

Hardware

The hardware base for the GIS 2000 will be a highly refined version of the present day work station. This work station will include high resolution color based systems for scanning, storing and displaying large detailed data bases. Large capacity mass storage devices will permit the user to store and retrieve detailed spatial data bases covering large geographic areas. Automated data redundancy systems will insure the safety and backup of the data. High speed data transfer devices will permit the routine transmission of large quantities of data between work stations. The CPU portion of the work station will be capable of working with the large spatial data bases and supporting the billions of operations associated with spatial data in the engineering field.

Data

The data component in the year 2000 will be characterized by the availability of a wide range of spatial data bases, an intelligent scanning system for entering hard copy maps into the GIS, and a universal exchange format for transferring spatial data between installations and software systems. Within the water resources field spatial data bases covering the entire country will be available containing topographic information (with sufficient detail to generate a continuous surface representation), soils, land cover, political jurisdictions, population, hydrographic elements, sub surface elements and infrastructure (roads, pipes, etc.). The information will be integrated so that, for example, hydrographic features such as streams will be consistent with topographic features such as ridge lines. The universal exchange format will facilitate the transferability of the data and remove the difficulties associated with different formats different projections, etc. For information available only as hard copy mappage, hardware-software systems will permit the intelligent scanning of paper maps and conversion of the data into vector based entities.

Software/Data Structure

In the formative years of GIS (1960's - present), a major emphasis in applying a GIS has been the mechanisms for storing spatial data and manipulating the data. By the year 2000, both the structures for storing the data and the methods of manipulating the data will be virtually invisible to the user. An intelligent 'front-end' to the GIS including a high level spatial command language and a 'Macintosh' style graphical interface will permit the user to combine, transform and manipulate spatial data with ease. 'Hooks' used to integrate the GIS with programs will use standard formats and data access methods allowing the custom programmer to easily access spatial data for use in their programs and to store spatially generated information back into the GIS.

Modeling

The advances in the field of spatial data handling will have a synergistic effect on models in the field of water resources. To date, the limited availability of spatial data and the cumbersome manipulation of such data has discouraged the development of truly spatial models which in turn has slowed down the requirements for spatial data. By the year 2000, the sophisticated GIS and greater availability of data will have spurred renewed development of models that can incorporate detailed spatial data. This will include highly distributed rainfall-runoff models using detailed representations of topographic surfaces, spatially distributed soils and land cover data, spatially varying rainfall data derived from radar systems, and most importantly, a better understanding of the spatially dependent physical processes affecting the runoff process. Other models in water resources which will benefit from improved spatial data include groundwater and groundwater - surface water models, non point source models, stream hydraulic and water quality models, sewer and water system analysis and design models. The spatial data management/display capabilities associated with GIS will also serve as a means of displaying voluminous data generated by highly distributed models.

Display

The final component in the GIS is the display mechanism; the means of displaying and producing maps and diagrams from the spatial data. In the year 2000, inexpensive devices for routinely displaying and producing high quality color outputs on paper, slides and video will be widely available. Additionally, the superposition of both photographic material such as an aerial photo and digital information such as a pipe network will be common in both hard copy and screen displays along with three dimensional display methods.

Research and Development Needs

Achieving a GIS which fulfills the needs of the water resources engineer by the year 2000 requires active participation by the engineer in the GIS/spatial data management field. Both research into the spatial aspects of water resources problems and influence in the GIS design decisions are needed.

Specific areas of research include (but are not limited to): spatial processes in hydrology, definition of spatial needs in water resources modeling, and recognition of the integration needs among the various spatial tools commonly used in the water resources area (GIS, CAD, AM-FM, modeling, computer cartography). Influence within the GIS design field can be exerted by the water resources engineer by communicating the needs within the water resources field to the GIS developers and pressuring them to provide a product which is responsive to these needs.

This view of the GIS in the year 2000 is achievable. However, without an organized effort by the water resources community to define their needs, to conduct the required research efforts, to communicate their needs to the GIS developers, and to pressure federal agencies to continue the data base development programs, the end product in 10 years will be much less than is described in this paper.

UTE MOUNTAIN UTE INDIAN WATER RIGHTS SETTLEMENT OF 1988

Steven C Harris (1)
Member, ASCE

Abstract

The Ute Mountain Ute Tribe, located in the southwest corner of Colorado, agreed to a negotiated settlement of Winters Doctrine Water Rights rather than pursuing litigation. The Tribe will receive, in lieu of Winters Water Rights, water supplies from two Bureau of Reclamation Projects and a cash Development Fund that can be used to construct and operate facilities to utilize the water supplies.

Introduction

The "Colorado Ute Indian Water Rights Settlement Act of 1988" provides for the settlement of Winters Doctrine water right claims by the Ute Mountain Ute and Southern Ute Indian Tribes. The two Indian tribes are located on two reservations in southwest Colorado; the Winters Water Right claims were on rivers and streams that pass through the reservations.

The Settlement was a negotiated agreement between the two Tribe's, local water users, the State of Colorado, and the United States Government. This paper is a synopsis of the Settlement for the Ute Mountain Ute Tribe. The author provided engineering expertise to the Ute Mountain Ute Tribe during the negotiation process from 1985 through 1988.

In order to understand the basis of the Winters Water Rights claims, a brief history of the Ute Indians is described. The Ute Indians occupied the area generally west of the Rocky Mountains in Colorado, east of the Wasatch Mountains in Utah, and from Wyoming on the north to New Mexico on the south. The Ute's were a nomadic people who primarily hunted for food and migrated according to the seasons.

The first treaty between the Ute's and the United States was in 1868 and provided that the Ute Reservation would be most of western Colorado. In

---

(1) Owner of Harris Water Engineering, 954 Second Avenue, Durango, Colorado 81301.

1895, another treaty was signed that reduced the reservation area significantly and separated the Ute people into three reservations. The reservation boundaries in the latter treaty are essentially the same today.

The Ute's were separated into the Southern Ute, Ute Mountain Ute, and Uinta Ute reservations. The Uinta Ute's are located in Utah while the other two tribes are located in southwest Colorado.

The Ute Mountain Ute Reservation is located in the extreme southwest corner of Colorado. The Reservation comprises the northeast quadrant of the Four Corners Monument. The Reservation is about 500,000 acres in size, receives an average of about 8 to 10 inches of precipitation per year and ranges in elevation from 8000 to 5000 feet above sea level. The major river on the reservation is the the Mancos River, entering the reservation near the northeast corner and exiting near the southwest corner. The San Juan River also traverses the reservation for about 3 miles in the southwest corner. There is one other small stream entering the reservation, Navajo Wash, that carries irrigation return flows from land to the north.

Winters Water Rights Claims

The Winters Doctrine was established in 1906 and says that the United States Congress implied that adequate water is reserved in rivers and streams traversing Indian reservations to meet the purposes of the reservation. In most cases the purpose of the reservations was to provide a homeland for the Indian Tribe where they can become farmers. The Doctrine says that an Indian Tribe is entitled to adequate water rights to irrigate all of the "practicably irrigable" land on the reservation and the water rights shall have a priority date when the reservation was established.

In the case of the Ute Mountain Ute Tribe the initial reservation was established in 1868 which was long before any non-Indians were irrigating. The result would be that the Ute Mountain Ute Tribe would have first priority to all water that can be shown, in court proceedings, to serve land that could be practicably irrigated.

The Federal Government filed suit against the State of Colorado in 1975 to quantify the Winters Water Rights that the Ute Mountain Ute and Southern Ute Tribes were entitled to.

The Winters Water Rights Claims of the Ute Mountain Ute Tribe are primarily on the Mancos River, with smaller claims on the San Juan River, Navajo Wash, small tributaries that originate on the reservation, and the Dolores and LaPlata Rivers that are off the current reservation but were within the 1868 reservation boundaries.

The Mancos River currently has an average annual flow of about 17,000 acre-feet per year after irrigation of about 10,000 acres north of the reservation. Non-Indians began irrigation in about 1890 with direct diversions from the Mancos River and its tributaries. In the 1940's the United States Government, through the Bureau of Reclamation constructed Jackson Gulch Reservoir to store Mancos River flows. The result is that the flows remaining in the Mancos River had a high salt content and are only adequate to irrigate about 100 acres without a very large reservoir to store flood flows.

The Ute Mountain Ute Tribe not only had Winters Water Right claims to most of the flows of the Mancos River but had a damage claim against the United States Government for constructing a dam that further depleted the water the Tribe was entitled to.

The present use of the Mancos River flows to irrigate 10,000 acres of land supports a small community which would be economically destroyed if the Ute Mountain Ute Tribe obtained first priority to the Mancos River flows, which all parties agreed was inevitable.

Negotiated Settlement

In 1985, the Colorado State Attorney General initiated talks to determine if the two Tribes, the federal government, and the local water users might be interested in negotiating a water rights settlement, rather than continuing with court proceedings. There were several reasons for the parties being interested in a negotiated settlement. From the State of Colorado's position, court proceedings would probably cost from $10 million to $20 million based upon other trials which could be better spent on building facilities to implement a settlement. Also, the Tribe would receive a first priority water right on rivers and streams in southwest Colorado and as a minimum could destroy the Mancos Valley economy.

From the Tribe's perspective, a negotiated settlement made sense because court proceedings very often result in a first priority water right but the Tribe's would probably not have the monetary resources to construct facilities to utilize the water. This is referred to as a "paper water right" as opposed to a "wet water right".

The potential parties of a settlement agreed that a negotiated agreement which utilized water resources from two Bureau of Reclamation projects, Dolores and Animas-LaPlata, would be beneficial to everyone, but they also understood that there were tremendous problems to be overcome. The foundation of the settlement would be to supply water to the Tribe's from the two projects in lieu of the potential Winters claims.

The key to negotiating a settlement for the Ute Mountain Ute Tribe was to determine what it wanted from the negotiations. The Tribe's basic premise was that water resources are essential to developing a self supporting reservation economy and a suitable homeland; neither water nor monetary resources were adequate alone but had to be available together. Generally, the Tribe determined that: (1) it wanted potable drinking water for the reservation residents, the present municipal water supply is not drinkable, (2) adequate water to develop a significant irrigation economy, and (3) the monetary resources to develop and operate the first two items.

Engineering studies were performed to evaluate all of the resources on the reservation that may require water. The resources include drinking water for the Tribal town of Towaoc, industrial water for coal reserves, and irrigation water for the arrable land.

The Bureau of Indian Affairs had prepared an arrable land classification for the entire reservation which was used to determine the amount of land that could be irrigated. Also, the Bureau of Reclamation classified lands for potential inclusion in the Dolores and Animas-LaPlata Projects. Cursory studies showed that there were some coal reserves. The most pressing need was for suitable drinking water in the Tribal Town of Towaoc. After these evaluations, the Tribe decided that some issues were non-negotiable and some could be modified.

The non-negotiable items were: (1) municipal water from the Dolores Project and the facilities to deliver the water to the reservation, (2) irrigation water from the Dolores Project to be delivered to 7,500 acres of land, (3) a development fund which would

INDIAN WATER RIGHTS SETTLEMENT 119

provide funds to construct and operate some of the water facilities, (4) industrial and irrigation water from the Animas-LaPlata Project but the water could be delivered at the reservation boundary rather than to a specific site on the reservation (the on reservation delivery facilties would be constructed from the Development Fund), and (5) water rights to unused flows on rivers and streams on the reservation.

The Ute Mountain Ute Tribe will receive from the Settlement:

* 1,000 acre-feet of municipal water delivered to the Town of Towaoc through a $6 million pipeline constructed by the State of Colorado. The water delivered will be treated by the City of Cortez through a contract with the Tribe. This water was available in 1989 and for the first time Towaoc has adequate potable water.

* 22,900 acre-feet of Dolores Project irrigation water delivered to each field. The Tribe must still finance the $35 million of on-farm facilities to utilize the irrigation water, with the Development Fund being used to help secure funding.

* A Development Fund in the amount of $34.5 million to be funded in 3 installments in fiscal years 1990, 1991, and 1992. The State of Colorado will spend $8.5 million in cash, $6 million for the pipeline and $2.5 million into the Development Fund. The Federal government will contribute the remainder. The Tribe will drop all damage claims against the Federal governement.

* 26,000 acre-feet of irrigation water and 6,000 acre-feet of industrial water from the Animas-LaPlata Project delivered at the reservation boundary. Approximately $100 million of facilities will be needed to distribute the water where it is needed on the reservation.

* Water rights to flows in the Mancos River not used by upstream users, 10 cfs from San Juan River, and about 10 cfs from Navajo Wash.

ADMINISTRATION OF THE PECOS RIVER COMPACT
BETWEEN NEW MEXICO AND TEXAS

Neil S. Grigg, M. ASCE[1]

Abstract

The Pecos River Compact specifies the allocation of water between New Mexico and Texas. Due to difficulty in reaching agreement Texas sued New Mexico in the Supreme Court. The Court issued an Amended Decree in 1988 to establish procedures for interstate water administration.

Introduction

Water of the Pecos River is shared between New Mexico and Texas according to an interstate compact which has recently been interpreted by the Supreme Court through an Amended Decree. This paper describes the background and the current status of annual administration of the compact.

Origins of the Compact and the Amended Decree

The Pecos River heads in the mountains of north-central New Mexico and flows about 900 miles to join the Rio Grande near Langtry, Texas. It drains about 25,000 square miles in New Mexico and about 19,000 square miles in Texas. The river can be viewed as having three major reaches: above Alamogordo Dam, between the dam and the New Mexico and Texas state line, and the reach in Texas. Precipitation in the basin is in the general range of 11-14 inches annually, and extensive irrigation is practiced, both from surface and groundwater diversions. There were about 210,000 irrigated acres in the two states in 1948, about 75 percent in New Mexico.

---

[1]Director, Colorado Water Resources Research Institute and River Master of the Pecos River.

Water development in the basin dates to before the Spanish conquest, as Coronado found irrigation practiced among indians in the upper reach in 1540. The Ft Sumner project was initiated in 1863 and rehabilitated by the Bureau of Reclamation in 1906. Irrigation in the Roswell area began from surface waters about 1889, from artesian waters about 1891 and from shallow wells after 1927. Irrigation in the Carlsbad area started about the same time with the use of McMillan and Avalon reservoirs (constructed in the 1890's) for storage. Alamogordo reservoir was constructed in 1937 to replace the deteriorated capacity of these reservoirs.

The controversy about interstate allocation of water dates back to about 1914 when a report by the Bureau of Reclamation commented on the need for a state line reservoir to regulate Texas' share of the water. Red Bluff reservoir was completed in 1936 as a Public Works Administration project. Details of the controversy can be traced in Supreme Court documents such as (Breitenstein, 1979).

A Compact Commission was organized in 1923. The compact it drafted failed due to a veto by the New Mexico governor. In 1931 the Texas legislature authorized a suit but it was not filed. The National Resources Planning Board completed a study called the Pecos River Joint Investigation in October 1942 and this report figured prominently in future compact negotiations (National Resources Planning Board, 1942).

The Pecos River Compact Commission was formed in 1942 and had its first meeting on February 9, 1943. The Compact was ratified by New Mexico on February 9, 1949, by Texas on March 4, 1949 and by the US Congress on June 9, 1949. Two key features of the Compact were the organization of the Pecos River Commission and a statement of New Mexico's obligation under Article III(a) of the Compact.

The Pecos River Commission has had difficulty resolving disputes due to the lack of tie-breaking vote and this problem led to the appointment in 1988 of a River Master.

New Mexico's Article III(a) obligation has been the subject of considerable litigation before two special masters and the Supreme Court. It is stated this way in the Compact: "Except as stated in paragraph (f) of this Article, New Mexico shall not deplete by man's activities the flow of the Pecos River at the New Mexico-Texas state line below an amount that will give Texas a quantity of water equivalent to that available to Texas under the 1947 condition."

The Court has approved the special master's elaboration of the 1947 condition which is stated this way: "The 1947 condition is that situation in the Pecos River Basin which produced in New Mexico the man-made depletions resulting from the stage of development existing at the beginning of the year 1947 and from the augmented Fort Sumner and Carlsbad acreage" (Breitenstein, 1984).

River Administration

The Engineer Advisory Committee to the Compact Commission recommended and the negotiators accepted an "inflow-outflow" method of apportioning waters. This is quoted by Special Master Breitenstein this way: "The inflow-outflow method involves the determination of the correlation between an index of the inflow to a basin as measured at certain gaging stations and the outflow from the basin" (Breitenstein, 1979).

Over the years there have been numerous hearings and activities to bring the case to its present status. The case was divided into two parts by the Court after a July 1986 report by Special Master Charles J. Meyers. One part concerned remedies for past shortfalls set at 340,100 acre-feet for the period 1950-1983. The status of this part of the case was that New Mexico was expected to make up this shortfall over a ten-year period, but there remain unsettled issues and a new Special Master, Monte Pascoe, was appointed due to the untimely death of Charles Meyers. After hearings in 1989 this part of the case was settled when New Mexico agreed to pay Texas a $14 million cash settlement.

For the future enforcement of the Compact an Amended Decree was issued by the Court on March 28, 1988. It sets forth the schedule for the administration of the Compact and the duties of the River Master. The following are some of the principal features of the Amended Decree:

- the concept of the water year and accounting year

RIVER COMPACT ADMINISTRATION 123

- adoption of the Pecos River Master's Manual
- annual calculation by the River Master of a shortfall or overage by New Mexico using the inflow-outflow method decribed in the Manual
- procedures for modifying the Manual
- requirement for New Mexico to submit a plan for making up shortfalls

In accounting year 1988 which covered water year 1987 the first calculation was made under the Amended Decree. Due to wet years in 1986 and 1987 the result for water year 1987 was an overage of 15,400 acre-feet delivered at the state line. These wet years carried over to the water year 1988 in which New Mexico had a calculated overage of 23,600 acre-feet.

References

Breitenstein, Jean S., Report of Special Master on Obligation of New Mexico to Texas Under the Pecos River Compact, Supreme Court of the United States, No. 65 Original, filed October 15, 1979

Breitenstein, Jean S., Report and Recommendation of Special Master, Supreme Court of the United States, No. 65 Original, filed February 27, 1984

Meyers, Charles J., Report of Special Master, Supreme Court of the United States, No. 65 Original, filed November 1987

National Resources Planning Board, Regional Planning: Part X, the Pecos River Joint Investigation in the Pecos River Basin in New Mexico and Texas, US Government Printing Office, Washington, 1942

WATER RIGHTS, WATER DEVELOPMENT, & GROWTH ISSUES IN GOLETA, CALIFORNIA
A Southern California Water Drama in Three Acts: Supply, Politics and the Law

Daniel Wendell [1]

ABSTRACT

The Goleta Valley and Santa Barbara areas of southern California are highly desireable places to live. In the past, relatively uncontrolled growth of the Goleta Valley area led to a gradual deterioration in the quality of for many of the residents. Unable to control growth of this unincorporated area through the County, a slow-growth group took control of the local Water Board and instituted defacto growth control via a moratorium on new water service connections. Costly litigation soon followed. Resulting battles over water have aggravated water supply problems and are in part responsible for burdensome rationing during the current drought. Growth control and water supply issues are becoming increasingly common in California, especially along the southern coast.

BACKGROUND

The Goleta Valley is an unincorporated area lying along the south-central coast of California, in Santa Barbara County. The major water purveyor for the area is the Goleta Water District which currently supplies a community of about 75,000 people with an average 14,500 acre-feet (AF) of water each year through 14,000 service connections. The District covers an area of about 30,000 acres. The District was formed by a vote of the people of the Goleta Valley area in 1944 in order to form an agency capable of contracting for a supply of imported water from the Bureau of Reclamation's then-proposed nearby Cachuma Reservoir. Water service from the Reservoir began in 1956.

The Goleta Valley and nearby Santa Barbara areas are highly desireable places to live. The climate is sunny and mild year round, its beaches are well known, and the area still has something of a small-town, and locally rural, atmosphere. Over the last 20 years, however, population growth along the coast has threatened the very qualities people sought when moving to the area. Housing prices are far beyond the reach of average workers, air quality has deteriorated, existing water resources are stretched beyond their sustainable limit, and existing roadways are choked with traffic during rush hours.

The changes that growth has brought to the Goleta Valley area have polarized much of the community into "slow-growth" and "pro-growth" camps. For the past 17 years the battle over growth within the valley has been fought within two main arenas, the County Board of Supervisors and the Goleta Water Board, but has spilled out into the community and led to numerous lengthy legal battles between the Boards and private property owners. For most of the past 17 years the slow-growth forces have controlled the Water Board, and have used that position to limit and shape growth within the community. During this same time the County Board of Supervisors was more supportive of development interests. It is significant that recent elections have brought a

---

[1] Associate Hydrogeologist, Goleta Water District, PO Box 788, Goleta, California, 93116.

solid majority of slow-growth Supervisors to the County Board.

This paper will present, in a non-technical manner, the effects the battle over growth has had on the area from the perspective of a water purveyor. Facts presented within this paper are not in serious dispute by local professionals; opinions and viewpoints expressed throughout this paper, however, are solely those of the author and do not necessarily represent those of the Goleta Water District, for whom the author works, or those of any other organization.

ACT I: THE SUPPLY

Local creeks and the Goleta Ground Water Basin (GGWB) were the only water resources for Goleta Valley from the time the area was first settled in the 1800's until Cachuma Reservoir was brought on line. Ground water production from the basin peaked in 1948, then dropped off as land was converted to urban uses and water from Cachuma Reservoir was imported into the area (Fig 1.; Loux, 1987). From 1956 until 1963, District service consisted solely of imported surface water from Cachuma Reservoir. In 1963 the District drilled its first well into the GGWB, the only major ground water basin located within the District. Since that time the District has become highly dependent on ground water production from this basin in order to meet demand. Currently, Cachuma Reservoir supplies about 70 percent (10,200 AFY) of the District's average annual demand, and ground water production from the GGWB most of the remaining 30 percent (4,100 AFY). Ground water from the basin is also used by private overlying land owners (1,000 AFY), and a large private water company (1,000 AFY). Ground water production from the basin is currently near historic highs (Fig. 1).

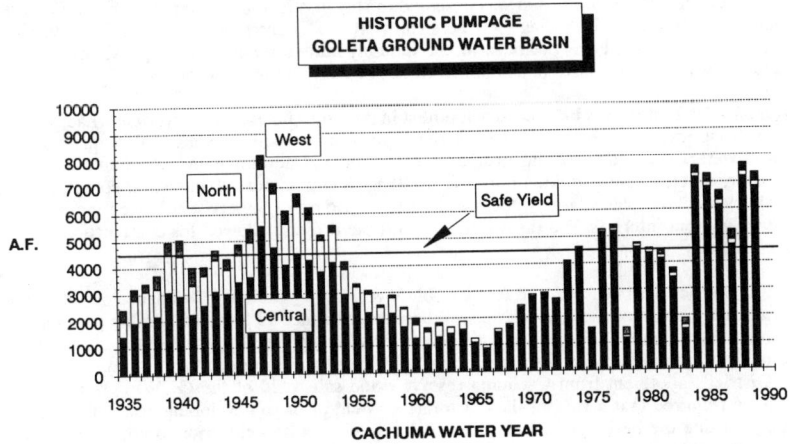

Figure 1

The GGWB is typically divided into three sub-basins: the North, Central and West Sub-basins. Most of the production from the GGWB, including all of the District's, comes from the North and Central Sub-basins. These two sub-basins are the most productive portions of the GGWB and contain the best quality water. Ground water from the West Sub-basin is generally not potable without extensive treatment.

The safe yield of the GGWB is about 4,500 AFY and basin overdraft is currently running about 2,000 AFY (TAC, 1989). Water levels in portions of the basin are currently dropping by as much as 10 feet per year, especially in the Central Sub-basin, and are below sea level over most of the basin. An uplifted wedge of bedrock has prevented seawater from intruding the aquifer. Production rates of District wells are being severely impacted by declining static water levels produced by the overdraft (GWD, 1988).

ACT II: THE POLITICS

Until the early 1960's land within the Goleta Valley area was used for agricultural purposes and water supplies from Cachuma Reservoir and the GGWB were adequate to meet the areas needs (Loux, 1987). During the 1960's the population of the valley tripled, increasing from about 19,000 in 1960 to about 60,000 in 1970 (Wright v. Goleta Water District, 1985). This growth altered the character of the community and began to tax the area's existing water supplies.

Because the area is unincorporated decisions regarding zoning and growth are made by the County Board of Supervisors. The Goleta Valley is one of the most populous unincorporated areas in the State, yet only two of the five County Supervisors represent the area. Unable to effectively control growth within the valley through County government, voters of the area elected a slate of Water Board candidates dedicated to slow growth policies. One of the campaign symbols for this group was the universal slow-growth symbol: a red circle and slash covering a bulldozer.

The new slow-growth Water Board declared a "Water Emergency Condition" within the District and adopted Ordinance 72-2, which severely restricted new water service connections, and limited the ability of existing customers to expand their service or change the use of existing service. The ordinance prohibited existing customers from drilling new wells in the basin, and customers with existing wells were limited to historic levels of extraction - - violators risked disconnection from District service. The moratorium was designed to stay in effect as long as the "Water Emergency Condition" existed. As of Spring 1989 no significant new sources of water have been developed, the emergency measure has not been lifted, and only limited numbers of applications for new or additional water service have been approved (such as agricultural conversions, Fig. 2).

Ordinance 72-2 effectively blocked development in the valley unless property owners had the money to construct a well and treatment system, and were lucky enough to overlie an adequate supply of ground water. The effect of this ordinance on residential development was immediate (Fig. 2). However, development of some multi-unit dwellings and commercial/industrial complexes within the valley still took place, largely because the County Board of Supervisors looked more favorably on development interests, and the economics of these projects allowed for construction of private water systems.

In 1973 District voters passed The Responsible Water Policy Initiative Ordinance placing a formal moratorium on new service connections. Whereas Ordinance 72-2 was vulnerable to being voided by later Water Boards, this later initiative could only be repealed by a vote of the electorate. The ordinance required that District service obligations not be any greater than the combined total of the District's allotment from Cachuma reservoir and safe yield of the GGWB. In addition, the initiative required that a vote of the electorate be held prior to developing new sources of water supply outside the basin, and emphasized that a vote must be held prior to importation of State water. In 1979 Santa Barbara County voters, including those in the Goleta Valley, soundly rejected a bond measure designed to finance facilities needed to import water from the State Water Project.

In 1973 the District found itself in the position of needing new water supplies simply to meet existing customer demand, but limited in its scope of authority to do so. The District took the only easy step it could and began aggressive development of the GGWB. In retrospect it is obvious that this would soon lead to overdraft of the GGWB and hence to litigation.

ACT III: THE LAW

California operates under a plural system of water rights, the most ubiquitous being riparian and appropriative (see, for example, Attwater and Markle, 1988). All water rights must be exercised in a "reasonable" manner. Riparian rights are senior to appropriative, and only surplus waters from the resource may be used by appropriators. Ground water surplus is defined as available yield, up to the safe yield of the basin, after riparian (overlying) demands are met. Hierarchy of appropriators (non-overliers) is on a "first-in-time, first-in-right" basis.

California also recognizes prescriptive water rights, which may accrue against private landowners by open and adverse use of the water resource by another party, public or private, for a period of five years. For example, if the District were to overdraft the GGWB for five years with resultant adverse impacts then prescriptive rights senior to overlying water rights could accrue in the District's favor. This fact was not lost on overlying land owners who had either no or only limited District service.

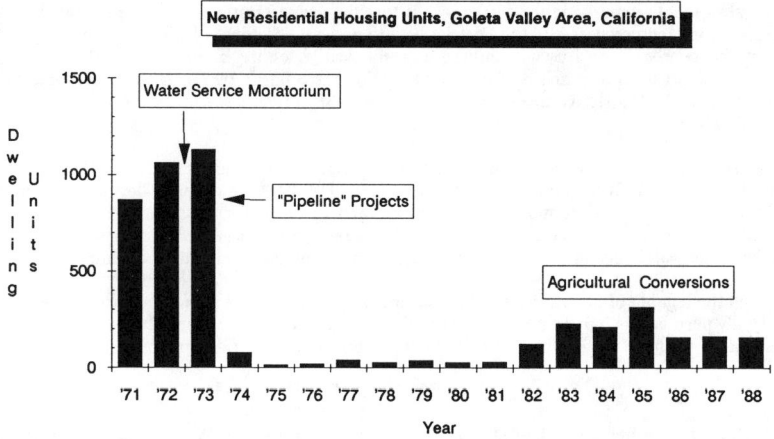

Figure 2

Faced with the possibility of losing their ground rights to the District via prescription, and finding themselves unable to readily develop their properties due to lack of water service from the District, property owners overlying the North and Central Sub-basins of the GGWB brought suit against the District in 1973 to determine relative rights to use of the ground water. These property owners included private parties, the County, and local school districts. The District cross-complained against about 220 overlying land owners that, "to the best of its knowledge", had a potential interest in using ground water from these sub-basins (Wright v. Goleta Water District, 1985).

The trial court decision was handed down in 1979. It established the safe yield of the sub-basins, the relative rights to ground water, and quantified the right of each party. The District was declared to be an appropriator, but due to a perceived legal precedent (the California Supreme Court's recent "Long Valley" decision, discussed in the next section) was granted the right to appropriate 1,103 AFY of the safe yield on a permanent basis. The trial court decision was appealed and overturned in the overlying landowners favor in 1986 ("Long Valley" was held not to apply), and the District's absolute right to 1,103 AFY of water was dissolved.

Because the courts had determined that the District was an appropriator, the District only had a right to use surplus ground water. This surplus would have amounted to about 2,000 AFY, much less that the District's average production of about 4,100 AFY. The District was basically required to chose between reducing its ground water production by about 50 percent in order to bring the basin back into safe yield, or compensate the overlying land owners for use of the land owners ground water.

In 1989 a settlement agreement was signed requiring the District to immediately provide the plaintiffs with their current water need of about 500 AFY. In addition, the District is required to supply plaintiffs an additional 500 AFY water by June 1992 to allow for potential development of the properties, or face paying "rent". Rent is defined as the difference in income for the property under its present usage versus its highest and best use *with full water service*. Rental would continue until the property is supplied the additional water, or until 1999. At that date the owner could require the District to buy the property at its fair market value *with full water service*, or take back the water right from the District. The total cost of purchasing plaintiff properties has been estimated to be about $55,000,000 to $110,000,000 in 1989 dollars. In exchange, the overlying property owners are required to convey their water wells and water rights to the District.

The legal rationale underlying the settlement is that the ground water of the basin is the property of the overlying land owners, not the District, and to prevent a "taking" of this property right by the District the overlying land owners must be compensated, either monetarily or through water service. Plaintiff legal fees arising from this litigation were borne by the District and amount to about $1,100,000. District counsel legal expenses for this litigation have been estimated to total about $500,000.

The court has retained jurisdiction over the case to ensure compliance with the settlement and to ensure that overdraft of the GGWB is brought to an end by 1999. In order to develop the supplies needed to fulfill the requirements of judgement, and to allow for possible future growth, the District is currently evaluating potential new water supply projects. These water supply projects include: waste water reclamation, sea water desalination, and enlargement of Cachuma Reservoir.

Although the legality of growth control via limiting water service is in some dispute, it appears that it is legally permissible only in exceptional cases (see, for example, Lemieux, 1977). A Grand Jury investigation of the Goleta Water District in 1989 concurred with this opinion.

THE RESULT

In Goleta, it can be seen that slow-growth domination of the Water Board helped slow development of the area, especially of single-family dwellings where property owners either did not have the money and/or did not have the water resource available to construct private water supply systems. However, significant numbers of large developments, especially commercial and industrial complexes, were able to overcome this barrier. This has resulted in a recent imbalance between residential and commercial development that the County is now addressing.

One of the prices paid for this political wrangling over the water supply has been a water shortage that amplified the impacts of the recent drought, leading to burdensome and financially costly water rationing. The slow-growth faction blames past Water Board decisions (primarily those occurring during a two year period when the "pro-growth" faction dominated the Water Board) to allow new water service connections for this problem. This group also blames past decisions by the County Board of Supervisors allowing development in the valley on private wells at a time when the areas water resources were already overtaxed and water rights issues not fully resolved. The pro-growth faction views the current water shortage as a product of the failure, often termed irresponsibility, of past Water Boards to develop new supplies. There is all too much merit in all of these criticisms.

Solution of the areas water and growth problems are inextricably linked. Formation of a Technical Advisory Committee (TAC) in 1987 between Water District and County staff allowed for a first-time consensus of opinion regarding water supply and demand figures for the area, and was the first step in more integrated management of the Goleta Valley area. More recently, the County has formulated a growth management plan that it appears will severely restrict development of the area. "Guaranteed" restricted growth would allow the area's water supply problems to be more easily solved. It is significant that slow-growth candidates have won all recent County and District elections. It is the author's opinion, however, that only incorporation of the area, with resultant municipal government, will be able to provide the strong and focused attention the area needs.

At least two significant legal questions arose from litigation of water rights within the GGWB. First, it is potentially significant that the District did not cross-complain against all overlying land owners, which would have included its own customers. In arriving at its decision the trial court followed the Long Valley decision, and gave exercised rights of the litigants a higher priority than currently unexercised rights of the overlying land owners. The appellate court overturned this decision stating that application of Long Valley was improper because a *comprehensive determination* of all ground water rights within the sub-basins was not being made - - the District had not cross complained against all overlying land owners. One must wonder whether if the District had attempted a full adjudication of the basin, if the Long Valley decision could have been applied and a different result in apportionment of water rights arrived at.

Another potentially significant legal point is whether the District could have exercised its *customers* overlying ground water rights. Although attorneys on both sides of the case suggested that this was not possible (due to resultant "severance" of land and water rights), it has been suggested that a legal instrument might be available that would allow a water district to serve their customers "their own" water, thereby exercising a defacto overlying right. Because Goleta Water District customers overlay 70% of the GGWB, this would have provided a right to a significant amount (possibly about 3,400 AFY) of water. This theory was not tested in this case.

Many coastal communities in California are currently undergoing the same growth-related and water supply problems discussed above. The slow-growth groups in these areas commonly argue that communities should "live within their local resource base", and often view control of water resources as an effective means of controlling growth. Pro-growth forces typically argue that water districts are obligated by law to develop the new water supplies that are required to meet service area demands, and that responsibility for growth issues legally reside elsewhere. Pro-growth groups also often claim that significant growth rates are necessary for economic vitality.

It is the authors opinion that what citizens basically want is a cap on growth that maintains the character of their community as well as the environmental integrity of the area, and that this is a reasonable and desireable goal. However, this cap must allow for importation of items not naturally present in the area, including water. It is important to note that the actual local water resource base of Goleta Valley is the GGWB and small local streams, which might barely support a third of the current population. Modern economies do not operate in a vacuum and do not function within local resource bases - - the exchange of goods and services across political and physical boundaries is the norm, and water should be no different.

REFERENCES

Attwater, W.R., and Markle, J., 1988, Overview of California Water Law; Pacific Law Journal, v.19, no. 4, p.957-1030.

Goleta Water District Staff Report, September 1988, Estimated Future Ground Water Production Capacity of District Wells, 29p.

Goleta Water District Staff Report, August 1989, Technical Advisory Committee Analysis, Water Supply and Demand in the Goleta Valley Area, 84p.

Lemieux, W.K., 1977, Land Use Control by Utility Service Moratorium: The Wrong Solution to the Right Problem; Los Angeles Bar Journal; v.53, no. 5, p. 262-269.

Loux, J.D., 1987, A Comparative Analysis of Local Groundwater Management Programs in California, Univ. of Calif., Berkeley, Unpub. PhD Diss., 318p.

Wright v. Goleta Water District, 1985, California Reporter, v.219, p.740-754.

Water Basins in the Middle East

Philippe W. Zgheib[1]

Abstract

In Middle Eastern factional scheming for power, water is viewed as a strategic resource. The distribution of surface waters constitutes the basis for water geopolitics, thus representing the way to national security. In this perspective, the value of water is economic, but also emotional. Water inspires a certain perception of wealth.

Unfortunately, water scarcity in most Middle Eastern countries is the central issue of animosity between many of them. Whereas economic benefit/cost analyses are blind to where benefits occur, the political process of water development involves the weighing of benefit distribution. But political decisions often overrun economic considerations, As a result, a project may not be acceptable economically, and still may get implemented.

Water Politics in the Middle East

Water seems to be the "hidden agenda" behind most Middle Eastern current political disputes, which are all too often attributed to religious diversity. Historically, groundwater has been the main supply in most of the Middle east. While competition for subsurface water is covert, it remains most vivid.

The following areas have been determined as regions of severe water shortage and declining water quality: Egypt, Jordan, Israel, West Bank, Gaza Strip, Syria, and Turkey. Of the whole Middle East region, Lebanon is the only country that is known for having a surplus of quality water supplies.

---

[1]Professional civil engineer, research assistant, Utah State University, Department of Civil and Environmental Engineering, Logan, Utah 84322-4110.

Water Basins in the Middle East

Four major Water Basins can be geographically identified in the Middle East:

1- The JORDAN RIVER BASIN. It encompasses the countries of: Jordan Syria, Israel, and Lebanon.

2- The TIGRIS-EUPHRATES RIVER BASIN. It encompasses: Turkey, Iraq, Syria, and Saudi Arabia.

3- The NILE RIVER BASIN. It encompasses the countries of Egypt and Sudan.

4- The LITANI RIVER BASIN. It is fully located within the international borders of Lebanon.

THE JORDAN BASIN (Jordan, Syria, Israel, Lebanon)

The Jordan River is a small river. It originates in southern Lebanon, and runs through Jordan, Syria and Israel. It provides 60 % of Israel's water and 75 % of jordan's water. All countries in this basin, except for Lebanon, suffer periodic water shortages. As a result, this basin has been the scene of most severe conflicts over water in the Middle East.

The Great Yarmuk Project proposed by Syria and jordan has constituted the hidden agenda of several wars between Syria, Jordan, and Israel. The Golan Heights in southern Syria, and the West Bank in western Jordan are considered vital to the water resources of Israel. This explains Israel's invasion of these regions in June of 1976. Since then, they have been formally annexed by the state of Israel.

West Bank surface waters are exploited in a ratio of 4.5 % to the West Bank and 95.5 % to Israel. This discrepancy has constituted a time bomb waiting to explode. The uprising of the local Arab populations in the West Bank and their determination to rebel is only a result of this discrepancy.

Although the Jordan River Basin is well suited to integrated development, all proposed schemes have failed. Israel's invasion of Lebanon in June of 1982, and its continued military presence in southern Lebanon allows the government of Israel to have full control of all sources of the Upper Jordan.

THE TIGRIS-EUPHRATES BASIN (Turkey, Iraq, Syria, and Saudi Arabia)

This is the only basin in the Middle East with markedly unused surplus of water. Although it is mostly developed by the individual countries within the basin: Turkey, Iraq, Syria, and Saudi Arabia, every one of these countries suffers periodic shortages and has little growth potential due to limited water resources.

The only noted crisis was in 1974 between Syria and Iraq. A new Syrian dam in the upper reaches of the basin reduced downstream flow by 25 %. Threats to bomb the dam from the Iraqi government were followed by troop action. After diplomatic efforts, Syria agreed to release more water. Currently, a Multinational Euphrates River Authority is being established.

THE NILE BASIN (Egypt, Sudan)

The Nile constitutes the longest river system in the world. It undergoes extreme climate variability. Therefore, its hydrologic regime is most complex. It drains 10 % of the African continent. However, it is the sole supply to Egypt, where water requirements dramatically underlie every facet of life.

In the early 1950s, political conflict was triggered between Sudan and Egypt by the Great Aswan Dam project. The conflict culminated in military confrontation in 1958. However, An agreement for full utilization of the Nile waters was signed in 1959.

THE LITANI BASIN (Lebanon)

The Litani lies entirely within the official boundaries of Lebanon, which is the only Middle Eastern country with a surplus of water resources. The Litani drains eastern and southern Mount Lebanon range. It originates in northeastern Lebanon and drains south towards the Israeli border. About 20 miles before it reaches the border it turns west towards the Mediterranean coast.

Currently, its lower course and rather developed basin area lies in Israeli-controlled territory. This is not surprising, since it represents the only surface water supply of high quality within reach of the Israeli Military Forces.

The "Israeli Security Zone" in southern Lebanon encompasses the developed lower reaches of the Litani.

Thus, it is interpreted by the central Lebanese government, as well as by the local political groups of Southern lebanon as an attempt to annex the Litani, then develop a diversion scheme into Israel. Further disputes seem inevitable.

Prospects for the year 2000

By the year 2000, water not oil, will be the dominant resource issue in the Middle East:

* Israel's needs will exceed supply by 30 %

* Jordan's water deficit will increase by 20 %

* Development of the Upper Yarmuk will increase salinity of the Lower Yarmuk.

* Decreasing quantities and deteriorating qualities in the Tigris-Euphrates basin will be dominant points of controversy between Syria, Turkey, and Iraq.

* Increased water pollution will exacerbate Egypt's total dependence on the Nile.

* Lebanon's civil strife, nurtured by external regional appetites for its water supplies will result in the total collapse of its water infrastructure.

References

Center for Strategic and International Studies. The politics of Scarcity, Water in the Middle East. 1985.

Foreign Affairs, chronology, summer 1987.

The Middle East Journal, Winter 1986.

Water Development Ideology: A New Status Quo

D. Clayton Brown[1]

Abstract
The old ideology of economic growth used to justify water resource development is no longer popular in the Southwest. A new ideology is developing, based on new circumstances.

Paper
Until the 1970s, the proponents of water development in the Southwest espoused the ideology of economic growth to justify their demands for projects. Their ideology was based upon industrial expansion, abundant jobs, and social improvements. Multipurpose benefits such as flood control, navigation, hydroelectric power and recreation were regarded as steps toward wealth and abundance, and they easily won public acceptance of their proposals. Thus, for about a half century water development encountered little resistance of importance, creating a status quo that went unchallenged. Projects were routinely authorized by Congress. That set of circumstances, described as the old status quo, has ceased to exist and a new ideology is evolving, one that is not fully shaped but that is, nonetheless, far enough along to be evident.

No better example of the old ideology can be found than the McClellan-Kerr River Navigation System, the largest civil works project built by the Army Corps of Engineers when it was finished in 1971. Business and political interests were, of course, the principal proponents of the waterway and they called for economic expansion. A river navigable to Tulsa, Oklahoma would, by making possible low transportation rates, allegedly attract new industries, thereby spurring employment, raising tax revenues and generally enhancing the well-being throughout the System's area of operations. Flood control was not

---

[1]
Professor of History, Texas Christian University, Fort Worth, Texas, author of <u>Rivers, Rockets and Readiness: Army Engineers in the Sunbelt</u> and <u>The Southwestern Division: 50 Years of Service</u>.

needed to make a project economically feasible. Navigation and the anticipated growth of industry were the heart of the push for developing the Arkansas River Basin.²

The Arkansas River system was the last hurrah for the old ideologists because their counterparts in Texas were resoundly defeated in an almost identical project within two years. In 1973 voters in seventeen Texas counties rejected a tax bond proposal tied to the proposed Trinity River Waterway, a 360 mile multipurpose navigation project from Fort Worth to the Gulf of Mexico. As was the case with the Arkansas River System, the sponsors of the Trinity River project represented business interests. They, too, envisioned industrial expansion, high employment and a general social and economic enhancement of the Trinity River basin if only the river were made navigable.

During the campaign for the bond approval, they met stiff grass-roots resistance that materialized suddenly and unexpectedly. Opponents attacked the ideologists of growth from three directions: (1) they effectively raised questions of cost, insisting the benefit-cost ratio of the waterway was inaccurate, and that significant hidden costs were also involved, (2) they deplored the environmental impact of the project, insisting on a new environmental study that conformed with the National Environmental Policy Act of 1969, and (3) they questioned the need for growth. New industries would bring more pollution, ruin the natural beauty of the Trinity River and worsen crowded living conditions in the north Texas area. These new arguments defied the standard definition for improving the quality of life which had been economic growth and supplied a new definition.³

Out of the fight over the Trinity River Waterway came part of the new ideology. Industrial expansion alone did not justify new taxes and the natural beauty of the environment should not be sacrificed for economic growth. And new growth should be planned so as to avoid overcrowding and pollution.

Almost a generation has passed since the 1973 bond election and few more new ideas have advanced. Water projects, at least those identified with the Corps of Engineers, will likely have to be planned and built to supply water--the old notion of impoundment for flood control and other benefits without water supply will not be acceptable. The Reagan administration emphasized water supply as a local responsibility, and given the constant concern over that subject in Texas, new single-purpose water supply lakes may be developed. In 1975 Southwestern Division Engineer General Charles McGinnis wrote: "We have reached the point where future projects addressing flood damage reduction are less and less likely. The challenge of water supply . . . is one which, will sustain the Corps well into the future."⁴

The concept of privatization may well be applied to water projects. If the process of de-federalization continues, and local entities become more responsible for water supply, a move might grow in Congress calling for the release of smaller federal projects to municipal governments. Such a move could be justified on the need for water supply. Retired Major General Hugh Robinson, one-time Southwestern Division Engineer predicted that de-federalization would continue.[5]

Perhaps the only survivor of the old ideology for justifying projects will be recreation-one that used to be a stepchild of water projects, but one which, though already much expanded, will undergo further expansion. Added to the traditional recreational practices of boating, swimming and fishing will be visitor interpretative centers similar to those in natural history museums, animal and wildlife refuges, archeological exhibits and outdoor displays for educational benefit. Nature centers with hiking trails and animal exhibits will likely have to be built along with picnic tables. To be sure, some federal water projects have already moved in this direction and new ones will have to incorporate such facilities to win approval.[6]

Indeed the old reasons for impounding rivers, building locks and dams, and appropriating millions of taxpayer funds are dead. Navigation of riverways, with its enormous costs, is dead. Impoundment of rivers for the generation of hydroelectric power, always a minimal benefit in the Southwest, is dead. Only flood control is likely to survive as a criteria for a large-scale project, and flood control has not been a problem in the Southwest for some time. And certainly the call for economic growth via massive federal water projects has lost its appeal. Future water projects will have to be justified on new grounds, and therein lies the new status quo.

ENDNOTES

2. Ironically the Army Corps of Engineers never officially declared the Navigation System to be economically feasible. The project's political sponsors, particularly Oklahoma Senator Robert Kerr, managed to bypass the Corps' standard procedures of review and obtain Congressional approval. See D. Clayton Brown, <u>The Southwestern Power Division: 50 Years of Service</u> (Washington, D.C., 1987), pp. 102-103.

3. For a discussion of the Trinity River Waterway, see D. Clayton Brown, "A Companion of the Trinity and McClellan-Kerr Navigation Projects," <u>National Waterways Roundtable</u>, Proceedings, <u>History, Regional Development, Technology, A Foot Ahead</u>, (U.S. Army Engineer Water Resources Support Center, Institute for Water REsources April 22-24, 1980).

4. Brown, <u>The Southwestern Power Division</u>, p. 150.

5. <u>Ibid</u>.

6. <u>Ibid</u>., pp. 41-44.

WATER FOR HOUSTON: THE WALLISVILLE CASE
Bonnie B. Pendergrass[1]

Abstract

The multipurpose Wallisville project included an industrial water supply for Houston. The project was nearly 70 percent complete when environmentalists succeeded in stopping construction in 1973. Wallisville, however, funded largely by the U.S. Army Corps of Engineers, proved to be a "legislative Lazarus" resurrected by the courts and Congress. With the passage of the 1986 Water Resources Act which requires local sponsors to pay a larger share of the cost than before, the project once again seems terminal. Nevertheless, it could come back to life once more.

The Early History

The Corps has always had critics, but after the 1969 National Environmental Policy Act (NEPA) the critics became increasingly vocal and influential. The Galveston District was affected more than many other Corps Districts because of the number of permits it processes and because of the environmentally sensitive coastline and wetlands in its jurisdiction. Perhaps no project in the District better reveals the throes attending change than the Wallisville project, which some critics viewed as an attempt to revive the aborted Trinity River project which would make Dallas-Fort Worth a seaport by linking it to the Gulf of Mexico 370 miles away.

Few projects prompted such scathing prose or, in the view of its proponents, such misguided diatribes as Wallisville. Opponents likened it to "a slowly growing cancer" and called it "a scam and a scandal." Proponents like the Galveston District, the Trinity River Authority (TRA), the City of Houston, and the Chambers-Liberty Counties Navigation District saw the project which would dam the Trinity River near the town of Wallisville, east of Houston, differently. Located 3.9 miles above the mouth of the Trinity, the shallow four-foot 19,700 acre reservoir created by the squat 39,200-foot long dam would store 58,000 acre-feet of water. The project also included a navigation lock at mile 28.3, and a ten-mile extension of a channel to Liberty, Texas.

Proponents claimed five major benefits from the project: (1) an industrial water supply for Houston; (2) control of saltwater intrusion; (3) improved navigation; (4) increased recreation; and (5) fish and wildlife enhancement.

---

[1]President, PenSEC, Inc., 14017 55th Avenue West, Edmonds, Washington 98020.

Congress authorized the project in 1961; construction began in 1966. The local sponsors' share would be $4.95 million; the Corps' share, $28.8 million. But Wallisville's fate became inextricably linked with NEPA when NEPA became law on January 1, 1970. NEPA required that the environmental effects of a project be thoroughly evaluated in an environmental impact statement (EIS). This became the basis for court challenges of water projects. NEPA introduced an era of litigation unequaled in Corps history.

The Court Battles Begin

The legal wrangling over Wallisville would occupy the Galveston District for over a decade and a half. In September, 1971, environmentalists, including the Sierra Club and the Audubon Society, sued to halt construction because the Corps had not filed an adequate EIS. At this time, the Wallisville project was nearly 70 percent complete. Three months later, the Galveston District completed the EIS and filed it with the District Court.

Construction proceeded through 1972. Then in February, 1973, the District Court enjoined the project because an EIS for the entire Trinity River project had not been prepared. The District and the sponsors appealed to the Fifth Circuit Court of Appeals in New Orleans, arguing that Wallisville was an independent project, not part of the Trinity River project.

Eighteen months after the District Court enjoined Wallisville, a Federal Appeals Court, second only to the U.S. Supreme Court in authority, in August, 1974, reversed and remanded the case, sending it back to the lower court. The Appeals Court held that the Wallisville project was not part of the Trinity River project, but was a separate project just as the Corps contended. However, the Court ruled that the District must prepare a final or supplemental EIS on Wallisville before construction could resume.

The plaintiffs who had filed the original suit requested a rehearing, but it was denied. Yet the fight was far from over. The District proceeded slowly and cautiously. In 1976 the District still was working on the supplemental environmental impact statement ordered by the Court. D. T. Graham, Chief of the Engineering Division in the District, seemed to feel personally responsible for the injunction. He wanted to make sure that all bases were covered before going back to the court with the revised or amended EIS. In hindsight, some within the Corps considered this a mistake. Instead of "throwing a patch on the environmental statement and getting on with the construction," Graham and his staff by deciding to review the entire project compounded the delay. The ways to calculate recreational and water

supply benefits changed. As a result, the District "found that the old project that we had under construction was really not the project to build to fit today's situation" and began to move toward redesign.
Finally on December 10, 1977, the District held a public meeting on the rewritten EIS. There the District presented information on alternative plans. Of these, Plan 2A which reduced the area of the reservoir from 19,700 acres to 5,600 acres received considerable support from the sponsors. At the same time, still another alternative, one incorporating a temporary non-impoundment barrier, emerged from the meeting. This, too, would have to be analyzed in the supplemental EIS. By July, 1978, the District reported that local sponsors were offering qualified support, contingent upon continuation of the existing cost sharing contract and acceptability of the project design.
The EIS for Wallisville was repeatedly delayed as the project was modified and redesigned. It was late 1981 before the EIS mandated by the Court was finally released to the public. The most important aspect of the Post Authorization Change Report (PACR) and the 200 page EIS accompanying it was that the heavily touted benefits of the Wallisville project dropped from five to three. Navigation and fish and wildlife enhancements were no longer listed as significant benefits.
Within three months it was clear that the District faced a new torrent of debate. The 1981 EIS was criticized for double-counting water benefits, exaggerating recreation benefits, failing to mitigate environmental damage, and neglecting to consider impacts on Galveston Bay. Local critics charged, for example, that the shallow reservoir would become clogged with weeds and other vegetation. The reservoir would then act as a settling basin keeping sediments and organic and inorganic nutrients from marshes around the Trinity River from reaching Galveston Bay. This threatened the food supply of fish and shellfish in the bay.
The changes and deficiencies in the 1981 report suggested that the redesigned Wallisville project was entirely new, meaning that the District would have to go back to Congress for reauthorization.
Reauthorization presented several potential problems for the Galveston District. First, it could suggest that Plan 2A was indeed an entirely new project requiring still another EIS and further delaying construction. Second, it raised questions about the validity of the cost sharing agreement reached between the Corps and local sponsors in the 1960's. Under new federal regulations, the local sponsors' contribution would significantly increase from 15 percent to 70 percent.
Opponents of Wallisville subsequently claimed that the Galveston District concluded that it had to "patch

things up" and reinstate the navigation and wildlife benefits. The Corps brought back the lost benefits in 1982 in a 17 page document providing Supplemental Information to the 1981 report (SIPACR).

The Controversy Escalates

The SIPACR became perhaps the most controversial document ever produced by the District for two reasons. First, it reinstated the navigation and fish and wildlife benefits without clearly spelling out the bases for the change. Second, the SIPACR was not circulated for public review. The District contended that it was a document for internal use only. Yet somehow the report got to Washington, D.C. Representative Jack Brooks of Beaumont introduced legislation in July, 1982, which referred to SIPACR. In 1983 Congress appropriated money for the scaled down Wallisville project, even though the injunction was still in place.

Wallisville critics were outraged by what they termed the Washington "short circuit." When the District and the local sponsors filed a request before Judge Carl E. Bue, Jr. in January, 1985 to lift the original 1973 injunction, environmental groups argued that the injunction should be continued.

One of the focal points of the hearing which began in August was how the SIPACR reached Congress. Among the witnesses was Maj. Gen. Robert J. Dacey, who as Division Engineer of the Southwestern Division at the time the SIPACR was prepared, had certified that the Corps had followed proper procedures on the project. He could not, however, explain how the SIPACR reached Congress. Nor could the Galveston District

A second focal point of the hearing was the validity of the conclusions in the SIPACR. Wallisville's contribution to fish and wildlife enhancement was especially controversial, particularly since the reservoir initially would be only two feet deep. Depth would gradually increase to four feet as the need for water in Houston grew more acute.

Courtroom debate also centered around the need for additional water for Houston and its cost. Supporters conceded that the cited costs of 3 cents per thousand gallons did not include treatment or delivery. The costs were also distorted because the cheap water reflected the federal government paying much of the cost of the project. Opponents pointed out that in 1979 the City of Houston voted down another source for water, a diversionary canal from Luce Bayou south of Lake Livingston to Houston, because it could not be demonstrated that the demand for water was there. They also argued that because the reservoir would be so shallow, the quality of the water would be poor.

In March, 1986, the injunction was continued with comments on procedural irregularities. In his ruling, Judge Bue, the same District Court judge in Houston who issued the original injunction, took the District to task for its "legislative legerdemain." He ruled that both Congress and the Corps failed to follow their own laws and regulations on environmental procedures. The judge concluded that the District still had not complied with NEPA because SIPACR had not been through prescribed public scrutiny before Congress acted.

The Corps and the local sponsors appealed to the 5th U.S. Circuit Court of Appeals in New Orleans, arguing that the environmental evaluation of Wallisville was adequate. By now other parties had joined the fray. The Texas Parks and Wildlife Department filed a friend-of-the-court brief arguing that key environmental findings on Wallisville were "unsound" and that the Corps should have to do further environmental study. The Department also charged that in violation of federal law, it had not reviewed the 1982 report before it went to Congress.

The appeal was filed in April, 1986. Briefs were prepared and oral arguments presented in February, 1987. In May, 1987, a three-judge panel of the 5th Circuit Court of Appeals in New Orleans gave the go-ahead to proceed on Wallisville after 15 years of delay. The panel ruled that the Corps handling of the supplemental information was reasonable, that the final impact statement was adequate; and that Congress did not have to reauthorize the project.

Environmentalists were shocked. An environmental lawyer concluded that Wallisville won "not so much in the courts as in the political process."

Wallisville's Future

There are signs that the battle may ultimately be decided by economics. In September, 1987 John Doyle, Jr., Acting Assistant Secretary of the Army, suggested that the Corps might no longer participate in Wallisville.

> Because of project modifications . . . , the project is now primarily a single-purpose water supply project. This type of project traditionally has been the responsibility of non-Federal interests. Accordingly, I am not optimistic that this type of project will gain the budgetary support it would need . . . for construction to be resumed.

While some observers saw this as a "trial balloon" floated to see what the reaction would be, it potentially could begin a whole new legal battle. Local sponsors could challenge the Corps' right to pull out of the project, though as of October 1989 a suit had not been filed.

The original 1967 cost-sharing contract called for local sponsors to pay about 16 percent of Wallisville's construction cost. When Congress reauthorized the project in 1983 after SIPACR, it specified that this contract would still apply. In 1986, however, Congress passed the first major omnibus water resource development authorization bill since 1970. The cost-sharing provisions of the Water Resources Development Act of 1986 marked a major departure from traditional federal water funding policies. If the new formula were applied to Wallisville, the local sponsors' share could be as high as 70 to 75 percent, or even 100 percent if the project were reclassified as being only a water supply project.

A number of historical factors underlie the controversy and help explain the District's position. The District clearly was caught off guard by the reaction Wallisville provoked in the aftermath of NEPA. In terms of the District's traditional mental set, Wallisville was one more project in a long chain of civil works projects endorsed by Texans and Congress. Faced with a newly vocal and well organized environmental contingent, the District initially did not know how to respond. They viewed environmentalists as anti-growth. Former Texas Governor Price Daniel, a Wallisville supporter, suggested that the same organizatios that opposed Wallisville would also have opposed the highly successful Houston Ship Channel and probably would have called it, too, "an idiotic venture of a pack of troglodytes playing engineers."

Wallisville was just one of a number of suits brought against Corps projects. Often these projects were conceived and justified under criteria of decades ago. As one Chief of Engineers pointed out, "At times the Corps has been placed in the position of defending the past against the present; trying to explain what were rational decisions at the time, but decisions vulnerable to present-day analysis." General Charles I. McGinnis, who served as the Corps' Director of Civil Works, argues that many environmental organizations, and even some federal agencies, "enjoy the luxury of a single point of view, a single mission and a single purpose." The Galveston District does not have this luxury in a state where "water is high-order politics."

References

This paper began with research funded by the Galveston District as part of a history of the District between 1976 and 1986. It is based upon interviews with former District Engineers, past and present District employees, and members of other federal agencies. The paper also draws upon newspapers and court documents.

ENVIRONMENTAL PERMITTING
A MAJOR EXPRESSWAY FACILITY IN FLORIDA

by Kenneth A. Carper[1], M. ASCE

Abstract

As general consultant to the Tampa-Hillsborough County Expressway Authority, HNTB was responsible for the environmental permitting required for the design and construction of the Northwest Hillsborough Expressway. The project design was completed by nine different engineering firms, and included approximately 18 miles of urban and rural limited access expressway, within and north of the City of Tampa. HNTB was responsible for the coordination of pre-permit application meetings; preparation and submittal of the permit application packages; and the development of a mitigation plan to offset adverse impacts. In this capacity, HNTB reviewed design drawings, data, and calculations prepared by the subconsultants, and determined their consistency with all applicable environmental regulations.

Introduction

The design of the Northwest Hillsborough Expressway was segmented into eight different lengths and subcontracted to eight different consulting engineering firms. A ninth design package was subcontracted for the design of all of the toll plaza facilities. The design section lengths varied from approximately 1.3 miles to 2.8 miles, and included areas of dense urbanization and coordination with existing development in the south, to areas of rural alignment development in the north.

Because of problems inherent to roadway design in developed areas, the first three Sections (Sections 1, 2 and 3) took considerably more time to design than Sections 4 thru 8. This time lag in the design necessitated grouping Sections 4 thru 8 together for environmental permitting purposes. These Sections contained approximately seventy (70) percent of the project length and approximately 75% of the impacted wetland areas. Therefore, the initial permit

[1] Senior Drainage/Environmental Permitting Engineer - Florida
HOWARD, NEEDLES, TAMMEN, AND BERGENDOFF, 5900 Lake Ellenor Drive, Suite 600, Orlando, Florida 32809 .

package application submittals included information regarding Sections 4 thru 8 only, and the environmental permit packages for the remaining Sections will be developed as the design is completed.

Agencies and Regulations

The environmental regulatory agencies having jurisdiction over the project area included the U.S. Army Corps of Engineers (USCOE), Florida Department of Environmental Regulation (FDER), Southwest Florida Water Management District (SWFWMD), Hillsborough County Environmental Protection Commission (HCEPC) and the Tampa Port Authority (TPA). The United States Fish and Wildlife Service (USFWS), National Marine Fisheries Service (NMFS), and United States Environmental Protection Agency (USEPA) were involved by commenting on the USCOE permit application submittals, and the Florida Game and Freshwater Fish Commission (FGFWFC) provided input to FDER and SWFWMD on protected species. Comments from each of these agencies had been solicited and received during the preparation of the preliminary environmental documents. Table 1 below lists these agencies, the basis for their authority, and the resources which they regulate regarding the Northwest Hillsborough Expressway.

TABLE 1

Summary of Environmental Permitting Effort

Activity Regulated	Agency(s)	Authority
Stormwater Discharge	FDER	Ch. 17-25,F.A.C.
	SWFWMD	Ch. 40D-4, F.A.C.
Surface Water Management	SWFWMD	Ch. 40D-4, F.A.C.
Wetlands Management	USCOE	CFR 33
	FDER	Ch. 17-3, 17-4, and 17-12, F.A.C.
	SWFWMD	Ch. 40D-4, F.A.C.
	HCEPC	Ch. 1-11
	TPA	Ch. 84-447, F.S.
Protected Species	USEPA, USFWS, NMFS	Section 404c of Clean Water Act, Fish and Wildlife Coordination Act
	FGFWFC	Ch. 39, F.A.C.

Stormwater discharge regulation focused on the requirement of retaining or detaining and filtering the appropriate volume (usually the first 1/2" to 1" of runoff) of stormwater runoff prior to outfall to a receiving water body. This criteria is based on the premise that approximately 80 to 90 percent of the pollutant loading is contained within this first flush volume (Wanielista 1977 and 1979).

Surface water management issues primarily addressed the prevention of flooding downstream or upstream property with increased peak flow rates resulting from the construction of the project. This problem was handled by demonstrating that post development flow rates leaving the project after construction would be equal to or less than pre-development (pre-Expressway) flow rates. Because of the low-lying terrain of West-Central Florida through which the Expressway traversed, the potential for increasing the 100 year floodplain elevation(s) was also addressed. If roadway embankment necessitated the placement of fill below the 100 year floodplain elevation, an equivalent compensating storage volume was required to be replaced within the same drainage basin from which it was taken.

Perhaps the most formidable obstacle to overcome in the design and construction of the Northwest Hillsborough Expressway was that of wetlands management concerns. Although every effort was made throughout the initial preliminary studies and environmental documents to avoid and/or minimize as many wetland impacts as possible, the final alignment for design included significant dredging and filling within wetland areas. These encroachments were minimized by the design and offset by incorporation within the contract documents of a comprehensive mitigation plan for environmental impacts.

Multidisciplinary Approach

HNTB contracted the services of Proctor and Redfern, Inc., in Tampa, as subconsultant to the general consultant to develop the mitigation plan and assist with the environmental permitting on ecological issues. Proctor and Redfern, Inc., contributed experience from work on the preliminary environmental studies, and experience with local environmental conditions to the project team. More specifically, Proctor and Redfern, Inc., assisted HNTB and the design section engineers in establishing wetlands jurisdictional lines early in design, conducting preapplication meetings with the regulatory agencies, and developing criteria for construction plans preparation.

In addition to the creation of a mitigation plan, Stormwater Management Facilities (SMF's) were integrated into the Expressway's drainage design at strategic locations. These facilities varied in concept from special treatment ditches which basically paralleled portions of the alignment to wet detention and dry retention basins which required additional right-of-way acquisitions specifically for surface water management purposes. Whenever feasible, the stormwater management facilities were designed to provide multiple drainage/environmental functions for the Expressway. Wet detention basins not only provided stormwater discharge treatment and attenuation of peak flow rates, but in some instances, compensated for 100 year floodplain fill and delivered mitigation credit through the implementation of planted littoral zones.

The drainage design criteria generally followed the guidelines established by the Florida Department of Transportation with the primary objective of constructing a safe, reliable, and easily maintained drainage system for the Expressway. Environmental design criteria was integrated into this standard drainage design criteria in order to minimize alteration of the natural hydrology and secure all applicable permits for construction (Carper and Churchill, 1988).

Permit Application Packages Preparation and Submittal

Final deliverables to the general consultant from each Design Section Engineer for use in the permit packages preparation included the following:

1. Stormwater Management (Drainage) Report which included stormwater treatment calculations, pre/post development hydrology, and drainage design hydraulic calculations.

2. Environmental Assessment Report which included a biological assessment and quantification of all proposed wetland impacts.

3. Dredge and Fill Permit which was required by the Florida Department of Environmental Regulation for activities conducted within "Waters of the State".

4. Stormwater Discharge Permit which was required by the Florida Department of Environment Regulation for the construction of stormwater facilities within or discharging to "Waters of the State".

5. Miscellaneous items which included construction plans, permit application forms, and aerial topographic maps depicting pre-Expressway conditions.

Additionally, the environmental subconsultant submitted the mitigation plan to the design section engineers for incorporation into the construction documents and environmental permitting packages. This element consisted of plan views and cross sections showing the topography and planting scheme(s) including planting specifications, and a narrative detailing the intended function, hydrology, and construction methodology for each mitigation area.

Conclusion

The Northwest Hillsborough Expressway was an example of one project which integrated the preservation of environmental quality with the transportation requirements of a growing metropolitan area. Final design and construction of this limited access toll facility will serve to alleviate many of Hillsborough County's transportation problems while maintaining the unique environmental features of the existing wetland areas native to West-Central Florida.

Appendix I. References

Carper, K. A. and Churchill, G. J. (1988). "Northwest Hillsborough Expressway Memorandum No. 5". Technical memorandum submitted to design section engineers.

Wanielista, M.P. (1977). "Manual of Stormwater Management Practices". Final report submitted to the East Central Florida Regional Planning Council.

Wanielista, M.P. (1979). Stormwater Management Quantity and Quality. Ann Arbor Science, Ann Arbor, MI.

Weighting Factors for Transferable Discharge Permit Programs
that Group Several Pollutants

Barbara J. Lence,[1] Associate Member, ASCE

Abstract
Transferable discharge permit (TDP) programs for controlling several pollutants may manage such pollutants as several individual commodities or as a single weighted sum of the various pollutants. Under the weighted sum permits program, however, administrators would not have direct control over the amount of each pollutant that is discharged, and environmental quality may be jeopardized unless the selected weighting factors induce a market equilibrium that also satisfies a set of individual environmental quality standards for the different pollutants. This paper presents an approach for estimating the cost effective weighting factors that satisfy environmental quality standards for TDP programs in which pollutants are grouped together. It is shown that estimates of these weighting factors require complete treatment cost and water quality information.

Introduction
Water quality management programs that employ TDPs may be used to control several pollutants at once (see, e.g., *Dales* 1968; *Mackintosh* 1973; *Russell* 1980; *Palmer and Quinn* 1981; and *Lence et al.* 1988). Under these programs, the right to discharge a certain quantity of pollution, once issued by the governing authority, may be transferred among the dischargers as a free market commodity, i.e., at a price agreed upon by buyer and seller. The total quantity of permits is controlled by the governing authority, ensuring that environmental protection is maintained, while permitting existing facilities to grow and new facilities to be established. Such innovative approaches may improve upon single pollutant management schemes by providing incentives to develop efficient waste treatment technologies that remove several pollutants at once.
Two types of TDP programs for managing multiple pollutants have been suggested: 1) programs that manage pollutants individually, where each permit is based on the quantity of one pollutant or on its environmental effect (see, e.g., *Roberts* 1976; *Tietenberg* 1980; *Russell* 1980; and *Lence et al.* 1988), and 2) programs in which weighting factors are employed to aggregate pollutants into a single measure (see, e.g., *Mackintosh* 1973 and *Palmer and Quinn* 1981). Under the weighted sum permit approach, weighting factors are used to group pollutants thathave a similar impact on environmental quality or to group pollutants that are removed by the same treatment processes. Regardless, the primary advantage of the weighted sum permits

---
[1] Asst. Prof., Water Resources Engrg., Civ. Engrg. Dept., Univ. of Manitoba, Winnipeg, MB, R3T-2N2, Canada.

program is that administrative complexity may be reduced because fewer permit markets are needed. However, under this type of program, environmental quality may be jeopardized unless the selected weighting factors induce a market equilibrium that also satisfies environmental quality standards for each of the pollutants. For example, a water quality manager may choose to operate a weighted sum permit program to control biochemical oxygen (BOD) and phosphorus discharges in a river basin. Since the marginal cost of removing phosphorus with chemical treatment is higher than that for BOD at some levels of removal, the water quality standard for phosphorus may not be achieved unless the weight placed on phosphorus is large enough to encourage dischargers to employ chemical treatment.

In the following section, it is shown that the cost effective weighting factors that satisfy environmental quality standards under a weighted sum TDP program are functions of the treatment costs and water quality impacts of the given pollutants and are difficult to determine without complete system information. The management implications of this observation are then discussed in the final section of the paper.

Choice of Weighting Factors In Aggregate Permit Markets

The mathematical models for individual and weighted sum "pollution" permit programs for noninteractive pollutants are employed here to evaluate the effective weighting factors for a weighted sum permit program. *Montgomery* (1972), defines "pollution" permits as the right to emit pollutants at a rate such that the water quality measured at a certain location is degraded by no more than a specified amount. *Beavis and Walker* (1979) characterize noninteractive pollutants as substances that exhibit an independent effect on different environmental quality parameters. (For a demonstration of the efficiency of "pollution" permit markets for controlling both interactive and noninteractive pollutants see *Lence* 1988).

The region being managed consists of $i = \{1,..., I\}$ industrial dischargers which are the sole sources of pollution in a river basin and are fixed in location. The waste sources discharge $m = \{1,..., M\}$ different pollutants, at the rate e_{mi}. It is assumed that these pollutants affect ambient water quality conditions through strongly separable pollution transport functions (i.e., the affect of discharge from a given firm is independent of the amount of pollution discharged from other firms in the region). For simplicity, it is also assumed that the appropriate water quality constraints are binding at only one water quality checkpoint in the water body.

The individual "pollution" permits management model for a region, as described by *Montgomery* (1972), is formulated as:

$$\text{minimize } z = \sum_{i=1}^{I} F_i(e_{1i}, e_{2i}, ..., e_{Mi}) \qquad 1$$

subject to:
Permit limited water quality conditions

$$\sum_{i=1}^{I} h_{mi} e_{mi} \leq L_m, \qquad \forall m = 1,..., M, \qquad 2$$

and $e_{mi} \geq 0, \qquad \forall m = 1,..., M, i = 1,..., I. \qquad 3$

Where $F_i(e_{1i}, e_{2i}, ..., e_{Mi})$ is the convex joint abatement cost function for firm i, h_{mi} is the contribution that one unit of pollutant m discharged by firm i makes to the pollution level at the binding water quality checkpoint, L_m is the number of individual "pollution" permits which are issued by the water quality management agency, these are chosen to comply with the environmental standard at the binding water quality checkpoint, and all other variables described above.

The optimal discharge levels, e^*_{mi}, for the individual permits program may be found by evaluating the Kuhn-Tucker conditions for general optimality for *Equations 1-3*. These conditions are:

$$\frac{\partial F_i(e^*_{1i}, e^*_{2i}, ..., e^*_{Mi})}{\partial e_{mi}} + u_m h_{mi} \geq 0, \quad \sum_{i=1}^{I} e^*_{mi}\left(\frac{\partial F_i(e^*_{1i}, e^*_{2i}, ..., e^*_{Mi})}{\partial e_{mi}} + u_m h_{mi}\right) = 0,$$

$$\forall m = 1, ..., M, \quad 4$$

$$L_m - \sum_{i=1}^{I} h_{mi} e^*_{mi} \geq 0, \quad u_m\left(L_m - \sum_{i=1}^{I} h_{mi} e^*_{mi}\right) = 0 \quad \forall m = 1, ..., M. \quad 5$$

The weighted sum "pollution" permits management model for a region, as described by *Lence* (1988), is formulated as:

minimize $z = \sum_{i=1}^{I} F_i(e_{1i}, e_{2i}, ..., e_{Mi})$ \hfill 6

subject to:
Permit limited water quality condition

$$\sum_{i=1}^{I} \sum_{m=1}^{M} W_m e_{mi} \leq L_{ws}, \quad 7$$

and $e_{mi} \geq 0$, \hfill $\forall m = 1, ..., M, i = 1, ..., I.$ \quad 8

Where W_m is the weighting factor for pollutant m, L_{ws} is the number of weighted sum "pollution" permits which are issued by the water quality management agency, and all other variables described above.

The optimal discharge levels, e^{ws}_{mi}, for this model are defined for the shadow price $u^{ws} \geq 0$ such that:

$$\frac{\partial F_i(e^{ws}_{1i}, e^{ws}_{2i}, ..., e^{ws}_{Mi})}{\partial e_{mi}} + u^{ws} W_m \geq 0,$$

$$\sum_{i=1}^{I} e^{ws}_{mi}\left(\frac{\partial F_i(e^{ws}_{1i}, e^{ws}_{2i}, ..., e^{ws}_{Mi})}{\partial e_{mi}} + u^{ws} W_m\right) = 0, \quad \forall m = 1, ..., M, \quad 9$$

$$L_{ws} - \sum_{i=1}^{I} \sum_{m=1}^{M} W_m e^{ws}_{mi} \geq 0, \quad u^{ws}\left(L_{ws} - \sum_{i=1}^{I} \sum_{m=1}^{M} W_m e^{ws}_{mi}\right) = 0. \quad 10$$

Since such programs give dischargers flexibility as to the amount of each pollutant that they discharge for each weighted sum permit they own, the weighting factors used to aggregate pollutants must be designed so that the resulting water quality under the weighted sum permit market is no worse than that allowed under the individual permit markets program. That is, the efficient discharge levels for the weighted sum permit program, e_{mi}^{ws}, must be equal to the efficient discharge vectors for the individual markets case, e_{mi}^{*}, defined by *Equations* 4 and 5. By comparing *Equations* 4 and 5 with *Equations* 9 and 10, it can be shown that in order for $e_{m}^{ws} = e_{li}^{*}$ for every m and every i, L_{ws} and W_m must be defined as:

$$L_{ws} = \frac{\sum_{m=1}^{M} u_m L_m}{u^{ws}} \quad \text{and} \quad W_m = \frac{u_m h_{mi}}{u^{ws}}, \quad \forall m = 1,\ldots, M.$$

Management Implications

In order to estimate u_m and u^{ws}, and therefore the weighting factors and the total amount of weighted sum permits to be issued, the administrator would need complete knowledge of the cost and environmental impact data for the region. Even with this information, operation of a weighted sum permit market for several pollutants may be problematic because, unless the pollutants are conservative, the weighting factors for the pollutants would need to be different for each discharger. For such programs, the best the water quality manager might do is approximate these data, estimate the appropriate weights, and accept some degree of inefficiency, or water quality degradation, as a result of inaccurate information. To guard against such inefficiencies, the manager might estimate values for the weighting factors that are robust to a wide range of water quality and treatment cost information.

Appendix I - References

Beavis, B. and M. Walker, "Interactive pollutants and joint abatement costs: achieving water quality standards with effluent charges," Journal of Environmental Economics and Management, 6, 275-286, 1979.

Dales, J. H., Pollution, property, and prices, University of Toronto Press, 1968.

Lence, B. J., Market policies for control of multiple pollutants: management issues and methods of analysis, Ph.D. Thesis, University of Illinois at Urbana-Champaign, Department of Civil Engineering, Urbana, Illinois, 1988.

Lence, B. J., J.W. Eheart, and E.D. Brill, Jr., "Cost efficiency of transferable discharge permit programs for the control of multiple pollutants," Water Resources Research, July, 1988.

Mackintosh, D. R., The economics of airborne emissions: the case of an air rights market, 61-73, Preager Publishers, New York, 1973.

Montgomery, W. D., "Markets in licenses and efficient pollution control programs," Journal of Economic Theory, 5, 395-418, 1972.

Palmer, A. R., and T. H. Quinn, Allocating chloroflourocarbon permits: who gains, who loses, and what is the cost, Rand Report No. R-2806-EPA, The Rand Corporation, Santa Monica, California, July, 1981.

Roberts, M. J., Environmental protection: the complexities of real policy choice, in Managing the water environment, edited by N. A. Swainson, 157-235, University of British Columbia Press, Vancouver, B.C., 1976.

Russell, C.S. Environmental policy and controlled trading of pollution permits, Discussion Paper D-65, Resources For The Future, Washington, D.C., 1980.

Tietenberg, T. H., "Transferable discharge permits and the control of stationary source air pollution: a survey and synthesis," Land Economics, 56, 391-416, 1980.

STORMWATER MANAGEMENT PLANNING
FOR THE RUSH CREEK WATERSHED
ARLINGTON, TEXAS

Duke G. Altman[1], M.ASCE
William H. Espey, Jr.[2], M.ASCE
David D. Gieber[3]
Jerome F. Ewen[4], M.ASCE

Abstract

Persistent planning focused through the City of Arlington and a Citizen Stormwater Management Implementation Committee has initiated the developed of a City stormwater management program that considers the unique characteristics of individual watersheds. Stormwater management plans are being developed for three of the City's major watersheds--Rush Creek, Johnson Creek, and the South Branch of Fish Creek.

Being the City's largest drainage basin, the 34-square mile Rush Creek Watershed is approximately 50% developed with a majority of the undeveloped area being located in upstream areas. Ongoing development of the Rush Creek Watershed Plan has required the balancing of a number of planning considerations such as legal/institutional issues, financial opportunities/constraints, environmental/open space concerns,

---

[1]Associate, Espey, Huston & Associates, Inc., P.O. Box 519, Austin, TX 78767

[2]President, Espey, Huston & Associates, Inc., P.O. Box 519, Austin, TX 78767

[3]Associate, Espey, Huston & Associates, Inc., 17811 Waterview Parkway, Dallas, TX 75252

[4]Asst. Dir., Community Development, City of Arlington, P.O. Box 231, Arlington, TX 76010

water quality conditions, identifying and solving flooding problems, making prioritization decisions, and implementation planning.

The proposed watershed plan utilizes a combination of structural and nonstructural measures to solve existing flooding problems as well as updating drainage policies and procedures aimed at preventing future problems from developing. To compliment and enhance the planning effort, the establishment of linear parks within the stream corridors has been identified as a major objective in maximizing utilization of the watershed's environmentally attractive features. Creation of an enterprise fund and bonding presently appear to offer the best mechanisms to provide funding for the needed programs and improvements.

Introduction

The City of Arlington is presently developing stormwater management plans for several of its major watersheds. One such watershed is the 34-square mile Rush Creek Watershed which is approximately 50% developed at present. The undeveloped areas are located primarily in the upstream portions of the watershed. Although somewhat slowed at present, ultimate development of these upstream areas will significant increase the flooding potential in the watershed's lower reaches. Additional concerns that convinced the City of Arlington to develop stormwater management plans for Rush Creek and its other major watersheds include the prevalence of existing flooding and erosion problems, the desire to utilize stream corridors for open space and parkland, the protection and enhancement of stream water quality and the establishment of a prioritization procedure that would insure that available funds would be spent where needed most.

Plan Development

Development of a stormwater management plan for the watershed was initiated with a watershed and stream corridor assessment that involved the collection and analysis of data related to climate, vegetation, wildlife, soils, subsurface geology, land uses, infrastructure, and archaeological/historical resources. A detailed hydrologic/hydraulic analysis was also performed as part of the assessment. In performing the hydrologic/hydraulic analysis, ultimate land use conditions were projected from the City's traffic survey zone data and utilized with the NUDALLAS rainfall-runoff model developed by the U.S. Army Corps of Engineers (Ft. Worth District) and the Corp's HEC-2 water surface profile model in developing future (potential) peak flood discharges and resulting flooding conditions. The future potential flooding conditions were then used as a base to analyze alternative plans of improvement.

The primary watercourses in the watershed were divided into reaches of similar flood damage and/or corridor utilization potential in order to evaluate the various alternative solutions using a reach-by-reach approach. Stream corridor utilization concepts and watershed nonstructural and/or structural alternatives were developed for the various reaches with the aim of allowing corridor utilization while providing flood correction and prevention. Watershed management planning opportunities varied between study reaches given their respective physiographic conditions, present development patterns and locations of flooding problems. Not surprisingly, alternative plans of improvement appropriate for the main branch of Rush Creek were not always well-suited for the creek's tributaries. A continual screening process was employed until the most promising comprehensive alternative plans were conceptualized. In general, an attempt was made to select up to three of the most feasible alternatives in each of eleven reaches and/or reach groupings. However, in certain reaches, or reach groupings, only one or two methods were selected due to limited applicability of the other methods.

Each of the eleven reaches, or reach groupings, were matched with one, two or three of the following alternatives:

(1) Selective Bridge and/or Channel Improvements
(2) On-site Detention Facilities
(3) Off-site or Regional Detention Facilities
(4) Levee Improvements
(5) No Action

Following selection of the most promising watershed management alternatives, a more detailed analysis and evaluation of the selected alternatives was made. With the goal of continuing the selection process and recommending an overall final watershed management plan for Rush Creek, improvements associated with the screened alternatives were conceptually located, sized, hydrologically/hydraulically analyzed and costed. The analysis results were then evaluated based on the number of structures removed from the 100-year full-development condition floodplain, the number of bridge/culvert crossings prevented from overtopping, the acreage removed from the referenced floodplain and improvement costs involved.

Each of the three final alternatives also include an overlay of regulations, programs, and open space policies that include floodplain storage preservation, elevated foundations of new structures, subdivision and/or zoning regulations, public acquisition/utilization of open space and flood insurance. These nonstructural components of each plan are aimed at controlling potential increases in flooding problems, while the structural components are primarily planned to alleviate existing flooding problems. Although existing and future flood control are the primary goals in establishing a watershed management plan, consideration was also given to associated open space opportunities, erosion control and water quality.

A set of base watershed conditions was utilized as a means of evaluating the three alternative plans. These base conditions assume that the entire watershed is urbanized and that a limited amount of floodplain valley storage has been lost due to development encroachment. Consistent with the Corps' 1988 "Record of Decision - Regional Environmental Impact Statement - Trinity River and Tributaries", a maximum of 15% valley storage loss was set to allow for a limited amount of future floodplain encroachment. The hydrologic/hydraulic analysis of each alternative accounted for the effect that the alternative improvements would have on the watershed's base condition flood potential. The cost of each of the various plan improvements is also a major concern. The total costs associated with each plan of improvement were developed utilizing the estimated quantities of various construction items and their associated unit costs.

The watershed management plan recommended for the Rush Creek Watershed consists of certain channel and bridge improvements and three regional detention facilities. Implementation of the recommended plan is estimated to remove all but 20 of 133 building/house structures and 6 of 24 roadway crossings expected to flood under 100-year full-development conditions. Utilization of three regional detention facilities also provides benefits additional to flood control such as control of peak flow increases due to future development, a reduced need for bridge and channel improvements, erosion and water quality benefits as well as increased recreational opportunities.

Although undergoing continued evaluation, certain funding options are being considered as part of the plan's implementation strategy. Funding is needed for the administrative, planning, engineering, maintenance, regulatory and capital improvement expenses associated with upgrading the City's overall stormwater management program and implementing watershed management plans. A storm drainage enterprise fund is presently considered the most viable primary funding method. This fund would be somewhat similar to a utility service charge for drainage. Several secondary funding methods appear feasible but need to be integrated with the drainage enterprise fund to be effective. The most viable methods presently appear to be plan review and inspection fees, special assessment districts as well as revenue and general obligation bonding.

LAKE ZEPHYR WATERSHED STORMWATER MANAGEMENT PLAN

By Elliot Silverston, M. ASCE,[1] C. Lynn Miller, M. ASCE,[2]
Stephen R. Noe, AM. ASCE[3]

Abstract

Zephyr Creek, located near the City of Zephyrhills in west-central Florida, annually experiences flooding caused by rainfall. Development has encroached into the floodplain causing homes, buildings, and roads to flood and emergency services to be impaired. Existing Federal Insurance Rate Maps grossly underestimated the extent of the floodplain along the creek. To correct this condition, a stormwater management plan (Plan) was developed for the watershed. This paper describes the matrix methodology used to develop the Plan and inter-government coordination required when a project encompasses many political and permitting jurisdictions.

Introduction

The Lake Zephyr Watershed is located in southeastern Pasco County, Florida. The watershed area is approximately 5 square miles (13 km^2). Zephyr Creek is approximately 8 miles (12.9 km) long with the headwaters being comprised of pastureland. The creek meanders through residential communities, parks and

---
[1] Associate, Greiner, Inc., 5601 Mariner Street, Tampa, Florida 33609
[2] Associate Vice President, Greiner, Inc., Tampa, Florida 33609
[3] Project Engineer, Greiner, Inc., Tampa, Florida 33609

pastureland prior to discharging to the Hillsborough River. A section of the creek traverses the City of Zephyrhills. Average annual rainfall in the Lake Zephyr Watershed is approximately 54 inches (1.37 m). The summer months are susceptible to hurricanes and tropical storms.

Stormwater Management Plan

The Lake Zephyr Watershed Stormwater Management Plan (Greiner, Inc. April 1989) was developed by assessing the acceptability and impacts of both non-structural and structural alternatives. A matrix methodology was used to rank these alternatives as to environmental, land use compatibility, socioeconomic, and hydrologic/hydraulic issues. A four-phase procedure was developed for selecting the Plan.

The first phase entailed developing a hydrologic/hydraulic model of the watershed in order to predict floodprone areas and ascertain how the system drains.

In the second phase, a matrix was developed for rating both the non-structural and structural alternatives with impacts or acceptability (Figure 1). The alternatives included special drainage performance criteria, channel maintenance, pumping, wetland creation, development restrictions in the floodplain, and detention and retention ponds. Each alternative was ranked with respect to environmental impacts (agricultural, archaeological, flora/fauna, hazardous waste, upland habitat, wetlands); land use compatibility (maintenance of traffic, neighborhoods, right-of-way, zoning); socioeconomics (community acceptability, construction cost, operation and maintenance, reliability, relocation); hydrology/hydraulic (flood reduction, recharge, pollution abatement); and opportunity (feasibility). These issues were then given a weighting factor which was related to the assumed client expectation for the project: flood reduction. The rating forms were distributed to a group of evaluators with diverse backgrounds. Included with the rating forms was a package of information with results

160 RESOURCES FOR WATER MANAGEMENT

FIGURE 1 - Strategy Matrix (Greiner, Inc., April 1989)

from the screening model and maps delineating hydrologic characteristics, water quality data (domestic waste, hazardous waste and gasoline storage tank, dumps, industrial wastes, and non-point source sites), zoning maps, subdivision locations, land use/vegetation maps and soil classification maps. This information was to be used by each evaluator when grading the relative benefit and suitability of an improvement strategy.

The third phase involved the selection of four candidate plans from the results of the matrix data.

The fourth phase entailed the selection by Pasco County and the Southwest Florida Water Management District (SWFWMD) (both agencies funded the project) of a preferred plan from the four candidate plans. The preferred plan includes the following elements: (1) Development restrictions within the 100-year floodplain; (2) Wetland creation; (3) Special drainage performance criteria; (4) Channel maintenance; (5) Structural improvements/replacements; (6) An on-line detention facility; and (7) Secondary drainage system improvements.

The objective of the structural improvements is to detain runoff in upstream reaches from flowing to downstream sections of the creek while improving the flow capacity of the channel throughout the watershed with the results being the reduction of flood stages. When this strategy is implemented, the total volume of water moving through the system will not significantly change; however, the change of flow rate in time will be modified. Culvert improvements at roadway crossings and some channel improvement and maintenance are required throughout the entire watershed, otherwise flooding problems would shift from one location to another.

Regulatory measures should be implemented as described in the Plan to permit future development to occur without increasing flooding along Zephyr Creek. Floodplain restrictions would provide for compensation when storage areas are encroached on within the existing floodplain. Special drainage criteria would serve to reduce the peak rates of discharge and volumes of runoff caused by increasing impervious area. The special drainage criteria would be more comprehensive than existing Pasco County and SWFWMD requirements.

The benefits of the Lake Zephyr Plan include: (1) Significant reduction of intensity and frequency of flooding in the watershed; (2) Improved water quality in the watershed; (3) Erosion control from upstream reaches and in stabilized reaches of the creek; (4) Improvement of emergency service facilities (roads) during severe storm events; (5) Creation of wetlands; and (6) Provision of accurate planning and design data for construction (such as floodplain elevations).

The impacts resulting from the Plan include: (1) Reduction of developable land in the watershed through acquisition for the pond and comprehensive regulatory criteria; (2) Reduction in some existing wetland areas near the creek.

Interagency Coordination

Coordination with regulatory agencies during the planning phase is necessary to develop an implementable plan. Environmental permits are required prior to construction of the Plan's structural features. The permitting agencies assess the project impacts on water quality, water quantity and wetlands. Two meetings were held with local, state, and federal agencies to keep them apprised of the study and allow for input. The Florida Department of Environmental Regulation (FDER), SWFWMD, City of Zephyrhills, and Florida Department of Transportation (FDOT) had the most concerns relative to the project so individual formal and informal discussions were held at later dates.

Public Involvement

The residents in the watershed had a major role in the project. They urged Pasco County to fund the study which would determine the cause of flooding to their homes and to develop a plan for remediating the flooding problem. Throughout the project, residents were supportive in providing information as to the extent of the flooding. They attended the Pasco County Board of County Commissioners and SWFWMD board meetings where they supported the Plan and requested it be implemented immediately. A Public Information Pamphlet (Greiner, Inc., May 1989) was prepared and distributed which described the Plan, implementation and costs in easily understood, non-technical terms. This pamphlet aided in the Plan's acceptance.

Conclusions

The matrix methodology was used to develop alternative plans for the Lake Zephyr Watershed. The Plan was well received because it gave the Pasco County and the SWFWMD decision makers a logical approach for the selection of a preferred plan. Coordination with regulatory agencies gave credibility to the Plan and should assist in permitting the structural phases. The project results have been accepted by Pasco County, the City of Zephyrhills and the SWFWMD as part of their regulatory programs. The public has accepted the Plan and supports its implementation.

References

Greiner, Inc., Lake Zephyr Watershed Stormwater and Flood Management Master Plan, Final Report, April 1989.

Greiner, Inc., Lake Zephyr Watershed Stormwater and Flood Management Master Plan, Public Information Pamphlet, May 1989.

Hydrology Review for Corps 404 Permit Process

Paul K. Rodman, Member ASCE[1]

Abstract

Since 1985 the Corps of Engineers has reviewed Section 404 permit requests in regard to hydrology and hydraulic impacts of developments in the mainstem floodplains of the Trinity River in the Fort Worth-Dallas Metroplex. A Regional Environmental Impact Study with multiple alternative mainstem floodplain development scenarios indicated very significant negative cumulative impacts on downstream land uses. Development of a significant part of the mainstem floodplain can occur without a Corps permit but does require approval of local governments. Local political entities are considering implementing a permit process in cooperation with the Corps for the entire mainstem floodplain.

Introduction

In the early 1980's development of the previously generally undeveloped floodplain of the Elm Fork and West Fork Trinity River began to accelerate upstream from the channel and levees of the Dallas Floodway. The Dallas Floodway was designed in the early 1950's to handle a Standard Project Flood (SPF) with four feet freeboard. The SPF is an estimate of flood discharges that may be expected from the most severe combination of meteorologic and hydrologic conditions that are considered reasonably characteristic of the geographical region involved, excluding extremely rare combinations. SPF discharges are generally equal to 40 to 60 percent of the probable maximum flood for the same basin. Hydrology and hydraulic studies during the 1970's indicated that for ultimate watershed development, the SPF discharge would increase to the point that the levees of the Dallas Floodway would have inadequate freeboard. The accelerated floodplain development of the early 80's raised concerns about the impacts of projects for which Corps Section 404 (Clean Water Act) or Section 10 (Rivers and Harbors Act of 1899) permits were required. While no one project was big enough to radically impact the SPF discharges at Dallas, there was

---

[1] Chief, Hydrologic Engineering Section, Fort Worth District U.S. Army Corps of Engineers, P.O. Box 17300, Fort Worth, TX 76102.

significant concern about the cumulative increase in SPF discharge from multiple floodplain projects occupying areas which previously stored water and attenuated flood peaks. These concerns resulted in the Corps starting a Regional Environmental Impact Study in December 1984.

Regional Environmental Impact Study

The Regional Environmental Impact Study (REIS) involved the North Central Texas Council of Governments (NCTCOG) as convenor of representatives of nine cities and three counties having jurisdictional authority for part of the developing floodplain of the Elm Fork and West Fork Trinity River. The U.S. Fish and Wildlife Service, the United States Environmental Protection Agency, and the Federal Emergency Management Agency (FEMA) were also involved study participants. Five alternative future development scenarios were formulated by the Corps and other study participants in the Draft REIS of 1986 in an attempt to define the range of options. The cities also supplied projections of ultimate watershed development within their jurisdictional areas and outside the mainstem Trinity River floodplain. Hydrology modelling indicates that urbanization of the tributary watersheds without developing or filling the mainstem floodplain results in an almost insignificant increase in the SPF discharges for the Trinity River at Dallas. Maximum development of the mainstem floodplain using channels and levees to maximize area "reclaimed" results in a radically increased SPF discharge which would overtop the Dallas Floodway levees. Other development options considered included a wider floodway with maximum development, full development of the FEMA floodway fringe, development of the floodway fringe except in areas where a 404 permit is required, and no additional mainstem development with environmental enhancement. Public comment on the Draft REIS resulted in the formulation of additional scenarios. As part of the Final REIS, a composite future was analyzed with limits of mainstem floodplain development defined by local governments staffs. This option represented the most likely development alternative if there were no major shift in regulatory policy. SPF discharge is increased so much that levee overtopping results at Dallas. A theoretical "modified floodway" option was considered with the target of allowing encroachment of the mainstem floodplain so that the 100-year water surface does not increase by more than approximately one foot. Full filling of the floodway fringe in the Draft REIS had resulted in increases in the 100-year and SPF water surface much greater than one foot. The Final REIS was published in October 1987. Comments were considered from numerous individuals, groups and agencies for consideration in the Record of Decision. District Engineer Colonel Schaufelberger signed the final Record of Decision on April 29, 1988, formalizing a set of criteria for evaluating environmental and hydrology and hydraulic impacts of projects being evaluated under the Corps Section 404 and Section 10 permit process.

RESOURCES FOR WATER MANAGEMENT

Corps' Permit Process, Hydrology Criteria

The permit criteria adopted in the Record of Decision evolved during the REIS study period. In August 1986, hydrology and hydraulics (H-H) criteria were written down based on impacts of alternatives evaluated in the Draft EIS and other previous technical studies. Prior to that time, H-H recommendations on 404 permits were made by experienced engineers based on data supplied by developer's engineers and whether "significant negative impacts" resulted locally or cumulatively from the project involved and similar projects. The H-H criteria were further refined in September 1987 to very nearly the same criteria as were adopted in the final Record of Decision. The following H-H criteria for mainstem projects are some of the primary ones included in the Record of Decision: (1) no rise in the 100-year or SPF elevation for the proposed condition; (2) the maximum allowable losses in valley storage (on-site and considering full valley cross-section) are 0% and 5% for the 100-year and SPF, respectively; (3) alterations of the floodplain may not create or increase an erosive water velocity on- or off-site; (4) and, minimum elevation for fills is the 100-year elevation plus one foot, while minimum top of levee is the SPF elevation plus four feet, unless a relief system is designed which prevents catastrophic failure. The H-H personnel of the Fort Worth District Corps of Engineers have spent many hours reviewing data from engineers for developers and discussing and explaining H-H criteria over the last few years in conjunction with evaluating 404 permit requests. Projects which have required Section 404 permits have been designed significantly differently than traditional projects. Significant areas have been set aside for valley storage mitigation, frequently with extensive excavation and wetland creation. Hydraulic impacts have generally been mitigated by relief swales or channel enlargement so that water surface profiles for the 100-year and SPF floods have not been raised significantly.

Beyond Section 404: "Common Vision"

While the Section 404 permit program offers some limitation of negative impacts of development of the mainstem floodplain, much of the floodplain can be developed without a 404 permit. Uncontrolled development of this part of the floodplain would result in significant negative impacts. The Corps has continued to meet with the NCTCOG and impacted cities and counties in developing a "Common Vision" whereby the local political entities and the Corps would use common criteria in evaluating floodplain development. The Corps and the cities are working on a Corridor Development Certificate (CDC) process to be followed by developers in seeking permits for any mainstem floodplain development. The Cities have each endorsed a resolution in support of the CDC process. A committee of local government staff representatives is working with Corps permit personnel on forms and procedures for implementing the CDC process. Much work is yet to be done. A draft manual and ordinance for implementing the CDC process are scheduled for July 1990.

Nonpoint Source Runoff and Urban Water Management

Michael A. Collins[1], M. ASCE
Roger O. Dickey[2], M. ASCE
Mark K. Boyd[3]

Abstract

Urban nonpoint source pollution can be viewed from physiochemical, source, and impact perspectives. These and its dependence upon runoff pose important problems for pollution control management, including allocation of pollution control monies between point and nonpoint source pollution, identification of the true pollution problem, definition of monitoring strategies, adequate attention to pollutant load variability, and coordination of pollution control activities across political boundaries.

Introduction

Urban nonpoint source pollution (NPSP) is a major contributor to today's water quality problems. Because most urban NPSP occurs during runoff periods, focus upon the runoff process can dominate thinking about NPSP control; but water pollution control management must have a broad perspective which recognizes not only the importance of urban runoff in NPSP, but also diverse technical factors that influence the ability to describe and control NPSP.

On The Nature of NPSP

There are alternate ways to view NPSP. These affect management perspectives in development of control strategies.
Early and continuing attention tends to describe NPSP in terms of the physiochemical composition of runoff waters. The disadvantage of a purely chemical description is that it is commonly not enlightening as to the reason

---

[1]Professor of Civil Engineering, Southern Methodist University, Dallas, TX 75275-0335
[2]Research Scientist, Institute of Environmental Sciences, University of Texas at Dallas, Richardson, TX 75080
[3]Graduate Student, Southern Methodist University, Dallas, TX 75275-0335

for the presence of a particular pollutant.
NPSP can be alternately characterized by its source
or cause. The US EPA has developed a master list of
sources and causes of NPSP, but such a list is not unique.
Furthermore, there are inconsistencies in the US EPA list
which tend to muddle management perspectives. For example,
urban runoff, including storm and combined sewers and
surface runoff, is identified as a specific category of
NPSP, yet other listed categories will be responsible for
the contamination in the urban runoff.

Impact characterization is a third way to describe
NPSP, though it is, in general, difficult because impacts
can be diverse, widespread, not always unique, and evidence themselves in different ways and over different time
periods. Some impacts are directly related to human health
but others are associated with aquatic ecosystems and consequently much more difficult to identify and quantify.

Variability, Similarity, and Monitoring

A source of major difficulty in controlling NPSP is
its extreme variability and the inability in many studies,
such as the National Urban Runoff Program (NURP), to trace
observed variability to specific factors such as land use,
geographic location, topography, precipitation patterns,
or population levels. Variability is, however, inherent to
the NPSP generation process, although it can be
demonstrated that inappropriate field sampling strategies
can measurably contribute to the apparent randomness in
estimated pollutant loads.

Management Issues

The first fundamental management issue in effective
NPSP control in the urban environment is the relation of
NPSP to point source pollution control. Presumably the
objective in water pollution control is reduction of water
pollution from whatever source. In different locals and at
different times NPSP may be more or less severe than point
source pollution. An effective management strategy would
be one which achieves the greatest reduction in pollution
from the money allocated for the pollution control effort.
However, quantification of NPSP is difficult. A major
benefit to be derived from better quantification of
nonpoint source pollution will be the ability to assess
its relative importance to point source pollution in a
particular setting. Effective pollution control therefore
dictates adequate attention to appropriate quantification
and comparison of both point and nonpoint source
pollution.

Compounding the difficulty in allocation of pollution
control dollars are regulatory programs which prescribe

the allocation of pollution control dollars to either point source control or nonpoint source pollution without an assessment of which deserves, in so far as water quality protection is concerned, the greater attention. Water management at the regional or local level is often dictated not solely by water pollution control needs but in considerable part by either the availability of funds or the politics of pollution control. Water pollution control management must be sufficiently flexible and cognizant of regional and local conditions to allow the most effective allocation of pollution control dollars.

The second fundamental management issue is to determine just what is the problem of NPSP. Is it merely NPSP or is it the adverse consequences produced by what is termed NPSP? The distinction is not trivial. Urban runoff, despite US EPA views to the contrary, is not NPSP; it is the materials contained in the urban runoff which present the potential pollution problem. A focus upon control of urban runoff because it is categorized from a regulatory standpoint as NPSP encourages an end-of-pipe mentality whose only goal is, at considerable cost, to limit urban runoff without consideration of what effect or noneffect that limitation may actually have on water quality conditions. Identification of appropriate goals in NPSP control management is essential for wise use of pollution control dollars.

Even with appropriate focus upon the impacts of the NPSP, we as a technical community have a difficult time identifying what are the adverse impacts. There are an enormous number of contaminates which have the potential for becoming a pollutant when certain thresholds are exceeded, but those thresholds and their synergistic interactions are often only poorly understood. This is certainly not unique to NPSP, but the difficulty is exacerbated by the fact that often the evaluation of effects from NPSP essentially focus upon in-stream ecosystems of considerable complexity. What is the effect of NPSP upon such ecosystems and, just as importantly, is that effect bad in some way? Meaningful, nontraditional monitoring strategies, such as biomonitoring, must become increasingly common in effective water pollution control efforts.

The third management issue is interwoven with a significant technical one. Even if we are able to quantify what are the adverse impacts of various types of pollutants, we have the considerable difficulty of determining what in fact is the amount of NPSP present and, furthermore, when it is present. This issue encompasses two basic management concerns:

The first concern is the more obvious. NPSP is very time dependent and time variable. Traditional sampling strategies for water pollution evaluation are geared toward dry weather or slowly time varying conditions. Water quality monitoring programs are frequently based upon some type of periodic sampling which may have little relation to the nature of the erratic occurrence of runoff. Continuous water quality monitoring, at least during key periods, must become more central to water quality management if effective control of NPSP is to be achieved.

The second concern, far less recognized, is the limited amount of good information that exists on the magnitudes of NPSP loads, despite years of effort and application of massive research funds. Periodic grab type sampling has by and large formed the data base upon which estimates of NPSP loads to streams and lakes have been deduced. But as the authors have found through their research employing continuous monitoring of both flow and suspended solids during runoff events, periodic sampling at what would seem reasonable frequency can not only radically overestimate or underestimate the pollutant load because of the erratic temporal behavior of the suspended solids but also lead to essentially a random, white noise type of estimated pollutant load variability.

Not only is the in-storm frequency of measurement important, but so also is the number of storm related events to be sampled. Little research has been done to assess the necessary duration of sampling programs for adequate quantification of NPSP loads and their variability. In their own research the authors have developed a stochastically based methodology to define necessary lengths of sampling programs to achieve various levels of assurance that the hydrologically based driving forces for generation of NPSP load are adequately measured. Nonpoint source pollution control must address the problem of just how long expensive sampling programs must be maintained to assure an adequate quantification of the NPSP loads and their variability. Water quality management, particularly that for NPSP, must move beyond dealing with only average loads and begin to more effectively address the issue of impacts of load variability.

Finally, there exists the very practical problem in NPSP control management arising from the generally large geographic dispersal of NPSP and its sources. NPSP sources contributing to a particular receiving water can extend across numerous political boundaries. The classical confrontation of upstream polluters vs downstream users is magnified because of the generally diffuse nature of the pollutant load generation. Furthermore, it becomes very easy for different entities to point fingers at each other or at different causes in an attempt to lessen potential responsibility for remedying the problems. NPSP management must be built upon an integrated, area-wide approach which can deal with diverse political entities in an equitable fashion in devising pollution control stategies and the methods for their funding.

IMPACTS OF EPA STORM WATER REGULATIONS ON THE DALLAS-FORT WORTH METROPLEX

Brent Larsen[1] and Wren Stenger[2]

Abstract

New storm water discharge permit application regulations proposed by EPA will have a significant impact on municipalities across the nation. Cities in the Dallas-Fort Worth metroplex are planning a regional approach to control storm water pollution. Comments received by EPA Region 6 provide insight into perceived impacts the regulations will have on municipalities in the area.

Introduction

Section 402(p) of the Clean Water Act (U.S. Congress, 1977), as amended by the Water Quality Act of 1987 (U.S. Congress, 1987), required the Environmental Protection Agency (EPA) to establish National Pollutant Discharge Elimination System (NPDES) permit application regulations for storm water discharges. These regulations were to address storm water discharges associated with industrial activity and discharges from medium municipal separate storm sewer systems serving populations of 100,000 or more but less than 250,000 and large systems serving populations of 250,000 or more.

On December 7, 1988, EPA public noticed the proposed rule in the *Federal Register* (EPA, 1987). The comment period was open through March 7, 1989. Additionally, EPA conducted six public hearings to discuss the proposed rule and its associated impact on both the industrial and municipal communities. Numerous municipalities and professional groups even journeyed to

---

[1]Environmental Scientist, Municipal Permits Section, Water Management Division, U.S. EPA Region 6, 1445 Ross Ave., Dallas, TX 75202
[2]Chief, Municipal Permits Section, Water Management Division, U.S. EPA Region 6, 1445 Ross Ave., Dallas, TX 75202

Washington, D.C., to discuss their concerns with EPA Headquarters representatives.

In our EPA Region 6 area, many municipalities have taken a proactive stance on storm water control. The Region has reviewed several storm water planning packages submitted by municipalities and returned comments and guidance. The Region sees the storm water initiative as a multi-faceted program that will require close coordination and communication between the agency and the regulated community.

Discussion

Formal and informal comments on the proposed storm water permit application regulations provide insight into perceived impacts the regulations will have on municipalities in the Dallas-Fort Worth area. Major areas of concern raised by commentors include uncertainty regarding exactly who will be required to get permits and when, storm water associated with industrial activity, application requirements, permit conditions, and costs of both the application and permit implementation. These same concerns are shared by many municipalities across the nation.

Section 402(p)(4) of the Clean Water Act requires NPDES permit applications prior to October 1, 1992, for municipal separate storm sewer systems serving a population of 100,000 or more. Section 402(p)(2)(E) authorizes designation of other discharges for early permitting. The municipal separate storm sewer system definition in the final regulations coupled with agency implementation of the designation authority will determine who will need to apply for a permit prior to October 1, 1992.

In the December 7, 1988, Notice of Proposed Rulemaking, EPA requested comment on several options for defining a municipal separate storm sewer system. These options were variations on two main approaches. The first approach relies on ownership or operation of the storm sewer system serving the appropriate population. The second approach would define the storm sewer system as all municipal storm sewers within a geographic area with all owners and/or operators as either individual or co-applicants. At this time, EPA appears to be leaning towards a geographical definition based primarily on all storm sewers within an incorporated area or census urban area meeting the population requirement. This would be supplemented by other storm sewers designated for interrelationships or pollutant contribution.

Most of the major cities in the Dallas-Fort Worth area are involved in a regional effort to coordinate storm water pollution control efforts. The North Central Texas Council of Governments (NCTCOG), the designated water quality planning agency for the Dallas-Fort Worth area, has been a driving force in this effort. Participating member cities in NCTCOG have developed a regional strategy (NCTCOG, 1989) based on a watershed approach. The regional strategy is intended to reduce costs and focus resources on the watersheds with the most problems. Cooperative, integrated storm water management plans would be developed watershed by watershed. Under this strategy, each city would submit individual Part I applications and then joint Part II applications by watershed. Comments received from NCTCOG request EPA provide the flexibility to issue storm water permits by watersheds. Region 6 is hopeful that flexibility to adapt to local conditions will be incorporated into the final regulations.

The statutory deadlines for permitting contained in Section 402(p)(4) of the Clean Water Act called for permit application regulations for large systems by February 4, 1989, and February 4, 1991, for medium systems. Applications from affected municipalities were to follow one year later. With final application regulations for both classes expected in the Spring of 1990, EPA will be a year late for the large systems and a year early for medium systems. If the proposed application deadlines become final, municipalities would be allowed up to two years to complete the two part application process, but medium municipalities would have less than one year to submit Part I. Commentors have requested municipalities be allowed the full time intended by Congress to submit applications.

EPA proposed that the discharge of storm water associated with industrial activity to a municipal separate storm sewer system be covered under the municipal permit. All cities cooperating with NCTCOG commented that cities should be able to designate, on a case-by-case basis, industries that would be required to get individual permits directly from EPA. On the other hand, several cities want to be able to exercise controls on direct discharging industries within city limits. The cities are concerned about the potential costs and liabilities of implementing a local control program for indirect industrial storm water discharges.

Municipalities across the nation have commented that EPA cost estimates for preparation of a municipal storm water permit are too low and do not even address program implementation. One potentially expensive application requirement is the proposed dry weather screen of all "major" outfalls for illicit discharges. With "major" outfalls defined as proposed according to a certain size pipe or its equivalent draining a given acreage, the City Of Dallas estimates they have over 10,000 outfalls. The COG and member cities commented that a maximum number of outfalls to be sampled for Part I of the application should be specified. A schedule for screening all outfalls could be included in the permit. The purpose of the proposed Part II characterization study is to gather data to estimate pollutant loadings from different land use classifications and the storm sewer system as a whole. Participants in NCTCOG's regional plan have proposed that cities be allowed to do required sampling on a regional basis and share the data, thus reducing the cost to each individual city.

In a departure from traditional end-of-pipe treatment permits, Congress declined to require a technology based treatment level for municipal storm water discharges. Instead, Section 402(p)(3) of the Clean Water Act requires controls to reduce the discharge of pollutants to the maximum extent practicable (MEP). The permit envisioned by EPA will incorporate a municipality developed storm water management program to achieve MEP. Commentors have expressed concern that neither Congress in the Clean Water Act nor EPA in the proposed regulations have further defined MEP.

Conclusions

With promulgation of final application regulations expected Spring 1990, municipalities in the Dallas-Fort Worth metroplex are well ahead of many other areas of the nation. With the coordination of NCTCOG, cooperating cities are trying to develop a cost effective means of controlling pollutants in storm water discharges. Each city realizes that an effective storm water management program will require a substantial commitment of resources. Region 6 EPA will be working with applicants to develop NPDES discharge permits that will effectively and efficiently control pollutants in storm water discharges.

Appendix I. References

Environmental Protection Agency. (1988). "National
  Pollutant Discharge Elimination System Permit
  Application Regulations for Storm Water Discharges;
  Proposed Rule." *Federal Register* 53(235), 49416-
  49487, December 7, 1988.

North Central Texas Council of Governments. (1989). Regional Strategy for Managing Urban Storm Water Quality 1989-92. North Central Texas Council of Governments, adopted February 23, 1989.

U.S. Congress. (1977). "Federal Water Pollution Control Act, as Amended by the Clean Water Act of 1977." 33 U.S.C. 1251, et. seq.

U.S. Congress. (1987). "Water Quality Act of 1987." Public Law 100-4

Application of a GIS to Storm Water Quality Monitoring

Steven J. Haness[1]
John J. Warwick[2], Member ASCE
Roger O. Dickey[1], Member ASCE

Abstract
Integration of an ARC/INFO GIS with hydrodynamic water quality models (HEC-1 and HEC-5Q) helps quantify the water quality impacts of urban storm water runoff. The system can identify municipal outfalls affecting surface water quality, classify watersheds based on sensitivity to storm water inputs, and assist the local community in meeting EPA proposed NPDES permit requirements for storm water discharges. Application of this integrated system provides an effective, affordable planning tool for cities interested in assessing the impacts of storm water problems and proposed mitigation projects.

Introduction
With the passage of the Water Quality Act of 1987, the U.S. Environmental Protection Agency (EPA) must formally regulate urban storm water runoff. The EPA has proposed regulations to issue discharge permits, by the early nineties, under the National Pollutant Discharge Elimination System (NPDES) for municipal separate storm sewers in all cities of at least 100,000 people (53 Federal Register 49416). The identification of storm sewers as a source of surface water quality degradation is a significant step in addressing a nonpoint issue with point source techniques. However, the permitting of storm water outfalls in metropolitan areas is an enormous task.

---
[1]Research Scientist, Institute for Environmental Sciences, University of Texas at Dallas, Box 830688, Richardson, TX 75083.
[2]Director, Institute for Environmental Sciences, University of Texas at Dallas, Box 830688, Richardson, TX 75083.

Because of the magnitude of the problem, the proposed EPA regulations encourage system-wide cooperation in assessing and regulating the quality of urban storm water runoff. Within the Dallas-Fort Worth Metroplex, the North Central Texas Council of Governments (NCTCOG) has developed a three phase plan for managing storm water quality. The first phase focuses on the assessment of current storm water conditions. The second phase centers on the development of reasonable approaches for the management of urban storm water. The last phase promotes the adoption of local storm water improvement programs.

Geographic Information Systems (GIS) are effective tools for environmental planning, and their application shows great promise for water resources management. This research demonstrates that GIS technology can be used to identify storm water problems and to assess the efficacy of storm water management programs. The work confirms that a GIS can be more fully utilized when its capabilities are effectively linked to other tools and models in the decision-making process (Davis, et al., 1989; Wright, 1989).

Integrating GIS and Hydrodynamic Modeling

This research integrates an ARC/INFO GIS with two hydrodynamic models to evaluate the surface water quality effects of storm water inputs. It is intended to help municipalities meet the requirements of the Water Quality Act of 1987 and to develop a comprehensive system which links the GIS with conventional water quality models. The two hydrodynamic models, HEC-1 and HEC-5Q (Hydrologic Engineering Center, 1981 and 1984), are used to quantify the water quality effects of the storm water on the receiving bodies of water. The GIS is used to direct the analysis and highlight the results.

The study area chosen is the upper segment of the Trinity River Corridor in the Dallas-Fort Worth Metroplex. This corridor is under study by the U.S. Army Corps of Engineers and the NCTCOG for the surrounding communities to assess development potential. A computer generated map of the area serves as the foundation for analysis.

The ARC/INFO GIS is used to process the data held in four data bases (Figure 1): topography; land use including runoff water quality; applied regional precipitation pattern; and location and flow characteristics of municipal outfalls.

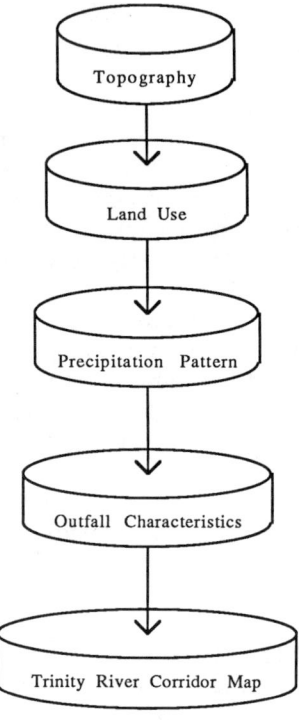

Figure 1. The data bases

The data bases are both input to and output from the two models, representing the effects of precipitation on flow (HEC-1) and the subsequent impact on receiving water quality (HEC-5Q). GIS manipulation of the data allows classification of storm water outfalls and identification of critical water quality areas.

HEC-1 is a hydrodynamic flood model which uses the applied precipitation pattern, topography, and municipal outfall data to adjust the flows of the Trinity River and its tributaries. HEC-1 modification includes the addition of pollutograph computation as currently performed within the Stormwater Management Model (U.S. EPA, 1981) and the Storage, Treatment, Overflow, and Runoff Model (U.S. Army Corps of Engineers, 1977). Through HEC-1, storm events of varying lengths and intensities can be simulated.

HEC-5Q is a hydrodynamic model used to predict water quality. The output flow data from HEC-1 is the flow data for HEC-5Q and is used with the storm water quality data in the GIS data bases. HEC-5Q is used to quantify receiving water quality parameters like dissolved oxygen, and it can be modified to include inorganic constituents like those targeted by the U.S. Geological Survey's National Water Quality Assessment Program (Hirsch, et al., 1988).

Conclusions

The integration of these three systems allows identification of sensitive watersheds and important storm water outfalls. This information can be used to simplify the NPDES permitting process by classifying storm sewers according to characteristics like land use and impact on surface water quality. NPDES permits can be issued based on the classifications.

The research complements the developmental efforts of HEC, a division of the U.S. Army Corps of Engineers, and expands the application of GIS technology into water quality monitoring. A GIS-hydrodynamic interface supports all three phases of the NCTCOG's regional plan for managing storm water quality and can help municipalities meet the forthcoming NPDES permit requirements for storm water runoff. More universally, it provides an effective, affordable planning tool for cities nationwide interested in assessing the effects of storm water mitigation projects.

References
Davis, Darryl W. and Walter M. Grayman, 1989. GIS in Water Resources: An Historical Perspective, in Water Resources Planning and Management. ed. Steven C. Harris, American Society of Civil Engineers, New York, pp. 141-144.

Hirsch, Robert M., William M. Alley, and William G. Wilber, 1988. Concepts for a National Water-Quality Assessment Program. U.S. Geological Survey Circular 1021.

Hydrologic Engineering Center, 1981 (Revised 1988). HEC-1, Flood Hydrograph Package Users Manual. Davis, CA.

Hydrologic Engineering Center, 1984. HEC-5Q, Simulation of Flood Control and Conservation Systems, Users Manual. Davis, CA.

U.S. Army Corps of Engineers, 1977. The Hydrologic Engineering Center, Storage, Treatment, Overflow, Runoff Model (STORM) Users Manual, U.S. Army Corps of Engineers, Davis, California.

U.S. Environmental Protection Agency, Sept. 1981. Stormwater Management Model, User's Manual, Version III.

Wright, Jeff R., 1989. The role of Rastor-based GIS Technology in Water Resources Planning and Research, in Water Resources Planning and Management. ed. Steven C. Harris, American Society of Civil Engineers, New York, pp. 145-148.

53 Federal Register 49416.

TUCSON, ARIZONA'S 110-YEAR WATER RESOURCES PLAN

By

Norm Brazelton, P.E.
Director, Water Resources
Southwest District
CH2M HILL
Denver, CO

and

Karen Dotson, AICP
Water Resources Planner
Tucson Water
Tucson, AZ

ABSTRACT

The desert community of Tucson, Arizona, has just completed a state-mandated 110-year water supply plan. The plan includes conjunctive use of local groundwater and surface water imported through the Central Arizona Project. Artificial groundwater recharge, an aggressive conservation program, and reuse are also incorporated to extend the basic sources of supply. This long-range planning effort was commissioned as a result of community recommendations and restrictions on groundwater pumping rates set forth in the state's recently enacted Groundwater Management Act. Tucson Water, the regional city-owned water utility, is totally dependent on groundwater to supply its service area population of nearly 600,000 people. The plan was developed to provide water supply for Tucson Water's estimated service area population of 2.8 million at the end of the planning period in 2100.

Tucson Water and its consultant worked closely with a community advisory committee to develop and analyze many potential plan elements. The elements were then categorized and combined into alternative plans, and the preferred plan was selected through a consensus building process. The plan will be updated at specified intervals to reflect changes in the regulatory environment, community values, and long-term population projections.

TUCSON'S WATER RESOURCES PLAN

INTRODUCTION

The City of Tucson encompasses 155 square miles in eastern Pima County, Arizona. The city, the second largest in Arizona, has a population of 397,000 (1988). The annual growth rate in the Tucson metropolitan area is 2.5 to 3 percent compared to the annual national growth rate of about 0.9 percent.

The Tucson metropolitan area is one of the largest urban areas in the United States that is totally dependent on groundwater. About 85 percent of the municipal and industrial water users in the metropolitan area are served by Tucson Water, the city's water utility. Tucson Water serves over 550,000 people within a 285-square-mile service area.

Tucson Water operates a dual system, serving both potable and reclaimed water (secondary effluent treated to open access irrigation standards set by the state). The potable system includes 196 active wells. Depth to water ranges from 50 to 400 feet, and without treatment, the water meets all state and federal regulatory standards.

Beginning in 1991, Tucson Water will begin receiving imported surface water from the Central Arizona Project (CAP). The city has contracted for an annual allocation of 148,420 ac-ft, Arizona's largest municipal allocation of Colorado River water. The city's first surface-water treatment plant, a direct filtration facility designed to ultimately treat 225 million gallons per day (mgd), is now under construction.

The reclaimed water system provided water to its first customer in 1984. Today, the system is the third largest and the fastest growing nonpotable water system in the United States. In 1988, 4,700 ac-ft of reclaimed water was provided for turf irrigation. Additionally 2,700 ac-ft of secondary effluent was used to irrigate golf courses.

It is estimated that the annual renewable supply of groundwater (safe yield) together with CAP allocations will meet the projected total municipal and industrial demand in Tucson Water's service area until about 2035, or when the population reaches 1,750,000.

INSTITUTIONAL SETTING

A complex and rapidly changing array of federal, state, and local laws, policies, and community preferences has shaped water service and long-range planning activities in the Tucson area.

In 1980 the Groundwater Management Act (GMA) was passed into law by the Arizona Legislature. The primary purpose of the law was to provide a framework for the comprehensive management and regulation of the withdrawal, transportation, use, conservation, and conveyance of rights to use the groundwater in the state.

The law established the Arizona Department of Water Resources (ADWR), which is empowered to manage groundwater, adjudicated unappropriated surface-water rights, and maintain jurisdiction over flood control, dam safety, interstate streams, the CAP, and, to some degree, water quality.

Four active management areas were also created by the legislation. These four geographic areas account for about 75 percent of the groundwater pumpage in Arizona and contain over 80 percent of the state's population. The Tucson Active Management Area (TAMA) includes eastern Pima County and parts of Pima and Santa Cruz Counties (see Figure 1).

In 1985, most of the estimated 300,000 ac-ft of total groundwater pumpage in TAMA was pumped in Pima County. Agricultural uses accounted for about 40 percent of the total pumpage; municipal uses accounted for about 40 percent; industrial uses, primarily mining, accounted for about 19 percent, and other uses accounted for about 1 percent. Nature and incidental recharge are currently the primary means for replenishing groundwater. It is estimated that the 1985 pumpage resulted in an overdraft of about 178,000 ac-ft.

The GMA also established five management periods between 1980 and 2025. For each management period, a management plan developed by ADWR is in effect for each Active Management Area. The main components of each management plan are water supply augmentation, water quality, and water conservation plans for all agricultural, municipal, and industrial users and providers.

The conservation plans include target per capita water use rates. Only pumped groundwater is included in calculating the target use rates; reclaimed water use is not included to

TUCSON'S WATER RESOURCES PLAN 183

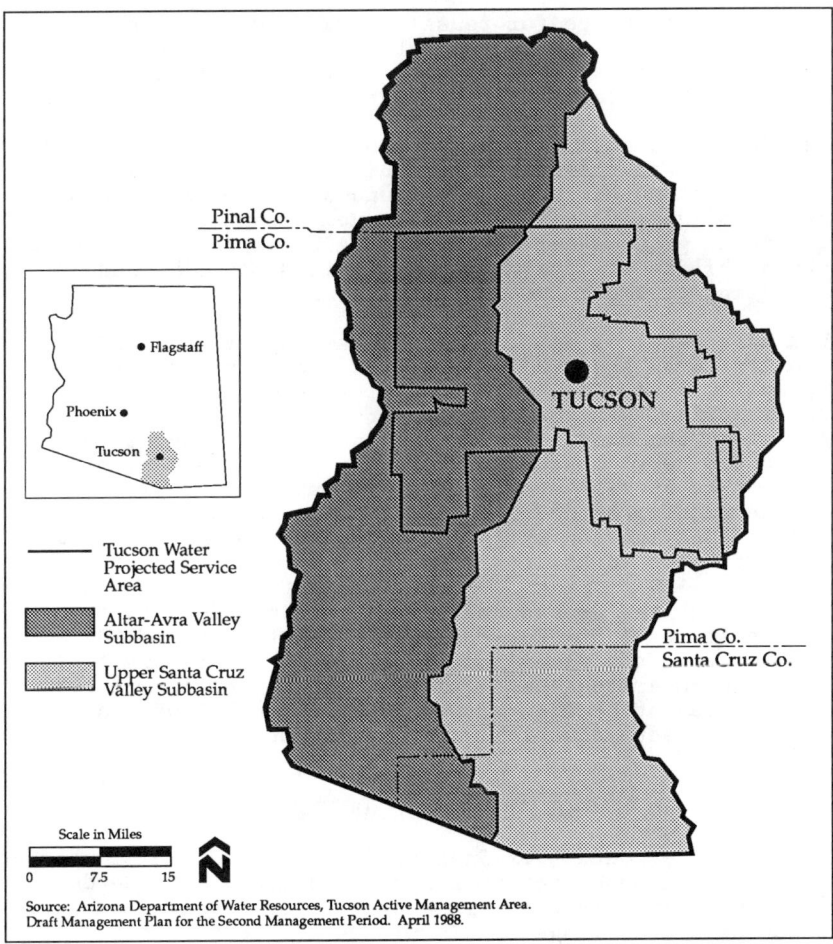

Figure 1. **Tucson Active Management Area**

provide an incentive for reuse. ADWR calculated the 1988 per capita use in the Tucson Water service area at 164 gallons per day (gpd) and the target use rate at 155 gallons per capita per day (gpcd).

The management goal for the Tucson Active Management Area is "to achieve and thereafter maintain a long-term balance between the annual amount of groundwater withdrawn in an Active Management Area and the annual amount of natural and artificial groundwater recharge." ADWR is charged with the responsibility of determining safe yield for TAMA and for allocating it among the area's water users.

ADWR also requires all water providers within the TAMA to demonstrate an assured 100-year water supply. An assured supply for a provider means that sufficient groundwater and/or surface water of adequate quality will be available to satisfy the needs of existing and proposed development within the service area for at least 100 years. Also, water use must be consistent with the TAMA management plan goals, and the water provider must demonstrate the ability to finance construction of the delivery system and any necessary treatment works.

In addition, the Groundwater Recharge and Underground Storage Act of 1986, Environmental Quality Act of 1987, policies of the Central Arizona Water Conservation District, the Southern Arizona Water Rights' Settlement Act of 1982, and numerous other federal, state, and local laws and policies impact potential water supply options.

110-YEAR WATER RESOURCES PLAN

It was in the context of increased regulation, the impending change from groundwater to a surface source, and the desire of varied community water interests to be involved in development of a long-range supply plan that Tucson Water initiated the development of a water resources plan with a 110-year planning horizon.

Recognizing the high level of community interest in local and statewide water issues, a community advisory committee (ADCOM) was formed. This 15-member committee reflected the diverse water interests in the community and advised the project consultant throughout the planning process. During its deliberations on the plan, the ADCOM worked with the city's Citizens' Water Advisory Committee, the county's Wastewater Management Advisory Committee, and an influential

TUCSON'S WATER RESOURCES PLAN   185

community organization, the Southern Arizona Water Resources
Association.

The plan was developed using goals and objectives agreed
upon by the ADCOM. Although the goals appeared to be
straightforward, it was found during the development of
alternative plans that the accomplishment of one goal often
ruled out or limited the effectiveness of another. The
ADCOM then had to weigh the importance of competing goals to
develop a plan. The agreed-upon goals were to:

o   Meet the demands of the projected service area
    with high quality water

o   Comply with the conservation, safe-yield, and
    assured water supply requirements of the GMA

o   Maintain rates at levels acceptable to the community by avoiding sharp rate increases and using
    funding mechanisms that distribute the costs among
    present and future ratepayers

o   Reduce groundwater pumpage

o   Make maximum use of effluent in the projected service area

o   Make maximum use of CAP water as soon as possible

o   Retain all TAMA CAP allocations with TAMA

A population of 2.8 million in the year 2100 was used to
project demand over the planning period. Factors likely to
increase or decrease future per capita water use appeared to
be in approximate balance. It was therefore assumed that
without the implementation of additional conservation
measures, a per capita use rate of 160 gpd was a reasonable
baseline demand. This assumption was consistent with the
general water use trends over the past 10 years.

Using these population and per capita use projections,
demand was projected to be approximately 500,000 ac-ft/yr in
2100. This represents 300,000 ac-ft/yr more than is currently available from existing supply sources.

To address this need, the sources likely to be available to
the projected service area by the year 2100 were analyzed.
Initially, approximately 30 potential supply sources and/or
management options were identified. These were grouped into

five categories ranging from highest priority to contingent sources. From these categories, combinations of sources were formulated for consideration as alternative plans.

An interactive, process involving the consultant, the ADCOM, and Tucson Water was used to develop and evaluate alternative plans. A spreadsheet-based, supply-demand-time computer model was developed to combine various water supply sources into alternative plans. The model allowed parameters such as constructions costs, operation and maintenance costs, population and demand projections, and implementation schedules to be varied. Using these inputs, the model estimated total plan costs, average costs, and the volume of water required from each source over the planning period.

Initially, two extreme or boundary-condition plans--the "Base Case" plan and the "Least Cost" plan--were developed to reflect the limits of the range of alternatives and the relationship between cost of the plan and difficulty of implementation. The Base Case plan could be implemented today with no institutional constraints, but at a relatively high cost. The Least Cost plan assumes that any institutional changes necessary to reduce plan cost (with the exception of safe yield pumping limitations) could be accomplished.

Next, three alternative, or compromise, plans were developed (see Figure 2). Over 40 variations of these plans were then modeled as a result of additional comments and suggestions received from the ADCOM and Tucson Water, and sensitivity analyses were performed to isolate the impacts of various plan modifications. This process was repeated until a consensus on the selection of a single plan was reached.

The agreed upon plan, the "Tucson Water Resources Plan, 1990-2100" was adopted by the Mayor and City Council on July 3, 1989. This plan uses a combination of seven sources to meet the 37.89 million ac-ft (maf) demand for the planning period. Figure 3 illustrates how conservation, nonpotable reuse of effluent, groundwater, direct use of CAP water, recharge and recovery of CAP water, in lieu recharge credits for pre-1980 retirement of agricultural land, and potable reuse of effluent are phased in to meet the growing demand.

The seven sources that compose the plan were selected based on their availability and cost. Table 1 summarizes the plan, and each element is described below.

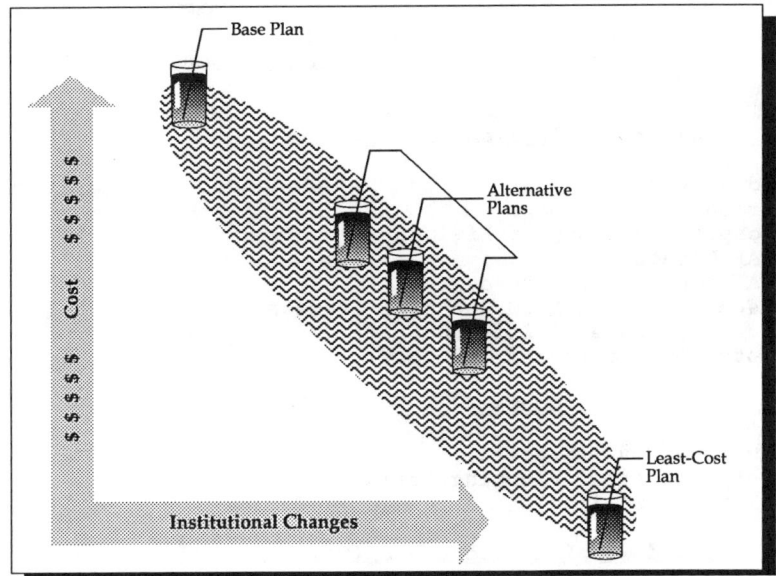

Figure 2. Relative Costs and Required Institutional Changes for Alternative Plans

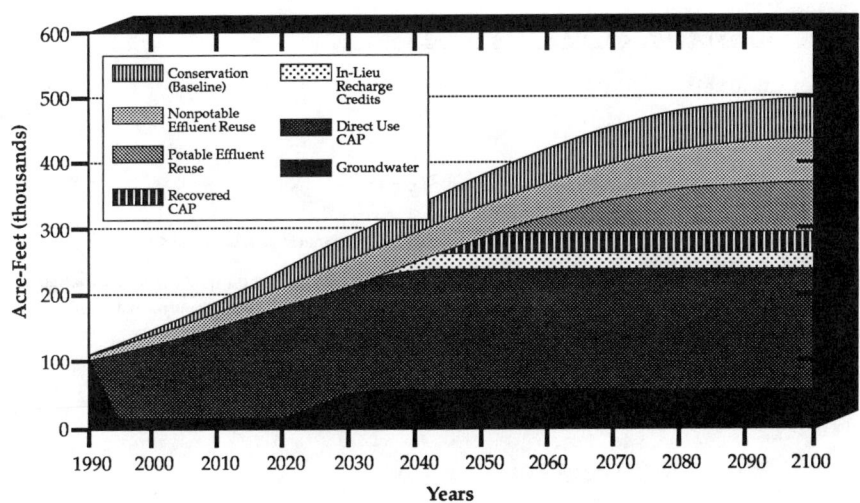

Figure 3. Tucson Water Resources Plan: Phased Use of Water Sources to Meet Projected Demand

Table 1
SUMMARY OF THE TUCSON WATER RESOURCES PLAN
1990-2100

Water Supply Elements (maf)	
Conservation	4.68
Groundwater Pumpage	4.18
Nonpotable Reuse of Effluent	4.88
CAP Direct Use	19.97
CAP Recharge and Recovery	1.39
Recovery of In Lieu Recharge Credits	1.52
Potable Reuse of Effluent[a]	2.27
Total Demand (maf @ 160 gpcd)	37.89

Costs	
Average Cost ($/ac-ft)	146
Total Cost for Planning Period ($ x 1 billion)	4.86

Breakdown of Effluent Use (maf)	
Amount Used	7.33
Not Used for M&I Purposes	
Southern Arizona Water Rights Settlement Act	3.33
Pima County	1.46
Tucson Excess	5.81
Total Available Supply	17.93

Breakdown of CAP Use (maf)	
Amount Used	20.36
Not Used	6.02
Total Available[b]	26.38
Initial Direct CAP Use (ac-ft/yr)[c]	87,430

[a] Includes a 15 percent loss as a result of the reverse osmosis water treatment process assumed to be used for one-half of the recovered water.
[b] Includes all TAMA CAP allocations. It was assumed in this study, however, that the three Green Valley private water companies, FICO, and the Indians (except ChuiChu) are planning to use their allocations (1.17 maf).
[c] Direct use will be phased in over a 5-year period.

TUCSON'S WATER RESOURCES PLAN

CONSERVATION

The plan includes significant water savings from conservation. By the year 2100, conservation is expected to reduce the total demand by 14 percent. Conservation (not including nonpotable reuse) will reduce the per capita use rate from the current 158 gpd to 138 gpcd by the end of the planning period. The recently adopted plumbing code requiring 1.6 gallons-per-flush toilets is expected to account for 51 percent of the water saved during the planning period.

GROUNDWATER

Between 1991 and 1995, Tucson Water will gradually reduce its groundwater pumpage from 100,000 ac-ft/yr to approximately 15,000 ac-ft/yr. Between 2020 and 2030, groundwater pumpage will increase to 45,000 ac-ft/yr, which is Tucson Water's assumed share of safe yield.

RECOVERY OF IN LIEU RECHARGE CREDITS

Credits for the purchase and retirement of agricultural land in the Avra Valley prior to 1980 are included in the plan. If the required state legislation is passed, these "in-lieu recharge credits" will allow additional groundwater to be pumped. The plan assumes that legislation will be passed allowing 3 ac-ft of groundwater to be pumped annually for each acre of irrigated agricultural land that was retired. Recovery of in lieu recharge credits will begin in 2035.

DIRECT USE OF CAP WATER

Fifty-one percent of Tucson Water's demands during the 110-year planning period will be met with the direct use of CAP water. Direct use will begin in 1991.

RECHARGE AND RECOVERY OF CAP WATER

During the early years of CAP availability, supply will exceed demand. This excess CAP water will be recharged to the underground aquifer beginning in 1992. Recharge will continue until approximately 2040. Recovery of CAP water will begin in 2045, continuing through 2100.

NONPOTABLE USE OF EFFLUENT

The reclaimed water system provides treated effluent for turf irrigation. In 1988, the system provided 4,200 ac-ft of water to customers with planned expansions; beginning in

2005, the system will be able to accommodate 15 percent of the total demand through the remainder of the planning period.

POTABLE REUSE OF EFFLUENT

Potable reuse of effluent will meet 6 percent of the demand during the planning period. Effluent will be recharged during the early years of the planning period and in later years, beginning in 2050, will be recovered and treated to drinking water standards.

UPDATING PROCESS

Any plan that looks 10 years into the future is subject to uncertainty. Anticipating the future technical, legal, and institutional uncertainties, the Tucson Water Resources Plan was designed to be flexible. The plan accounts for uncertainties by relying on seven different water supply sources. Changes in the availability of supply from any single source can be compensated for by increases or decreases in others. In addition, processes to annually review and update the plan and to conduct comprehensive revisions at least every 5 years are in place. The annual reviews will be performed by the city's Citizen's Water Advisory Committee. The comprehensive revision process will include the formation of a community water resources advisory committee similar to the one that assisted in developing the Tucson Water Resources Plan, 1990-2100. It may also use the services of a consultant.

SUMMARY

The Tucson Water Resources Plan provides a plan for developing water supplies to meet the water demand in the projected service area from 1990 to 2100. The plan represents a broad community consensus on how competing water supply objectives should be addressed at this time. It is the starting point for additional research, data collection, and community participation. The total projected demand for municipal supply, without additional conservation measures, is 37.89 million ac-ft (maf) over the planning period.

Flexibility is provided by using seven sources to meet the demand. The demand will be satisfied through residential conservation (about 4.7 maf), nonpotable effluent reuse (about 4.9 maf), groundwater pumpage (about 5.7 maf) including in lieu recharge credits, Central Arizona Project surface water (about 20.4 maf) for direct use and recharge and recovery, and potable effluent reuse (about 2.3 maf). Groundwater recharge and recovery is planned for a portion of the Central Arizona Project water and for both potable and nonpotable effluent reuse.

The plan also provides a process for periodic updates, including an annual review as part of the city's capital improvement program and a comprehensive update every 5 years, or whenever events occur that could significantly affect the plan.

A METHODOLOGY FOR ANALYZING ALTERNATIVE RESERVOIR SIZING, SHORTAGE, AND OPERATING CRITERIA

George Oamek[1], Larry Schluntz[2],
Loren Bottorff, Member ASCE[3], and Eldon Johns, Member ASCE[4]

ABSTRACT

The Bureau of Reclamation's shifting emphasis from a construction oriented agency to a water management agency has initiated the development of analytical tools for estimating marginal benefits of alternative reservoir sizes and operating criteria. This paper presents a portion of a new methodological approach for estimating marginal benefits and applies it to a case study.

The modeling system developed from this effort links a spreadsheet-based model of reservoir operations to economic models of various demand sectors, including irrigation and M&I uses. Linking the models results in quick response in estimating the annual marginal economic benefits of alternative reservoir sizes (for prosposed projects) or alternative reservoir operating criteria (for existing facilities).

When applied to a case study of an existing Southern California reservoir, the modeling system estimated the annual benefits of reservoir enlargment.

---

[1] Economist, CH2M Hill, 3840 Rosin Court, Suite 110, Sacramento, CA, 95834

[2] Economist, Bureau of Reclamation, D-5442, Box 25007, Denver, CO, 80225

[3] Water Resource Engineer, CH2M Hill

[4] Hydrologist, Bureau of Reclamation

ALTERNATIVE RESERVOIR SIZING

INTRODUCTION

The Bureau of Reclamation's shifting emphasis from a construction oriented agency to a water management agency has initiated the development of analytical tools for estimating marginal benefits of alternative reservoir sizes and operating criteria. Of increasing importance is the nation's demand for high quality water and the necessity for effective, efficient water resource project development and management. Current objectives are to improve management and use of facilities, which, in many cases are already in place. Accordingly, Reclamation is developing new analytical tools to aid in the planning of new projects and the management of existing ones.

The process of measuring marginal economic benefits of alternative reservoir sizes and operation criteria is an example of where such an analytical tool is appropriate. The Bureau of Reclamation has traditionally considered marginal benefits across a range of project alternatives for a proposed reservoir site. However, Reclamation has used heuristic rules to link the measurement of economic benefits with changes in reservoir size and operations, rather than an economic modeling analysis.

In response to the need for consistency and to examine the relationship between reservoir characteristics and economic benefits, Reclamation is developing a modeling framework in which to estimate total and marginal benefits of alternative reservoir sizes. Benefits estimated within this framework can then be matched against marginal cost of reservoir construction to arrive at an economically optimal sized reservoir. Moreover, the methodology is flexible enough to examine alternative operating and shortage criteria with a fixed reservoir size.

The economic benefit of a reservoir, as a whole, is the sum of benefits to individual sectors using water, whether their demand be for consumptive or nonconsumptive uses. The marginal benefits of alternative reservoir sizes are the changes in total benefits as the reservoir size gets incrementally larger. Marginal benefits of alternative operating criteria is the change in total benefits from the current, or baseline criteria to the proposed criteria. Model development described here concentrates on 2 project purposes, irrigation and municipal and industrial (M&I).

Several goals for the modeling system, intended to maximize its usefulness were specified prior to model development. The goals which had a significant impact on design of the modeling system included:

(1) The models should be able to address annual and seasonal variation in water deliveries, and any priority of uses in times of shortage.

(2) All model sectors, or components, should be separable. For instance, the irrigation component should be able to stand alone without the other components.

(3) The methodologies used for each component should be consistent with Bureau of Reclamation procedures and guidelines for project planning.

The remainder of this discussion focuses on development of model components and their application to a case study.

MODEL COMPONENTS

Reservoir operations model

The first of the above goals required the construction of a spreadsheet-based reservoir operations model to simulate annual and seasonal deliveries to the demand sectors considered. It uses a homogeneous hydrologic sequence (adjusted for historical use) to construct a monthly time series of reservoir inflows. Using this, and data regarding the physical characteristics of the reservoir site, including area-capacity, rainfall, and pan evaporation, a monthly time series of deliveries to each sector is constructed for each reservoir size considered. Operating criteria concerning priority of use and shortage criteria for each user group are explicitly considered, and can be altered to consider a range of criteria. The operations model uses fixed rules to allocate shortages among the various uses.

Figure 1 contains a flowchart of the overall reservoir sizing modeling system. The first 3 levels of the chart summarize input and output of the operations spreadsheet and the linkages between the model components.

Figure 1. Flowchart of modeling system

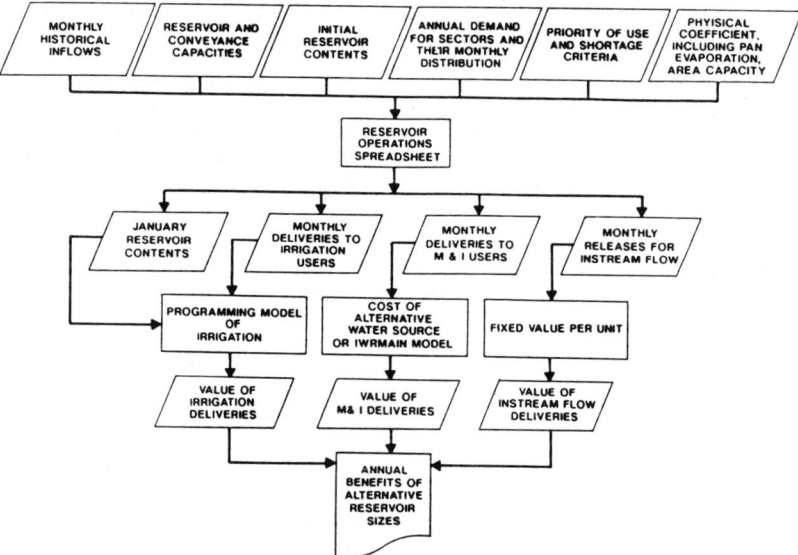

Irrigation component

For each reservoir size and period of record considered, the operations model passes monthly, per acre-foot water deliveries, and other data, to the irrigation component. The irrigation component optimally distributes monthly water supplies over a range of crops in the project service area, using a profit maximizing mathematical programming approach. The output of this process is a time series of net farm income corresponding to each scenario considered. Marginal benefits can be derived from the time series by examining the changes in net farm income from one series to the next.

The irrigation component recognizes that many agricultural production decisions, such as cropping patterns, input usage, and capital requirements are based on expected deliveries of irrigation water for the coming year. As the crop year progresses and actual deliveries are realized, irrigators are "locked-in" to the cropping patttern decisions made before planting. Additional data passed on by the operations model, beyond monthly water deliveries, are end-of-year (previous year) reservoir contents and the actual criteria used by the operations model to allocate shortages. It is assumed that, on January 1, irrigators observe the contents of the reservoir, and by knowing the actual criteria used by the reservoir operator, develop an expectation of project water deliveries for the coming year. They then base their crop production decisions, regarding crop acreage and water application levels, on this expectation. Later in the year, the irrigators realize the actual water deliveries and, if an unanticipated shortage occurs, they can either conjunctively use groundwater (if available) to make up the deficit, cut back water applications, abandon some irrigated acres, or use any combination of the 3 adjustments.

The irrigation model, then, is run twice for every year in the period of record. Once using anticipated water deliveries to lock in crop acreages for the coming year and set preliminary rates of water application, and a second time to update this information using actual deliveries. Figure 2 illustrates this process. End of year reservoir contents and shortage criteria are used to develop expected monthly deliveries. This, along with regional crop production data are used by the optimization model to set preliminary values of land use (LU), project water use (SU), and conjunctive groundwater use (GU). Actual monthly deliveries are then used in the model to arrive at updated values of LU, SU, and GU. Regional net farm income is calculated from the model solution. As previously stated, a series of net farm income results when this process is run over a period of record for a given reservoir size.

Regional crop/water production function information is incorporated to allow crop yields to move down the production function when water is in short supply (CH2M Hill, 1987). Other data used in the irrigation model include variable crop production costs (from crop enterprise budgets), crop yields, monthly crop water requirements, water delivery and application efficiencies, land availability, and availability of alternative sources of water. The irrigation component is coded and solved using GAMS/MINOS ver. 2.04. software designed for solving mathematical models on an IBM-compatible personal computer.

M&I Component

In contrast to the relative complexity of modeling the irrigation component, the M&I component uses a single value measure to calculate the benefits of project deliveries. Specifically, the per unit cost of the next cheapest single purpose alternative available to the municipality is used to measure M&I benefits. In other words, the municipality's per acre-foot avoided cost. This approach is consistent with Bureau project planning procedures, although little consideration is given to seasonal variabilities in delivery. As a result, only annual deliveries from the reservoir to the M&I sector are transferred from the operations model to the M&I component.

CASE STUDY

A preliminary application of the reservoir sizing modeling system addressed the issue of enlarging an existing reservoir, Lake Cachuma, California. It is important to note that the case study is only for illustration of the methodology and is not intended to accurately represent the actual situation in the study area. Lake Cachuma is a 205,000 acre-foot, multi-purpose reservoir

Figure 2. Flowchart of irrigation component

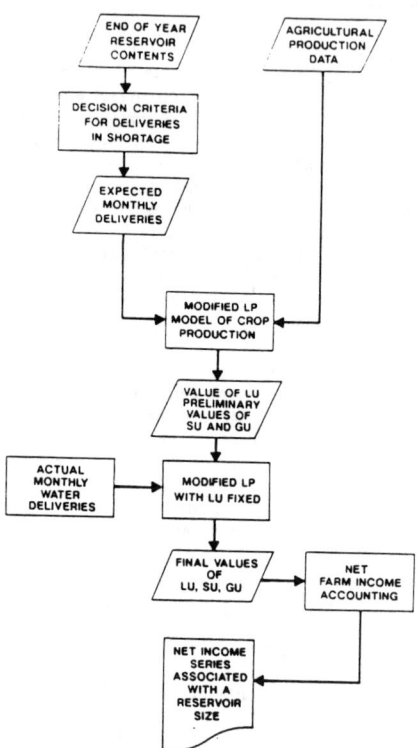

located about 30 miles northwest of Santa Barbara. Its annual average release of approximately 30,000 acre-feet is distributed to irrigation in the Santa Ynez valley (3,300 AF), irrigation along the Pacific South Coast (13,300 AF), and municipal supply for Santa Barbara. No releases are made specifically for maintenance of instream flows. This is an area of extremely tight water supplies, and the geography makes it very difficult to import additional water supplies. Groundwater is fully utilized. Pumping in excess of annual safe yield will result in salt water intrusion within a very short period of time.

The Santa Ynez region is characterized by a ranching economy, where project water is dedicated (in order of magnitude) to irrigated pasture, grass hay, alfalfa, barley, wheat, dry beans, and tomatoes. Conversely, irrigation in the South Coast area concentrates on high valued tree crops, such as avocados and lemons. There was sufficient difference in the two regions to segregate them from a modeling standpoint, resulting in two irrigation models rather than one.

A 30 year period of record, using the flow years 1945-1974 were used to generate a baseline series of monthly deliveries to the irrigation and M&I components, assuming the current reservoir size of 205,000 acre feet. An exteme drought during the late 1940's and early 50's

ALTERNATIVE RESERVOIR SIZING

TABLE 1
Net farm income for Lake Cachuma reservoir size alternatives

Reservoir size AF	Avg. annual shortage %	Avg. annual net farm income $	Change from baseline /1 $	Total net farm income /2 $	Standard deviation $
Santa Ynez service area, 1945-1974 period of record:					
154,000	22%	7,501	(5,703)	225,016	17,828
179,000	19%	10,704	(2,500)	321,122	18,313
205,000	14%	13,204	0	396,118	15,741
231,000	12%	15,462	2,258	463,864	14,664
256,000	10%	16,366	3,162	490,981	14,365
308,000	7%	19,502	6,298	585,047	12,617
410,000	1%	25,069	11,865	752,068	5,687
South Coast service area, 1945-1974 period of record:					
154,000	22%	(2,928,203)	(2,022,271)	(87,846,087)	4,791,821
179,000	18%	(1,916,178)	(1,010,246)	(57,485,333)	5,054,432
205,000	14%	(905,932)	0	(27,177,947)	4,888,243
231,000	11%	(122,889)	783,043	(3,686,660)	4,858,537
256,000	10%	356,286	1,262,218	10,688,585	4,623,197
308,000	7%	1,503,814	2,409,746	45,114,421	3,755,999
410,000	1%	3,788,441	4,694,373	113,653,219	836,274

1/ The baseline size is 205,000 AF, the current capacity of Lake Cachuma
2/ This is the undiscounted sum of annual net incomes over the period of record

TABLE 2
M&I benefits for Lake Cachuma reservoir size alternatives

Reservoir size AF	Avg. annual shortage %	Avg. annual M&I benefit $	Change from baseline /1 $	Total M&I benefits /2 $	Standard deviation $
1945-1974 period of record:					
154,000	9%	3,414,341	(182,604)	102,430,229	720,676
179,000	6%	3,523,919	(73,026)	105,717,569	475,215
205,000	4%	3,596,945	0	107,908,335	284,776
231,000	3%	3,639,617	42,672	109,188,518	228,734
256,000	2%	3,674,162	77,217	110,224,858	187,973
308,000	1%	3,722,934	125,989	111,688,013	69,535
410,000	0%	3,744,000	147,055	112,320,000	0

1/ The baseline size is 205,000 AF, the current capacity of Lake Cachuma
2/ This is the undiscounted sum of annual incomes over the period of record

TABLE 3
Summary of annual benefits for alternative reservoir sizes
1945 - 1974 period of record

Reservoir size (AF)	M&I benefits	change from base /1	South Coast net farm income	change from base	Santa Ynez net farm income	change from base	Cumulative change
154,000	$3,414,341	($182,604)	($2,928,203)	($2,022,271)	$7,501	($5,703)	($2,210,578)
179,000	$3,523,919	($73,026)	($1,916,178)	($1,010,246)	$10,704	($2,500)	($1,085,772)
205,000	$3,596,945	$0	($905,932)	$0	$13,204	$0	$0
231,000	$3,639,617	$42,672	($122,889)	$783,043	$15,462	$2,258	$827,973
256,000	$3,674,162	$77,217	$356,286	$1,262,218	$16,366	$3,162	$1,342,597
308,000	$3,722,934	$125,989	$1,503,814	$2,409,746	$19,502	$6,298	$2,542,033
410,000	$3,744,000	$147,055	$3,788,441	$4,694,373	$25,069	$11,865	$4,853,293

1/ The baseline case is the reservoir's current capacity of 205,000 AF

resulted in over 40 months of zero reservoir inflows. In addition to a reservoir size of 205,000 acre-feet, 6 other sizes were evaluated for comparison purposes: 154,000, 179,000, 231,000, 256,000, 308,000, and 410,000 acre-feet. There is a common operating criteria throughout the range of sizes. It dictates a 50 percent reduction in irrigation deliveries when the reservoir level falls below 90,000 acre-feet. M&I deliveries are reduced 20 percent when the reservoir falls below 50,000 acre-feet.

The South Coast portion of the irrigation model was modified to better recognize longer term effects that drought periods have on avocados and citrus fruits. Contact with area horticulturalists and water district personnel indicated that, when expecting a water shortage, avocado growers will cut back acreage to give a full irrigation to remaining acres rather than attempt to practice deficit irrigation. Additionally, a full two year post-drought recovery period is needed before a yield can be expected from avocados. Lemons can be deficit irrigated and the recovery period for non-irrigated acreage is a single year.

RESULTS AND CONCLUSIONS OF CASE STUDY

Table 1 summarizes the results of alternative reservoir sizes on the irrigated regions served by Lake Cachuma. As expected, average shortage levels and their variability are reduced, and income levels increase, as reservoir size increases. It is of interest to note the wide variation in income in the South Coast area. More frequent and severe shortages are economically very disastrous to growers here. Examination of annual results (not included) indicated a dramatic drop in income after the first year of successive drought years. Table 1 also suggests that South Coast growers are, on the average, losing money under the current reservoir size. This is probably due more to the severe nature of the period of record used than the actual situation in this area in recent years.

Table 2 presents results of various reservoir sizes on the M&I sector, assuming an avoided cost by the municipality of $240 per acre-foot. Due to the high priority given M&I uses in the operations model, there is only approximately a 10 percent difference in benefits between the smallest and largest size.

The final column of Table 3 aggregates the sectors to arrive at a measure of cumulative changes in net benefits across the irrigation and M&I sectors. At reservoir sizes larger than 205,000 acre-feet, the cumulative change can loosely be interpreted as the maximum annual payment the irrigation and M&I sectors could afford to make to enlarge Lake Cachuma. Of course, these figures would have to be matched against the marginal costs of enlargement, including marginal O&M costs.

REFERENCES

CH2M Hill, "A Quick Reference Guide for Selecting Crop Water Production Functions", Bureau of Reclamation Delivery Order 5-PD-20-13110, Engineering and Research Center, Denver, CO. December, 1986

Howitt, Richard and Phillip Mean, "Positive Quadratic Programming Models", Working Paper, unnumbered. Departmemt of Agricultural Economics, University of California, Davis. December, 1985.

OPTIMIZATION OF WATER RESOURCES ALLOCATION USING THE MODSIM MODEL
By L. Philip Graham[1], David M. Frick[2],
Daniel L. Law[3], and Peter D. Binney[4]

Introduction

The Fraser River Basin, shown in Figure 1, is located in north central Colorado west of the Continental Divide in an alpine basin with elevations ranging from 8,000 to 12,000 feet. The heavily forested, steep, mountainous upper basins are primarily National Forest lands. Open meadows and rangeland dominate at the lower elevations in the basin. The climate is typical of the Rocky Mountain region with short summers and cold winters experiencing heavy snowfall. A large spring snowmelt runoff results with peak flows occurring primarily in May and June. Apart from thunderstorm runoff in the summer months, the streams in the basin exhibit low baseflows.

Existing permanent resident population density is relatively low throughout the basin. Several small towns are located along the Fraser River and are interspersed with ranch lands and large tracts of undevelopable public lands. Wide seasonal population fluctuations occur in both summer and winter due to tourism. Close proximity to the Denver metropolitan area enhances the likelihood that tourist populations will increase as both winter ski activities and summer outdoor destinations are expanded and marketed.

Current Water Demands

Existing water development projects in the basin are primarily associated with transbasin diversion of water for municipal use in east slope communities. Lake Granby to the north stores water for transmission through the Adams Tunnel to Northeastern Colorado. The Windy Gap Project provides additional yield to this system by pumping water from the Fraser River to Lake Granby. Both the Ranch Creek and Moffat Collection Systems divert runoff from upper portions of the basin to the Moffat Tunnel for delivery to the Denver metropolitan area. The Vasquez Tunnel supplements flows in the Moffat Collection System with transbasin water from the adjacent Williams Fork basin to the southwest.

Future Water Demands

Water resources in the basin have long been diverted to the east slope of the Continental Divide to satisfy extensive out-of-basin municipal demand. These coupled with senior downstream demands on the Colorado River result in a scarcity of water resources to satisfy both existing and future in-basin municipal demands.

---
[1] Water Resources Engineer, Resource Consultants, Inc., Fort Collins, Colorado
[2] Vice President for Engineering, Resource Consultants, Inc., Fort Collins, Colorado
[3] Associate Director, Colorado Water Resources and Power Development Authority, Denver, Colorado
[4] Director, Water Resources Engineering, CH2M Hill, Denver, Colorado

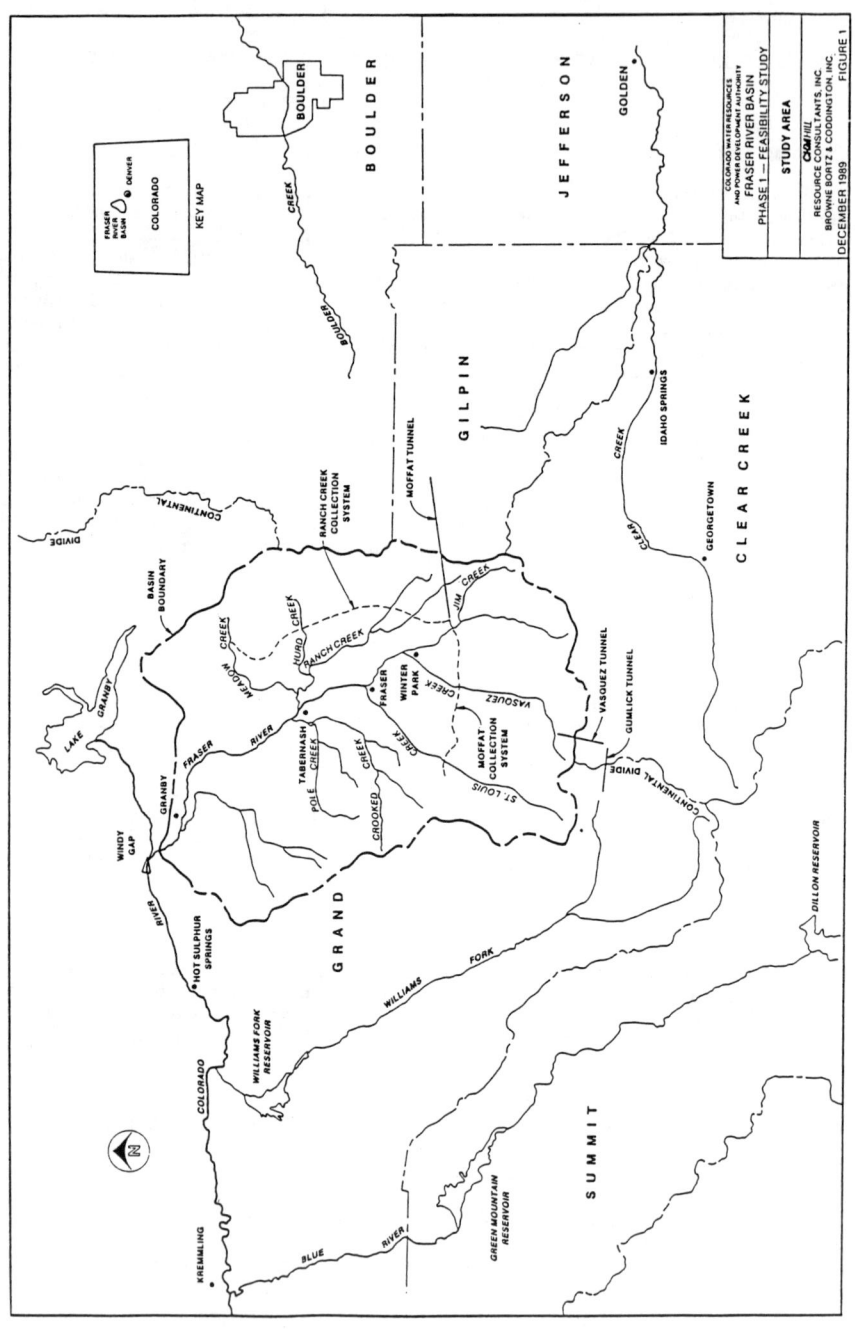

WATER RESOURCES ALLOCATION

The Colorado Water Resources and Power Development Authority was approached in late 1986 by a group of sponsoring agencies to perform this Phase I Feasibility Study. The sponsors included the following organizations:

- Colorado River Water Conservation District
- Denver Water Department
- East Grand County Water Quality Board
- Middle Park Water Conservancy District
- Municipal Subdistrict-Northern Colorado Water Conservancy District

The Phase I study is a precursor to a full feasibility study of the recommended alternative and is designed to identify the conceptual framework of how plan elements should be combined to meet the identified needs. The Phase II evaluation would include detailed engineering, geotechnical, environmental, and financial analyses along with the associated permitting activities.

Specific goals of the study were as follows:

- Developing a firm water supply for in-basin municipal and industrial demands expected under ultimate development conditions
- Protecting efficient operation and firming up the absolute and conditional yield of the Denver Water Department's Moffat and Ranch Creek Collection Systems (DWD)
- Providing carryover storage for Middle Park Water Conservancy District's allotment of water currently stored in Lake Granby (MPWCD)
- Protecting and/or enhancing the yield of the Windy Gap Project
- Protecting existing absolute and conditional water rights
- Protecting water quality
- Developing reservoir-based, stream-based, and stream corridor recreation
- Enhancing fish and wildlife resources
- Mitigating flood damages

Hydrologic Model Selection

Three model choices were initially evaluated for this study. One possibility was using the existing CORSIM or BESTSM Colorado River models. As these two river-specific models cover a large portion of the Colorado River mainstem, it was felt that they would not provide sufficient detail for a study of the Fraser River alone. A second option was to develop a basin-specific model for the Fraser, but was not considered to be economically justified for this level of study. Use of the river basin simulation model, MODSIM, featured the operation of Colorado's prior appropriation water rights system in an easily usable network format and was considered the most favorable option. Other models such as HEC-3 and HEC-5 were rejected because they do not adequately consider Colorado water administration and the Prior Appropriation Doctrine.

MODSIM, developed at Colorado State University, is a network flow simulation model utilizing linear programming for its solution. It is a generalized model that allows for the representation of the complete flow morphology of a river basin system. It is specifically geared toward evaluation of a complex water rights structure including direct flow rights, storage rights, instream minimum flows and water exchange possibilities. The model user inputs the various administrative priorities and hydrologic data to represent both physical and legal constraints that exist or may be imposed for a given river basin. Flow throughout the system is optimized to satisfy formal water rights structures as well as informal water exchange mechanisms under operational plans. In this manner, MODSIM can be used as a planning tool to evaluate the impacts of proposed water development projects at various locations within a basin.

Model Structure

The initial MODSIM network developed for the Fraser River basin contained 59 nodes and 70 links to represent stream linkages, major demand points within the basin, instream flow requirements and potential reservoir locations. The years 1947-1986 were chosen as the period of record for analysis; this included average, extreme dry and extreme wet years as well as operational records of import and export facilities. Data available to establish baseline conditions included gages with uninterrupted records, gages with sparse records and areas with no records at all. Agricultural diversion records for the basin were considered to be unreliable.

Model Operation

The annual baseline water yields were derived by three methods. This included gaged runoff prior to diversions at the Moffat Tunnel, evaluations using a subalpine water balance model (WATBAL) and regional correlations. Three hydrologic yield zones were identified as follows:

upper zone - above Moffat or Ranch Creek Collection Systems,
middle zone - below the collection systems and above 8600 feet, and
lower zone - below 8600 feet (most of the irrigated areas).

Inflows to each model node were determined by:

1) Aggregating monthly yields for upper and middle zones and distributing them according to spatial and elevational factors(results of WATBAL).

2) Estimating monthly irrigation demands and returns based on decreed ditch capacities, irrigated acres, and consumptive use for hay crops.

3) Estimating municipal demands and returns (provided by other tasks in the study).

MODSIM runs were made with these inflows and demands and modified to minimize the difference in flows after comparison with downstream gages were redistributed to lower elevation node yields.

WATER RESOURCES ALLOCATION

Calibration runs were made after diversions through Moffat Tunnel and imports from Williams Fork were incorporated into the model. Initial results for years with complete records indicated deviations from historical conditions. The total flows at the mouth of the basin were reasonable but distribution among the upper basins did not agree with gage records. Additional operating constraints were then introduced to the model in terms of artificial prioritizing conditions applied to the links representing the Ranch Creek and Moffat Collection Systems. Iterations of the model were made until conditioned values were established which satisfactorily simulated observations and records. These artificial conditions served to prohibit the model from using the links in question during times when flows were not historically available at these locations (ie: winter months when no snowmelt runoff occurs). The final MODSIM calibration results for the full study period simulated historic records within three percent at both upper and lower gages.

Senior downstream water right "calls" on the Colorado River constitute a major driving force for the allocation of water in this model. Summer flows are subject to calls by the Cameo demand which is an aggregation of senior irrigation water rights near Grand Junction. In winter, the primary downstream demand is Shoshone power plant that forces minimum instream flows on the Colorado River near Glenwood Springs. For representation of future operating conditions, the full conditional water rights for Denver, maximum pumping rates at Windy Gap and the proposed filing of minimum instream flows by the Colorado Water Conservation Board were imposed on the model.

Alternative Plan Simulation

Preliminary investigations identified 78 potential reservoir sites in the basin. Subsequent screening of location and physical features reduced these to 11 sites. MODSIM was used to perform a "storable flow" analysis at each of these 11 sites. This was accomplished by simulating a reservoir in the network at the location of each of these sites and making individual runs to determine the availability of storable water at each site. The reservoirs were assigned a large demand with no return to the system, unlimited storage capacity and were junior to all other demands in the basin with the exception of the Windy Gap project. Results of this analysis provided an initial estimate of the gross storable water supply potential at each reservoir site.

Results of these storable flow simulations indicated further refinement in the number of reservoir sites acceptable for potential projects; additional runs of MODSIM were then used to consider specific reservoir alternatives. The MODSIM storage alternatives network is shown in Figure 2. Three reservoir sites were identified as preferable based on available flow, economics and geotechnical considerations. Reservoir operations were further defined to more closely simulate future conditions. Storage operating rules were modified and future municipal, MPWCD and DWD scheduled demands were included. These demands were modeled as three separate storage pools at the same reservoir site so that the different priorities could be assigned to each pool. Evaporation losses based on records from nearby Lake Granby were included. As there are legal questions concerning the interpretation of previous agreements with the

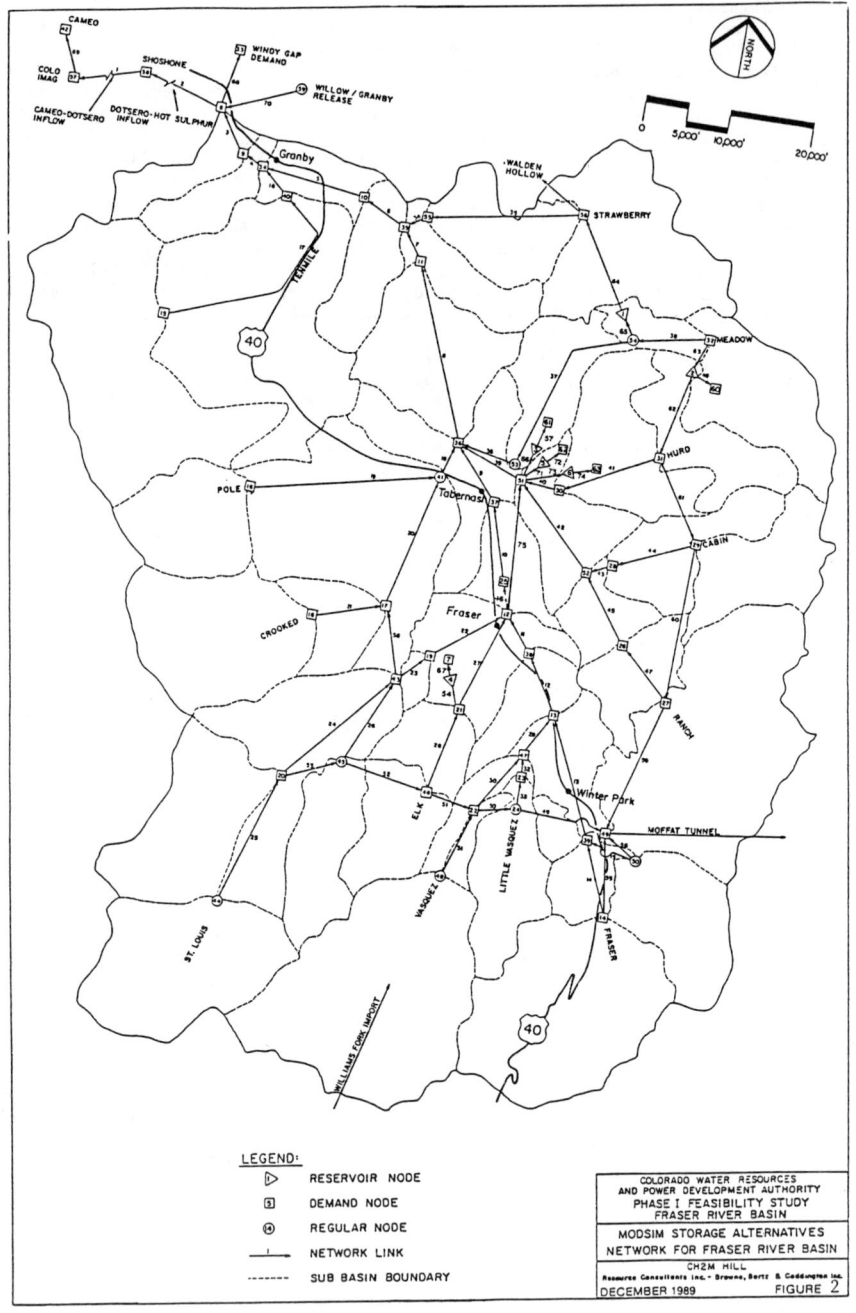

MODSIM STORAGE ALTERNATIVES NETWORK FOR FRASER RIVER BASIN, FIGURE 2

WATER RESOURCES ALLOCATION 205

Windy Gap Project, computer runs were made with Windy Gap both junior and senior in priority to demands from the water stored at new projects in the Fraser Basin. To effect the necessary changes listed above the model network was extended to 75 links and 63 nodes.

Model Results

The general results of the storage alternative runs indicated that a single reservoir with a capacity of 20,000 acre-feet could meet future municipal demands in the basin and provide firm yield for MPWCD without adversely affecting operations of transbasin diversions to east slope communities. Typical monthly storage summaries for the 40-year modeling period are shown in Figure 3.

This study was a pre-feasibilty effort designed to identify and evaluate conceptual water development projects in the Fraser River Basin. Additional studies would be required to investigate more detailed water management constraints for the scenarios proposed. This should include, but not be limited to, more detailed reservoir operations, representation of releases considering extreme wet and dry conditions, detailed operation of possible exchange scenarios and specific inclusion of pumpback operations. Weekly or daily operations (versus monthly operation, as done in this study) should be conducted at the design stage.

As a planning tool, MODSIM proved valuable in reducing a complex water system to a manageable but reasonable representation as a network model. Specific incorporation of both direct flow water rights and storage rights together with representation of reservoir operations and exchange scenarios reasonably simulates allocation of water under Colorado's Prior Appropriation Doctrine. It is particularly useful to private consultants in its current PC format which is cost effective and convenient to use.
The modeling period for this study was divided into two 20-year segments. As an indication of efficiency, run times for each 20 year period for the final version of the model took approximately 25 minutes to execute on a 286, 12mhz PC.

Model Limitations

There are some practical problems to consider when constructing and operating this model. Some agencies may not be willing to release operational records and policies of the water structures that they administer. As with all models of this type, inaccurate operational rules can significantly detract from the accuracy of the results obtained. MODSIM requires that reservoir nodes always come first in the network numbering schematic. One should always think ahead and add extra "dummy" reservoirs for later use if unsure of the eventual structure of the model as it is time consuming to reorder the nodes. Furthermore, data input due to modifications can be challenging if the number of nodes needs to be changed. This requires revision of the larger of the two input files used by the model which contains hydrologic and demand information. One possible solution to this is external manipulation of the data with situation-specific programming codes created by the user.

206 RESOURCES FOR WATER MANAGEMENT

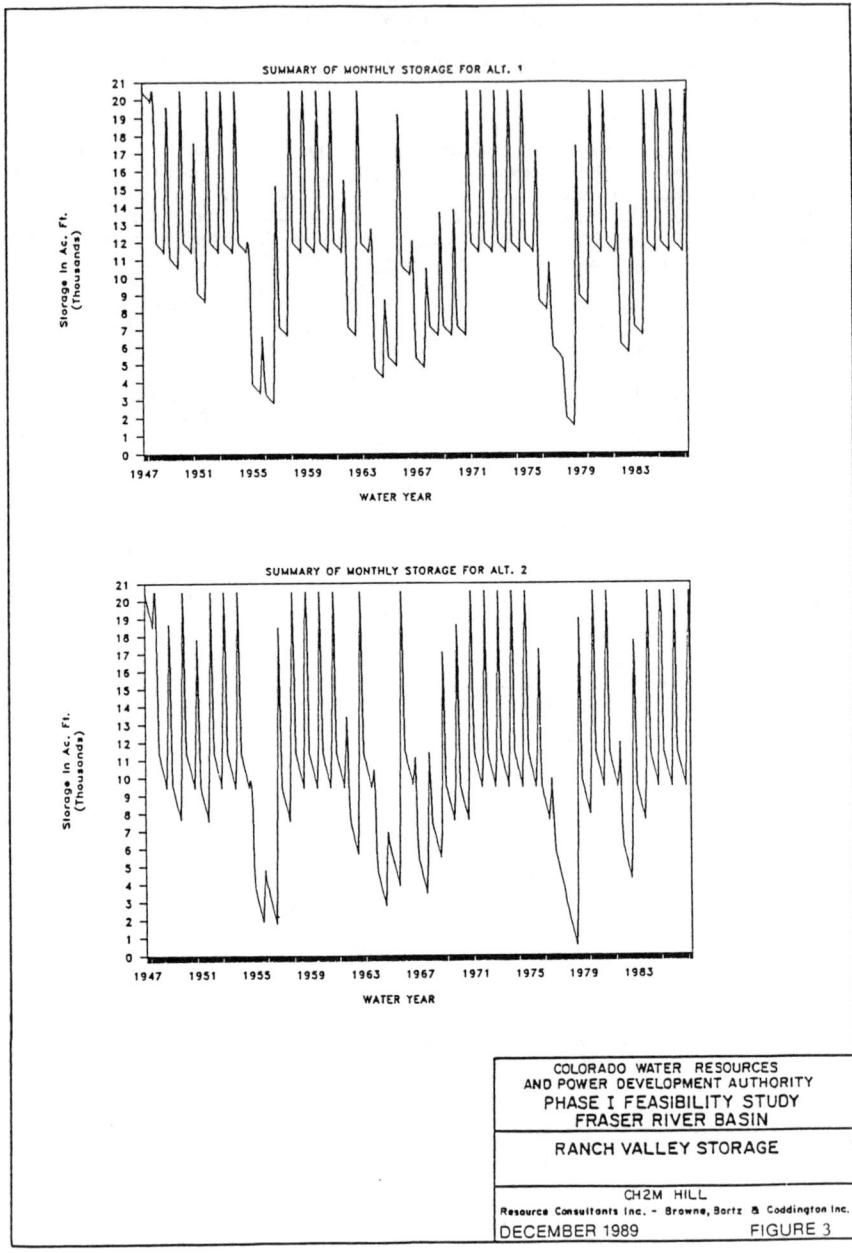

Convergence problems can occur within the linear programming algorithm. Troubleshooting by the user generally consists of pinpointing the location in the network of the problem and slightly adjusting the input values (upward or downward) till convergence can be obtained. While this does not greatly affect the results, it certainly can be a source of headache to the user, particularly a new user. Current MODSIM output is cumbersome, especially when dealing with multiple years. There is considerable information placed in an ASCII file that may not always be pertinent to the analysis at hand. As there is no way to direct the model to provide summary output, a postprocessor is essential to adequately and efficiently locate the results of interest. Under the Fraser study, a specific programming application was developed by the consultant to achieve this end. There exists the possibility within the model to limit the amount of demand that can be placed at a specific node in a given month or week, but no easy way to limit annual or periodic deliveries. This becomes a factor in the case of agreements which are based on an annual maximum delivery as with the Windy Gap Project where monthly maximums are irrelevant.

Summary

MODSIM has served as a useful conceptual planning tool capable of simulating a complex water resource system overlain by various consumptive and diversion demands as well as institutional constraints. The model has allowed efficient analysis of a large array of potential projects and provided the decision makers with information that will allow them to identify a development project that does not conflict with the established interests of other parties. As water resources have greater demands placed on them, the ability to consider these various and often conflicting needs is essential.

Application of Remote Sensing to Flood Forecasting

N. Kouwen[1], E.D. Soulis[1], A. Pietroniro[1] and R.A. Harrington[2]

Abstract

Forecasting flood flows caused by severe rainfall events relies heavily on a knowledge of the surface characteristics of a watershed and precipitation inputs. This information can be obtained from remotely sensed data, namely, satellite derived land use/land cover information and precipitation measured by radar. The paper provides a description of a flood forecasting system that has been designed specifically to make maximum use of remotely sensed data, both in the calibration and operational stages of the application.

Introduction

In this paper, flood-flow forecasting is viewed as a data management and rainfall-runoff simulation process for watersheds having drainage areas of approximately 1000 to 10,000 square kilometers. The activity involves rainfall excess estimation and runoff routing which depend heavily upon accurate and timely rainfall estimates and the character of the watershed surface respectively. It is generally accepted that the rainfall-runoff process is highly non-linear. While this non-linearity can be accounted for in various ways, a process based model can automatically account for this and allows a flood forecaster to make maximum use of remotely sensed data. The data management system is called WATFLOOD and the rainfall-runoff model is called SIMPLE.

The WATFLOOD system uses radar precipitation measurements or raingauge data to provide frequent areal distributions of rainfall intensities and Landsat data to provide the distribution of the various land use/land cover classifications in a watershed. The data

---

[1]Department of Civil Engineering, University of Waterloo, Waterloo, Ontario, Canada, N2L 3G1
[2]Conservation Authorities and Water Management Branch, Ontario Ministry of Natural Resources, Queen's Park, Toronto, Ontario, Canada, M7A 1W3

is organized in a square grid co-ordinate format. SIMPLE is a distributed mode that uses a square grid approximation of a river basin that corresponds to the WATFLOOD data base. The paper describes both systems and presents both time and space validation results.

Data Management System

WATFLOOD is a menu driven data input and file management system. At present, the system will operate on an IBM PC/AT or compatible system in a completely independent mode if radar data is not used or not available. If radar precipitation measurements are used, a communications link is required to acquire the voluminous radar data. Rainfall, streamflow and reservoir release data can be entered or corrected through a spreadsheet type user interface in real time. The menu allows for various operating modes, namely: parameter optimization, which is done on historic data; a forecast mode, which automatically up-dates the model's soil moisture parameter and produces a flow forecast; and a single run mode, which can be used for a "what if" exercise during a flood event.

The Rainfall-runoff Model

SIMPLE can use any square grid system having a minimum interval of one kilometer and models only the dominant short duration processes such as interception (the exponential relationship with accumulated precipitation in Linsley et al. 1949); infiltration (Green and Ampt, 1911; Philip 1954); depression storage; interflow (linear storage-discharge function); base flow (recession curve); overland flow (storage routing and Manning's formula); and channel flow (storage routing and Manning's formula). The entire routing sequence is based on storage (simple) routing, which is one of the reasons for naming the model SIMPLE. It should be noted that those processes which are modeled occur primarily at the surface, and are thus most likely to benefit from a more detailed land cover description (Tao and Kouwen, 1989).

In SIMPLE, runoff is calculated separately for each land cover class in each element, and the modelling parameters are identical throughout the whole watershed for a particular land cover class. In other distributed models, such as the Systeme Hydrologique Europeen (SHE) model, a watershed is subdivided into square grid elements but each element has just one land use/land cover class and other runoff affecting characteristics (Abbot et al., 1986). Bathurst (1986) determined that the model should be subdivided into elements no larger than 1 percent of the basin area in order to ensure that each element is more or less homogeneous. Such a fine mesh results in great demands on computer resources.

In contrast, SIMPLE is not very sensitive to grid size. This is because up to six land use/cover classifications can be specified for each element, negating the requirement that each element has to represent a homogeneous hydrologic response classification. The main assumption in SIMPLE is that a given land use/cover classification results in certain hydrologic response, irrespective of the location in the basin. This results in substantial savings in computer time because large elements can be used and the number of channel routing computations are reduced. Even more important, it appears the same hydrologic response can be expected from the same land use/land cover classifications in watersheds in the same geographic region. This greatly reduces the calibration effort required to configure the WATFLOOD system for other watersheds and improves the prospect that the system can be more reliably used on ungauged areas, where the model calibration cannot be verified.

Calibration and Validation Watersheds

The Grand River watershed above Cambridge (Galt) in Southwestern Ontario, Canada, was used for the development and calibration of the flood forecasting system. The drainage area is 3520 km². In general, flood flows take about 4 hours to travel from upper reaches to the three flood control reservoirs, and 3 to 5 hours from the reservoirs to the main damage areas.

The WATFLOOD system was validated on three areas in Southern Ontario, namely the Saugeen River, Humber River, and four small watersheds just east of Metropolitan Toronto. The system was applied to these areas without further calibration. Only raingauge data was used for the simulated flood forecasts. The Saugeen River drains an area of 4056 km². There are no significant flood control reservoirs in the Saugeen River basin. The Humber River drains an area of 570 km², with its headwaters on the east side of the Niagara escarpments, and its outlet in Lake Ontario at the west side of Toronto. The lower part of the watershed is heavily urbanized. The third area studied includes four separate watersheds, each individually draining into Lake Ontario. The rivers are: the Rouge River with a total drainage area of 328 km²; Duffin Creek with 288 km²; Lynde Creek 112 km²; and Oshawa Creek with 122 km². These are relatively small streams descending the south slope of a glacial moraine.

Results

Figures 1 and 2 show the graphical output produced by the WATFLOOD system. In each figure, the number is the peak flow and the station name is also given. Figure 1 is a validation in time for the Grand River watershed. Figure 2 is a validation in space, using an event on the Saugeen Watershed. These results are typical of a number of simulations

on each of the watersheds. In the figures, the thin solid line is the computed flow while the heavy line is the flow recorded up to the time the forecast is made. The time of forecast is denoted by a vertical line crossing the hydrographs. The duration of the hydrographs is five days. Considering that the hydrographs for the

Grand River are for an event having a peak flow at Galt of five times the largest peak in the calibration events, and that the hydrographs were applied to the Saugeen without calibration, the results are deemed very good.

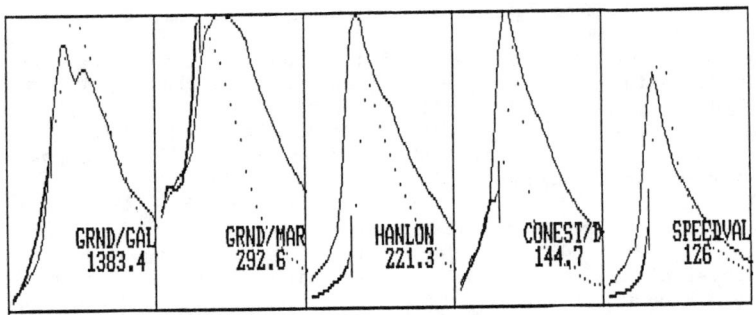

Figure 1 - Validation in Time for the Grand River Watershed. Showing peak flow in m³/s. Hydrograph duration is 5 days.

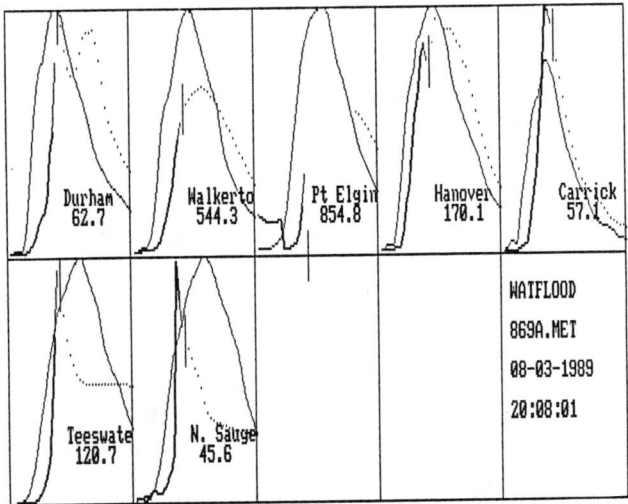

Figure 2 - Validation in Space for the Saugeen River Watershed Showing peak flow in m³/s. Hydrograph duration is 5 days.

References

Abbot, M.B., Bathurst, J.C., Cunge, J.A., O'Connell, P.E., and Rasmussen, J., 1986, "An Introduction to the European Hydrological System - Systeme Hydrologique Europeen, 'SHE', 1: History and Philosophy of a Physically-based, Distributed Modelling System", Journal of Hydrology, Vol. 87, pp. 45-59.

Bathurst, J.C., 1986, "Sensitivity Analysis of the Systeme Hydrologique Europeen for an Upland Catchment", Journal of Hydrology, Vol. 87, pp. 103-123.

Green, W.H., and Ampt, G.A., 1911, "Studies in Soil Physics, 1, The Flow of Air and Water through Soils", Journal of Agricultural Science, Vol. 4, pp. 1-24.

Linsley, R.K., Kohler, M.A., and Paulhus, J.L.H., 1949: Applied Hydrology, McGraw-Hill, 689pp.

Philip, J.R. 1954: "An infiltration equation with physical significance", Soil Science, Vol.77, January-June.

Tao, T. and N. Kouwen, 1989, "Remote Sensing and Fully Distributed modelling for Flood Forecasting", Journal of Water Resources Planning and Management", ASCE, Vol. 115, No. 6, November, pp. 809-823.

Use of Remote Sensing and G.I.S. in the
Economic Analysis of Flood Damage
Reduction -- Three Recent Case Histories

Peter H. Shaw[1]

Abstract

Three recent studies of the Trinity River in the nine-city Dallas-Fort Worth metroplex have been based on a regional geographic information system (G.I.S.), using digitized satellite imagery and other sources to characterize land use to a very high degree of accuracy. This system has been used to model potential flood damages for a highly-developed floodplain of over 70,000 acres (175,000 hectares), almost entirely without the traditional labor-intensive field surveys and manual encoding of economic data.

Introduction

G.I.S. techniques have been used by the Fort Worth District Office of the U.S. Army Corps of Engineers in the accomplishment of three major water resources planning studies in as many years. These studies are the Trinity River Final Regional Environmental Impact Statement (U.S. Army Corps of Engineers, 1987), a draft reconnaissance-level review of the existing Dallas Floodway system (U.S. Army Corps of Engineers, 1989), and on ongoing reconnaissance-level investigation of the Upper Trinity River.

It is beyond the scope of this paper to discuss the overall purposes and methodologies of these studies, or technical details of the geographic information system developed to accomplish them. Rather, the focus will be on the integration of G.I.S. into the traditional economic analysis of flood damage reduction measures in the specific context of these studies.

The Economic Analysis of Flood Control

The analysis of potential damages in a floodplain is,
----
1. Regional Economist, U.S. Army Corps of Engineers, 819 South Taylor Street, Fort Worth, Texas 76102-0300

conceptually, a simple matter. Once the boundaries of the floodplain have been defined, information is gathered about the nature of the economic activities in the floodplain that would suffer loss in the event of a flood. This information largely consists of site-specific land use data. These data are traditionally collected by on-site visual inspection of the affected structures, often supplemented by interviews with owners or proprietors, local government officials, and other knowledgeable individuals -- a highly labor-intensive task. For small floodplains, every structure is usually counted individually, but for large study areas, structures may be considered in homogeneous groups by property type, or statistical sampling may be employed. However they are collected, the data are then encoded and debugged (another labor-intensive task) for use in a computer program that performs the actual calculation of potential flood damages.

Given the typically limited time and funds available for the work, it is highly desirable to minimize the labor-intensive task of performing the field survey, without compromising the accuracy of the study's findings. To this end, many key data items can successfully be given assumed values, or generalized from previous studies, without compromising the accuracy or usefulness of the results.

Once the existing condition data are established, the evaluation of alternatives for flood damage reduction becomes a matter of recalculating potential flood damages with changed hydraulic conditions, or changes in floodplain land use, or both. With a well-constructed data base and a friendly computer model for calculating the damages, this is relatively quick and easy.

Case 1: The Trinity River Final Regional E.I.S.

This study, referred to below for brevity as the REIS, considered the cumulative effects on future flood elevations resulting from floodplain development activities individually underway in the nine cities in the Dallas-Fort Worth area, given several generalized floodplain land use scenarios. Each scenario was evaluated with respect to the potential damages that would occur in the event of a 100-year flood and a standard project flood (SPF).

The land use data base consisted of digitized Landsat thematic mapper imagery, recorded in 1984, with a ground resolution (effective grid cell size) of 40 meters. This was demonstrated to be capable of identifying water, wetlands, a variety of vegetative cover types, transportation (roads, highways, parking lots, etc.), residential, and commercial/industrial land uses with a very high degree of accuracy, even in the absence of additional information. Of the ten categories of land use provided by the data, three were pertinent to the economic analyses: residential, commercial/industrial, and "other non-vacant".

The land use data were related within the G.I.S., cell-by-cell, to overlays of topographic elevation and water surface elevations for the 100-year and SPF events, to arrive at the number of acres of each land use category, in each city, under one foot of water, two feet of water, and so on.

Each city's planning staff was requested to provide information on the market value per acre of lands and structures, by land use category, within their part of the SPF floodplain. These data were supplemented as needed with comparable information from the U.S. Census and the North Central Texas Council of Governments.

Weighted average depth-damage relationships for structures and contents, a weighted average proportion of contents value to structure value, and a weighted average floor correction for each of the broad categories of land use were derived from data developed in the course of urban flood control studies previously performed by the Fort Worth District office of the Corps of Engineers.

For each land use class, contents values were determined by applying the weighted average relationship of contents value to structure value to the value of structures per acre. The composite depth-damage relationships were then applied to the acreage of each land use class under each successive foot of flood depth, to compute damages to structures and contents, adjusted for the weighted average floor correction appropriate to the land use class. Damages were then summed over the range of flood depths to arrive at total damages for the flood event.

Case 2: Dallas Floodway Review Reconnaissance Study

One of the findings of the REIS was that, under the most aggressive regional floodplain land use scenario, the elevation of the SPF at Dallas would be raised enough to overtop the existing Corps of Engineers levees protecting the city of Dallas, which would result in their catastrophic failure. Accordingly, this study was undertaken under the authority of Section 216 of Public Law 91-611, which provides for review and modification of completed projects in response to changed conditions.

For this study, field inspection was used to confirm the land use identifications of the remote-sensed data used in the REIS and differentiate them further (from three categories to seven), and to refine the estimated values of damageable development per acre. The composite depth-damage relationships for these land use categories were calculated from the same base of previous flood control studies as in the REIS, but without so great a degree of aggregation.

Representative data on structure value per square foot of gross floor area, per story of building height, was adduced for each land use category from publications of the Marshall Valuation Service. This was adjusted on the basis of field observation, and combined with an assumed floor area ratio (the proportion of a gross acre occupied by structures), and the weighted-average ratio of contents value to structure value (see above), to calculate the total value of damageable development per acre for each land use category.

As in the REIS, the land use data were related within the G.I.S., cell-by-cell, to overlays of topographic elevation and the water surface elevation for the levee-failure event, to arrive at the number of acres of each land use category, behind each of the three levees, under one foot of water, two feet of water, and so on. For each land use category, contents values were determined by applying the weighted average relationship of contents value to structure value to the value of structures per acre. The composite depth-damage relationships were then applied to the acreage of each land use category under each successive foot of flood depth, to compute damages to structures and contents, adjusted for the weighted average floor correction appropriate to the land use class. Damages were then summed over the range of flood depths to arrive at total damages for the levee-failure flood event, under the baseline condition, for each of the three levees in the Dallas Floodway system.

Case 3: Upper Trinity River Reconnaissance Study

This study is still underway at this time. Like the Dallas Floodway Review Reconnaissance Study, it has its origins in the REIS, which not only demonstrated the need for a coordinated regional approach to flooding problems along the Trinity River, but also helped to establish the institutional framework for doing so.

This study is an initial reexamination of recommendations by the Corps of Engineers for the upper Trinity

FLOOD DAMAGE REDUCTION ANALYSIS					217

River, as previously authorized by Congress. It covers the Trinity River and its major forks upstream of the confluence of the East Fork, below Dallas. Further work on the Dallas Floodway Review beyond the reconnaissance phase has been absorbed into this study. It also provides for a review of the existing Fort Worth Floodway project: unlike the REIS, whose upstream limit on the West Fork was the downstream end of the Fort Worth Floodway, the current study includes the West Fork, Clear Fork, and Marys Creek through the city of Fort Worth.

The study is using several sources of land use information for the G.I.S. data base: late-1988 Landsat thematic mapper imagery, aerial photography, and digitized land use data for the nine-city study area compiled by the North Central Texas Council of Governments. The land use classifications used in the economic analyses in the present study are similar to those used in the Dallas Floodway Review, but with greater differentiation among residential development. Except for this increased level of detail, the methodology is essentially the same as used in the Dallas Floodway Review. Once specific areas have been selected for consideration of potential projects, two refinements to the data base will be made in those areas: on-site field inspection will be used to verify and refine the generalized structure and contents values per acre for each land use classification, and aerial photographs will be either digitally scanned or planimetered to refine the assumed floor area ratio used for each land use classification.

One notable procedural change from the earlier efforts is that the calculation of economic damages has been integrated into the G.I.S. software itself, instead of being a stand-alone application on a different computer. This not only saves time and labor, but provides the opportunity for economic outputs to be produced directly by the G.I.S. in tabular or graphical form -- for example, a color-coded map of flood damages by grid cell for any desired area, for use in identifying promising areas for potential structural and nonstructural flood control measures.

Discussion

These three studies display a growing degree and sophistication of use of G.I.S. methods, in lieu of on-site visual inspection and manual encoding of data, in the economic analysis of flood damages. In fact, the cost of doing these analyses in these three studies by traditional methods would have been altogether prohibitive.

Once the initial investment in hardware, software,

and learning time has been made, G.I.S. offers a tool for economic analysis of tremendous flexibility and untapped potential. It is not claimed that remote sensing and G.I.S. techniques are a panacea, replacing all need for on-site field work, but they do allow for field work to be enormously more selective, and for professional judgment to be used more efficiently and effectively, than has been the case with traditional methods.

More generally, G.I.S. techniques can manipulate and present any economic, demographic or social data correlated or visually mapped against each other, elucidating relationships that might be otherwise unnoticed. As relatively inexpensive desktop hardware and software for this purpose become more generally available, this will provide an analytical tool for the social scientist of unprecedented richness and power.

REFERENCES

1. U.S. Army Corps of Engineers, **Final Regional Environmental Impact Statement, Trinity River and Tributaries, Dallas, Denton, and Tarrant Counties, Texas**, U.S. Army Engineer District, Fort Worth, 1987.

2. U.S. Army Corps of Engineers, **Dallas Floodway, Dallas, Texas, Review of Completed Projects, Draft Reconnaissance Report**, U.S. Army Engineer District, Fort Worth, 1989.

Applying a Simple GIS to PMP Analysis
In a Microcomputer Environment

Mark W. Killgore 1/

INTRODUCTION

The analysis of probable maximum floods (PMF) in the Northwestern United States requires the inclusion of a snowmelt component combined with probable maximum precipitation. The National Weather Service's "Hydrometeorological Report No. 43" (HMR 43) (NWS,1981) is the standard approach required by the Federal Energy Regulatory Commission (FERC) in conducting such analyses. A significant factor required by FERC "Engineering Guidelines" for the Evaluation of Hydropower Projects" (FERC, 1987) is the 100-year snowpack appropriate to the month under consideration. A rainfall-runoff model is required to simulate the effect of probable maximum precipitation (PMP) when combined with this severe snowpack condition.

Traditionally the approach has been to planimeter the area by bandwidth for each subbasin included in the model to develop a curve of area below a certain elevation versus elevation. This process is laborious and mundane for the technician who develops this essential data for the runoff model. Based on such an experience in developing area-elevation data for a 6,000 square mile basin in the states of Washington and Idaho it was decided to seek an alternative approach for the evaluation of the 7,100 square mile Flathead River Basin in Western Montana. The study area was subdivided into 15 subbasins based on USGS gaging stations and widely varying snowpack conditions within the Flathead River Basin.

OPTIONS FOR INPUTTING TOPOGRAPHIC DATA

The company had standardized on "AUTOCAD" software installed on 386 personal computer workstations for engineering design. This represented the initial constraint for topographic data input.

1/ Senior Engineer, Ebasco Services Incorporated
10900 NE 8th St., Bellevue, WA 98004-4404

Three alternatives were considered. Two were on a small scale basis to determine the most economic approach to develop the topographic data base. The first method utilized a scanner to input USGS topographic maps at 1:250,000 scale. It was estimated that the effect to "cleanup" the superfluous data would be excessive and an alternate method was chosen.

A large table digitizer was used to enter contours at 1000 foot intervals for each drainage subbasin as well as the watershed boundaries, major rivers, key climatological station, and USGS gaging stations. Each item as well as each contour band was entered on a separate layer. This service was provided by Wichai Engineering Services.

A third alternative method rejected due to time constraints was the use of USGS digital terrain data files. This approach may have offered superior economy but was not evaluated. Future studies will explore this option.

IMPLEMENTATION

Having essentially developed a topographic database, the next step was to interpret the data into areal bandwidth. Though simple in principal, no commercial software was located to make the analysis. Preliminary trials in the autocad environment defining contour bands as objects and computing consecutive areas of the objects using the area command proved to be time consuming and uneconomical. It was decided to develop a macro written in LISP which met specific functional criteria. Each contour band which intersected the drainage basin boundary was defined as an object using a pointer. Similarly, each internal closed contour band was defined as an object and had its area computed. The result was written to an ASCII file and given an identity in sequence. The difference was then computed such that the total area by bandwidth was determined.

As a check, the sum of the areas of each bandwidth was compared to the total subbasin area.

A final check was made by combining the 15 smaller subbasins into four major subbasins which had previously been investigated by the Pacific Division of the Army Corps of Engineers. The results indicated excellent agreement with the earlier Corp's study. Some minor differences were manually spot-checked and the AUTOCAD method was determined more accurate.

The resulting snowband area-elevation relationships were successfully integrated into the Army Corps of Engineers

"Steamflow Synthesis and Reservoir Regulation" (SSARR) model (COE, 1987). Subsequent verification of model parameters proved successful and the data was ultimately used to estimate the probable maximum flood for the Flathead River.

RECOMMENDATIONS AND CONCLUSIONS

The total time committed to this approach probably exceeded the traditional planimeter approach. However, development time of the macro and the learning curve factor would probably be overcome in future applications resulting in less costly snowband analyses.

The ideal future approach may also include the use of USGS digital terrain data. Because of the nature of flood studies in the west, with most requiring some form of snowmelt analysis, it would appear economically feasible to develop a program which would read the x-y coordinates of the drainage basin boundaries and overlay the results on digital terrain data. Provided a regular grid was used, such that each elevation point carried equal weight, the elevation values could then be sorted within the drainage basin and the distribution of elevation versus percentage of area below that elevation could be determined.

REFERENCES

U.S. Army Corps of Engineers, North Pacific Division (1987 draft). "User Manual, SSARR Model, Streamflow Synthesis and Reservoir Regulation".

U.S. Department of Commerce, Environmental Science Services Administration, Weather Bureau (1966, reprinted with revisions of 1981). "Hydrometeorological Report No. 43, Probable Maximum Precipitation, Northwest States"

U.S. Federal Energy Regulatory Commission, Office of Hydropower Licensing (1987). "Engineering Guidelines" for the Evaluation of Hydropower Projects".

ACKNOWLEDGMENTS
Montana Power Company
Wichai Engineering Services
Alacrity Company

Stochastic Optimization of Conjunctive Use in Pakistan

Christine A. Shoemaker and Carolyn J. Logan[1]

Abstract

This paper describes an optimization analysis of conjunctive use of ground and surface water that incorporates stochastic inflows and regional variations in groundwater quality and availability. The objective function includes the effects of salinity, water deficits and/or waterlogging on expected crop production as well as income from the sale of water and hydroelectric power. The model is applied to a very large irrigation system in the Indus Plains in Pakistan, which has saline and fresh groundwater regions and a random surface water inflow. The results for the Indus Plains indicate that crop losses can be substantially reduced by replacing the historical policy, which involves constant pumping rates, with a "flexible" policy that modifies groundwater pumping and surface water allocations among regions in response to fluctuations in the surface water supply.

Introduction

Conjunctive use of surface and groundwater supplies is a key to future improvements in the management, timing and distribution of water supplies in many areas. Our analysis will consider an area composed of one or more regions, which are distinguished from one another in some of the following aspects: a) location on different parts of the water supply network, b) variations in groundwater quality or availability, c) differences in capacity for aquifer use and control, or d) substantially dissimilar cropping patterns or practices. Our goal is to maximize the objective function, which is the expected value of the sum of the costs in crop losses over N time periods. The analysis is described in more detail in Shoemaker and Logan (1989).

The transition equations incorporate the changes in the values of state variables due to changes in pumping policies, surface allocations, and in random inputs like weather. The equations for water table depth and soil salinity are based on mass balances. The state variable $x^1_{i, t+1}$ describing the water table depth in region i at time t is computed as a function of the water

---

[1]Professor and graduate research assistant, respectively, School of Civil and Environmental Engineering, Cornell University, Ithaca, N.Y., 14853.

table depth in the previous time period plus the amounts of water entering the groundwater from seepage (of precipitation and of surface water in the canal and of water applied to crops in the field) minus the amounts of water leaving the groundwater due to capillary rise into the root zone or evaporation. The state variable $x^2_{i,t+1}$ describing the soil water salinity is computed as a function of the soil water salinity in the previous time period plus the salinity due to water entering the root zone from irrigation water or from capillary rise minus the salinity lost to water seeping from the root zone into the groundwater.

The cost function includes the effects of water deficits, water logging and salinity on crop production. The effect of water deficit on crop yields is based on the work of Doorenbos et al. [1979] and Stewart et al. [1977]. This relationship assumes that the crop loss is a function of the ratio of the actual water received by the plant to the optimal amount of water for plant growth. The effect of salinity on crop yields is based on work by Doorenbos et al. [1979]. This model assumes that if if salinity is below a lower threshold, there is no effect on crop yield. If the salinity is above a higher threshold, there is no crop yield. In between these two thresholds the effect declines linearly as the salinity level increases. The effect of water logging on crop yields indicates a linear decline in yield as the water table elevation increases beyond a minimum level related to the root zone depth [World Bank, 1984]. Since the optimization method being used is a nonlinear procedure, it is possible to replace the linear crop loss models above with alternative nonlinear models if that is deemed necessary for a particular situation.

The amount of crop loss is a multiplicative function of the losses from each of the three losses: water deficit, salinity and water logging. Each of these loss equations are based on parameter values that are crop specific. Hence the total crop loss function is a weighted average of the losses for each crop. The weights are determined by the percentage of acreage planted to each crop and the economic value of each crop.

Application to Indus Plains Irrigation System in Pakistan

The Indus Plains of Pakistan has one of the world's longest irrigation histories, having seen a variety of irrigation systems for some 5000 years. The Indus River irrigation system that currently serves the basin is the world's largest contiguous system, distributing over 12.5 million hectare meters of water across 14 million hectares of agricultural land each year. Surface water is provided from the Indus River. Groundwater is of varying quality and in some areas it is so saline that it cannot be used for irrigation purposes. In these areas the addition of surface water for irrigation coupled with no groundwater pumping has resulted in gradual increases in water table elevation to the point where waterlogging is seriously affecting crop losses. To address this problem there has been a massive construction project to build the Left Bank Outfall Drain (LBOD) to drain excess water from this region. In the areas underlain by fresh groundwater, pumping can provide valuable irrigation water. In addition the fresh groundwater aquifer can be used for inter-year storage.

In our analysis the study area is divided into two regions: a fresh groundwater (FGW) region and a saline groundwater region (SGW). The boundaries used to differentiate the these two areas were taken from Duloy and O'Mara (1984). The data on seepage rates and evaporation rates were also from the Duloy and O'Mara study. The time horizon is 25 years. Within each year there is a summer and winter season. The cropping pattern and the seepage and evaporation rates vary between seasons. Data on sub-irrigation rates due to capillary rise were from Gardner and Fireman [1958]. The World Bank [1984] provides estimates of the optimal water needs for each crop in each season.

Figure 1 compares the total crop losses with the optimal dynamic programming solution (Strategy 2) to the traditional policy (Strategy 1). We see that the traditional policy has 76% more crop losses than does the optimal policy. In the traditional policy the rates of pumping from the fresh groundwater region and the fraction of surface water going to the FGW are constant in each year. In the optimal Strategy 2, the ground and surface water use varies each year as a function of the surface water availability

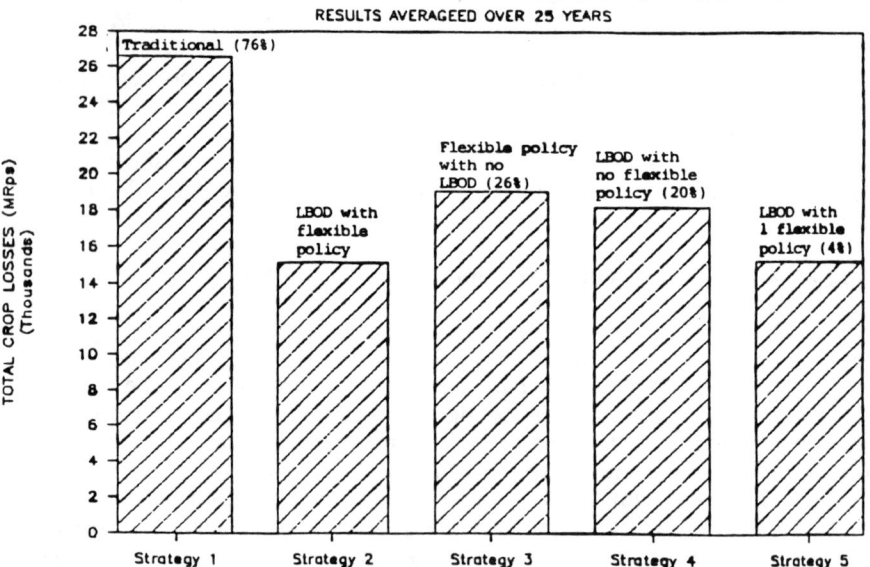

Figure 1. Results of the stochastic dynamic programming analysis of conjunctive use in the Indus Basin over 25 years.

(a random variable) and as a function of groundwater tables and salinity levels. The traditional policy does not make use of the LBOD drainage capacity because this facility is not yet operational and hence has not been utilized in previous water resource management strategies. Strategy 3 indicates the best that could be done without the LBOD using a DP solution and Strategy 4 indicates the best that could be done with the LBOD if an inflexible (i.e. time invariant policy is used). Strategy 5 is a simpler policy in which the only decision variable in the DP is the freshwater pumping. Sensitivity analysis of the results and limitations in the data base are discussed in Logan and Shoemaker (1989).

Conclusion

The results of the analysis for the Indus Plains suggests that crop losses can be substantially reduced by replacing the historical policy, which involves constant pumping rates, with a "flexible" policy that modifies groundwater pumping and surface water allocations among regions in response to fluctuations in the surface water supply. The dynamic programming analysis was also used to determine the best constant policy for the Indus Plains irrigation system when the LBOD becomes operational. The results indicate that the LBOD achieves only about 80% of its full economic value if a constant rather than a flexible policy. Strategy 5 is a very desireable policy because it is easier to compute, explain and implement than the optimal (Strategy 2) and yet there is little difference in crop losses.

The dynamic programming solutions represent a significantly improved operating system for the area in the Indus Plains studied in this analysis. These results support the value of a systems analysis approach to conjunctive use in large irrigation systems.

References

Doorenbos, J. et al., "Yield Response to Water", **Irrigation and Drainage paper No. 33**, Food and Ag. Org., Rome, 1979.

Gardner, W.R. and M. Fireman, "Laboratory Studies of Evaporation From Soil Columns in the Presence of a Water Table", **Soil Sci.**, 85, 244-249, 1958.

Shoemaker, C.A. and C.J. Logan, "Managing Conjunctive Use Irrigation Systems I: A Stochastic Dynamic Programming Model Incorporating Water Deficits, Salinity and Waterlogging" (submitted manuscript)

Logan, C. and C.A. Shoemaker, "Managing Conjunctive Use Irrigation Systems II: A Case Study in the Indus Plains of Pakistan" (submitted manuscript)

World Bank, "Pakistan LBOS Stage 1 Project", Staff Appraisal Report, Report No. 5185-Pak, Washington, DC 1984.

Evaluation of Conjunctive Use and Drainage Reduction Strategies

Nigel W.T. Quinn [1] Assoc. M, ASCE

Abstract

Optimal drainage management strategies for control of salt and selenium contamination problems in the San Joaquin Valley of California must recognize subregional differences in groundwater chemistry and aquifer characteristics. Modelling analysis has shown that these optimal strategies involve various levels of surface water use, groundwater use and recycled drainage in combinations depending on the costs of the water and its salt concentration. Conjunctive use strategies are responsive to policy options which might involve increased water prices or the imposition of drainage treatment and disposal fees.

Introduction

Problems associated with drainage of irrigated agricultural lands on the west side of the San Joaquin Valley result from the necessary leaching of accumulated salts from the crop rooting zone. These salts, which threaten the future productivity of irrigated agriculture in the valley, also include toxic and potentially toxic trace elements such as selenium, boron, arsenic and molybdenum which are eliminated in subsurface drainage water. Impacts associated with the storage and disposal of this subsurface agricultural drainage include degradation of surface and ground-water quality, contamination of fish and wildlife habitats, and risks to public health.

Studies have been conducted over the past several decades by public agencies and researchers seeking a technically feasible, economically justified, environmentally sound, and politically acceptable approach to managing agricultural drainage problems on the west side of the San Joaquin Valley (SJVDP, 1989).

The need to address toxic constituents in drainage water has complicated the drainage issues significantly beyond just "salt disposal." The scale and urgency of the problem call for creative approaches in formulating and evaluating alternatives for source control and drainage management.

---

[1] Research Associate, Cornell University, Ithaca, NY.
Water Resources Planner, San Joaquin Valley Drainage Program, Sacramento, CA.

Conjunctive Use Options

One of the options that will likely be part of any comprehensive plan to manage drainage water is selective pumping of the semi-confined aquifer which would be used to lower regional water tables and provide a source of supplemental irrigation water supply. Planning an optimal long term conjunctive use program in the western San Joaquin Valley is complicated by the heterogeneity of the groundwater aquifer both in terms of its hydraulics and its chemical stratification. Hence, long term solutions to the agricultural drainage problem will need to recognize the dynamic nature of contaminant movement in the groundwater aquifers.

Management plans involving groundwater pumping should aim to maximize the longevity of the groundwater resource and not accelerate degradation of the aquifer. Continued pumping of wells, completed at depth within strata of high quality water in the semi-confined aquifer and overlain by strata of poorer quality water, will eventually yield groundwater with an increased concentration of salts or other contaminant elements. The utility of the groundwater diminishes as its quality declines - hence groundwater pumping within aquifers where the zone of good quality water is relatively limited in extent is a fragile resource.

Modelling Approach

The analysis of conjunctive use of groundwater and surface water for irrigation in those areas of the San Joaquin Valley that are affected by drainage problems is proceeding in three phases. The first phase involves a reconaissance of the chemical stratification of the semi-confined aquifer and the confined aquifer so as to discern zones of groundwater low enough in dissolved salts and boron to be usable as an irrigation water supply, or sufficiently low in TDS, boron, arsenic and selenium to be usable as a supplemental water supply for wetlands. This calls for an extensive survey of the depth distribution of salts, selenium and other contaminants of concern and the hydraulic characteristics of the semi-confined aquifer throughout the western San Joaquin Valley and a compilation of records which describe the screened depth of existing wells in the study area.

Only two observation well cluster sites exist where the chemical stratification of groundwater can be directly observed. The only other source of data are water quality samples drawn from active pumping wells. Interpretation of the depth distribution of TDS and trace elements is difficult using these data, since the screened interval of these wells is extremely variable and in many cases is not known. The streamlines generated by each pumping well may draw water from a large vertical interval in the aquifer - hence it is difficult to discern the nominal interface between zones of suitable and unsuitable groundwater quality in the semi-confined aquifer.

Interpretation of well pumping records, pumpage water quality data and well logs is currently being performed to estimate the depth distribution of groundwater high in TDS and trace elements. A regression model is being developed within a Geographic Information System (ARC-INFO) to allow the extrapolation of this analysis to areas that have not been surveyed. The depth to which the contaminated groundwater has moved is considered to depend on the following factors:

o   time since the onset of irrigation
o   specific yield of semi-confined aquifer
o   average, long-term irrigation water use efficiency
o   historic groundwater pumping from the semi-confined and confined aquifers
o   lateral flows of groundwater within the semi-confined aquifer
o   rate of groundwater leakance through the Corcoran Clay layer

Evaluation of pumping scenarios.

Evaluation of the water quality of agricultural pumpage is being made under a range of possible long term pumping scenarios including: pumping at various screened depths in the semi-confined aquifer; pumping in regions where the semi-confined aquifer is stratified by chemistry or by texture; and pumping at various extraction rates relative to the annual recharge of the semi-confined aquifer.

A finite element model, SOLTRAK, which simulates groundwater pumping and radial flow to a single well, has been developed by Matanga (Frind and Matanga ,1985). The model generates a series of stream tubes into a pumped well and allows the tracking of solute particles. Hence the arrival time of solutes, originating from a zone of high concentration within the aquifer, can be estimated. The solute discharged through each stream tube is mixed at the well - hence the concentration of the pumped water increases over time as more of the solute from the zone, higher in solute concentration, is displaced toward the pumped well.

The model will be applied to each of a number of aquifer zones - these aquifer zones divide the regional aquifer into subunits on the basis of shallow groundwater conditions, water table height, depth and concentration distribution of contaminants with depth and boundary conditions. Boundary conditions include the lower boundary flux (leakance across the Corcoran Clay layer, upper boundary flux (rate of irrigation recharge) and lateral flows in to and out of the system. The model will help to set constraints on pumping strategies, as a function of aquifer physical and chemical characteristics, to promote long term viability of the groundwater resource.

Economic and policy considerations

To evaluate the regional impacts of groundwater pumping, where shown to be feasible, a second model is being used. The Westside Agricultural Drainage Economics (WADE) model is an optimization model that attempts to simulate long-term behavior and response of the coupled surface irrigation - groundwater system to a variety of management strategies and policy options (Hatchett et al., 1989). The WADE model can be considered as three interacting submodels. One is an agricultural production model which simulates cropping decisions, farm revenue and profit, and water management technology selection, and the others are hydrology and salinity models which estimate the effects of these management decisions on the water table, salinization in the crop root zone, and drainage quantity and quality.

The WADE hydrology model considers four layers within the groundwater aquifer one of which is below the Corcoran Clay and the others divide the semi-confined aquifer into a root zone, a 20 ft layer and a deep semi-confined layer. The deep semi-confined layer recognizes a zone of contamination and zone beneath this zone of contamination of higher quality groundwater. The salt concentration of pumped groundwater from the deep semi-confined layer is initially assumed equal in concentration to the zone containing higher quality groundwater, which in most cases is located immediately above the Corcoran Clay layer in the semi-confined aquifer. Changes in the concentration of this zone over time, as affected by various pumping regimes will be directly determined using the SOLTRAK model.

The objective function to the agricultural production submodel of the WADE model maximizes net returns to land and management for each of the five proxy crops and 180 polygon cells considered by the model, taking into account all irrigation, drainage and agronomic costs associated with production. These include annualized cultivation and harvest costs; annualized costs of tile drain installation; annualized system costs for various irrigation management practices and technologies; surface water delivery costs; groundwater pumping costs; fees assessed on subsurface drainage flows and drainage recycling costs. The model takes account of the yield decrement associated with the use of saline irrigation water. The model can irrigate with a blended water supply which includes surface sources, groundwater, irrigation and drainage return flows to meet a target salinity level (EC) - the model considers the cost of water obtained from each source as well as the potential yield decrement associated with its use. In areas where shallow water tables exist, upflow from the water table is considered in the volume and salinity mass balance in the crop root zone.

Local variations in costs and management practices are difficult to account for in these types of models, and thus they often fail to predict actual farmer behavior. Using a calibration technique known as Positive Mathematical Programming (PMP), the WADE agricultural production submodel is adjusted to more closely match observed grower responses. Thus PMP matches model results to observed conditions, taking into account social, institutional, and other factors not commonly accounted for in a grower's crop budget.

Constraints

The linear constraint set to the objective function sets limits to a number of model parameters which include : the total irrigable area within each polygon cell (region); the total area allocated to individual irrigation technologies by crop; the total amount of available surface and groundwater resource; the maximum allowable proportion of drainage recycled; the permissible quantity of irrigation water applied to each crop; the maximum installation rate of subsurface tile drains; total drained area; and crop acreage.

Projections of future agricultural crop acreages made by the WADE model determine future water requirements which need to be met by surface water deliveries, groundwater pumping and drainage recycle. Average annual ET losses, established by the irrigation water districts such as the Westlands Water District, are used to establish seasonal water requirements to be met from these sources. In areas with high concentrations of salts in the groundwater, the model will utilize surface water and employ surface and subsurface recycle systems in preference to groundwater pumping. In these areas, the cost of pumping is added to the incremental loss in benefits associated with irrigating with saltier water, to determine the best strategy. In general, groundwater quality tends to improve from east to west across the western half of the San Joaquin Valley.

Regional strategies of groundwater pumping can reduce drainage production by reducing groundwater tables during the irrigation season. In areas which produce large quantities of drainage water and where the costs associated with drainage treatment and disposal are high, the benefits gained by this strategy may far outweigh any costs associated with irrigating with more saline water and power requirements of pumping.

Summary of findings

Initial results show that conjunctive use of groundwater declines as the salinity of groundwater increases under a system of restricted irrigation water supply. The WADE model continues to make use of groundwater until the salinity of the root zone causes crop yields to slip below target levels. This reversal occurs faster in areas subject to evapoconcentration of salts due to shallow groundwater levels - in these areas groundwater pumping helps to reduce the rate of upward movement of salts during the growing season by lowering water tables. This can offset the increase in salinization of the root zone due to salts contained in irrigation applications of pumped groundwater.

A decline in groundwater use may be accompanied by changes in cropping patterns to allow recovery of soil salinity to within target concentrations. Should future policy options for management of contaminated drainage lead to the imposition of drainage treatment and disposal fees or an increase in water prices, groundwater pumping will become more cost effective and will increase in those areas presently subjected to shallow water tables, before the switch is made to alternative salinity management strategies.

APPENDIX

References

Frind E.O. and G.B. Matanga, 1985. The Dual Formulation of Flow for Contaminant Transport Modeling. 1. Review of Theory and Accuracy Aspects, Water Resources Research, Vol. 21, No.2, pp 159-169.

Hatchett S.A., N.W.T. Quinn, G.L. Horner and R.E. Howitt, 1989. A Drainage Economics Model to Evaluate Policy Options for Management of Selenium Contaminated Drainage. Paper presentation at the Second Pan-American Regional Conference on Irrigation and Drainage, Ottawa, Canada.

San Joaquin Valley Drainage Program, 1989. Preliminary Planning Alternatives for Solving Agricultural Drainage and Drainage-Related Problems in the San Joaquin Valley. Final Report.

CRANES ROOST
LAKE LEVEL MANAGEMENT PROJECT

By Thomas R. Sear [1], P.E., Member, ASCE
and Nicolas E. Andreyev [2], P.E., Member, ASCE

Abstract

An internally drained water body has historically experienced a wide range of lake level elevations due to its function as a regional aquifer recharge area, and due to the urbanized nature of its watershed. A lake level management plan was developed that incorporates the use of treated wastewater effluent for lake level augmentation, and pumped discharges for high lake level control. A hydrogeologic/hydrologic study was conducted to investigate recharge responses to various constant lake level conditions.

Introduction

The City of Altamonte Springs is a rapidly growing Central Florida community located in Seminole County, approximately five miles (8 km) north of the City of Orlando. The principal drainage feature of the downtown area is the land locked Cranes Roost water body; which has a surface area of about 45 acres (18 ha) and is the terminal receiving lake for an approximately 2.74 square mile (7.10 square Km) watershed that contains a variety of urban land uses. Cranes Roost has historically experienced a wide range of lake level elevations due to the lack of a natural drainage outlet and its function as a regional aquifer recharge area; and due to the urbanized nature of its watershed, which can produce high volumes and rates of stormwater runoff. Historic lake level elevations in Cranes Roost have varied over a 20 foot (6.1m) range since December, 1970, when routine lake level recordings began. The City constructed a pump station and force main system for Cranes Roost that can provide discharges to a river located about 1.3 miles (2.1 km) to the west. This pumped discharge system has a capacity of 15.7 cfs (0.445 cms), and is intended to draw down water levels in Cranes Roost following a major rainfall event.

[1]Project Engineer, HOWARD NEEDLES TAMMEN & BERGENDOFF, 5900 Lake Ellenor Drive, Suite 600, Orlando, Florida 32809

[2]Vice President, JAMMAL & ASSOCIATES, INC., 1675 Lee Road, Winter Park, Florida 32789

The City has recently promoted the redevelopment of the downtown area into an attractive urban environment that will feature a park surrounding Cranes Roost. The variable nature of water levels in Cranes Roost, together with the City's concerns relating to aquifer recharge and stormwater management has led to the preparation of the Cranes Roost Lake Level Management Plan. This management plan will allow the city to stabilize lake levels within the Cranes Roost water body, and optimize recharge volumes to the Floridan Aquifer. Lake level augmentation during periods of low water level shall be accomplished through the addition of treated wastewater effluent obtained from the City's reuse water system. The objectives of the Cranes Roost Lake Level Management Plan are summarized below.

1. Establish a set of optimal water level elevations that address aquifer recharge, stormwater management, and urban park aesthetics.

2. Prepare a set of management rules that will recommend the addition of reuse water during low water levels; and pumped discharges during high water levels.

Cranes Roost Watershed

The Cranes Roost watershed is a rectangular shaped drainage area containing approximately 2.74 square miles (7.10 square Km), which drains land surface runoff in a southwesterly direction to the Cranes Roost water body, located near its western limits. The Cranes Roost watershed contains four significant water bodies, numerous wetland areas, and a variety of urban land use types. Stage vs. storage and stage vs. discharge relationships for the various water bodies and wetland areas within the Cranes Roost watershed were created using the best available mapping; and information obtained from a detailed field survey of hydraulic control structures and drainage features.

Historic Lake Level Recording Analysis

Water level elevations in the Cranes Roost water body have been recorded since December, 1970 by the U.S. Geological Survey (USGS), Altamonte Springs, and/or Seminole County. These 18-1/2 years of periodic lake level elevation recordings were plotted versus time, and the resulting graphs were used to determine an average water level elevation for each month of record. The monthly averaged water level elevations were then used to calculate the mean annual lake level elevation for each year from 1971 through 1988. These 18 years of yearly averaged water level elevations were used to create a "cumulative relative frequency distribution diagram" for mean annual lake level elevations in Cranes Roost. Based on this information, average monthly water level fluctuations were determined for low water years (lower 25 percentile years); typical water years (middle 50 percentile years); and high water years (higher 25 percentile years). The resulting monthly averaged water year values for low, typical, and high water years could then be used for long term hydrologic analysis.

Hydrogeologic Modeling

A three-dimensional groundwater flow model was developed to estimate infiltration losses under variable lake levels, and under proposed controlled lake levels. The groundwater flow model utilized was the "Modular Three-Dimensional Groundwater Flow Model" developed by Michael McDonald and Arlen Harbaugh, (USGS, 1984). The Cranes Roost watershed was incorporated into the groundwater flow model, which was subdivided into a grid system that incorporates lake water bodies and upland areas. The model simulated two aquifer systems. The surficial aquifer consisted of the sandy portion of the unconfined aquifer. Layer 2 consisted of the underlying highly transmissive limestone aquifer (Floridan aquifer). The intervening clayey sands and clay layers, where present, were simulated by a leakance value between Layer 1 and Layer 2. Initial hydraulic parameter values for each layer were obtained from site soil investigation and regional geologic data. The model was then calibrated using recorded lake water level fluctuations under both short-term and long-term rainfall runoff conditions. The contributing runoff component from the watershed was estimated from short-term measurement of lake level response to measured rainfall.

After calibration, numerous individual computer runs were conducted to develop a relationship between lake level, potentiometric surface of the limestone aquifer and the associated total infiltration loses out of the lake. From this relationship, an estimate was made of total infiltration losses out of Cranes Roost for variable lake level and potentiometric surface elevation, and for controlled lake level and variable potentiometric surface elevation. This estimate was then tabulated on a monthly basis for a low, typical, and high water year. Depending on the lake level control, the total infiltration losses were calculated for each month and summarized graphically for each of the three statistical years. These results are presented on Figure 1. Comparing the total monthly infiltration losses under uncontrolled lake level conditions with the three proposed controlled lake levels, provides an estimate of the required lake augmentation volume and/or pumping volume out of the lake. The area above the uncontrolled lake level curve on Figure 1 presents the total estimated augmentation volume while the area below the uncontrolled lake level curve indicates the total pumping volume for each statistical year. The control lake levels used in these analyses were elevations 50.0 feet (15.2m), 52.5 feet (16.0m), and 55.0 feet (16.8m).

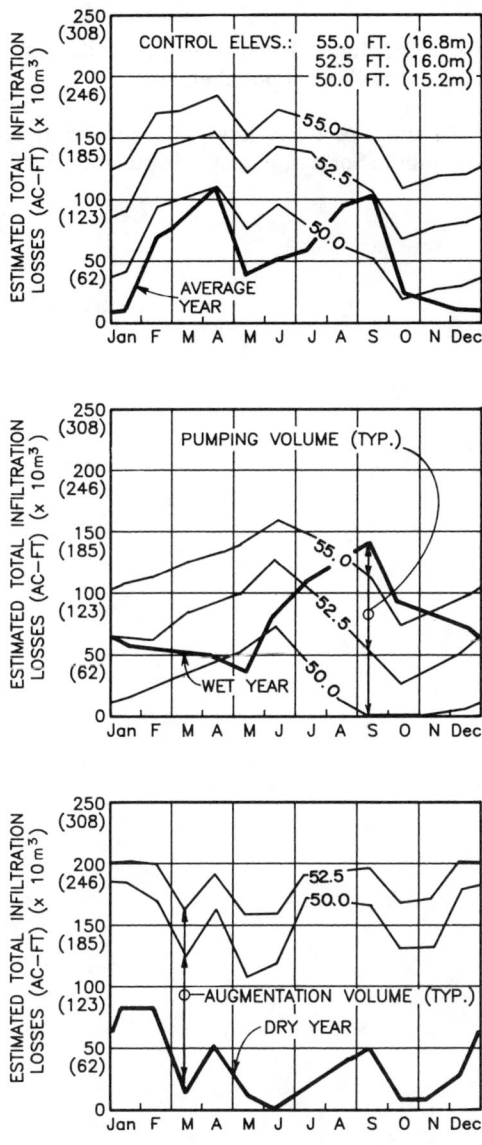

FIGURE 1. RELATIONSHIP OF INFILTRATION, PUMPING, AND AUGMENTATION FOR CRANES ROOST

Appendix I. References:

Jammal and Associates, Inc., "Hydrogeologic Study, Cranes Roost Basin Regional Drainage Facility Plan", September, 1989.

Howard Needles Tammen & Bergendoff, "Cranes Roost Regional Drainage Facility Plan for Altamonte Springs, Florida", September, 1989.

NONPOINT SOURCE POLLUTION CONTROL & LAND USE
William Whipple, Jr., FASCE*

Abstract

Nonpoint source pollution control requires dealing with city, suburban and rural activities, and controlling pollution either at source, by detention basin quality control or by treatment of runoff. New forms of land use planning featuring clustered development may require different solutions for waste disposal and nonpoint source control.

Introduction

Control of nonpoint source pollution (NPS) is basically a reactive process. Research indicates that NPS pollution occurs from a variety of sources, such as automobiles, urban runoff and fertilizer use. Such pollution may be dealt with by stopping it at the source, by settling particulates out in detention basins or, occasionally, by some form of treatment of runoff. Since there has been relatively little done to control NPS (despite the 17 years which have elapsed since passage of the Clean Water Act) there has been relatively little experience in its implementation.

*Coordinator, Nonpoint Source Control
Division of Water Resources, NJDEP
CN-029, 401 East State Street, Trenton, NJ 08625

Land Use and NPS

NPS pollution depends very largely upon land use. Various studies have pointed out or provided data indicating the correspondence between water quality of runoff and land use. (Fam et al 1987; Najarian et al 1986; Heaney 1986; Whipple et al 1987). Multiple family housing, per acre of development, has more pets, more garbage cans, and more automobiles; and, not unexpectedly, it has higher concentrations of bacteria, biochemical oxygen demand, lead and petroleum hydrocarbons than single family housing. City runoff also is relatively highly polluted; but the causes are more complex. City storm sewers generally carry either leakage or storm overflow of sanitary sewers; also there are usually a variety of dispersed spills and leakages from commercial and industrial facilities. In general, however, the same relationship exists: the more intensive the development, the more pollution in the runoff.

Patterns of Development

New patterns of population growth and economic development are now arising, due to the general dissatisfaction with the pattern of big city decay and suburban sprawl. In heavily populated states, housing developments spread across the landscape, have been an unacceptable loss of farmland and open space. For example, from 1970 to 1985, the population of New Jersey grew by almost 5.5 percent; but the six largest cities lost 13 percent (New Jersey, 1988). Between 1950 and 1985, New Jersey lost over half of its farmland; and in the following two years the rate of loss was doubled. Forests, open space and wooded areas were also greatly reduced.

Faced with these trends in New Jersey and elsewhere, planners are advocating new forms of development to replace "suburban sprawl". These plans aim to revitalize the cities and to concentrate suburban development along transportation corridors and in selected hamlets and closely-packed clusters of houses, surrounded by open space.

The principal aspect of this type of development which concerns nonpoint source pollution will be the substitution of clusters of housing developments

separated by open space rather than further
proliferation of more uniformly spaced family
dwellings, each on its own lot. These new planning
patterns are based upon the conviction that closely
packed clusters of housing, surrounded by open
space, are environmentally and socially preferable
to having the same amount of open space divided
among large lots of individual home owners.

Impact of Development Patterns

The immediate impact of such subdivision plans upon
the concentration of pollutants in storm runoff will
be to increase the problem. As brought out above,
the runoff from heavily developed areas and multiple
family dwellings has a much higher concentration of
contaminants than that from single family
dwellings. By appropriate layout of normal single
family dwellings, allowing runoff to flow overland
rather than through curbs, gutters and storm sewers,
the pollution of surface streams can be largely
avoided; and properly dispersed and maintained
septic systems can avoid contamination of
groundwater. To the extent that houses are
clustered, the surface water will be more
contaminated by automobiles, pets, garbage cans and
other family activities; and septic tanks, if used,
may fail.

However, these relative disadvantages can be
overcome. Although closely clustered dwellings
should not have septic tanks, they can be served by
sanitary sewer connections. Storm runoff will need
to be collected and processed through detention
basins with water quality features.

The extra cost of providing these features will be a
normal part of the construction costs, which will
counterbalance savings that would otherwise be made
in the building of streets and layout of utilities.
Therefore, the new types of development are not
inconsistent with nonpoint source pollution control;
provided that the types of NPS control and waste
disposal are appropriately adapted to the
situation. The conditions favoring the new type of
development are social and environmental, and the
cost of adapting to NPS control requirements does
not appear likely to constitute a substantial
impediment to the new concepts. However, provisions

for NPS control will undoubtedly affect layouts.
Some of the preliminary suggestions indicate close
groupings of perhaps 10-15 family dwellings in a
park-like setting. (See Figure 1.) This may prove
to be an inconvenient size. The storm runoff from
such a cluster would contain undesirable
concentrations of various pollutants. The use of
septic tanks would probably be disallowed; while the
provision of sanitary sewage arrangements would be
relatively expensive, due to the small scale. It
will probably be found that larger clusters, or
groupings of a number of clusters not too far apart,
would have considerable cost advantages. The ideal
layouts from an architectural viewpoint may have to
be compromised in some respects. The problems will
not be greater than for the more dispersed layouts;
but they will be different; and engineers and
planners will have to rethink some of the
traditional approaches.

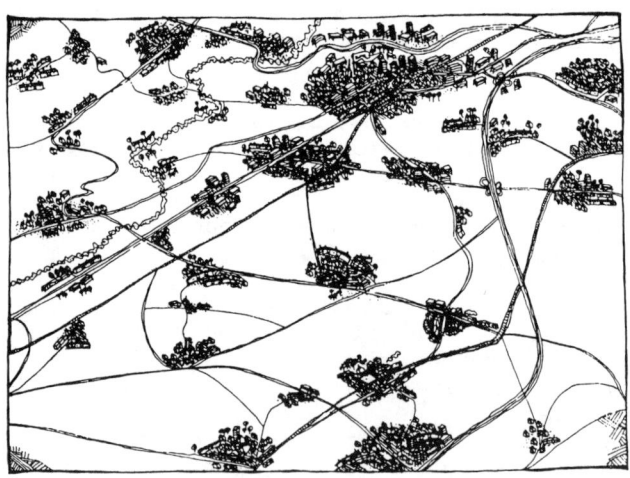

Plan Development Pattern

APPENDIX REFERENCES

1. Fam, Sami, Stenstrom, Michael K and Silverman, Gary "Hydrocarbons in Urban Runoff" Jour. Environmental Engineering 1987 113, 5, 1032-1046.

2. Heaney, James P., "Research Needs in Urban Stormwater Pollution" Journal Planning and Management ASCE 112,1, pp36-47 (1986).

3. Najarian Tavit. O., Griffin, Thomas T., and Gunawardana, Vajiro K., "Development Impacts on Water Quality: A Case Study" Jorunal Planning and Management ASCE 112, 1, 20-35 (1986).

4. State of New Jersey "The Preliminary State Development and Redevelopment Plan for the State of New Jersey" Vol. I. p7, 1988.

5. Whipple, William Jr., Richard Kropp and Susan Burke "Implementing Dual-Purpose Stormwater Detention Basins" Journal of Water Resources Planning and Management, ASCE, 113, 6, Nov. 87 779-92.

Land Use Considerations
and the Siting of Water Facilities

Jeanne Muñoz, Ph.D.[1]

Abstract

Land uses are an important considerion of water districts in the process of facilities siting. The methodology used to evaluate land use sensitivities in a large pipeline alignment study area in southern California is described, and findings are presented in summary form.

Introduction

Water districts in California frequently conduct alternative studies prior to beginning the environmental impact report process required by the State of California Environmental Quality Act (CEQA). These alternative studies or environmental opportunities and constraints analyses provide data and findings for informed decision making to select or refine a project description or to reduce the number of alternative sites or rights-of-way under consideration for a project. The studies may address the full range of environmental issues, but often are limited to those issues that are most constraining, including land uses.

Land uses were recently considered in the evaluation of proposed pipeline alignments for a major southern California water distribution system. The evaluation included the mapping of existing and future land uses and the preparation of a land use sensitivity map for the 1300 square mile pipeline study area. The evaluation resulted in the narrowing of the proposed alignments from 17 to 5 alternatives; additional engineering and environmental review will result in the selection of 1 of those routes as the preferred alternative.

This paper presents the methodology used in the evaluation of the 17 pipeline alignments, including sources of data, mapping

---

[1] Senior Project Manager, ERC Environmental and Energy Services Company, 5510 Morehouse Drive, San Diego, California 92121.

assumptions, criteria for evaluating land use sensitivity, and values assigned to various land uses. The evaluation and ranking of alignments in terms of land use sensitivity is also discussed.

Sources of Data

The primary sources of data for land use evaluations are the land use elements of General and Community Plans within a study area, focusing on present (i.e., 1990) and future (the year 2000, 2005, or 2010, depending on the Plan) land use designations. General Plans and their accompanying map(s) guide future growth and development. Some General Plans are very detailed and contain numerous maps, yet do not provide maps of land use designations for unincorporated communities; other General Plans are very general, but may be accompanied by maps that show land use designations in detail.

Mapping

The maps that accompanied the pipeline alternatives report were prepared under the following assumptions:

- Land uses of less than 100 acres were not mapped, except for known hazards or severe restraints (e.g., hazardous waste disposal sites) and linear facilities (e.g., transportation and utilities corridors).
- Land use development above a particular density presents a constraint for pipeline rights-of-way of 100 feet or more and for trenching for large diameter pipelines; there is no planning benefit in dividing such land uses into refined categories. For this reason, industrial and commercial land uses were treated together as one land use designation, and the categories of residential land uses were combined, resulting in fewer land use designations than is found in many general plans.
- All agricultural lands provide opportunities for buried pipeline projects because the land is largely vacant and can revert to agricultural use following construction.
- Aggregation of land uses that are predominant but discontiguous within a minimum 100-acre area provide useful information at the constraints level of analysis and were therefore mapped as that one land use.
- In cases in which there was a conflict between boundaries mapped by a county and those mapped by a city, the city maps were utilized.
- In cases in which there was a conflict between land use designations mapped by two different jurisdictions, the most restrictive land use (the "worst case") was used.
- Existing residential or commercial land uses that are more constrained than future designated land uses were mapped to represent the existing conditions.

Criteria for Evaluation of Land Use Sensitivity

The land use designations shown on the maps prepared for the report are described below. Included in the descriptions are discussions of sensitivity. The data provided in the available documents were varied, and the use of some of the data required generalization, largely in the form of combining classes or categories that had been divided into disparate units by one agency compared to another.

- **Open Space 1 (OS-1)**. This designation was applied to open spaces that are likely to have relatively few restrictions/constraints, such as United States Forest Service (USFS) land and vacant, undeveloped parcels or golf courses. This land use is less restrictive than uses of other land, and these lands therefore provide an opportunity for large pipeline projects.
- **Open Space 2 (OS-2)**. General plans typically include maps showing lands with physical or other constraints, and designate their use as Open Space. On the map/overlay accompanying the case study report, these constrained lands were labeled OS-2. The category includes landform restrictions (e.g., slopes, floodplains) and restrictions related to resources found in or on the land (e.g., biological, cultural, mineral resources). Many OS-2 lands present constraints that would be prohibitive for a pipeline project.
- **Agriculture/Range Land (AG)**. All agricultural and range lands were mapped under one designation. This category also includes lands that are designated for a maximum density of 1 dwelling unit per 5 acres of land. This land may provide the most opportunity for a pipeline alignment.
- **Government Land 1 (GL-1)**. Local government land is designated GL-1. Land uses include community parks, schools, and civic uses. Some of these lands may provide opportunity for pipeline projects.
- **Government Land 2 (GL-2)**. Federal and state government lands, including military bases, National Monuments, National Parks, designated wilderness areas, state parks and recreation areas, correctional institutions, universities, and Indian lands, were designated GL-2. These lands, by their dedicated nature and use, are more constrained than other government lands.
- **Industrial/Commercial (I/C)**. Industrial and commercial land uses were mapped together because both land uses are intense and both are restrictive for projects requiring wide rights-of-way and large-scale trenching operations.
- **Rural Residential (RR)**. This designation was applied to lands designated for a maximum development of 1 dwelling unit per 2 acres. These lands provide potential opportunity for large pipeline projects.
- **Low Density Residential (LD)**. The low density designation was applied to land on which 1, 2, or 3 dwelling units per acre may be built. This land may be less constrained than that allowing for higher densities of residential development.

- **Low/Medium Density Residential (L/M)**. The low/medium residential land use designation allows for 3 or 4 to 6, 7, or 8 dwelling units per acre (refinement of the number of dwelling units per acre to a more precise classification was impossible because of the variety of criteria used by the various jurisdictions for such classification). Land developed to this density presents constraints for large construction projects of any nature.
- **Medium/High Density Residential (M/H)**. Land on which more than 7 or 8 dwelling units per acre are allowed was designated medium/high residential. Residential land use of this density severely constrains concomitant use of the land for large-scale projects.

Those areas identified as undesignated land use by various jurisdictions were mapped in accordance with existing (1990) land use conditions because existing conditions within these areas are not likely to change in the near future. Other land uses, such as transportation facilities, utility corridors, and waste disposal facilities, were individually designated by name on the maps prepared.

Sensitivity Values

Relative values were assigned for each of the land uses described above to quantify comparisons among the proposed alignments such that higher sensitivity areas received a higher quantitative scoring than lower sensitivity areas. The following were considered in determining value assignments:

- restrictions and constraints associated with open space (OS-2)
- restrictions and constraints associated with government land (GL-1, GL-2)
- number of residents potentially affected (RR, LD, L/M, M/H, SP)
- potential for economic loss (AG, I/C, SP)

The values assigned to the land uses ranged from 0 (lowest sensitivity) to 4 (highest sensitivity). An additional point was added in cases in which an especially sensitive land use occurred. A summary of assigned values by land use designation is shown below:

0	tunnel under nonresidential land
1	OS-1, AG, RR
2	GL-1, LD
3	GL-2, L/M
4	OS-2, M/H. I/C
+1	added to any of the above when an especially sensitive land use (landfill or other disposal site, cemetery, freeway, railroad, airport) occurred within an area; added to tunnels under residential areas (this latter may be an adverse effect that is more perceived than real, but it is ERCE's experience with other water distribution system projects that the public has

Table 1. Summary of Land Use Scores

PIPELINE ALIGNMENT	LENGTH (MILES)	TOTAL SCORE	RANK	NORMALIZED SCORE	RANK
1	40.50	66.75	3	37.45	2
2	40.00	85.50	8	47.97	7
3	37.00	77.75	6	43.62	5
4	37.25	78.75	7	44.18	6
5	37.00	85.50	9	47.97	7
6	36.75	76.50	4	42.92	3
7	37.00	77.50	5	43.48	4
8	43.50	66.75	2	37.45	2
9	43.50	61.50	1 *	34.50	1 *
10	36.25	102.25	10	57.36	8
11	35.75	111.25	11	62.41	9
12	39.25	122.75	12	68.86	10
13	45.50	139.75	15	78.40	13
14	41.25	126.50	13	70.97	11
15	47.50	161.00	16	90.32	14
16	52.75	178.25	17	100.00	15
17	43.75	131.00	14	73.49	12

* least environmentally sensitive, i.e., preferred alignment

serious concerns about construction by tunneling under homes)

These relative values were multiplied by the number of lineal miles of each land use designation within 0.5 mile (on either side) of the proposed alignments in order to compare the relative sensitivity of each alignment. When more than one land use occurred within 0.5 mile of a proposed alignment, the land use with the highest value was recorded for that portion ("worst case" analysis).

Estimates of potential number of residents affected by construction of the pipeline were also provided. The estimates were based on 25.3 acres fronting each lineal mile and on an average parcel depth of 0.5 acre (approximately 100 feet). It was assumed that dwelling units would be constructed on both sides of the alignment. It was also assumed that buildout would be 100 percent, that both sides of a roadway or alignment would be affected equally, and that 20 dwelling units per lineal mile for rural, 100 per lineal mile for low, 160 per lineal mile for low/medium, and 300 per lineal mile for medium/high density residential land uses would be affected. It was assumed that 3.5 persons would reside in each dwelling unit. The values assigned to the various residential land uses include, by definition, these estimates, and therefore no additional weight was assigned to the residential land uses.

Evaluation/Ranking of Alignments

The total value for each alignment was broken down by land use designation and number of miles of each type of land use crossed by each alignment. Values were increased by an additional point for added segments containing especially sensitive land uses. The alignments were ranked comparatively, with the least environmentally sensitive alignment ranked as the preferred alignment (Table 1).

Normalized scores were derived by dividing scores by the highest total score for any one alignment. It was necessary to normalize scores in order to combine the land use findings with the findings from biological, cultural, and paleontological resource analyses. The normalized scores were weighted to reflect potential mitigation factors (land use was allocated 30 percent of the total), and the 17 alignments were reduced to 5 alternatives based on the combined findings.

Conclusions and Recommendations

Existing and future land uses have been and will continue to be an important consideration in the siting of water and other facilities. The analysis of values assigned to land uses should be used in combination with conclusions from similar studies on biological, cultural, and paleontological resources. The combined quantified findings can then be used for informed and defensible decision making.

Real-Time Optimized Control of a Water Distribution System

Bryan Coulbeck[1] and Chun-Hou Orr[2]

Abstract

The paper presents the design of a fully automated real-time computer control scheme for least cost operation of a water distribution system. The scheme includes modules for optimized pump scheduling, water demand prediction, and complete system simulation. A set of real-time modules complement the applications modules to form a sophisticated on-line computer control procedure. The scheme has been implemented as part of an overall management facility for a city distribution network in the United Kingdom.

System Description

Water supply and distribution networks generally consist of large numbers of inter-connecting pipes with occasional control valves, all of which have non-linear relationships between flow and head loss. Reservoir are connected at strategic points throughout the network to provide storage capacity and maintain required pressure levels for the consumer demands. In many regions, boreholes are a typical source of water supply with pumping to the network via pump stations using parallel combinations of fixed and/or variable speed pumps. Booster pumps, together with control valves are normally used for transfer of water between reservoirs of differing pressure zones. In both cases the pump flows are dependent upon the reservoir levels and the costs upon electricity unit and demand charges

---

[1] Professor of Water Control Systems, School of Engineering and Manufacture, Leicester Polytechnic, PO Box 143, Leicester LE1 9BH, England

[2] Director of Water Control Unit, School of Engineering and Manufacture, Leicester Polytechnic, PO Box 143, Leicester LE1 9BH, England

(Coulbeck and Orr, 1988a).

Control Scheme

The basic requirements are for control of pumps and valves in order to supply demand at minimum cost. In addition, reservoir levels must be maintained within prescribed limits to meet emergencies and cater for future demands. The cyclic nature of the demand sets a minimum control period of 24 hours and, for typical reservoirs, control actions need only be considered every one or two hours. Suitable controllers must rely on the limited monitoring of reservoir levels, and pump and pipe flows in order to derive the consumer demands.

For the present system, an optimal control strategy can be calculated which will facilitate control actions over the future 24-hour period, based on the predicted consumer demands and the simplified network model reservoir levels. To cater for errors, the actual values of reservoir levels and derived demands provide up-to-date corrections to the control process. If additional optimization calculations are performed whenever a significant error is detected, the resulting control strategy should be optimal to the end of the control period (Coulbeck and Orr, 1988b).

Demand Prediction

Optimization over a future time period can only be performed for known consumer demands, and a prediction scheme is required which will estimate demand throughout the optimization period. The data available on which to base such estimates are essentially past consumption records, together with an allowance for expected future industrial and domestic demands. The automated demand prediction scheme which has already been developed as part of the project will be briefly described in the presentation.

Optimized Scheduler

The successful application of optimization methods depends significantly upon the formulation of a simplified dynamic network model, together with associated computational procedures, for rapid and repeated evaluation of the effect of control strategies upon the network reservoir levels. Simplified static network solutions are readily available for determination of reservoir flows for known reservoir levels and pumping and demand flows. The slowly varying nature of the reservoir levels allows simplified dynamic solutions to be obtained by repeated static solutions with reservoir levels updated by integration of the reservoir flows.

Since water networks contain storage the optimization problem reduces to minimization of electricity charges over the entire optimization period. The optimized pump scheduler which has been developed as part of the project will be briefly described in the presentation.

Computer Control Implementation

An interface is required between the supply system and the control computer. For fully automated operations, Supervisory Control And Data Acquisition (SCADA) systems can provide a convenient means of transferring measurements and control signals.

Selected telemetry data are supplied to the controller at regular and frequent intervals. Typical data include: quarter-hourly measurements of critical supply pressures, reservoir levels, pump and trunk flows and system control states.

Computed pump schedules are returned to control the supply system operation via the supervisory control actions. Under normal conditions, schedules are transferred every 24 hours, but allowance has been made for intermediate re-computed schedules under abnormal conditions.

Results

Figure 1 gives a typical result for real-time optimized control of the system. The presentation will further illustrate the benefits, which include: least-cost pumping, automated system operations, together with instantaneous and predicted system assessments.

Acknowledgements

The authors would like to acknowledge the financial support of both the Severn-Trent Water Authority and the Science and Engineering Research Council. Thanks are also due to all contributors to the project, with particular reference to: Mr M F Williams, Mr A Elton, Mr L Brammer, Dr M A Parkar, Mr S T Tennant and Miss A E Cunningham.

References

Coulbeck, B and Orr, C H (Ed), *Computer Applications in Water Supply, Vol 1, Systems Analysis and Simulation*. Research Studies Press and John Wiley and Sons, 1988a.

Coulbeck, B and Orr, C H (Ed), *Computer Applications in Water Supply, Vol 2, Systems Optimization and Control*. Research Studies Press and John Wiley and Sons, 1988b.

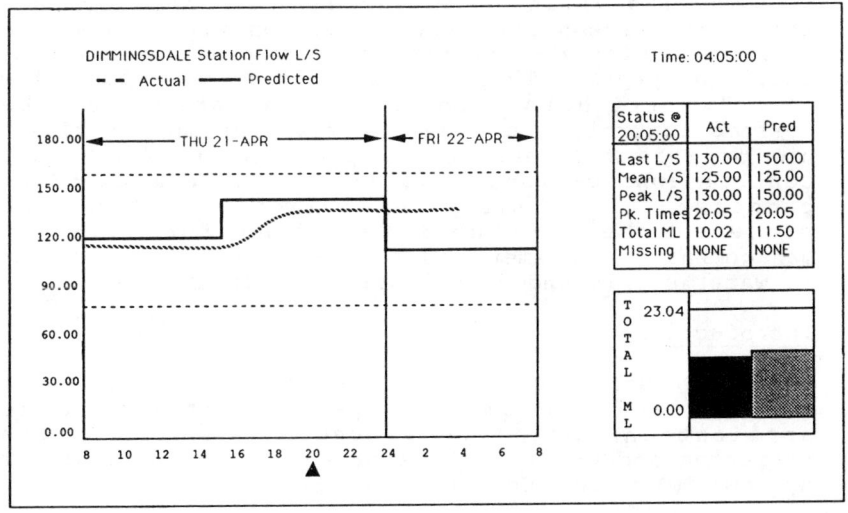

Figure 1

Typical display: actual vs predicted station flow

Telemetry Data Considerations in Water Systems Control

Chun-Hou Orr[1], Bryan Coulbeck[1], Masud Parkar[1] and Steven Tennant[1]

Abstract

The installation of increasingly sophisticated telemetry systems for data collection within the water supply and distribution networks has progressed rapidly in recent years. This has resulted in vast quantities of telemetry data being made available for water systems control. In order to make the most efficient use of this telemetry data, particularly for on-line control applications, the data must be managed and processed efficiently and reliably. This paper presents the main considerations for effective management of telemetry data for control applications in water supply and distribution systems.

Introduction

The establishment of sophisticated, intelligent and reliable telemetry systems has led to new applications being developed for the efficient operation and control of water supply and distribution systems (Orr and Coulbeck, 1989).

The efficient management and reliable processing of telemetry data is vital in order to develop and maintain a cost-effective and robust operational control strategy for water systems. Telemetry data provides the key information required to implement operational strategies. Moreover, for on-line control applications, the problem of processing and managing telemetry data is compounded, since data is received at regular intervals and it needs to be processed within this time interval. There may also be a need to

---

[1] Water Control Unit, School of Engineering and Manufacture, Leicester Polytechnic, PO Box 143, Leicester LE1 9BH, England

prepare time-critical data for transmission to outstations via the telemetry system.

Telemetry Data Management

The processing and management of all activities relating to telemetry data is not a straightforward task. The overall procedure of processing incoming raw telemetry data, archiving the data and transmitting control signals is complex. The complete process of regulating this two-way flow of data needs to be coordinated efficiently in order to maintain a reliable, up-to-date status of the system.

The main considerations for telemetry data management include the type of data coming in, the applications using the telemetry data and the resulting outgoing telemetry data.

Incoming Telemetry Data

The type of incoming telemetry data from water systems would generally include pipe flows, reservoir levels, pump states (ON or OFF), pump speeds, valve positions and pressures. The format of the incoming data is usually system-dependent but, in most cases, this would require reorganizing for interpretation and efficient archiving purposes. The frequency of incoming data can vary from continuous data to daily data on a regular or irregular basis.

It is important to archive telemetry data as received, including any spurious data and null values. The main reason for this is the interpretation relating to each particular data item. It may be, as is often the case, that the raw telemetry data needs to be calibrated prior to being used for analysis purposes. This calibration procedure must be kept separate and applied to the archived data as and when required.

The storage structure for the telemetry data archive must be designed in such a way that access to the most recent data is immediate while access to historical telemetry data can be compromised. In addition, system data, which is not directly related to telemetry data, but may require rapid access must be taken into account when the telemetry archive database is designed. The vast quantity of data associated with telemetry can only be used effectively if a well-designed, robust and efficient database is implemented for storage and retrieval.

Telemetry Data Applications

The incoming telemetry data provides an invaluable information system covering all aspects of the water system and, as such, the applications that can be derived from this database is limitless.

At the basic level, an important application for telemetry data is to provide an information system. The information system can be established to provide operators with an up-to-date system status covering all measurements. There are two main levels of operating an information system. Firstly, the current status of all, or a set (eg on a zonal basis) of data, can be displayed. This is useful for assessing the immediate status of the network and would be the normal mode of operation. The second level of the information system would contain the most recent data regarding each quantity. This would normally be from the start of the current operational period so that any quantity can be investigated in more detail.

The next level up in telemetry data applications includes extensive data processing for demand prediction and system simulation purposes. These applications usually require detailed data covering extensive and varied time periods, so that the particular system can be identified, calibrated and modelled accurately. The demand prediction and system simulation can be carried out in an off-line mode or integrated into an on-line operations environment. For on-line applications, the integrated environment can include the basic information system facility which can be extended to include monitoring.

At the top level of applications using telemetry data, the demand predictor and system simulator can be linked up with a system control procedure for cost-effective and reliable system operation. This level of application can be carried out on-line in order to maximize the benefits offered by implementing such schemes. The most significant difference at this level of systems operation, compared with the first two levels, is that a closed-loop structure for operational control can be implemented. Any discrepancies between actual and predicted system responses can be monitored immediately and cost-effective remedial measures applied promptly in order to maintain an efficient system. Such applications provide a focal point for the incoming telemetry which is rapidly processed to provide control instructions for subsequent operations. This type of closed-loop control application, using standard demand prediction and system simulation techniques, makes the most efficient use of telemetry data, and its implementation is potentially the most beneficial to water systems operation.

Outgoing Telemetry Data

The processing and management of outgoing telemetry data is invariably linked with incoming telemetry data. Control signals, which may need to be transmitted to remote outstations within the network, are derived as a result of incoming telemetry data. The type of outgoing telemetry data may include pump speed settings, valve positions and alarms.

There may also be a need for sending out predicted system parameters such as reservoir levels, pipe flows and pressures, so that local monitoring and regulation strategies can be implemented. In such cases, appropriate alarms can be generated and transmitted in order to signal critical discrepancies between predicted and actual system behaviour.

Conclusions

Recent advances in computer technology have resulted in the implementation of reliable and sophisticated telemetry systems within existing water networks. This single development has resulted in the application of advanced modelling techniques for system simulation, optimization and control. The main purpose of such applications is to implement cost-effective operational control strategies while maintaining an acceptable level of service to consumers (ORR et al, 1988). The key link between the physical water network and advanced control strategies is telemetry data. In order to implement control schemes or improve system operating performance, the telemetry data must be processed and managed efficiently.

Although the management of telemetry data may seem a straightforward task, careful consideration must be given at the design stage to its subsequent use. It is often necessary to determine the ultimate operational strategies in advance so that the telemetry data management can be designed accordingly. Telemetry data is a relatively recent development in water systems and it is imperative that it is used effectively in order to improve the overall operational efficiency of water supply and distribution systems.

References

Orr, C H and Coulbeck, B, <u>Computer Applications in Water Systems in the UK</u>, in Water Resources Planning and Management, ASCE, 1989, pp 653-656.

Orr, C H, Coulbeck, B, Brdys, M and Parkar, M A, <u>Computer Control of Water Supply and Distribution Systems: Structures, Algorithms and Management</u>, in Computer Applications in Water Supply, Vol 2, Research Studies Press, John Wiley and Sons, 1988, pp 392-420.

MetaSite:
Water Distribution System Analysis Software

Ed P. Odom, Jr., P.E.[1], Associate Member, ASCE

Abstract

Many local municipalities now require a network analysis for all proposed additions to their water distribution systems. A graphically oriented, user-friendly program is being developed to aid the engineer in these analyses. The program is currently under development, and its initial use will be to model the water distribution system of Brunswick County, North Carolina. After model calibration and validation, it will be used to provide a masterplan for the system improvements to be implemented over the next twenty years to accommodate this coastal county's rapid development.

Introduction

A new approach to network modeling of water distribution systems is being developed by Stephen Dedalus Incorporated in affiliation with its parent company, the civil engineering consulting firm of William G. Daniel & Associates, P.A.

The computations required for network analysis, while not difficult, are extremely tedious. This has meant that many water system improvements and additions have not been as thoroughly examined as they might have been had an easier technique been available. With the development of the initial generation of computer programs to perform water system analysis, the actual time spent in number-crunching decreased substantially. However, the time required to set up, debug, and evaluate the output from these programs tended to significantly offset the productivity gained by the increased computational speed.

---

[1]Project Manager, William G. Daniel & Associates, P.A., 8000 Regency Parkway, Suite 140, Cary, North Carolina 27511

Computational Method

The Nodal Method (Brater and King, 1976) was chosen to compute pressures and flows throughout the system instead of the more frequently used Hardy Cross algorithm. This avoids the need for the Hardy Cross required loops and pseudo-loops. The Nodal Method also eliminates the need for system initialization with continuity-respecting pipe flows. Its only required initialization consists of junction pressures which are randomly assigned within the normal operating range of a water distribution system.

User Interface

The difficulties associated with describing the water system geometry and analysis parameters as a graphical representation using card images and data fields are eliminated. The entire piping network is shown to-scale on the screen and is a true graphical illustration. Any portions of the system geometry can be viewed in greater detail by zooming and panning the screen image.

Analysis options are selected via mouse-driven menus created for the MetaSite® software package. One menu applicable to the current operation is displayed on the screen. This eliminates the need to search a digitizer tablet containing every system command or having to enter a cryptic keyboard command. A "heads-up" style of operation is achieved which greatly increases productivity.

Model Setup

The system geometry database can be created by digitizing existing system mapping, importing a file from another software or GIS package (*e.g.* AutoCAD® DXF® or Intergraph® SIF), or utilizing the drafting capabilities within the MetaSite package. The only data required for the system piping are the diameters and Hazen-Williams coefficients which can be assigned individually or as a user-specified default. Because the system is drawn to scale, the line lengths and network connectivity are automatically determined from the system's geometric elements and need not be entered. The network model can be as detailed as desired and include all valves, hydrants, *etc.*, or the user can "skeletonize" a major system to model only the larger trunk mains.

Demands are entered as flowrates at discrete points by placing the cursor near the appropriate node and clicking the mouse button. The cursor "snaps to" the nearby node, and the user enters the demand flow. Demands can also be tied to land uses or development levels in defined geographic areas. Future system performance can easily be modeled by changing the population or land use within a specific area to reflect future conditions.

Pump curves from various manufacturers can be viewed on-screen from the built-in library of pumps. These are the standard curves as they appear in the manufacturers' catalogs complete with NPSH, horsepower, impeller and efficiency curves. The user can add or delete pumps in the library.

When a node is specified as a pump station, its pumps can either be selected from the pump library or by entering the pump performance data directly. For a particular analysis scenario the user will specify which impeller is to be used and which pumps will be "on." The individual pump curves are combined to create the composite curve for the pump station. After the analysis run, the pump station operating point can be displayed if desired.

Analysis Results

The resulting network pressures can be displayed as 2-D plots superimposed over the system map on the screen. Areas of low pressure are easily identified. The various system boundary conditions (pump combinations, valve openings, pressure settings for control devices, tank water levels, *etc.*), network geometry, and computed results can be saved for each scenario analyzed for later comparison. Several system improvement scenarios can easily be analyzed in a single session. The system geometry and pressure contours can be plotted for inclusion in an engineering report.

To construct the system improvements, the final design's geometry is annotated and easily converted into plan and profile sheets. Any other project components such as pump station or storage tank site details (fences, drainage works, and access drives) can be added. These can be plotted and used for the construction drawings necessary to bid and build the project.

If the original information was imported from from a municipal GIS database, it can be updated by exporting back to it the details of the system improvements as designed with MetaSite.

Hardware/Software Configurations

The software runs on the Silicon Graphics™ IRIS™ series workstations. This provides extremely rapid computational speeds for the largest networks plus full color, 3-D graphics capabilites.

The water system program is available in a stand-alone version containing the drafting, plotting, and computational capabilities to lay out and analyze a distribution system. Or, if a firm requires the complete MetaSite civil engineering package, the water system analysis program is contained as one of its design components.

Future Versions

The first revision to the initially released program will be a minor modification to account for fitting losses. Standard user-changable coefficients will be included in a library to model the minor losses from fittings such as throttled valves, reducers, and bends. Also, provisions for user-specified additions to the fitting library will be added. While not necessary for the Brunswick County study where fitting losses are a negligible portion of the overall head loss, this will allow smaller networks such as a building's sprinkler system to be modeled where these losses are significant.

The ability to view the computed pressure contours in 3-D will be added utilizing the graphics capabilites of the hardware and MetaSite.

Another feature will allow a node to be declared a pump station but without specifying the particular pumps. The pump library would be searched and the most appropriate combination selected based on user-specified parameters. For example, the parameters could require that a minimum of three pumps from the same manufacturer be selected.

A major enhancement will add an extended period simulation modeling capability. After incorporating the ability to model pressure switches, changing tank and reservoir water levels, pump starts and stops, and demands varying over time, the designer can simulate the operation of a system through an extended period.

Summary

The MetaSite analysis program will significantly increase the efficiency of analyzing water distribution systems. The capability to graphically modify system components will greatly contribute to the program's ease of use and to the user's productivity. The ability to immediately review analysis results, modify the system accordingly, and immediately reanalyze the revised system will allow the parameters of an optimum system for a particular set of boundary conditions to be very quickly determined.

References

Brater, E. F., and King, H. W. (1976). *Handbook of Hydraulics*. McGraw-Hill, New York, N.Y.

MetaSite is a registered trademark of Stephen Dedalus Incorporated.
Silicon Graphics and *IRIS* are trademarks of Silicon Graphics, Inc.
AutoCAD and *DXF* are registered trademarks of AutoDesk, Inc.
Intergraph is a registered trademark of Intergraph Corporation.

On Obtaining Best Compromise Solutions for
Municipal Water Use

Ronald K. Williams [1] M.ASCE and G. Padmanabhan[2] M.ASCE

Abstract

Providing water and wastewater services to industries at acceptable costs is a major concern for industrializing municipalities. Approaches to determine the "best" use of available resources, including reuse of treated effluent streams have frequently relied on optimization techniques which seek to minimize one desision parameter, such as cost to the city. In a real-world situation however, several competing decision parameters must be weighed simultaneously to find a "best compromise" solution. Such an optimization problem was formulated as a multiple objective decision making (MODM) model using surrogate worth trade-off (SWT) approach. Solutions of the non-linear optimization problem were obtained for SWT analysis by using a powerful and very user-friendly optimization package, General Algebraic Modelling System (GAMS). The model was applied to the city of Moorhead, MN.

Introduction

Urban water use has been an engineering concern historically. The problem is to provide an adequate supply of water, meeting demands for both quality and quantity, at an acceptable cost to the user. When an industry considers locating in a city, it must consider levels of treatment required in that area and whether the local government can help it meet those requirements, either using existing treatment facilities, or through a program of water reuse by participating industries. To be competitive, the city must offer a package of incentives which might include a city-wide plan for water use, wastewater treatment and potential reuse of waste streams. The developemnt of such a plan and the methodology to optimize it is addressed in this paper. Given the quantity and quality of all sources, process demands and waste streams generated by industries, a model is developed to provide

---

[1]Lecturer and [2]Associate Professor, Department of Civil Engineering North Dakota State University, Fargo, ND 58105

the city with a plan to meet each demand and ensure adequate treatment for each effluent prior to discharge, at a cost acceptable to the city and the participating industries (best compromise solution). Such a model will be useful for industrializing cities which have a small tax-base and a greater need for low-cost alternatives in offering incentives to industries.

The model developed is demonstrated using the City of Moorhead, Minnesota as a typical example. Moorhead presently has only two industries of significant size - American Crystal Sugar (ACS) processing sugar beets and Anhueser-Busch malting barley; but would like to attract more. The locations of sources, industries and water/wastewater treatment facilities of the city are shown in Fig. 1. The major sources are Red River of the North, Moorhead aquifer and Buffalo aquifer. A schematic representation of the system is shown in Fig. 2.

Multiple Objective Model

The problem was formulated as a multiple objective nonlinear programming problem with three objectives - minimizing total cost of water and wastewater services to the City, Busch and ACS. Total costs included costs of delivery and treatment of raw water, pumping of treated water to other industries, pumping untreated effluent or treated wastewater from another industry for reuse and costs to treat wastewater. Costs also included payments made to another industry less payments received from other industries. Capital costs of existing facilities were not included since the recovery of the capital is a part of each industry's cost of normal operation. The constraints included total available flow from all sources in relation to total demands, continuity of flows through the system, reuse of effluent streams by industries and required quality of influents to and effluents from different industries. The model itself is not presented here for want of space.

Surrogate Worth Trade-off method is used for obtaining the 'best-compromise' solution. However, to obain such a solution, one of the objectives must be optimized holding the other two at several fixed levels and the solutions thus obtained will have to be ranked based on the preference of decision makers (DM). Solutions for the ranking were obtained by using a powerful and very user-friendly optimization Personal Computer package, General Algebraic Modeling System (GAMS).

Surrogate Worth Trade Off Decision Making

The objective levels and marginals obtained by optimizing the city's cost, keeping the costs to the other two industries at different fixed levels were presented to a DM and his preference on a scale of -5 to 5 were recorded as shown in Table 1. Then, multiple linear regression was used to fit two linear equations relating the costs to city and Busch with SWT and costs to city

MUNICIPAL WATER USE 263

CITY	BUSCH		CRYSTAL	
LEVEL	LEVEL	SWT	LEVEL	SWT
1,131,000	800,000	-5	400,000	0
933,000	800,000	-5	600,000	0
876,000	700,000	-5	700,000	-5
1,049,000	700,000	-3	500,000	-4
946,000	500,000	1	700,000	-3
1,226,000	500,000	0	400,000	0
1,024,000	430,000	3	700,000	-4
1,100,000	430,000	5	600,000	-1
1,305,000	430,000	0	400,000	0

Table 1. Ranking by DM

Regression Output:	City/Busch		City/Crystal	
Constant	5.207481		4.583337	
Std Err of Y Est.	0.771109		3.142407	
R Squared	0.851348		0.525147	
Observations	9		9	
Degrees of Freedom	6		6	
Ranking related to:	Busch	Crystal	Busch	Crystal
X Coefficient(s)	-9.8E-06	-3.8E-06	3.39E-06	-1.4E-06
Std Err of Coef.	1.71E-06	2.06E-06	4.75E-06	5.7E-06

$0 = -9.8E-06 \times BUSCH - 3.8E-06 \times CRYSTAL + 5.207481$
$0 = 3.39E-06 \times BUSCH - 1.4E-06 \times CRYSTAL + 4.583337$

Solving simultaneously yields: BUSCH = 368,540
CRYSTAL = 426,961

Table 2. Multiple Regression Equations

	CITY	BUSCH	CRYSTAL
Raw Water Drawn From:			
Red River	3.068		
Moorhead Aquifer	0.343		
Buffalo Aquifer	-----		
Total	3.410		
Available treated volume	3.137		
Sanitary Water Use	2.678	0.001	0.012
Plus I/I	0.787	0.000	0.004
Less consumption	0.733		
Less WPR	0.028		0.008*
	-----	-----	-----
Discharge to city	2.704	0.001	0.000
Process Water Use			
Drawn from city		0.001	0.447
Effluent reuse		0.006	0.052
Treated waste reuse		0.000	0.000
Reuse from other ind.		0.907	0.000
		-----	-----
Demand Volume		0.914	0.499
Plus generated			0.547
Less consumption		0.055	0.465
Less effluent reuse		0.006	
		-----	-----
Discharged to city		0.853	
Discharged to Crystal			0.581
Waste Volume Treated	3.557	0.000	0.581

Note: Crystal's flume process is not shown. This process draws all it's demand flow from in-house effluent reuse.

* Effluent reuse to flume process

Table 3. Best Compromise Solution Flows

and ACS with corresponding SWT. These equations were solved simultaneously to obtain Busch's cost = $365,500 and ACS's cost = $427,000 (Table 2). These values can be entered back into GAMS and a new minimum of city's cost can be obtained. Strictly this should be the 'best compromise' solution. However, in this case since the DM selected rankings of zero for both trade offs when the costs for Busch and ACS were $430,000 and $400,000 these values were returned to the DM as the model's choice of 'best compromise' solution. The corresponding values of major decision variables are given in Table 3.

Conclusions

The model developed in this study seeks the 'best compromise' solution to a problem of optimizing the cost of water and wastewater services to more than one water user in an interconnected water system of a city. The model is generic enough to include prospective industries considering to locate in the city. Although studies were made by including at least one prospective industry considered highly likely to locate in the city, no discussion of that part of the study is included here. However, the usefulness of the approach to optimize the cost of providing municipal water for major users in an industrializing city has been demonstrated.

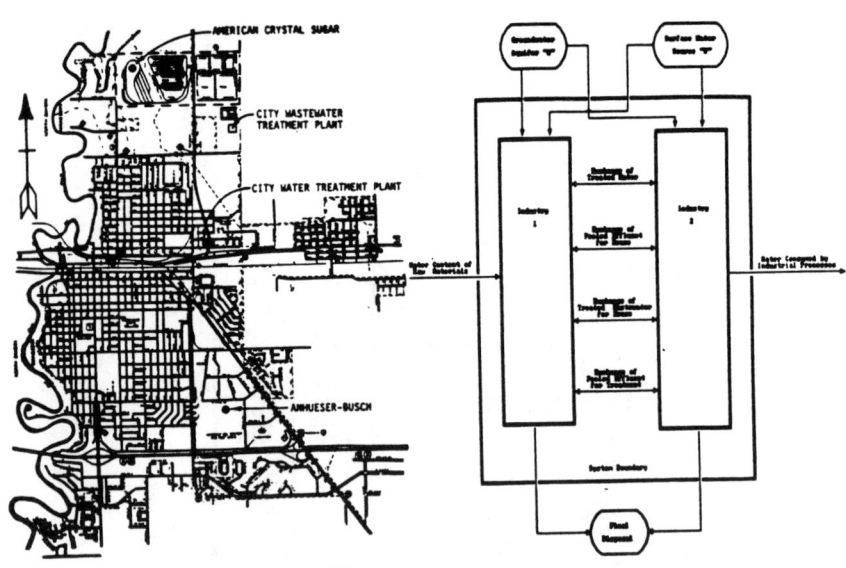

Figure 1. Location Map   Figure 2. Schematic

THE IMPACT OF THE MORRIS SHEPPARD DAM EXPERIENCE ON BUTTRESS DAM SAFETY EVALUATIONS

Jerry L. Foster, 1/ M.ASCE

Abstract

The stability problems encountered at the Morris Sheppard Dam have had an impact upon the Federal Energy Regulatory Commission's (FERC) dam safety program. This paper describes FERC's involvement in the evaluation of the project's stability and discusses the increased emphasis placed upon the evaluation of all buttress dams under FERC jurisdiction inspired by the Morris Sheppard experience.

Introduction

FERC's Part 12 inspection program requires the owners of licensed and exempted non-federal hydropower projects to retain a qualified independent engineering consultant to inspect all dams more than 32.8 feet (10 meters) in height; or which impound more than 2000 acre-feet (2.5 million cubic meters); or which have been rated as having a high hazard potential. The Morris Sheppard Dam was inspected under this program by Freese and Nichols, Inc. Observations made during this inspection, a concern for the optimistic design assumptions, and questions concerning the validity of existing piezometer data led the consultant to request that additional piezometers be installed. This was the beginning of a comprehensive geotechnical, hydrologic and structural evaluation of the dam which ultimately led to remedial measures to stabilize the structure. In addition, The experience gained at the Morris Sheppard Dam led FERC's Division of Dam Safety and Inspections (D2SI) to begin an in-depth review program of all buttressed dams aimed at identifying licensed or exempted project structures which may have similar problems.

---
1. Structural Engineer, Division of Dam Safety and Inspections, Federal Energy Regulatory Commission, Washington, D.C.

History of Buttress Dams

Buttressed dam, and a special type of buttressed dam the Multiple Arch (Multi-arch) dam, construction was popular in the United States between 1900 and the end of World War II. The popularity of buttressed dams relative to other types of concrete dams was due primarily to two factors: The savings in material costs, especially cement, coupled with the low cost of labor during this period; and the development of reinforced concrete design techniques.
The flat slab buttressed dam, or Ambursen Dam, was by far the most common type of buttress dam built in the United States. It was usually comprised of a simply supported reinforced concrete face slab, inclined at 45 to 50 degrees in the downstream direction. Buttresses were initially designed as cantilevered beams and later as bearing walls with consideration given to lateral buckling. Struts, or other measures, were often placed between buttresses to reduce the unbraced lengths of the buttress and thereby mitigate buckling concerns.
Approximately 400 concrete buttress dams of all types were constructed in the United States, of that number only 207 are in existence today, many of which are less than 30 feet (9.15 m) in height. There are about 35 multi-arch and 64 flat slab dams over 30 feet in height still in operation. (Legas, 1988). 2.6 percent of the buttress dams built prior to 1969 failed, and 46 percent of all concrete dam failures were buttress dams. This failure rate exceeds by far the rate for all other types of dams, including embankments (NRC, 1983).

Morris Sheppard Dam

The Morris Sheppard Dam is owned and operated by the Brazos River Authority (licensee) and is located on the Brazos River approximately 70 miles (112.7 km) west of Ft. Worth, Texas. It is an Ambursen dam, with an overflow spillway that utilizes a downstream face slab and an embankment section that forms the right abutment of the dam. The dam was inspected under FERC's Part 12 program during the period December 9-12, 1986 by Freese and Nichols, Inc. On April 3, 1987, the licensee informed FERC that the consultants' preliminary investigations, conducted in accordance with the requirements of Part 12, had revealed potential stability problems which made it prudent to take immediate action to increase the factor of safety against sliding. The licensee noted that they were in the process of lowering the lake level to elevation 992 feet (302.43 m) msl, or 8 feet (2.44 m) below the normal operating level of 1000 feet (304.80 m) msl, as an immediate measure to reduce the loads on the structure. The Director, Division of Dam Safety and Inspections, after reviewing the available field data, ordered the lake drawn down an additional 5 feet (1.52 m) to elevation 987 feet (300.83 m) msl, and that a minimum of four spillway gates be maintained in an open position. The lake was maintained at the 987 feet msl level until April 26, 1988, when the required remedial measures had progressed sufficiently to allow the lake to be safely raised to elevation 995 feet (303.3 m) msl, and was ultimately allowed to return to normal level on June 6, 1989.

The problems encountered at Morris Sheppard were unusual; The spillway portion of the buttress dam had moved downstream as much as 4.5 inches (11.43 cm) since construction; high uplift pressures existed on a nearly horizontal weak shale zone approximately 30 feet (9.14 m) beneath the buttress footings, and a significant portion of the passive resistance downstream of the spillway had been eroded away during a flood in 1941.

Problems Unique to Buttress Dams

Several other buttressed dams under FERC jurisdiction were under evaluation at about the same time as the Morris Sheppard dam. Many of the problems encountered at these projects were the same as those experienced at other types of dams and hydraulic structures, i.e. stability problems; maintenance problems; increased loading conditions due to changes in criteria; foundation problems; etc.. However, it was discovered that buttressed dams suffer from a unique set of problems due primarily to the nature of their design and the concrete technology available during the period they were constructed.

The most common problem encountered is extreme concrete deterioration due to freeze/thaw cycles, environmental conditions, corrosion of reinforcement or alkali reactivity. This is a critical problem for buttress dams since they are constructed of relatively thin reinforced members where the loss of even a few inches of concrete to deterioration can have a great impact upon the strength and safety of the structure. Unfortunately, many of the techniques used in modern concrete structures to control cracking and increase durability were not developed at the time most buttressed dams were built. Use of the water-cement ratio as a tool for estimating strength and its impact on the heat of hydration was recognized about 1918, and the effect of air entrainment upon durability was not recognized until the 1940's. Since many buttressed dams were built during the early 1900's, the lack of air entrainment explains many of the freeze/thaw problems, and the lack of control of heat of hydration explains many of the cracking problems observed.

Uplift theory was evolving during the early 1900's, and many dam designers felt that buttress dams were not subject to uplift loads because of the relatively narrow buttress footings, and the lack of a slab between the footings. The assumption was made that any head differential below the footings would be rapidly dissipated to atmospheric pressure at the rock surface between footings. This assumption does not have a significant effect on the stability analyses of these structures as long as the critical potential failure plane is at the rock-concrete interface. However, for dams were the post construction investigations have revealed critical failure planes within the foundation, or slabs constructed between buttresses, this assumption has had an adverse impact upon stability. The uplift force on the failure plane in the foundation, or on the slab between buttresses at the interface, can be large enough to reduce the net vertical forces on these relatively light structures to a level at which sliding failure is indicated.

Most older dams evaluated by current hydrologic standards are found to have inadequate spillway capacity resulting in higher reservoir levels than anticipated in the original design. Buttress dams subjected to higher than design reservoir levels and possibly overtopping during flooding are especially susceptible to damage. The thin buttress footings transmit higher stresses to the foundation than conventional gravity structures, therefore the loss of bearing area due to erosion could result in overstressing of the footing leading to a sliding or overturning failure of the buttress. Even small differential movement between buttresses could cause failure of the upstream slab or significant leakage at the joint between the slab and buttress. In addition, Surcharging the reservoir to a level above the design elevation can result in increased stress in the upstream slab. These slabs are usually designed to be of variable thickness to coincide with the load on the slab which is a function of the reservoir depth. Therefore the upper portion of the slab is usually thinner than the lower portion. The upper portion of the slab is also more susceptible to freeze-thaw damage and erosion due to reservoir operation, so even a small increase in load coupled with the loss of a few inches of concrete to deterioration can lead to a significant change in slab stresses from the design conditions (Foster, 1988).

Impact on FERC Projects

Based upon the experience gained at the Morris Sheppard dam and other projects with similar problems, The Division of Dam Safety and Inspections began a detailed program of re-evaluation of all buttressed dams under FERC jurisdiction. This was accomplished by first conducting a survey of all existing concrete dams in the dam safety inventory to identify the slab and buttress or multi-arched dams. A tracking system was developed to monitor these dams. Secondly, a revision to the "Operating Manual for Inspection and Supervision of Licenses, Permits and Exemptions" was issued which outlined the experience recently gained and documented procedures for evaluating the safety of constructed slab and buttress dams. Finally, the regional offices were asked to review the dams in their area of the country and increase the level of inspection by examining the potential problem areas identified at other projects.

In addition to the increased inspection emphasis by FERC staff, owners of licensed buttress dams were notified by letter that these structures were undergoing a reevaluation. This letter emphasized FERC's concern that there were some inherent problems with buttress dams and cited specific problem areas. The owners were also informed that additional analyses and, concrete and/or foundation drilling may be necessary to satisfy FERC concerns in upcoming Part 12 inspections.

Table 1 shows the current status of buttress dams in the tracking system. This table shows that more than 60 percent of the high or significant hazard buttress dams surveyed have been, or are under, repair. It should be noted that the survey only included dams covered by the Part 12 Inspection program, therefore many low hazard or small dams which have been repaired, or which are badly deteriorated are not included in the repair numbers.

Table 1

Buttress Dams Under FERC Jurisdiction 1/

Type Dam	Number	High Hazard 2/	Dams Repaired 3/
Slab and Buttress	83	53	31
Multi-Arched	22	20	13
Totals	105	73	44

1/ Dams Licensed, exempted or application pending.
2/ Includes significant hazard dams. Low hazard dams may not fall under Part 12 Inspection Program.
3/ Includes dams repaired prior to survey and dams under repair.

The majority of the dams requiring repair suffered from extensive concrete deterioration. Table 2 shows the primary cause of the remedial repairs to the high or significant hazard dams identified in the survey.

Table 2

Primary Cause of Repairs to Buttress Dams

Type Dam	Concrete		Foundation		Other
	Freeze/Thaw	Cracking	Uplift	Erosion	
Slab and Buttress	20	5	1	2	6
Multi-Arched	9	2	1	-	1
Totals	29	7	2	2	7

Deterioration of concrete has resulted in a wide range of remedial measures including: guniting of buttress and slab surfaces; epoxy grouting of cracks; complete replacement of slabs and/or buttresses; filling of the area between buttresses with concrete and complete dam replacement. Foundation problems encountered range from erosion of buttress footing support due to overflow, to the discovery of zones of high uplift pressures along failure planes below the dam-foundation interface.

Conclusions

The generally poor condition of buttress dams built in the Untited States prior to the development of modern concrete technology demonstrates the need to carefully evaluate the safety of these structures. Any safety evaluation of a buttress dam must consider their unique design concepts including; varying the upstream slab thickness to coorespond with the loading and the assumption that uplift below buttress footings is rapidly disapated due to the relative thinness of the footing.

References

1. Foster, J.L., "Rehabilitation of Buttress Dams", Proceedings of the Structural Engineers Conference, Corps of Engineers, St. Louis, Mo., July, 1988.

2. Legas, J, "Concrete Buttress Dams", Section 4 of "Development of Dam Engineering in the United States", Edited by W.L. Chadwick and E.B. Kollgaard, Pergamon Press 1988.

3. National Research Council, "Safety of Existing Dams, Evaluation and Improvement", National Academy Press, Washington, DC, 1983.

RESTORATION OF A BUTTRESS DAM

Mr. Robert A. Thompson, III, P.E., Fellow ASCE[1]
Dr. Ronald H. Waters, P.E., Member ASCE[2]

Abstract

Morris Sheppard Dam is a major dam on the Brazos River some 25 miles northwest of Mineral Wells, Texas. It is licensed to generate electrical power and, therefore, subject to the regulation of the Federal Energy Regulatory Commission (FERC). In compliance with FERC's Part 12 Inspection Program, the Brazos River Authority (BRA) employed Freese and Nichols, Inc., as an independent consultant to perform a complete site inspection of all project works. This inspection, conducted in December of 1986, and subsequent investigations revealed serious defects in the dam and its foundation. Piezometric pressures below the spillway buttresses greatly exceeded the assumptions of no uplift used in the original design. Certain buttresses along the south side of the spillway had moved downstream as much as 4.5 inches. This movement had sheared the connection between the upstream toe wall/water seal and transition beam forming the footing for the upstream deck panels. This movement was enough to crack the hearth and its deflector toe wall downstream of these buttresses. Erosion downstream of the hearth had weakened the sliding resistance of 7 buttresses and the spillway was inadequate to pass the Probable Maximum Flood. This paper summarizes the major features of the investigation and restoration effort for this high hazard classification dam.

Introduction

Morris Sheppard Dam is one of the first massive buttress flat-slab dams constructed in the United States (Figure 1). It is 190 feet high and 2,740 feet long (including the terminal dike) and was designed to raise the water 130 feet from the original river level to

---
[1]Vice President, [2]Project Manager, Freese and Nichols, Inc., 811 Lamar St., Ft. Worth, Texas 76102

MORRIS SHEPPARD DAM
(POSSUM KINGDOM PROJECT)
FIGURE I

BUTTRESS DAM RESTORATION

a normal pool elevation of 1000. The non- embankment portion of Morris Sheppard Dam is 1,626 feet long and includes a 720 foot longservice spillway. The dam was constructed for the Brazos River Authority by Lytle-Johnson Construction Company at a cost of $9 million. Possum Kingdom Lake, which is formed by the dam, was first filled in May of 1941, and is used primarily for water supply, electrical power generation and recreation.

The design of Morris Sheppard Dam utilizes the weight of the structure and impounded water to stabilize the dam against overturning and sliding. This concept was first employed for reinforced concrete buttress dams by Nils F. Ambursen at Theresa, New York, in 1903. This basic type of flat-slab and buttress dam has since borne the name of its inventor and has been used on over 390 dams in the United States and around the world.

The principal structural components of the buttress dam include reinforced concrete flat-slab lake wall panels and massive concrete buttresses (Figure 2). The 40 triangularly shaped massive buttresses are spaced on 40-foot centers and form thick concrete walls proportioned to transmit the water load and the weight of the structure to the foundation rock. The base of each buttress is integrally connected to a thick concrete spread footing designed to interface with the foundation rock and sustain the dam's gravity and overturning loads. The lake wall panels are supported at the buttresses on thickened corbels and span between the buttresses. These panels are keyed into the buttresses and thus transfer their water load and weight entirely to the buttresses. The lake wall panel and buttress connections at the corbels are articulated to allow for temperature expansion and some vertical or horizontal displacement between buttresses without losing the water seal or inducing moments in the buttress corbels. The lake wall panels tie into a transition beam which serves as a seating for these panels and a cap for the upstream toe wall.

The dam's 720-foot service spillway is controlled by nine roof-weir crest gates. The downstream side of the spillway buttresses is covered by reinforced concrete deck panels, similar in design to the lake side panels. The concrete spillway utilizes a combination of raised and flat roller buckets with a hearth and deflector to dissipate the velocity head generated during spillway discharge.

The rock strata in the vicinity of the dam is comprised of several thick beds of hard limestone, grading into the Wolf Mountain shale. The buttress footings were usually set on the blue shale, but along the south abutment many footings are on the sandstone overlying the shale. To control seepage under the dam, a 35-foot deep concrete toe wall was saw-cut into the shale at the upstream toe of the dam.

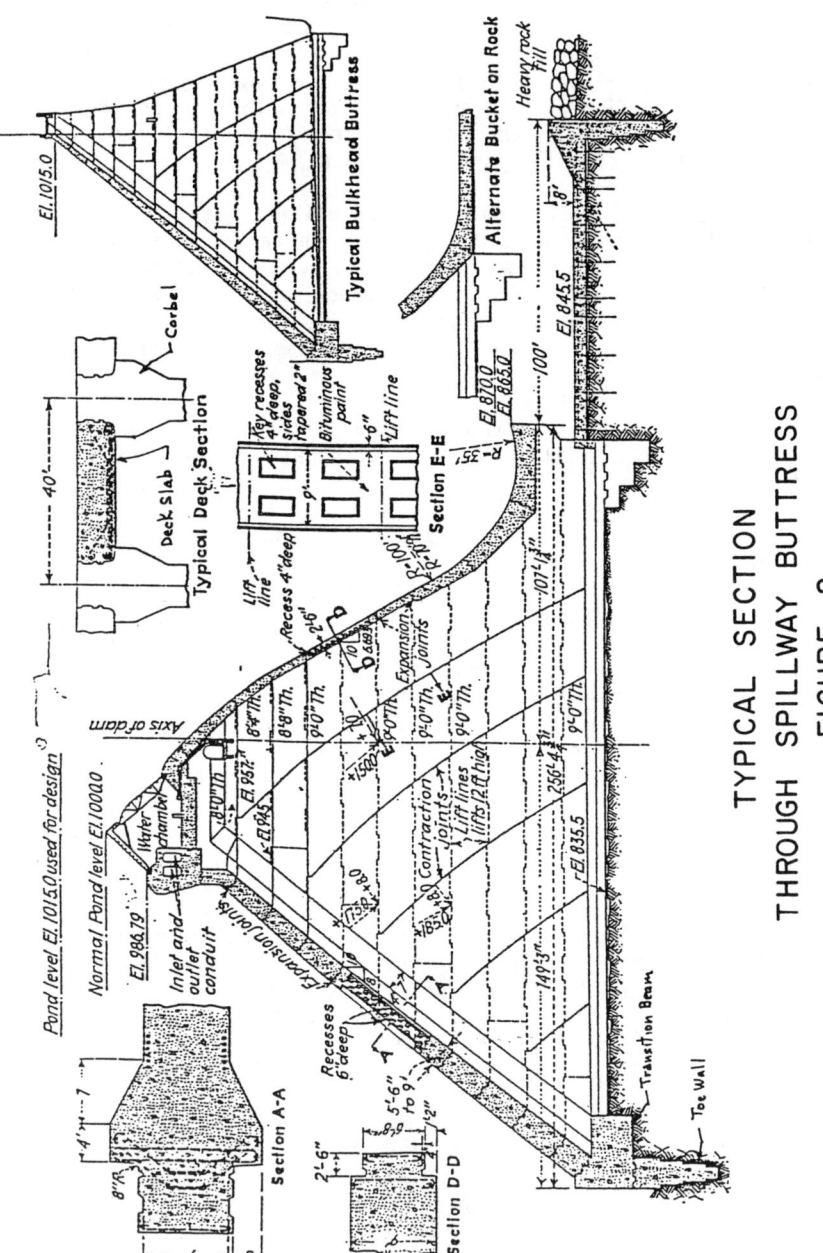

TYPICAL SECTION
THROUGH SPILLWAY BUTTRESS
FIGURE 2

Weep holes and foundation drains for the buttress footing were also provided.

Findings and Restoration Work

In April of 1987, the Brazos River Authority lowered the lake level of Possum Kingdom from the normal pool elevation of 1000 to elevation 987 after the routine 5-year inspection found excessive piezometric pressures in the foundation shale and indications that portions of the spillway had shifted downstream as much as 4-1/2 inches from its original alignment. The reservoir was lowered to reduce the driving force acting on the dam and immediately increase the dam's stability. Concurrent with this lowering of the reservoir, the BRA initiated emergency construction and geotechnical contracts to access the spillway bays, extend the geotechnical investigation and install relief wells across the service spillway.

The construction and geotechnical investigation proceeded concurrently. A footing level 8-foot diameter passageway was drilled through the buttresses into the enclosed spillway bays. Once the passageway had been constructed, each bay was mucked out and filled with crushed gravel to form a working platform for relief well and instrumentation installation. As the working platform was constructed, additional instrumentation and piezometers were installed further upstream in the spillway bays. In total, 132 piezometers, 10 inclinometers and 18 extensometers were installed to monitor the dam's piezometric pressure and movement.

The progression of the access passageway and the gravel working platform allowed the installation of a relief well curtain across the upstream end of the bays forming the service spillway. The relief well curtain was designed to consist of 6-inch diameter relief wells spaced every 13 feet; however, as the wells were installed in the region of buttresses 14 to 19 high pressure flows of up to 500 gallons per minute were encountered which necessitated installing additional wells in these bays. A total of 146 wells, some as large as 12 inches in diameter, were installed without effectively stabilizing the piezometric pressures.

A series of exploratory core holes were drilled into the upstream end of Bays 14 and 15 in an attempt to isolate the entry point of the relief well flows. These holes indicated that the flow was entering the dam's foundation in the vicinity of Buttress 14. These core holes also encountered a high pressure flow and diagonal crack at the interface of the concrete transition beam and toe wall. After considering the various grouting techniques available for sealing this crack, the use of a sodium silicate grout accelerated by cement was selected and a series of primary and secondary grout holes were installed. The typical set time for the primary grouting effort was approximately 1 minute. Prior to beginning the primary grouting effort, the total flow from the relief wells in Bays 14, 15 and 16 was on the order of 550 gallons per minute. After the primary grouting effort these flows were reduced to 12 gallons per minute. The reduction in flow was accompanied by a corresponding reduction in the foundation piezometric pressures as measured by numerous piezometers. The secondary grouting effort further reduced the relief well flow from 12 gallons per minute to 2 gallons per minute. In some of the secondary grout holes which exhibited low flows, neat cement was used to seal off the crack and flow zone. This combination of sodium silicate and neat cement grouting was very successful in sealing off the flow zone entering the foundation near Buttress 14 and did not affect the existing relief well curtain or the piezometers monitoring the foundation conditions.

In June of 1989 permission was obtained to raise the lake back to the normal pool elevation. While the service spillway piezometric pressures are stabilizing and the grouting program is being evaluated for long-term effectiveness under full lake head, the BRA has elected to proceed with construction of a new 1,400-foot wide emergency spillway and the stabilization of the eroded area downstream of the south section of the service spillway. This construction effort will also modify the 9 spillway gates to accommodate the loads consistent with a probable maximum flood. The construction effort involving the new emergency spillway is currently scheduled to begin in November 1989. The remaining portion of the construction effort involving adding additional ballast to the service spillway will follow under separate contract, possibly beginning as early as May of 1990. The total cost of this restoration effort could exceed $30 million.

Summary

The restoration effort at Morris Sheppard Dam is an outstanding example of how a thorough 5-year inspection, performed as part of the BRA/FERC inspection program, led to the detection of the failure in progress of a major high hazard dam. The problems encountered were complex and involved many disciplines such as public relations, hydrology/hydraulics, structural engineering, geology, geological engineering, civil engineering, precise surveying, grouting, biology, geophysics and construction technology. The success of the program to date is due in large measure to the responsible, timely and open action of the Brazos River Authority.

Morris Sheppard Dam:
A Rational Approach to Stability Analysis

John A. Focht, Jr., P.E., Fellow, ASCE[1]
Robert P. Ringholz, P.E., Associate Member, ASCE[2]

Abstract: This paper details the excessive foundation piezometric conditions found during a routine five-year inspection which are believed to have caused a section of the dam to move downstream and presents the results of an "as is" backfigured stability analysis of a critical buttress using the dam's performance as a full-scale load test for determining strength parameters. It then summarizes the multiple sets of design stability criteria established by the design team to be achieved by the corrective measures. This rational approach using the Terzaghi observational method in conjunction with detailed analyses is believed to have provided a better balance of risk and certainty than is normally achievable with new construction. Analyses of corrective measures undertaken are presented to show that adequate stability of this 50-year old dam can be accomplished by grouting, development of good foundation drainage, and placement of substantial ballast within the dam.

Introduction

After an initial investigation revealed excessively large piezometric pressures in the shale foundation of Morris Sheppard Dam and evidence that a section of the spillway moved downstream, the reservoir was lowered from El 1000 to El 987 and a more intensive investigation was undertaken. Based on 125 borings, 132 piezometers, and 146 relief wells, the most likely position of the near-horizontal failure surface and the

---

[1]Chairman of the Board, Fugro-McClelland, Inc., Houston, Texas.
[2]Project Engineer, McClelland Consultants (Southwest), Inc., Houston, Texas.

most probable piezometric profile for a full reservoir (at El 1000) were determined for each buttress. The most likely position of the sliding surface, measured piezometric levels with the reservoir at El 987, and the piezometric profile extrapolated to El 1000 as established early in the investigation for Buttress 21 are shown on Fig. 1. The most critical buttress was later found to be Buttress 19, with a piezometric profile and likely failure surface as shown on Fig. 2.

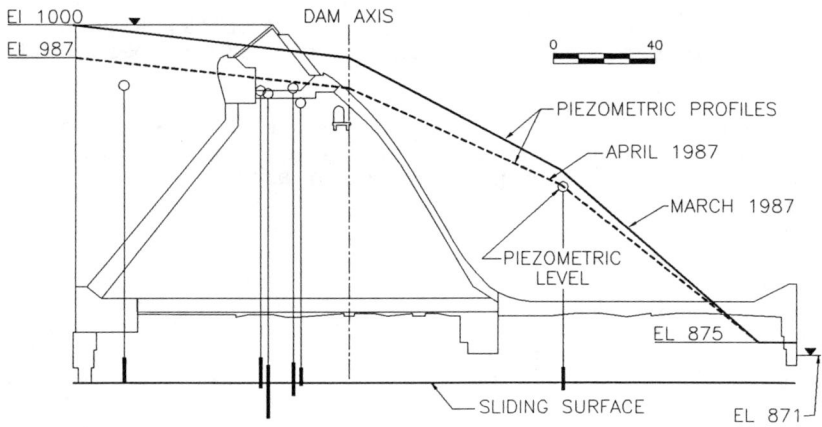

Fig. 1 Piezometric Profiles, Buttress 21

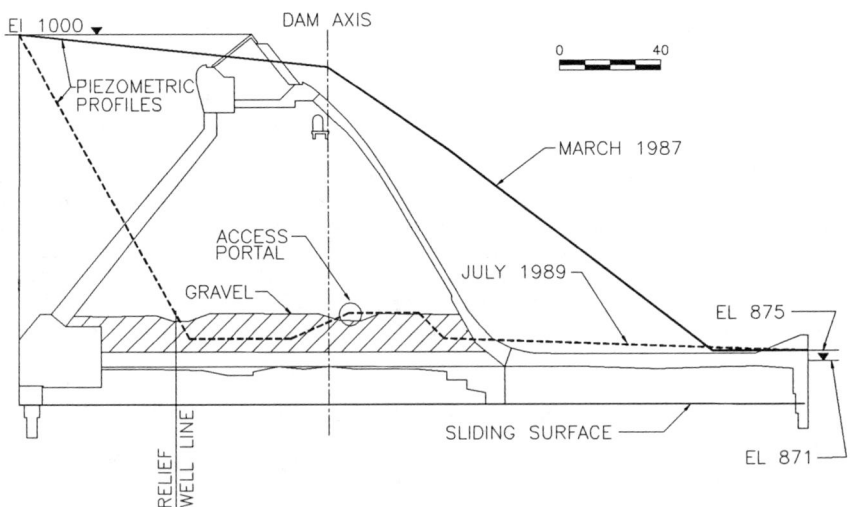

Fig. 2 Piezometric Profiles, Buttress 19

Design Criteria

To provide strength parameters for use in stability analyses of potential and design corrective measures, Buttress 19 was assumed to have a factor of safety of 1.0 for the piezometric profile and sliding surface shown on Fig. 2. Extensive evaluation of probable frictional strength, including interpretation of 1938 field direct shear tests, lead to the selection of $\tan \phi = 0.4$ as the frictional strength parameter. Sliding analyses then indicated that a nonfrictional resistance equal to an average value of 1.79 ksf on the horizontal sliding surface was necessary for equilibrium. Preliminary analyses using Buttress 21 as the critical buttress had indicated that a nonfrictional resistance of 1.69 ksf was required for equilibrium. Because it was slightly more conservative, 1.69 ksf was used for the analysis for final design of corrective measures. With this value, a minimum factor of safety of 1.75 was established as the design criteria for corrective measures using piezometric uplift values determined by actual observations and modestly adjusted for potential decrease in efficiency of the pressure relief system as installed.

A second criterion was established to consider only the anticipated frictional resistance. The frictional resistance on the horizontal sliding surface for $\tan \phi = 0.4$ and the design piezometric uplift (based on actual piezometer data) divided by the net driving force was defined as the sliding ratio. In March 1987, the sliding ratio for the critical buttresses was only about 0.1. For acceptable design, the minimum sliding ratio was selected as 1.0, a ten times increase in this "partial factor of safety."

A third stability criteria was also established in the planning process. This criterion states that the factor of safety with the additional weight must be greater than 1.2 if the piezometric condition was to return to its March 1987 position.

Corrective Measures

The high piezometric pressures were lowered substantially by a line of 6-in.- to 16-in.-diameter relief wells drilled 40 to 80 ft upstream of the dam axis. These wells were nominally 13.7 ft apart and 50 to 110 ft deep. Additional wells were installed in Bays 15 and 16 after large flows were encountered. All wells had slotted risers encased in graded sand filters.

A direct connection to the reservoir was found to exist that permitted lake bottom organisms to pass through the foundation and clog the sand filter of the wells. As a result, grouting of the open joint system near the upstream edge of the structure from inside the dam was initiated working against the reservoir head of El 987. The grouting was successfully accomplished using a sodium silicate cement grout mixture with a very fast set injected in 32 holes drilled in three bays. Flow from the relief wells was reduced from about 550 gpm to less than 1 gpm by the three-stage grouting program. The grouting also further reduced piezometric pressures. The profile shown on Fig. 2 for Buttress 19 is typical of the total piezometric pressure reduction accomplished by the relief wells and grouting.

Approximately 179,600 cu yds of crushed gravel were placed in the interior of the dam to permit the investigation, drilling of relief wells, and grouting. The gravel fill at Buttress 19 is indicated on Fig. 2. At this buttress, the additional weight of the gravel fill and the lowering of the piezometric profile has resulted in a substantial increase in the normal force on the horizontal sliding surface. Nevertheless, the computed factor of safety and sliding ratio are still both less than the established criteria of 1.75 and 1.0. An additional 17,200 kips of weight must be placed in the bays adjacent to Buttress 19 to achieve a sliding ratio of 1.0 and a factor of safety of 1.87. With this additional weight, the factor of safety with the March 1987 piezometric condition will be 1.28. This amount of additional weight, called "ballast," is to be created by placement of concrete or ashcrete in the bays.

A total of 326,500 kips of ballast will be required to complete the stabilization of Morris Sheppard Dam. The maximum to be placed at a single buttress will be 23,200 kips at Buttress 9. No ballast is required for the south bulkhead section because the existing weights provide adequate stability.

Conclusion

The procedure of measuring actual piezometric pressures, determining by investigation the most likely sliding surface, and backfiguring the combination of strength parameters to represent the shale foundation is a logical, rational procedure that has practically eliminated the uncertainties involved in routine pre-construction design. Consequently, the choice of a

DAM STABILITY ANALYSIS

factor of safety could be made without having to consider that the strength parameters might be too large, the piezometric pressures might be assumed too small, and the modelled critical failure surface might differ from the actual. We believe that corrective measures based on this integrated analytical and observational approach provide adequate stability on a balanced and most rational basis for this critical situation.

To convert unit	to SI unit	Multiply by
kip per square foot (ksf)	kilopascal (kPa)	47.88
inch (in)	millimetre (mm)	25.4
foot (ft)	metre (m)	3.048×10^{-1}
cubic yard (cu yd)	cubic metre (m^3)	7.645×10^{-1}
kip (k)	Newton (N)	4.448×10^3
gallon per min (gpm)	cubic metre per second (m^3/s)	6.309×10^{-5}

Possum Kingdom Lake: The Impact of Releases for Fish and Wildlife

by Thomas C. Gooch[1]

Background

Possum Kingdom Lake is a 570,000 acre-foot reservoir on the Brazos River in Palo Pinto County, Texas. It has been owned and operated by the Brazos River Authority (BRA) since its completion in 1941. Under Texas Water Commission permit 1262, the lake is operated to supply water for municipal, industrial, irrigation, and mining use, for hydroelectric power generation, and for recreation. In 1938, the BRA was granted a fifty year license by the Federal Power Commission (now the Federal Energy Regulatory Commission, or FERC) to construct Morris Sheppard Dam, which forms the lake, and to generate hydroelectric power.

In 1985 the BRA applied to FERC for a renewal of its license to generate hydropower at Morris Sheppard Dam. The U. S. Fish and Wildlife Service (FWS) recommended to the FERC that the renewed license should require the BRA to make continuous, controlled releases from the dam for the benefit of fish and wildlife in the Brazos River downstream. The FWS proposed releases of 50 cfs from October through February, 100 cfs from March through June, and 75 cfs from July through September.

In response to this recommendation by FWS, the BRA authorized a study of the impact of these proposed release requirements on the operation of Possum Kingdom Lake. The impacts considered in the study include reductions to reservoir yield, stage, and hydroelectric generation. A computer model of daily operation of Possum Kingdom Lake was developed to determine how the proposed release requirements would have affected reservoir stage and hydroelectric generation if they had been in effect in the past.

As the relicensing of Morris Sheppard Dam proceeded, the computer model of daily lake operation was used to analyze the impact of a number of alternative release programs. Several of these alternative programs included

---

[1] Member, ASCE. Principal with Freese and Nichols, Inc., 811 Lamar Street, Fort Worth, Texas 76102.

drought contingency provisions which decrease the impact on other uses of Possum Kingdom Lake by curtailing releases when the water level in the lake is low.

Determining the Impact of Releases on Reservoir Yield

In water-short Texas, the most important use of Possum Kingdom Lake is water supply. The Brazos River Authority was concerned that the releases proposed by the FWS would affect the lake's yield, decreasing the amount of water available on a reliable basis.

Most of the water used from Possum Kingdom Lake is committed to downstream users, many of them near the mouth of the Brazos River. These users rely on the flow of the river most of the time, calling for releases from Possum Kingdom only during the most severe droughts, when the natural flow of the river is depleted. As a result, water supply use of Possum Kingdom Lake requires holding water in storage until it is needed downstream. The release requirements proposed by the FWS would result in a continual release from the dam. Any water released when it was not needed by downstream users would be wasted for water supply and would not be available later, when the downstream users did need it.

The impact of the proposed releases on reservoir yield was computed by monthly operation studies comparing the yield with a given release program to a base case of yield without releases.

Computer Model of Daily Operation of Possum Kingdom Lake

The computer model of daily reservoir operation was intended to determine how the proposed release requirements would have changed historical water surface elevations and hydroelectric generation if they had been in effect. The model used a methodology suggested by a previous analysis of the impact of releases from Possum Kingdom Lake (7). For each day of operation, a cumulative total of the difference between the historic content and the content with the proposed releases was computed as follows (2):

1) The historical total discharge from the project is (turbine releases + spills + leakage).

2) The total discharge from the project with the proposed release requirements is (turbine releases + spills + leakage + releases for fish and wildlife).

3) The difference in evaporative losses is caused by differences in water level between historical operation and operation with the release requirements.

4) The difference in content caused by the release requirements for

the current day is (historical total discharge - discharge with release requirements + difference in evaporative losses).

5) The cumulative difference in content is (the cumulative difference for the previous day + the difference for the current day).

6) The content with the proposed release requirements is (the historic content - the cumulative difference).

7) The stage and surface area with the proposed release requirements are determined from the content.

The most complicated step in the computation of impact of the releases was Step 2), determining the total discharge with the proposed releases. Three basic rules were followed within Step 2):

    a. During historical releases for energy generation, operate the turbines so that the energy produced equals historical levels.

    b. During periods of historical releases for water supply, release the same amount of water as was released historically.

    c. During historical flood control operation, attempt to operate the project so that the stage with the proposed releases is equal to the historical stage.

The initial analysis of the releases proposed by the FWS showed a pattern to the impact of the releases on reservoir stage. When the reservoir is full and spilling, it would generally also be full with the proposed releases. However, during historical periods of low flow, when the reservoir is drawn down below its full content, the proposed releases would begin to have an impact on stage. Although the change in stage caused by the releases in any single day is small, the cumulative impact would become quite pronounced during extended periods of low inflow, when the lake was historically at its lowest levels. As a result, the most severe impact on reservoir stage caused by the initial FWS proposal occurred during the most critical drought situations.

Alternative Proposals and Their Impact on Possum Kingdom Lake

In the course of the FERC relicensing process, several alternative release programs were proposed by the FWS, the BRA, and FERC staff. Some of the proposals include provisions limiting release requirements to current inflows to the reservoir. This is significant because the release of stored water for the benefit of fish and wildlife is not authorized by the BRA's Texas Water Commission permit for Possum Kingdom Lake. There was some question of the FERC's authority to overrule the state permit and require such releases. The release programs proposed during permitting are described briefly below:

a. FWS Initial. The initial proposal described above, with releases varying seasonally from 50 cfs to 100 cfs and with no drought contingency.

b. 985 Cutoff. A second proposal put forward by the FWS, with releases limited to leakage (about 20 cfs) when the reservoir is below elevation 985 (15 feet below full).

c. Inflow Contingency. A third FWS proposal, with releases limited to current inflow to the reservoir but with no drought contingency based on elevation.

d. 994.5/990 Cutoff. A proposal of FERC staff, with releases limited to current inflow and with required flows cut in half when the reservoir is below 994.5 and limited to leakage (about 20 cfs) when the reservoir is below 990.0.

e. 997/995 Cutoff. A proposal of the BRA, with releases limited to current inflow, and with required flows cut in half when the reservoir is below 997.0 and limited to leakage (about 20 cfs) when the resevoir is below 995.0.

Table 1 shows a comparison of the impacts of the various release proposals.

Results and Conclusions

The FERC has now issued a renewed license for Morris Sheppard Dam, with release requirements based on the 994.5/990 cutoff proposal. Some of the release requirement programs proposed during relicensing would have severely curtailed other uses of Possum Kingdom Lake, including water supply, hydroelectric generation, and recreation. The BRA's ability to analyze the impacts of those proposals, and to make those impacts clear to the FERC, was instrumental in the development of an acceptable set of requirements, which benefit downstream fish and wildlife without intolerable harm to other project purposes.

Table 1

Comparison of the Impacts on Possum Kingdom Lake
of Alternative Flow Release Proposals

	Proposal				
	FWS Initial	985 Cutoff	Inflow Contingency	99.5/990 Cutoff	997/995 Cutoff
Change in Average Stage (Feet)	-1.5	-1.1	-0.9	-0.4	-0.2
Greatest Change in Stage (Feet)	-10.5	-5.6	-3.9	-2.8	-1.3
Average Loss of Power Generation (kWh)	845,000	750,000	632,000	443,000	243,000
Annual Value of Lost Power[b]	$ 33,800	$ 30,000	$ 25,280	$ 17,720	$ 9,720
Loss of Yield (Acre-Feet per Year)	33,700	21,900	6,400	3,600	2,000
Annual Value of Lost Yield[c]	$4,044,000	$2,628,000	$ 768,000	$ 432,000	$ 240,000

Notes:

a. Impacts are taken from the FERC Environmental Assessment (1) and from reports and letters describing analyses by Freese and Nichols (2, 3, 4, 5, 6).

b. Lost power is valued at 4¢ per kWh.

c. Lost yield is valued at $120.00 per acre-foot, or 36.8¢ per thousand gallons.

APPENDIX - REFERENCES

(1) Federal Energy Regulatory Commission, Office of Hydropower Licensing, Division of Project Review, "Environmental Assessment for Hydropower License, Morris Sheppard Dam Water Power Project, FERC Project No. 190-003, Texas," Washington, December 1988.

(2) Freese and Nichols, Inc., "Possum Kingdom Reservoir: Impact of the Required Releases Proposed by the U. S. Fish and Wildlife Service," prepared for the Brazos River Authority, Fort Worth, February 1987.

(3) Freese and Nichols, Inc., "Possum Kingdom Reservoir: Impact of the Required Releases Proposed by the U. S. Fish and Wildlife Service, Supplemental Report," prepared for the Brazos River Authority, Fort Worth, March 1988a.

(4) Freese and Nichols, Inc., "Possum Kingdom Reservoir: Impact of the Draft Releases Requirements Proposed by the Federal Energy Policy Commission in May of 1988," prepared for the Brazos River Authority, Fort Worth, July 1988b.

(5) Freese and Nichols, Inc., Letter Report from Thomas C. Gooch to Carson Hoge dated July 26, 1988, "Re: Impact of the BRA Counterproposal on Possum Kingdom Reservoir," prepared for the Brazos River Authority, Fort Worth, July 1988c.

(6) Freese and Nichols, Inc., Letter Report from Thomas C. Gooch to Carson Hoge dated March 1, 1989, "Re: Impact of the New FWS Proposal on Possum Kingdom Reservoir," prepared for the Brazos River Authority, Fort Worth, March 1989.

(7) URS/Forrest and Cotton, Inc., "Simulation of Effects of Minimum Discharge Requirements Proposed by U. S. Fish and Wildlife Service for Morris Sheppard Dam (Possum Kingdom Lake)," prepared for the Brazos River Authority, Dallas, December 1979.

Planning the Development of the OASIS Advisory System
By Vinio Floris[1] and Gary F. Goforth[2], Members, ASCE

Abstract

This paper describes the evolution of the Operations Advisory and Simulated Intelligence System (OASIS). In its first phase, already concluded, a prototype was developed for testing the applicability of Artificial Intelligence to water management operations. OASIS' second phase, in progress, follows a five-year strategic plan to develop and deploy a full-scale knowledge-base advisory system for the real-time water operations management activities within the limits of the South Florida Water Management District.

Introduction

Making real-time water management decisions is a complex duty that requires a full staff of individuals with very special training and broad experience, and the utilization of varied resources. The South Florida Water Management District (District) is no exception. The District, under the direction of its Operations Division, operates more than 200 water control structures along 2,000 miles of primary canals and 25,000 miles of secondary drainage canals within its 1,600 square mile domain. Environmental protection and enhancement, water supply, flood protection, and water quality protection are the key elements of the mission of the District and combine to create a very complex decision-making arena. Responsive operation of these facilities ensures the perennial protection of the estimated $185 billion in property value in the 16 counties that compose the District.

The decision-making process continues to become more complex because of the increased water management demands, while the water conditions in South Florida vary substantially from season to season and

------

[1]Senior Water Resources Engineer, Operations and Maintenance Department, South Florida Water Management District, P.O. Box 24680, West Palm Beach, FL 33416.

[2]Director of Project Management, Department of Construction Management, South Florida Water Management District, P.O. Box 24680, West Palm Beach, FL 33416.

year to year. To exacerbate an already difficult situation, the turnover of key operations staff due to retirement and alternate jobs represents a problem for the future. There is a need to ensure the quality of all decisions at all times, now and in the future.

Water management experts use a combination of empirically-derived heuristics and relationships, operating constraints brought about by physical guidelines. This enables them to rapidly and accurately reduce the countless possibilities of operating hundreds of water structures (gates, pumps, reservoirs, canals, etc.) down to a few appropriate solution paths. Thus, a viable approach to creating a reliable advisory system to ensure the quality of decision-making and to avoid loss of valuable knowledge is to develop a knowledge-based system. Not only does the knowledge-based system provide the highest level of expertise to real-time decision-making, but it also helps document the expert's heuristic knowledge and problem solving strategies making it available to other people for study and examination.

Definition and Evolution of OASIS

In the fall of 1985, the District formalized a commitment to develop an Artificial Intelligence application in the Operations and Maintenance Department. Based on the needs specified in the introduction, in 1986 the District started an Artificial Intelligence Program called OASIS (Operations Advisory and Simulated Intelligence System). Two major development phases have been identified in the evolution of OASIS: the prototype phase and the development and deployment of the advisory system.

Phase I: Development of an OASIS Prototype.

The main objective of the prototype was to evaluate the applicability of Artificial Intelligence to water management tasks. Consistent with other major applications of a new technology, a reduced scale prototype was designed for OASIS to evaluate the technical feasibility of a decision support tool with an integrated expert system. This expert system is an advisor that captures expert knowledge of water control operations.

The OASIS prototype incorporates four fundamental elements; specifically, the real-time display of hydrologic and meteorologic data, continuous trend analysis of incoming data for alarm conditions, graphical presentation of recent and historic data, and an operations advisor expert system. This prototype is implemented on a Symbolics LISP machine using the Genera operating system in Common LISP. The Automated Reasoning Tool (ART) from Inference Corporation acts as the inference engine using a rule based paradigm and the *schema* capability for modeling.

OASIS is interfaced with an operations environment consisting of a control facility, a data acquisition system, and an information storage facility. Real-time operational data is provided by a Modcomp data acquisition system. A Micro VAX II with an Oracle database provides data sensing in a real-time basis.

The prototype was required to provide the means to develop and test a knowledge base for basin operations. The prototype concentrated on the development of OASIS features for the Everglades Agricultural Area, one of the 12 major hydrologic basins that comprise the District's jurisdiction, and was selected as the prototypical region because of the variety and operational complexity of its component stations. The Everglades Agricultural Area is bounded by Lake Okeechobee on the north and three large Everglades water conservation areas to the south and southeast. In all, 31 stations are located within this area, encompassing over 80 sensors, more than 50 control gates, and eight major pump stations located on four primary canals.

When the prototype was completed, it basically recreated the domain experts' toolkit used in the operational decision making. This included access to available data sources, appropriate data analysis techniques, and a compilation of the extensive set of operational rules which govern the operation of the water control structures.

Both internal and external reviews of the prototype were initiated after its release in the summer of 1988. The evaluation effort was concentrated in system requirements, development methods, operations environment, system design, prototype implementation and future plans. All evaluators agreed that, in general, the OASIS prototype was a successful experience and the conclusions obtained provided a good base for developing and deploying a full scale system.

Plan II: Development and Deployment of an OASIS Advisory System.

The goal of OASIS is to allow the District to leverage its water management expertise to ensure the highest level of decision-making in the short term as well as in the long term. OASIS enables the District to bring to bear levels of expertise consistently across all situations at all times and applies this valuable expertise on a real-time basis. OASIS also allows the District's water management expertise to be documented and communicated to others, allowing new personnel to be trained off-line and assists the District in rationalizing decision-making and justifying decisions. OASIS, as well as the Supervisory Control and Data Acquisition (SCADA), the Meteorological Analysis Display and Modeling (MADAM), and the Information Management System Divisional Database (DAB) are subsystems of the future Consolidated Real-Time Operations Support System (CROSS). All the subsystems mentioned above are a set of functioning components which interact in various ways.

OASIS, in support of its goals, is composed of five subsystems (See Figure 1): Intelligent Warning System, Intelligent Advisory System, Data Abstraction Management System, Maintenance and Configuration System, and Quantitative Models.

OASIS Phase II was started at the end of 1989 and is an on-going project.

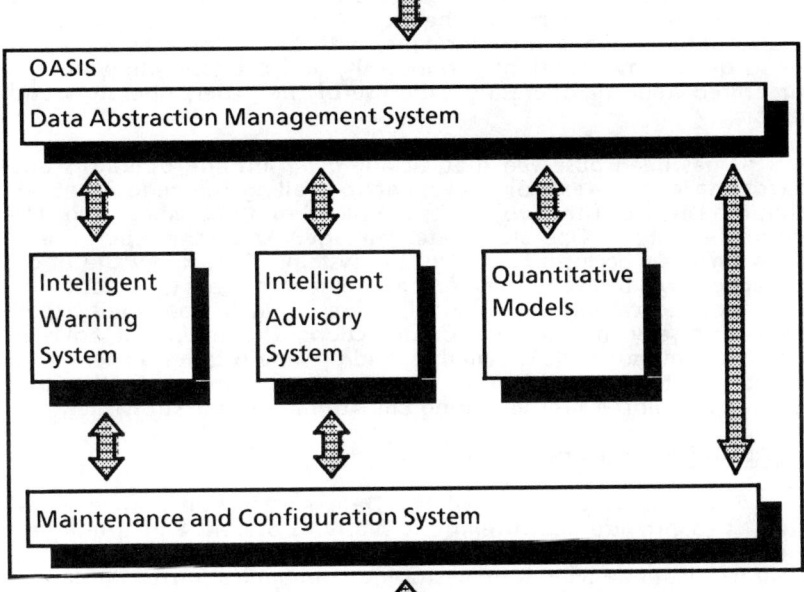

Figure 1: OASIS Subsystems

Intelligent Warning System

The primary objective of the Intelligent Warning System is to focus operator attention on potential problems. The Intelligent Warning System will perform checks consistently, vigorously, tirelessly, and quickly to identify potential abnormalities.

It has been observed that both the operators and water managers continuously maintain an overall view of the status of the District operations. New data helps them extend/modify their view on an incremental basis. They use predicted forecast data to mentally simulate future conditions. This enables them to identify situations that require preventive and/or remedial actions. The Intelligent Warning System will support this human activity by alerting the operator to existing and developing abnormal conditions. The Intelligent Warning System will help focus attention on abnormalities that are detected through vigorous, consistent, and rapid application of operations expertise.

Intelligent Advisory System

The primary objective of the Intelligent Advisory System is to provide solicited advice to the operator. This subsystem makes sure that the advice is consistent with existing operations guidelines formulated by the operations manager, reflects the accumulated experience in handling similar situations, and is in conformance with current objectives - and it does so quickly by consistently, rigorously, and tirelessly applying the enumerated heuristic operating expertise of the expert operators and directors.

It has been observed that, at any given instant, operators and directors have short-term objectives for controlling the various entities within the District. These objectives are based on the existing/predicted state of the system. Operators/water managers know the repertoire of actions they can perform to control the system. They know the effect these actions will have and they can determine if they are consistent with the current tactical objectives. Finally, they bring to bear their expert judgment in selecting the appropriate action. The Intelligent Advisory System will embody such knowledge, and provide it to less experienced operators (or to the experienced operators/water managers in the form of a quick reference/refresher during times of fatigue and stress).

Data Abstraction Management System

The primary objective of the Data Abstraction Management System is to provide the Intelligent Warning System and Intelligent Advisory System with a single, consistent, reliable, high level view of data. It abstracts the underlying format, storage, communication, computation, and retrieval of data. In addition, this module is required to maintain and communicate to the CROSS Information Management Subsystem the description of various entities being managed by the OASIS system like canals, stations, sites, lakes, etc.

Maintenance and Configuration System

The very nature of expertise requires that the knowledge bases be continually updated to leverage new insights learned by the expert managers and operators. This capability enables the District to document and use its most valuable asset, operating expertise. The primary objective of the Maintenance and Configuration System is to provide the maintainer of OASIS with an intuitive user interface for modifying the underlying knowledge bases, entity descriptions, and day-to-day system configuration. In addition, the ability to quickly and easily configure OASIS to reflect existing operating conditions is key to ensuring that operators will use its results with a measure of trust essential to its long-term acceptability.

The ability to edit the knowledge base is simplified by the use of a structured knowledge-base editor that is based on the problem-solving paradigm used by the water managers and operators.

Quantitative Models

Quantitative models or numerical models have been successfully applied to water management for many years. The primary objective of the numerical models is to enhance the predictive power, and correspondingly, the accuracy and richness of Intelligent Warning System and Intelligent Advisory System conclusions. Combining the use of numerical models with heuristic models for providing control advice is a powerful approach that allows the system to harness the benefits of two complementary methods of providing computer-based decision-making assistance. Using real-time numerical models can greatly enhance the ability to predict future water conditions and can prove crucial to the selection of appropriate control advice. On the other hand, heuristic representation techniques provide the best vehicle for capturing and using operator judgment of when to use such models and how to weigh the pros and cons of executing a particular control action.

Qualitative modeling or model-based reasoning refers to generally non-quantitative causal models and not mathematical modeling techniques. It is intended to investigate and use some qualitative modeling techniques right after a major part of the heuristic system is fully operational.

Conclusions

OASIS leverages the District's valuable water management expertise to ensure the highest level of decision-making consistently across all situations at all times. OASIS enables the District to transform a very valuable but intangible and volatile asset, operating expertise, into a tangible asset.

The planning process has defined goals, rules, benchmarks, and tasks to be carried out during the development and real-time deployment of such system. The strategic plan embodies state-of-the-art software, tools, techniques, and computer platforms at appropriate evolution levels. OASIS' modular design provides the required functionality of incrementally merging its subsystems and is envisioned to be implemented as an integral component of CROSS. The development, deployment and evolution of a real-time full-scale system like OASIS represents, because of its complexity and magnitude, a challenge to the practical applications of Artificial Intelligence.

References

Arthur D. Little, Inc. (1989). *Detailed Evaluation of OASIS (Phase I)*. Cambridge, MA.

Mc Donnell Douglas Space Systems Company (1989). *OASIS - Results of Review and Evaluation*. Orlando, FL.

South Florida Water Management District (1989). *Strategic Plan of the Operations Advisor and Simulated Intelligence System (OASIS)*. West Palm Beach, FL.

AN EXPERT SYSTEM FOR
CONTROL CURVE EVALUATION DURING DROUGHT

Shinji Nishida[1], Richard Palmer[2], Carol Slaughterbeck[1], and Susan Walker[3]

ABSTRACT
This paper presents ongoing research into the automation of control curve generation and the development of an expert system for reservoir management for North West Water of Warrington, England. The paper begins with a brief introduction to the NWW and their use of control curve analysis for planning and operation. Next, a procedural computer program entitled SCREEN (Simulation Model for Control Curve Generation and Evaluation) is described that automates all phases of control curve analysis to increase the speed and ease with which control curves can be developed and evaluated. The paper then describes an expert system, ESCORT (Expert System Control Curve Analysis and Reservoir Tracking) that guides water managers through the development of operational strategies during droughts. A discussion of the knowledge acquisition process used to develop the expert system is also presented. The remainder of the paper addresses the incorporation of operational rules into the expert system and experience to date.

Introduction
In the United Kingdom, the Water Act of 1973 consolidated approximately 1600 river authorities, town water commissions, and other public water supply and wastewater treatment systems into ten water authorities. North West Water (NWW - formerly the NorthWest Water Authority) is one of the largest of these. NWW provides water to the northwest portion of England, stretching from the Scottish border in the north to Chesire in the south. A total of approximately seven million consumers are served, spread over 14,500 square kilometers, and demanding approximately 2,500 megaliters of water per day (Ml/d). Numerous aqueducts connect the reservoirs and provide flexible solutions to water supply problems. Water sources include a number of upland impounding reservoirs as well as systems for pumped transfer of lake or river water, and extraction from boreholes. NWW operates approximately 120 reservoirs.

The project described in this paper serves as a feasibility study and prototype for the overall system. The current project deals with three reservoirs; Clowbridge, Cloughbottom, and Haslingden Grane, located in the Rossendale District, and built in the 1850's. These three sites supply water to Manchester and the surrounding area. The total active capacity of the three reservoirs is 3,910 Ml and they supply around 28 Ml/d.

Research Assistant[1] and Associate Professor[2], Department of Civil Engineering, FX-10, University of Washington, Seattle, Washington 98195, and Hydrologic Services Manager[3], North West Water, Warrington, England

Control Curve Planning

Like other water authorities in England, the NWW uses control curves as their primary approach to protect system reliability. NWW defines a reservoir control curve as a set of values of the storage required at the beginning of each month to meet a specified demand during a design drought without failure. Operational policy is then developed based upon the minimum and probabilistic inflow volumes from historical records. The derivation of the control curve ordinates can be divided into two steps. First, the inflows that might occur during the design drought are calculated from a probabilistic analysis. Second, these probabilistic inflows can be converted to values of storage required by simple continuity equations balancing inflow and release.

It is interesting to note that synthetic streamflow generation is not used as a planning tool. An important reason for this is the length of rainfall and inflow records available to use in probabilistic analysis. Instead, the minimum historic and probabilistic inflows (1, 2, 5, 10, and 20%) for periods of 1 through 36 consecutive months starting in each month of the calendar year are calculated based on sixty-one years of data (1927 through 1987) for Stocks reservoir. These 432 sets of data are examined and fit to a 2-parameter log-normal distribution. Based on the continuity equation, the storage requirement at the beginning of each calendar month is calculated for the 2% reliability level to give the operational control curve.

Three simple operational rules are derived from these curves. If the storage level remains above the control curve for the target supply value, supplemental releases can be made. If the storage is below the control curve for the target supply value, only the target value can be released. If storage falls below the control curve evaluated at 85% of the target supply value, further analysis is usually undertaken to determine if drought actions are necessary.

Automation of Control Curve Generation (SCREEN)

Prior to the initiation of this research, the generation of all control curves and drought management analyses were performed on a main-frame computer run in a batch format. Interpretation of the control curves and the evaluation of simulation results was a time consuming and tedious process that required several distinct stages of analysis, some of which were performed on the computer and some with calculations and graphs created by hand. One individual was responsible for developing the control curves and projected storage of the system. During periods of low flow, when extended analysis of the situation is required, the requirements of this task exceed the available resources of one person.

One objective of this research, therefore, is to automate this process and augment the current procedure by providing extensive database and graphic functions to improve the planning environment. SCREEN (Simulation Model for Control Curve Generation and Evaluation), the system developed by researchers at University of Washington, to perform this function operates on IBM PC compatibles. The system is written in the C language and is currently 3000 lines in length. SCREEN is capable of processing information for three individual reservoirs; Clowbridge, Cloughbottom, and Haslingden Grane; and summarizes of all three reservoirs. The system currently has the following capabilities:

(1) Facilitate analysis with a Menus system and appropriate Help screens
(2) Graph existing rainfall and inflow data
(3) Calculate and present 432 sets of rainfall and streamflow data using 3-parameter
    log-normal distributions using quantile scheme
(4) Generate control curves based on minimum historic flows and the 1, 2, 5, 10, and 20%
    probabilistic inflows with various assumptions concerning default values

(5) Simulate and graph reservoir storage for any specified historic record or probabilistic inflows given initial storage, starting month, and demand

(7) Generate reservoir storage simulation summary tables, including the safe yield, critical period, minimum and maximum storage, spill and month of failure for various probability levels for all reservoirs

Expert System for Operational Guidance (ESCORT)

The development and interpretation of control curves and selection of the appropriate management response requires considerable expertise. This expertise is typically gained through several years of experience in evaluating control curves, discussing operational policy with managers and others with extended experience, and using simulation models of the water supply system. A second goal of this research is to develop an expert system that guides less experienced engineers through this process and allows managers to transfer the responsibility of developing initial drought plans to their subordinate engineers. ESCORT was developed to provide such guide through the interpretation of the results of SCREEN and to allow engineers to pursue analysis in an orderly and complete fashion.

Expert systems are computer programs that provide expert quality solutions or advice in a specific domain. Generally, the knowledge contained in expert systems is obtained from the experience and expertise of human experts. Expert systems differ from more conventional engineering programming in that they are more transparent, allowing the user to understand the logic of the program easily. Because expert systems separate the knowledge from the solution procedure, they are more easily modified.

ESCORT is a rule-based system primarily composed of IF/THEN type rules from which procedural and subjective paradigms used in drought decision making operational guidance are inferred. ESCORT was developed using VP-EXPERT, a relatively low-end expert system shell that is written in C.

Knowledge Acquisition for ESCORT

Knowledge acquisition (KA) is the process of gathering information and translating it into a format suitable for incorporation into an expert system. KA has often been cited as the major bottleneck in expert systems development. The authors have had similar experiences with other expert systems and were determined to perform this phase of research as efficiently and effectively as possible. The authors' experience suggests that no single technique for KA is "best" and that one must be familiar with a variety of methods to apply the one that is most appropriate. The following general categories were used in this project: structured interviews, unstructured interviews, interruption analysis, protocol/case study analysis, questionnaires, and documentation analysis. Each of these techniques was used in this project at various times.

The geographic distance between the researchers and the water supply managers and hydrologists in this project increased the normal problems of KA. This problem was overcome with the use of electronic mail, telephone calls, the FAX messages, and several in-person visits. The KA process in this project can be divided into four phases. Phase I included initial meetings between the principal investigators and the water supply managers to provide a general overview of the system. A number of documents written at North West Water also aided in providing the researchers an understanding of the system to be modeled and existing operational policy. In addition, second and third in-person interviews were made to define the parameters of the system to be developed. Phase II included a series of interviews conducted using Fax messages and telephone calls from the US to England. These interviews allowed a detailed understanding of the system to be obtained and a prototype expert system to be developed. Phase III included a third visit to England for in-depth interviews concerning operating procedures and a review of all software developed to that point. Phase IV, yet to be conducted, will include a final visit to NWW to ensure that all the concerns of the authority have been incorporated into the program.

System Operation

After the knowledge acquisition process, the rules obtained from NWW personnel were incorporated into ESCORT. Although the expert system is not yet complete, a prototype has been developed and software specifications and requirements have been established. The expert system will function in the following general manner: ESCORT begins by requesting fundamental operational data from the user such as the time of year, current reservoir storage, supply targets, compensation values, and desired probability levels to be used for the analysis. This information constitutes the basic components of the expert system rule base and is used to execute the portion of the SCREEN program that calculates basic control curve values. ESCORT then evaluates the results and determines whether or not a more detailed analysis is necessary. If the analysis suggests that storage will not fall below the rule curve for the desired probabilistic forecasts, ESCORT informs the user of this fact and the session is terminated. If the analysis suggests that storage could fall below the control curve at selected probability levels, ESCORT classifies the relative severity of the drought scenario and suggests that further analysis is required.

The relative severity of the drought scenario is used to determine both the extent to which further analysis is required and the type of analysis that is needed. Situations in which the drought potential is low requires only cursory review of system operation. For potentially more serious situations, more complete analysis is needed. It should be noted that such classification can save considerable time by preventing needless analysis and requiring analysis when it is appropriate. The severity is also used to determine the type of operational strategies that are available and their likelihood of success given the time of year, demands, and other considerations. Potential drought management strategies that the system can advise include balancing releases from primary reservoirs, obtaining water from alternatives (ie., more expensive) sources, pressure reductions, and hosepipe bans.

An extremely important aspect of this research that has not been completed is the validation and verification of the expert system. These phases are essential in the development of any successful expert system. They will be accomplished through a series of drought scenario games in which specific events are described, water managers are requested to suggest the type of analysis needed and the drought action that they would initiate. These results will then be compared to those generated by ESCORT.

Summary and Conclusions

This paper has described the development of two computer models to be used to automate and improve drought management planning for North West Water of Warrington, England. When used jointly, the models allow engineers to generate control curves for a variety of conditions, track reservoir operation using probabilistic inflow data, and to suggest drought management responses when appropriate.

Acknowledgements

The authors wish to acknowledge the funding support of North West Water, the Department of Civil Engineering of the University of Washington, and the Valle Scholarship and Scandinavian Exchange Program of the University of Washington. The authors also wish to acknowledge the research efforts of Dr. Paul Jowitt and David Howarth who have served as co-investigators in this research in the Department of Civil Engineering at Heriot-Watt University, Edinburgh, Scotland.

Closing the Gap between Water Resources Systems
Education and Practice

Mohammad Karamouz*, M. ASCE

Introduction:

This paper is focused on teaching system analysis and its water resources applications to engineers and architects. Although, the principles of system analysis is known to civil engineer students in general, their familiarity is limited to a course that they might have had, entitled system analysis for civil engineers. The content of those courses that were offered under this title or similar titles all over U.S., indicates that they are structured around the application of linear programming in solving general civil engineering problems. The real water resources systems problems such as operation and expansion of water distribution and treatment systems, reservoir operations, design and location of sedimentation and drainage systems, monitoring and managing groundwater systems, decision making under uncertainty, and flood control management, etc. are briefly explained or completely ignored.

For the last six years, attempts have been made by this author to teach the techniques and the applications of system analysis to water resources and environmental problems. The result of this education have already been observed and tested in actual cases.

The Site, the Sound, and the Echo:

The Site -- New York City, with its unique socio-economic characteristics, has been an excellent place for bringing together the university education and water resources practice. A good portion of graduate students in this field are practicing engineers striving to get a leading edge by using analytical techniques in their work place especially if it can help them or
----
* Associate Professor, Department of Civil Engineering, Pratt Institute, Brooklyn, New York 11205.

their supervisor to make better decisions at a lower cost. Diverse and expanded structure of engineering corporations and city agencies engaged in operation, expansion, maintenance, and development of massive infrastructure, national and international projects, makes the graduate student body working in these organizations interested in multi-deciplinary problems/projects often with a water resources component.

The Sound -- Three courses have been taught by this author in this subject:
- Systems Analysis for Civil Engineers
- Analytical Methods in Decision Making
- Computer Applications of Systems Management

The students taking these courses are graduate students in water resources/hydraulic engineering program,graduate students in environmental systems management, undergraduate and graduate students in other programs, and continuing education/special students at Polytechnic University and Pratt Institute.

The Echo -- A number of students who enrolled in these courses used linear programming/systems approach to one or more water resources problems in their work place. Although most of these applications were directed to small project of capacity expansion, sewer design, facility locations, solid waste disposal, eight cases are consider to be significant. In these cases, the systems approach to decision making were implemented and even changed the way certain problems were being looked at and solved in the past. The details of these studies are not discussed here to avoid obtaining official clearance from certain agencies.

Case 1 - A comprehensive flood control study has been done to determine the optimal elevation of the crest of the Pompton lake Dam in New Jersey and also to identify the most cost effective level of flood protection. The study includes the use of mathematical and optimization models. Flood damage assessment, hydrologic analysis, hydraulic analysis, development of a cost and a profit relationships were performed before analysing a two stage optimization plan. The result of this study affected 340 homes and 18 business susceptable to inundation by flood flows.

Case 2 - Development of a test model of new sources of supply for large water utility in New York has been studied to explore the range of decision making methods available for actual planning studies. A Linear/Mixed Integer Programming has been used. The objective function is to maximize the net economic benefit from additional water supply.

Case 3 - The problem of valve changes at Cannonsville Reservoir in New York has been studied. The objective of the study is to minimize the number of valve changes each day subject to meeting the target flows within specified margins and to avoid flow changes of more than specified amounts in specified time period.

The objective function is also subject to a variety of technical constraints relating to the valve system. The formulation are designed to minimize the number of valve changes and the river fluctuation.

Case 4 - A power plant sitting problem to determine the type, size and location of plants was studied for hydropower systems in Syria. The Analytical technique to solve this problem was a mixed integer programming (MIP). Comprehensive sensitivity runs displayed an interesting result showing that decision for construction of aggregate capacity at all sites is influenced significantly by spacial factors.

Case 5 - A Systems approach to managing well operation in the context of salt water intrusion has been investigated for Truro, Massachusetts well field. A finite element model is coupled with systems interface to identify the parameters and the best way to design wells and analyze upcoming problems.

Case 6 - The selection of optimum installed capacity of small hydropower plant projects in New York State were investigated. Both the preliminary and final turbine setting, running diameter, and other plant features are determined and the trade offs are established.

Case 7 - Capacity expansion of a water distribution system in New Jersey has been studied. The growing demand level and the population growth have been considered and the available surface and groundwater resources and the pressure loads requirements at each node were studied in order to meet the demand for the year 2020.

Case 8 - A systems approach to design, expansion and optimization of water distribution system at a sub-post station at Pedricktown, New Jersey was implemented. A combined simulation, optimization model was used to determine the pressure distribution and the cost associated with the presence of pumps, pressure reducing valves, check valves and multiple supply points. The optimization portion was intended for the sizing of the pipes within the network.

In cases 5 and 6 students had a water resources planning course at Polytechnic University taught by Alvin S. Goodman.

Closing the Gap:

Certainly the gap is still very well in place. We are moving steady but slowly to close the gap. There are a number of barriers: text books in the subject of water resources planning and management, although technically sound, have not been designed for practical applications and came short of realizing this gap; the class attendance is low and forces the departments to revise course outlines to attract students from other areas;

computer illiteracy and students lack of interest to use computer even at this age of automation are stumbling factors; middle and upper manager's unquestioning reliance on traditional engineering approaches in decision making.

Neverthless, the need for using analytical methods in decision making has been realized by both private and public agancies. State and city agencies, with the pressure induced from lack of resources, are willing to try and started to encourage their staff to implement these techniques. A growing demand for planning and management courses especially in the area of environmental systems led to the establishment of a number of related programs with a comprehensive campaign for attracting students. This resulted in better public awareness of the need for existence and support of such programs. We need programs that are tailored for training managers for water resources and environmental systems. We also need continuing education courses for middle managers in governmental agencies. we need to write more technical articles in professional magazines and newsletters. The echo is not very loud but it is increasing.

Minimizing the Risk of Unsuccessful Modeling Exercises

John J. Warwick[1] Member ASCE

Abstract

Monte Carlo simulation techniques were employed to relate input parameter uncertainties to the characteristics of model output accuracy and reliability, and to the probability of successfully applying a calibrated model. A simple Streeter-Phelps dissolved oxygen (DO) model was chosen as an exemplar. Application of these techniques allowed for optimization of the field monitoring (sampling location) and mathematical modeling (selection of calibration data set) exercise. The best average probability of attaining a DO model with an accuracy of ± 0.10 mg/L was only 37%. Using the "wrong" data set for model calibration greatly reduced this probability to only 7%.

Introduction

Water quality models are commonly used to compute wasteload allocations into receiving bodies. Results of these simulations often lead to significant capital expenditures which increasingly must be borne by the local community. Unfortunately, water quality management decisions are often made with little or no knowledge of the uncertainty associated with the numbers upon which these decisions are based. It is therefore crucial to quantify a model's predictive capability and develop strategies which will enable researchers to improve that capability to an acceptable level.

Methodology

The classic Streeter-Phelps equation was assumed to perfectly simulate in-stream dissolved oxygen (DO):

$$D = D_o e^{-(K_a/V)X} + \frac{K_d L_o}{K_a - K_d}[e^{-(K_d/V)X} - e^{-(K_a/V)X}] \quad \ldots (1)$$

[1]Director, Inst. for Environmental Sciences, University of Texas at Dallas, Richardson, TX 75083-0688.

in which D = DO deficit (mg/L) = C_s - C; C_s = DO saturation (mg/L); C = DO (mg/L); D_o = initial DO deficit (mg/L); K_a = reaeration rate (day^{-1}); V = velocity (miles/day); X = distance (miles); K_d = deoxygenation rate (day^{-1}); and L_o = initial ultimate biochemical oxygen demand (mg/L).

The empirical expression developed by Tsivoglou and Neal (1976) is used to define reaeration (K_a):

$$K_a = ESC * V' * S \qquad (2)$$

in which ESC = escape coefficient (ft^{-1}); V'= velocity (ft/day); S = channel bottom slope. The expected (true) mean value for D is calculated for a particular X location by using the assumed true value for K_d (0.20 day^{-1}) and the mean values for D_o, L_o, V, ESC, and S.

Table 1 presents two different data sets; Data Set A characterizes a high loading situation, while a low loading condition is represented by Data Set B. Standard deviation values were computed as one-half the magnitude reported by Chadderton, et al. (1982) and "Methods for Chemical Analysis of Water and Wastes" (EPA, 1976).

Table 1: Input Parameter Characterization

Parameter	Dist.	Data Set A Mean	Std. Dev.	Data Set B Mean	Std. Dev.
D_o (mg/L)	Normal	1.00	0.10	1.00	0.10
L_o (mg/L)	Normal	100.	10.0	20.0	2.00
D (mg/L)	Normal	Computed	0.10	Computed	0.10
V (ft/sec)	Normal	0.50	.025	0.50	.025
ESC (ft^{-1})	------	0.0540	----	0.0540	----
S	Normal	0.0010	.00005	0.0010	.00005
K_d (day^{-1})	Computed	0.20	Computed	0.20	Computed

K_d was selected as the calibration parameter. A Monte Carlo technique was used to determine the expected frequency distribution of K_d as a function of input parameter uncertainties. Monte Carlo simulation included running the model 100,000 times and subsequently grouping the computed K_d values into 41 equally sized subintervals in the range $0.10 \leq K_d \leq 0.30$ day^{-1}.

Model application involved using the calibrated model to predict future system state. Monte Carlo simulation techniques were again employed to computed the reliability of model predictions. Reliability is defined as the probability that the model will predict, to within some prescribed level of accuracy, the correct location and magnitude of the critical DO deficit (D_c). An accuracy tolerance limit of ±0.10 mg/L was selected. Model reliability was computed for the average K_d value associated with each of the 41 intervals used in the previous frequency distribution calculation. The number of successful model projections (predicted D_c within ±0.10 mg/L of the true D_c) were counted over 20,000 trials per interval.

Likelihood is defined as the probability that an individual can attain, through the calibration process, a model which will perform at or above some specified level (reliability and accuracy). After specifying an acceptable reliability, a range of K_d values can be found which provides the required reliability. Integration of the K_d frequency distribution curve over this range of K_d values results in a probability which is called the attainment likelihood. Further details can be found in an earlier work (Warwick and Cale, 1987).

Results and Discussion

Two different scenarios were investigated. Scenario I was created by using Data Set A for model calibration and Data Set B for model application. The order of data set utilization was reversed in Scenario II.

Figure 1 presents the results of model calibration for Scenario I, and illustrates the importance of location for the downstream site. The optimum sampling location is the point where the frequency distribution is most concentrated about the true system behavior (K_d=0.20 day^{-1}). This point occurs at X=2.5 miles.

The reliability of model application, for Scenario I, is shown in Figure 2. Maximum model reliability occurs at the true K_d value (0.20 day^{-1}) and is equal to 48.0 %. This result indicates that the analyst would actually fail to accurately (±0.10 mg/L) predict D_c 52.0 % of the time for a perfectly calibrated model. The magnitude of the resulting reliabilities is directly related to the assigned accuracy criteria. Selection of a larger accuracy level (e.g. ±0.50 mg/L) would have caused a significant increase in model reliability.

A likelihood surface is presented in Figure 3. The area underneath the surface at any X value is equal to the total probability that an analyst will successfully calibrate and apply the model (L_{total}). The maximum L_{total} value occurs at X=2.5 miles, and is equal to 37%. Therefore, any individual who calibrates the model using Data Set A stands only a 37% chance, on the average, of also predicting the correct D_c value to within ±0.10 mg/L for Data Set B.

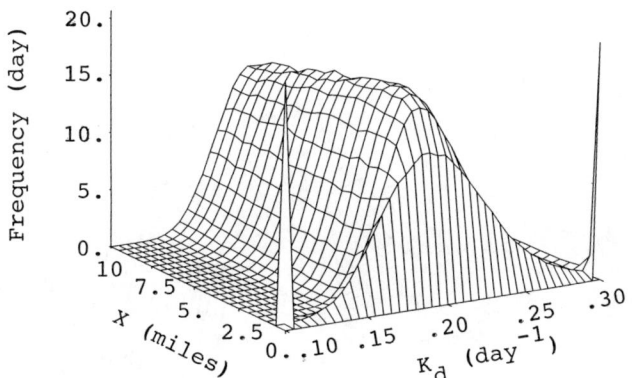

Figure 1: K_d Frequency Distribution for Scenario I.

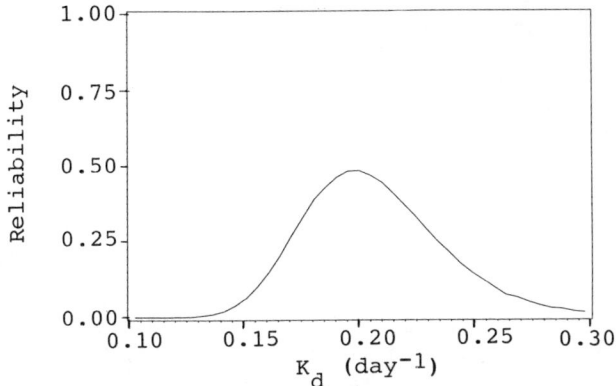

Figure 2: Model Reliability for Scenario I.

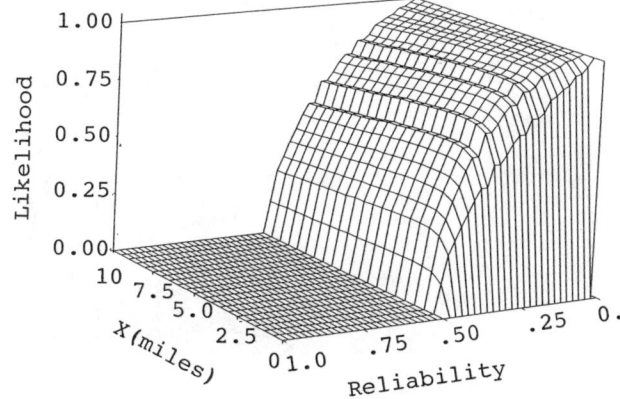

Figure 3: Likelihood Surface for Scenario I.

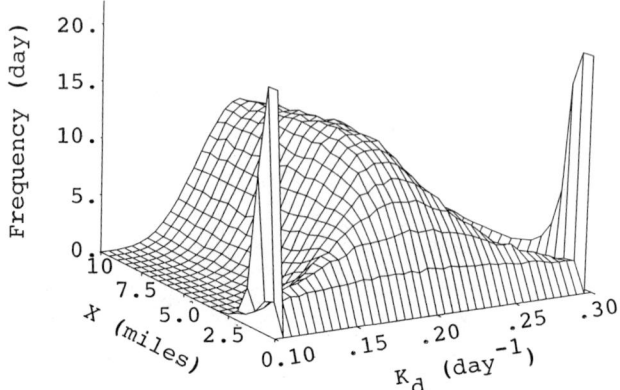

Figure 4: K_d Frequency Distribution for Scenario II.

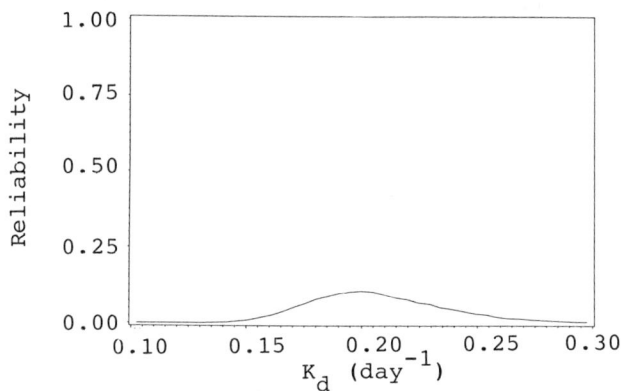

Figure 5: Model Reliability for Scenario II.

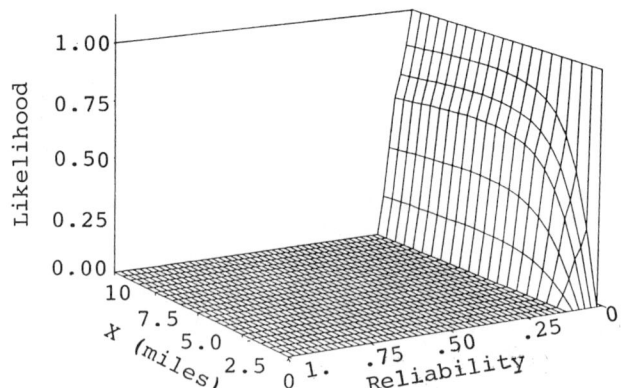

Figure 6: Likelihood Surface for Scenario II.

Figures 4 through 6 present the results for Scenario II. The order of data set analysis has a dramatic impact on the entire modeling process. Using Data Set B for model calibration (Figure 4) results in an increased amount of variability in computed K_d values. The optimal location for collecting the downstream data is 5.5 miles. Model reliability is greatly reduced when Data Set A is used for model application (Figure 5). The maximum model reliability is only 11.%. This reduction in reliability is directly related to the increased magnitude of L_o. The overall impact of reversing the order of data set usage is quite negative (Figure 6). The maximum L_{total} value occurs at X=5.5 miles and has a value of only 7%.

Conclusions

The effectiveness of the overall modeling process can be quantified as the average probability (L_{total}) of attaining a model with stated performance characteristics (reliability and accuracy). Improving the modeling process involves increasing L_{total}. Judicious selection of downstream sampling site location results in an optimal expenditure of monies. Model application (reliability) was extremely sensitive to the magnitude of L_o. Therefore, the order of data set usage had a dramatic impact on the success of the overall modeling process. If further improvements are required measurement uncertainties associated with both the calibration and application data sets must be reduced.

References

1. Chadderton, R.A., Miller, A.C., and McDonnell, A.J., "Uncertainty Analysis of Dissolved Oxygen Model," *Journal of the Environmental Engineering Division, ASCE*, Vol. 108, No. EE5, 1982, pp 1003-1013.

2. "Methods for Chemical Analysis of Water and Wastes," Environmental Research Center, United States Environmental Protection Agency, Cincinnati, Ohio, 1976, 298pp.

3. Tsivoglou, E. and Neal, L., "Tracer Measurement of Reaeration: III. Predicting the Reaeration Capacity of Inland Streams," *Journal Water Pollution Control Federation*, Vol. 48, No. 12, pp. 2669-2689.

4. Warwick, J.J., and Cale W.G., "Determining the Likelihood of Obtaining a Reliable Model," *Journal of Environmental Engineering Division, ASCE*, Vol. 113, No. 5, 1987, pp. 1102-1119.

BEYOND BASIC MODELING

Daniel H. Leighton, Craig Von Bargen[1]

ABSTRACT

Computers have long been used in water engineering to model hydraulic distribution networks. In recent years, computer technology has exploded, yielding computers that are powerful and accessible, and software tools for data management, graphics, and mapping.

This paper looks at the evolving use of computer technology to do water planning studies, and proposed a revised approach to building analysis environments that go beyond basic modeling.

A HISTORICAL PERSPECTIVE

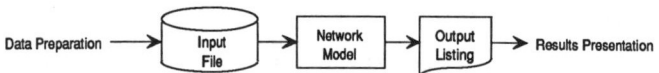

Figure 1: Traditional Water Modeling Process

Figure one shows the steps performed in a traditional modeling project, as it has been done for over 20 years. Although the network model does the mathematically complex operation of balancing flows in a distribution system, considerable work remains in the data preparation and results presentation and review steps.

When FORTRAN was the primary programming language available for modeling, it was reasonable to expect that these data preparation and presentation tasks would be done by hand. Today, with modern CAD, database, and mapping products, one can envision a system that has far more functionality. Such a system is presented in figure two.

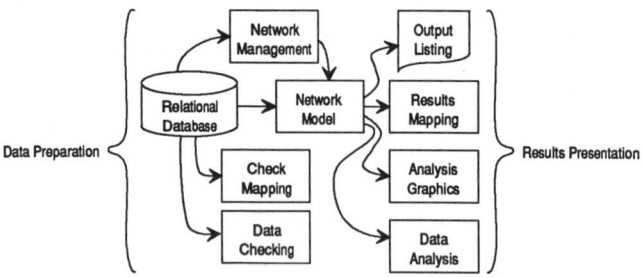

Figure 2: Adding Preparation and Presentation Functions

---

1. Camp Dresser & McKee, Inc., 100 Pringle Ave, Suite 300, Walnut Creek, CA 94596

of altering records for different analysis scenarios far more reliable. We have the ability to do SQL (structured query language) calls into the database, making it easy to integrate with other software packages.

- Database Structure ("schema") – The structure of the database itself determines the ease in which graphics, models, and other analyses can be done. We used a modified "object oriented" approach, where each feature (pipe, junction, pump, etc) has knowledge of how it behaves and relates to other features.

- Open Approach – Links to other software packages should be designed in an open, general purpose fashion. For example, routines in our environment for automated mapping will work for both facility attributes (pipe diameter for example) and model results (flow velocity). Designing an open interface is more work, but pays off in future flexibility.

- Modular Architecture – Computer technology is still moving forward at a rapid pace. The approach we selected emphasized a modular architecture with well defined interfaces between each component. As a result, any component shown in figure three can be replaced without effecting other components as long as the interfaces are maintained.

APPLICATIONS TO DATE

To date, variations on this system have been used successfully in several cities across the United States. Examples include:

- A transmission study for San Francisco, California

- A master planning study for Forth Worth, Texas

- A planning study for Arlington, Texas

As our environment for water analysis expands, new possibilities keep suggesting themselves. In the future, we hope to add modules to interface with GIS software, perform water quality review and energy utilization analysis, and more. We have found that the data-centric approach to water analysis yields a robust platform for new technology and tools as they become available.

Site Specific Hydrological Model
for Permaculture Application
by
William Blatner and Reza Khanbilvardi*

Abstract

This paper presents results of a study conducted on a small pond and watershed in Waterbury, Connecticut,(2). The Soil Conservation Service method presented in Technical Release #55 (TR 55),(3), and the "Puls method",(1), were used to estimate runoff and the effect of storm events on pond stage and storage. A means of monitoring and measuring pond outflow was devised. Current and historical weather data, together with interviews, site history, direct observations and the collected flow data were used to construct a conceptual model of the site's hydrology. Preliminary evaluation of the pond's potential for utilization under a specific agricultural philosophy is presented.

Introduction

The study presented in this paper began formally in September, 1988, and continues at present. The evaluation of a pond and watershed as hydrological resource was conducted as part of a larger ecological survey to be used in the design of a small, low input, sustainable farm operation.

Standard runoff and flood routing analyses were performed to obtain estimates of the effects of storm events. The attitude of the owners, together with the type of farm enterprise envisioned, however, suggested development of a structural model. This allowed utilization of a wide range of data, observation and historical information. The model provides a framework through which to view the effects of expected seasonal changes in weather, as well as extreme events or perturbations imposed by the agricultural operation.
----
*Research Assist. & Assoc. Prof., Dept. of Civil Engineering, City College of New York, Convent Ave. New York, N.Y. 10031

Flood Analysis

Figure 1 shows the location and topography of the site. The enlarged version of the U.S.G.S. topographic map, as well as on site inspection, were used to delineate watershed boundaries, area and other characteristics. Runoff analysis was performed for the 2, 5 and 10 year, 24 hr. storm events using TR 55. The synthesized flood hydrographs were routed through a two foot wide, rectangular weir using a finite difference form of the continuity equation. Significant results are summarized below.

Storm Return Period(yrs)	24-hr. Rainfall (in)	Peak Runoff (cfs)	Peak Routed Outflow (cfs)
2	3.25	10.3	4.2
5	4.25	19.5	9.1
10	5.00	31.3	17.2

Flow Measurement

The purpose of this part of the study was to devise an economical means by which the net flow into the pond could be measured on an ongoing basis. The pond is fed continuously by the surrounding water table and intermittently by small streams and surface springs. Surface flow out of the pond, however, occurs at a single point, making this the logical place to locate a metering device.

Outflow was channeled through a 16" pipe into a wooden box with a V-notch weir cut into one end. The weir was calibrated by measuring the head on the weir and the time to fill a known volume, then solving the weir equation,

$$Q = CH^{5/2} \qquad (1)$$

for the calibration constant, C. A ratcheted float was devised to indicate maximum head on the weir between readings. Average flow for the period between readings could then be calculated using three values instead of two.

The volume of flow for the period between readings was calculated using the average flow, Qave, and the formula,

$$V = Q_{ave}(cfs) \times time(hrs) \times 3600(sec/hr). \qquad (2)$$

314 RESOURCES FOR WATER MANAGEMENT

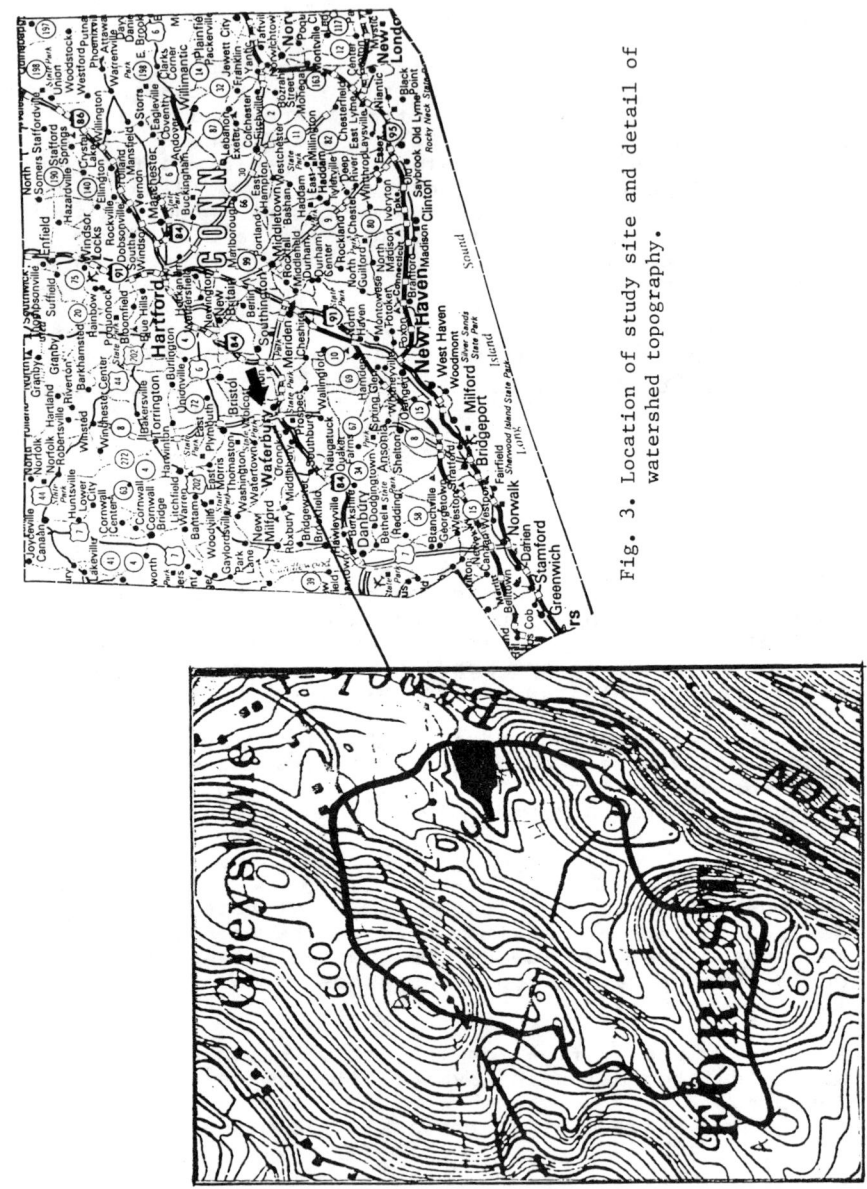

Fig. 3. Location of study site and detail of watershed topography.

SITE SPECIFIC HYDROLOGICAL MODEL

Significant results are summarized below.

Period of record	12/22/88-5/16/89
No. of days in period	144
Qmax(cfs)	1.3
Qmin(cfs)	0.003
Qave(cfs)	0.18
Total Cumulative Volume	2,250,000 cubic ft.
	51.65 acre-ft.

Model Development

The period over which flow data were kept and the nature of the data itself are too limited to form the basis for conclusions in and of themselves. When taken together with various climatological data, qualitative observations and information from discussions with residents familiar with the site's history, however, some reasonable conclusions may be drawn.

The most dominant characteristic of the site is the continuous year round supply to the pond of ground water. Several observations support this conclusion. First, the Greystone area has a characteristically high water table. Outcroppings of granite dominate the landscape and depth to bedrock is, according to one water well contractor and several excavation contractors, generally less than 20 feet. The water table aquifer sits atop bedrock and often presents difficulty in placing septic tanks and soil absorption fields. During the summer, surface flow into and out of the pond may cease, as it did in the summer of 1988, but frigid water welling up from the bottom can always be felt along a deep trench running roughly through the middle of the pond. Finally, the streams feeding the pond remained dry well into January, 1989, yet the stage began to recover in September and continuous outflow established itself by November, 1988.

The feeders streams are indicative of the water table level. They flow continuously once established, even with weeks of little or no precipitation. The streams delineate lines along which the water table intersects the ground surface. As the water table rises, they extend further upslope.

An idea of the extent to which the water table fluctuates can be gotten from observations of a dug well nearby. The well has not been used for many years so it should indicate the water table level in its vicinity. Between August, 1988 and January, 1989, the level in the well rose 9 feet.

From these observations, two extreme, qualitative

pictures emerge of conditions dictating seasonal
variations in base flow into and out of the pond. The
first, occurring in late summer, is characterized by a
low water table (see Fig. 2). Vegetation is at its
height in summer and much of the precipitation is
intercepted and evaporates before reaching the ground.
Much of that which does reach the ground is absorbed by
plants and encorporated into tissue or returned to the
atmosphere by evapotranspiration. Recharge of the water
table is minimal to zero. Though the pond continues to
receive ground water in its deeper sections it is
probably leaking in shallower areas. Direct surface
evaporation is maximum and pond stage may actually fall
as it did in the summer of 1988.

The second picture is dominated by a high water table
(see Fig.3). In fall and winter, temperatures drop and
plants lose their foliage and become dormant.
Evaporation, interception, and evapotranspiration are all
minimal. The water table rises, ground water inflow
overcomes leakage and direct evaporation losses, pond
stage recovers and outflow begins. As the water table
continues to rise, small gaining streams form that
increase the rate of ground water flow into the pond.

Theoretical Safe Yield

The model, together with the short term flow record,
can be used to estimate a theoretical safe yield. Many
factors influence water table levels and hence, inflow to
the pond. To obtain a statistical return period for the
combination of rain, snow and snowmelt, soil cover,
evaporation rates, solar radiation and intercepting
foliage during and leading up to the period of flow
record is probably impossible. Examining these factors
chronologically through the framework of the model and
relative to historical data, however, gives a reasonable
idea of the "typicalness" of the flow record.

In May, 1988, the streams feeding the pond are
running, indicating the water table at its normal high
spring level. All snow, however, has long since melted,
foliage is well established and temperatures begin to
exceed 90 degrees F. The water table is probably
beginning to recede.

During the 77 days between May 31 and August 15,
1988, temperatures exceed 90 F on 33 days, 100 F on 2
days, and record high temperatures are recorded on 17
days. Average monthly temperatures are .8, 4.3 and 5.4
degrees above historic averages for June, July and
August, respectively. June rainfall is a 20 year low.
In the first week of June, feeder streams dry up. In

SITE SPECIFIC HYDROLOGICAL MODEL 317

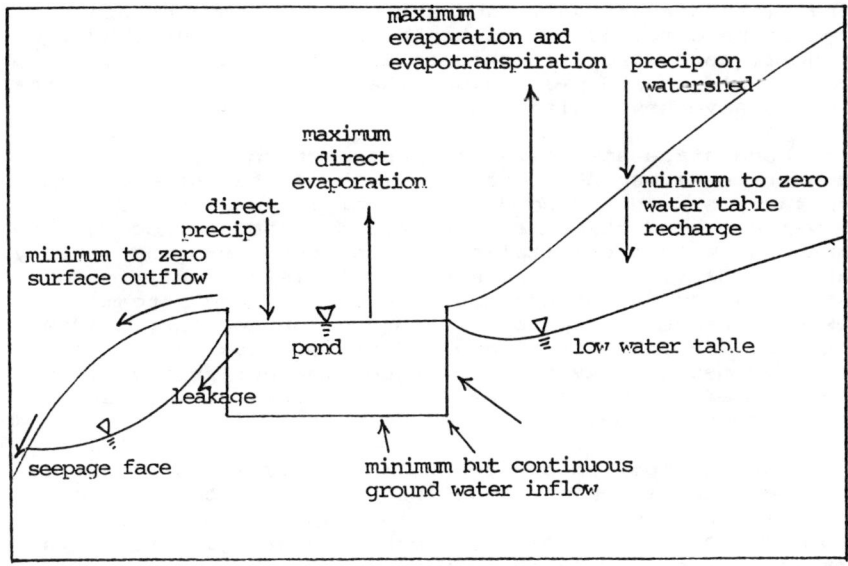

Fig. 2. Dominant aspects of hydrological model, mid-summer and early fall.

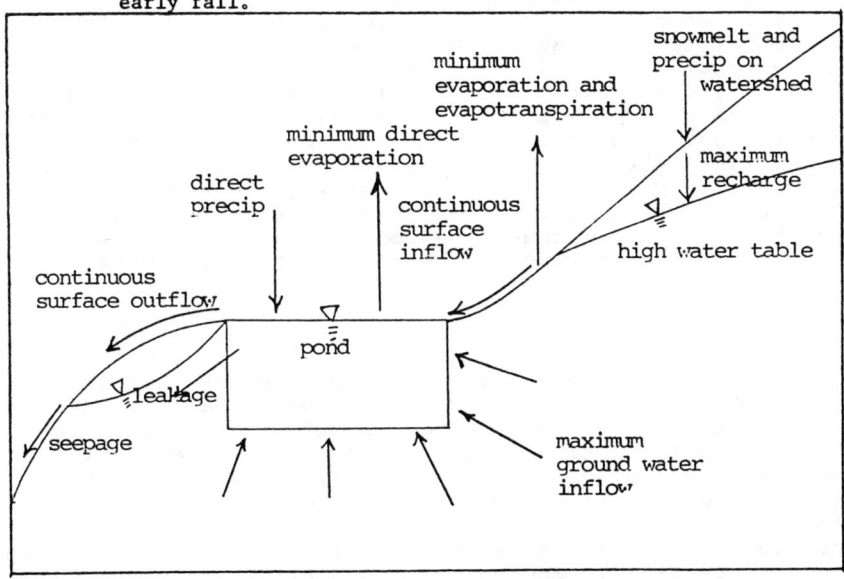

Fig. 3. Dominant aspects of hydrologic model, winter and spring.

the first week of July, surface outflow from the pond
ceases as combined losses begin to exceed gains. By mid
August, pond stage has dropped 2' below the overflow
point. In the 35 years since the pond was first dug, the
owners have never witnessed such a drop.

Pond stage stabilizes in September and October as
temperatures begin to drop and much of the intercepting
foliage is shed. Record high rainfall is recorded in
November, pond stage recovers rapidly and surface outflow
begins. With precipitation in December, 1988 and January
and February, 1989 below average, it is not until mid-
January that feeder streams reappear. These streams
extend themselves upslope through March and April, 1989.
Rainfall in the first 7 days of May exceeds the total
monthly median. Average recorded flow during the first
16 days of the month is over 5 times that of the rest of
the record period.

That the period considered may be taken as an extreme
of low flow is supported by these data and observations,
seen through the framework of the model. Under more
normal conditions, one could expect a net gain to begin
earlier, possibly by as much as two months, than it did
in 1988. The water table would then reach its highest
level earlier and average flows over the entire period
would be greater. Finally, recorded snowfall in the
winter of 1988-89 was 28" below normal for the state of
Connecticut. Snowmelt could normally be expected to make
a significant contribution to flow gains into the pond.
Net gains began in October, 1988, as pond stage began to
recover and have continued through the entire summer of
1989. The total cumulative volume recorded from December
22, 1988 to May 16, 1989, would seem to be a very
conservative estimate of the theoretical safe yield for
one year. The 51 acre-ft. also gives a feel for the
amount of flow through that can occur over a 5 month
period.

Utilization

The actual safe yield is dependent on the use or uses
to which the resource is put. The objective here varies
from that of a typical engineering study in that those
uses are not predetermined. The pond is viewed by the
owners as a living ecological entity, deeply bound up in
the natural cycles of the surrounding land. The use to
which it is put must respect that integrity rather than
reduce it to a simple vessel capable of yielding so many
gallons of water. Ecological enhancement, as opposed to
minimal environmental damage relative to arbitrary,
exteriorly imposed criteria, is an important design
parameter for the farm operation.

Three possible uses have been identified so far. The first is as a source of irrigation water. Here the actual safe yield is determined by the time at which it would be most needed and the total storage capacity of the pond. The pond's surface area is about one acre and its maximum average depth between 10 and 12 feet, so that storage capacity is 10-12 acre-ft. With the potential for a 2 acre-ft. loss in storage during summer, when irrigation would be most needed, the maximum safe yield becomes 8-10 acre-ft., about 1/5 of the theoretical safe yield. This practice however would rule out any other use and would certainly violate the ecological integrity of the pond by pumping it dry. During a more normal or wet year, on the other hand, it may be possible to withdraw more than this amount of water without effecting pond stage or storage.

In order to take advantage of good years and at the same time preserve the integrity of the resource in bad ones, the farm design will encorporate diversity and flexibility in its choice of crops. Hardy, low maintenance, perennial fruit and nut crops may form the basis of such a design. Frost hardy spring and winter crops provide another hedge against a dry summer season. By staggering plantings in general, an entire year's crop is not made or lost by one or two dry months. By watching the water table level, as indicated by the feeder streams and the observation well mentioned earlier, one may make prudent judgments as to whether a given plot should be planted or left in cover.

The second use being considered for the pond is raising fish. The effects of withdrawal, pond storage and flow through on water temperature and chemistry must be determined in order for this to be integrated with a successful irrigation plan. By examining seasonal fluctuations through the framework of the hydrologic model it may be possible to predict the effects of these perturbations. This ability can only be gained and improved through experience, but the model provides a basis against which to compare seemingly isolated phenomena and upon which to build a more complex ecological one. In order for the process to be sustainable, fish raising should begin on a small scale as one component of a diverse, integrated agricultural system.

Finally, the owners have begun experimenting with the harvest and composting of submergent plants and organic sediments from the pond. This process may, by its effect on BOD and dissolved oxygen, have important implications for the other two uses. The accumulation of dead organic material is the basis for the process of eutrophication, which would eventually make the pond unlivable for many types of fish and other organisms requiring cooler waters and high levels of dissolved oxygen. By arresting this process, the long term maintenance of the fish pond and irrigation reservoir may be achieved,in addition to securing a renewable source of fertilizer.

In order to maximize storage without flooding portions of the surrounding land, an adjustable weir was originally designed. When fully open, the weir would allow for routing of the 10 year storm event without loss of storage. Adjustment consisted of adding or removing one of several wooden slats to increase or decrease the weir height. The owners are currently allowing a beaver that lives in the pond to perform this function. The height of the beaver dam is adjusted every few days with a hay fork to prevent flooding. Branches are tossed in a separate pile, while leaves, algae and various soft stemmed emergents and submergents are collected and eventually hauled away to be composted or used directly as a mulch. So far the arrangement appears to be satisfactory.

References

Bedient, Philip and Huber, Wayne, Hydrology and Floodplain Analysis, Addison-Wesley Pub. Comp., 1988.

Blatner, William, Site Specific Hydro/ecological Model for Permaculture Application, 1988, Civil Engineering Dept., City College of New York, Convent Ave. New York, N.Y. 10031.

U.S. Dept. of Agriculture, Soil Conservation Service, Technical Release 55, Urban Hydrology for Small Watersheds, June, 1986.

Land-Water Management: Theory and Practice

Warren Viessman, Jr.[1], M. ASCE

Abstract

Land use and water use are inseparable. Almost everything that is done on the land surface affects the associated water resource in one way or another. Policies for land and water management should be consistent and coordinated. Traditionally, land use and water management decisions have been made by different levels of government and/or agencies. The resulting conflicts and inconsistencies this creates are well known but progress in overcoming them has been slow. Topics of concern include facilities and industrial siting; urbanization of land, agricultural development and operations; flood management; and environmental protection.

Introduction

The long-established tradition of dealing independently with land, water, and air resources management issues has been a major contributor to the degradation in quality of natural and developed areas and to the difficulties now being faced in handling problems that are regional, intergovernmental, and interdisciplinary in nature. Concerns about landforms, plants, animals, fish, and humans should be dealt with collectively. A 1989 comment by acclaimed land planner Ian McHarg is relevant. He said: "Science remains obdurately in the late phase of 19th Century reductionism, resistant to synthesis or holism". We must stop manipulating components in a vacuum, and begin to explore and foster interactive management approaches.

---

[1]Professor and Chairman, Department of Environmental Engineering Sciences, 217 black Hall, University of Florida, Gainesville, Florida 32611

In the final analysis, it is how we configure and collectively manage the parts that will spell the difference between poorly and well-managed systems. The need for reform is well documented, but the key to accomplishing it is elusive. There is no generalized strategy that can be expected to work everywhere, and change will have to be tailor-fitted to the locality in question, be it a state, county, or some other subdivision. The setting for managing land-water systems includes geographic, political, economic, and social attributes. The challenge is to skillfully blend these traits into a coordinated management effort.

Land-Water Cross-Impacts

Water resources development affects associated lands, and land use practices affect related waters. Reservoir developments change land use patterns for better or worse; management of solid wastes may affect associated water quality; land treatment residues appear in runoff waters; channelizing streams affects their flood plains and wetlands; watershed management can affect the amount and quality of water available for use; attitudes of landowners are reflected in the impacts they make on water quantity and/or quality; and facilities siting can have significant spillover effects on water resources, particularly on water quality. These examples of close ties between land-water management practices underscore the need to coordinate water resources planning and management with land use planning and regulation. The need has long been recognized, but overcoming the institutional barriers to it has lagged (NWC, 1973). A creative exercise of land use control powers, such as zoning, could, however, go a long way toward mitigating this problem.

The Issues

There is a need for better coordination and consistency among the governments and agencies engaged in land-water management (Viessman and Welty, 1985). In general, there is no pervasive mandate or organizational arrangement that provides for these elements. Without question, planners and managers should be sensitive to the impacts their proposals may have on other governments, agencies, and programs, but there are few formal structures for requiring this. Viewing problems in all of their dimensions is crucial to effective resource management, and yet we continue to operate principally along strict disciplinary or agency lines.

The public's desire for optimal use of its lands and water resources is not being reflected consistently in the reality of agency, or agency approved, plans and their implementing actions. Legal reforms are needed to accomplish this task. Even when fragile lands, such as wetlands, are in state ownership and subject to public trust rights, damages from developmental activities such as drainage sometimes occur. Usually this is due to poor record keeping on ownership, lack of coordination of agency missions, and narrowly-scoped planning processes.

Effective, authoritative, regional, institutions must be designed and put into operation. Cities, counties, and states are often too limited in jurisdiction to deal appropriately with land-water issues that transcend their boundaries. More often then not, locally perceived problems have regional, if not global, dimensions. The management of waters that cross political boundaries, particularly international boundaries, is a case in point. Both land and water attributes are involved and good solutions to such problems cannot be devised by narrowly focused agencies.

Water planning must not be considered an end in itself (NWC, 1973). Water planners operating independently of those engaged in efforts related to land use, transportation, housing, and industrial development cannot be expected to produce plans that adequately incorporate these dimensions. The same may be said for their counterparts in other agencies. Important land or water use decisions are often constrained, or even precluded, because a narrowly conceived functional plan has been implemented. And while the representation of other interests on water resources planning bodies may aid in reducing conflicts, this practice is more akin to a band-aid than a prescription. There is a need for some umbrella to pull time frames and differing interests together. The strong interrelationships between water and land use planning suggest the need for formal coordinating machinery at federal,state, and local government levels. An example is Florida's State planning system. It requires that state, regional and local government plans be consistent. It mandates that water elements in local government comprehensive plans be in conformance with broader state and regional policies, an important link in coordinating land-water planning elements.

Land-Water Management Initiatives

Florida's Kissimmee River restoration program is a

unique land-water management undertaking (SFWMD, 1986). It proposes to modify the Kissimmee river system from its present canalized state to one having the features of a meandering stream with wide floodplains and extensive wetlands. Changes in both form and function are part of the scheme. Because land use practices in the upper basin influence downstream hydrologic events so significantly, their modification is the key to an effective project design.

A Save Our Rivers Program (SOR), addressing land-water management, was initiated in 1981 to protect Florida's natural waterways, wetlands and the state's drinking water (Lewis, 1986). The program is designed to remove fragile river-related lands from private ownership so that they can be managed in a manner that maximizes their utility for water supply, and for the conservation and protection of water resources. Under this program, the Water Management Districts (WMD's) buy lands they think are the most critical for the protection of the water resources in their regions.

Lake Okeechobee, is one of the largest freshwater lakes in the U.S. It is an integral part of the Kissimmee-Okeechobee-Everglades ecosystem. The lake's functions are in jeopardy, however, because of substantial nutrient loadings from dairy farms, cattle ranches, sugar cane fields, and vegetable farms. Unless this situation is alleviated, Lake Okeechobee could become unable to support the delicate balances resident in a healthy lake. A Lake Okeechobee Technical Advisory Committee has recommended a 40 percent reduction in phosphorous loading to the lake. This goal is to be achieved using a combination of approaches including: fencing farm/dairy cow operations off from close proximity to waterways; preventing the direct discharge of runoff into waterways; retaining runoff from areas of intense animal use; the purchase of land; and chemical and biological treatment of nutrient-rich surface waters. The mix is one of joint land-water management practices.

Lake Apopka, once a famous Florida sport fishing lake, is now hyper-eutrophic. As one approach to dealing with this problem, the St. Johns River Water Management District (SJRWMD), recommended that about 8,000 acres of muck farm land adjacent to lake Apopka be exchanged for a similar land holding in South Florida (Dean, 1987). The exchange would have been on a value for value basis, based on appraisals. The Trustees of the Internal Improvement Trust Fund would have retained ownership of Apopka lands and the SJRWMD would have leased and restored these lands in cooperation with several other institutions. Although the land exchange proposition was not implemented, it is indicative of a growing movement toward exploring new, non-traditional approaches to land-water management.

Conclusions

The key to coordinated land-water management must be found. Interagency and intergovernmental coordination and cooperation must be improved. Political processes must be better understood and shaped to focus on holistic land-water management approaches. Land-water management policies must take on a unified dimension. Few contemporary problems are local in nature. More emphasis must be placed on regional planning and management, and regional institutions to accommodate this must be devised. It is time that we began to focus on preventive rather than remedial approaches to land-water issues.

APPENDIX I. REFERENCES

Dean, H., Lake Apopka Land Exchange. St. Johns River Water Management District. Memorandum. Palatka, Florida, 1987.
Lewis, J., Save Our Rivers. Executive Office of the Governor. Tallahassee, Florida, 1986.
National Water Commission (NWC), Water Policies for the Future, U.S. Gov't. Printing Office, Washington, D.C., June 1973.
South Florida Water Management District (SFWMD), Annual Report 1986. West Palm Beach, Florida, 1986.
Viessman, Jr., W. and Welty, C., Water Management: Technology And Institutions. Harper and Row Publishers, Inc. New York, New York, 1985.

Changing Land Uses in The Platte and Arkansas Basins

Gary L. Lewis[1]   Ph.D., P.E., M. ASCE

Abstract

Several water disputes among various parties in the Platte and Arkansas River Basins may have significant impacts on future land use practices. This paper describes five cases being litigated in either state water courts, the United States Supreme Court, or federal district courts. Aspects of the cases are reviewed, and the implications on near and long-term water management and land use practices are discussed.

Kansas v. Colorado - Arkansas River Flows

Kansas has filed a Supreme Court action against Colorado, asserting that groundwater pumping has depleted the flows into Kansas and violated apportionments established in the 1948 Arkansas River Compact. The states have litigated the river flows twice before, and Kansas has been the "loser" both times. One case spanned the years from 1928 to 1943 and produced 385 exhibits and over 7000 reports and documents. News accounts indicate that each state may expend in excess of $3 million on the upcoming litigation. A special master has been appointed by the Supreme Court to hear the case in mid-1990.

Prairie Bend Unit

This case study involves an expanded version of an original 1976 permit for a water right from the Platte River to store water in two reservoirs and irrigate 70,000 acres in central Nebraska. A failed 1950's referendum on the U.S. Bureau of Reclamation (USBR) Mid-States project included many of the current project

---

[1]Principal Engineer, Boyle Engineering Corporation, 165 South Union Boulevard, Suite 200, Lakewood, CO 80228.

CHANGING LAND USES 327

objectives and components. Nebraska's water officials feel one more project on the Platte can be built.

The 1976 project was a traditional USBR storage and surface irrigation proposal. Today's requirements for expanded environmental considerations resulted in abandonment of the traditional concept in favor of a multipurpose project with habitat and instream flow components. After considerable review by a public values committee, the proposal was eventually transformed to a groundwater recharge, storage and recovery project, with half the $500 million costs dedicated to environmental components. This also changed the point of diversion and the number and locations of the reservoirs. Even with these components, numerous objections were filed by downstream water users and environmentalists.

After prolonged delays, the Director of the Nebraska Department of Water Resources issued an order in September, 1989 setting aside the 1976 approval (so that other junior project applicants can be heard) and denying the proposed revisions. Whether the Prairie Bend Unit or some other project is built, it will need to incorporate similar environmental considerations and land use components.

Nebraska v. Wyoming and Others

In several separate actions, Nebraska is objecting to existing and proposed upstream water uses in the Platte River. In one case Nebraska has asked the Supreme Court to enforce a 1945 decree regarding the three-state apportionment of flows in the North Platte River. Nebraska officials feel that Wyoming is already violating the decree by operations of the Greyrocks reservoir on the Laramie River (a tributary to the North Platte) and fear that development of the $52 million Deer Creek dam on another tributary could further impact the apportionment. Wyoming contends that deliveries made since 1914 to three regulating reservoirs in Nebraska are without a legal right, and that tributaries are not covered by terms of the decree. Wyoming in turn has filed a counterclaim in the Supreme Court alleging decree violations by Nebraska. Wyoming has also filed a Federal District Court action for an injunction against the USBR, who operate several major reservoirs in Wyoming, to stop deliveries of water to the three Nebraska reservoirs.

The U.S. Army Corps of Engineers (Corps) granted a 404 permit in 1988 to Wyoming for construction of the

Deer Creek dam. Nebraska objected to both the Draft and Final EIS, claiming numerous flaws in the hydrologic models, and flaws in mitigation requirements that trade land in Nebraska for flow reductions in upstream reaches. A lawsuit filed in U.S. District Court names both the Corps and Fish and Wildlife Service as violators of procedural requirements for evaluation of the project. The state later requested that the original suit be expanded to include a recognition of critical wildlife habitat for threatened and endangered (T & E) species in the central Platte valley. This, plus Wyoming's request for Summary Judgment, and requests for intervention by several other parties, have been denied.

Nebraska has also taken exception to the 404 permit for the Two Forks dam (see below) but cannot take formal action because of language in the 1923 South Platte River Compact between Colorado and Nebraska.

EPA v. Corps of Engineers - Two Forks Dam

A 1.1 million acre foot Two Forks Reservoir just West of Denver has been proposed to meet long-term water needs of some 30 communities in the metropolitan area. It will be located several hundred miles upstream of the critical habitat areas in Nebraska, and will store water derived in greatest proportions from sources outside of the Platte River Basin. Opponents have threatened lawsuits if construction is ever approved. Controversy has been so intense that opponents have resorted to publishing domestic water-use amounts by key local dam backers as a way of suggesting personal avarice as a motive (Ref. 1).

A Systemwide Environmental Impact Study (EIS) begun in 1982 and completed in 1987 set a new cost record for such studies. Participants in the $40 million EIS inventoried and tagged just about every frog, bird, fish, butterfly, deer, invertebrate, kayaker, fisherperson, relic, rock and fault line in the region. An intent to issue a 404 permit was announced by the Corps after extensive Endangered Species Act consultations and National Environmental Policy Act public hearings.

As one of his first campaign-promise tests in office, and faced with the Alaskan oil spill, President Bush's new administrator of EPA has announced intentions to veto the Corp's proposed permit. The Denver regional EPA administrator had earlier concurred with the EIS, leaving the project sponsors disappointed, stunned, and

CHANGING LAND USES 329

with $40 million in expenditures to date. Public and political pressures are being vigorously applied, and legal proceedings are likely.

Colorado v. U.S. Forest Service

In this case, Colorado and other water users are opposing water court applications by the U.S. Forest Service (USFS) seeking to acquire instream water rights for channel maintenance in alpine areas of a large portion of Colorado. If granted, the USFS claims would amount to about half the flow in most of the streams. Long-standing state-permitted rights to divert these flows for Front Range communities would presumably be abandoned in the public interest. The USFS basis for the claim in the 1897 Organic Administration Act. Colorado and other impacted interests disagree with the legal interpretation and technical procedures for quantifying the claim.

Effects on Future Land Use

All but the first case involve debate over effects of flow changes on channel morphology in mountain streams or the central Platte River. Land use policies and practices in the subject reaches are likely to be governed in growing proportions by habitat and channel capacity considerations. In two cases, Deer Creek and Two Forks, the U.S. Fish and Wildlife Service rendered non-jeopardy opinions if tracts of land in the Platte valley would be purchased, cleared, and maintained as habitat for T & E species. Large portions of the testimony at hearings and trials related to these projects have been apportioned to debate over alluvial channel morphology and the viability of these proposed water, habitat and land management practices. Scientists are far from agreement over these issues.

A significant potential land use impact of the outcome of several of these disputes is the conversion of irrigated agricultural rights to municipal and industrial rights, and the subsequent permanent retirement of lands previously irrigated. In the Arkansas Basin, farmers have been yielding to disastrous economic conditions (and lucrative financial offers) by selling their water rights to urban areas. Aurora, Colorado, for example responded to an early 1980's development boom by negotiating two purchases totalling nearly 15,000 acre feet of Arkansas River water rights from half as many acres for amounts approaching $50 million. These lands would revert to dryland uses, resulting in potential for increased erosion, weed

growth, dust, and loss of aesthetic values. In an
effort to control dust bowl conditions in the Arkansas,
the water rights transfers to Aurora can commence only
after a one or two year state-mandated diversion of the
acquired water to first establish a cover of dryland
grasses.

Such water rights transfers are politically
supported by a wide range of interest groups. The fact
that the transfers offer an alternative to large dams
makes them palatable to environmentalists. Key
legislators in Nebraska are working to cautiously allow
water right transfers as a means of bolstering a
declining farm and ranch economy in areas where almost
any farm could offset the entire Two Forks impacts, and
where the depth of high-quality underlying groundwater
has yet to be measured.

Reallocation of water stored in existing
reservoirs, and reuse of water, will become even more
popular as water battles continue. These changes may
alter land uses. The reorganized USBR, and other
agencies such as the Corps, are actively studying
reallocation options. Corps and Bureau reservoirs in
Kansas are undergoing investigation as high-potential
candidates for increased efficiencies through
reallocation, and studies of other systems demonstrate
similar possibilities throughout the region.

Declines in groundwater levels in western Kansas
have already invoked significant land use changes. The
first "Intensive Groundwater Use Control Area" has been
designated along a 150 mile reach (Ref. 3) of the
Arkansas River. This closes the area to all new
appropriation, including domestic uses. A Supreme Court
decision in favor of Kansas over state line flows would
have several possible impacts on water and land
management practices. Modified water rights to well
irrigators in Colorado could force abandonment of some
lands and may deprive junior surface water appropriators
of supplemental supplies during most years. Crop
patterns could change, and winter flow diversions may
recur. Operations of key reservoirs may also be
altered.

A decision for Colorado would mean that the wells
are not the cause of depleted flows into Kansas, and
little land or water management changes would likely
occur. Regardless of the outcome in court, Kansas' own
allowance of heavy well-irrigation may result in
increased land and water use controls for Kansans and
other downstream irrigators.

Construction of the Two Forks dam will provide water for continued growth in 30 or more communities. Failure of the project would likely result in land development restrictions and/or aggressive acquisition of agricultural water rights by communities that were to be served by the project. Project proponents argue that in the absence of Two Forks, a raid on other supply-limited rivers and aquifers would occur, and Colorado's agricultural economy would be severely impacted. Opponents argue that greater water conservation and cooperation will result. Either outcome will result in a change in water and land use practices for many Coloradoans.

Bibliography

1. Obmascik, M. "Key, 2 Forks Backers Top List of Water Users", Denver Post, Sept. 19, 1989.

2. Two Forks for Nebraska Association, "What Two Forks Reservoir Does for Nebraska", 1989.

3. U.S. Water News, "Kansas Restricts Wells Along Western Arkansas R. Valley", Feb. 1987.

Optimizing Dallas' Multiple Reservoir Supply System

Robert M. McCarthy[1]

Abstract

Dallas Water Utilities (DWU) applies a mathematical computer model of its reservoir supply system to assist in making operational decisions to optimize supply operations. The model considers projected water demands, permit constraints on reservoir withdrawal rates, hydrological data, power costs, chemical costs, and treatment and distribution system constraints.

Introduction

Dallas Water Utilities provides raw and treated water service to over 1.6 million people over a 719 square mile service area. Water system demands have continued to increase rapidly in recent years, increasing from 235 MGD in 1978 to 374 mgd in 1988. DWU holds water rights in seven major reservoirs spread over three major river basins. These rights total 580.9 mdg. Additionally, DWU can purchase up to 10 mgd of treated water from the North Texas Municipal Water District bringing the total supply available to 590.9 mgd. Projections made as part of DWU's 1989 Long Range Water Supply Study indicate the above water rights will supply DWU system needs through year 2018. Use of return flows would extend the time for when a new supply is needed. Although two reservoirs are currently not connected to treatment plants, both will be needed to meet system demands soon after year 2000. Having supplies in excess of demands gives DWU great flexibility in operating its supply system.

A traditional approach to supplying water demands has been to draft supplies up to an amount calculated to be the dependable yield of a supply. Dependable yield is defined to be that constant rate of withdrawal that would just empty a reservoir during a repeat of conditions experienced during the worst historical drought. Consistant with this approach, many

---
[1]Water Scientist, Dallas Water Utilities, 1500 Marilla Room 5AS, Dallas, Texas 75201

consultants have recommended that DWU operate each lake at its dependable yield. However, pumping costs from remote supplies are substantially higher than those for nearby supplies. Also, there are many sequences of years when the inflows to the nearby supplies are relatively high resulting in much more than the dependable yield of these lakes being available. The competing needs of minimizing operating costs versus ensuring adequate supplies are available during a drought led Dallas to develop a mathematical model of its supply system. The model allows analysis of alternative operations in an effort to optimize the use of available supplies.

Operational Considerations

Figure 1 shows the reservoir supply system used by DWU. Dallas' western reservoirs, Lakes Lewisville, Ray Roberts and Grapevine, release water which flows by gravity via river channel to raw water pumps which low-lift the raw water approximately 40 ft to the Elm Fork and Bachman treatment plants. Water from eastern reservoirs is pumped up to 55 miles through pipelines to the East Side treatment plant. The required lift from Lake Tawakoni, the most distant eastern supply currently connected to the DWU system, is approximately 200 ft. Reservoirs held for future use will require even higher pumping heads. For example, plans for connecting Lake Fork call for first pumping the water to Tawakoni and then repumping it to Dallas. Lake Palestine water will be pumped to a new Southeast Treatment Plant. Obviously pumping eastern water instead of western water incurs high energy requirements and costs. However, water from eastern reservoirs is of better quality than the water reaching treatment plants from the western reservoirs. This is primarily because western water is conveyed from the reservoirs via open creek and river channels where suspended solids and point and non-point pollution degrades water quality. Therefore, the cost for chemicals for treating eastern water is normally cheaper than for treating western water. However, the total cost for pumping and treating western water is still cheaper than for eastern water.

Many other complicating factors exist. For example, evaporation is higher in western supplies making it desirable to draw these reservoirs down to reduce evaporation and to provide space for capturing runoff from rain events. Diversion permits for western supplies allow for annual diversions far in excess of their dependable yields (overdrafting), while permits for eastern supplies limit annual diversions to near firm yields. Overdrafting is normally a prudent operation since overall costs are reduced and in most years rainfall, and thus inflows, are above those which would occur during a drought. This results in water being available in western reservoirs in most years in excess of yields calculated for conditions experienced during

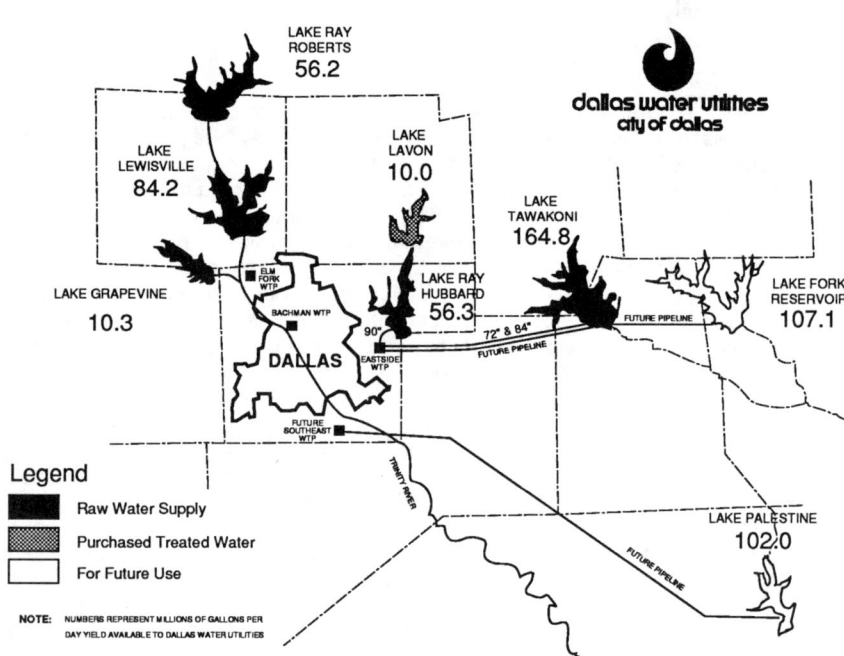

Figure 1. DALLAS WATER SUPPLY SOURCES

the most severe recorded drought. However, to take advantage of the cost savings and still guarantee demands could still be supplied throughout a drought equal in severity to the most severe recorded drought, a practical limit on overdrafting must be set. If western supplies are drawn too far down, eastern permits would not allow overusing eastern supplies to make up for their earlier underuse during a significant drought. While a shift to eastern supplies results in an immediate dramatic increase in power costs, the savings from overdrafting cheaper western supplies in most years offsets the increased cost from the infrequent shifts to eastern supplies and, therefore results in net savings over the long term.

The supply system changes through time and no one operation is optimal under all conditions. For example, in periods when the connected supply is at or near actual system demand, little overdrafting can take place without the risk of running out of water in western supplies late in a drought and then being unable, due to distribution and permit constraints, to supply enough water to meet system demands from eastern supplies. DWU periodically develops operational guidelines which take the above factors into account. For example, in 1988 DWU had the same total connected supply as it did in 1978, approximately 382 mgd. Having 382 mgd supply versus a 235 mgd demand in 1978 allowed DWU to heavily overdraft western supplies while maintaining the ability to cut back western usage in winter months and pump water from eastern sources. Computer simulations made in 1978 determined that DWU could safely overdraft western supplies until they were almost 50% depleted. Once 50% depletion occured operations would shift to maximizing pumpage from eastern supplies and, to the extend possible, holding western supplies for peaking during summer months. Conversely, in 1988, when demand was 374 mgd versus the same connected supply of 382 mgd, simulations showed DWU could only overdraft western supplies until they were 5% depleted without danger of being unable to make up pumpage from the east should a drought equal in severity to the worst recorded drought recur.

The ability to transfer water to and from treatment plants also changes with time. Pump station, pipeline and purification plant expansions increase the amount of water that can be delivered from a lake into the distribution system. What once prevented the ability to make up water from eastern supplies late in a drought may dramatically change with any of the above improvements. In particular, as new lakes are connected to the system, there are periods of time when total supply is greater than demand. During these periods a substantial savings can be realized by overdrafting western supplies. However, just prior to connecting a new lake by long expensive pipelines, it is best to operate lakes not to minimize costs, but rather to maximize the available supply. Shifting operations to maximize eastern water usage much sooner than needed to ensure drought demands could be met is more expensive operationally but results in a slightly higher system yield. When connected supplies are close to actual demands, such an operation can still save money by delaying as long as possible the need for large capital expenditures to connect a new supply since cost differences resulting from different lake operations are small compared to debt service expenses for large capital expenditures.

DWU uses a mathematical computer model to consider the above factors and to assist in finding what is hopefully a near optimum operation that saves money over the long term. This model is applied periodically as system conditions change or as demands increase. Operational costs of alternative operations are computed and compared by simulating each alternative operating rule over the entire hydrologic period of record. The period of record is used because simulating costs of an average operation may be far different than simulating the costs from widely varying conditions ranging from wet to drought periods and then calculating what the average would be. Comparing the costs of numerous trial operating rules can quickly find an operation that is near the cheapest cost and which still ensures drought demands can be supplied. In addition to costs, monthly drafts, and lowest and average individual lake levels can also be compared.

Model Overview

The model consists of three basic modules. The first module performs monthly mass-balance computations for each lake using monthly hydrologic records of inflows and evaporation, storage-surface area relationships and monthly withdrawal rates calculated in the second module. The second module is the decision making routine. This routine considers purification plant, distribution system, and lake permit limitations together with each lake's water level at the beginning of the month, advanced knowledge of which lakes have more expensive pumping costs and other information input as data to the model to determine a trial set of monthly withdrawals from each lake. These routines are run on a trail-and-error basis with many simulations normally required to find one that would work. Once several feasible operations are identified their costs can be compared by the third program module. The third module computes what the operating costs over the hydrologic period of record would have been for each feasible operation by estimating what monthly power and chemical costs would have been. A more detailed explanation of the model and how costs are computed is contained in another paper (McCarthy, 1989).

Summary

Periodic application of a reservoir operation computer model assists DWU in analyzing and optimizing supply system operations under various conditions. In applying the model DWU tries to balance the ability to supply demands that would occur should the historic drought of record be repeated in the future versus minimizing operational costs over the long term.

APPENDIX I. References

McCarthy, R.M. (1989). "Computer Modeling to Develop Annual Reservoir Operation Guidelines." <u>Proceedings of the specialty Conference on Computers and Automation in the Water Industry (in press)</u>, American Water Works Association, Denver, CO.

APPENDIX II. Conversion To SI Units

To Convert	To	Multiply By
mgd	m^3/d	3785.4
ft	m	0.3048
sq mi	sq km	2.59

MICROCOMPUTER TOOLS FOR THE MANAGEMENT OF A MULTIPLE RESERVOIR WATER SUPPLY SYSTEM

Charles I. Moore, A.M. ASCE
and
Christopher C. Clarkson, A.M. ASCE (1)

Abstract

In a Raw Water Management Plan study performed for the City of Newport News Waterworks, Camp Dresser & McKee developed a series of micro-computer programs that allow the City to effectively manage the raw water system. One component is a Safe Yield Model that evaluates the effects of changes in reservoir storage volume, pumping capacity, and conveyance capacity on the safe yield available during severe droughts. The second component is an expert decision support system that evaluates the cost, water quality, and risk of depletion impacts of various available pumping configurations to meet specified demand conditions and assists Waterworks staff in selecting the optimum configuration. This paper provides an overview of these two management tools and of the results of the Raw Water Management Plan.

Introduction

The City of Newport News, Virginia, relies on a series of six water supply reservoirs, augmented with a run of the river pumping station, to provide water to about 350,000 persons in the York-James

---

(1) Water Resources Engineers, Camp Dresser & McKee, 7535 Little River Turnpike, Suite 200, Annandale, Va, 22003

River Peninsula. Present water use averages about
45 mgd. A system of force mains and pumping
stations connect the various reservoirs. The
conveyance system contains a total of 80 miles of
pipe ranging from 24 to 48 inches in diameter, 17
pumps with a combined pumping capacity of 151 mgd,
and extends a maximum distance of 31 miles.

Safe Yield Model

The Raw Water Management Plan required a
computer model that could simulate the interaction
of the raw water reservoirs and conveyance system
and the effects of changes in this system on its
ability to meet water supply demands during critical
droughts. A further requirement was that the
program be user friendly so the client could
frequently use the model and also make required
modifications to the data input as changes occur in
the system. The Newport News Safe Yield Model was
developed specifically to meet the needs of this
study.

The model uses methodologies similar to those
used by the U.S. Army HEC-3 and HEC-5 models (1981,
1982). The Safe Yield Model simulates reservoirs
system operation using algorithms that balance the
reservoir stages and limit the transfer rates to the
constraints imposed by the system and by minimum
instream flowby rules. The driving inputs to the
program are the long-term flow records at a USGS
gaging station on the Chickahominy River (1927-
present). Reservoir characteristics and default
data that do not change often are read from input
files. During a simulation the user provides input
interactively where required and may override many
of the default inputs.

The Safe Yield Model has three modes of
operation. The first provides detailed information
on the simulated reservoir stages and inter-
reservoir transfer volumes for the period of record.

The second mode determines the safe yield of
the system. In this study, the safe yield is
defined as the maximum constant rate that can be
delivered to the treatment plants without depleting
available storage in the reservoir system. The safe
yield of the present system is estimated to be 57.8
mgd. Analysis shows that the safe yield is

constrained by the long drought that occurred in the mid- through late-1960s and that the safe yield can be increased to 66 mgd by increasing the pumping capacity at the Chickahominy Pump station by 30 mgd. If this modification is made, additional increases in safe yield are attainable only through increasing the available storage capacity by adding new reservoirs or by increasing available storage in existing reservoirs.

The third mode of operation of the Safe Yield Model uses a "Position Analysis" methodology (Hirsch, 1978) to determine the risk of reaching certain reservoir stages based on today's reservoir levels. Reservoir levels are reset to the defined initial position for each drought in the period of record and the safe yield for each drought is determined. The drought safe yield estimates are ranked to produce a probability curve from which the risk of reaching a percent full stage given a rate of demand is determined. This is used as a drought management tool to evaluate the risk of reaching certain alert levels for water conservation program implementation.

Expert System

An expert decision support system was also developed for the Newport News Raw Water Management Plan. This system was designed as a drought management tool and as a means to evaluate the water quality and pumping cost implications of selective pumping from the water sources to the terminal reservoirs that supply the water treatment plants.

The system manager enters information on the current status of the system including reservoir stages, demand, the forecast for rain in the future, and water quality in the reservoirs. This data is summarized in report format by the expert system. The safe yield position analysis risk is then computed by the Safe Yield Model. Based on the risk and the current status of the system, recommendations are provided as to the drought management activities that should be undertaken.

The program also selects five pumping configurations that meet the current water supply demand. The quality of the water being delivered to the terminal reservoir for up to three constituents is evaluated and ranked. Of particular interest in the Newport News study is the trihalomethane formation potential in the raw water. Using this tool, the concentration of trihalomethane in the finished water may be managed by selectively operating the raw water system during critical periods. The cost of pumping is also computed and ranked. From this information the manager can make informed decisions on how to operate the system to meet water supply demands, maintain water quality, and minimize pumping costs.

Conclusion

Microcomputer tools were developed to allow the City of Newport News to manage its water supply effectively. These included the following:

o   Safe Yield Model

o   expert decision support system.

These tools will be used regularly by Waterworks managers to:

o   manage the day-to-day operation of the system,

o   manage the system during drought or other emergency conditions,

o   evaluate the effect of changes in the system on the safe yield.

References

Hirsch, R.M., Risk Analysis for a Water-Supply System: Occoquan Reservoir, Fairfax and Prince William Counties, Virginia. U.S. Geological Survey, Open File Report 78-452, Reston, Virginia, 1978.

U.S. Army Corps of Engineers, HEC-3 Reservoir System Analysis for Conservation, Users Manual, Computer Program 723-030, Davis, California, 1981

U.S. Army Corps of Engineers, HEC-5 Simulation of Flood Control and Conservation Systems, Users Manual, Computer Program 723-X6-L2500, Davis, California, 1982.

OPTIMAL OPERATION OF MULTIPLE RESERVOIR SYSTEMS

Qinghui Zhong and Kevin E. Lansey[1], A.M. ASCE

INTRODUCTION

Determining the optimal operation of multiple reservoir systems for hydropower production has been an area of continuing interest. Dynamic programming and its extensions have been widely used to solve both deterministic and low dimension stochastic models. In their review articles both Yakowitz (1982) and Yeh (1985) point out the inability of solving large problems by DP or the so-called curse of dimensionality. Several methods have been proposed to overcome this problem (Turgeon (1981) and Foufoula-Georgiou and Kitanidis (1989)) with some success but with their own limitations.

Nonlinear programing (NLP) has not enjoyed the popularity of DP in this area although several applications have appeared in the literature (Hanscom et al. (1980) and Dembo, et al (1989) and others). In most cases a single large NLP problem is solved which requires long computation times for large-scale systems. Another limitation of NLP is the difficulty in incorporating the uncertain nature of inflows. Turgeon (1988) and others, however, have discussed the potential of solving an implicit stochastic program by adding chance constraints to the model and determining optimal operation rules to account for the stochastic inflows. Unfortunately this requires solving for long-term operations which increases computation efforts.

In this paper a temporal decomposition approach is presented to solve a long term deterministic model for a multi-reservoir system. Through relaxation the long term problem is broken into several smaller subproblems; each of which can be solved relatively quickly using standard NLP codes. Coordination between subproblems is accounted for by a Lagrangian penalty term in the objective function of each subproblem. Overall convergence is achieved through an iterative process by updating the Lagrange multipliers.

---

1. Graduate Assistant and Assistant Professor, respectively, School of Civil Engineering, Oklahoma State Univ., Stillwater, OK, 74078.

The method has been applied to a nine-reservoir system in central China. A technique to improve overall convergence and the potential to consider inflow uncertainty are discussed.

PROBLEM FORMULATION

In a multireservoir system containing n reservoirs which are primarily used for power generation, we wish to maximize the total electrical production from the system subject to satisfying the required relationships of conservation of mass and physical limits on the system. This problem can be written as;

$$\underset{\{X_j,Y_j\}}{Max} \sum_{j=1}^{M} N_j(X_{j-1}, X_j, Y_j) \tag{1}$$

$$X_{min} \leq X_j \leq X_{max} \tag{2}$$
$$Y_{min} \leq Y_j \leq Y_{max} \tag{3}$$
$$Q_{min} \leq Q_j \leq Q_{max} \tag{4}$$
$$N_{min} \leq N_j \leq N_{max} \tag{5}$$
$$X_0 = X_m \tag{6}$$
$$V(X_j) = V(X_{j-1}) + q_j - B(Q_j + Y_j) \tag{7}$$

where j is the number of time periods, say months or years. Each variable is a vector of n elements corresponding to n reservoirs. The objective function is to maximize the total power generation N which is a function of the decision variables, X_j and Y_j, the reservoir water levels and spillages, respectively. q_j and Q_j are the direct runoff into each reservoir and controlled reservoir releases, respectively, and B is a matrix describing the configuration of the reservoir system. Eqs. (2-5) impose bounds on the decision variables, the reservoir discharge and power production for each period. The initial and final water levels are defined as being equal in Eq. (6) although any target value can be used. Eq. (7) is the conservation of mass relations for the system where V is the water storage associated with water levels, X. These can typically be expressed as exponential functions. For simplicity of notation, Eq. (4, 5, and 7) can be written as functions of X and Y;

$$G(X_{j-1}, X_j, Y_j) \geq 0 \tag{8}$$

SOLUTION ALGORITHM

If a long period of study is considered, say 10 years of monthly data, this problem is becomes very troublesome to solve directly. To overcome this difficulty a temporal decomposition approach is applied to break the original model into a number of submodels according to time index which can be quickly solved. Coordination between subproblems is then made through a Lagrangian function. To make the original problem separable a pseudo-variable, Z_j, is introduced and defined as the vector of water surface elevations at the beginning of period j. This must be equal to the ending water level for period j-1, therefore, the constraint, $X_{j-1} = Z_j$ is added to the model which becomes;

$$\underset{\{Z_j, X_j, Y_j\}}{Max} \sum_{j=1}^{M} N_j(Z_j, X_j, Y_j) \qquad (9)$$

$$X_{min} \leq X_j \leq X_{max} \qquad (10)$$
$$Y_{min} \leq Y_j \leq Y_{max} \qquad (11)$$
$$Z_{min} \leq Z_j \leq Z_{max} \qquad (12)$$
$$G_j(Z_j, X_j, Y_j) \geq 0 \qquad (13)$$
$$X_0 = X_m = Z_1 \qquad (14)$$
$$Z_j = X_{j-1} \qquad (15)$$

Only the new constraint (Eq. 10) contains variables from more than one time period. Relaxing the constraint by incorporating it in a Lagrangian term, the objective function becomes;

$$L = \sum N_j(Z_j, X_j, Y_j) + \sum P_j^T (X_{j-1} - Z_j) \qquad (16)$$

where P_j is a vector of multipliers for each reservoir. The proper values of P_j are unknown prior to the optimization and must be determined. Since Z_j and X_j are used to compute power production and in the mass balance equations (Eq. 7) during each subperiod, the model is separable by time period. The solution approach is then to decompose the model by time period and solve each submodel (Eq. (9-14)) for X_j, Y_j and Z_j. Coordination among submodels is accomplished in the Master problem which works to find the correct values for P_j. The Master problem is written as;

$$\underset{\{P\}}{Min} \sum_{j=1}^{M} L_j(P_j) \qquad (17)$$

where
$$L_j = N_j(.) + P_{j+1}^T X_j - P_j^T Z_j \qquad (18)$$
and $P_1 = 0$, $P_{m+1} = 0$, P unrestricted

After the subproblems are solved the optimum X and Z are passed to the Master problem, this unconstrained minimization is solved using a steepest descent scheme. The resulting update relationship for P_j is

$$P_{ij}^{(k+1)} = P_{ij}^{(k)} - K_i(X_{i,j-1}^{(k)} - Z_{ij}^{(k)}) \qquad (19)$$

The new $P_j(k+1)$ is passed to the submodels which determines a new set of optimum X and Z which are returned to the Master problem. This iterative process continues until the difference, $X_{j-1} - Z_j$, is less than acceptable limit. With K>0, this algorithm can be shown to converge to the global optimal if the initial problem is concave. Local optimum will be found in general nonlinear problems.

The approach has been employed to determine annual operations of a nine-reservoir system in central China which is dominated by Three-gorge hydropower station. A schematic map of the system is shown as follows. The nonlinear optimization code, GRG2, developed by Lasdon and Waren (1986) is used to solve the subprob-

RESERVOIR SYSTEMS OPERATIONS   345

lems. Preliminary results have shown that the   initial   selection
and updating of the multipliers, P, are critical for convergence of
the overall algorithm. The linear updating scheme   provides   good
initial results but poor convergence.

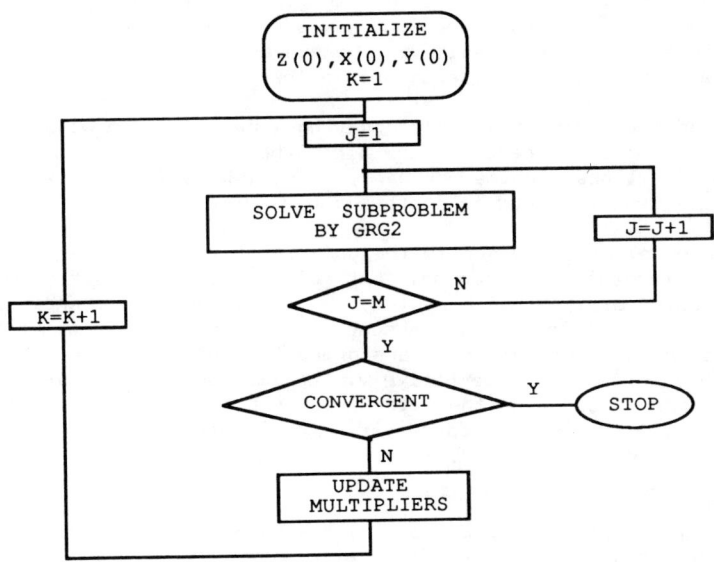

Fig. 1 Flowchart of Computation

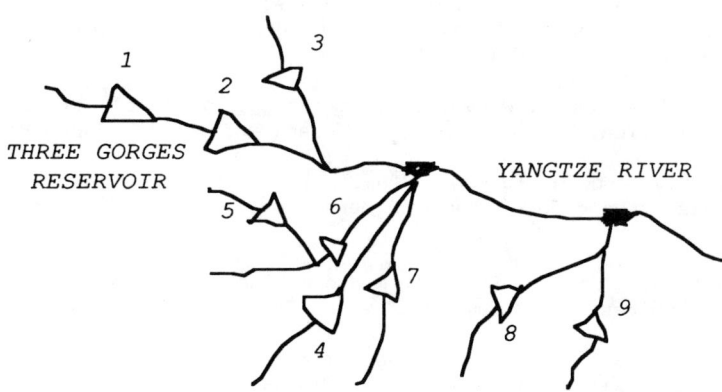

Fig. 2 Schematic Map of Central
       China Hydrosystem

DISCUSSION
A temporal decomposition approach has been presented to determine the optimal release policy for a multireservoir system using deterministic inflows. The model has been implemented to select the optimal operations for a nine reservoir system in central China.

(a) The model can be applied to long term operations by using a long time step for each subperiod, say a season or year. A trade-off exists between the length of the subperiod (i.e., the time to solve) and the number of iterations in the coordination phase.

(b) The penalty weights and the updating scheme for the weights are important for convergence of the algorithm. We are investigating the use of a linear scheme for early iterations and later switching to a quasi-Newton method to improve convergence.

(c) The model can incorporate the uncertainty of inflows through implicit stochastic programing. For reliable operation, firm power requirements of the entire system can be included as chance constraints. If the inflows are assumed to be log-normally distributed these constraints can be transformed to nonlinear inequalities in each subproblem. Alternatively, "optimal operation rules" can be devloped based upon the deterministic problem results. These "rules" will supply guidance for future operations and should adjusted for real-time conditions.

REFERENCES
Dembo, R., J. Mulvey, and S. Zenios, "Large-Scale Nonlinear Network Models and their Application," Operations Research, 37(3), 1989.

Foufoula-Foufoula, E., and Kitanidis, P.K.,"Gradient Dynamic Programing for Stochastic Optimal Control of Multidimensional Water Resources Systems", Water Resources Res., 24(8), 1988.

Hanscom, M. A., et al, "Modeling and Resolution of the Medium Term Generation Planning Problem for a Large Hydro-electric System," Management Science, 26(7), 1980.

Lasdon, L., and A. Waren, GRG2 User's Guide, School of Business Administration, The University of Texas, Austin, TX, January, 1986.

Saad, M., and A. Turgeon, "Application of Principal Component Analysis to Long Term Reservoir Management," Water Resources Res., 24(7), 1988.

Turgeon, A., "Optimal Short-term Hydro Scheduling from the Principle of Progressive Optimality," Water Resources Res., 17(3), 1981.

Yakowitz, S., "Dynamic Programming Applications in Water Resources," Water Resources Res., 18(4), 1982.

Yeh, W., "Reservoir Management and Operations Models: A State-of-the Art Review," Water Resources Res., 21(12), 1985.

STORAGE REALLOCATION EVALUATION FOR
RESERVOIR SYSTEM
M.ASCE

Patrick Carriere[1]

Ralph Wurbs[2]

Abstract

Reservoir storage capacity is allocated to various purposes prior to project construction. However, changing needs and conditions may warrant later conversion of storage capacity from one purpose to another. A simulation modeling strategy for evaluating potentialities for permanent and seasonal storage reallocations and other related strategies is presented in the paper. Application of the modeling and analysis approach to a system of twelve reservoirs in the Brazos River Basin is discussed. The study focused primarily on increasing water supply yields while minimizing impacts on other purposes.

Introduction

Reservoir operation is based on the conflicting objectives of maximizing the amount of water available for conservation purposes and maximizing the amount of empty space available for storing future flood waters to reduce downstream damages. The conservation and flood control pools in a multipurpose project are fixed by a designated top of conservation pool elevation. Conservation pools may be shared by various purposes, such as water supply, hydroelectric power, and recreation, which involve both complementary and conflicting interactions.
Public needs and objectives and numerous factors affecting reservoir operation change over time. An increasing necessity to use limited storage capacity as effectively as possible warrants periodic reevaluations of operating policies. Reallocation of storage capacity between purposes represents a general strategy for optimizing the beneficial use of limited storage capacity in response to changing needs and conditions.

---
[1] Assistant Professor., Department of Civil and Mechanical Engineering., Texas A&I University, Kingsville, Tx. 78363.

[2] Associate Professor., Department of Civil Engineering., Texas A&M University, College Station, Tx. 77843.

The Hydrologic Engineering Center (HEC) recently conducted an investigation to identify opportunities for reallocation of storage capacity at Corps of Engineers reservoir nationwide (USACE, HEC 1988). Although given relatively little consideration in the past, storage reallocations will likely be proposed more frequently as demands on limited resources increase.

The paper would summarize an investigation of: (1) the potential of storage capacity reallocation and other related modifications in operating policies for optimizing the beneficial use of existing reservoirs in Texas and (2) modeling capabilities for formulating and evaluating such changes in operating policies (Wurbs and Carriere, 1988 and Carriere, 1988) The paper describes a modeling and an analysis approach which was adopted for evaluating storage reallocations for a reservoir system in the Brazos River Basin. Although the discussion is from the perspective of a particular case study, the reservoir operation strategies and simulation modeling approach should be applicable to similar studies of other reservoir system as well.

Modeling and Analysis Approach

A system of 12 reservoirs in the Brazos River Basin provides an illustrative case study for the discussion of modeling and analysis of storage reallocations. The Brazos River Basin extends across the state of Texas from eastern New Mexico to the Gulf of Mexico.

Readily available, state-of-the-art, generalized simulation models were applied, and various analyses of simulations results were performed. The following models, which are available from the Hydrologic Engineering Center (HEC) of the USACE, were used in the study; HEC-5 simulation of flood control and conservation system; HEC-3 reservoir system analysis for conservation; MOSS-IV monthly streamflow simulation; and STATS statistical analysis of time series data. The various HEC generalized computer programs are described by Feldman (1981).

Basin hydrology was represented in the models by inputed 85-year monthly streamflows and reservoir net evaporation rates. Reservoir water surface elevations versus area and capacity relationship, sedimentation estimates and operating criteria were obtained from USACE and BRA files and reports.

The study focused on the following types of storage reallocations: (1) permanent reallocations of storage capacity between flood control and water supply (2) seasonal rule curve operations (3) reallocations of storage capacity between hydroelectric power and water supply; and (5) temporary use sediment reserve for other purposes. Although not actually a type of reallocation, multireservoir system operation was also a major consideration. The emphasis was on improving water availability and reliability while minimizing adverse impacts on flood control and hydroelectric power operations.

A broad array of data was generated by the simulation study. A key aspect of the study was to organize the numerous HEC-5 simulation runs and the various analyses of the voluminous output data in such a manner as to provide meaningful information.

Alternative storage reallocation plans and related modifications in reservoir operating policies were evaluated using HEC-5 and HEC-3 with the monthly hydrologic input data covering the 85-year simulation period. Two types of simulations were performed based on alternative approaches for representing withdrawals of water for beneficial use: (1) computation of yield versus reliability relationships, particular firm yields, for alternative reallocation plans: and (2) simulation of actual 1984 and projected 2010 water use conditions, with alternative reallocation plans combined with various analyses of the simulation output.

The yield demonstrates the increases in water supply yields and reliabilities which potentially could be achieved by alternative modifications in reservoir operations. The individual reservoir and multireservoir system yields were determined for years 1984 and 2010 sediment conditions. The results of the present study indicated that yields reflecting system operation are significantly greater than the sum of the yields computed for each individual reservoir.

System Simulation for Specified Water Use Scenarios

The yield study discussed above provided some quantitative measure of the potential for alternative storage reallocations to improve the water supply capabilities of the reservoir system. The system simulations and associated analyses of simulation output data discussed below provide additional information regarding potentialities for improving water supply capabilities and also provide a measure of the impacts that reallocations would have on flood control capabilities.

The objective of the investigation was to evaluate reallocation potentialities in general, not to design a specific reallocation plan for implementation. A number of alternative hypothetical reallocation plans were simulated. The present discussion focuses on the existing allocation of storage capacity and three alternative reallocation plans. The three reallocation plans involve changing the designated top of conservation pool elevation. One plan involves permanent reallocation of flood control storage capacity to water supply. The other two plans involve adoption of seasonal rule curves. The results of system firm yield for the three reallocation plans are presented in Table 1.

The simulation specified water use scenarios provides a data base for performing frequency analyses of conservation pools drawdowns, flood control encroachments, water supply shortages, and hydroelectric power shortages as well as other types of analyses for alternative reallocation plans.

Reallocation Plan	(m^3/s)	(%)
No Reallocation	48.2	100.0
Permanent USACE Limit	51.1	106.0
Seasonal USACE Limit	50.5	104.8
15% Seasonal Rule Curve	49.5	102.7

Table 1. 12-Reservoir System Firm Yield

Conservation Storage Drawdown Frequency Analysis

The frequency of drawdowns which resulted in depleting conservation pools to specified levels were used to compare alternative water use scenarios and reallocation plans. For example, the number of drawdowns resulting in a completely empty conservation pool are tabulated in Table 2 based on simulations for each of the four alternative storage allocation plans, using year 2010 conditions of water use and reservoir sedimentation. A drawdown is defined here as beginning with a full conservation pool and ending with an empty conservation pool. The frequency of drawdowns decreases significantly with the three storage reallocation water use and reservoir sedimentation, none of the reservoirs emptied with the existing storage allocation or the three reallocation plans. Therefore, assuming a repetition of historical hydrology, 1984 water demand levels can be met, thus implying storage reallocation are not presently needed. However, projected future demands cannot be met without shortages occurring. The selected storage reallocation plans reduce but do not completely alleviate the shortages.

Flood Control Storage Frequency Analysis

The study addressed the task of developing a statistical approach for evaluating flood control capabilities using the same 85-year monthly HEC-5 simulations used to evaluate water supply capabilities. Although the procedure presented here involves significant approximations, the estimated exceedence probability or recurrence interval of filling the flood control storage to capacity was adopted as an index for comparing alternative storage reallocation plans. The recurrence interval computed for the existing storage allocation and three storage reallocation plans are shown in Table 3. With the existing allocations of storage capacity between flood control and conservation purposes, estimated recurrence intervals vary from 39 years at Whitney Reservoir to 132 years at Waco Reservoir. Either permanent or seasonal reallocation of flood control to water supply to the USACE discretionary authority limit, which is the lesser of 50,000 ac-ft or 15% of the total capacity, reduces the recurrence intervals as indicated in Table 3. The seasonal reallocation plan results in only slight reductions, which are much less severe than the permanent reallocation plan. The last reallocation plan included in Tables 1, 2, and 3 involves setting the top of conservation pool elevation equal to, above, and below the existing elevation during selected months of the year. This seasonal rule curve plan results in slightly greater recurrence intervals than those for no reallocation. The three measures of reservoir effectiveness reflected in Tables 1, 2, and 3 are all improved by this last reallocation plan.

Reservoir	Reallocation Plan			
	A*	B*	C*	D*
	Number of Times Reservoir Emptied in 85-year simulation			
Hubbard Creek	0	0	0	0
Possum Kingdom	7	7	7	7
Granbury	0	0	0	0
Whitney	1	0	0	0
Aquilla	8	3	5	3
Waco	13	8	9	7
Belton	8	3	5	3
Stillhouse	8	3	5	3
Granger	10	3	5	3
Somerville	8	3	5	3
Limestone	8	3	5	3

Table 2. Number of Drawdowns in Conservation Pool Based on 2010 Sediment Conditions

	Reallocation Plan			
Reservoir	A*	B*	C*	D*
Whitney	39	37	38	40
Aquilla	72	56	69	81
Waco	132	88	131	150
Belton	46	35	46	72
Stillhouse	115	63	115	174
Granger	112	50	112	145
Somerville	51	30	44	53

Table 3. Recurrence Interval for Filling Flood Control Pools

A* = No Reallocation
B* = Permanent USACE Limit
C* = Seasonal USACE Limit
D* = 15% Seasonal Rule Limit

Conclusion

Optimizing the beneficial use of existing reservoirs is becoming a major emphasis of water supply planning and management. The results of the study reported here indicate that storage reallocations and related reservoir management strategies can be effective in responding to changing conditions and increasing demands on limited resources. An enhanced understanding of the effects of changes in operating policies can be developed through simulation studies.

APPENDIX I. - REFERENCES
Carriere, P.E. (1988). "Hydrologic and Statistical Evaluation of Storage Reallocation for Multiple Purpose Reservoir Operation," Ph.D. Dissertation, Texas A&M University, College Station, Texas

Feldman, A.D. (1981). "HEC Models for Water Resources Systems Simulation," Advances in Hydroscience, Vol. 12, pp. 297-423, Academic Press, New York, N.Y.

U.S. Army Corps of Engineers, Hydrologic Engineering Center (1988). "Opportunities for Reservoir Storage Reallocation," IWR Policy Study 88-PS-2, Davis, California.

Wurbs, R.A., and Carriere, P.E. (1988). "Evaluation of Storage Reallocation and Related Strategies for Optimizing Reservoir System Operations," Technical Report 145, Texas Water Resources Institute, College Station, Texas.

ECONOMIC BENEFITS OF A FLOOD WARNING SYSTEM
THE VENTURA COUNTY, CALIFORNIA EXPERIENCE

By Dolores B. Taylor,*
Senior Hydrologist

ABSTRACT

Since the spring of 1979, Ventura County has been receiving the benefits of a growing Flood Warning System (FWS). Beginning with six self-reporting raingages, two untested flow models, and a Nova 3c computer, the pilot system worked so well for the City of Fillmore in the February 1980 flood that the U.S. Navy funded an 11-gage expansion which included two self-reporting streamgages and two more flow models. The Navy had experienced $15,000,000 damage to the Pt. Mugu Missile Test Center from the Calleguas Creek levee failure, a three day closure, evacuation of personnel housing, and the trauma to those evacuated. The cost of closing the Base is more than $300,000 per day, so an advance flood warning or even the estimate that there is no potential danger of flooding from a storm, saves many times over the original FWS cost of $46,000. A third expansion to the Ventura County Flood Warning System included the capability of increasing water supply from the Ventura River through real-time operation of a diversion canal that carries flows from the Ventura River headwaters into Casitas Reservoir. As water value continues to increase, the conservation impact as a dual use of a self-reporting system more than offsets the $38,000 price tag.

The essential involvement of the National Weather Service CA-NEV River Forecast Center in Sacramento cannot be overstated: Calibration of models, free PC software, coordination of radio frequencies, and timely weather forecasts of quantitative precipitation are all a part of the current operation that aids not only Ventura County, but 18 other counties in California, Nevada, and several federal agencies for better stormwater management.

*Ventura County Public Work Agency, Ventura, CA

INTRODUCTION

Often a disaster occurs before measures are taken which could have relieved the disaster. This was certainly the situation in establishing a flood warning system for Sespe Creek. In February of 1978, the highest peak of record occurred at the USGS gaging station on Sespe Creek approximately three miles north of the City of Fillmore. The Creek banks were able to contain most of the water; however, the resulting deposit of sediment reduced creek capacity. A considerably smaller peak a month later resulted in overbank flows and disastrous flooding of the Los Serenos area of the City. A flood warning system would not have held back the water, but it would have provided time for defensive measures to reduce personal property damage, and time to effect an orderly evacuation. This event provided the impetus to get the wheels moving. Within a year, through the joint efforts of The Ventura County Flood Control District and The National Weather Service, an automated flood warning system was in operation for the Sespe Creek and Santa Paula Creek watersheds.

ELEMENTS AND OPERATION

Basically, the Flood Warning Operation application consists of five elements:

1. Self-reporting rain and stream gages at strategic points in the watershed. These gages collect the rainfall data and water-level data and transmit signals via radio waves whose frequencies have been reserved for this special function. This equipment meets National Weather Service Standards for ALERT, an acronym for Automated Local Evaluation in Real Time.

2. Local Flood Warning Center equipped with a receiver to receive signals from the gages and two computers which convert the signals into inches of rain, stage levels in streams to flow rates, and store the data relative to the time of occurrence. Models of 17 watersheds generate local flood condition reports every 12 minutes for flood warnings or assurance of no danger to users. The two computers are networked together to share tasks under normal circumstances. If one computer should fail, the other will take over all the necessary functions.

3. The California-Nevada River Forecast Center in Sacramento, a branch of the National Weather Service, which, by use of its hydrologic models and rainfall data from the local center, forecasts peak discharges to be expected for various amounts of additional rain. The redundant analysis serves as a quality assurance tool.

4. A weather consultant charged with forecasting the amount of rain that can be expected over the next 24 hours along with the maximum 6-hour amounts for different watersheds. In the event that the rainfall amount expected would generate a peak discharge that would exceed the capacity of the stream channel, it is the local center's responsibility to notify the proper authorities in the threatened areas to initiate whatever precautions and evacuation warnings are judged to be appropriate.

5. A technician assigned to keep the system equipment regularly maintained and calibrated to assure reliability. The value of regular maintenance on the gages cannot be underestimated: battery replacement; tipping bucket cleansing; stream gage base-setting and ratings; weather station calibration and accuracy are all critical to the credibility of the System.

   Ventura County uses a skilled hydrographer full time to keep the system in good working order. With 123 sensors to maintain, it is indeed fortunate that most of the gages operate with only an annual visit to clean tipping buckets and change out the battery. The new weather stations are much more complex to install, operate, calibrate, and maintain than rain and stream gages. There is a need for the manufacturers to provide improved manuals for the weather station maintenance.

ECONOMIC BENEFITS OF SUCCESSFUL APPLICATIONS

Local officials who approve budgets that contain funds for new equipment or improved software need to see successful applications. For example, the very close agreement between the model prediction and the actual flow in the 1980 flood in Sespe Creek, and the ensuing successful implementation of the response plan, gave us the confidence to present the ALERT concept to the Navy officials at Point Mugu. This same storm caused flooding of personnel housing at the base resulting in 15 million dollars in damages plus closing of the base for three days at a cost of $300,000 per day. In six months, the 11-gage System was designed, implemented, and functioning with a duplicate computer at the Navy base. The County computer interrogates the base computer constantly by direct phone line to exchange data received, flood forecasts, and weather reports.

During the winters of 1981 and 1982, enough streamflow occurred on Calleguas Creek and Revolon Slough to allow the National Weather Service RFC to recalibrate the urbanizing stream model both for peak flow and time to peak on the two streams impacting the Navy base. The River Forecast Center also provided the models to be running in-house as our local officials funded the expansion of our computer memory.

On March 1, 1983, we were watching rainfall gages and stream levels for cities of Fillmore and Santa Paula, the U. S. Navy at Point Mugu, and our own Flood Operations Department. Not only were National Weather Service personnel watching this large Pacific storm, but our private forecaster for meso-scale quantitative precipitation forecast was very concerned. At that time, models used six-hour QPF, and engineering judgment caused "sweaty palms" among us as we looked at the models.

Armed with a 24-hour forecast, local OES officials assisted in bringing together response people from sheriff, fire, cities, public works, the Red Cross, and radio reporters. Each agency outlined for the others the boundaries of their response saving much personnel overlap and money.

Severe flooding to a areas and flood damage occurred due to the runoff from Calleguas Creek along its route, but the U. S. Navy was able to close its tidegates and flood gates several hours before breakout. In Fillmore, local police and firemen notified affected occupants of the potential for a flood, giving them time to move cars to higher ground. Satisfaction was the general acclaimer.

The third event that has acquainted not only local officials but also the public to the use of our Flood Warning System was the Wheeler and Ferndale fires of 1985. Over 17 percent of the County of Ventura was burned, including brush that had stood for over 50 years. The Wheeler fire was started on July 2, 1985, by an arsonist.

By July 11, the fire rehab team from the U. S. Forest Service had identified that nearly 70 percent of the fire area was in a hydrophobic condition. Recognition of the fireflood cycle was addressed before the fire was b. Twenty-six agencies of local, state and federal officials worked together to prepare a response plan. During public meetings, the ALERT System expansion to cover the fire area was explained to public groups and taped by television stations to be shown over and over during the fall months. ALERT gages purchased as spares, and others furnished by the State Department of Water Resources, were sited and installed among the charred chaparral skeletons. The National Weather Service RFC completed additional calibrations for selected canyons, as well as the main Ventura River, impacting towns along its banks. In Santa Paula, a breakout of Santa Paula Creek would inundate 60 percent of the urban area. Concern that the Ferndale fire that burned 70 percent of Santa Paula Creek would mirror expected flooding predicted for Ojai from the Wheeler fire.

Many service clubs who had heard about ALERT following the 1980 flood and 1983 flood invited Flood Control officials to return and explain what could happen. Slides of the denuded areas, debris control structures and potential flood plain maps were shown and explained. Service clubs in Ojai and Santa Paula manned sandbag and sand distribution centers for several weekends.

Early rains served as training exercises for the response team, now well versed in "buzz" words like hydrophobic soils, flood plain, debris production and saturation.
By February 10, 1986, the 5-day forecast from both the National Weather Service QPF forecaster in Los Angeles and our private forecaster was for a major event with several severe bands of rain over a period of four days. Adrenalin ran high, as did the "media-hype" from all over Southern California. Predictions by our hydrologists of a 10-year storm producing the 100-year flood plain due to debris loading had reached everyone. Maps were hung in libraries, schools, fire stations, and city halls. Hour after hour it rained, but never did any gage detect

more than 0.5 inch per hour intensity. Fortunately, the rain stopped before the soil reached its water saturation limit. The value of this exercise which forced the development of a shared response plan cannot be overemphasized.

Further expansion to our system in 1986 moved us from a Floodwarning System to a Public Safety System. The County Fire Department has a "fire response plan" to any incident that occurs depending on the current "Burn Index" for that area of the County. Real-time weather stations with 30-minute readings of temperatures, humidity and wind data are polled several times per day to determine the current burn index. Thousands of dollars per incident can be saved by not sending trucks and crews to an incident where the weather is helping suppress the fire. To date, ten weather stations are operating from the National Forest Boundary to the coast. Additional money is saved since fire stations personnel are no longer required to make the periodic readings used to determine the burn index. The dispatcher using a modum on a computer terminal can collect the data in moments.

BENEFITS TO FLOOD CONTROL OPERATIONS

With a limited work force to patrol nearly 2000 square miles of Ventura County and over 50 linear miles of flood control channels to maintain, storm-time deployment to critical areas is essential. The real time rainfall and stream levels allow decisions to be made that put equipment where it is much needed.

BENEFITS OF AN INTER-AGENCY NETWORK

The Ventura County Flood Warning Center located in the County Government Center Administration Building in Ventura is in communication, either by phone line or radio transmission, with gages in the Sespe/Santa Paula Creek Network, gages in the Calleguas/Revolon Network, gages in the Ventura River Network, Santa Barbara County precipitation stations, Los Angeles County precipitation stations, the Point Mugu receiving station, the NWS River Forecast Center (RFC) in Sacramento and Pacific Weather Analysis, Weather Consultants in Santa Barbara. The direct line between Ventura and Point Mugu allows either agency to receive rainfall data from stations that cannot transmit directly to the respective receivers, as well as providing for the exchange of messages and forecasters between the two centers. An auto-answer phone link to Sacramento transmits data received by the Ventura Center to the RFC, and river peak stage forecasts from the RFC to Ventura. The weather analyst in Santa Barbara, being tied into the Ventura Center, receives all data and messages the Center receives and can send updated rainfall predictions back to the Ventura Flood Warning Center. Thus, a complete network exists allowing each of the cooperating agencies to receive data and messages and to transmit data and messages to all other agencies comprising the system.

BENEFIT OF A CA-NEV ALERT USERS GROUP

The most important interest level generator and stimulation comes from the ALERT Users Group. Since 1982, we have met annually, and in recent years, quarterly, to share concerns, innovations and hear of new developments by vendors, both hardware and software.

The Western Region of the National Weather Service has contributed greatly by facilitating those meetings which allow weather forecasters, hydrologists, technicians. manufacturers and River-Forecast-Center personnel to participate and share problems, ideas, and experiences. At Asilomar, most participants stay on the cloistered grounds to eat together, meet formally together for presentations or workshops and share informally at breaks. The group has been effective in modifying standards, encouraging design improvements, and monitoring the use of the real-time technology throughout California.

A second group of ALERT systems have banned together to form SAAS (Southwestern Association of ALERT Systems) covering Texas, Oklahoma, Colorado, New Mexico and Florida. Both groups are incorporated as Non-profit corporations with bylaws and officers.

SUMMARY

The Ventura County Flood Warning/Public Safety system is being operated for the benefit of Ventura County in general, and in particular for the residents of the areas in the county where there is the potential for serious flooding. The value of the system, 'however, does not stop at the County line. This interconnected network of gages and agencies provides data to the National Weather Service Forecast Office in Los Angeles, which is of value to them in improving their forecasting capabilities for all Southern California.

BENEFIT/COST ANALYSIS OF STORMWATER DETENTION SYSTEMS

Richard H. McCuen and Glenn E. Moglen[1]

INTRODUCTION

Land development and the accompanying flood, erosion, and water quality problems have fostered a variety of stormwater management practices, including the detention basin. In the past, detention basins have been designed to control peak discharge rates. However, there is considerable interest in using the detention basin for control of nonpoint source pollution. The cost of the pollution associated with increases in both erosion and nonpoint source pollutants must be recognized.

While the technical details of detention basin design are reasonably well established, there are many unanswered questions related to the economics of detention basin design for flood and water quality control. To approach these problems, a framework was developed for evaluating the economic benefits of water quality control using detention basins.

PRODUCTION FUNCTIONS FOR DETENTION BASINS

An economic production function is a relationship or process that transforms resources of specified forms into other resources that are considered to be more useful for purposes of consumption or additional production. In terms of detention storage for the management of stormwater quantity and quality, the input resources would be construction materials and manpower, engineering knowledge, and the funds that are necessary to administer, maintain, and operate the basin. The output resources would be storage for social objectives such as flood and water quality control, aesthetical improvements, increases in land values, and the control of sediment. The production function should be formulated to reflect resources applied at various times, both short- and long-term.

To illustrate the compilation of production functions for detention basins, a hypothetical watershed of 100 acres was assumed. To reflect various levels of land development, after development curve numbers over the range from 70 to 95 were assumed, with a CN of 65

---
[1]Dept. of Civil Eng., Univ. of Maryland, College Park, MD 20742

used for the before development condition. The SCS Graphical method was used to calculate the peak discharge rates for all exceedence frequencies. A stormwater management policy that required control to the before-development 2-year peak discharge rate was assumed.

An economic analysis was performed for various levels of watershed development, with flood damages computed for the stream reach immediately downstream of the detention basin. For each after-development watershed condition the flood control benefits were assumed to equal the difference between the damages incurred without detention storage and the damages with storage. The damages were computed for floods of all exceedence frequencies. The integration of the flood frequency curve with the stage-discharge and damage-discharge curves were performed using a tabular approach. Table 1 illustrates the tabular calculation of the expected damages with and without the detention basin, with a CN of 70 used for the after development condition. The computed before- development 2-year peak discharge of 25.8 cfs, was used to size the detention basin.

Flood damages were assumed to be dependent only on river stage. Bankfull flow was assumed to occur for the before development 2-year event. Since after-development peak discharge rates are greater than the before-development rates, out-of-bank flows will occur after development for events more frequent than the 2-year event. For the after-development with detention storage case out-of-bank flows do not occur for events smaller than the 2-year magnitude since the detention basin limits the discharge to the before-development 2-year peak discharge rate. The damages incurred as a result of the flooding are based on an average of previously reported findings. The property value density was assumed to be $200,000/acre.

The expected damages are determined as the product of the damages and the weight assigned to the particular flood exceedence frequency range. The production function for flood control is derived with a reasonable cost function. The benefit-cost ratios were well above 1.

A simple model for the sediment yield from a given drainage area was developed. The off-site damages from soil erosion are quite varied. Recreation, including freshwater and marine fishing, water storage, navigation, commercial fishing, water conveyance facilities such as drainage ditches and irrigation canals, water treatment facilities, municipal and industrial users, and stream electric power plants are adversely affected by the presence of excessive sediment in runoff. Off-site damages of erosion from all sources total $7.0 billion per year in the United States, which yields an average damage of $1.38 per ton, but is considerably larger in urban areas. For this analysis an average value of the damage caused by eroded sediment was assumed to be $7 per ton. Therefore, for each of the detention basins, which were designed for flood control rather than sediment control, the water quality benefits in terms of sediment control were calculated as a function of the sediment yield, the trap efficiency, and the area.

In assessing the magnitude of a project, the benefit-cost criterion is adequate for project justification. However, in project evaluation, the decision on the level of the project must be based on both the benefit-cost ratio being greater than one and the ratio of the marginal benefits to the marginal cost being at least one. For an individual project, such as the design and construction of a detention basin, the project is justified when the benefit-cost ratio exceeds 1; however, if the design and construction for water quality control requires costs beyond those required for flood control, then they may not be justified if the marginal costs exceed the marginal benefits. For the conditions used in this analysis, the marginal benefits for sediment control did not exceed the marginal costs.

CONCLUSIONS

From preliminary results for on-site detention basins designed for peak discharge control, it does not appear that water quality benefits from small on-site detention facilities are significant when compared to the economic benefits from flood control. While only selected benefits for sediment control were considered in assessing water quality benefits, they were several orders of magnitude less than the flood control benefits. Therefore, from an economic standpoint decisions should be based on flood control considerations rather than a joint consideration of water quantity and quality control.

For almost two decades, the debate over on-site versus regional detention control has persisted. Some localities have adopted policies that require regional detention facilities rather than on-site facilities. Support for this policy orientation was provided in two ways. First, an analysis of an isoquant diagram suggests that, as the storage volume increases, water quality control becomes more cost effective. The greater slope in the direction of water quality benefits indicates an increase in the marginal benefits and, therefore, the marginal rate of transformation of water quality control for flood control. Second, which is based on theoretical concepts of settling suggest that detention times much longer than those that occur in on-site detention facilities are required for significant reductions in water pollutants. Detention times of 10 or 20 hours are required in order for significant reductions in pollutant concentrations; these are detention times that would be appropriate for regional detention facilities, not on-site facilities as they are currently designed. Detention basins intended to control channel erosion must be considerably larger then basins designed to control peak discharge rates.

At the present time, the benefits that result from trapping pollutants, including sediment, are one of the most difficult elements of the water quality production function to assess. Public goods, or non-marketed resources, are difficult to assess, in part, because of the many beneficiaries involved and because many of the benefits are value-based. The benefits are also a function of the flow level, with greater water quality benefits accruing during low flows, which compounds the problem of estimation.

TABLE 1. Expected Damages With and Without the Detention Basin (CN=70)

EXCEEDENCE EXPECTED FREQUENCY RANGE (%)	With Detention Basin			Without Detention Basin		
	DISCHARGE (CFS)	STAGE (FT)	EXPECTED DAMAGE ($)	DISCHARGE (CFS)	STAGE (FT)	EXPECTED DAMAGE ($)
99.9 - 100.0	1	0.41	0	5	0.64	0
99.0 - 99.0	2	0.51	0	8	0.75	0
95.0 - 99.0	4	0.62	0	13	0.86	0
90.0 - 95.0	6	0.70	0	18	0.94	0
85.0 - 90.0	9	0.76	0	21	1.00	0
80.0 - 85.0	10	0.81	0	25	1.05	0
75.0 - 80.0	12	0.85	0	28	1.09	1,954
70.0 - 75.0	15	0.89	0	32	1.13	4,424
65.0 - 70.0	17	0.93	0	35	1.16	6,847
60.0 - 65.0	19	0.97	0	38	1.19	9,232
55.0 - 60.0	21	1.00	0	42	1.23	11,670
50.0 - 55.0	24	1.04	0	46	1.26	14,175
45.0 - 50.0	27	1.08	1,283	50	1.29	16,785
40.0 - 45.0	31	1.12	4,015	55	1.33	19,547
35.0 - 40.0	35	1.16	7,022	60	1.37	22,515
30.0 - 35.0	40	1.21	10,355	66	1.40	25,732
25.0 - 30.0	46	1.26	14,218	73	1.45	29,372
20.0 - 25.0	53	1.32	18,754	81	1.50	33,541
15.0 - 20.0	63	1.39	24,504	92	1.55	38,685
10.0 - 15.0	78	1.48	32,069	107	1.62	45,248
5.0 - 10.0	103	1.61	43,664	131	1.73	54,935
1.0 - 5.0	158	1.83	51,784	178	1.89	57,313
0.1 - 1.0	298	2.21	19,048	282	2.17	18,343
0.0 - 0.1	618	2.75	3,425	480	2.55	2,920
		TOTAL	$230,141		TOTAL	$413,237

Reliance on Structural Controls for
Water Supply Protection in Urbanizing Watersheds

John P. Hartigan, M. ASCE, Thomas F. Quasebarth,
Kelly A. Cave, A.M. ASCE, and David A. Nailor[1]

Introduction

Over the next few years, it will become increasingly important to minimize contamination of water supply reservoirs to help water supply utilities meet the new EPA drinking water standards while minimizing treatment costs. Because of the increases in nonpoint pollution loadings which accompany urbanization, it will be most difficult to achieve these goals in urbanizing watersheds. For example, compared to undeveloped land uses like forest land, annual runoff pollution (lbs/acre/year) from urban development in the mid-Atlantic region is as much as 10 to 20 times greater in the case of nutrients and as much as 10 to 50 times greater in the case of toxicants like heavy metals.

The watershed is the "first line of defense" for protecting a drinking water supply, and therefore effective watershed management is the logical first step to meet EPA's new drinking water standards. This is because the watershed is the source of pollutants which can contaminate the water supply reservoir. It is far preferable to implement an affordable watershed management plan that keeps contaminants out of the water supply reservoir, than to rely solely on water treatment plants to treat a contaminated supply in order to meet drinking water standards. The watershed management approach offers a greater factor of safety because it is an additional pollution "barrier" deployed to ensure high quality drinking water at the source. A watershed management plan is also desirable because it is a proactive approach which focuses on the cost-effective prevention of future water quality problems. In the absence of a watershed management plan, there is a greater risk that uncontrolled future development will result in serious contamination of the water supply.

---

[1] Camp Dresser & McKee, Inc., 7535 Little River Turnpike, Suite 200, Annandale, VA 22003.

This paper describes a watershed management plan developed to protect two water supply reservoirs which serve the City of High Point in central North Carolina.

Description of Study Area

The watershed management plan covers Oak Hollow Reservoir (3.0 billion gal) and City Lake (1.3 billion gal) which have drainage areas of 31 sq mi and 61 sq mi, respectively (see Figure 1). The development of the watershed management plan was complicated by the significant amount of urban development which has already occurred in the two watersheds. Both watersheds currently have urban development on 25%-30% of the total area. City Lake watershed is characterized by commercial development on almost 10% of the total area. In addition, several large tank farms for storage of oil refinery products are also located in the headwaters of the watershed. Major petroleum pipelines and an interstate highway traverse both watersheds.

Future land use plans call for urban development on about 80% of the total area in both watersheds, with overall imperviousness projected to increase from the existing level of 10%-13% to 30%-45%. The watershed management plan considered both structural and nonstructural alternatives for mitigating the nonpoint pollution impacts of future increases in urban runoff.

Impacts of Urban Nonpoint Pollution

A nonpoint pollution loading model (NPS-CDM) was used to screen 5 different future land use plans for the two watersheds. In the absence of any urban nonpoint pollution controls, future annual loadings of total phosphorus and lead were projected to be, respectively, 60%-140% and 130%-450% greater than existing conditions. These loading projections indicated the potential for significant water quality degradation under future development options.

Evaluations of the sources of raw water in each water supply also indicate the significant impacts of future runoff increases. For Oak Hollow Reservoir, future runoff from urban paved areas would contribute 2 to 3 gal out of every 5 gal of drinking water compared to 1 out of every 6 gal under existing conditions. For City Lake, future pavement runoff would contribute 3 to 4 gal out of every 5 gal of drinking water, compared to 1 out of every 3 gal for exisitng conditions. The significant levels of pavement runoff for future conditions indicate a relatively high risk level for loadings of toxic contaminants which predominate within paved areas.

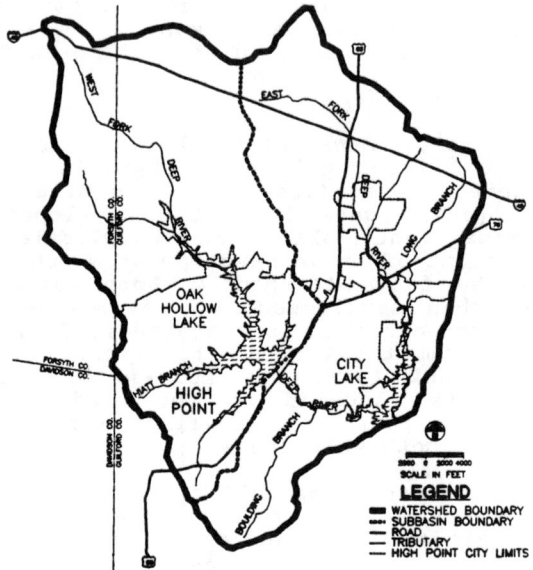

Figure 1

Pollutant	Existing		Future Without BMPs		Future With BMP Plan	
	CL	OHR	CL	OHR	CL	OHR
Total-P (mg/L)	0.05	0.05	0.07-0.08	0.06-0.07	0.05	0.05
Total-N (mg/L)	1.0	1.1	1.3-1.4	1.3-1.4	0.9	1.1
Chlorophyll-a (ug/L)	14	15	16-17	19-20	12	16
Lead (ug/L)	7	4	20-35	10-20	7	4
Zinc (ug/L)	28	22	75-100	50-70	30	29

CL = City Lake
OHR = Oak Hollow Reservoir

Table 1. Water Quality Model Projections of Mean Concentrations for Alternate Land Use Conditions and Management Alternatives

Table 1 summarizes projections of receiving water quality developed with an input/output model. Under the future land use plans, mean concentrations of toxicants are projected to increase by 100%-400%, with average lead levels in excess of proposed drinking water standards. Increases in total P of 20%-60% under future conditions are projected to result in 20%-30% increases in mean summer chlorophyll-a. Increased chlorophyll-a is likely to make it more difficult to meet future drinking water standards for disinfectant byproducts (e.g., trihalomethanes [THM's]) without the use of expensive new treatment processes. Because of the more intensive development pattern projected for City Lake watershed (e.g., up to 32% of the total area in commercial and industrial development) and greater future metals concentrations in the reservoir, it was concluded that the control of future toxic loadings was more critical than eutrophication management for City Lake. In constrast, eutrophication management was assigned a higher priority for Oak Hollow Reservoir.

Watershed Management Plan

The recommended management plan consists primarily of "regional" wet detention basin best management practices (BMPs) strategically located to serve future development and some existing development in the two watersheds. A total of 72 regional BMPs with drainage areas averaging about 300 acres were sited within the watersheds, with the total service area representing almost two-thirds of the total watershed area. A regional approach was used to deploy BMPs due to the significantly reduced costs (capital and O&M), greater reliability, and feasibility of retrofitting existing as well as future urban development. To supplement the regional BMP system, the use of smaller onsite detention BMPs is recommended for about 20% of the area in the two watersheds. As indicated in Table 1, the recommended BMP plan is capable of maintaining future water quality levels at or near existing levels. Approximately 75%-90% of the future water quality improvements projected in Table 1 is achieved by the regional BMP system alone. The annualized total cost (capital and O&M) of the regional BMP facilities is about $1.8 million per year. The construction costs for the regional BMPs will be recovered from future development through a "fee-in-lieu-of" program, with the average fee on the order of $3,400 per impervious acre. Because it is a higher quality water supply and more options for land use controls are feasible, the plan for Oak Hollow Reservoir watershed also includes nonstructural BMPs for areas within about one mile from the Lake.

A spill containment plan was also developed for the two watersheds. The plan provides multiple barriers to protect the water supply reservoirs, including the following: (a) temporary spill containment devices; (b) dedicated containment facilities located immediately downstream of a potential spill site; (c) design of selected regional wet detention basins to serve as multi-purpose spill containment structures; and (d) automated spill detection monitoring.

Considerations for a Multiple-Use
Stormwater Detention Facility

David P. Smith,[1] M. ASCE, and Barend W. Meiling[2]

Abstract

A 60-year-old neighborhood provides the unusual setting for the City of Tulsa's Turner Park - Will Rogers High School Stormwater Detention Facility. The 20-acre site is located within the heavily wooded park and the playing fields of the school. A large floodwater detention basin is excavated on the school grounds to protect over 80 homes in the existing 100-year floodplain. Several at-grade hydraulic structures and a small embankment are constructed in the park along the alignment of the existing underground storm drain. Relatively few trees are removed. The facility is designed to be consistent with the historic use of the park and school grounds. Cooperation with the City of Tulsa Park and Recreation Department, the Tulsa Public Schools, and the surrounding community is essential to project development.

Background

The City of Tulsa has been a proponent of stormwater management since the mid-1970's. Two devastating Memorial Day floods in 1976 and 1984 led to the master planning of all watersheds in the City by the Stormwater Management Department. The Coal Creek Master Drainage Plan, adopted by the City Commission in 1986, recommends the construction of a regional stormwater detention facility to protect approximately 80 structures and a portion of

---

[1]Formerly Project Engineer, W.R. Holway and Associates. Current address: 317 E. Carrillo Street, Suite 200, Santa Barbara, CA 93101.

[2]Project Engineer, W.R. Holway and Associates, 5314 S. Yale Avenue, Tulsa, OK 74135.

Interstate 244 from 100-year flood damage. In the 1984 flood, over $1,000,000 in damages occurred in the Coal Creek Basin.

The proposed site of the detention facility is within the boundaries of both the City of Tulsa's Turner Park and the Tulsa Public School District's Will Rogers High School. Flows exceeding the capacity of the existing 14-foot diameter semi-circular storm drain are diverted into the park. Although the capacity of this conduit is approximately 1,100 cfs, the estimated 100-year peak discharge from the 830-acre urban drainage area is over 3,500 cfs!

Engineering Considerations

To reduce the peak discharge in the existing storm drain and eliminate surface flooding, a minimum of 130 acre-feet of flood storage is necessary. Although the entire runoff volume could have been controlled by the detention basin, this method would have been hydraulically inefficient. Instead, only the runoff volume which exceeds the capacity of the storm drain is to be diverted. This concept is commonly referred to as "side-spill" or "off-line" detention.

Complicating the diversion technique is the constraint that, to preserve the large number of existing trees, the park should not be excavated. This constraint requires that the headwater must rise 12 feet above the invert of the storm drain using a 108-inch diameter circular orifice. A series of concrete baffle walls upstream of the orifice dissipate the inflow velocity in the storm drain. The diversion structure is 265-feet long to produce the required weir flow with minimum headwater.

The overflow from the diversion structure proceeds through the existing park to a 7-foot high embankment and an 8-foot x 2-foot concrete headwall which serves as the principal outlet to the storm drain. Overflows which exceed the 1-year recurrence interval must also travel down a concrete-lined drop structure (faced with native stone) into a 10-acre excavated detention basin over 15-feet deep.

The excavated detention basin on the school grounds provides almost all of the 130 acre feet of flood storage. A 24-inch concrete pipe with a flap gate, combined with the principal outlet, is designed to drain the school grounds within 48 hours of the initial inflow event. Both the flap gate and a subdrainage system with twin 10-hp pumps are necessary because the finished grade of the detention basin is at approximately the same elevation as the invert of the storm drain.

The embankment is protected on the downstream face by a precast concrete flexible revetment which lines the emergency spillway. Because of the high risk associated with overtopping the embankment, the emergency spillway is designed to control 50 percent of the probable maximum discharge.

Institutional Considerations

Since the Turner Park - Rogers High School site has multiple uses, individual design requirements are necessary. For example, one objective is to avoid excavation or removal of trees in the park; the numerous large elm, pecan, and sycamore trees provide a natural resource for the community. To replace the few trees located in the embankment fill, almost 40 elm, oak, and pear trees are planted.

The embankment is sculptured to provide an non-engineered appearance. Revetments for erosion control at the diversion structure and emergency spillway are backfilled and covered with grass sod. These aesthetic qualities are incorporated into the project as a result of several public hearings and the concerns expressed by the Park and Recreation Department.

Requirements for the school site are quite different. Although excavation of the detention basin is permitted, a maximum side slope of 3:1 provides for maintenance, egress, and the convenience of spectators at athletic events. The existing 6-lane, 1/5-mile running track will be upgraded by the school to 8 lanes and 400 meters using a synthetic porous running surface. With these amenities, plus a new irrigation and subdrain system, the detention basin doubles as a first-rate athletic facility.

Numerous discussions were held by the Stormwater Management Department with the school administration, athletic department, and maintenance staff. Negotiations were then conducted to acquire the drainage easement, assign maintenance responsibilities, and determine construction requirements. Routine maintenance will be provided by the school while floodwater debris and silt will be removed by the City. Flashing warning lights operate as a safety measure during an inflow event.

Summary

Over 200,000 cubic yards of excavation is required for construction. The Turner Park - Will Rogers High School Stormwater Detention Facility is scheduled to be completed by June 1990 at a construction cost of over $2,900,000, not including the running track.

As older, undersized drainage systems require retrofitting of detention storage facilities, competing uses for available real estate will impact the design concept. Engineers and planners must realize that political or institutional constraints are actually opportunities for the enhancement of multiple-use projects.

The authors would like to thank the staff of the City of Tulsa Stormwater Management and Park and Recreation departments and the Tulsa Public Schools for their contributions to this project.

Appendix - Conversion of English Units to SI Units

1 inch = 0.02540 m
1 foot = 0.3048 m
1 mile = 1,609 m
1 acre = 4,047 m^2
1 cubic yard = 0.7646 m^3
1 acre-foot = 1,233 m^3
1 cubic foot per second (cfs) = 0.02832 m^3/s
1 horsepower (hp) = 0.7457 kw

FORT WORTH: WHERE THE WEST BEGAN WITH WATER

Roxanne L. Pillar[1], Member ASCE

ABSTRACT

"The river with no name never quite knew what to do with the land that sprawled away from the minnows and mud, whether to punish it or baptize it. So the river did a little of both."

This paper presents a historic overview of the impact the Trinity River has had on the development of Fort Worth with regard to fire protection, water supply and flood control.

INTRODUCTION

The river with no name was christened the "Rio de la Santisima Trinidad" - the sacred Trinity in 1690 by Alfonson de Leon, a Spaniard sent to found a mission. The three forks of the Trinity, the Clear Fork, the West Fork and the Elm Fork in Dallas make the trine of the Trinity.

The first Anglo-American attempt at settlement came with the establishment of Bird's Fort in 1841 but was abandoned. In 1843 the abandoned fort was the site of the signing of a treaty establishing a line separating Indian land from territory open for colonization. This line gave Fort Worth its reputation as the city "Where the West Begins."

MANUSCRIPT

On June 6, 1849 Brevet Major Ripley Arnold, under orders from General William Jenkins Worth, was sent to establish a military post. The troops climbed a bluff that overlooked the valley to choose a camp site at the confluence of the Clear Fork of the Trinity. Arnold decided on a strech of flat land at a bend on the south side of the river, one that offered a plentiful supply of water. Arnold named the fort after General Worth who had, unknown to

---

[1] Project Engineer, Freese and Nichols, 811 Lamar Street, Fort Worth, Texas 76102

Arnold, had died from cholera three days before in San Antonio.

In July the menancing Trinity flooded, sending the soldiers scrambling for higher ground and bringing malaria. The higher ground is believed to be the site of the present Tarrant County courthouse. The soldiers fought Indians and the River but a permanent settlement had been established. Fort Worth dug in and survived.

From initial conception to modern day, the river has been an ever present force to be dealt with. The river gave and it took away. It provided a water supply which attracted people. More people generated a need for reliable fire protection, water supply, and flood control. The first influx of population came to Tarrant County and Fort Worth after the Civil War. Next came the cattle drives from south Texas to the railhead in Kansas. Then the railroad came to Fort Worth, making it one of the wildest towns in the West. In the twentieth century the livestock, aviation, and oil industries have been the backbone of the economy.

The first water distribution systems in Fort Worth were for fire protection, not water supply. The motto of the town was "Burn and pray for the bucket brigade." The idea for a volunteer fire department was first proposed in 1873 by B.B. Paddock. The first mayor donated a site. A hand drawn pumper was purchased for $600 and rubber buckets replaced leather ones. Large cisterns were used to hold water. There was a 1000 gallon cistern at the courthouse and two 500 gallon tanks, one at the site of the present day Hilton Hotel. The first fire station was built in 1883. So much money was spent on the building there were not enough funds to pay firemen. Fire Station No. 1 located at 2nd and Commerce has been restored and is a museum today.

More water supply was needed during the fire that destroyed the Texas Spring Palace May 30, 1890. The palace was similar to the present day Michell Corn Palace in South Dakota. The palace designs, made of natural material, provided ample flammable material for the fire that destroyed the Palace on the last night of the second season. Alfred S. Hayne, an English civil engineer, was the only fatality of the fire. Mr. Hayne returned to the burning structure helping others out and saving many lives. He died the next day from burns received during his heroic effort. There is a water fountain and monument located at the intersection of Lancaster and So. Main dedicated to Alfred S. Hayne.

In 1913 the Southside fire, which destroyed Hell's Half Acre site of the present day Tarrant county Convention Center again demonstrated that there was not adequate fire protection for the growing town.

Fort Worth's first artesian well was drilled in 1878 at Florence and May Street and a second on Peach near Hampton. Prior to that time, water for domestic use was obtained from shallow wells, springs or diresty from the Trinity River. Most sewers were merely open ditches that were flushed with water periodically.

The first water works, a private system, was built in 1888 and consisted of a 4 MGD pump station and six miles of pipe. This station was located on the east bank of the Clear Fork just upstream of the confluence with the West Fork. By 1890 the plant had been expanded to 5 MGD but was unable to meet the demands for municpal water and fire protection. In 1892 McArthur Brothers of New York City contracted to install two large Holly steam pumps on the bank of the Clear Fork at the location now known as the Holly Water Treatment Plant. The pumps were installed in a stone lined pit on the river bank. In 1973 the pits were still being used by the Water Department to house electric pumps and motors. The Holly Plant was completed in 1892 with a pumping capacity of 16 MGD. A prolonged drought in 1901 and the disastrous Southside fire of April 3, 1909 indicated a need for additional water supplies. A dam was built on the West Fork of the Trinity River in 1914, creating Lake Worth with an original capacity of approximately 40,000 acre-feet.

In April of 1922 both forks of the Trinity River flooded, taking 37 lives, causing $3 million in property damage, shutting down the pumping and filter plant and leaving three quarters of the City without water and shutting down the Texas Utility power and light plant which is still located at the junction of the two forks of the River. The flood was spawned when 7.54 inches of rain fell in six hours. The peak flow from 2615 square miles of drainage area was 85,000 cubic feet per second. A detailed study conducted by John B. Hawley soon after the calamity showed that most of the runoff had been from the smaller Clear Fork watershed and a maximum storm on the West Fork and Clear Fork could produce runoff two-and-one-half times the record flood of April 1922.

The result of the flood was the formation of a water district and the construction of Eagle Mountain and Bridgeport Dams. The voters created the Tarrant County Water Improvement District Number One, a water conservation district in 1924. Texas laws were created in 1925 to adequately address the dual problem of flood control and water supply. The Tarrant District was confirmed in 1926, becoming the first such district in Texas. The district moved into action and in 1930 and 1032 constructed the Eagle Mountain and Bridgeport Reservoirs above Lake Worth on the West Fork of the Trinity. The two reservoirs were constructed under the watchful eye of Marvin C. Nichols. Eagle Mountain, completed in October 1932 had a flood control capacity of 368,000 acre feet and a consrevation capacity of 214,000 acre-feet. The larger Bridgeport Reservoir in the upper watershed of the West Fork was built to have a flood control capacity of 632,000 acre-feet and a conservation capacity of 291,000 (4).

The Flood of 1949 resulted in the loss of ten lives, flooding of the Holly Water Plant, and $15 million in damages partly due to the failure of the railroad to close the track opening through the levee system. Flood waters rose to two feet below the second floor of the Montgomery Ward Building on 7th Street. Eleven inches of rainfall in nine hours produced the damage. The Clear Fork flow of 107,000 cfs breached the Clear Fork levees and pondage. The flow was constricted at the Main Street bridge reducing the flow from 107,000 to 64,300 cfs as the water split and spilled behind the levee. When the flood occurred the City was under contract to replace a steam pump. The motor was hauled to Fort Worth in short order by a dedicated truck driver who drove day and night. The City honored the man by presenting him with cowboy boots and hat. With the construction of the flood control and conservation storage in Lake Benbrook by the Corps of Engineers, and the widening of the river channel by the Water District, the levee system was considered safe. Today the levee system protects homes and businesses while citizens watch "Shakespeare in the Park". Present day projects include moving 1.4 miles of the Trinity, construction of a levee and reclamation of 600 acres of floodplain.

The drought of the 1950's had united efforts to lay the foundation for future water supply. In May 1954 the City Council and Mayor Garrison created the Fort Worth-Tarrant County Water Commission and charged it with finding a suitable supply for the City to meet the anticipated demands through the year 2000. In October 1973 the Rolling Hills Water Treatment Plant and the Cedar Creek Lake, Pump Station and Water Transmission Facilities were dedicated. The Reservoir, with a capacity of 679,000 acre feet, was completed in 1965 and filled in December 1967, with a safe yield of 133 million gallons per day. In November 1988 the Richland Chambers Reservoir, pump station and facilities were dedicated. The Reservoir, with a capacity of 1,183,400 acre feet will serve Fort Worth until 2010. The safe yield of Fort Worth's water system today is 383 MGD. Beginning with the wells in 1878, Fort Worth has had an adequate water supply and no water shortages of supply for the last century.

(1.)　Fort Worth The Civilized West. Caleb Pirtle III, Continental Heritage Press 1980

(2.)　Fort Worth & Tarrant County. Ruby Schmidt, Texas Christian University Press 1984

(3.)　Report on Water Supply for Fort Worth and Tarrant County. Tarrant County Water Control and Improvement District Number One, May 1957

(4.)　Diaries of Simon W. Freese 1922-1987. Freese and Nichols, 1988

(5.)　USGS Flood of May 17, 1949 at Fort Worth, Tex., June 1949

(6.)　Where the West Begins, Janet L. Schmelzer, Windsor Publications, 1985.

The Genesis of Surface Water for San Antonio

William C. Allanach, Jr., P.E.[1]
Barbara A. Nickerson[2]

Abstract

San Antonio is the ninth largest city in the United States and the only one of that group that relies exclusively on groundwater. The Applewhite Water Supply Project is the first surface water reservoir proposed to supplement groundwater from the Edwards Aquifer. This paper discusses the project approval process and the engineering, environmental and political issues involved.

****

"Remember the Alamo" was the rallying cry in 1836 for Texas independence. Today, the citizens of San Antonio are seeking independence of another kind-independence from relying on a single source of water. In 1891, the first well was drilled and water was found at 890 feet in the Edwards Aquifer. From this first man-made well, the City has relied exclusively on the Edwards Aquifer for its water. Currently, water use by the City averages about 160 MGD, with a maximum draw of more than 300 MGD in 1986.

Questioning the infinite capacity of the aquifer, the City Water Board (Board) began to look for a supplemental supply of water for San Antonio as early as the 1930s. First mentioned as an alternative in the 1950s, the Applewhite Water Supply Project has been studied repeatedly for almost 30 years. The Board authorized the preliminary design of the project in 1973. The proposed project consisted of a dam and reservoir on the Medina River and a dam on Leon Creek, with a diversion canal to transport high flow water from Leon Creek to Applewhite Reservoir.

---

[1]Project Manager, City Water Board, P.O. Box 2449, San Antonio, Texas 78298.

[2]Environmental Project Manager, Freese and Nichols, Inc., 811 Lamar Street, Fort Worth, Texas 76102.

A City Council resolution in 1979 authorized the Board to secure a Texas Water Rights permit for Applewhite. The application was submitted later that year and the permit was finally granted in September 1982. The permit allowed the Board to divert 70,000 acre-feet/year; 57,700 acre-feet from the reservoir, and 12,300 acre-feet from Leon Creek.

The Section 404 permit application was filed with the Corps of Engineers (Corps) in October 1982. With the issuance of the Water Rights permit, the Board's consultants prepared to begin land surveying and geotechnical investigations. However, denial of access by landowners made this impossible. The Board approached the City Council to intervene, but it was perceived that support for Applewhite had diminished. Rather than pursue the issue at this time, the Board requested the Corps to suspend action on the 404. In February 1983, the Corps published a notice stating that the scheduled scoping meeting was cancelled at the request of the applicant.

Ly late summer the City Council showed a renewed interest in the project. In October 1983, the Board requested the Corps to proceed with processing of the 404 permit application. In November the Corps published the Public Notice scheduling the scoping meeting for January 1984.

With renewed political support, the Board initiated new work on the Applewhite Project in 1984. A water quality sampling program on the Medina River and Leon Creek was begun and the second phase of the archeological study was authorized. An inter-agency team of the Corps, U.S. Fish and Wildlife Service (USFWS), Texas Parks and Wildlife Department (TPWD) and the Board performed a Habitat Evaluation Procedure (HEP) on the reservoir site in May. The Corps prepared a baseline HEP analysis and proposed six potential mitigation plans, all of which were rejected by the USFWS in June. The Board also filed for an extension to the water rights permit, since the permit required construction to begin within two years of the 1982 date of issuance.

In 1986, the Corps had not yet published the draft environmental impact statement (DEIS) and the Board once again requested an extension for the water rights. While the engineering design had moved slowly ahead, land surveys and acquisition had not begun.

Three years after the initial scoping meeting, the DEIS was finally issued and the public hearing was held in April 1987. Based on letters received during the public comment period and comments at the hearing, the Corps requested additional information from the Board in September. The Board provided the information in November. In December the Corps again requested more information, which was sent in February 1988.

The DEIS contained a proposed mitigation plan prepared by the Corps. The Fish and Wildlife Coordination Act requires the federal wildlife agency to propose a mitigation plan to satisfy the habitat losses of a project. However, the USFWS proposed that the Board prepare the plan. The Board rejected this request. Finally, to break the impasse, the Corps proposed a mitigation plan. The proposed plan impacted a narrow riparian corridor upstream of the reservoir to Castroville, affecting a large number of farm operations. Release of the DEIS prompted the landowners to hold a meeting to voice their opposition. The public comments were sufficient to cause the agencies to look for another mitigation tract.

In the summer of 1988, the Joint Committee on Water Resources, representing the San Antonio City Council and the Edwards Underground Water District Board of Directors, released the Regional Water Resources Plan. The plan addressed the water issues of the region, including conservation, reuse, groundwater allocations and surface water development. In July 1988, the City Council passed an ordinance supporting Applewhite and directed the Board to take all steps necessary to complete Applewhite dam and reservoir.

Despite the ordinance and mandate to proceed, the Council did not endorse the whole Applewhite project. The water quality of Leon Creek had been an issue with opponents of the project, who perceived the water to be unsafe. Since their concerns were based on 20 year old data, the Board decided to implement a new water quality sampling program to abate the concerns. However, the new data was disregarded by the opponents. Their outcry was enough to convince the City Council to defer the Leon Creek dam and diversion canal from the ordinance for the present.

The project was finally moving ahead. Access for land surveys, geotechnical and archeological investigations had been obtained. The interagency team performed a HEP on land downstream of the reservoir, and were in agreement with the proposed tract and management of the land for mitigation. Design of the dam was progressing, and the final environmental impact statement (FEIS) was nearing completion. However, two years had passed since the Board received an extension on the water rights permit, so another request for an extension was filed in October 1988.

Unlike the two previous requests, the 1988 request was formally opposed by project opponents at the Texas Water Commission (TWC) hearing in Austin. The opponents argued that the Board had dragged its feet over the past six years and should not receive the extension. The Commissioners remanded the issue to a hearing examiner for an adjudicated hearing in March 1989, with the scope limited to due diligence. In August, 10 months into a 24-month extension, the TWC found the Board had been diligent and granted an extension to begin construction by October 1990.

The FEIS was released in January 1989 and the public hearing was held in February. In March, based on public comments and concerns, the Corps again requested additional information from the Board. The information requested required extensive research, and the detailed response was provided in June.

Concurrently, the TWC was processing the 401 water quality certification for Applewhite, the first reservoir project in the state requiring such certification under the Clean Water Act. The TWC received numerous comments and requests for a public hearing on the water quality of the project. The agency held a public hearing in April 1989. In June, the TWC denied the 401 certification for the Leon Creek portion of the project, and conditionally granted certification for the Medina River portion. The Leon Creek certification was not denied because of the perceived water quality problems voiced by the opponents. It was denied because the minimum release from the diversion dam would violate the dissolved oxygen values in the river downstream of the Leon Creek wastewater plant.

The City Council deferred the Leon Creek portion of the project in July 1988; the wastewater permit section of the TWC denied 401 certification for the Leon Creek portion and approved, with conditions, the Medina River portion of the project in June 1989; the water rights section of the TWC granted an extension of the water rights permit for both portions in August 1989. How would all of this impact the 404 being processed by the Corps?

Again, the Corps requested more information from the Board in early August 1989. On August 28, 1989, the district engineer signed the Section 404 permit for the Applewhite Reservoir project. But the permitted project was different from that proposed seven years earlier. The Corps denied the Leon Creek Diversion dam without prejudice based on the denial of the TWC 401 certification. The Board retains the water rights for 12,300 acre-feet/year from Leon Creek, but construction of any portion of the Leon Creek diversion dam and canal cannot occur at this time.

With both State and federal permits in place, work on the project is progressing. Land surveying and archeological investigations in the project area are continuing. Construction is scheduled to start May 1, 1990, five months before the water rights permit extension expires. And the Corps has just received a letter of "Intent to Sue" over its issuance of the Applewhite 404 permit. Despite all of the problems, the Board remains optimistic that the Applewhite Water Supply Project will be built and surface water will become a reality for San Antonio.

THE DALLAS FLOODWAY
PAST AND PRESENT SUCCESSES IN FLOOD PROTECTION BENEFITS

by

Nancy E. Begel[1], A.M. ASCE and Gary M. Pettit[2], M. ASCE

ABSTRACT

This paper explores the history of the Dallas Floodway, past performance of the project under various flood conditions and, most recently, the present successes in flood protection provided during the record rainfalls of May and June 1989. The Dallas Floodway, as an integral part of the U.S. Army Corps of Engineers' flood protection plan for the Trinity River, has provided direct and indirect benefits to the City of Dallas throughout its history of almost 60 years.

INTRODUCTION

The Dallas Floodway is often referred to as the most significant flood control and floodplain reclamation project in Dallas history. It was the calamitous, costly and tragic inundation of 1908 which spurred Dallas' leaders and engineers into action to free the City from future ravages of the Trinity River. The Trinity River, a usually calm stream 548 miles (882 km) long and draining a total area of approximately

---

[1] Director of Engineering, Stevenson Engineering Associates, Inc. 10617 Jones Street, Suite 201-A, Fairfax, Virginia 22030.

[2] President, Nationwide Water Resource Services, Inc., 17304 North Preston Road, Suite 800, Dallas, Texas 75252.

17,900 square miles (46,360 sq km) [6,106 square miles (15,814 sq km) at Dallas] would periodically become a raging torrent, isolating the east and west sections of Dallas and inundating all in between.

Historical records indicate major floods in 1844, 1866, 1871, 1890, and the most catastrophic flood of 1908, which resulted in a peak discharge of 184,000 cfs (5,210 m^3/sec) and a maximum stage of 52.6 feet (160 m) at the Commerce Street bridge. With floodwaters extending two miles wide, Oak Cliff could be reached only by boat, and trips to Fort Worth had to be made via Terrell and Ennis. Loss estimates from the disaster reached $2.5 million, a considerable figure in 1908. Damages from a similar flood today, without the existing flood protection levees, would reach into the billions.

Following the devastating 1908 flood, Dallas' planners in 1910 began to masterplan the construction of levees to protect the City from such flood damages. George E. Kessler, a Dallas engineer who drafted the first city plan for the proper development of Dallas, and of the land adjacent to the Trinity River, recognized as early as 1910 the potential growth possible to the City of Dallas if the river could be tamed. He was persistent in his belief that a great city could spring up immediately upon construction of a flood control project.

During the decade following the 1908 flood, Dallas expanded rapidly, but growth stopped on its western edge due to the flood-ravaged Trinity. In 1920, an extensive study of the Trinity River was initiated by Myers, Noyes & Forrest Engineers. By 1926, plans were complete enough to permit the establishment of an assessment district, which was to become the City and County of Dallas Levee Improvement District (DLID). Engineering plans showed that the cost of the flood control and reclamation work alone would exceed $6.5 million. The total cost of related improvements, including railroads, utilities, roads and bridges, would total approximately $21 million. Construction of the flood control improvements, which took place between June 1928 and November 1931, included widening, straightening and diversion of the old channel, 35-ft (10.7 m) high levees, and a floodway approximately 2,200 feet (671 m) wide. In all, the project encompassed some 25 miles (40.2 km) of levees, with 14 miles (22.5 km) of new diversion channel and floodway (DLID, 1931).

In terms of benefits to real estate, land development and overall growth, the Trinity River flood control project spurred growth of the Trinity Industrial

District, 1,150 acres (465 ha) located adjacent to downtown Dallas. In terms of health, safety and welfare, thousands of acres of flood-prone land were protected from periodic floodwaters, including a significant portion of the Dallas Central Business District. There is doubtless no single project which has meant as much to Dallas, in terms of the City's development into a major metropolis and in both direct and indirect economic benefits.

The effectiveness of the Dallas Floodway and other flood control works in the upper Trinity River Basin was demonstrated in the April 1942 flood, in which a discharge of 111,000 cfs (3,143 m^3/sec) was experienced at the Commerce Street gage. The 1942 flood represents the second largest discharge of record for the Trinity River at Dallas. A major regional flood in the spring of 1957, which resulted in a peak discharge of 75,300 cfs (2,132 m^3/sec) at the Commerce Street gage and caused extensive flooding over the entire upper basin, resulted in damages estimated at approximately $19.5 million. However, it is estimated that the flood control projects in operation in the basin at the time of the 1957 flood prevented an additional $85 million in damages. Based on the estimates of flood damages prevented, the projects more than repaid their total initial costs by preventing losses from this single flood.

The most recent major improvements to the Dallas Floodway were made in 1958 by the U.S. Army Corps of Engineers. These improvements included raising the levees to provide for conveyance of the Standard Project Flood (SPF) with four feet (1.2 m) of freeboard. To improve interior drainage, additional pump stations, including pumps and gravity sluices, were constructed and the pilot channel within the floodway was modified by excavation to an average depth of 25 feet (7.6 m), with a 50-ft (15.2 m) bottom width, to provide a design capacity of 13,000 cfs (368 m^3/sec) (USCE, 1986). Additional studies of the Floodway and adjacent sump areas have recently been completed in anticipation of future improvements.

The effectiveness of the Dallas Floodway was again tested in the spring and summer of 1989, when North Texas experienced more rainfall than during any six-month period since 1957. A series of storms began on May 3, 1989, and resulted in weeks of flash flooding on local watersheds and prolonged high stages on the Trinity. The storms caused extensive damages, took 25 lives, and caused hundreds of residents to lose their homes and valuables. The Metroplex flooding of May and

June 1989 resulted primarily from three major storm systems. The first storm, on May 3-5, saturated the watershed and caused area Corps of Engineers reservoirs to go into their flood pools. The total rainfall reported for the Dallas-Fort Worth area was approximately 5 inches (0.13 m) with approximately 8.7 inches (0.22 m) in portions of the West Fork watershed (USCE, 1989).

The second storm occurred on May 16-18, and brought an additional 4 to 9 inches (0.10 to 0.23 m) of rainfall to an already saturated watershed. This storm caused Lake Arlington to flow over its spillway, inundating parts of southwest Arlington, a golf course, and several major roads. Dallas' Five Mile Creek flooded extensively, destroying homes and everything along its banks, including 150 new police cars parked in a lot near the creek. Floodwater releases from Lake Ray Hubbard on the East Fork of the Trinity River breached three downstream levees, causing vast areas of agricultural land to flood. Approximately 13 inches (0.33 m) of rainfall were reported in the Upper West Fork of the Trinity River Basin (USCE, 1989).

The Dallas-Fort Worth area had slightly over one week to recover from the second storm before the third major storm arrived, bringing a two-week period of heavy rainfall throughout the Upper Trinity River Basin. From June 1 through June 14, rainfall occurred virtually every day in some portion of the Dallas-Fort Worth area. Total rainfall varied from 9 to 12.5 inches (0.23 to 0.32 m), with up to 17 inches (0.43 m) in some areas of the watershed above Lake Grapevine (USCE, 1989).

Many longtime residents of Dallas and Fort Worth remember the disastrous floods of May 1949, when widespread flooding occurred on the Trinity, with the exception of the area protected by the Floodway. While more significant rainfall occurred in 1957 and again in the spring of 1989, these storms did not result in the extent of flood damages that would be expected from floods of this magnitude due to protection by the levee system and upstream flood control structures in the Upper Trinity River Basin (including the recent additions of Joe Pool and Ray Roberts Lakes). The flood protection works prevented extensive economic losses in the Dallas area (including the Trinity Industrial District and portions of the Central Business District). These benefits were realized in a time when Dallas' slow economic recovery from the recession of the late 1980's could have been dealt a severe blow.

As of 1990, the City of Dallas boasts a population of approximately one million, and the City and surrounding suburbs within the Trinity River Basin have experienced major growth and expansion since the initial construction and subsequent improvements to the Dallas Floodway. The project was designed based on historical flooding from a watershed which was largely undeveloped and agricultural in nature. Recent hydrologic and hydraulic studies by the U.S. Army Corps of Engineers indicate that the future integrity of the levee system may now be threatened by increased flows under certain projected growth and flood plain encroachment scenarios within the watershed (USCE, 1986). Additionally, siltation of the pilot channel within the floodway has reduced its conveyance and caused problems in draining adjacent sump areas. Engineering has been completed for restoration of the pilot channel capacity through approximately ten miles of the floodway. In addition, the applicability of the Dallas Floodway design flows is also being reevaluated due to significant changes in the watershed characteristics, including extensive urbanization in the Dallas-Fort Worth area and alteration of the hydrologic regime by various reservoirs in the upstream basin.

In conclusion, the Dallas Floodway, in conjunction with other flood protection works which have been constructed in the Upper Trinity River Basin, has proven itself as an effective means of flood damage prevention and a major catalyst to the growth of the City of Dallas, which would not have been possible otherwise due to the frequent inundation of the Trinity River flood plain. Ongoing maintenance and modifications of the Floodway, as required to offset the effects of urban growth and other alterations in the Upper Trinity River Basin, will ensure the long-term protection of the City whose infrastructure and economic base are so heavily dependent upon this major flood control project.

REFERENCES

City and County of Dallas Levee Improvement District. 1931. Facts Supporting the Coordinated Program Involved in the Dallas County Flood Control and Reclamation Project. Dallas, Texas.

_____. 1951. First Southwest Company. Dallas, Texas.

Trinity Improvement Association. 1968-1969. The Trinity River: New Vistas of Opportunity for Texas and the Great Southwest. Dallas, Texas.

U.S. Army Corps of Engineers. 1986. Draft Regional Environmental Impact Statement, Trinity River and Tributaries. Fort Worth District. Fort Worth, Texas.

_____. 1989. Dispatch, Vol 7, No. 8. U.S. Army Corps of Engineers, Fort Worth District. Fort Worth, Texas.

WATER REUSE IN LAS COLINAS, IRVING, TEXAS

Mark R. Ernst[1] and Stanford W. Lynch,[2] Member, ASCE

Abstract

The largest urban water reclamation project in Texas that involves reuse of treated wastewater was implemented in July, 1987, to provide an economical and drought-free supply of water to the master planned 12,000 acre Las Colinas Development in Irving, Texas. This area experiences routine water rationing and is predicted to see significantly increased potable water rates. This project, coined the Raw Water Supply Project, provides for the contractual right to 8000 ac-ft/yr of secondary treated effluent from Trinity River Authority's 100 MGD Central plant and the appropriative right to up to 5034 ac-ft/yr of raw water from the Elm Fork of the Trinity River to irrigate four golf courses, boulevard medians, and open spaces while also providing for evaporative makeup in 158 acres of man-made lakes. The RWSP is operated by Dallas County Utility and Reclamation District and allows for mixing of the effluent and river waters in select reservoirs to produce high quality irrigation water. The Project presently has an annual demand of approximately 2500 ac-ft from five customers. Project facilities include eight pump stations, 15 miles of low pressure transmission mains and nine miles of high pressure (40 - 80 psi) distribution system. This paper will describe the RWSP infrastructure, supply and demand statistics, O&M procedures, financial characteristics and water quality considerations.

---

1   Water Supply Manager. Dallas County Utility and Reclamation District. Irving, Texas 75016
2. General Manager. Same as above.

Introduction

Las Colinas is a 12,000 acre, master planned development located wholly within the City of Irving, Texas. This development is denoted by elegant highrise offices, luxury hotels and exclusive residential areas as well as for distinct attention to landscaping. Greenbelt areas, parks, manicured road medians, numerous lakes and four golf courses provide significant landscaped open space in which to work, live and play.

The Las Colinas Developer and the Dallas County Utility and Reclamation District (the District), realized that there was a definite demand for a long term, economical and drought free water supply. The District was asked to develop a plan for a drought free water supply which eventually became known as the Raw Water Supply Project (RWSP). The basic premise for the RWSP was the contractual commitment with the Trinity River Authority (TRA) for up to 8000 ac-ft/yr of secondary treated effluent. This guaranteed source of water, coupled with limited and regulated authorization to divert water for the Elm Fork of the Trinity River, provide a drought-free water supply for irrigation and evaporative make-up in area lakes.

Infrastructure

A 10.2 mile, 30" RCP waterline from the TRA Central Wastewater Treatment Plant to the District's 23 acre Lake Remle was completed in July 1987. Lake Remle is an off-channel reservoir that acts as a temporary storage basin with detention times of approximately 35 days. Water within Lake Remle is either pumped to Hackberry Creek Lake which serves as a reservoir for the 18-hole Hackberry Creek Country Club (HCCC) golf course or to a second storage reservoir, the 125 acre, manmade Lake Carolyn. Lake Carolyn is the largest reservoir within the Development and is the direct recipient of waters diverted from the Elm Fork. Distribution pump stations on Lake Carolyn supply water to the Las Colinas Country Club's (LCCC) 18 hole golf course and the Las Colinas Sports Club's (LCSC) Cottonwood Valley and Tournament Player's golf courses, which are each 18-holes respectively. The water is also diverted for irrigation of miscellaneous open spaces and area lake evaporative makeup.

The majority of the distribution system is low pressure main whereby large volumes are transported to remote reservoirs. These reservoirs are the sites of high pressure pump stations, owned and operated by the respective golf courses for irrigation. Golf course irrigation is principally at night, while District supply is continuous. Minor fluctuations in reservoir water levels are typical.

Supply and Demand

In 1988 a total of 730 mgal (2240 ac-ft) of water were procured from the two supply sources, with the majority (82%) being purchased from TRA. Figure 1 depicts the annual trend in supply. Elm Fork diversion is governed by two (2) permits from the Texas Water Commission and is based on the river's elevation downstream of two water treatment plants. If the river exceeds elevation 407.0 msl, the District is authorized to divert at a rate of 3200 gpm. If the river is less than or equal to 407.0 msl, diversion is limited to only 221 ac-ft per year. These constraints make river diversion common only during spring and fall months.

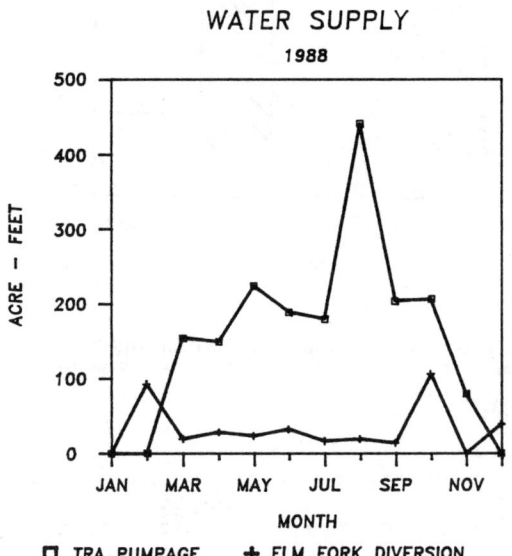

FIG. 1. Annual Trend in Supply of Water to District Reservoirs from TRA (Effluent) and the Elm Fork of the Trinity River.

Figure 2 shows the 1988 demand for the four customers. A fifth customer has been contracted for 1989 and a sixth will participate in 1990. The District's demand in Figure 2 represents evaporation on 158 acres of man-made lakes. Evaporation is calculated daily based on local Corp of Engineers pan evaporation statistics. The remaining three customers are golf courses representing about 140 acres for every 18 holes. Golf course demand is measured by metering golf course pump stations. These meters are read weekly to assure they are performing properly. Note that variation among golf course irrigation quantities is typical, but a million gallons per 18 holes is a good rule-of-thumb for summer irrigation.

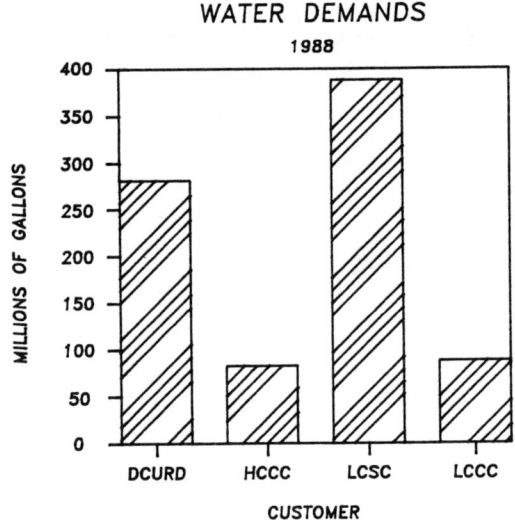

FIG. 2. 1988 Demand by Four Major Customers for Irrigation Water. DCURD Represents Evaporation Makeup, Others Represent Golfcourse Irrigation.

Cost of Water

Contracts are structured for customers to make two types of payments to the District. The first type of payment reflects the capital charge or payback of debt associated with construction of facilities necessary to serve that particular customer. The second type of payment is the commodity cost which is based on monthly meter reading at golf course pump stations or summation of daily evaporations. The commodity charge covers RWSP O&M costs.

The capital charge will be retired in 20 years. The commodity charge is approximately $0.50/1000 gallons. Projections for the Fiscal Year 1989-90 incorporating both capital and commodity charges into an average cost per 1000 gallons range from $0.91 to $1.30. The District is presently encumbered with the highest rate because of the expense of reserve capacity within the system. Nevertheless these rates are significantly below that of the City of Irving's $1.68/1000 and are free of any rationing.

Water Quality

High salt content is often a concern with effluent irrigation. The District monitors water quality monthly at select sites within the Development to determine the suitability of our waters for irrigation. It appears that dilution is a solution to the salt problem. Effluent directly from the plant has moderate irrigation restrictions, but detention in various lakes and intentional mixing with river and storm water ameliorate the salt concentrations. Chemical analysis shows that water delivered to the golf courses often reveals no similarity to that of effluent at all.

Dilution and detention, coupled with an annual rainfall of 29.46 inches seems to lessen the problems associated with effluent reuse water quality common to more arid parts of the country.

TABLE 1: Abbreviations and Conversions Used in This Paper

Million gallons (mgal)	= 3785 Cubic meters (m3)
Gallon per minute (gpm)	= 0.004 Cubic meters per minute (m3/min)
Acre-foot (ac-ft)	= 1230 Cubic meters (m3)
Pound per square inch (psi)	= 6.89 Kilopascal (kPa)
Acre	= 0.405 hectare (ha)
Mile	= 1.61 Kilometer (Km)
Foot	= 0.305 Meter (m)

Evaluation of Global Warming Impact on Soil Moisture and Water Runoff in Texas

Juan B. Valdés* M. ASCE, Gerald R. North[†] and Timothy Raines[‡]

Abstract

In this paper a numerical evaluation of the variability of soil moisture and surface runoff due to global warming is carried out. An analytical model of the soil moisture balance based on our previous work (Valdés et al, 1989; Diaz-Granados et al, 1984) is used to evaluate the probability distribution of the soil moisture concentration and resulting surface runoff. The input of hydroclimatic values is based on point precipitation models but modifications were carried out to account for the other variables following the approach suggested by Richardson (1981,1988). Preliminary results show that not only the mean of the distribution of both soil moisture and runoff change, as expected, but the variability of the values around the means also does. The results of our research have applications on the planning of reservoir operation for irrigation demands and to evaluate the change in surface runoff expected due to global warming.

1 Introduction

Global warming is expected to increase the intensity of the global hydrologic cycle (MacCracken and Luther,1985; Mitchell, 1989). Precipitation and temperature patterns, soil moisture requirements, and the physical structure

---

*Associate Professor, Environmental and Water Resources Engineering,
Department of Civil Engineering and Climate System Research Program,
Texas A&M University, College Station, TX 77843-3136

[†]Distinguished Professor and Director, Climate System Research Program,
College of Geosciences, Texas A&M University,
College Station, TX 77843-3146

[‡]Student, Environmental and Water Resources Engineering,
Department of Civil Engineering, Texas A&M University,
College Station, TX 77843-3136

of the vegetation canopy play important roles in the hydrologic system of drainage basins. Changes in these phenomena, because of a buildup of CO_2, have the potential to affect the quantity, quality, timing, and spatial distribution of water available to satisfy the many demands placed on the resource by society (Callaway and Currie,1985). In addition, the location and magnitude of many different types of demand for water may be quite sensitive to the effects of CO_2 buildup on temperature and vegetation.

2 Mathematical Models

Several models of the components of the hydrologic process were used in our work. To model the climatic variables required in the soil moisture analysis the mathematical representation suggested by Richardson (1981) was used to obtain the daily values of temperature, radiation and precipitation, all of them correlated among themselves. These daily values were then disaggregated to hourly values by the use of constant coefficients that reflected the characteristics of the sites under study. Finally the hourly temperature and radiation were used to estimate the potential evapotranspiration at each hour. The climatic variables were then used in a mathematical model of the one-dimensional soil layer, that accounted for the soil moisture and surface runoff at each time interval. To describe the soil moisture concentration, mathematical representations for the different water balance components were needed. This was done by dividing the events in two possible types. The rainfall (or infiltration) event will be described here. The interstorm periods (or exfiltration events) are similar and the reader is referred to the references mentioned below for a thorough discussion of them. Several assumptions were made in the development of these models. First, the rainfall intensity was assumed to be constant during the duration of the storm. The infiltration and exfiltration models proposed by Eagleson (1978) were adopted here to evaluate the actual evapotranspiration $e_T(t)$ and the surface runoff $R_s(t)$. Finally, percolation was assumed to be constant throughout the duration of the event (infiltration or exfiltration), although its magnitude was determined by the initial soil moisture of the corresponding event.

During a rainfall event, it was assumed that no evapotranspiration, $e_T(t)$, occured. Precipitation, $i_r(t)$, was taken as a rectangular pulse of constant intensity, i_r, and duration, t_r. The difference between rainfall, $i_r(t)$, and surface runoff, $R_s(t)$, is the infiltration that contributes to soil moisture. The infiltration rate capacity is defined as Philip(1969):

$$f_i^*(t) = \tfrac{1}{2} S_i t^{-1/2} + a \tag{1}$$

where the term a is the gravitational infiltration rate (it also takes into account the water table influence), and S_i is the infiltration sorptivity, embodying capillarity.Both parameters may be expressed as a function of soil characteristics (Eagleson, 1978) and for different soil textures, Eagleson and others give typical values of the parameters. This work uses three hypothetical soils with parameters representing the areas of San Antonio, Temple and Amarillo in Texas. At the beginning of the storm event, the infiltration capacity of the soil will commonly be greater than the intensity of the rainfall. The soil moisture content will increase up to some time, t_o, at which time the soil surface may reach saturation and $f_i^* = i_r$. For t between t_o and t_r, surface An approximate expression for t_o is (Eagleson, 1978):

$$t_o \simeq \frac{S_i^2}{2(i_r - a)^2} \qquad (2)$$

Two cases were considered in our previous work (Diaz-Granados et al, 1984; Valdés et al, 1989):

i) No Surface Runoff occurs ($0 \leq t_r \leq t_o$), thus the soil moisture final state is equal to the value at the beginning of storm j plus the precipitation depth minus the percolation losses thoroughout the storm, i.e.:

$$s_1(j) = s_o(j) + [i_r t_r - K(1)s_o^c(j)t_r]/nZ, \quad 0 \leq t_r \leq t_o \qquad (3)$$

ii)Surface Runoff occurs ($t_r > t_o$), thus the soil moisture concentration , $s_1(j)$, at the end of storm j is equal to the value at the beginning of the storm plus the infiltration amount minus the percolation losses thoroughout the storm, i.e.:

$$s_1(j) = s_o(j) + [i_r t_o + S_i(t_r^{1/2} - t_o^{1/2}) + a(t_r - t_o) - K(1)s_o^c(j)t_r]/nZ, \quad t_r > t_o \qquad (4)$$

where s_1 is the final value of the degree of saturation for the infiltration process, j is a relative index of the location of the event j in time, and Z is a measure of the penetration depth of the wet and dry fronts during storm and interstorm periods, respectively.

3 Analysis of Results

Three examples cases with climatic and soil data representing different parts of Texas were modeled : they correspond to the areas of Temple, San Antonio and Amarillo. Five years were simulated both for the actual climate and with an assumed warming of $5°C$. Of these time series the mean and standard deviation were computed. These moments were then used to evaluate the parameters of a Beta probability distribution for both the soil moisture concentration levels and surface runoff. For example, in the Temple area the mean decreased, as expected, around 10% but more interestingly the standard deviation also changed by around 20% making the distribution more tighter than the actual values. Similar results were also flound for surface runoff, supporting the statement that global warming will have a significant impact on Texas water resources.

Acknowledgements

J. B. Valdés was partially funded through the TEES Engineering Excellence Fund- Civil Engineering. T. Raines participation was funded through the TEES Undergraduate Summer Research Program. C. Graves and J. Tessendorf at the Climate System Research Program (CSRP) and S. S. P. Shen of the Department of Mathematics, all at Texas A & M University gave invaluable comments. All contributions are gratefully acknowleged.

References

⋄ Callaway, J.M., and Currie, J.W., "Water Resource Systems and Changes in Climate and Vegetation", Publication DOE/ER-0236, U.S. Department of Energy, Washington, D.C., 1985.

⋄ Delworth, T.L. and S. Manabe, "The Influence of Potential Evaporation on the Variabilities of Simulated Soil Wetness and Climate", Journal of Climate, Vol. 1, pp.523-547, 1988.

⋄ Diaz-Granados, M.;J. B. Valdés and R. Bras, "A Physically Based Flood Frequency Distribution for Ungaged Catchments," Water Resources Research, Vol. 20(7), 995-1002, 1984.

⋄ Eagleson, P.S., "Climate, Soil and Vegetation 1-7 ," Water Resources Research, 14(5), 705-776, 1978.

⋄ Mitchell, J.F.B., "The Greenhouse Effect and Climate Change", Reviews of Geophysics, Vol. 27(1), 115-139, 1989.

⋄ Richardson, C.W., "Stochastic Simulation of Daily Precipitation, Temperature and Solar Radiation", Water Resources Research, vol.17(1), 182-190, 1981.

⋄ Valdés, J. B.; M. Diaz-Granados and R.L. Bras, "A Derived PDF for the Initial Soil Moisture in a Catchment," in press, Journal of Hydrology, 1989.

GROUNDWATER CONTAMINATION
FROM AN UNLINED, POORLY CAPPED LANDFILL

Alejandro J. Gonzalez[1], Ching-Pi Wang[1], and Hideo Fujita[1]

Abstract

This paper presents a case study of groundwater and surface water contamination from a major, unlined, and poorly capped municipal landfill located in Western Washington. The landfill has been in operation for nearly 25 years and is in need of significant work to mitigate the environmental concerns. Specifically, approximately 0.95 million cubic meters (250 million gallons) of leachate saturate the lower portion of the landfill. This paper reviews past disposal practices, describes geologic and hydrogeologic conditions affecting leachate migration, and examines the results of field investigations conducted to evaluate the feasibility of leachate head reduction using horizontal and/or vertical wells.

Background

The Cedar Hills Landfill is the largest municipal landfill in the state of Washington. The landfill opened in 1963, is located in south-central King County in Western Washington (Figure 1) and covers an area of approximately 3.7 million square meters (920 acres). The landfill is operated by the King County Solid Waste Division (KCSWD) and is projected to receive about 2.7 million metric tons per year by closure date in the year 2006 (CH2M Hill - 1987).

---

[1]Respectively, Environmental Engineer, Senior Hydrogeologist and Groundwater Hydrogeologist, State of Washington, Department of Ecology, 4350 - 150th Avenue N.E., Redmond, WA 98052

GROUNDWATER CONTAMINATION

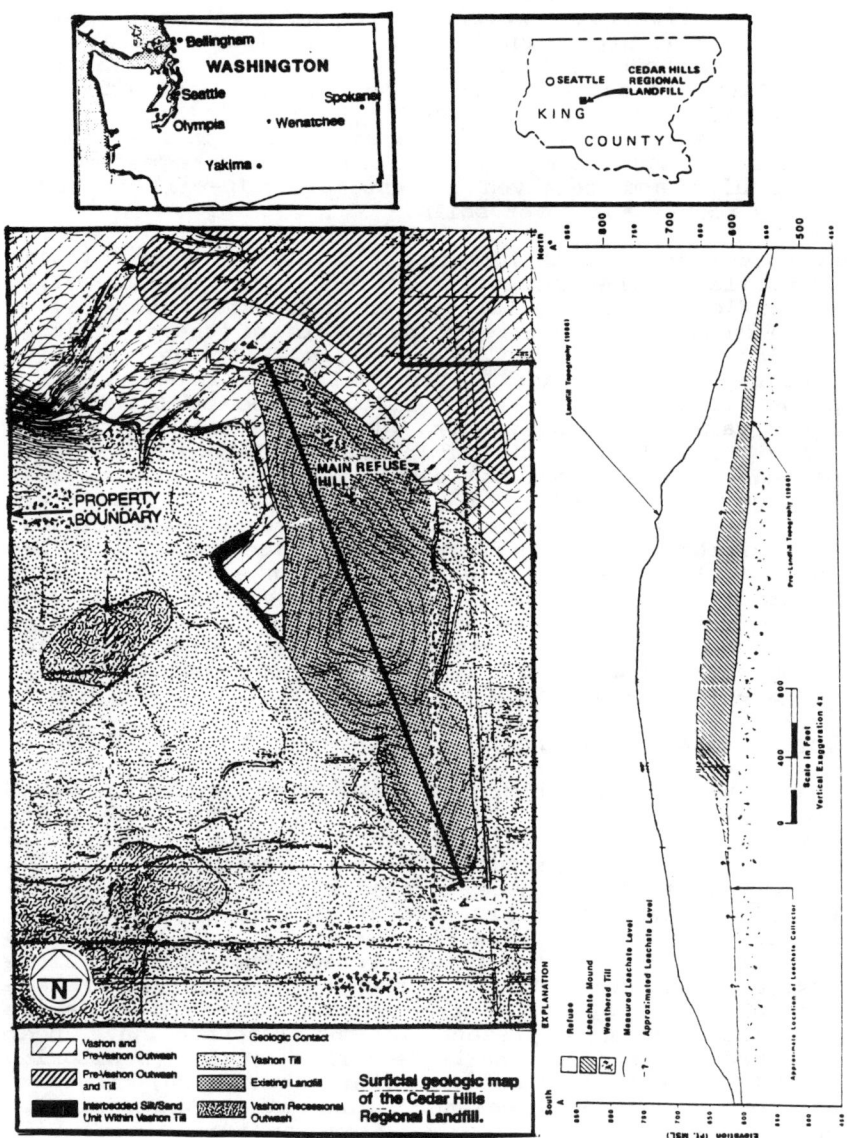

Figure 1. Location Maps and Main Hill Cross-Section Cedar Hills Landfill, Washington

Twelve million cubic meters of refuse were landfilled in four unlined areas until 1987 when lined refuse cells were constructed. Between 1963 and 1987, the landfill operation did not meet the present federal definition of a sanitary landfill. The Main Refuse Hill (Figure 1) is the largest unlined landfill area. The Main Hill covers an area of approximately 0.64 million square meters, is 80 m high and received an estimated 10-million cubic meters refuse and cover soils.

Hydrogeologic investigations by R.W. Beck (1983) identified three hydrostratigrafic units: Vashon Till, Stratified Glacial Drift and Outwash sands and gravel. The Vashon Till, the least permeable of these stratas, mantles most of the Main Refuse Hill pre-landfill topographical surface. The Till thickness with a permeability ranging from 0.000036 m/sec to 0.000000051 m/sec varies from 5m to 19m. Perched water collects on top of the Till. The Till is underlain by the more permeable advance outwash sand and gravel deposits with average permeability of 0.00024 m/sec. These are multiple layers of discontinuous perched water zones. Local recharge and discharge points have been identified onsite. Shallow ground water flows in a radial pattern toward the boundaries of the site. Beneath the outwash deposit is the deep regional aquifer. The top elevation of the deep aquifer is estimated to range from 80 to 100 m above mean sea level, approximately 60 m below the Till surface (CH2M Hill-1987).

Environmental Concerns

The environmental concerns associated with the past landfill practices are leachate contamination of soils, surface water and ground water. This concern is heightened by the presence of an estimated 0.95 million cubic meters of leachate mounded within the Main Refuse Hill on top of the Till layer (CH2M Hill-1988). A high BOD/COD ratio of 0.61 (26,311 ppm of BOD) and high metals concentration (100 ppm of Total Recoverable Zinc) indicate that acid forming bacteria are active and metals leachability is an environmental concern. Volatile organics compounds present in the leachate have been detected in samples collected from onsite monitoring wells. Site investigations (Parametrix-1986) indicate shallow ground water contamination within the landfill. The contaminated ground water flows on tops of the Till layer toward springs and offsite. Although the Till layer is an aquitard, its permeability may not prevent leachate from moving downward toward the regional aquifer. The threat to the regional aquifer is a great concern because it is the source of drinking water for the people in the vicinity of the landfill.

Leachate Removal Investigations

A pilot study of leachate extraction has been conducted to evaluate the feasibility of vertical and horizontal wells (CH2M Hill-1988). Three six-inch diameter leachate pumping wells and three observation wells were completed for this study. Results of this study indicate that the thickness of the leachate mound fluctuated as much as 1.50 m during the period of measurements. Gas pressure interferences of up to about 7 m (12.5 psig) appear to play an important role in leachate depth variations. In fact, a criterion prescribed to obtain representative drawdown and recovery data from both pumping and observation wells during pump test was to maintain a constant gas pressure in the wells. Pumping test results indicate that initial pumping rates of about 0.13 lps (2 gpm) decreased gradually to less than 0.6 lps in 4 to 13 hours after the test started. Small drawdowns or no response at the observation wells indicate that the cone of influence may not have extended beyond a few meters from the pumping wells.

The development of the cone of influence may have been affected by the daily solid waste disposal operations, interlayers of refuse with low permeability compacted cover material, which has resulted in a heterogenous anisotropic saturated solid waste media. Average values for the hydraulic conductivity and storage coefficient are 0.0024 cm/sec and 0.00069 respectively for the saturated solid waste media. The confining conditions indicated by the low storage coefficient value are thought to be due to the high gas pressure and the interlayering of compacted soil cover.

A more recent Main Hill Head Reduction Investigation by Harper Owes (1989) was conducted to evaluate the performance of vertical extraction wells and horizontal drains. The pumping test results indicate the leachate discharge rates from vertical wells are much lower than previously predicted. Reasons for this include: lower hydraulic conductivity, well screen clogging, dissolved gases interfering with the pumping system and leachate foam affecting liquid levels.

Pumping test results indicate air driven pumps designed for highly corrosive liquids are the most efficient for leachate extraction from the vertical wells. Electrical pumps may fail because the 60 C temperature of the leachate exceeds the maxiumum design operation of the pump. Bladder pump efficiencies are adversely affected by the presence of leachate foam. Based on the results of pumping tests, it is proposed that vertical wells equipped with air driven pumps be used to extract leachate at a maximum rate of 0.10 lps (1.5 gpm) for an eight-hour period and allowing 16 hours for recovery. Thus, each well should produce 2.7 cubic meter per day (720 gpd).

Based on information gathered during this study, it is proposed that horizontal drains of about 200 m in length be installed. The drains will be constructed of 3.18 cm diameter (1.25 inch) stainless steel pipe. A flow of about 0.06 lps (1 gpm) is expected from each drain. The low leachate removal rate of the horizontal wells is in part explained by the low vertical hydraulic conductivity of the solid waste media due to the perching effect of the cover soils used to create refuse lifts. Therefore, a perimeter drain system is also proposed to collect the leachate seeps occurring at the Main Hill sideslopes. The drain system will be built in conjunction with the closure construction. The drain system will consist of a layer of gravel placed underneath the impermeable liner, which will drain leachate toward the Main Hill perimeter where it will be combined with the leachate extracted by the vertical and horizontal wells, and then enter the transmission system.

Summary

The purpose of this paper is to examine the results of field investigations conducted to evaluate the feasibility of leachate head removal using horizontal and vertical wells. Information provided shows that leachate removal rates are low. Initial pumping rates steadily decreased and recovery time is necessary between pumping periods. Pumping equipment is adversely affected by the physical properties of the leachate and air driven pumps are recommended. Results of the undergoing field activities are expected to provide more data on the proposed leachate removal system performance.

Observations

This paper has been prepared based on information contained in the references, for which no representations are made. Conclusions, observations and recommendations contained constitute only the opinion of the authors, for which no assurances are made.

Appendix-References

R.W. Beck, (1983). <u>Ground Water Geology/Quality Investigations for the Cedar Hills Regional Landfill</u> Seattle, Washington.

CH2M Hill, (1988). *Cedar Hills Regional Landfill Site Development Plan, Task 45.0- Investigation of the Feasibility of In-waste Leachate Head Reduction*: Report to King County Solid Waste Division, Seattle, Washington.

CH2M Hill, (1987). *Cedar Hills Regional Landfill Draft Site Development Plan*: Report to King County Solid Waste Division, Seattle, Washington Vol. I.

Parametrix, (1986). *Cedar Hills Regional Landfill Baseline Report*: Report to King County Solid Waste, Seattle, Washington.

Harper Owes, (1989). *Cedar Hills Regional Landfill Leachate Head Reduction Draft Engineering Report*: Report to King County Solid Waste Division, Seattle, Washington.

The Market Value of Water in the Ogallala Aquifer
as Implied by Recent Farm Sales

L. Allen Torell, James D. Libbin, and Robert R. Lansford[1]

Abstract

As indicated by farm sales in the Ogallala region, the value of water in the Ogallala Aquifer has fallen. Market values have declined by 30 to 60%, following the recent downward trends in land values. Estimates of in-storage water values in the aquifer range from a high of about $9.50/acre-foot in New Mexico in 1983 to a low of $1.09/acre-foot in Oklahoma in 1986.

Introduction

As irrigated farms overlying the Ogallala Aquifer return to dryland production because of declining water levels, an important economic impact for landowners will be falling land values. It was the need for the land-water value allocation for claiming an income tax deduction for depletion of the groundwater resource that motivated the research reported here. This study estimates water value as the price differential between irrigated and dryland farm sales.

Conceptual Model and Procedures

The standard methodology to estimate the value of irrigation water can be characterized as the income appraisal approach to valuation, whereby the marginal or average value of water is based on crop-water production functions, enterprise budgets and/or dual solutions of linear programming analyses. This study departs from previous work in that the valuation procedure used is the market data appraisal approach, which captures all factors influencing farm value. We develop separate single-equation price models for dryland and irrigated farms. This two-equation procedure was necessary because explanatory variables are not the same in the two models.

Ordinary least squares (OLS) regression was used to estimate an equation for predicting farm sale price through time for both dryland and irrigated farms. Explanatory variables included in both models were the value of buildings and

---

[1]/Department of Agricultural Economics and Agricultural Business, New Mexico State University, Las Cruces, NM 88003-3169.

structures on the farm, time of sale, size of the farm, and expected farm earnings. Additionally, the dryland model included average precipitation amount expected at the farm, and, the irrigated model included the net irrigation requirement for the primary crop grown on the farm, and aquifer characteristics at the farm including depth to water and the saturated thickness of the aquifer. Torell, Libbin and Miller (In Press) provide more detail about the modelling procedures and model specification.

With definition of the two land price models, the value of water was estimated as the per acre difference in farmland value for a farm of similar characteristics. A basic assumption made was that the price differential between the two farm types is the result of increased income earning potential because water is available on irrigated farms, and that as the Ogallala Aquifer is depleted, irrigated farms will revert to dryland farming as the next highest value of land use.

Data Sources

A rich data set comprised of detailed sales information on more than 7,200 farm sales were obtained from Farm Credit Services for use in the empirical model estimation. For each farm sale, the data set included township and range location, farm size in acres, sale price, irrigation water source (well or surface), sale date (month and year), house and other building values, acres cultivated, acres irrigated, and many other descriptive qualitative variables. Data included farm sales in Colorado, Kansas, Nebraska, New Mexico, Oklahoma, South Dakota and Wyoming. Because of a limited number of farm sales in South Dakota and Wyoming, these two states were not included in model estimations. Texas was also excluded because sales data were not available.

In addition to data defining the terms of various farm sales, data were also gathered from various government agencies that defined for each farm sale the average amount of precipitation for the area, net irrigation requirements for crops grown on the farm, and expected farm earnings. Various U.S. Geological Service (USGS) and state engineer publications and Ogallala maps were used to define additional hydrological coefficients.

Results

The wide variation in farmland values between different geographic areas overlying the Ogallala Aquifer were found to be largely explained by differences in farm income, irrigation requirements, precipitation amounts and farm characteristics. Also important were state level variations in time trends of land prices to which no definite cause can be attributed.

Differences in aquifer characteristics between areas were also found to be important in explaining irrigated land values. Regression results indicated that the saturated thickness of the aquifer and degree of aquifer recharge at the farm were important considerations in setting the value of irrigated farms.

Figure 1 shows the estimated trend of dryland and irrigated farm values by state when evaluated at state level means. By January 1986, the estimated decline in dryland farm values from peak levels ranged from 50% in Nebraska to only 8% in New Mexico. Similarly, irrigated farmland values were estimated to decline by 23% in New Mexico, by about 40% in Oklahoma, Kansas and Colorado, and by 51% in Nebraska.

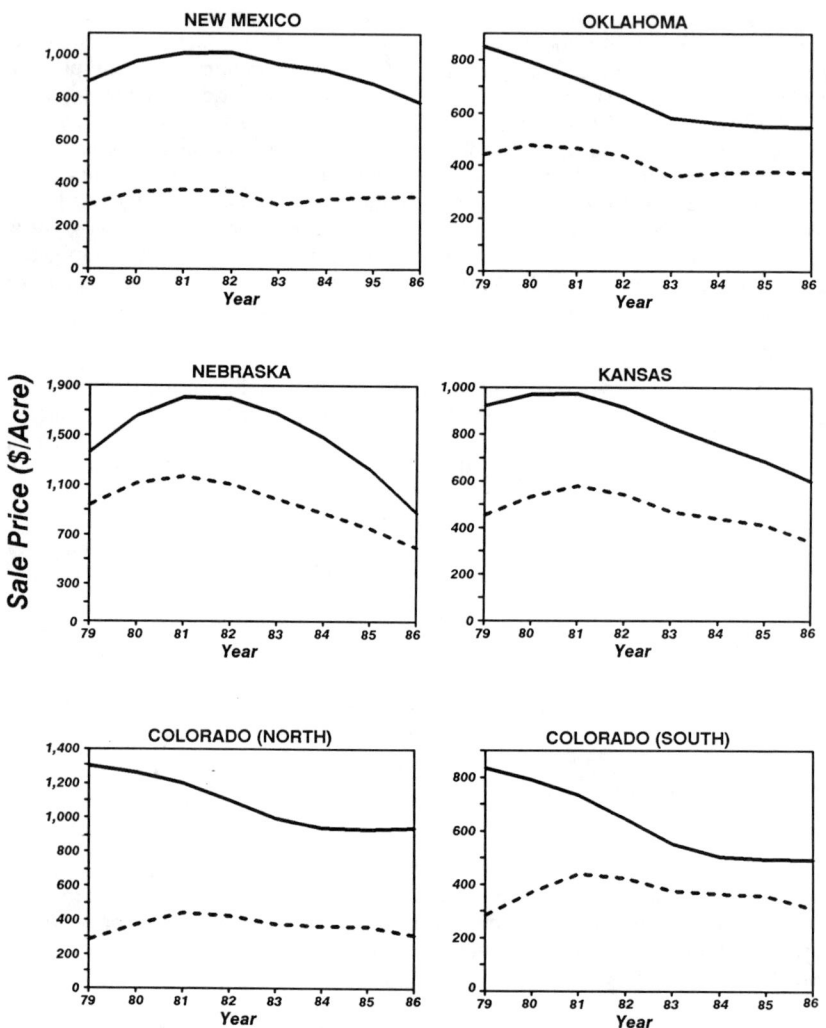

**FIGURE 1
TIME TREND OF FARMLAND VALUES
(—— Irrigated, - - - Dryland)**

Source: Torell, Libbin and Miller (In Press). Reprinted with permission of *Land Economics*.

As shown in Figure 1 and Table 1, the price differential between dryland and irrigated farms, which is considered to be the value of the water including irrigation equipment, has fallen through time. The valuation of water in the marketplace has declined by 30% in New Mexico and 60% in Nebraska and northern Colorado.

The average water value in-storage was estimated to be highest in New Mexico, peaking at $9.49/acre-foot in 1983 and declining to $6.64 by January 1986 (Table 1). This amounts to 64% of the total average irrigated farmland sale price in the state.

As shown in Table 1, the percentage of land price attributed to water value by state is variable and falling. The estimated water value as a percentage of total irrigated farm value was estimated to average more than 60% for New Mexico, and Colorado north of the Republican River, to only 30 to 40% in Oklahoma, Colorado south of the Republican River, Kansas and Nebraska.

Table 1. Average Value of Water In-Storage by State ($/acre-foot)

Year	New Mexico[a]	Colo. Okla.[a]	Colo. North[b]	South[a]	Kansas[a]	Nebr.[b]	Avg.
Water Value as % of Total Irrigated Farmland Price (%)							
1979	66	49	78	67	51	31	57
1980	63	41	70	54	45	33	51
1981	63	37	63	41	40	35	47
1982	64	34	61	36	40	39	46
1983	68	39	62	34	43	41	48
1984	65	34	61	30	41	41	45
1985	61	31	61	30	39	39	44
1986	57	32	67	39	43	32	45
Average	64	38	66	44	43	37	48
Value of Water In-storage ($/acre of irrigated farmland)							
1979	579	431	1,004	567	467	429	580
1980	610	325	878	437	432	542	537
1981	639	271	749	312	386	633	498
1982	648	224	668	238	365	695	473
1983	657	226	615	193	349	688	455
1984	603	187	571	156	308	610	406
1985	530	168	569	154	266	476	361
1986	442	173	622	200	253	285	329
Average	589	251	710	282	353	545	455
Value of Water In-storage ($/acre-foot of saturated thickness)							
1979	7.66	2.54	7.62	5.94	3.07	2.29	4.85
1980	8.24	1.93	6.69	4.58	2.87	2.88	4.53
1981	8.89	1.63	5.73	3.28	2.61	3.38	4.25
1982	9.20	1.36	5.14	2.52	2.49	3.71	4.07
1983	9.49	1.39	4.73	2.06	2.40	3.65	3.95
1984	8.84	1.16	4.41	1.68	2.12	3.23	3.57
1985	7.87	1.05	4.41	1.66	1.85	2.51	3.22
1986	6.64	1.09	4.85	2.18	1.77	1.49	3.00
Average	8.35	1.52	5.45	2.99	2.40	2.89	3.93

Source: Torell, Libbin and Miller (In Press). Reprinted with permission of Land Economics.
[a]/South of the Republican River.
[b]/North of the Republican River.

Literature Cited

Torell, L.A., J.D. Libbin, and M.D. Miller. In Press. The Market Value of Water in the Ogallala Aquifer. J. of Land Economics.

CONTRIBUTIONS OF SATELLITE IMAGERY TO WATER RESOURCE EVALUATIONS

Aubie J. Oslin, Ph.D.[1]

Abstract

The utility of satellite imagery for resource inventory, land use evaluation, environmental impact assessment, and facility siting is being recognized by engineering and planning communities. Satellite images may also facilitate the development and maintenance of regional Geographic Information Systems (GIS) by providing both a source of base map creation and update, as well as a method for evaluating land use changes through time. Landsat TM, SPOT MS and SPOT Panchromatic data have been registered to State Plane or UTM coordinates using two methods, either control points are taken from U.S.G.S. 7.5' quadrangle maps or control points are taken from computer base maps developed from controlled aerial surveys. Land cover information is often combined with soils data then summarized according to sub-drainage area and used as input to the hydrology model for various watersheds under study.

Introduction

Planning and engineering applications of Geographic Information System (GIS) and remote sensing technology are being identified by the resource management community. GIS provides a vehicle, whereby map, image, and textual data are correlated and spatial information is analyzed. Quantitative information derived from analysis is being used in Wetland-404 Permit applications and mitigation, environmental impact assessments, Flood Insurance Studies, and watershed management, as well as for feasibility studies, highway routing, infra-structure alignment and facility siting (Oslin 1988).

Geographic Information Systems are being developed using both vector (CADD) and raster (image) data forms. Vector graphic display and storage is

---

[1]Environmental Scientist, Albert H. Halff Associates, Inc., 8616 Northwest Plaza Drive, Dallas, Texas 75225

most efficient when the spatial conditions are accurately defined as lines, points,or polygons with definite edges, such as property parcels, jurisdictions, and the center lines of roads, pipelines or streams. A vector based GIS is useful for many applications where these features are mapped and the spatial relationship analyzed. A raster based GIS is useful for managing and analyzing a database that relies upon remote sensing as a principal source of database development and update. Raster GIS has been used to evaluate change in land use, to model non-point source pollution potential and to map erodible soils using the Universal Soil Loss Equation. The user community is thus promoting the development of integrated systems that incorporate the best features of each data form (Logan and Bryant 1987, Robinson and Frank 1987).

Satellite images provide an economic data source for evaluating land cover and determining changes in land use through time. Land cover classification and change analysis require careful registration of the satellite image to the GIS base. Research was conducted to compare image to map registration accuracies of the three principal sources of satellite imagery; Landsat Thematic Mapper (TM), SPOT Multi-Spectral (MS) and SPOT Panchromatic data.

Landsat TM images (30 Meter pixel resolution) have repeatedly been geo-coded to fit a 50 by 50 ft. raster grid cell size using control points taken from either U.S.G.S. 7.5' quadrangle maps or computer base maps generated from controlled aerial surveys. The images have been processed to depict a variety of land cover types. Land cover information tabulated using this grid cell size compares closely to area calculations using vector based GIS and CADD systems. Initial results for SPOT imagery indicate that in geographic areas with little topographic relief, images can be registered to 1:24,000 scale (1"=2000') base maps with horizontal displacement errors less than forty feet and to 1:4,800 scale (1"=400') base maps with horizontal displacement errors less than twenty feet.

Method

A similar method is employed for processing either Landsat TM, SPOT MS, or SPOT Panchromatic images for resource inventory, watershed and flood plain management studies. The raw image data and subsequent land cover products are registered to map coordinates by one of two methods. Either ground control points from the image are matched to points on U.S.G.S. 7.5' quadrangle maps or the processed image is registered to control points from digital base maps.

Image classification is the process whereby image picture elements (pixels) are assigned into one of a predetermined set of categories. When applied to multispectral imagery the result is usually an image that maps categories of land cover, vegetation, and soil type. Prior to classification the computer must be trained to recognize the class signatures. There are two basic types of image classification, the supervised approach and the unsupervised approach.

Supervised training requires representative areas for each designated class be located in the image. Field surveys, aerial photography, and existing maps are typically used to verify the training sites. The term training field is a field site that has been selected as representative of some object or land cover the image analyst desires to train the computer to identify. Class signatures are calculated for these identified pixels. Once the computer has been trained to recognize the spectral signature of a land cover type it can locate similar land cover types throughout the remainder of the image.

In the unsupervised approach the image is submitted to clustering algorithms that determine statistical groupings of the data. For example, in the cluster analysis the computer arbitrarily locates a predetermined number of cluster centers, then iteratively repositions them until they are optimally located. The optimum locations are those in which the clusters have maximum spectral separability. Each grouping is assumed to represent the signature probability for one class. In order to relate these groupings to meaningful classes or land cover types the clusters are evaluated using field survey data, aerial photography, and other reference data.

Accuracy of the classification map can be quantitatively assessed through error analysis similar to manually photo-interpreted inventories. A general scheme for determining classification accuracy involves; first, the selection of representative test areas and second, calculation of an estimated percentage of correctly classified pixels in each class.

Case Studies

Supervised and unsupervised classification methods have been used in many environmental and engineering projects to establish the existing land cover and provide a raster GIS base for site suitability analysis, environmental impact assessment, and hydrology modeling. Two development projects are presented to illustrate the use of this data as input to the hydrology model and for watershed resource inventory.

The first project is a 2,500 acre development site situated northeast of Atlanta, Georgia. SPOT MS imagery was geo-referenced to state plane coordinates taken from a digital base map created by a $1" = 200'$ scale controlled aerial survey. A small part of the CADD design file is illustrated in Figure 1. A few image registration points are shown in the figure. The two ft. elevation contours and planimetric features created in the mapping process comply with National Map Accuracy Standards.

SPOT MS imagery was registered to the 1" = 200' scale digital base map using the cubic convolution method and a 20 by 20 ft. grid cell size. Resulting horizontal displacement errors for all check points were less than 15 ft. compared to the map coordinates from the CADD design file. Figure 2 illustrates the geo-coded image and the client's property boundary. Registration points are indicated throughout the image.

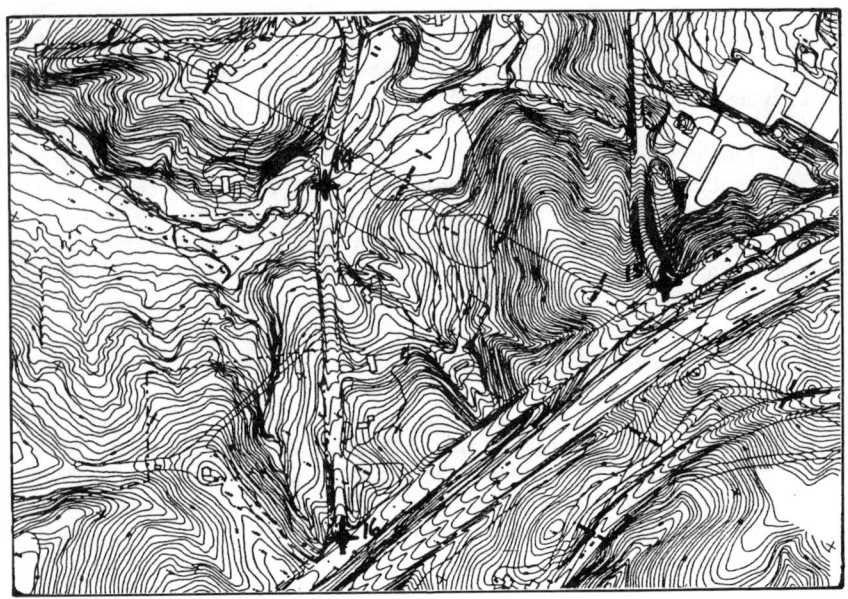

Figure 1. A Portion of the 1" = 200' Scale
Digital Base Map Used to Register SPOT MS Image Data

Existing land cover information was produced from the raw satellite data to assist site suitability study and hydrology modeling. A supervised classification was performed to provide the following land cover categories; Hardwood, Pine, Mixed Hardwood-Pine, Grass Field, Grass-Shrub, Cleared Land, Impervious Surfaces, and Water. Rural Homesteads, Residential, Public Services, Commercial-Retail-Industrial and Transportation Route Land Uses were added to the GIS and incorporated into the land cover map. Soils were categorized as to their hydrologic condition then digitized into the GIS. Soil categories were indexed to the class map to provide a new map that was then summarized by sub-drainage area. The final watershed land cover map used for hydrology modeling provide summary information that indicated the acreage of each land cover category on a particular soil type by sub-drainage area.

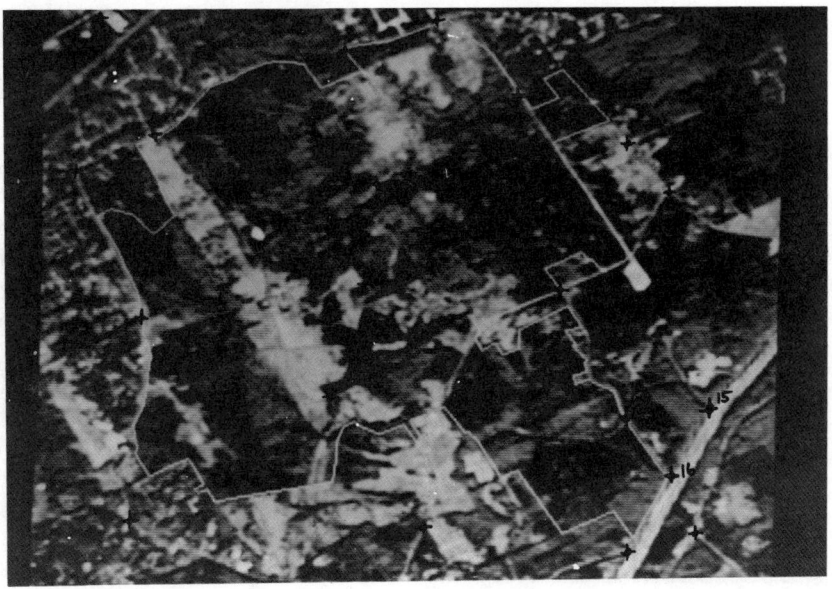

Figure 2. Client's Property Depicted upon the Satellite Image Registered to the 1"=200' Scale CADD Base Map

A similar study was conducted for a development project in the Raleigh and Durham, North Carolina area. The development site was located in the Brier Creek watershed which covers approximately 7,300 acres just north of the Raleigh-Durham Airport. SPOT MS imagery was registered to the 1" = 400' scale digital base map using the cubic convolution method and a 20 by 20 ft. grid cell size. Resulting horizontal displacement errors for all check points were less than 15 ft. compared to the map coordinates from the CADD design file. Planimetric features on the CADD map comply with National Map Accuracy Standards which require less than 13 ft. horizontal displacement error.

Existing land cover information was produced from the raw satellite data over the entire watershed to assist site suitability study and hydrology modeling. As in the previous example, soils were categorized according to hydrologic condition and included in the land cover map summarized for the hydrology model. Figure 3 illustrates the first land cover product produced from the supervised classification of the SPOT MS data.

Figure 3. Initial Land Cover Map
Produced from the Satellite Image

References

Logan, T.L. and Bryant, N.A., 1987. "Spatial Data Software Integration: Merging CAD/CAM/Mapping with GIS and Image Processing", Photogram. Engineering & Remote Sensing, Vol.53, No.10, pp.1391-1395.

Oslin, A.J., 1988. "GIS to Integrate Remote Sensing and CADD for Engineering and Environmental Studies", *in proceedings*, GIS/LIS '88 Accessing the World, San Antonio, Texas Nov.30 - Dec.2, Vol. 1, pp.407-416.

Robinson, V.B. and Frank, A.U., 1987. "Expert Systems for Geographic Information Systems", Photogram. Engineering & Remote Sensing, Vol.50, No.10, pp.1435-1441.

Old Ideas, New Applications:
Expanding the State of the Practice

Dean Randall[1], M. ASCE and Daniel P. Sheer[1], M. ASCE

Abstract

This paper describes three projects in which analytical tools were developed to assist decision makers in operating large-scale water resource systems. Position analysis models were developed for the Central Valley in California and the Savannah River in South Carolina. These models are being used to access the risk of reservoir storage falling below desired levels. A simulation model was developed for the lower Colorado River to schedule hourly releases through the powerhouses, considering the operations of Hoover, Davis and Parker dams and the grid to which power is delivered. Preliminary testing of the model indicates a huge potential to increase the value of power generated.

Introduction

The field of water resources systems analysis has been an active area of research since the early 1960's. There have been innumerable articles, papers and reports describing and promoting the use of some technique, or set of techniques, to enable improved use of a water resource. The ideas have typically included a synthesis of standard operations research tools: mathematical programming, statistical and stochastic analysis, and simulation. Much of the research effort has been in developing models that optimize the use of the resource.

The models described in this paper were developed to address real-world problems. The ideas certainly aren't new, but they represent a decided step forward for the state of the practice.

Water Resources Management, Inc.
6310 Steven's Forest Road
Columbia, Maryland 21045

There are at least three roadblocks in expanding the state of the practice of water management using systems analysis tools. One problem is the amount of time for technology transfer from the research community to the practitioners often takes ten to twenty years. Part of that problem is fear, lack of understanding, and hesitation on the part of engineers and managers to accept proposals which are unfamiliar and may be deemed as "witchcraft." This fear is understandable. In many cases, water managers don't even realize that there is potential to operate the system more efficiently.

A second inherent problem in developing optimization models is that they rely on a formal objective function. Our experience is that it can be difficult to get the water managers to articulate their objectives. Sometimes, after seeing results of a model which uses their stated objectives, the water managers may realize that there are other objectives that were not stated, perhaps weren't even understood. It is important that a model be robust enough to incorporate new objectives, or have output that will shed light on unspoken objectives.

The third roadblock is cost. Effective water resource system analytical tools are not cheap to develop. In some cases the data required by a model are very expensive to synthesize. This has been our experience working with the Central Valley Project in California. Optimization models tend to require a lot of computing horsepower and may have a prohibitively long solution time.

Position Analysis

Position analysis is a risk analysis technique that determines the probability of a system being at a certain state, given it's current state (position). This is useful, for example, if you want to estimate the risk of a water supply reservoir being drawn below a given level, given the current state of the system and likely inflows. The position analysis models we have developed use synthetically generated traces of streamflow coupled with an operation simulation model of the system to quantify the risk of drought.

Hirsch's (1981) technique was used to generate multiple traces of equally likely, monthly streamflows for a 2-year period. The number of traces is the number of years of streamflow record minus 2. Each trace is run

independently through the operation model, starting with
the current conditions. The results of the multiple runs
are compiled to generate a cumulative distribution
function of flows, storages or deliveries.

Briefly, Hirsch's technique works as follows. The
model parameters are estimated monthly. The synthetic
flows are generated in two year sequences by adding the
random component of each monthly flow value in the
historic record to the expected value of the flow in that
month. The random component of each monthly flow value
is the historic error term. The expected value of the
flow is the expected value of the time series model. The
use of the historic error as the random value maintains
the cross-correlation among the inflow points. Of course
any serial correlation between flow in two consecutive
months is maintained through the lag-1 autoregressive
term that appears in both time series models. Each of
the monthly flow values generated in this way are
considered to be equally likely.

Water Resources Management, Inc. has developed two
position analysis models that are in use: one for the
Central Valley in California and the other for the
Savannah River in South Carolina.

Central Valley. The U.S. Bureau of Reclamation, Mid-
Pacific Region, was concerned about another drought in
1988. They wanted to be able to quantify the risk of
drought to determine if the deliveries to users should
be cut back. We developed the Central Valley position
analysis model using an operation model of the Central
Valley previously developed for the Metropolitan Water
District of Southern California in 1987. It includes
the main features of the Central Valley Project and the
State Water Project. An example of the model results is
shown in Figure 1. It shows the probability of Shasta
Reservoir storage with full deliveries made to Bureau
water users and with 25% shortages.

Savannah River. The Southeast began experiencing a
prolonged drought beginning in 1986. The users of the
Savannah River needed to analyze the risk of running low
on water during the summer of 1989. We wrote a position
analysis model to quantify that risk. The managers of
the river were only concerned about the maintaining a
flow below the downstream-most reservoir, so the model
lumped all five major reservoirs on the river into one.
The model was used to show how the probability of
achieving given reservoir storage levels changed through

time and with different outflow values. The example shown in Figure 2 indicates how the probabilities of achieving certain storage levels at the end of May changes from February to April.

Hydropower Scheduling

The Lower Colorado River, with Parker, Davis and Hoover dams, provides an enormous amount of hydropower to the Southwest. Scheduling releases to maximize the value of power is very difficult. One of the difficulties is the institutional framework in which two different agencies, the Bureau and WAPA, are involved in scheduling releases and selling the energy. To improve their efficiency, the Bureau and WAPA wanted a mid-term model that would consider weekly power operations on an hourly time step.

We chose to build a simulation model rather than an optimization model because of the large number of constraints, and the corresponding long solution times, given 168 time steps. A heuristic was used to "maximize" the value of power produced. The constraint set considered minimum and maximum reservoir storages and releases, maximum transmission capacities, and minimum and maximum energy loads. In addition, the Bureau had a preset daily release schedule for Parker Dam (the downstream-most dam). The hourly releases from Parker could follow any arbitrary pattern, provided that the volume for the day followed the schedule.

The heuristic works as follows. An envelope of minimum and maximum cumulative releases from Parker Dam is computed. Given this envelope, similar envelope curves are computed for Davis Dam, then Hoover. Next we go back down to Parker and recalculate going upstream, this time adding power constraints to the calculations.

The model provides a systematic way to schedule releases through the powerhouses to take advantage the temporal fluctuation of the value of power. The model is currently being enhanced by the Bureau with improved front and back ends, and by adding Glen Canyon Dam to the system.

Conclusion

The models described in this paper illustrate the emerging technology of real-world applications of water resources systems analysis. The continuing growth of similar applications will result in better decision making by water managers.

Reference

Hirsch, Robert M. "Stochastic Hydrologic Model for Drought Management" *Journal of the Water Resources Planning and Management Division*, Vol 107, No. WR2, October, 1981.

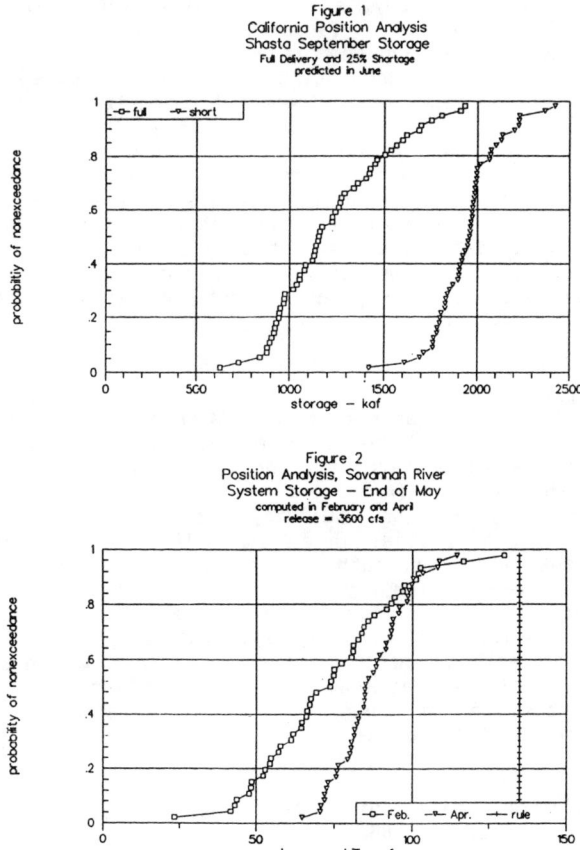

Figure 1
California Position Analysis
Shasta September Storage
Full Delivery and 25% Shortage
predicted in June

Figure 2
Position Analysis, Savannah River
System Storage — End of May
computed in February and April
release = 3600 cfs

IS THERE A FUTURE FOR VACUUM SEWERS ?

DONALD D. GRAY, M. ASCE*

Introduction

Vacuum sewers collect and transport sanitary sewage using pressure difference rather than gravity as the primary motive force. Compared to conventional gravity sewers, they use smaller pipes, are less constrained by topography, are mechanically more complex, and require electrical power. Vacuum sewers are economically competitive in residential and commercial areas of low to moderate population density, flat or undulating topography, rocky soil, high water table, water shortage, or any combination of these conditions.

More than forty vacuum sewer systems are now operating in the U.S., yet this number is small compared to the other alternatives - grinder pump, septic tank effluent pump, and small diameter effluent sewers. As the era of preferential treatment for alternative sewers in the EPA municipal construction grant program draws to an end, it is natural to ask if the vacuum sewer can compete, or whether it is destined for extinction. This paper presents my personal answer to this question.

The Past

Charles T. Liernur was the first to propose the use of vacuum to transport sewage. Liernur was born in Holland in 1828 and served as a Captain in the Confederate Army during the American Civil War. An article in The Engineer (Anonymous, 1866) describes his plan to remove excrement from the buildings surrounding a street intersection. Special privies in each building were connected by pipes to a tank buried beneath the intersection. At night a steam-powered, self-propelled wagon bearing a vacuum pump and sewage tender was used to suck the excrement from the privies to the tank and then into the tender. Manually operated valves were used to supply vacuum to each building in turn. Liernur was granted a German patent in 1886; and at least three systems were constructed, although the dates are not known. The system at Stanstead, U.K., was still in use in 1904 (Foreman, 1985).

---

*Associate Professor, Department of Civil Engineering, West Virginia University, Morgantown, WV 26506-6101.

Joel Liljendahl, a Swedish engineer, invented the modern automatic vacuum interface valve and installed the first residential vacuum sewer system in Sweden in 1959.

The earliest U.S. patent for a vacuum sewer system was issued in 1887 to Adrian LeMarquand, but it was not until 1970 that the first U.S. residential vacuum sewer was constructed. Many of the early installations failed due to faulty components or incorrect design concepts, but many improvements have been made during the last two decades. With more than forty U.S. systems in operation, the technical viability of the vacuum sewer is now beyond question.

The Present

A modern vacuum sewer system has three major subsystems: the central collection station, the collection network, and the on-site facilities. Vacuum is generated at the central collection station and is transmitted by the collection network throughout the area to be served. Sewage from conventional plumbing fixtures flows by gravity to an on-site holding tank. When about 10 gallons has been collected, the vacuum interface valve opens for a few seconds allowing the sewage and a volume of air to be sucked through a service pipe and into the main. The difference between the atmospheric pressure behind the sewage and the vacuum ahead provides the primary propulsive force. The fact that both air and sewage flow simultaneously produces high velocities which prevent blockages. Following the valve closure, the system returns to equilibrium and the sewage comes to rest at the low points of the collection network. Further transport occurs each time a valve opens. After several cycles, the sewage reaches the central collection tank, which is under vacuum. When the tank fills to a certain level, a conventional sewage pump discharges the sewage through a force main to a treatment plant or gravity interceptor.

The vacuum interface valve is the unique component of a vacuum sewer system. These valves operate automatically using pneumatic controls. The on-site facilities do not use any electricity. The valve is placed in a valve pit which is usually buried above the holding tank. A single valve may serve several houses or small businesses. Vacuum toilets which use about 1.2 liters of water per flush may be used when water conservation is crucial. They contain their own manually activated interface valves and have their own service lines.

Plastic pipe is used throughout a vacuum sewer system. The gravity flow house sewer is usually 4-inch pipe; typical service connections are 3-inch pipe; and mains range from 4 to 10 inches depending on the flow and layout.

The profile of the collection network makes use of the limited ability of vacuum propulsion to flow upward in order to avoid excessive excavation. Where the ground slopes in the flow the pipe is laid with a downward slope of about 0.2 % until the depth becomes excessive. When this occurs, a lift formed by two 45-degree elbows and a short length of pipe is inserted to gain elevation. The typical lift raises the pipe by 2 feet or less, but higher lifts have been used. Division valves are usually placed at main junctions and at 1500 foot intervals to facilitate troubleshooting and repairs. Service lines or tributary mains always join the continuing main from above through a wye.

Several mains may be served by a single collection station. Each main is connected to the collection tank independently through a division valve. Air flows from the collection tank through a vacuum reserve tank to the vacuum pumps, which discharge to the atmosphere. Both liquid ring and sliding vane pumps have been used. Automatic controls cycle the dual vacuum pumps alternately to maintain the vacuum in the desired range, usually 18 to 23 feet of water. A backup diesel-generator set is used to maintain service during electrical outages, and an autodialing telephone alarm is provided to summon the operator in case of malfunctions.

In addition to residential applications, vacuum plumbing is used in office buildings, hospitals, factories, and on both naval and passenger ships.

The Future Of American Society

There is often a strong linkage between the development of a technology and the society it seeks to serve. In this case the trends in society will control the future of vacuum sewers with only minor feedback. Thus it is necessary to forecast the future of American society before considering the future of vacuum sewers. I am not a professional futurist, and my opinions concerning the future of society are not based on original research or modeling. They are my considered judgements based on discussions with my associates, reports in the popular and technical media, the literature of science fiction, and the futurist books American Renaissance (Cetron and Davis, 1989) and Megatrends (Naisbitt, 1982). The responsibility for these predictions is mine alone. Caveat emptor!

The accuracy of predictions tends to deteriorate rapidly as the prediction period grows, so I have chosen to limit my predictions to the twenty years ending in 2010. In the interest of brevity, I have generally omitted the obvious qualifier, "I believe that...," in what follows.

There will be no major war in the next 20 years. The nuclear stalemate of the last 45 years has contained Soviet expansion long enough for the inherent economic weakness of the communist system to become manifest. As the old antagonisms subside, money which would have gone into military spending will be spent on civilian projects; but the health care system, the war on drug abuse, and environmental problems will preclude any massive Federal spending for wastewater collection. The states will play an increasing role in funding and regulating collection and treatment systems.

The general trend of the U.S. economy will be one of growth, prosperity, and increasing internationalism. The percentage of dual income households will rise, and the average work week will drop to 32 hours. This will lead to an increase in the number of vacation homes in rural areas. The percentage of workers engaged in information processing as opposed to manufacturing will continue to increase. Improvements in telecommunications and mass transit will allow more people to work at home or commute long distances, thus bringing further growth to suburban and rural areas. These relatively affluent and sophisticated new residents will demand a higher level of public services, including sewerage, than now exists in rural areas.

The U.S. population will grow from 227 million in 1980 to 280 million in 2010, with much of the growth attributable to recent or future immigrants and their offspring. The performance of the U.S. educational system will remain far below that of other developed nations. There will be an increasing shortage of native-born scientists, engineers, and technicians. Immigrants from third world countries will fill many of the science and engineering positions, but robots will substitute for technicians in many cases. Much of the nation's growth will continue to be in the Sunbelt, including the arid Southwest where water conservation measures will be pushed to new levels.

Concern for the environment will continue to increase. The problems of acid rain and global warming will force growing restrictions on the use of fossil fuels. The energy shortfall will be made up through conservation, solar energy, and a new generation of inherently safe nuclear reactors. Neither "hot" fusion, "cold" fusion, nor solar power satellites will produce commercial electricity during this period. The NIMBY (Not In My Back Yard) reaction will force most new power plants to be built on the sites of existing plants. These trends (and the constantly increasing number of lawyers) will cause the cost of energy to escalate, and will force ever higher levels of public participation and ever more Byzantine regulatory structures on utilities of all kinds.

Robot usage will soar in manufacturing and will become widespread in construction and maintenance. Fiber optics will allow great advances in the transmission of data. Artificial intelligence (AI) will be widely used for control systems; but neural network chips, which can learn through experience, will largely supplant expert system programs. Personal computers which can respond to speech will be found in a majority of homes. New upper income houses and apartments will use artificial intelligence to control their mechanical and electrical systems and to monitor them for impending failures.

The Future Of Vacuum Sewers In America

Many of the trends I predict for America are favorable to the expanded use of alternative sewers in general and vacuum sewers in particular. The increased residential and commercial development of rural areas will naturally require new systems to handle the sanitary waste produced. Although on-site treatment will be feasible in many cases, I expect that more difficult sites will be developed as time goes on, and that increasing numbers will require collection and central treatment of sewage. Concern for groundwater pollution will accelerate this trend. The fact that vacuum mains leak inward rather than outward will be a deciding factor in many environmentally sensitive areas, particularly around resort lakes. In arid regions, the water conserving potential of vacuum plumbing will finally be realized.

Other trends will be less favorable to vacuum sewers. One problem arises from the fact that vacuum systems require more energy than the other alternatives. As the cost of electricity rises, the operating costs of vacuum systems will become less competitive than at present. On the other hand, the energy needed to service an average 1987 household of 2.66 persons is about 416 kWh/year, which is 4.4 % of the average household's electrical consumption (Gray and Gidley, 1987; Hoffman, 1989; DOE, 1988). Since this electricity is billed at the commercial rate, the financial burden is somewhat less. It seems unlikely that energy costs alone could render vacuum systems unaffordable.

As current research programs (such as the one I am conducting for the David Taylor Research Center) lead to a better understanding of the fluid mechanics of vacuum sewers, less conservative design techniques will allow the design of more energy-efficient systems. Additional energy savings may be possible if special purpose vacuum pumps become available. Present systems generally use pumps designed to produce vacuums of up to 29 inches of mercury, even though most systems require 20 inches or less. If the vacuum sewer market becomes large enough, the manufacture of special purpose pumps will become profitable.

The other Achilles' heel of vacuum sewers is their relatively high need for maintenance. This is a drawback which could become more serious if the availability of technicians drops. The most maintenance-intensive component of present systems seems to be the vacuum pump. If special purpose pumps are designed, low maintenance should be a primary design goal. Another possibility lies in the use of ejector vacuum pumps, which are mechanically simpler than conventional types. Vacuum ejectors are multiphase jet pumps which have no moving parts. The primary fluid (recirculated sewage) is driven by a conventional centrifugal pump.

Many of the monitoring and troubleshooting functions presently performed by maintenance personnel will be taken on by a microcomputer with an artificial intelligence chip. With actuators for the division valves, the computer could even perform the major steps in locating a vacuum leak before summoning a repair crew. Going further, an AI chip powered by a watch battery may be built into each vacuum valve. In case of a malfunction or anticipated malfunction, the chip could tell the household computer to transmit a service request by telephone to the collection station computer. The ultimate step of using a repair robot to perform field maintenance lies beyond the time horizon of this paper.

Incremental improvements to present vacuum valve designs will further improve reliability and reduce the need for preventive maintenance. New designs will be introduced, including additional 3-inch valves. The prospect of designing and operating a custom vacuum station is intimidating to many engineers and utilities. Larger package vacuum stations will be introduced to overcome this hurdle. As vacuum technology becomes more widely understood, more engineers and regulators will be willing to consider the possibility of using a vacuum system.

Conclusions

The coming years will bring many changes in the social, political, economic, and technical factors which impact on the choice of a sewage collection system. Vacuum sewer technology has its share of advantages and drawbacks, but I predict that the advantages will predominate in an increasing number of situations.

References

Anonymous, 1866. The Pneumatic Sewage System, The Engineer, Dec. 7, 1866, pp 437-438.
Cetron, M. and Davis, O., 1989. American Renaissance, St. Martin's Press, NY.
DOE, 1988. Energy Facts 1987, U.S. Department of Energy, DOE/EIA-0469(87), 55 pp.
Foreman, B. E., 1985. Vacuum Sewers - the First 100 Years, Airvac Division, Burton Mechanical Contractors, Inc., Rochester, Indiana, 6 pp.
Gray, D. D. and Gidley, J. S., 1987. Operating Experience of Alternative Sanitary Sewers, Proceedings of the Water Resources Symposium, ASCE, Environmental Engineering and Water Resources Division, Rosemont, Illinois, 18 pp.
Hoffman, M. S., Editor, 1989. The World Almanac, Scripps Howard, NY, 928 pp.
Naisbitt, J., 1982. Megatrends, Warner, NY, 333 pp..

Appendix: Conversion to SI Units

```
            1 ft           = 0.305 m
            1 inch         = 25.4 mm
            1 gallon       = 3.79 liters
  1 inch of mercury        = 3.39 kPa
  1 foot of water          = 2.99 kPa
```

Combining Groundwater Simulation and Nonlinear Optimization Models

James G. Uber[1], Associate Member, ASCE

Abstract

An approach is presented for linking groundwater simulation models with nonlinear optimization algorithms. The approach involves the solution of a reduced optimization model in which the simulation model equations are included implicitly in the constraint set. The reduced model is much smaller than an equivalent formulation that includes the simulator equations explicitly, and thus should be applicable to large-scale problems.

Introduction

Mathematical models for groundwater quality management and for geohydrologic parameter estimation can be expressed as constrained nonlinear optimization models (see, e.g., Gorelick [1983], Wanakule et. al. [1986], Yeh [1986], and Ahlfeld et. al. [1988a,1988b]). In addition, approaches for estimating the reliability of groundwater contaminant transport predictions can also be expressed in a nonlinear optimization framework [Shinozuka, 1983]. Such nonlinear programming models include physical constraints that describe the mass conservation and mass transport of both fluid and contaminant. For practical problems, these physical constraints are the finite difference or finite element simulation model equations that approximate the transport of fluid and contaminant for the domain of interest.

As a finite difference grid or a finite element mesh can include hundreds of nodes, nonlinear optimization models that contain the simulation model (or "simulator") equations in the constraint set can include thousands of variables and nonlinear equality constraints (for transient problems). Such optimization models may be difficult to solve using general nonlinear programming algorithms. Rather than embed the simulator equations in the constraint set, an equivalent "reduced" optimization model may be formulated and solved in which the model functions are fewer in number but are implicit (this is a decomposed formulation). A general reduced formulation is presented here, as well as techniques for evaluating the implicit functions and

---

[1]Assistant Professor of Civil Engineering, The University of Alabama in Huntsville, Huntsville, Alabama 35899

their gradients (this first order information is required by general nonlinear programming techniques). Some advantages and disadvantages of the reduced formulation are discussed.

While this paper focuses on theoretical issues, future work will emphasize practical numerical results. Alternative methods for combining groundwater simulation and optimization models should be evaluated by applying them to practical problems in groundwater management, parameter estimation, and reliability analysis. In particular, approaches that use large-scale nonlinear optimization algorithms (e.g., MINOS [Murtagh and Saunders, 1987]) to solve the explicit embedded formulation should be compared with those that use general purpose algorithms to solve the implicit reduced formulation that is presented here.

Nonlinear Optimization Framework

Groundwater quality management models (e.g., models for optimal remediation of contaminated aquifers) may be expressed as general nonlinear optimization models:

$$\min_{\mathbf{x},\mathbf{y}} f_o(\mathbf{x}^1,\ldots,\mathbf{x}^p,\mathbf{y}^1,\ldots,\mathbf{y}^p,\theta) \tag{1}$$

subject to: $\mathbf{g}^k(\mathbf{x}^{k-1},\mathbf{x}^k,\mathbf{y}^k,\theta) = 0, \quad k=1,\ldots,p$

$f_i(\mathbf{x}^1,\ldots,\mathbf{x}^p,\mathbf{y}^1,\ldots,\mathbf{y}^p,\theta) = 0, \quad i=1,\ldots,neq$

$f_i(\mathbf{x}^1,\ldots,\mathbf{x}^p,\mathbf{y}^1,\ldots,\mathbf{y}^p,\theta) \geq 0, \quad i=neq+1,\ldots,nc$

where: $\mathbf{f} = (f_o,\ldots,f_{nc})^T$ is a vector of objective and constraint functions (e.g., functions expressing the total system cost or the concentration of a contaminant); $\mathbf{g}^k=(g_1^k,\ldots,g_m^k)^T$ is a vector of simulation model equations that describe the physics of the problem at time level k (i.e., at time $t = k \cdot \Delta t$, where Δt is the time step); $\underline{\mathbf{x}} = (\mathbf{x}^1,\ldots,\mathbf{x}^p)$, where $\mathbf{x}^k=(x_1^k,\ldots,x_m^k)^T$ is a vector of model variables that define the state of the groundwater system at time level k (these are dependent variables, e.g., heads and contaminant concentrations); $\underline{\mathbf{y}} = (\mathbf{y}^1,\ldots,\mathbf{y}^p)$, where $\mathbf{y}^k=(y_1^k,\ldots,y_n^k)^T$ is a vector of model design variables (these are independent variables, e.g., flow rates for individual injection or extraction wells); $\theta=(\theta_1,\theta_2,\ldots,\theta_r)^T$ is a vector of model parameters (e.g., aquifer permeability and dispersivity, or boundary condition parameters); and p is the number of time steps, so that $p \cdot \Delta t$ defines the planning or management time horizon. The simulation model equations for the kth time step depend on the state variables $\mathbf{x}^{k-1}$ and $\mathbf{x}^k$, and the design variables $\mathbf{y}^k$ ($\mathbf{x}^o$ are the assumed initial conditions). Thus the formulation in equation (1) is general for any simulation model that uses forward differencing in time.

Included in equation (1) are, for example, optimal hazardous waste remediation design models. Such models seek the minimum cost spatial and temporal distribution of injection and extraction well pumping rates so that the model estimate of the spatial and temporal contaminant concentration satisfies certain minimum design criteria (e.g., the estimated concentration of a contaminant at a drinking water well must be less than a threshold concentration within a specified maximum time for remediation).

Only the model variables are optimized in equation (1); the parameters θ are assumed to be known constants (equal to some nominal parameter values $\hat{\theta}$ that are assumed for design purposes). If the model parameter values are uncertain (this is usually the case), then the formulation in equation (1), and the solution techniques that follow, could be extended to include sensitivity-based measures of the system reliability, robustness, variance, and the like. Eheart and Valocchi [1986], Wagner and Gorelick [1987], Uber et. al. [1988], and Uber and Brill [1989] consider various formulations and solution techniques that consider uncertainty in the model parameter values.

Nonlinear optimization models are also used in geohydrologic parameter estimation [Yeh, 1986] (the inverse problem), and in reliability analysis [Shinozuka, 1983] (the advanced first-order second moment approach). These optimization models are similar to equation (1), except that the model parameters are optimized and the model design variables are held fixed:

$$\underset{\underline{x},\theta}{\text{minimize}}\ f_o(x^1,\ldots,x^p,y^1,\ldots,y^p,\theta) \tag{2}$$
$$\text{subject to:}\ g^k(x^{k-1},x^k,y^k,\theta) = 0, \qquad k=1,\ldots,p$$
$$f_i(x^1,\ldots,x^p,y^1,\ldots,y^p,\theta) = 0, \qquad i=1,\ldots,neq$$
$$f_i(x^1,\ldots,x^p,y^1,\ldots,y^p,\theta) \geq 0, \qquad i=neq+1,\ldots,nc$$

Included in equation (2) are, for example, weighted least squares nonlinear parameter estimation procedures. Such procedures seek values of geohydrologic parameters (e.g., the spatially distributed values of permeability or hydraulic conductivity), so that the spatial and temporal model estimates of heads and concentrations are as close as possible to the values measured in the field (in a weighted least squares sense).

Equations (1) and (2) may be written as equivalent *reduced* models, in which the functions depend implicitly on the design variables and the parameters. For example, the reduced model corresponding to equation (1) is expressed:

$$\underset{\underline{y}}{\text{minimize}}\ f'_o(x^o,y^1,\ldots,y^p,\theta) \tag{3}$$
$$\text{subject to:}\ f'_i(x^o,y^1,\ldots,y^p,\theta) = 0, \qquad i=1,\ldots,neq$$
$$f'_i(x^o,y^1,\ldots,y^p,\theta) \geq 0, \qquad i=neq+1,\ldots,nc$$

where the reduced functions $\mathbf{f}' = (f'_o,\ldots,f'_{nc})^T$ include the dependence of $\mathbf{f}$ on $\underline{y}$ and θ through the state variables $\underline{x}$. The reduced functions are defined mathematically:

$$f'_j(x^o,y^1,\ldots,y^p,\theta) = \tag{4}$$
$$f_j(x^1(x^o,y^1,\theta),\ldots,x^p(x^o,y^1,\ldots,y^p,\theta),y^1,\ldots,y^p,\theta), \qquad j=1,\ldots,nc$$

The functions $x^k(x^o, y^1, \ldots, y^k, \theta)$ define the dependence of the state variables at the kth time step on the initial conditions, the design variables through the kth time step, and the model parameters. In general these functions are not known explicitly, but are defined implicitly by the simulation model equations, $g^k(x^{k-1}, x^k, y^k, \theta) = 0$, $k=1,\ldots,p$; thus the reduced functions f' are also implicit.

The reduced optimization model in equation (3) may be solved by a variety of iterative methods for constrained nonlinear optimization (see, e.g., Gill et. al. [1981]). Such methods use first-order information about the problem functions (i.e., function and gradient evaluations at the current iterate) to determine a search direction vector **d** that will yield an improved feasible design. Thus, for example, the design variable values for the i+1th iteration are obtained from the design variable values and the search direction at the ith iteration: $\underline{y}^{i+1} = \underline{y}^i + \alpha d^i$, where α is a scalar step size. The efficiency and robustness of the optimization algorithms depend in large part on the efficiency and accuracy of the function and function gradient evaluations. Since the reduced functions f' are defined implicitly by the simulation model equations, the evaluation of f' and the gradients of f' is not straightforward. In particular, the gradients of f' require methods of system sensitivity analysis.

The value of f' at the ith iteration is obtained by solving the simulator equations $g^k(x^{k-1,i}, x^{k,i}, y^{k,i}, \theta^i) = 0$, $\forall k$, sequentially in time for the unknown state variables $x^{k,i}(x^o, y^{1,i}, \ldots, y^{k,i}, \theta^i)$, $\forall k$, given the current values of the design variables $\underline{y}^i$ and model parameters θ^i (either the design variable or the model parameter values will be constant - see equations (1) and (2)). The reduced functions are then evaluated directly from equation (4).

The gradients of f' (with respect to $\underline{y}$ and θ) at the ith iteration are obtained by differentiating both sides of equation (4):

$$\left(\frac{\partial f'_j}{\partial y^k}\right)^T = \sum_{m=k}^{p} \left(\frac{\partial f_j}{\partial x^m}\right)^T \left(\frac{\partial x^m}{\partial y^k}\right) + \left(\frac{\partial f_j}{\partial y^k}\right)^T, \quad \forall j,k \qquad (5a)$$

$$\left(\frac{\partial f'_j}{\partial \theta}\right)^T = \sum_{m=1}^{p} \left(\frac{\partial f_j}{\partial x^m}\right)^T \left(\frac{\partial x^m}{\partial \theta}\right) + \left(\frac{\partial f_j}{\partial \theta}\right)^T \quad \forall j \qquad (5b)$$

where all derivatives are evaluated at the current iterate $(x^{1,i}, \ldots, x^{p,i}, y^{1,i}, \ldots, y^{p,i}, \theta^i)$. The *state variable sensitivity coefficients*, $(\partial x^m / \partial y^k)$ and $(\partial x^m / \partial \theta)$, are Jacobian matrices of the implicit functions $x^m(x^o, y^1, \ldots, y^m, \theta)$.

Although the functions $x^m(x^o, y^1, \ldots, y^m, \theta)$ are implicit, their derivatives can be obtained by differentiating both sides of the system equations, $g^m(x^{m-1}, x^m, y^m, \theta) = 0$, with respect to y^k and θ (this is a practical result of the implicit function theorem from calculus - see, e.g., Kaplan [1984]). Differentiating the system equations leads to a system of *linear* algebraic equations in the unknowns $(\partial x^m / \partial y^k)$ and $(\partial x^m / \partial \theta)$:

$$\left[\frac{\partial g^m}{\partial x^m}\right] \cdot \left[\frac{\partial x^m}{\partial y^k}\right] + \left[\frac{\partial g^m}{\partial x^{m-1}}\right] \cdot \left[\frac{\partial x^{m-1}}{\partial y^k}\right] + \left[\frac{\partial g^m}{\partial y^k}\right] = 0 \quad (6a)$$

$$\left[\frac{\partial g^m}{\partial x^m}\right] \cdot \left[\frac{\partial x^m}{\partial \theta}\right] + \left[\frac{\partial g^m}{\partial x^{m-1}}\right] \cdot \left[\frac{\partial x^{m-1}}{\partial \theta}\right] + \left[\frac{\partial g^m}{\partial \theta}\right] = 0 \quad (6b)$$

and, solving for the unknowns $(\partial x^m/\partial y^k)$ and $(\partial x^m/\partial \theta)$:

$$\left[\frac{\partial x^m}{\partial y^k}\right] = -\left[\frac{\partial g^m}{\partial x^m}\right]^{-1} \cdot \left[\left[\frac{\partial g^m}{\partial x^{m-1}}\right] \cdot \left[\frac{\partial x^{m-1}}{\partial y^k}\right] + \left[\frac{\partial g^m}{\partial y^k}\right]\right] \quad (7a)$$

$$\left[\frac{\partial x^m}{\partial \theta}\right] = -\left[\frac{\partial g^m}{\partial x^m}\right]^{-1} \cdot \left[\left[\frac{\partial g^m}{\partial x^{m-1}}\right] \cdot \left[\frac{\partial x^{m-1}}{\partial \theta}\right] + \left[\frac{\partial g^m}{\partial \theta}\right]\right] \quad (7b)$$

where, again, all derivatives are evaluated at the current iterate $(x^{1,i},\ldots,x^{p,i},y^{1,i},\ldots,y^{p,i},\theta^i)$. In parallel with the calculation of state variable values, the needed gradients of the reduced functions f' can be accumulated using equations (5) and (7) in an iterative procedure that steps through time (note that, from equation (7), the state variable sensitivity coefficients at time step m are functions of the sensitivity coefficients at the previous time step). Thus a particular simulation model can be used in conjunction with equations (5) and (7) to evaluate the reduced functions and the reduced function gradients; the reduced model (e.g., equation (3)) may then be solved by a variety of gradient-based, general nonlinear optimization algorithms.

Discussion of Reduced Nonlinear Optimization Framework

One significant practical advantage of the reduced formulation is the separation between simulation and optimization. A variety of existing optimization and simulation algorithms could be used to solve the reduced models, depending on the availability of software and persons familiar with its use; the only requirement is that appropriate reduced function and reduced function gradient values are calculated and communicated properly.

The reduced formulation may also have a computational advantage over the explicit embedded formulation because it is significantly smaller (although it may be more nonlinear). The computational efficiency and robustness of solution methods for the reduced formulation depends largely on the method of computing the gradients of the reduced functions [Lasdon et. al., 1989]; thus a significant computational issue is the manner in which equations (5) and (7) are implemented (e.g., are the derivatives calculated analytically or by finite differences, and is the sparsity pattern of the matrices in equation (7) known and used to advantage). The reduced functions themselves are evaluated efficiently using the simulation model, since simulation models usually exploit any special structure in the equations g^k (e.g., the use of banded matrix solvers). This special structure would be ignored if the simulation model equations were embedded in the constraint set.

References

1. Ahlfeld, D. P., Mulvey, J. M., Pinder, G. F., and Wood, E. F., "Contaminated Groundwater Remediation Design Using Simulation, Optimization, and Sensitivity Theory, 1, Model Development," *Water Resources Research*, Vol. 24, No. 3, March, 1988.
2. Ahlfeld, D. P., Mulvey, J. M., and Pinder, G. F., "Contaminated Groundwater Remediation Design Using Simulation, Optimization, and Sensitivity Theory, 2, Analysis of a Field Site," *Water Resources Research*, Vol. 24, No. 3, March, 1988.
3. Eheart, J. W., and Valocchi, A. J., *Multicriterion Management of Groundwater Quality*, Research Report to the University of Illinois Water Resources Center, July, 1986.
4. Gill, P. E., Murray, W., and Wright, M. H., *Practical Optimization*, Academic Press, 1981.
5. Gorelick, S. M., "A Review of Distributed Parameter Groundwater Management Modeling Methods," *Water Resources Research*, Vol. 19, No. 2, April, 1983.
6. Kaplan, W., *Advanced Calculus*, Addison-Wesley, Reading, Massachusetts, pp. 110-121, 1984.
7. Lasdon, L. S., Waren, A. D., and Sarkar, S., *Interfacing Optimizers with Planning Languages and Process Simulators*, working paper, The University of Texas at Austin, 1989.
8. Murtagh, B. A., and Saunders, M. A., *MINOS 5.1 User's Guide*, Tech. Report SOL 83-20R, Systems Optimization Lab, Stanford University, Stanford, CA, 1987.
9. Shinozuka, M. "Basic Analysis of Structural Safety," *Jour. of Structural Engineering, ASCE*, Vol. 109, No. 3, March, 1983.
10. Uber, J. G., Kao, J-J., Brill, E. D., Jr., Pfeffer, J. T., *Sensitivity Constrained Nonlinear Programming: A General Approach for Planning and Design Under Parameter Uncertainty and an Application to Treatment Plant Design*, Final Technical Report to the Department of the Interior, U.S. Geological Survey, U.S.G.S. Grant No. 14-08-0001-G1144, 163 pp., 1988.
11. Uber, J. G., and Brill, E. D., Jr., "Design Optimization with Sensitivity Constraints," submitted to *Engineering Optimization*, September, 1989.
12. Wagner, B. J., and Gorelick, S. M., "Optimal Groundwater Quality Management Under Parameter Uncertainty," *Water Resources Research*, Vol. 23, No. 7, pp. 1162-1174, July, 1987.
13. Wanakule, N., Mays, L. W., and Lasdon, L. S., "Optimal Management of Large-Scale Aquifers: Methodology and Applications," *Water Resources Research*, Vol. 22, No. 4, April, 1986.
14. Yeh, W. W-G., "Review of Parameter Identification Procedures in Groundwater Hydrology: The Inverse Problem," *Water Resources Research*, Vol. 22, No. 2, February, 1986.

Fuzzy Sets in Civil Engineering - A Tutorial

Jean-Lou Chameau[1]

This tutorial is an introduction to the theory of fuzzy sets and its applications in Civil Engineering, including its use within the framework of knowledge-based systems (KBS). The techniques to be discussed have not had a major impact on civil engineering practice yet; they represent recent technology and time is needed for their transfer to and acceptance in practice. A parallel can certainly be made between this situation and the development of finite element computer codes in the 60's and early 70's.

The tutorial will be composed of two main parts: (1) presentation of the basic concepts and mathematical tools used in fuzzy sets theory; and (2) overview of typical applications in engineering. An increasing number of recent applications relate to the development of knowledge based systems. Examples will be presented in the last part of the tutorial, including systems that relate to the field of water resources. The following discussion serves as background information for this tutorial. It addresses some of the issues that led engineers and researchers to consider the use of fuzzy sets.

Engineering Knowledge

The knowledge engineers can apply to problem solving is composed of three parts: science; feedback from applications to other similar or related problems; and experience and rules of thumb. Although this distinction is convenient for discussion purposes, its boundaries are often fuzzy! Science from an engineering standpoint may incorporate analysis techniques that have been modified through applications; "experience" and "rules of thumb" have their bases in observations made during previous applications. Incorporating feedback and experience in knowledge has an important implication: qualitative

---

[1] Professor, School of Civil Engineering, Purdue University, West Lafayette, IN 47907

information often plays a major role in the decision process. In civil engineering, we lump all the pieces of qualitative information under "engineering judgment". As soon as engineering judgment is part of the game, two important issues arise: (1) how do we insure that it is consistently applied? and (2) how can we preserve and transfer it?

State-of-the-Art and State-of-the-Practice

"State-of-the-art" refers to all the knowledge enclosed within the expanding frontier of understanding in a field. On the other hand, "state-of-practice" is a subset of the state-of-the-art that includes the knowledge frequently applied. The advances in both states are mutually dependent and made stepwise. In some cases practice is at the frontier developing the state-of-the-art, however it usually lags behind. One can speculate on the reasons for this phenomenon: inertia to continue old practice, reluctancy to new ideas, difficulty and cost involved in implementing changes, unwillingness to take risks, and need for further verification of new techniques. Many times the reason for this lag is simply the lack of awareness of new alternatives. For example, the gap between art and practice in geotechnical engineering was clearly stated by Peck (1981) after reviewing the failure of dams; he concluded that "nine out of ten recent failures of dams occurred not because of inadequacies in the state-of-the-art, but because of oversights that could and should have been avoided..."The necessary knowledge existed; it was not used". Could better communication methods or systems be developed to preserve the state-of-knowledge and enhance its transfer to the state-of-practice?

Systems, Failures, and Acceptable Risk

The actual probability of failure of engineering systems is often two or three orders of magnitude higher than theoretically predicted. For example, studies conducted in different parts of the world show a consensus value of about 1% for the probability of failure of dams. This is a striking fact, particularly if one considers that the above observations correspond to very different systems, and various historical and geographical contexts. Peck (1981) made the following observations from the study of dam failures:

- Most causes are unthought of events
- Improvement is within the state-of-the-art
- Sophistication in the analysis does not necessarily help
- Best engineering judgment is needed
- Problems are non-quantitative

- Solutions are non-numerical

These remarks suggest that practice, and thus the performance of constructed systems, could be improved by providing tools that systematically remind engineers of all facts to be considered, give easy access to the knowledge in the state-of-the-art, stimulate the use of best judgment, and help make allowance for non-quantitative parameters.

Precision/Imprecision-Reliability-Context

It is often convenient to represent the steps or the decisions involved in an engineering project (or part of a project) in a tree of information. Information can be in terms of goals one wants to achieve (e.g., economical design), or rules (e.g. factor of safety FS > 1.30), or technical findings (e.g., FS = 1.35). When one has to make decisions or evaluate a design based on such information, it has to be recognized that the nature of the information and its precision depends upon its level within the tree. The lower the information is in the tree, the more precise it is, however, the less likely it is to be true, i.e. the less reliable (probable) it is. On the contrary, the higher it is within the tree, the less precise (i.e. vague) the information will be, however the more likely it is. In other terms, the more precise information becomes the less reliable its contents is. Imprecision (or precision) is also a function of context, i.e. it depends upon existing information and goals to be achieved. A simple but illustrative example was given by Blockley (1983) for the term "tall man". In everyday language this is a sufficient term to communicate an idea (i.e. there is no need for additional information). However, a "truth seeking" scientist may not be satisfied until the man's height is measured to the nearest micron.

Uncertainty

It is common to equate uncertainty with randomness. Randomness involves uncertainty about propositions, events or systems that are precisely defined and described. For engineering applications, the uncertainty of the system output can be entirely derived from a stochastic definition of the system and the uncertainty of input parameters. Assuming randomness as being the unique source of uncertainty implies that one can define the system precisely. This may be true for a simple beam subjected to specified random loading, or for the toss of a coin. However, it is rarely the case; for example, the modeling techniques used in slope stability or for earthquake occurrences are at the best approximations of reality. Uncertainty arises from the systems themselves, or from our understanding (or lack) of these systems. System uncertainty would exist even if all parameters used in a model could be precisely defined. It is clearly related to the complexity of the system. System uncertainty can be viewed as critical in civil engineering since we often design "one-of-a-kind" systems, thus we use solutions that do not quite fit the problems and do not have the chance to test them. Human uncertainty is part of (or possibly the cause of) system uncertainty since the latter has to do with complexity and man's limited understanding of it. However, it goes beyond that and involves issues such as lack of consistency, biases (Santamarina and Chameau, 1989) and "gross" errors. Preventing gross errors can by itself be a partial justification to the use of computerized techniques.

There are several models/techniques that have been proposed to represent uncertainty, e.g. probability, fuzzy sets, or Dempster-Shaffer's theory of evidence. While it is possible for any of them to be applied to a particular case, context specific characteristics should favor the use of one over the others (or a combination). Researchers in fuzzy sets have indicated that fuzzy models are dedicated to solving complex situations. But this criterion is not sufficient since both the stochastic and fuzzy approaches may serve as models of complex phenomena. Then, what is the difference between these tools? In essence, they are different languages to express uncertainty, each of them with their own axiomatic framework, advantages, and disadvantages. Guidelines for selecting among the methods that model uncertainty are limited and even contradictory. There are three main reasons; first, the choice depends strongly on the analyst's perception of the problem and previous experience; second, it is domain-dependent; and lastly, there are combinations between probability theory and fuzzy sets (e.g. "fuzzy probabilities" and the "probability of fuzzy events") that make the transition less pronounced. The following conditions tend to support the use of fuzzy sets: vagueness and imprecision, linguistic variables, qualitative information, lack of sufficient physical measurements, need for a "real" model instead of a "normative" one (like Bayes Theorem), values of variables restricted to ill defined ranges, complex causal hierarchies. It is important to note that these conditions characterize a number of knowledge-based systems already built, or in the process of being built.

Tutorial: Fuzzy Set Theory in Water Resources Systems

Lucien Duckstein[1], Istvan Bogardi[2], Andras Bardossy[3]

Abstract

Principles of using fuzzy set theory (FST) to describe imprecision (or vagueness) in water resources systems are provided. The main tool of FST, the membership function, measures the degree of pertinence to a given set such as a water supply failure event. A brief survey of fuzzy set applications is provided. Three main challanges of fuzzy set applicability are discussed: 1, to recognize the type of imprecision and assess the membership function accordingly, 2, to select the appropriate fuzzy set algebra and 3, to identify potential application areas in water resources systems.

Introduction

A distinction is made between randomness and uncertainty, on the one hand, and vagueness and imprecision, on the other hand. Taking a Bayesian decision theoretic viewpoint, (Raiffa and Schlaifer, 1961) randomness refers to hydrologic quantities which fluctuate in a uncontrollable way according to some probabilistic model; and uncertainty is concerned with, for example, model selection and parameter estimation. To a certain extent, uncertainty may be reduced by obtaining more information; thus, the prior information on a parameter vector is transformed into posterior information through observation.

---

[1] Lucien Duckstein, Department of Systems and Industrial Engineering, University of Arizona, Tucson, AZ 85721.

[2] Istvan Bogardi, Department of Civil Engineering, University of Nebraska-Lincoln, Lincoln, NE 68588-0531.

[3] Andras Bardossy, Institute for Hydrology and Water Resources, University of Karlsruhe, Karlsruhe, FRG D-7500.

In contrast with, or in complement to, a probabilistic approach, we consider the treatment of imprecision (or vagueness) in water resources. Consider, for example, the statements "runoff increases with higher antecedent moisture" or "the water supply is less than the demand in midsummer" or "transmissivity is greater near the foothills" or "salt water intrusion may occur if pumpage gets close to capacity" or "high intensity rain". How can such imprecise information be used to describe hydrologic phenomena in a reliable or at least reproducible manner, and how can decisions be made under these conditions? Also, is a trade-off possible between imprecise criteria such as cost or risk? More generally, how can fuzzy logic be applied to help or complement human judgment? These are the questions we wish to pose from a tutorial viewpoint.

Background

Fuzzy sets were first defined as an intellectual discipline by Zadeh (1965). Fuzziness is meant to represent situations where membership of an object in a set cannot be defined on a binary (yes-no) basis. Thus, let the deficit in water supply be $h = D - Q$, where D = demand and Q = supply.

If we simply defined a failure F as the event $h>0$, then we have an ordinary set inclusion. If, however, we define a default incident I* as an ordered pair defined on the real numbers R: If I* = $\{(h, mF(h)): h.E.R\}$; $mF(h)$ is the membership grade function of h in F with values in [0,1], then I* is a fuzzy set (h.E.R. means h is an element of R).

Such a definition makes it possible to accept an imprecise definition of a failure: incident I(h) may still represent only a fair supply condition leading to a 10% deficit. Thus any value of deficit h belongs to the set F of supply failures with a non-negative membership function $mF(h)$, with values in the unit interval.

If $mF(h)$ satisfies the so-called convexity and normality conditions for fuzzy sets, then the pair (h, $mF(h)$) is a fuzzy number (Kaufmann and Gupta, 1985). Operations such as additions and multiplications can be defined on fuzzy numbers, as shown in Zimmermann (1985).

For almost two decades, the applications of fuzzy sets to hydrology were quasi non-existent; the main thrust had been in theoretical developments, with applications to control and social sciences. In particular, an increasing number of "hi-tech" and artificial intelligence applications have appeared, especially in Japan.

Existing Applications

Fuzzy logic is already applied in Japan to control underground railway systems (metro) (Yasunobu et al, 1987) and in stock trading. It is also applied to embed short term flood forecasting into medium-term forecasting. Kalman filtering is used for the short term component, while fuzzy logic operates on the medium term, leading to a complete real-time forecasting system (Kojiri, 1988). Many references on fuzzy sets can be found in the journals (*Fuzzy Sets and Systems*, and *Systems, Man, Cybernetics*, among others). Basic references include Dubois and Prade (1980), Zimmermann (1985), Kaufmann and Gupta (1985). Hydrologic applications include regional water management (Bogardi et al, 1983; Nachtnebel et al, 1986), fuzzy regression (Bardossy et al, 1988a), fuzzy set geostatistics (Bardossy et, 1988b, 1989), multicriterion forest management (Duckstein et al, 1988), fuzzy risk analysis (Bogardi et al, 1989), and reservoir operation planning (Savic and Simonovic, 1988). Finally, it should be mentioned once again that the "father" of fuzzy sets is Zadeh, who has produced a long string of distinguished papers, books and reports on the subjects since his original 1965 paper.

Three Methodological Steps

As pointed out in Duckstein et al (1989), a fuzzy set membership function depends on the type of imprecision considered. Consequently, membership functions may be similar to: (1) a value function, (2) a subjective probability, say a Bayesian prior, (3) both (1) and (2), or (4) neither one. The first step is to recognize which type of imprecision one deals with. In any case, the arithmetic of fuzzy sets is completely different from probability calculations or the ordinary algebra used in multiattribute value functions. In fact, there is only one way to define probabilistic quantities; for example, if A and B are two events.

$$P(A \cup B) = P(A) + P(B) - P(A \cap B)$$

Also, if $x_1, \ldots, x_J$ are attributes, the multiplicative form of a multiattribute value function, valid under preferential independence condition, is written as

$$1 + kv(x_1, \ldots x_J) = \prod (1 + k\ k_j\ v_j\ (x_j))$$

In contrast, the membership function of $A \cup B$ and $A \cap B$ may be written as, respectively, $m(A \cup B)(x) = \max \{mA(x), mB(x)\}$ and $m(A \cap B)(x) = \min \{mA(x), mB(x)\}$, but other definitions are possible. Thus, as pointed out in Bardossy et al (1989), the membership function in a given set A of a time series of criteria $\underline{c} = \{c(t); t = 1, \ldots, T\}$ may be taken as

FUZZY SET THEORY 437

$$mA(\underline{c}) = \min_t \{mAc(t)\}, \text{ or, } mA(\underline{c}) = \frac{1}{T} \sum_t mAc(t), \text{ or else}$$

$$mA(\underline{c}) = \min_t (mA\ c(t) + \sum_t mA\ c(t)).$$

A similar problem occurs in fuzzy regression; several measures of vagueness can be selected as well as several reference points (Bardossy et al, 1988a). The second methodological step is thus to select the appropriate fuzzy set algebra, i.e., fitting the problem on hand.

The third step is to examine potential areas of application of fuzzy logic in water resources systems, including: weather circulation models and detection of climatological change; fuzzy geomorphology; fuzzy flood forecasting and control; groundwater pollution, transport, salinity intrusion; water requirements analysis under fuzzy conditions; fuzzy reliability of water supply; and, fuzzy regression when it is known that a causal relation exists, but only very few imprecise data points are available. This point is now illustrated further.

Generally speaking, any water problem involving imprecise or vague elements may be analyzed by fuzzy logic (Duckstein et al, 1986; Bardossy et al, 1986). Thus, discharge curves corresponding to time invariant hydrological conditions are often based on a few data points. Discharge measurements may be inaccurate. Then, critical hydrologic decisions must be made over such parts of the discharge curve where no data points are available. Fuzzy regression may be used to express the uncertainty in discharge curves.

The modeling of various relationships between variables describing water quantity and quality provides other examples. For instance, the dissolved chemical concentration such as phosphorus stemming from non-point sources is often related to the peak flow or total volume of runoff events (Wetzel, 1975). Often, the number of such measurements is not sufficient to perform standard statistical regression analysis.

Similarly, sediment transport relationships may use river flow quantities to estimate suspended sediment concentration or bed-load. Since the river regime may change quite fast, often there is time to obtain just a few observation points. In addition, sediment measurements are quite imprecise.

In groundwater systems, several examples can be mentioned. To estimate aquifer parameters using expensive tests, time constraints may lead to the availability of a relatively small amount of data points. Further, dispersion coefficients, which are quite difficult to measure directly, may be estimated indirectly from other aquifer parameters (Fried, 1975). Though the calculated pollution concentration may be quite sensitive to the dispersion coefficient, the inaccuracy involved is rarely accounted taken into consideration. Fuzzy regression may thus be helpful in this regard.

Rate constants for dissolved oxygen models may be estimated from average water depth and flow velocity (Biswas, 1981). However, measured rate constants may be available at only a few points; thus the use of statistical regression analysis is difficult, whereas fuzzy regression may be applicable.

Flow in fractured rocks is strongly related to the geologic properties of the material. In fact, parameters governing such flow can be estimated indirectly from geologic quantities which, however, are often difficult and time consuming to measure. As a result, the relationships may have to be modeled from just a few data points (Bogardi et al, 1982); another potential area of application of fuzzy regresssion.

Health risk analyses use dose-response relationships based on a few animal experiments over a dose region which considerably exceeds doses occurring, say in contaminated groundwater. Health risk estimated from such uncertain relationship may be the basis of environmental regulation. Fuzzy regression offers a possibility to express health risk under uncertainty and to select cost-effective risk reduction alternatives (Bogardi et al., 1989).

Finally, fuzzy set analysis necessitates that membership functions be assessed. Surprisingly, very little work has been done on this subject (Turksen, 1986; Chameau and Santamarina, 1987). Statistical data may be used in certain cases (Civanlar and Trussel, 1986) and a value function transformation may be applicable in other cases (Duckstein and Heidel, 1989). Furthermore, data need to be given with a measure of vagueness or imprecision (Kruse and Meyer, 1987).

Acknowledgements

Research leading to these notes has been partially supported by a National Science Foundation Grant Nos. ECS-8802350 and 8802920.

References

Bardossy, A., Bogardi, I., and L. Duckstein. Analyse multicritere "floue" de la gestion d'use nappe karstique regionale: II. Application numerique. *Review Internationale des Sciences de l'Eau*, 2(1):7-12, February 1986.

Bardossy, A., Bogardi I., and L. Duckstein. Fuzzy regression in hydrology. Working paper 89-5, Systems and Industrial Engineering Department, The University of Arizona, Tucson, AZ 85721, 1988a.

Bardossy, A., Bogardi I., and W.E. Kelly. Imprecise (fuzzy) information in geostatistics, *Math. Geology*, 20(4):287-311, 1988b.

Bardossy, A., Bogardi, I., Duckstein, L., and P. Nachtnebel. Fuzzy decision-making to resolve regional conflicts between industry and the environment, Chapter 3, C.W. Evans, W. Karwowski and R.M. Wilhelm (eds.), *Fuzzy Methodologies for Industrial and Systems Engineering*, Elsevier, Amsterdam, 1989.

Biswas, A.K. (eds.). *Models for Water Quality Management*, McGraw-Hill, p 348, 1981.

Bogardi, I., Duckstein, L. and F. Szidarovszky. Bayesian analysis of underground flooding, *Water Resources Research*, 18(4):1110-1116, August 1982.

Bogardi, I., Duckstein, L., and A. Bardossy. Regional management of an aquifer under fuzzy environmental objectives. *Water Resources Research*, 19(6):1402-1994, December 1983.

Bogardi, I., Bardossy, A., and L. Duckstein. "Uncertainties in Environmental Risk Analysis," in *Risk Analysis and Management of Natural and Man-made Systems*, Edited by Y.Y. Haimes and E.Z. Stakhiv, ASCE, 1989.

Chameau, F.L. and F.C. Santamarina. Membership functions I and II. *International Journal if Approximate Reasoning*, 1:287-316, 1987.

Civanlar, M.R. and H.F. Trussel. Constructing membership functions using statistical data, *Fuzzy Sets and Systems*, 18:1-13, 1986.

Dubois, D. and H. Prade. *Fuzzy Sets and Systems: Theory and Applications*, Academic Press, New York, 1980.

Duckstein, L., Krzysztofowicz, R. and D.R. Davis. To build or not to build: A Bayesian analysis, *Journal of Hydrological Sciences*, 4(1):55-68, 1978.

Duckstein, L., Bogardi, I., and A. Bardossy. Analyse multicritere "floue" d'une nappe karstique regionale: I. Theorie et cas de la Transdanubie (Hongrie), *Review Internationale des Sciences de l'Eau*, 2(1):1-6, February 1986.

Duckstein, L., Korhonen, P. and A. Tecle. Multiobjective forest managment using a visual, interactive and fuzzy approach, *Proceedings*, 1988 Symposium on Systems Analysis in Forest Resources, USDA Forest Service, Fort Collins, Colorado, pp. 68-74, April 1988.

Duckstein, L., and K. Heidel. Estimation of fuzzy set membership functions using value function transformations, in press, *Proceedings*, Fourth International Conference on the Foundations and Applications of Utility, Risk and Decision Theory, Budapest, Hungary, 1989.

Duckstein, L., Bogardi, I., and A. Bardossy. Fuzzy set membership, prior probabilty and value function, Working paper, University of Nebraska-Lincoln, Lincoln, Nebraska 68588-0531,1989.

Fried, J.L. *Groundwater Pollution*, Elsevier, p. 330, 1975.

Kaufmann, A. and M.N. Gupta. *Introduction to Fuzzy Arithmetic: Theory and Applications*, Van Nostrand Rheinhold, New York, 1985.

Kojiri, T. Real-time reservoir operation with inflow prediction by using fuzzy inference theory, Seminar on Conflict Analysis in Reservoir Management, Session F, Asian Institute of Technology, Bangkok, Thailand, December 1988.

Kruse, R. and D. Meyer. *Statistics with Vague Data*, D. Reidel Publishing Co., p. 279, 1987.

Nachtnebel, H.P., Hanish, P. and L. Duckstein. Multicriterion analysis of small hydropower plants under fuzzy objectives, *The Annals of Regional Science*, 20(3):86-100, 1986.

Raiffa, H. and R. Schlaifer. *Applied Decision Theory*, Harvard University Press, Cambridge, Massachusetts, 1961.

Savic, D.A. and S.P. Simonovic. Fuzzy linear programming and reservoir operation planning, Working paper, Civil Engineering Department, University of Manitoba, Winnipeg, Canada, 1989.

Turksen, I.B. Measurement of membership functions, pp. 55-67 in W. Karwowski and A. Mital (eds.), *Application of Fuzzy Set Theory in Human Factors*, Elsevier, Amsterdam, 1986.

Wetzel, R.G. *Limnology*, W.G. Saunders, London, p. 743, 1975.

Yasunobu, S., Sekino, S. and H. Toshitsugu. Automatic Train Operation and Automatic Crane Operation Systems Based on Predictive Fuzzy Control, *Proceedings* (preprint), Second Congress of the International Federation of Fuzzy Sets and Applications, Tokyo, pp. 835-838, July 1987.

Zadeh, L.A. Fuzzy sets, *Information Control* 8:338-353, 1968.

Zimmermann, H.J. *Fuzzy Set Theory and its Application*, Martinus Nijhoff, p. 363, 1985.

Risk Management for Groundwater
Contamination: Fuzzy Set Approach

Istvan Bogardi[1], Andras Bardossy[2], Lucien Duckstein[3]

Abstract

A methodology is developed for health risk management under uncertainty, using fuzzy sets. Groundwater nitrate contamination illustrates the methodology. A risk management framework (Travis et al., 1987) is used, in which regulatory action should be taken above a "de manifestis" risk line, no action taken under a "de minimus" line, and action taken between the two lines if the cost is below $2 million per life saved. In cases when the "pyramid" representing the joint membership function of individual risk (from the possiblity tree analysis) and population risk falls on one of the lines, an appropriate technique is developed for regulatory decision-making.

Introduction

The purpose of this paper is to develop a risk managment methodology, using fuzzy sets, for groundwater contamination. The example of cancer risk of nitrate exposure illustrates the methodology.

Risk analysis in general can be formulated as the description of an exposure and the consequence of this exposure. In most cases, both the exposure and its consequence are uncertain, and probabilistic methods can be used to account for the uncertainties involved.

---

[1] Istvan Bogardi, Department of Civil Engineering, University of Nebraska-Lincoln, Lincoln, NE 68588-0531.

[2] Andras Bardossy, Institute for Hydrology and Water Resources, University of Karlsruhe, Karlsruhe, FRG D-7500.

[3] Lucien Duckstein, Department of Systems and Industrial Engineering, University of Arizona, Tucson, AZ 85721.

GROUNDWATER CONTAMINATION RISK 443

In health risk analysis, including cancer risk, the consequence of an exposure dose is analyzed by a dose-response relationship providing the probability of an event such as cancer development in an individual given an exposure dose. If the exposure dose, x, is probabilistic, the so-called individual (health) risk can be expressed as an expected value. Let HR = (individual) Health Risk.
$$E(HR) = \int DR(x) \, g(x) \, dx,$$
where DR(x) is the dose-response relationship and g(x) is the density function of x. When combined with the size of the exposed population, this individual risk yields population risk. Population risk may be measured by the incidence of cancer in the exposed population per year.

During the last couple of years, health risk assessment has been performed according to EPA guidelines finalized in 1986 (EPA, 1986). These guidelines have been used to assess cancer risk for a number of specific chemicals. The development of the guidelines required several years and involved many scientists from every area of cancer risk analysis. The procedure and the underlying assumptions reflect the state-of-the-art up to the mid-eighties. The guidelines explicitly acknowledge the various uncertainties involved and recommend (but not specify) procedures to incorporate new scientific results. There is one main controversial feature of the procedure which has provoked most of the criticisms: this is the "worst case scenario" approach leading to the definition of an upper-bound unit risk instead of the "actual" (average) risk.

Health risk management uses both case-by-case decision making and standards or regulations. Travis et al. (1987) present regulatory guidelines summarized in Fig. 1: Above line A ("de manifestis" individual lifetime risk), regulatory action should be taken; below line B ("de minimus" individual lifetime risk), regulatory action need not be taken; between the two lines regulatory action is taken if the cost is below $2 million per life saved.

These guidelines are clear and easy to implement. However, they assume that the risk estimates (individual and population) are accurate. The question arises how the guidelines can be interpreted when risk estimates are uncertain. Fig. 1 illustrates this situation. Seven hypothetical groundwater contaminants with uncertain risk estimates are considered: Chemical 1: located above Line A, regulatory action should be taken; Chemical 2: located below Line B, no regulatory action; Chemical 3: further analysis is necessary to find out if regulatory action is warranted; Chemical 4 and 5: it is not straightforward to declare whether or not these chemicals are above or below

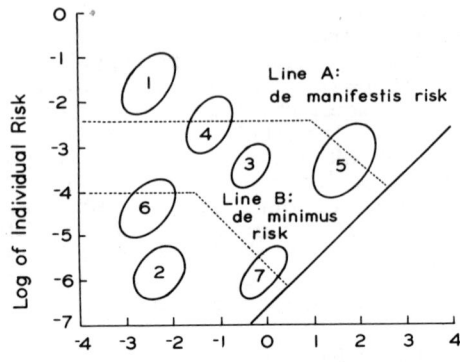

Log of Population Risk (cancer/yr)

Figure 1. Problem of regulation under uncertainty.

Line B; Chemical 6 and 7: Similarly to chemicals 4 and 5; it is not straightforward to decide if these chemicals are below Line B, in which case no regulatory action would be necessary. Many of the contaminants have the characteristics of hypothetical chemicals 4, 5, 6, or 7. The next section provides an approach to decision making in such situations.

Uncertainty Analysis

The fuzzy set methodology used in the present investigation to account for uncertainties in risk management is briefly described in this section; further technical information is provided in Duckstein et al. (1990).

The simplest method of considering uncertainty is to perform an interval analysis. An uncertain parameter of risk assessment, such as interspecies correction factor, can take on any value within such an interval. With more information on the uncertain parameter, the interval model can be "sharpened", that is, we determine the possibility that the parameter can take on certain value(s) within the interval. If the axioms and hypotheses of probability theory are verified, then the probabilistic procedure is simply an extension of interval analysis. However, in the present study, considerably weaker hypotheses than those of probability theory are warranted.

GROUNDWATER CONTAMINATION RISK

The propagation of uncertainty characteristics measured as intervals is the basis of traditional sensitivity analysis. The arithmetic of intervals is straightforward and functions of interval numbers are easy to calculate (Dong and Wong, 1986). To utilize additional information on an uncertain parameter, multi-intervals can be defined. Fuzzy sets represent situations where membership in sets cannot be defined on a yes/no basis; in other words, the boundaries of sets are vague.

Health risk management

Both population risk and individual risk are estimated under uncertainty (Bogardi et al., 1989a), and expressed as fuzzy numbers. Then, each contaminant can be represented as a two-dimensional membership function called a membership "pyramid" (Fig. 2). Now the relative location of such pyramids can be determined with respect to Line A or Line B. Two decision problems can be formulated: (1) to use the actual location to decide whether to regulate (hypothetical contaminants 4 and 5 in Fig. 1), or not to regulate (contaminants 6 and 7); (2) to decide if the cost of regulation is below $2 million per life saved. The first decision problem can be solved by comparing a fuzzy number (the location pyramid) with a crisp level (Line A or Line B) using the technique developed in Bardossy (1989).

The approach to solve the second decision problem is illustrated in Fig. 3. Assume that it has already been decided that the actual location is between Lines A and B. Two levels (1 and 2) of regulatory actions are considered.

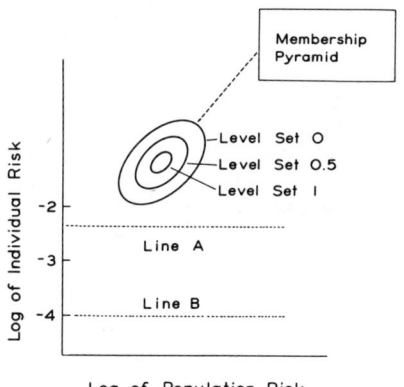

Figure 2. Characterization of cancer risk for chemical 1 (Fig. 1) with membership pyramid.

At either level, the population risk PR* and the cost of regulation C* are uncertain. No other cost than regulation costs is considered. Then, a cost-effectiveness index for each regulation is calculated. The cost-effectiveness at Level 1 is: $\dfrac{C_1^*}{PR_0^* - PR_1^*}$. At Level 2 regulation the cost effectiveness is: $\dfrac{C_2^*}{PR_0^* - PR_2^*}$. Fuzzy number arithmetic (Duckstein et al., 1990) is used to calculate the two ratios, which are also fuzzy numbers. Now the order relation: cost-effectiveness $\leq 2 \times 10^6$ will be checked according to the method given in Bogardi et al. (1989). A regulatory action (1 or 2) will be selected if either ratio is smaller than 2×10^6. If both are smaller, then the smallest between them is the better one according to this simple decision rule.

Illustrative Example

Cancer risk management for nitrate in drinking water is considered by locating that case in Fig. 4. The individual risk corresponding to an imprecise nitrate exposure dose of "around 20 mg/day" is calculated in Bogardi et al. (1989b) as a fuzzy number. The population risk is calculated by multiplying the individual risk by an assumed (crisp) size of exposed population of 10,000. Thus the population risk is also characterized by a fuzzy number. Note that variation in exposure dose within the population is not considered in this example. As a result, the population risk as a fuzzy number can be directly

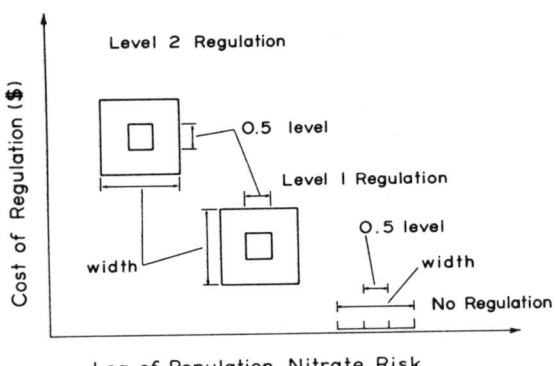

Figure 3. Regulation problem under uncertainty.

GROUNDWATER CONTAMINATION RISK   447

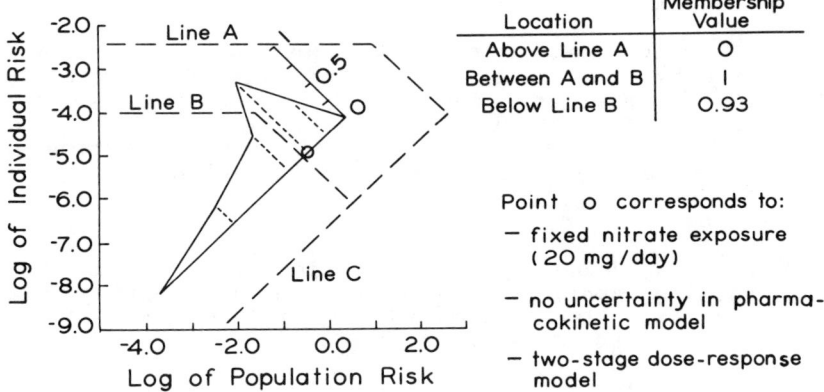

Figure 4.   Characterization of nitrate case in view of regulation.

calculated from the fuzzy individual risk. In this case the membership pyramid collapses into a line (trace of a plane).

Conclusions

   The conclusions of this paper can be drawn from Fig. 4. First, there is a possibility that the corresponding individual and population risk is located either under line B (no regulation) or between lines A and B (regulation depending on economics). Second, there is no straightforward way to decide on the actual location. Third, the traditional analysis (no uncertainty considered) would correspond to a location represented by the unit membership value. Based on this single point, one may decide that the regulation should be considered depending on economics. The method described in Bogardi et al. (1989) has been used to determine the location under uncertainty. Evidently, in this case, the risk cannot be located above Line A. However there is almost equal possibility that the location is between A and B (membership 1), or under B (membership 0.93). Such a situation may lead to the consideration of a threshold, and seems to justify the correctness of an allowable nitrate content of 10 ppm in drinking water. Finally, note, however, that the location is case-specific and would certainly move if any of the influencing quantities change. Among others the effect of the size of exposed population can be studied with the above methodology. The joint membership is then represented by a non-regular pyramid, since individual and population risk are in any case functionally related.

Acknowledgement

Research leading to this paper has been partially supported by a National Science Foundation Grant No. ECS-8802350, by a grant from the U.S. Geological Survey, Department of the Interior, No. 14-08-0001-G1631, and funds from the Science-Policy Integration Branch, Office of Policy Analysis, U.S. Environmental Protection Agency.

References

Bardossy, A., "Combination and siting of fuzzy numbers," Working Paper, Department of Civil Engineering, W348 Nebraska Hall, University of Nebraska-Lincoln, Lincoln, NE 68588-0531, 1989.

Bogardi, I., Duckstein, L. and A. Bardossy. "A framework for assessing uncertainties associated with cancer risk assessment." Working Paper, Department of Civil Engineering, W348 Nebraska Hall, University of Nebraska-Lincoln, Lincoln, NE 68588-0531, 1989a.

Bogardi, I., Bardossy, A., and B. Curtis, "Risk analysis for nitrate contaminated groundwater supplies," Working Paper, Department of Civil Engineering, University of Nebraska-Lincoln, Lincoln, Nebraska, 68588-0531, 1989b.

Dong, W.M. and F.S. Wong, "From uncertainty to approximate reasoning, Part 2," *Civil Engineering Systems*, December 1986.

Duckstein, L., Bogardi, I., and A. Bardossy, "Fuzzy set theory in water resources systems," *Proceedings*, Specialty Conference of the Water Resources Planning and Management Division, ASCE, Fort Worth, Texas, 1989.

EPA. "Guidelines for Carcinogen Risk Assessment," *Federal Register* 51:33992-34054, 1986.

Travis, C.C., S.A. Richter, E.A.C. Crouch, R. Wilson and E.D. Klema, "Cancer risk management," *Environ. Sci. Technol.*, Vol. 21, No. 5, 1987.

Bayesian Decision Theory and Fuzzy Sets Theory
in Systems Operation

Mohammad Karamouz*   M. ASCE

Abstract:

Operation of Water Resources Systems involves complex set of human decision. Many of the parameters involved in systems operations are random functions of time. Sometimes, the data needed is inadequate and inaccurate which introduces a very significant degree of uncertainty in the model. Furthermore, in the course of developing a model we come across subjective information with a very large degree of imprecision and with different linguistic impressions. In this paper, attempts have been made to differentiate between uncertainty and imprecision and to realize certain similarities and ambiguities in the use of two terms. Application of Bayesian Decision Theory and Fuzzy Sets Theory are also discussed.

Uncertainty and Imprecision

It has been stated that if there is uncertainty in the analysis of a system, it can only be the result of one's limited comprehension of the phenomenon and its complexity. The drawback could be in man's cognitive capabilities. In most cases the information is not available, and even if it were, modeling of the whole process would be cumbersome if not impossible. In modeling, it should be realized that the natural tendency should be directed towards the maximization of the performance, and not to the maximization of the precision. Hence, although cognitive components could improve comprehension of a complex phenomenon, simple but uncertain or imprecise abstraction can be used to represent the process. This could be the best alternative in a complex world with limited resources (Santamarina, 1987).

The uncertainty of the system output, in an engineering sense, could be entirely derived from a stochastic definition of the

----

* Associate Professor, Department of Civil Engineering, Pratt Institute, Brooklyn, New York, 11205 - (718) 636-3440.

system and the uncertainty of input parameters. In contrast, imprecision can not be characterized by probabilities and should be defined by qualification measures (linguistic, reasoning). The imprecision is a function of context, it depends upon existing information and goals to be achieved. Imprecision can be referred to vagueness in the boundary of a variable. The more precise information becomes the less probable it is. This is similar only in definition with the probability of one single point as it is described by the probability density function of a continuous variable.

Example of uncertainty in real time operation can be stated as follows: The inflow at time t+1 is not known and must be forecasted at time t. The decision maker faces a joint uncertainty about the actual realization of the streamflow (natural uncertainty) and about the accuracy of forecasts (forecast uncertainty).

Example of imprecision can be stated as follows:
- The reservoir is approximately full
- The groundwater table is about 10 feet from ground surface
- The demand for water will not be much greater than 4 units.
- The demand is about average and the Reservoir level is almost full.

The two terms are similar in some respects -- imprecision has been considered as a form of uncertainty with qualitative measures that can be handled through fuzzy logic and sometimes through fuzzy probabilities. Fuzzy probabilities are combinations of probability and fuzzy theory, (see Dubois and Prade 1980). Uncertainties with sufficient physical measurements can be treated with probability theory and Bayes Theorem.

- Bayesian Decision Theory application -

Bayesian decision theory can be of significant value to systems operation because of its flexibility in being able to incorporate new information and/or opinions and judgments of decision makers or operators in the interpretation of probability.

Bayesian procedures not only optimally account for forecast uncertainty, but in contrast to other decision procedures, ensure a nonnegative economic gain from a real time forecast no matter how great the uncertainty may be [see Degroot(1970)]. The iterative nature of Bayesian analysis would seem to provide a mechanism by which parameter uncertainties and new data can be incorporated into assumptions concerning inflow processes to reservoir systems.

Example 1 - The discrete Markov process assumed to describe the streamflows is based on the probabilities of transitioning to an inflow in season t+1 conditioned on the inflow for season t. Thus if a set of conditional probabilities, P[I(t+1) | I(t)], which relate each inflow in season t+1 to the inflows in season t can be found, the discrete lag-one Markov process can be included in the model.

In this example, a forecast series {H} can be used jointly with actual historical inflow series {I}. The sequence of {I,H} is assumed to form a periodic Markov process. Under Markov assumption, the density functions and conditional density functions characterize completely the forecast process. The effects of forecast series on the probability statements can be explained as follow: The behavior of streamflow physical phenomenon whose state effects the decision outcome is described in terms of a prior distiribution $P[I_{(t+1)}]$ and prior transition probabilities $P[I_{(t+1)} | I_{(t)}]$. The behavior of the system that forecast the uncertain state is described in terms of joint probabilities $P[I_{(t+1)}, H_{(t+1)}]$. This independent information can be combined through Bayes theorem and the results is a family of posterior distribution of the state condition (see Krzystofowicz 1985).

$$P[I_{(t+1)} | I_{(t)}, H_{(t+1)}] = \frac{P[H_{(t+1)} | I_{(t)}] P[I_{(t+1)} | I_{(t)}]}{\sum_{\text{all } I(t+1)} P[H_{(t+1)} | I_{(t)}] P[I_{(t+1)} | I_{(t)}]}$$

The forecast system is characterized by the likelihood functions. The likelihood function describes probabilistically the conditional error of the forecast H(t+1) of the actual streamflow I(t+1) (see Krzysztofowicz, 1983). The density functions can be derived for the process with the assumption of normal prior forecast error or with any other assumptions that can be justified. Combining the forecast and its error one can optimally revise the prior distribution of {I} using Bayes theorem.

- **Fuzzy Sets Theory applications -**

The theory of fuzzy sets is based on the concept of degree of membership. It is also known as degree of belongingness. In standard set theory the membership is either 1.0 or 0.0 wether it belongs or does not belong to a set. A set of pairs of elements and their membership constitutes a fuzzy set.

In fuzzy set theory this requirement is relaxed (Santamarina 1987). A set of pairs of elements and their membership constitute fuzzy sets. If two fuzzy sets A and B are given, the union of two (A or B) defines a maximum operator and the intersection of two (A and B) defines a minimum operator. In decision making with fuzzy sets a mini-max operator has been used through the use of extension principle, (Zadeh, 1965).

Example 2 - A fuzzy window can be used which relates a dependent variable to an independent variable X with an assigned membership value. Let Y to be monthly demand of "about' 9 Mm^3 for the month of November (X). Then within the range of 4-13 Mm^3 monthly demand for the year, a fuzzy window of (0,0,0,0,.1,.8,1.0, 9,.2,0,0) can be defined. The demand of 9 gets a value of 1.0 and as we deviate from 9 the membership value is reduced. The window can be selected based on the analyst judgement and familiarity with the case. There is no specific rules except that the membership weight will be around the stated values, in this case 9. A stack of windows for all Y values of each month X provides the so called "Fuzzy Constraints". Any problem-case along the dimension X with defined membership can filter the stack of windows to compute the minimum (intersection) of the two values. Then the strongest of the weakest link at different Y levels can be found by selecting the maximum values (union). These values have the highest overall acceptability level, (Zimmermann, 1985) and represent the fuzzy sets for Y. For example the membership of the reliability of a reservoir in different months of the year can filter the stack of fuzzy windows of demand vs. time of the year in order to define fuzzy sets for the monthly demand, if one follows the above procedure. These output fuzzy set could provide a means for assessing the reliability of a reservoir to meet certain demands.

References:

DeGrout, M.M., Optimal Statistical Decisions, McGraw Hill, N.Y., 1970.

Dubois, D., Prade, H.J., Fuzzy Sets and Systems: Theory and Applications, Academic Press, 1980.

Karamouz, M. "Analysis of error and Uncertainty in Groundwater Quality Monitoring", Pollution, Risk Assessment and Remediation in Groundwater Systems, Scientific Publications, 1987.

Krzysztofowicz, R., "A Bayesian Markov Model of flooded Forecast Process", Water Resources Research, 19(6), pp.1455-1465, December 1983.

Krzysztofowicz, R., "Bayesian Models of Forecasted Time Series", Water Resources Bulletin, Vol. 21, No. 5, pp.805-814, Oct. 1985.

Santamarina, C. J., "Fuzzy Sets and Engineering Applications", Special Lecture Series, Polytechnic University, Nov. 1987.

Zadeh, L., "Fuzzy sets", Information Control, Vol. 8, pp.338-353, 1965.

Zimmermann, H.J., Fuzzy Set Theory, and Its Applications, Kluwer-Nijhoff, 1985.

BAYESIAN DECISION PRINCIPLES
FOR FLOOD WARNINGS

Roman Krzysztofowicz[1]

Overview

A Bayesian theory of flood warning systems has been formulated. The theory offers principles for mathematical modeling of warning systems. The objectives of modeling are (i) to find the optimal decision rule for issuing a flood warning to the public based on a hydrometeorologic forecast of the flood, and (ii) to obtain an ex ante evaluation of system performance under uncertainties about the actual flood events and public response to warnings.

Flood Warning System

The theory is tailored to a class of systems which can be conceptualized as a cascade coupling of three components: **monitor, forecaster,** and **decider.** The operation of such a warning system can be idealized as follows.

Floods occur intermittently. For economic reasons, a flood data collection network, forecasting procedure, and emergency management do not operate continuously. Rather, their operation is triggered only when potential flood conditions are detected. To enable such detections, a system monitoring hydrometeorologic conditions operates continuously. When a set of pre-defined conditions is observed, the monitor triggers operation of the forecast system. The flood data collection network is activated, and a forecast of the flood hydrograph is prepared. This forecast is supplied to the decision system -- a flood preparedness organization, or a floodplain manager -- who must then decide whether or not to issue a warning to the public.

Bayesian Warning Theory

The theory of flood warning systems is derived from Bayesian decision theory. It enables one to model statistically the performance of a monitor and a forecaster, and on that basis to

---

[1]Professor, Department of Systems Engineering, University of Virginia, Thornton Hall, Charlottesville, Virginia 22901.

formulate an optimal decider and determine the performance of the total warning system. The principal outputs from the theory are general expressions for the following four elements:

1. The **optimal decision rule** for issuing a flood warning to the public based on an imperfect forecast of the flood crest.

2. The **receiver operating characteristic** (ROC) of the warning system, showing a relationship among (i) the probability of detection, (ii) the probability of a false warning, and (iii) the expected lead time of a warning.

3. The **performance tradeoff characteristic** (PTC) of a warning system, displaying a relationship among (i) the expected number of detections per year, (ii) the expected number of false warnings per year, and (iii) the expected lead time of a warning.

4. The **annual value** of a given warning system, and the **potential annual value** of a warning system for a given floodplain. The expressions for the values are general and may be used to estimate the expected annual reduction of monetary losses, the expected number of lives saved per year, or any other quantity of interest. When the annual value is in monetary units, it may be termed the **annual economic benefit** of a flood warning system.

Optimal Decision Rule

The optimal rule for deciding whether or not to issue a flood warning to the public based on a hydrometeorologic forecast depends upon preferences of the decision maker -- an individual or an organization in charge of the warning system. The theory offers two alternative procedures for expressing and quantifying the preferences. The first procedure directs the decision maker's attention to the statistical characterization of system performance. The decision maker is shown the PTC, and his task is to decide on the most preferred **tradeoff point** among those feasible to attain in a given system. The second procedure directs the decision maker's attention to social and economic outcomes of decisions and flood events: (no warning, flood), (warning, no flood), (warning, flood). The **disutilities** of these outcomes are assessed, and the optimal tradeoff point on the PTC is found by minimizing the expected disutility of outcomes, conditional on the forecast. This coupling between the statistical and socio-economic characterizations of system performance is a hallmark of Bayesian decision analysis.

RESERVOIR OPERATIONS BY FUZZY GOAL PROGRAMMING

G.V. Loganathan,[1] Associate Member, ASCE, and D. Bhattacharya[2]

Abstract

The reservoir operations problem is composed of obtaining optimal releases, and storages of a reservoir and downstream reach routed flows based on forecasted inflows and precipitation. The formulation in general involves two difficulties: (i) estimation of objective function coefficients, and (ii) use of point estimates of targeted storages and flows. Goal programming formulation overcomes the first difficulty by minimizing the deviations from targets. Fuzzy goal program allows for a range for a target instead of a point estimate. The solution is compared with that of a preemptive goal program. These schemes are applied to the Green River basin, Kentucky data reported previously in literature.

Fuzzy Goal Programming(FGP)

Fuzzy goal programming utilizes the concept of membership function which defines degrees of belonging of various elements of a set. In conventional goal programming problem, an objective function made up of deviational variables from the crisply stated goals is minimized. In fuzzy goal programming the objective is to achieve all goals (in max min sense) as permitted by the functional form of the membership function. The fuzzy goals are related to the targets through a fuzzy decision D. Consider a set of linear fuzzy goals, expressed as

$$Ax \cong b \qquad (1)$$

where : b is a vector of targets, A is a matrix of coefficients, and x is a vector of decision variables. The symbol ' $\cong$ ' is a 'fuzzifier' representing the imprecise fashion in which goals are stated. Let $(Ax)_i$ represent the i th row of Ax, and b_i be the i th component of the right hand side vector or the target. The degree to which $(Ax)_i$ is close to b_i can be represented by means of a fuzzy membership function which attains a value of unity when $(Ax)_i = b_i$, and zero when either $(Ax)_i > b_i + \Delta_i$ or $(AX)_i < b_i - \delta_i$ where Δ_i and δ_i are prespecified deviations from the target b_i. For $b_i - \delta_i < (Ax)_i < b_i + \Delta_i$, the membership function for $(Ax)_i$ denoted as $\mu_i(Ax)$ assumes values between zero and one, indicating the degree of closeness towards b_i. That is

$$\mu_i(Ax) = 1 \qquad \text{if } (Ax)_i = b_i$$
$$= f[\ (Ax)_i, b_i\ ] \quad \text{if } b_i - \delta_i < (Ax)_i < b_i + \Delta_i \qquad (2)$$
$$= 0 \qquad \text{if } (Ax)_i < b_i - \delta_i \text{ or } (Ax)_i > b_i + \Delta_i \quad \text{for } i = 1, \ldots, p$$

---

[1] Associate Professor, Department of Civil Engineering, Virginia Polytechnic Institute and State University, Blacksburg, VA 24061

[2] Engineer, Whitney, Bailey, Cox, and Magnani Consulting Engineers, Timmonium, MD 21093

The membership function for an element x belonging to a fuzzy set A is denoted by $\mu_A(x)$. Let A be the intersection of two fuzzy sets B and C. Then $\mu_A(x)$ is defined as $\mu_A(x) = \min \{\mu_B(x), \mu_C(x)\}$. Therefore, if we have p fuzzy goals expressed as $[A]_{pxn}\{x\}_{nx1} \cong \{b\}_{px1}$, then $\{x:(Ax)_i \cong b_i\}$ may be denoted as the fuzzy set B_i, and the set $D = [\ x: [A]\{x\} \cong \{b\}\ ]$ denotes the intersection of sets $B_1 \cap B_2 \cap \cdots \cap B_p$. Therefore, the membership function $\mu_D(x)$ can be written as

$$\mu_D(x) = \text{Min} \{\mu_{B_1}(x), \mu_{B_2}(x), \ldots, \mu_{B_p}(x)\} \quad (3)$$

From the definition of the membership function, higher the membership function value, the element is closer to the target. Therefore, one would like to maximize $\mu_D(x)$, subject to : $x \in X$ so that the resulting decisions will yield objective function values close to the prespecified targets. It should be noted that such an approach will not differentiate between two solutions in terms of the value of $\mu_D(x)$ in which one may yield objective values close to b_i's in every i except for some b_j which is binding for $\mu_D(x)$ and the other may yield poor b_i values, but may yield the same b_j. Therefore, one might say that the fuzzy goal programming concentrates on the worst goal and provides little incentive for the remaining goals. The fuzzy goal programming formulation may be difficult to solve in general. However if the goals, the constraints and the membership functions are linear, then the problem can be solved using the available linear programming packages. Consider the following symmetric piecewise linear membership function

$$\mu_i(Ax) = 0 \qquad \text{if } (Ax)_i < b' = b_i - \Delta_i \quad (4a)$$

$$\mu_i(x) = \frac{(Ax)_i - b'_i}{\Delta_i} \qquad \text{if } b'_i \leq (Ax)_i \leq b_i \quad (4b)$$

$$\mu_i(x) = \frac{b'' - (Ax)_i}{\Delta_i} \qquad \text{if } b_i \leq (Ax)_i \leq b''_i = b_i + \Delta_i \quad (4c)$$

$$\mu_i = 0 \qquad \text{if } (Ax)_i > b'' = b_i + \Delta_i \quad (4d)$$

where, Δ_i's are the subjectively chosen constants for deviations from the target b_i. The domain of positive values for the membership function is given in the interval (b'_i, b''_i). Using the membership functions in Eq.(4) the fuzzy goal program may be solved as

$$\underset{x \in X}{\text{Max}} \ \underset{i}{\text{Min}} \ \frac{(Ax)_i - b'_i}{\Delta_i} \qquad \text{for } i \in D_1 \quad (5)$$

$$\underset{x \in X}{\text{Max}} \ \underset{i}{\text{Min}} \ \frac{b''_i - (AX)_i}{\Delta_i} \qquad \text{for } i \in D_2 \quad (6)$$

where : X = Feasible region of linear constraints , $D_1 = \{i: \ b'_i \leq (AX)_i \leq b_i\}$. and $D_2 = \{i: \ b_i \leq (AX)_i \leq b''_i\}$. Narasimhan (1980) suggested the following formulation for the solution of expressions (5) and (6).

Problem P1

$$\text{Max} \quad \lambda \quad (7)$$

subject to :
$$\lambda \leq \frac{(Ax)_i - b'_i}{\Delta_i} \qquad \text{for } i \in D_1 \quad (8a)$$

$$b'_i \leq (Ax)_i \leq b_i \qquad \text{for } i \in D_1 \quad (8b)$$

$$\lambda \leq \frac{b''_i - (Ax)_i}{\Delta_i} \quad \text{for } i \in D_2 \quad (9a)$$

$$b_i \leq (Ax)_i \leq b'' \quad \text{for } i \in D_2 \quad (9b)$$

$$x \in X \quad (10)$$

Because there are two possibilities for each i namely, either $i \in D_1$ or $i \in D_2$ and for p goals there are 2^p different problems of the type (P1). Each such problem has 3p goal constraints which are given by expressions (8) and (9). Let $\lambda_* = \max \{\lambda_i\}$ for $i = 1, 2, \ldots, 2^p$ be the maximum of objective function values for the 2^p problems. Hannan (1981) formulated a single equivalent linear program with 2p constraints capable of yielding the same optimal objective function value, λ_*. Hannan's formulation is given as
Problem (P2)

$$\text{Max} \quad \lambda \quad (11)$$

subject to:
$$\frac{(Ax)_i}{\Delta_i} + d_i^- - d_i^+ = \frac{b_i}{\Delta_i} \quad \text{for } i = 1, 2, \ldots, p \quad (12a)$$

$$\lambda + d_i^- + d_i^+ \leq 1 \quad \text{for } i = 1, 2, \ldots, p \quad (12b)$$

$$d_i^-, d_i^+, \lambda \geq 0 \quad \text{for } i = 1, 2, \ldots, p \quad (12c)$$

$$x \in X \quad (13)$$

Another formulation of the fuzzy linear program is given by Zimmerman (1978). Zimmerman uses maxima and minima of the various objective functions (as if they were optimized individually) to choose the Δ_i and δ_i allowance factors in defining the membership functions. However, such an approach removes the 'fuzziness' associated with the targets (Hannan, 1982).

The three major advantages of using the fuzzy subsets concept to formulate a goal programming problem are : (i) the suggested methodology has the advantage of dealing in a formal manner with the imprecision in defining targets; (ii) the solution approach reduces to solving a single linear program; (iii) the method doesn't require assignment of preferences for the various objectives. However, there are some drawbacks associated with the fuzzy goal programming approach : (i) the form of the membership function is open to question; (ii) poor choice of targets may also lead to infeasibility of the problem, i.e.,there may not be a nonnegative λ for problem (P2). With regard to reservoir operations, the targets are based on the demands of the system which are fuzzy. Therefore, the decision maker would prefer to have some flexibility in his imprecisely defined targets. This aspect can be easily incorporated into a fuzzy goal program.

Preemptive Goal Programming(PGP)

A goal program with prioritized objective functions may be stated as
Problem (P3)

$$\text{Minimize} \sum_{i=1}^{p} P_i(d_i^+ + d_i^-) \quad (14)$$

subject to : $G_i - Z_k(x) = d_i^- - d_i^+$ for $i = 1, 2, \ldots, p$ (15)

$x \in X$ (16)

$d_i^-, d_i^+ \geq 0$ (17)

Can and Houck(1984) formulated the reservoir operations problem as a preemptive goal program. In preemptive goal programming P_j 's are *not* numerical weights but hierarchical priorities assigned to different objectives or goals such that $P_1 >> P_2 >> P_3 \ldots >> P_p$. They simply indicate the order in which the various goals are to be considered. For a linear preemptive goal program the procedure consists of solving a series of linear programming sub-problems by using the solution of the higher priority problem as the starting solution for the lower priority subproblem.

Green River basin system

The system is located in the Green River Basin(GRB) in Central Kentucky which is a subbasin of the Ohio River Basin and lies largely in West Central Kentucky. The data provided by Can et al.(1982) have been used. There are four reservoirs in the GRB, namely Green, Nolin, Barren and Rough. The primary objective of the reservoir operation is flood control. The secondary objective is low flow augmentation and water quality.

The following notation is used :

R(i,j) - Release from reservoir i during day j (cfs)
S(i,j) - Storage volume of the reservoir i at the beginning of day j (cfs-day)
I(i,j) - Inflow to reservoir i during day j (cfs)
Q(k,j) - Flow at control station k during day j (cfs)
TF(l,j)- Tributary flow at station l during day j (cfs)
P(m,j) - Precipitation for reach m during day j (cfs)
i   - Reservioir index;
1. Green   2. Nolin   3. Barren   4. Rough
j   - Time index; t-2, t-1-past; t-current; t+1, t+2 -future
k   - Station Index
1. Greensburg 2. Munfordville 3. Brownsville 4. Bowling Green
5. Woodbury 6. Paradise 7. Fall of Rough 8. Dundee 9. Calhoun
l   - Tributary station index
1. Gresham 2. Alvaton 3. Glen Dean 4. Horse Branch
m   - Reach index; m = 1, 2, … , 9

The values for the inflows, I, tributary flows, TF, and precipitation, P, are either known or forecasted. For the decision variables namely, storage, S, release, R, and routed flow ,Q, only the past information is known. The storage at the begining of the current day is known.

The optimal releases and reach routed flows for the current day, denoted as, R(i,t) and Q(i,t) respectively, along with the optimal storage values at the end of the current day, denoted as S(i,t+1), are shown in Table 1. The solutions for the preemptive and fuzzy goal programs are listed as PGP and FGP respectively. The target values are listed as Target. PGP focusses on prioritized goals. The first two priorities of achieving storage levels for reservoirs 4 and 1 and maintaining flows in reaches 5,9 and 2 are achieved. Deviations occur starting from the third priority. FGP approaches the targets more uniformly and focusses on the most preferred values of the targets for all goals.

Table 1. Optimal Solutions

	PGP	FGP	Target
S(1,t+1)	82145.0	77596.9	82145.0
S(2,t+1)	31295.6	31528.5	32180.0
S(3,t+1)	32621.0	32621.0	32621.0
S(4,t+1)	15063.0	13181.9	15063.0
R(1,t)	1199.3	3747.4	-
R(2,t)	1000.0	767.1	-
R(3,t)	403.4	403.40	-
R(4,t)	118.9	2000.0	-
Q(1,t)	680.5	2001.0	4000.0
Q(2,t)	105.6	105.6	12000.0
Q(3,t)	1175.0	1005.7	13000.0
Q(4,t)	306.6	306.6	6800.0
Q(5,t)	1216.8	1210.8	17000.0
Q(6,t)	827.3	826.8	26000.0
Q(7,t)	163.5	1599.1	1200.0
Q(8,t)	272.0	701.7	2000.0
Q(9,t)	2044.2	2335.0	31000.0

Summary

The heart of the reservoir operations problems is the set of linear constraints generated by the continuity equations. If the routing equations and the objective function are chosen to be linear, one obtains a valid linear program. Fuzzy goal program provides for an interval about the most preferred point target values. However, it may select an inefficient point (there exist another solution which can improve at least one other goal without hurting the other goals) if the alternate optima are not examined.

References

Can, E.K., Houck, M.H., and Toebes, G.H., "Optimal Real-Time Reservoir System Operation : Innovative Objectives and Implementational Problems," Purdue Water Resources Research Center, *Technical Report*, 150, 1982.

Can, E.K., and Houck, M.H., "Real-Time Reservoir Operations by Goal Programming," *Journal of Water Resources Planning and Management*, ASCE, 110(3):297-309, 1984.

Hannan, E.L., "Contrasting Fuzzy Goal Programming and Fuzzy Multicriteria Programming," *Decision Sciences*, 13:337-339, 1982.

Narasimhan, R.,"Goal Programming in a Fuzzy Environment," *Decision Sciences*, 11:325-336, 1980.

Zimmerman, H.J.,"Fuzzy programming and linear programming with several objective functions," *Fuzzy Sets and Systems*, 1:45-56, 1978.

USING AN INDEX STREAM TO MAKE INSTREAM FLOW DECISIONS
Daniel R. Harvey and Peter F. Brooks, Members ASCE[1]

Abstract

The Cedar River basin water in Western Washington has experienced an increasingly competitive demand during low-flow periods for water to support M&I use and and a valuable fishery. In addition, the Seattle District, Corps of Engineers (USACE) has a major navigation lock and dam facility (the Lake Washington Ship Canal, LWSC) which relies on Cedar water for its operation. This has prompted USACE to develop an Integrated Operating Plan (IOP) to determine, on a daily basis, what flow should be provided in the Cedar River below the City of Seattle's Chester Morse Reservoir (CMR). The IOP uses an unregulated (natural) stream in the upper Cedar basin as an index of overall hydrologic status of the Cedar River system. The real-time index stream flow is compared, on a daily basis, to a set of three switching, or triggering flow levels of the index stream to determine to which of four instream flow regimes at the downstream control point the Cedar River should be adjusted. The IOP uses a 90-day daily moving average of the index stream flow and switching levels, which most accurately characterizes the critical low-flow duration period for CMR. The plan integrates the storage requirements of both Lake Washington and CMR such that critical storage rule curves are not required for either impoundment. This all but eliminates the potential for the perception of a "man-made" drought due to inappropriate management of either storage facility.

Introduction

The Cedar River on the western slope of the Cascade Range in Washington State provides 70 percent of the M&I

---

[1]Hydraulic Engineers, Hydrology and Hydraulics Branch, U.S. Army Corps of Engineers, P.O. Box C-3755, Seattle, WA 98124-2255.

water for distribution by the City of Seattle's Water Department (SWD) which witnessed an eight-fold increase in total system demand from 1901 to 1980. In addition, the Cedar supports a valuable anadromous fishery and provides 50 percent of the average annual inflow to Lake Washington which is used by USACE to store water for operation of the Lake Washington Ship Canal (LWSC). The competitive demand on Cedar River water during the low-flow season (usually June through October) makes the understanding and unbiased management of that resource critical. Development of an integrated water operating plan involved the uniting of a set of flow regimes at the Renton gage (the control point near the mouth of the Cedar River. USACE believed that the flow regimes were adequate from a volume standpoint but deficient in the timing of their delivery. A redistribution of the Renton flows to increase them early in the conservation season (July) with a corresponding reduction in October was made to ensure that Lake Washington's annual minimum level would not fall below its authorized project minimum level more often than historically. The effects of this "flow shifting" would be evaluated once the IOP was fully developed to see if the Seattle Water Department could still meet its water demands and that the Cedar River anadromous species fishery would not be adversely affected.

Development

There are a myriad of indexing methods developed to determine the flow rates to supply in a stream or from a reservoir to meet various water demands. Most of these methods involve a variety of hydrometeorologic and groundwater inputs to establish when the water supply is in a critical situation and, subsequently, what action is to be taken. The most widely used index of low flow at a site is the 7-day, 10-year low flow, which is the discharge at a 10-yr recurrence interval taken from a frequency of the lowest average flow for seven consecutive days in each year (Riggs, 1980). This is primarily used in regulating waste disposal to streams and for planning of water detention facilities and cannot be used on a daily real-time basis. Palmer's Drought Severity Index (Palmer, 1965) is a meteorologic index used to reflect both moisture deficiencies and excesses and requires several different kinds of hydrometeorologic data for its operation. The Pennsylvania Department of Environmental Resources (Kibler, et al 1987) uses five indicators to establish the severity of drought. Because of the many interested agencies, a dearth of data other than streamflow in the Cedar River, short-term groundwater changes, and that CMR refill has not been a problem historically (i.e, CMR's storage is relatively small compared to its contributing basin), USACE believed that the procedure for the IOP could involve a single index parameter and should be pre-disposed to be almost "hands-off" and simple to use. Before the development of the IOP, the SWD and USACE mutually agreed to a few criteria to guide the IOP's development: at least current M&I yield from the Cedar would be preserved; Lake Washington would not fall below its authorized project minimum annual elevation more than it had historically; flow reductions (as dictated by the IOP) to critical or lower at the control point would occur in only 10 percent of the years analyzed; no reservoir storage rule curves could be used; only existing demands on Cedar water would be considered (all parties subscribing to the IOP would be responsible for their own future demand and growth); there would be no significant impact to fisheries; and water conservation activities were the responsibility of each agency, i.e., no conservation strategy would be woven into the fabric of an IOP.

The first consideration was to select the critical low-flow duration period for CMR and use it throughout the development and use of the IOP. Preliminary analysis showed that a 30 or 60-day daily moving average of the index stream frequently indicated short-term water deficit situations that had little impact on CMR storage and would cause premature reductions in Renton flows. Conversely, a 120-day daily moving average reacted too late both within the model and historically, which caused a late reduction in Renton flows - in some cases after the reservour was already depleted. From this analysis, a 90-day daily moving average was selected as the most representative of the critical low-flow duration period for CMR. Hence, all future references to the index stream should be assumed to be 90-day moving averages. Daily frequency curves using a graphically fit lognormal distribution were developed from 74 years of unregulated daily streamflow data (43 years gaged, 31 years estimated) on the main stem of the Cedar above CMR. A daily flow was read from these frequency curves for each of three agreed-to exceedance frequencies (10, 5, and 1 percent). These three sets of flows for each day make up a set of continuous annual curves and are termed switching levels. Some adjustments to the exceedance frequencies were made to consider seasonal hydrology in a manner that would weigh critical periods of the year more heavily than non-critical periods as discussed in the study results. Currently there are two flow regimes (normal and critical) at the Renton control point on the Cedar. If flows are reduced from the normal to critical, in some months, this reduction can be quite large and potentially damaging to spawning anadromous fish.

Because the Renton flow regimes were being adjusted as part of the aforementioned "flow-shifting" aspect of the

in some months, this reduction can be quite large and potentially damaging to spawning anadromous fish. Because the Renton flow regimes were being adjusted as part of the aforementioned "flow-shifting" aspect of the IOP, USACE believed that an intermediate flow regime (subnormal) and a regime lower than critical (extreme) could be inserted to mitigate damages resulting from having to reduce flows at Renton. Simply, any required flow reductions at Renton would be smaller and less drastic.

Finally, the index stream switching levels were tied to the Renton flow regimes, and the IOP calibrated using a process discussed in the study results. On a daily basis, the index stream flow is compared to each of the switching levels and if the index stream falls below switching level I (see Figure 1) and stays below such that a downward trend is established, flows at Renton must be reduced to no less than subnormal. If the index stream continues to recede and falls below switching level II, Renton flows must be reduced from subnormal to no less than critical. And if the index stream falls below switching level III, Renton flows must be reduced to no less than extreme. A converse procedure is followed when flows are to be increased. Bounds about the switching curves are being developed to prevent switching back and forth when the index stream tends to closely follow a switching curve.

Results

The calibration process using the 74 years of daily streamflow data for the index stream consisted of three phases. An initial run was made to assess the number of switches to critical or extreme at Renton. The number of this type of switch was much greater than the maximum allowable of eight or fewer (10% of 74 years, rounded up) as established in the IOP development guidelines. This was due primarily to winter low-flow occurences (usually caused by cold weather), which do not impact water supply except in extreme situations. In addition, the minimum annual Lake Washington elevation was checked to ensure that its historical reliability was preserved. To reduce the number of switches, especially those in the winter, the daily frequency curves from which the switching levels were derived were manually reshaped within the bounds of hydrologic reason, e.g., the winter switching curves lowered. The historical sequence was rerun, and the number of switches and the minimum annual Lake Washington elevation were rechecked. This process was repeated until the developmental criteria were met or exceeded. The SWD then checked what effect the switching levels would have on the Cedar River yield. There was no

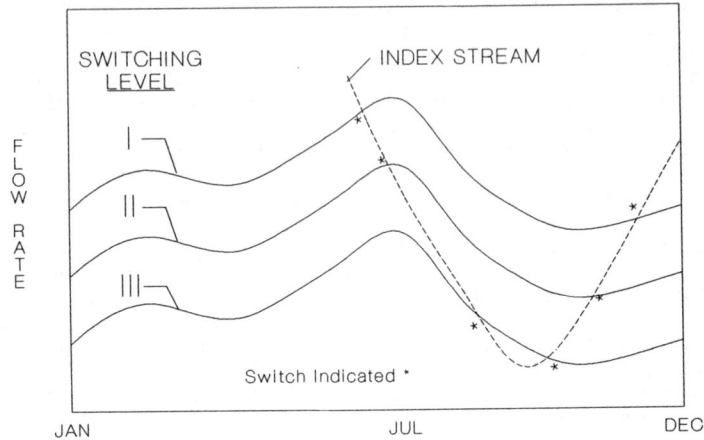

Figure 1. Schematic of Integrated Operating Plan
90-Day Moving Average

problem meeting this criteria; however, if a reduction in the Cedar River yield had occured, then the proposed Renton flow regimes would need to be modified and the Lake Washington criteria rechecked.

Because of the flow-shifting at Renton and the effectiveness of the index stream as an indicator of hydrologic status of the Cedar River basin, the proposed instream flows at Renton should provide more reliability in meeting the instream flows throughout the entire conservation season than the current method of operation which is more reactive than preventive; however, the monthly volume would be slightly lower later in the conservation season. Although the IOP and its associated flow regimes are still being negotiated with the fisheries agencies, indications are that a flow reduction as part of a new operating plan would be acceptable as long as the reliability of those flows is maintained at favorable levels.

References

Kibler, D.F., Shaffer, G.L., and White, E.L., "Analysis of Drought Indicators in Pennsylvania", Proceedings: Engineering Hydrology, Symposium sponsored by Hydraulics Division, ASCE, Williamsburg, Virginia, pp. 595-600, August 3-7 1987.

Palmer, W.C., "Meteorological Drought", U.S. Weather Bureau, U.S. Department of Commerce, Research Paper No. 45, February 1965.

Riggs, H.C., "Characteristics of Low Flows", ASCE, Journal of the Hydraulics Division, Vol. 106, No. 5, pp. 717-731, May 1980.

Estimating Lake Inflows for Storage by Linear Programming
Quentin W. Martin[1]

Abstract

The Lower Colorado River Authority (LCRA) recently completed a Water Management Plan for the lower Colorado River Basin in Texas. In developing the Plan, a daily river flow routing procedure, based on Linear Programming, was used to determine the maximum portion of each estimated daily historical inflow to the reservoirs in the LCRA Highland Lakes which could be held in storage without impacting downstream senior water rights. The Linear Programming procedure is described, and the resulting estimates of inflows available for storage are discussed.

Introduction

The Lower Colorado River Authority (LCRA) is a water conservation and reclamation district created by the State of Texas in 1934. It has a statutory service district of ten counties in Central Texas, covering approximate 10,000 mi^2 (Figure 1). LCRA operates a major reservoir system, called the Highland Lakes, on the lower Colorado River, and provides approximately 650,000 acre-feet of surface water annually for municipal, manufacturing and irrigation purposes. Approximately 80% of that supply is used for agriculture, specifically the irrigation of rice.

The State of Texas recently completed an adjudication of the water rights in the lower Colorado River Basin. As part of the settlement of a lawsuit over that adjudication, the LCRA was given the right to sell up to 1.5 million acre-feet annually - an amount far in excess of the firm yield of the Highland Lakes. This water may be sold as either firm or "interruptible" supplies, with firm water being supplies guaranteed to be available throughout the duration of the critical drought of record. LCRA may not contract to sell interruptible supplies in a given year in amounts which will impact the ability of LCRA to meet the

---
[1] Manager, Water and Wastewater Utilities Program, Lower Colorado River Authority, P.O.Box 220, Austin, Texas 78767.

current and near future demands for firm supplies.

LCRA was charged with preparing a Water Management Plan which would describe how it would manage this combination of firm and interruptible supplies. The Plan would also calculate the estimated firm yield from the Highland Lakes based on fully honoring all senior downstream water rights. The Plan was completed in April 1989 (LCRA, 1989) and scheduled for review and possible approval by the Texas Water Commission in September 1989.

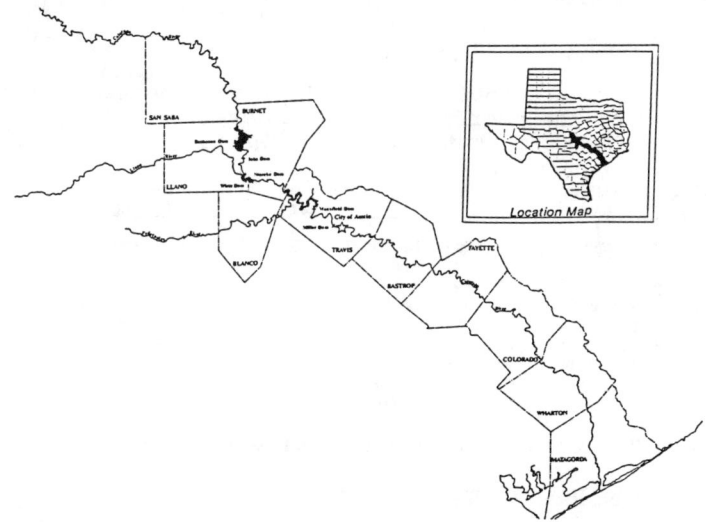

Figure 1. Lower Colorado River Authority District

All surface water diversions for senior downstream water rights to those of LCRA must first be satisfied by inflows to the Colorado River from drainage areas downstream of the Highland Lakes. Only the remaining portion of the senior water rights become the downstream demands for which inflows are passed through the Highland Lakes. Determining the required reservoir releases of inflow depends upon the results of the routing of the unregulated, daily inflows below Mansfield Dam.

Hydrologic Routing Relationships

The basic method proposed to determine the minimum reservoir inflows allowed to move downstream is to simulate, on a daily basis, the hydrologic conditions in all reaches of the river downstream of the Highland Lakes. Five river sections are considered, based upon the location of streamflow gaging stations. Figure 2 indicates the location of streamgages and water diversion demands used in the routing. The maximum flow travel time from Mansfield Dam to Bay City is about eight days during the irrigation season. Any channel losses, lateral inflows, or water diversions are considered at the junction points between reaches, as shown in Figure 2.

The outflow (O) of each river reach on day t is represented as a linear combination of the daily inflows (I) to the reach on the current or preceding days. A example daily outflow equation is

$$O_t = a_1 * I_{t-1} + a_2 * I_{t-2} \dots \dots \dots \dots \dots \dots \dots \dots \dots [1]$$

where a_1 and a_2 are coefficients which vary between reaches. The values of the coefficients were developed by LCRA staff using the QFIT-I computer program (Martin, 1986).

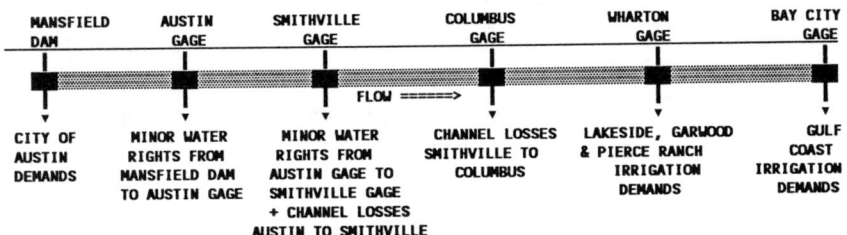

Figure 2. Location of Diversion Points

Flow Routing Optimization Problem

The problem of determining required pass through of daily reservoir inflows is to find the minimum reservoir releases that satisfy, to the maximum extent possible, the water demands of senior water rights holders adjusted for diversion of all inflows to the Colorado River below the Highland Lakes, while satisfying the following constraints:

- The movement of water downstream in the lower Colorado River is governed by a linear flow routing equation on each river section.

- The daily reservoir release cannot exceed the corresponding daily reservoir inflow.

- Flow is conserved at all stream junctions.

- The maximum daily demands of downstream senior water rights holders.

- Upstream channel flow losses must be satisfied fully

ESTIMATING LAKE INFLOWS 471

before any downstream water rights diversion deficits can be satisfied.

- All river flows and diversions are nonnegative.

Linear Programming Technique

The daily flow release problem can be solved approximately as a sequence of minimum daily releases problems with a parametrically varying penalty cost associated with all flows spilled from the Colorado River into the Gulf of Mexico. Each minimum release problem is formulated as a Linear Programming (LP) problem. LP is a mathematical solution technique for maximizing a linear function while satisfying a set of linear equality or inequality constraints (Taha, 1971).

The LP formulation for the daily reservoir release problem is given as finding the value of the reservoir release in day t which maximizes, over days t through t+7, the total water demands meet plus the total channel losses minus a penalty cost for water passing the Bay City gage. The solution must satisfy all constraints noted above for all eight days. After solving the LP for a given day, the LP is formulated and solve for the next day. This continues until all the days in the given simulation period have been considered.

The spill penalty cost is given by α times the total flow past Bay City in the eight days, where α is a constant coefficient. The penalty factor is needed to keep from releasing more water than is absolutely necessary to meet the downstream demands. By varying the value of α parametrically, it is possible to assess the tradeoffs between increasing the inflows available for storage and shortages that occur at the downstream water rights.

Simulation Results

The solution process described above was used to determine the inflows needed to be passed to downstream water rights holders on a daily basis for the 25 year simulation period 1941 through 1965, inclusive. Table 1 gives a summary of the inflows, demands, channel losses, and spills for the period using a variety of spill penalty values.

As would be expected, as the penalty value increases, there is a decrease in the water spilled past Bay City. However, as the spill penalty increases, the downstream water diversions do not drop proportionally. They remain essentially constant. Thus, the additional water available for storage is actually water that would otherwise spill from the Colorado River Basin.

An α value of 2.0 was selected as a reasonable penalty for spilling water past Bay City without unduly reducing the inflows released and actually diverted for downstream senior water right holders. The reservoir inflows calculated as available for storage were then used to estimate a combined firm yield of the Highland Lakes.

Table 1. Summary of Simulation Results

CATEGORY	SIMULATED TOTAL VOLUMES FOR PERIOD 1941-1965 (1,000,000 ACRE-FEET)					
	SPILL PENALTY COEFFICIENT (α)					
	.00	.10	.40	1.0	2.0	3.0
RESERVOIR INFLOW	24.445	24.445	24.445	24.445	24.445	24.445
WATER DIVERSION DEMANDS	13.012	13.012	13.012	13.012	13.012	13.012
CHANNEL LOSSES MET	.121	.121	.119	.119	.119	.105
DIVERSION DEMANDS MET FROM PASS THROUGH RESERVOIR INFLOWS	4.631	4.615	4.591	4.553	4.466	4.440
FLOW PAST BAY CITY RESULTING FROM PASS THROUGH OF INFLOWS	4.524	1.723	.670	.458	.127	.075
TOTAL PASS THROUGH OF RESERVOIR INFLOWS	9.276	6.459	5.380	5.131	4.712	4.621
INFLOW AVAILABLE FOR STORAGE	15.169	17.986	19.065	19.314	19.733	19.824

Appendix: References

1. Lower Colorado River Authority (1989). Water Management Plan for the Lower Colorado River -Volumes I and II, Austin, Texas.

2. Martin, Q. W. (1986). "Surface-Water Resources Optimal Daily Operation Model: MONITOR-I, Appendix B," Report UM-49, Texas Water Development Board, Austin, Texas.

3. Taha, H. A. (1971). Operations Research: An Introduction, The MacMillan Company, New York.

RESERVOIR REEVALUATION IN TVA

Jack L. Davis, Member ASCE[1]

Abstract

Demands for the use of dams and reservoirs tend to change after the projects are completed. The Tennessee Valley Authority (TVA) works with State and local groups to try to increase the range and magnitude of benefits without adversely impacting the purposes for which they were built. This is achieved by modifying operations and adding additional features as appropriate.

Introduction

TVA is interested in increasing the benefits that can be realized from the multiple-purpose system of dams and reservoirs managed by the agency. Certain projects are in progress in cooperation with two states and two local groups that are attempting to increase benefits without adversely affecting project purposes. These investigations are being conducted under current policies and procedures and are briefly described in the following material.[2]

Cooperative Effort with Tennessee

In 1988, TVA and the State of Tennessee agreed on a phased approach to improving water quality and water flow immediately downstream of TVA dams. In addition, the formulation and implementation of effective non-point source control measures were recognized as a crucial component of a comprehensive reservoir and tailwater management strategy. Under this agreement TVA would incorporate into this effort work already underway to improve conditions below selected dams.

Dissolved Oxygen: A principal component of each tailwater improvement scheme is an increase in the dissolved oxygen content of released water. Increases in dissolved oxygen will be achieved through use of turbine venting devices and devices designed to aerate the water in the reservoir before it enters the turbine. Oxygen injection will be added incrementally where aeration devices do not achieve desired levels of improvement.

---

[1]Manager, Navigation and System Modification, TVA, Evans Building, Knoxville, Tennessee 37902

[2]Also in progress is a study entitled "Tennessee River and Reservoir System Operation and Planning Review," which is determining whether the operating priorities for TVA dams and reservoirs, set out in the TVA Act over 50 years ago, still make sense given all the changes that have taken place in our society over this period. The results of this study are expected to be available in 1990.

Minimum Flows: A certain amount of flow must be sustained continuously in the tailwater reaches to support aquatic life, make the river area more attractive, and provide for higher levels of recreational use. Minimum flows will be sustained by schemes that generally involve one or more of the following techniques: (1) turbine pulsing, (2) reregulating weirs, and (3) small hydro-power additions.

Active Projects

Norris Project: Hub baffles are installed each year on the hubs of both turbines. The baffles increase air flow from the existing turbine aeration systems over the full range of operations and thus increase the DO of the water being released downstream. A 400-foot long, 5-foot high reregulating dam has been built in the Clinch River about two miles below Norris Dam. This dam in combination with turbine pulses is being used to sustain a minimum flow in the Clinch River.

Tims Ford Project: A small hydropower addition has been installed for use in sustaining a minimum flow. The small unit operates whenever the larger unit is not operating which is about 75 percent of the time. One large and two small air compressors have been installed to aerate releases from the turbines.

Douglas Project: Three surface water pumps and an oxygen injection system have been installed just upstream of unit 4 to increase the amount of dissolved oxygen in the releases during the low DO season. A year round minimum flow is being sustained in the downstream reaches by turbine pulsing.

Cherokee Project: A year round minimum flow is being sustained in the downstream reaches by turbine pulsing.

Tellico Project: Cold water is released from the project to help provide a refuge for stripped bass. Normally all flows coming down the reservoir are routed through a canal into Fort Loudoun Reservoir and then passed on downstream. A syphon discharges cool water onto one of the ogee sections of the spillway. The flow ducks under the tailwater surface water because of its greater density, travels downstream and backs up behind an underwater barrier dam constructed near the mouth of the river. The refuge consists of the deeper cool water behind the barrier dam.

South Holston Project: Work has been initiated to develop an alternative scheme to sustain a minimum flow in the river below South Holston Dam. An agreement has been reached with the City of Bristol, Tennessee to use $500,000 in funds remaining from a project to expand water lines on this minimum flow scheme as it will increase the amount of water that will be available to the city.

Recreational Floating: Flows selected to provide desirable conditions for recreation floating are being released from five TVA dams during the summer. The releases are provided for six hours on one weekend day each month for the months of June, July, and August. The flows are guaranteed barring certain emergencies and enable floaters to make plans well in advance with assurance that adequate water will be available.

Cooperative Study with North Carolina

In 1986, staff from the North Carolina Department of Natural Resources and Community Development contacted TVA staff for assistance in developing State capability to assess the impacts of potential operational changes in the TVA reservoir system. Over the years the State has received inquiries concerning the desire for higher pool levels for the reservoirs in western North Carolina. Previously they have essentially used answers provided by TVA to respond to these requests. The State was not taking issue with the

TVA answers, but at this time the State felt that a State appraisal of alternatives was needed to be fully responsive to their citizens.

TVA has provided the State with its Weekly Scheduling Model (Model) which is used both in planning and operating the reservoir system. The Model can be used to assess proposed changes on the entire system which enable estimates of impacts to project purposes to be evaluated including those accruing to navigation, flood control, and power.

North Carolina and TVA are both contracting with the U.S. Forest Service to provide confirmation of recreation benefits that will accrue with alternative operational schemes. Essentially the work is set up to have the collection of data in the field funded by North Carolina and analysis of the data funded by TVA. Visitation surveys were conducted during the summers of 1988 and 1989. The final report, including analysis of the data, is scheduled for completion in 1990.

In 1989, North Carolina requested TVA's review of a draft report containing reservoir management alternatives for the Chatuge, Fontana, and Hiwassee projects. Recreational zones were developed for these reservoirs to define an upper and lower lake level for the recreation reason. For these alternatives the recreation season extends from Memorial Day through Labor Day. It is expected that the final report will be published once the U.S. Forest Service completes its analysis of the recreation benefits.

Belgreen Bassmasters Club

In December 1986, the Belgreen Bassmasters Club requested that TVA provide more moderate water level fluctuations for the Little Bear Creek and Cedar Creek Units of the Bear Creek Project. A scheme was identified that would enhance recreational pool levels at a favorable benefit cost ratio. A two year introductory implementation period which concludes on September 30, 1990 is being used as a final test of feasibility before the change becomes permanent. The proposed changes would delay the initiation of the fall drawdown and raise the normal minimum pool levels.

Blairsville, Georgia

The town of Blairsville, Georgia is located near the upper end of Nottely Reservoir. In the winter when the reservoir is drawn to recover flood storage, there is little or no water in the reservoir opposite the town. The community leaders believe that this condition is having a detrimental impact on the area's capability to attract year round residents as well as second home developments. In cooperation with local representatives TVA is identifying and evaluating alternatives directed at enhancing winter pool levels to include possible construction of a collapsible dam in the upper end of the reservoir.

Comparison between the Field and Laboratory
Measured Properties of a Clay Liner

Andrew S. Rogowski[1]

Abstract

Hydraulic conductivity (K) and bulk density (BD) of an experimental clay liner were evaluated at a large number of locations using standard methods. They were then compared to laboratory values obtained on cores removed from the same locations. Although there was little difference among the means of different methods, all showed much variability. Even though the largest K measured was less than 0.1m/day, breakthrough was observed at numerous locations 2 days after ponding a 0.3m thick liner.

Introduction

A study was begun in 1983 (Rogowski, 1990) to characterize the areal variation in hydraulic conductivity of a compacted clay liner. A field-scale research facility was constructed and clay soil was compacted in three lifts to specifications commonly used in constructing clay liners. The facility was instrumented to measure infiltration, drainage, and soil properties at 250 data collection points. Preliminary studies were initiated using sections of small barrels and larger caissons to verify the performance of monitoring systems. Results from these prototype studies showed that any perforations of the compacted soil may result in preferential water movement by gravity down the walls of these perforations. To avoid this situation in the field-scale facility, access tubes were placed horizontally

---

[1]Soil Scientist, U.S. Department of Agriculture, ARS, Northeast Watershed Research Center, 110 Research Building A, University Park, PA 16802. This work was in part supported by the U.S. EPA through Interagency Agreement DW12930303-01-0 with USDA.

to accommodate the nuclear probes used to measure changes in clay density and porosity. Underdrains were embedded in the concrete support structure to collect outflow, infiltration cylinders were installed at the surface to monitor infiltration, and metal pedestals were placed on the clay to assess swelling by measuring elevation changes. Quality control observations during the construction showed that on the average water content and density of the compacted clay were close to the design specifications, but spatial variability in these values was large. Measured infiltration rates and outflow rates obtained following ponding the field-scale facility were poorly predicted by the prototype data. Initial data showed rapid breakthrough of percolate near the confining walls, a feature that was also observed earlier in prototype studies.

Field Scale Studies

Based on the design and preliminary studies a field scale facility was constructed and a 0.3m thick clay liner was installed. After the site was instrumented, inflow, outflow, evaporation, changes in density, and changes in surface elevation were continuously monitored for a year. Figure 1 shows the field scale facility which consisted of an elevated bridge-like platform supported by reinforced concrete beams which rested on compacted level subgrade. This arrangement allowed a crawl space under the platform for collection of percolate which passed through the liner. A 0.9 x 0.9m grid of collection drains was complemented by a similar grid of 0.3m diameter buffered infiltration rings at the surface.

Embedded in the floor of the platform, horizontally across the facility were the lower of the 24 access tubes to measure density using a dual gamma probe, their tops protruding 0.06m above the level of the floor. Positioned on top of the clay and situated exactly 0.3m above the lower ones were the upper access tubes. The attenuation measurements were made with a gamma source (Cs^{137}) in the lower tube and the detector in the upper tube.

Figure 2 shows measuring grids used in the study. Their origin (0,0) was in the southwest corner of the platform shown in Figure 1. After the liner was compacted the facility was covered with a building, and heat and light systems were installed. To account for evaporation from infiltration rings, 35 small evaporation pans, same size as the rings, were installed (Figure 2c) in addition to one large class A evaporation pan used to correct for evaporation from water ponded on

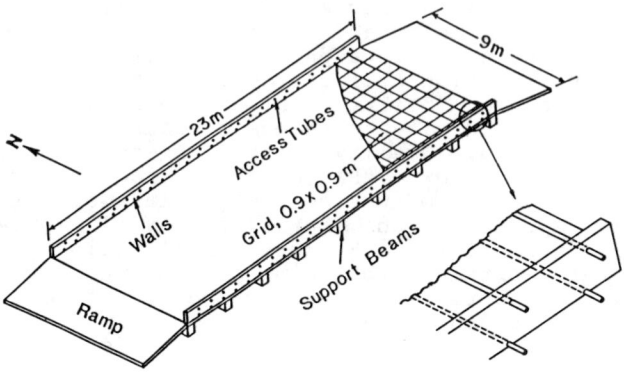

Figure 1. Clay Liner Testing Facility.

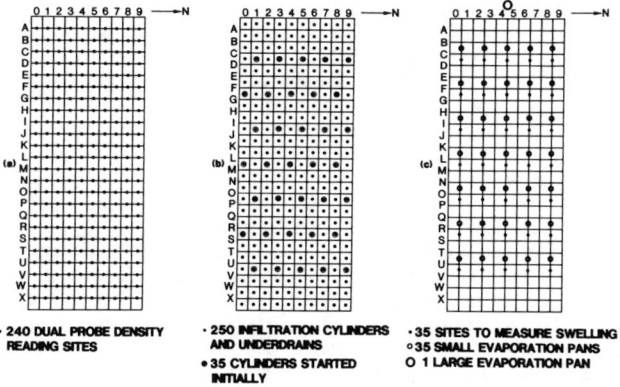

Figure 2. Experimental measuring grid for (a) bulk density, (b) infiltration and drainage, (c) swelling and evaporation.

the liner surface. In addition, 35 metal pedestals and a wooden walkway supported by access tubes were placed on the clay surface (Figure 2c) to monitor swelling, to keep access tubes from being forced up, and to provide access to instrumentation.

Methods and Materials

The field methods of hydraulic conductivity assessment included ring infiltrometer studies and outflow monitoring of the ponded liner. Bulk density and water content were measured first during construction with a nuclear surface probe on top of each lift, and subsequently, with dual gamma probe during ponding. Following ponding, density was evaluated using depth density probe, sand cone, and excavation of different diameter holes. Specific gravity and coarse fragment content of the clay material were also determined. Laboratory measurement of hydraulic conductivity was performed using flexible wall permeameter. The cores used for the measurement of hydraulic conductivity were subsequently coated with wax and their density was determined by immersion.

Results

Flux values, computed from observed infiltration and outflow measurements were compared to effective flux values based on breakthrough time distributions for water and tracer over the same area. Results suggested that both water and tracer move at similar rates, but considerably faster than expected on the basis of outflow flux alone, and that only a small fraction of the total pore space is involved in active transport. The ramifications of these findings were explored against the background of effective porosity, degree of compaction, and observed changes in bulk density with time.

The experimental clay liner was ponded for 1 year. During that time inflow, outflow, and changes in density were routinely monitored. Results suggested that initial increase and final leveling off of the density values could be associated with water passing into the clay matrix and attainment of the steady state. Observed increases in density initially were accompanied by increases in outflow which subsequently declined and leveled off at twelve months. Tracer breakthrough times were consistently faster than water flow rates, although initial water breakthrough times following ponding were similar to tracer breakthrough times. Results suggest that water and solutes move in the clay through only a small portion of total porosity.

Statistics for the hydraulic conductivity and bulk density are given in Table 1. Results show that mean values of hydraulic conductivity determined by several methods were quite similar though somewhat lower than mean laboratory values, and that average bulk density as determined by the dual probe method was larger than values obtained by other means.

Despite the statistics in Table 1 hydraulic conductivity distribution based on laboratory measurements underestimated field measured hydraulic conductivity distribution by a factor of five and comparisons of individual values at the same location could differ by several orders of magnitude. It was found that the distribution of water content and density in the compacted clay was adequately described by core samples and nuclear surface moisture-density probe data. However, such water content and density data appeared to have little relationship to average values of spatially distributed hydraulic conductivity.

The large bridge-like platform facility and a compacted clay liner provided satisfactory data about the performance of clay liners and relationship of field

TABLE 1.--Selected statistics for inflow flux, outflow flux, hydraulic conductivity, and bulk density.

Variable	N	Mean	Std Dev	Min	Max	W[1]
		($\times 10^{-9}$ m/s)				
Q_{inflow}	184	21/6[2]	40/5	0.09	235	0.54/0.98
$Q_{outflow}$	184	24/8	31/6	0.04	164	0.74/0.95
K_{inflow}	144	20/6	35/6	0.08	188	0.58/0.97
$K_{outflow}$	184	19/7	24/6	0.00	129	0.75/0.94
K_{lab}	162	29/4	121/4	0.45	973	0.24/0.87
		(Mg/m^3)				
BD_{avg}	250	2.18	0.07	1.94	2.37	0.97
BD_{wax}	181	1.98	0.08	1.73	2.57	0.82
$BD_{s. cone}$	59	1.84	0.12	1.45	2.10	0.96
$BD_{lift\ 1}$	39	1.95	0.62	1.84	2.07	0.96
$BD_{lift\ 2}$	39	1.99	0.77	1.78	2.11	0.96
$BD_{lift\ 3}$	39	1.96	0.50	1.82	2.05	0.97

[1]Shapiro-Wilk W statistic.

[2]Untransformed/Log$_{10}$ transformed.

hydraulic conductivity to lab values. In the course of
analysis the soil was found to contain a larger than
expected number of coarse fragments. However, no evidence was found of preferential layering, or preferential distribution of these rock fragments either because
of natural tendencies or mechanized compaction of the
three lifts.

The considerable variability observed in the spatially distributed infiltration and outflow may have
been affected by the presence of preferential pathways
of leachate flow through the clay liner. Higher flow
rates which originated in apparently unsaturated areas
suggested the presence of the preferential flow pathways.
Such pathways potentially pose a grave threat to underlying ground water quality even in the presence of a
clay liner.

There was no correlation between laboratory and
field derived values of hydraulic conductivity on the
point to point basis when values from the same locations
were compared. However, when the distribution of laboratory values was compared with the distribution of field
values the results appeared to be linearly correlated.
Laboratory hydraulic conductivity values were not a good
indicator of the clay liner behavior. Ring
infiltrometers, despite problems, appeared to provide
better estimates of potential outflow from below the
compacted clay. Best estimates of clay liner performance were obtained by following a conservative tracer
movement, and breakthrough history.

There was little change in clay liner density with
time suggesting a very limited movement of water into
the clay matrix. Initial change, however, just after
flooding could be indicative of the extent of
macroporosity. A surface moisture-density probe was
found to be a quick and satisfactory method of
determining field distribution of moisture and density
for individual lifts during construction. There
appeared to be no relationship between density and water
content of the clay and the observed values of hydraulic
conductivity. The flow regime, as perceived by changes
in density, consisted of concurrent alternating, filling
and draining episodes distributed in space.

Appendix 1.--References

1. Rogowski, A. S. 1990. Relationship between the
   Field and Laboratory Measured Hydraulic
   Conductivity. Final Report to the U.S. EPA,
   Cincinnati, Ohio.

Measuring Performance of Clay Containment
Barriers

Walter E. Grube, Jr.[1]

Abstract

Clayey soils compacted to engineering specifications are widely used as structures for hydraulic containment. Current applications include landfill liners, landfill covers, pond liners, and containment dikes; groundwater control using slurry trench cut-off walls is a closely related application. Regulatory requirements for performance specify low permeability. Compatibility is most commonly measured by noting changes in laboratory hydraulic conductivity during permeation by selected liquids. Research has provided reliable methods to evaluate the performance of compacted soil liners. Hydraulic performance evaluation of barrier dikes and groundwater cut-off walls is more complex than with broad expanses of relatively flat compacted soils.

Introduction

Laboratory characterization of liner candidate soil materials follows standard engineering criteria and ASTM methods, but includes permeability measurement. Grube, et al, 1987, have summarized and interpreted a large volume of published soil liner permeability research. Bowders, et al, 1986, offer a decision tree approach to liner/leachate compatibility testing, with a discussion of the factors which influence the results of various permeability test methods, and other important measures such as solubility, adsorption, and ion exchange. Daniel, 1989, has summarized methods available for measuring the hydraulic conductivity in-situ, in the field.

----
[1]Soil Scientist, Office of Research and Development, U. S. Environmental Protection Agency, Cincinnati, Ohio 45268

The Universe of Clay Containment Barriers

The U. S. Environmental Protection Agency has issued a Minimum Technology Guidance (USEPA, 1985a) which describes design, construction, and performance testing of liner systems underlying hazardous waste disposal facilities. Recommendations for soil liners, with minor modifications, form the basis for Agency approval of compacted soils in landfill covers, municipal solid waste landfills, and other similar applications.

Landfill liners---

Current regulations require that the compacted soil be part of a liner system which includes a flexible membrane liner (FML) of very low permeability overlying the compacted soil. The flexible membrane is designed, constructed, and tested independently of the soil liner component of the system.

Agency guidance specifies that a soil liner test section be constructed separately from the waste disposal facility, and that this test section be tested for hydraulic properties. The test section should be built using full scale equipment, of the same type and using the same soil material that is proposed for the full-scale waste management facility. The hydraulic conductivity of the test section is measured using an approved field method, such as described by Daniel, 1989. Additional measurements and characterization can be applied to provide supportive data, e.g. see Albrecht, et al, 1989.

Impoundment liners---

Surface impoundments of industrial process wastes, tailings from mineral processing, sludges and other waste waters require the same multi-component liner systems as do "dry material" landfills; with particular designs appropriate to the degree of hazard or toxicity of the impounded materials.

Particular attention needs to be placed on the results from liner/leachate compatibility tests. This is essential because a reservoir of liquids is ready to penetrate the compacted soil if failure occurs in an overlying leachate collection system and FML. Industrial process waters or saturation extracts of sludges or tailings should be used in compatibility testing. In addition, long-term exposure data should be obtained to verify that no unforseen geochemical interactions degrade the compacted soil liner material.

Clay caps---

The USEPA has developed a Technical Guidance Document which describes design, construction, and performance monitoring of cover systems for hazardous waste landfills (USEPA, 1989). The guidelines in this document can be modified for covers on waste facilities containing less hazardous materials. USEPA, 1985b, describes many details of cover designs to be applied at closure of remedial action sites under the Superfund program.

Several aspects of compacted clay layer performance in a cover need emphasis. The compacted soil may be constructed on a foundation designed to function as a gas venting layer; this may be porous soil or a geosynthetic filter material. The structural integrity of this type of foundation must be assured. The compacted soil in a cover must not be intruded upon by roots of plants seeking moisture for survival. The compacted soil layer in a cover is often the first structure where cost savings are sought by reducing the thickness of this layer. "Equivalent materials" or soil additives or amendments are frequently suggested as replacement for part or all of the soil barrier component of a cover system.

Industrial dikes---

Numerous commercial companies and industrial plants are required by federal, state, or local regulations to surround bulk storage tanks with earthen dikes adequate to contain any spillage from damaged tanks. These sites may contain crude petroleum, refinery products, motor oils, motor fuels, aviation oil and fuels, industrial solvents, agricultural pest control chemicals, agricultural fertilizers, and a variety of other liquids in very large volumes at one location. Design, construction, and containment performance criteria for these structures are primarily made on a case-by-case basis.

Slurry walls---

Backfill materials placed in slurry-trench cut-off walls to control groundwater commonly are composed of a mixture of soil materials. Bentonite clay is usually added to both contribute fines and form a filter cake on the trench sidewalls. Portland cement is included in some wall designs where structural integrity is needed. Some of the newest groundwater barrier designs included vertical sections of FML materials. Standard construction specifications used for site dewatering applications are usually the basis for contracts involving pollution control service; however worker safety standards are more stringent.

Clay amendments---

Where the properties of native borrow soils are judged unsuitable for construction of soil-based barriers, addition of small percentage amounts of commercially available clay minerals is practiced. The sodium-form of bentonite clay occupies by far the largest portion of the marketplace for clay amendments to lower soil permeability. There are no widely recognized standards for determining the mixing homogeneity obtained when incorporating clay additives into a borrow soil. Sampling techniques, sample sizes, sample numbers, areal and/or volume distribution of samples, and clay assay procedures are specified by site-specific design engineers.

Amended soils that are compacted to soil barrier engineering specifications can be expected to perform similarly to unamended native soils with similar physical and chemical properties. Therefore no unique testing methods are specifically recommended for measuring permeability of soils containing clay additives. Where the application, such as impoundment for chemical processing wastewaters, demands evaluation of the leachate/liner compatibility, care needs to be exercised in conduct of compatibility tests and data interpretation. It is well known to physical chemists that sodium-bentonite is quite chemically active. It exchanges the sodium for any multi-valent cation available in water films surrounding the clay mineral. It also may adsorb selected organic compounds. These reactions change the expansive character of sodium bentonite minerals, nearly always leading to reduced effective volume and physical shrinkage of the macroscopic soil mass containing the bentonite.

Measures of Performance

Hydraulic conductivity is the primary measure of performance of soils compacted for service as liners for waste landfills and surface impoundments. Legislation in the U.S. and other countries requires a hydraulic conductivity of less than 1×10^{-9} m/s for soil-based hazardous waste landfill liners. Laboratory permeability measurements are essential to document (1) the engineering suitability of a candidate liner soil material and (2) that incompatibilities of leachate and soil do not lead to future degradation of the compacted soil barrier. Numerous data confirm that the type of laboratory test apparatus does not significantly affect the value for compacted soil permeability when the permeant liquid is water alone. The modified compaction mold is the most sensitive geotechnical laboratory method to detect changes in hydraulic flow as an indicator of liner/leachate compatibility.

Measurement of hydraulic conductivity of a compacted soil test section, in the field, is recommended to demonstrate that design and construction techniques are adequate to meet regulatory requirements. Research has shown that preferential flow pathways, resulting in very low values of effective porosity, are features of serious concern in compacted soil barriers. This characteristic mandates the use of flow measurement systems that evaluate as large a compacted soil mass as possible, within practical limits. Large-area, carefully designed and operated, infiltration monitoring devices have been shown to provide reliable flow data in test sections of compacted soil liners and covers. Collection of seepage from a liner has been documented both experimentally (Rogowski, 1988) and in routine practice (Kmet and Lindorff, 1983). As recognized by many authors, seepage collection should require a very long time if the compacted soil is a tight as required, therefore relegating the pragmatic utility of this approach to long-term monitoring. Sample size, statistical array of sampling sites, acceptable levels of variance among replicate samples and analyses, and other areas of statistical data treatment are not yet well defined for containment barrier performance characterization.

Standardized methods to measure the performance of compacted soils in resisting penetration of aggressive plant roots are not available. Likewise, routine procedures for evaluating the hydraulic barrier equivalency of soil additives and amendments have not been developed nor accepted by regulatory agencies. The adequacy of soil barrier performance in arid climates where net infiltration of precipitation is absent has not been well documented in published reports. Data which document the experience with soil-based containment structures in dry climates rests largely with a few state agencies and private design engineering firms.

Means to test the hydraulic containment of a compacted soil dike only a few meters in height and width have not been published. Traditional construction techniques of soil compaction can be expected to result in leaky dikes when roadbase contractors routinely but falsely assume that structural test results demonstrate the hydraulic competence of their products. Performance testing of completed structures has not been rigorously practiced because of the short time that these structures are expected to be exposed to liquids from spill episodes. Field testing of sloping surfaces built to possess very low permeability is a problem that has not been addressed by credible research or practice. Questions regarding the as-constructed hydraulic integrity of soils compacted on slopes as steep as 4:1 to 2:1 remain also because of the increased difficulty of adequate compaction on slopes.

The permeability of a slurry wall backfill soil mixture is normally measured in laboratory tests using a triaxial cell permeability apparatus. Regulatory agencies accept laboratory hydraulic conductivity values which fall below 1 x 10 E-09 m/sec. Several authors have described application of routine triaxial cell permeability testing to backfill soil mixtures.

Compatibility of the groundwater and cut-off wall backfill is considered an integral part of backfill design. It is important to test the backfill for compatibility not only with site groundwater, but also with "NAPL", the non-aqueous phase liquid which may be floating upon the piezometric surface or resting in pockets on the aquitard underlying the pervious geologic formation.

Cut-off wall designs can be hydraulically tested by construction of a "slurry wall test cell" prior to implementing a full-scale project contract. Typically, a barrier several tens of feet deep, or down to a suitable aquitard, and perhaps 50-feet square is constructed using design equipment and backfill formula. Data from pumpdown tests on wells within the confined area are applied to calculate the permeability of the total barrier wall area. A few cut-off wall installations are known to contain an array of monitoring wells on each side of the wall, where drawdown or slug test data are used to calculate wall permeability. There are no known standardized or Agency-approved procedures for handling these well data. Routine hydrologic models are applied by geohydrologists, and where data show an acceptably low permeability, they are usually accepted by clients and agencies.

References

Albrecht, K. A., B. L. Herzog, L. R. Follmer, I. G. Krapac, R. A. Griffin, and K. Cartwright. 1989. Excavation of an Instrumented Earthen Liner: Inspection of Dyed Flow Paths and Morphology. Haz. Waste and Haz. Mat., Vol. 6, No. 3, pp. 269 - 279.

Bowders, J. J., D. E. Daniel, G. P. Broderick, and H. M. Liljestrand. 1986. Methods for Testing the Compatibility of Clay Liners with Landfill Leachate. in Hazardous and Industrial Solid Waste Testing: Fourth Symposium, ASTM STP 886, J. K. Petros,Jr., W. J. Lacy, and R. A Conway, Eds. American Society for Testing and Materials, Philadelphia, PA pp. 233-250.

Bureau of Reclamation. 1974. Design of Small Dams. USGPO, Washington, DC. 816 pp.

Daniel, D. E. 1989. In Situ Hydraulic Conductivity Tests for Compacted Clay. J. Geotech. Eng. ASCE, Vol. 115, No. 9, 1205 -1226.

Grube, W. E., Jr., M. H. Roulier and J. G. Herrmann. 1987. Implications of Current Soil Liner Permeability Research Results. in Proc. Thirteenth Annual Research Symp. on Land Disposal, Remedial Action, Incineration and Treatment of Hazardous Waste, EPA/600/9-87/015, NTIS No. PB 87-233151/A, pp.9 - 25.

Hammer, D. P. and E. D. Blackburn. 1977. Design and Construction of Retaining Dikes for Containment of Dredged Material. USACE, WES, Technical Report D-77-9.

Kmet, P and D. E. Lindorff. 1983. Use of Collection Lysimeters in Monitoring Sanitary Landfill Performance. presented at Nat'l Water Well Ass'n Conf. on Characterization and Monitoring of the Vadose(Unsaturated) Zone, Las Vegas, NV. December, 19pp.

Rogowski, A. S. 1988. Flux Density and Breakthrough Times for Water and tracer in a Spatially Variable, Compacted Clay Soil. J. Contam. Hydrol., 3:327-348.

USEPA. 1985a. Draft Minimum Technology Guidance on Single Liner Systems for Landfills, Surface Impoundments, and Waste Piles--Design, Construction, and Operation, EPA/530-SW-85-013 (see also companion document EPA/530-SW-85-014). Office of solid waste, USEPA, Washington, DC 20460.

USEPA. 1985b. Covers for Uncontrolled Hazardous Waste Sites, EPA-540/2-85-002, NTIS No. PB 87-119483. USEPA, Cincinnati, Ohio 45268.

USEPA. 1989. Technical Guidance Document: Final covers on Hazardous Waste Landfills and Surface Impoundments, EPA/530-SW-89-047. USEPA, Cincinnati, Ohio 45268, 39 pp.

A Rational Basis for Determining Safety of Containment

David E. Daniel[1]

Abstract

Design of waste containment facilities may follow one of three tacts: (1) the liner and cover systems may have prescribed components of predetermined minimum thicknesses and hydraulic properties; (2) the liner may be sized to prevent release of any chemical constituents within a set time; and (3) the system may be designed to prevent chemical concentrations in groundwater from exceeding established limits. The third alternative has the most rational basis and is a goal for which engineers should be striving.

Introduction

Containment of buried waste is accomplished with liner and cover systems that are designed to restrict infiltration of liquids into the waste and to minimize release of chemicals out of a disposal unit. For hazardous wastes, the U.S. EPA requires a double liner system consisting, as a minimum, of a flexible membrane liner (FML) for the primary liner and an FML-soil composite for the secondary liner (Fig. 1). Double composite liners are being used increasingly because of the added containment capability of a composite primary liner compared to an FML liner alone.

For municipal solid wastes, designs of liner and cover systems vary considerably. Figure 2 shows two recent designs. The design in Fig. 2A is for a landfill in South Dakota, where annual rainfall is only 350 mm (14 in). Water balances analyses indicate that no leachate will be produced after the cover is placed. The design in Fig. 2B is for a landfill in New York state, where annual rainfall exceeds 1200 mm (50 in). The two designs have different levels of sophistication, which is appropriate considering the differences in climate and geology.

A relevant question is: What shall be the basis for design of liner and cover systems for waste disposal units? In particular, what is a rational

---

[1] Associate Prof. of Civil Engineering, University of Texas, Austin, TX 78712

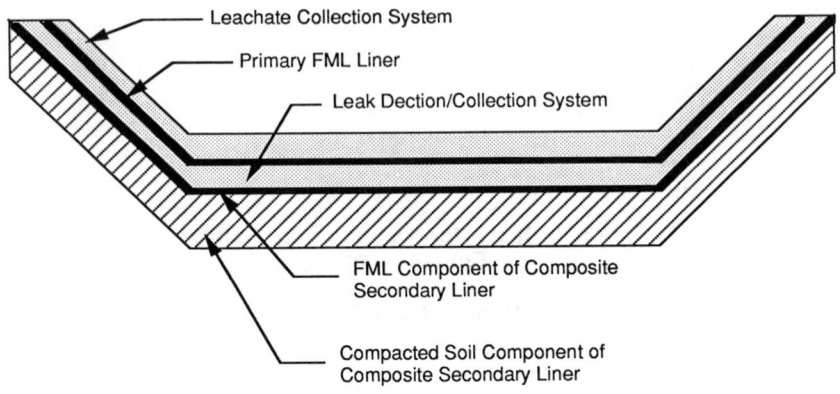

Figure 1. Double Liner System Required by EPA for Disposal of Hazardous Waste.

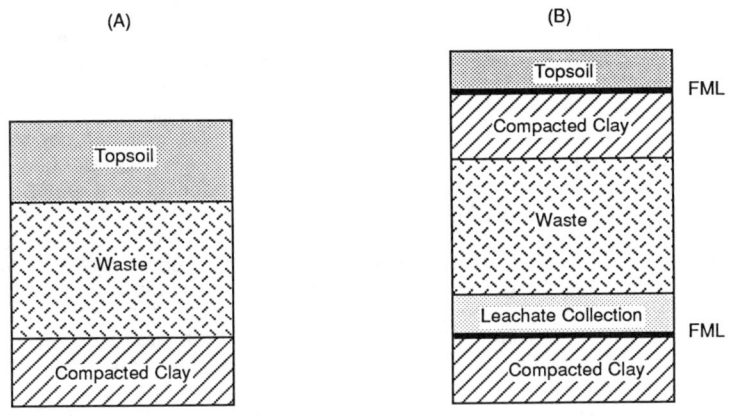

Figure 2. Landfill Liner and Cover Systems Recently Designed for Sites in (A) South Dakota and (B) New York State.

DETERMINING CONTAINMENT SAFETY 491

design framework to provide environmentally responsible and safe designs? The purpose of this paper is to explore these questions.

Three Design Approaches

Three approaches can be used for design of liner and cover systems:

1. The minimum thicknesses and hydraulic properties of required components of the liner and cover system can be prescribed with the assumption that the liner system will safely protect groundwater.

2. The liner can be designed to ensure containment of the waste within the liner system for a prescribed period, e.g., 30 years, under the assumption that very slow release of chemicals ensures adequate environmental control.

3. The design can be based upon a groundwater quality standard at a point of compliance, e.g., a down-gradient monitoring well at the property boundary.

Prescribed Liner System. The approach taken by the U.S. EPA for hazardous waste is to establish minimum requirements for a liner system (Fig. 1). This approach enjoys the advantages of simplicity in the regulatory process (the owner/operator and the regulatory authorities know precisely what is required) and ensures that a grossly inadequate design does not somehow slip through the regulatory process. On the negative side, this approach stifles innovation and ignores climatic and geologic factors that should be considered in the design process.

The critical question is: Does the prescribed design (Fig. 1) ensure that groundwater impact will be environmentally acceptable? This question has seldom been addressed quantitatively for long post-closure periods. There is a substantial body of data showing that FML's are often flawed by tiny holes, tears, or imperfect seams, and that organic chemicals can diffuse through intact FML's. Further, soils are inherently permeable and therefore are capable of allowing passage (although very slowly) of leachate. Thus, eventual release of chemicals from nearly all land disposal units is inevitable. Whether or not such release will occur is not the issue; the issue is whether there will be an adverse impact upon groundwater.

Some simple calculations may help to illustrate the situation. Assume a liner system such as shown in Fig. 1. Often, leak detection zones beneath primary FML liners collect and remove several tens liters per hectare per day of liquid. It is assumed, for the sake of this example, that the leak detection zone is successful in removing 99% of the liquid entering it. If the flow rate into the detection system is 50 L/ha/day (5 gallons/acre/day), then 1%, or 0.5 L/ha/day (0.05 g/a/day) leaks into the underlying composite liner. It is assumed that eventually the flux (V) into the aquifer reaches 0.5 L/ha/day, as shown in Fig. 3. If the landfill has a width (W) of 300 m (984 ft) and the flux of fresh water (F) in an underlying aquifer with a thickness (H) of 10 m is 20 m/yr (65 ft/year), then, by dilution, the concentration of a chemical (c) in the aquifer at the edge of the landfill, divided by the concentration (c_0) in the leachate, is 3×10^{-5}. For example, if the concentration of a chemical in the leachate is 1 mg/L, then the concentration in the aquifer at the edge of the landfill is 3×10^{-5} mg/L, or 0.03 μg/L. The key question is whether this concentration is acceptably low. Many assumptions were made in this illustrative example, e.g., no attenuation or degradation of chemicals in the leachate. Nevertheless, the example illustrates that if the concentration c_0 is high enough, c may reach a level of concern.

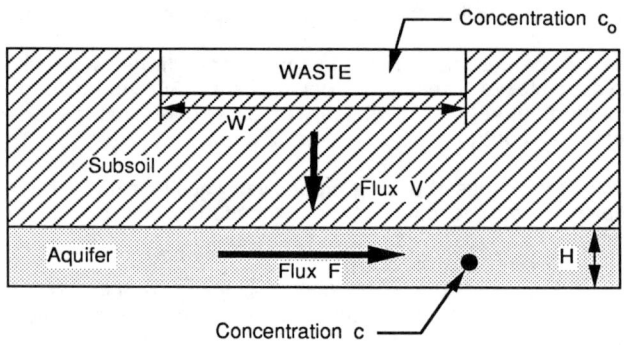

Figure 3. Example Analysis of Migration of Waste-Derived Chemicals to an Aquifer beneath a Waste-Disposal Facility.

<u>Containment for Set Period of Time</u>. The second approach is to design the liner system for no release of chemicals for a prescribed period of time, e.g., 30 years. This approach allows the designer more flexibility and, assuming the liner performs as designed, will provide environmentally safe landfills for at least some period.

Several problems diminish the tractability of this approach. First, prediction of travel times of chemicals is a difficult task that is fraught with uncertainties. Second, the time required for the first molecule of waste-derived material to pass through the liner is not environmentally relevant because dilution of that molecule will render it undetectable. Third, one can almost always envision a scenario in which the containment time for the first molecule of waste-derived material is relatively short, thus making rational design difficult or impossible. Finally, how does one select the design containment time? No matter what time is chosen, some are likely to argue that it should be larger; eventually, the design containment time could approach infinity, which creates an impossible design criterion.

<u>Water Quality Standard</u>. The third approach is to design cover and liner systems so that the expected concentrations of waste-derived chemicals in groundwater at some point of compliance, e.g., the property boundary, do not

exceed prescribed values based on water quality considerations. The water quality standard that should be applied might be based on drinking water standards, health risk considerations, or some other basis. Nevertheless, once such standards are established, the designer has a performance standard on which to base the design.

This approach has several advantages: it is logical, allows flexibility in design, and permits change as more knowledge is developed concerning health effects from water-born contaminants. On the negative side, detailed factual data and several assumptions are needed to calculate the probable concentration of chemicals in groundwater. The cost of design is much higher than with other methods (because of the information and analyses that are needed), and a much higher level of knowledge and expertise is required of the regulator who must evaluate the adequacy of the design. Finally, the water quality standards that should be applied are vague at this time due to lack of information concerning the health risks for some of the thousands of chemicals that might be found in landfill leachate.

The use of this approach is illustrated with the example in Fig. 3 and the parameters cited earlier for this case. It is assumed that the leachate contains 1 mg/L of some organic chemical (c_0). The maximum allowable concentration (c) in groundwater is assumed to be 0.1 µg/L. The earlier calculation showed for this example that the concentration in the aquifer was 0.03 µg/L at the edge of the landfill. The design is acceptable based on the assumed water quality standard. However, the analysis assumed that liquid was pumped from the leak detection system. Eventually, one can assume that pumping from this system will cease, but at the same time, the concentration of waste-derived chemicals in the leachate will probably decrease substantially, as well. The long-term case would also have to be considered. If the calculations had shown that the concentration in groundwater was unacceptably large, then additional engineering controls on the liner system, more exhaustive controls on the source material (waste), or a geohydrologically superior site might be needed.

Conclusions

Three approaches for design of liner systems have been discussed. The specification of a minimum liner system offers the simplest design methodology and is the easiest to regulate. However, this approach does not necessarily ensure that groundwater standards will be met in all cases. Design based on a minimum containment time suffers from several problems and is not recommended. Design of liner systems to meet a water quality standard at a point of compliance is the most logical approach because it is based on the need to ensure adequate protection of groundwater. Problems with this approach include lack of a consensus on acceptable concentrations of waste-derived chemicals in groundwater, a need for detailed data and analyses, and an increased level of sophistication required in regulatory review. The water-quality-based approach, while perhaps often intractable at present, is the approach for which designers and regulators should be striving.

Estimating Earthquake Hazard of Municipal Water Systems

Howard Hwang,[1] M., ASCE and Otto Helweg,[2] F., ASCE

ABSTRACT

Estimation of seismic hazards is the first essential task in performing the seismic risk assessment of a municipal water delivery system. This paper uses the City of Memphis as a case study to present the the seismic hazard evaluation of a municipal water delivery system. The horizontal peak bedrock accelerations resulting from large New Madrid earthquakes have been estimated and presented in contour maps. In addition, existing boring logs, collected from various sources, have been compiled and analyzed to establish the subsurface conditions for the entire Memphis area. The site response analysis and the evaluation of the liquefaction potential in Memphis and Shelby County have also been initiated. The results of the seismic hazard analysis will be used to evaluate the vulnerability of the water delivery systems due to a severe earthquake.

INTRODUCTION

The safe and serviceable operation of a water delivery system, immediately after a severe earthquake, is of crucial importance to the welfare of the general public. The seismic hazard estimation is the first essential task to be performed in order to evaluate the vulnerability of water delivery systems, to assess the economic loss and societal impact and to prepare an emergency response plan. A municipal water delivery system is very complex consisting of intersecting pipelines, storage facilities, pumping stations, treatment plants, wells and electrical equipment. The

---

[1] Associate Research Professor, Center for Earthquake Research and Information, Memphis State University, Memphis, TN 38152

[2] Professor and Chair, Department of Civil Engineering, Memphis State University, Memphis, TN 38152

system reaches almost every corner within the city boundaries. Thus, the seismic hazard estimate is not just for a site. It is necessary to cover a large area. This paper uses the City of Memphis as a case study to present the seismic hazard estimation of a municipal water delivery system.

BEDROCK MOTION MODEL

Memphis and Shelby County are geographically close to the southern segment of the New Madrid seismic zone (NMSZ) as shown in Figure 1. The NMSZ is regarded by seismologists and earthquake engineers as the most hazardous zone in the eastern United States.

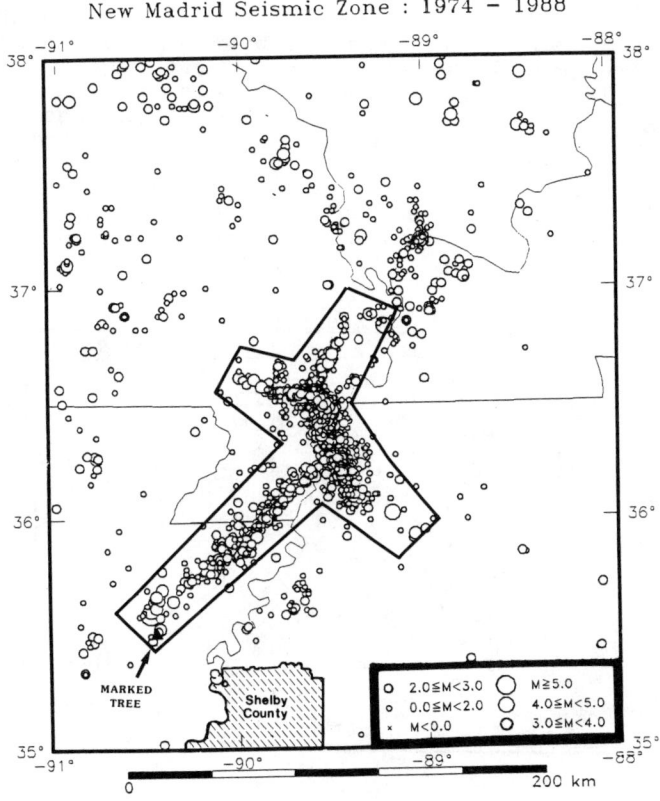

Figure 1   New Madrid Seismic Zone

In this study, a seismologically-based stochastic model is utilized to describe the horizontal bedrock motions primarily due to shear waves generated from a seismic source. This stochastic model is centered on a power spectral density function (power spectrum) which is developed from a seismologically-based Fourier amplitude spectrum. From the power spectrum, earthquake time histories and probability-based response spectra can be generated directly. Based on the extreme value distribution of a random process, the power spectrum can also be used to estimate the peak earthquake accelerations. Detail of the seismologically-based stochastic model is shown in Hwang et al. (1989b).

CONTOUR MAPS OF HORIZONTAL PEAK ACCELERATION

The peak values of the horizontal bedrock accelerations in Memphis and Shelby County are computed for two New Madrid earthquakes of moment magnitudes 7.5 and 6.5. Two different cases of seismic sources are considered: (1) a single source at Marked Tree, Arkansas, and (2) the southern segment of the NMSZ. The results are presented in contour maps (Hwang et al. 1989b). For example, if an earthquake of moment magnitude 7.5 occurs at Marked Tree, Arkansas (see Figure 1), the contour map of the mean peak acceleration is shown in Figure 2.

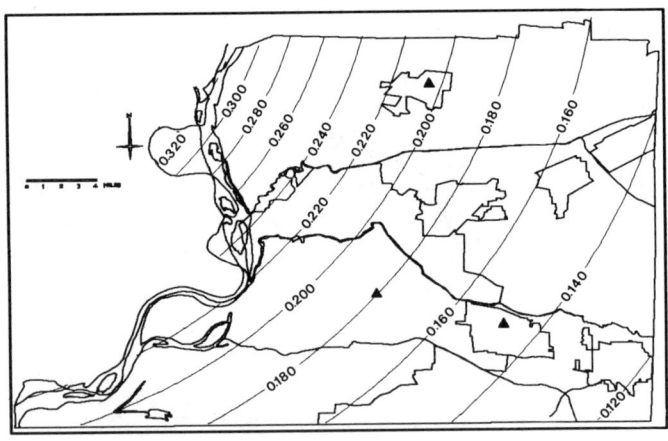

Figure 2 Contour Map of Mean Peak Accelerations

SOIL CONDITION

The effects of soil conditions on earthquake ground motions have been well demonstrated by many actual earthquakes such as the 1964 Niigata earthquake, the 1967 Caracas earthquake, and the 1985 Mexico earthquake. The bedrock motions can be greatly modified, both in amplitude and frequency characteristics, as the seismic waves are transmitted through the overlying soil deposits. Memphis and Shelby County are located in the Mississippi embayment which is composed of relatively unconsolidated soils up to about 3,000 feet thick. A recent study by Hwang et al. (1989a) has shown that the soil conditions in the Memphis area have significant effects on the amplification of strong earthquake acceleration.

Having recognized the significant influence of soil conditions on the earthquake ground response and the high seismic hazard potential in Memphis and Shelby County, an effort has been made to investigate the subsurface conditions of Memphis and Shelby County. About 8500 boring logs in the Memphis area have been collected from several soil testing companies, A/E firms and government agencies. Supplementary geotechnical data are also gathered from water-well logs, soil surveys, and technical publications. These data have been compiled and analyzed to establish a representative soil log for each cell, which results from applying a grid system to the entire area of Memphis and Shelby County. On the basis of these representative soil logs, the subsurface conditions for the entire Memphis area can be established (Ng et al. 1989).

CONCLUDING REMARKS

Estimation of seismic hazards is the first essential task in performing the seismic risk assessment of a municipal water delivery system. Sponsored by the National Center for Earthquake Engineering Research, a research project on the seismic risk assessment of Memphis water delivery systems is being carried out at Memphis State University and Princeton University.

This paper presents the evaluation of the seismic hazard in Memphis and Shelby County. The horizontal peak bedrock accelerations resulting from large New Madrid earthquakes have been estimated and presented in contour maps. In addition, existing boring logs, collected from various sources, have been compiled and analyzed to establish the subsurface conditions for the entire Memphis area. The site response study for Memphis and Shelby County is being carried out to evaluate the soil effects on earthquake ground motions. The evaluations of the liquefaction potential in Memphis and Shelby County has also been initiated.

The results of the seismic hazard analysis will be used to evaluate the vulnerability of the water delivery systems due to a large earthquake, to assess the economic loss and societal impact, and to prepare an emergency response plan.

ACKNOWLEDGMENTS

This paper is based on the research sponsored by the National Center for Earthquake Engineering Research (NCEER) under contract number NCEER-88-3016. (NSF Grant No. ECE-86-07591). Any opinions, findings and conclusions expressed in the paper are those of the authors and do not necessarily reflect the views of NCEER or NSF of the United States.

REFERENCES

Hwang, H., Low, Y. K., and Chang, T.-S. (1989a). "Seismic response study of two Memphis sites", in Foundation Engineering: Current Principles and Practices, F. H. Kulhawy, Editor, ASCE, 1, 786-798.

Hwang, H., Chen, C. H. S., and Yu, G. (1989b). "Bedrock accelerations in Memphis area due to large New Madrid earthquakes", NCEER Technical Report, (in preparation).

Ng, K. W., Chang, T.-S., and Hwang, H. (1989). "Subsurface Conditions of Memphis and Shelby County", Tech. Rept. NCEER-89-0021, National Center for Earthquake Engineering Research, State University of New York at Buffalo.

EFFECTS & RISK ANALYSIS FOR TIME VARIABLE EXPOSURES

John L. Mancini[1] and Peggy W. Glass, Ph.D.[2]

I. INTRODUCTION

The effects of toxicants on organisms in natural settings are a function of both the variations in exposure concentrations and durations of exposure. This paper presents analysis procedures which use bioassay results to generate quantitative predictions of the effects that would result from exposures to time varying concentrations and durations.

II. CONCEPTUAL FRAMEWORK

Data obtained from lethal bioassays usually consist of tabulated values of the percent mortality observed at various times of exposure for several concentration levels of a contaminant. The laboratory procedures (APHA, 1976) employed consist of exposure of a random sample of organisms to a constant concentration of contaminant in an experimental chamber with periodic observations of organism mortality. Organisms are observed to die at different times indicating that there is a distribution of sensitivity, within the organism population. In this context, the percent mortality can be viewed as a measure of population sensitivity.

Organisms at a given sensitivity level in each of the constant concentration experiments can be assumed to have similar characteristics with respect to the effects of the chemical being tested. By contrast, the organisms which represent two different sensitivity levels at the same exposure concentration have different characteristics. Lethal bioassay data can often be represented (Sprague, 1969) as illustrated in Figure 1. The log of time can be plotted against the percent mortality on the

---

[1]President, John Mancini Consultants, Inc., 12 Ginger Cove, Valley, NE 68064

[2]Manager of Environmental Services, Alan Plummer and Associates, Inc., Building II, Suite 300, 1120 Capital of Texas Highway South, Austin, TX 78746

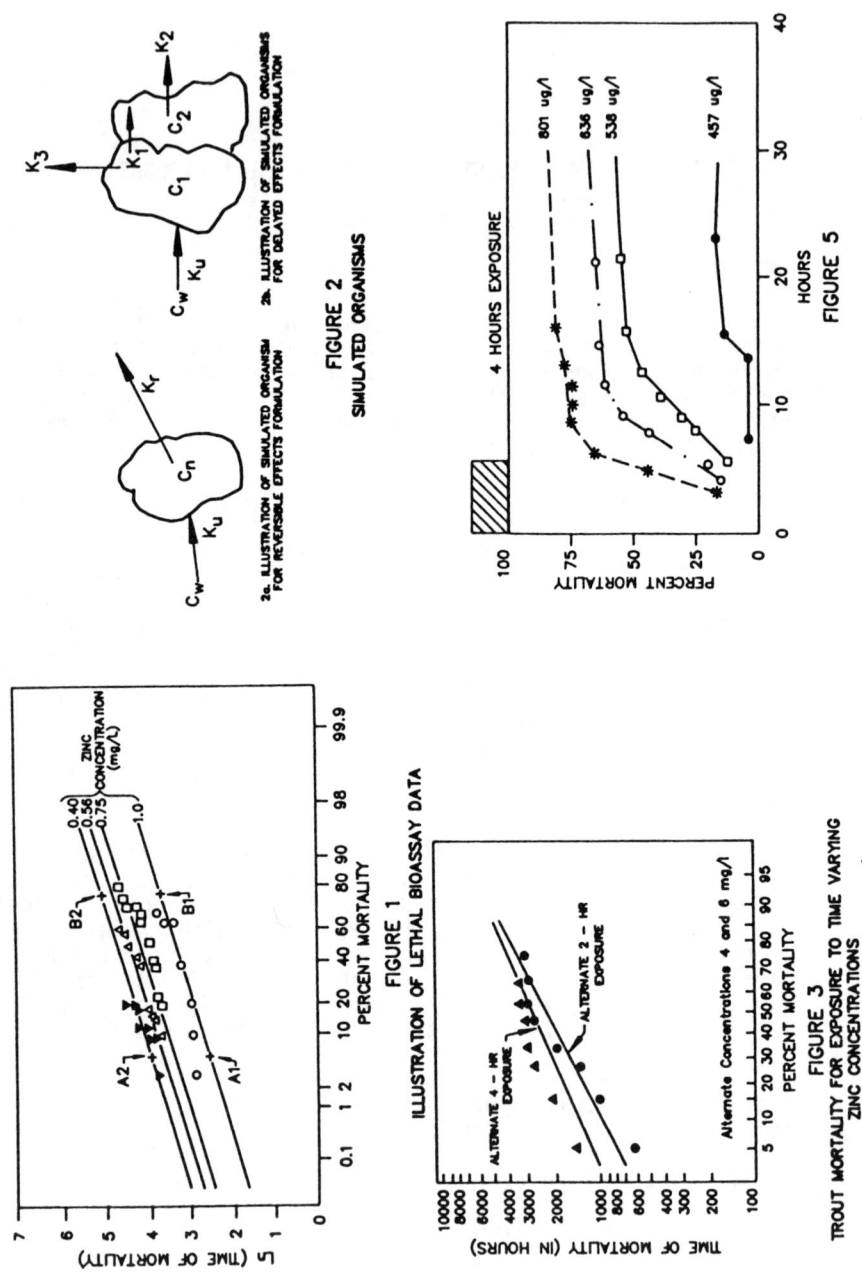

probability scale with a separate line for each concentration. The organisms represented by points A_1 and A_2 represent the five percent sensitivity level for the experiments at 1 and 0.40 mg/l of zinc and therefore have common response characteristics. By contrast, the organisms represented by points A_1 and B_1 have different response characteristics; since they represent two different sensitivity levels within the total population. Employing similar reasoning, the organisms represented by points B_1 and B_2 have common characteristics.

There are three concepts which are central to the analysis frameworks which will be presented. These are:

(1) variations in survival times between individual organisms, of the same species, indicate and define a distribution of sensitivities to a toxicant;
(2) over a range of exposure concentrations, the same percentile survival defines a common sensitivity level; and
(3) individual organisms at the same sensitivity level have common characteristics which regulate response to the toxicant.

III. REVERSIBLE EFFECTS FORMULATION

The characteristics and processes that distinguish various sensitivity levels in the population can include the rate of entry of the contamination, the rate of detoxification, and the concentration, in the organism, which results in mortality.

A first approximation considers uptake of the toxicant accompanied by detoxification as illustrated in Figure 2a. Equation (1) (Mancini, 1983) can be used to compute the effects of exposures.

$$\frac{C_D}{K_u} = \frac{C_w}{K_r} [1 - \exp(-K_r t_D)] \tag{1}$$

where:

C_N = organism related concentration of toxic (mass toxic/mass organism)
C_w = concentration of toxic (mass toxic/volume)
K_r = detoxification rate (time^{-1})
t = time of exposure (time)
K_u = toxic uptake rate (volume/mass organism-time)
C_D = organism related concentration at death
t_D = time of organism death

Equation (1) contains two coefficients which can be evaluated from bioassay data (Mancini, 1983).

The coefficient k_r represents the rate of detoxification. The value of the coefficient C_D/K_u is associated with the time of organism mortality. The units of the quantity C_D/K_u are toxic mass multiplied by time and divided by volume. This is an equivalent product of exposure time and concentration. Therefore, the coefficient C_D/K_u can be viewed as the equivalent toxic dose required for mortality and has a physical/biological interpretation.

The value of the equivalent mortality dose, C_D/K_u, is reached only at the time of organism mortality. For all exposure times, t, less than that required for mortality, and for a sequence of dosages in time, equation (1) becomes equation (2) where the variables are as defined previously and $C_{N(t)}/K_u$ is the calculated equivalent dose after exposure t.

$$\frac{C_{N(t)}}{K_u} = \frac{C_W}{K_r} [1 - \exp(-K_r t_1)] + \frac{C_{N(t-1)}}{K_u} \exp(-K_r t_1) \tag{2}$$

Examination of equation (2) indicates that the effects of all exposures are reversible. The equivalent mortality dose will decrease if C_W is equal to zero.

Data from constant concentration experiments were used to evaluate the coefficients in equation (1). Equation (2) was then employed to calculate the time of mortality for time variable exposures. One of the several comparisons used to test the approach (Mancini, 1982, 1983) are illustrated in Figure 3.

IV. DELAYED EFFECTS FORMULATION

Data from bioassay tests for some combinations of toxicants and organisms indicate that the effects of exposure to a toxicant can be delayed. The data presented in Figure 4 (Erickson, 1983) (Yurk, 1983) illustrate this type of response. It can be seen that fish mortality continued after exposure to the toxicant was terminated.

A two compartment analysis will accommodate delayed mortality and is illustrated in Figure 2b. The results of formulation development employing the same procedures and concepts indicated previously yield equations (3) and (4).

Summary Delayed Effects Formulation:

Compartment 1

$$\frac{C_1}{K_u} = \frac{C_W}{K_1+K_3} (1 - e^{-(K_1+K_3)t}) + C_{1p} e^{-(K_1+K_3)t} \tag{3}$$

Compartment 2

$$\frac{C_2}{K_u} = \frac{C_w k_1}{(K_1+K_3)K_2} (1 - e^{-K_2 t}) + \frac{K_1 C_{1p}(K_1 + K_3) - K_1 C_w}{K_2(K_1 + K_3) - 1} *$$ (4)

$$[e^{-(K_1+K_3)t} - e^{-K_2 t}] + C_{2p} e^{-K_2 t}$$

where:

- C_w = water concentration (C_w = 0 clean water exposure)
- K_u = uptake rate from water to compartment 1
- C_1 = concentration in compartment 1
- K_3 = detoxification plus other transport from compartment 1
- K_1 = transport from compartment 1 to compartment 2
- C_2 = concentration in compartment 2
- K_2 = detoxification rate for compartment 2
- C_{1p} = C_1/K_u from previous exposure, compartment 1 [C_{1p} = 0 initial exposure]
- C_{2p} = C_2/K_u from previous exposure, compartment 2 [C_{2p} = 0 initial exposure]
- C_1/K_u = equivalent dosage compartment 1
- C_2/K_u = equivalent dosage compartment 2. This controls mortality and an equivalent C_{2p}/K_u at which mortality occurs can be defined from bioassay data.

The coefficents required in equations (3) and (4) were developed by analysis of the data in Figure 5. These equations and coefficients were then employed to examine 21 additional data sets with the results indicated in Table 1.

V. DISCUSSION AND CONCLUSION

Formulations for the analysis of the effects, on organisms, of time variable toxicant concentrations and exposure durations have been developed. These formulations have been tested employing independent data sets.

The methodologies can be employed to establish environmental criteria (Mancini, 1986, 1988); carryout effects analysis, and risk characterization considering a variety of circumstances which have not been experimentally observed.

REFERENCES

APHA (1976) <u>Standard Methods for the Examination of Water and Wastewater.</u> 14th Edition. American Public Health Association, Washington, D.C.

Sprague, J.B. (1969) "Measurement of Pollutant Toxicity to Fish - I. Bioassay Methods for Acute Toxicity" Water Res. 5, 793-821.

Mancini, J.L. (1982) "Development of Methods to Define Water Quality Effects of Urban Runoff" EPA Cooperative Agreement No. 806828.

Mancini, J.L. (1983) "A Method for Calculating Effects, on Aquatic Organisms, of Time Varying Concentrations" Water Res. Vol. 17, No. 10, pp 1355-1362, 1983.

Erickson, R. (1983) 'Personal Communication.' College of St. Stolasticah.

Yurk, Linberg (1983) 'Personal Communication of Data.' University of Wisconsin at Superior, Wisconsin.

Mancini, J.L. and Plummer, A.H. (1986) "Urban Runoff and Water Quality Criteria;" Proceeding Urban Runoff Quality, Engineering Foundation Conference, June 23-27, 1986; pp 133-149.

Mancini, J.L. (1989) "Urban Discharges and Receiving Water Quality Impacts;" Edited by J.B. Ellis; Pergamon Press, "Urban Discharges and Water Quality Criteria: Towards the Development of Wet Weather Criteria;" pp 65-73.

TABLE 1

COMPARISON OF OBSERVED AND CALCULATED CONCENTRATIONS REQUIRED FOR MORTALITY

EXPOSURE		CONCENTRATION FOR MORTALITY ug/l		% ERROR
Toxicant	Clean	c_0 (calculated)	c (observed)	$(c-c_0)/c \times 100$
5.7	0	531	761	30.9
7.7	0	377	455	17
6.2	0	482	600	19.6
8	3.2	326	480	39.7
6.2	0	482	800	14.6
3.8	0	866	787	-10
6.9	0	426	463	7.7
4.6	0	685	821	16.5
5.5	0	555	620	10.5
7.7	0	377	468	19.4
8	.5	347	395	12
2.5	5	1039	818	-27
2.5	8	1038	699	-48.6
2.5	11	1041	602	-73.1
2.5	8	1038	778	-33.5
4	7.5	649	571	-13.7
4	8.5	650	490	-32.6
4	5.6	649	561	-15.6
8	4.5	324	584	44.4
8	7	325	495	34.3
8	9.5	326	327	.3

Water Measurement and Accounting
of Lake Michigan Diversion

By

W. H. Espey, Jr.[1] M.ASCE,
Harry H. Barnes, Jr.[2] F.ASCE,
David E. Westfall[3] M.ASCE

Introduction

The diversion of water from Lake Michigan and the Lake Michigan Basin into the Mississippi River Basin has been regulated since the turn of the century. In 1908 the United States brought action to enjoin the Sanitary District from diverting rates greater than the 4167 cfs previously authorized. Much of the time since has been marked with controversy, litigation, and Supreme Court actions concerning the allocation and use of Lake Michigan water, and the techniques used to measure and account for the diversion flow.

Lake Michigan is an integral part of the Great Lakes Basin whose waters are administered by the U.S.-Canadian International Joint Commission. Thus the development and use of the water resources of Lake Michigan are legitimate concerns of all States bordering the Great Lakes. Neighboring Wisconsin has long held a crucial interest in Illinois' use of its Lake Michigan diversion because both states share in the management and use of an important groundwater aquifer which lies beneath the two states.

---

[1]President, Espey, Huston & Associates, Inc., Austin, TX.

[2]Consultant, Meridian, MS.

[3]Vice-President, Parsons, Brinckerhoff, Quade & Douglas, Inc., Chicago, IL.

Historically Lake Michigan and the tributary watersheds of the Chicago and Calumet Rivers have played a key role in the infrastructural scheme for water supply and sewage disposal for metropolitan Chicago. From its beginning, Lake Michigan was the primary water supply and the stream system was used for sewage and waste disposal. The polluted discharge of the Chicago and Calumet Rivers had an increasingly adverse effect on the quality of Lake Michigan water in the vicinity used for supply. Water was first diverted from the Lake Michigan Basin at Chicago in 1848 through the Illinois and Michigan Canal. The canal joined the Chicago River with the Illinois River Basin near the present site of the USCE Lockport Lock and Dam.

Serious outbreaks of typhoid during the 1870's and 1880's were attributed largely to the water and sewage systems which had a common source and sump. This led to the Illinois State Legislature's creation of the Chicago Sanitary District in 1889 to correct the problem. The District constructed a canal system which reversed first the flow of the Chicago River in 1900, and later the Calumet River in 1922, away from Lake Michigan into the Illinois River system and the Mississippi River Basin. This scheme also provided a means to manage the concentration levels of sewage effluent in the canal by dilution using lake water and also provided an important navigation link between the Great Lakes and the Mississippi River. The flow of water from Lake Michigan at Chicago is presently controlled at the lakefront by three structures and by two structures at Lockport where the canal joins the Illinois River waterway.

The U. S. Supreme Court Decree of 1967, Wisconsin vs Illinois, enjoined the State of Illinois from diverting waters of Lake Michigan and its watershed into the Illinois River system, whether as domestic sewage effluent or as storm runoff diverted into the Sanitary and Ship Canal or by way of direct diversion from the lake into the canal, in excess of a combined total of 3,200 cfs. The decree also provided in detail for the method of determining the amount of flow diverted.

In 1980 the Court amended it's decree to adopt changes to the methodology and criteria for compliance. Included was the provision for the determination of <u>best current engineering practice and scientific knowledge</u> by a three-member technical committee to be appointed by the U. S. Army Corps of Engineers at intervals of five years. The first and second technical committees were conven in 1981 and 1986, respectively.

The committee evaluation reports provide a prospective of the growing complexities associated with the measurement and accounting of the component diversion flows in a dynamic hydraulic and hydrologic environment.

Diversion Criteria

The 1980 amendment to the 1967 Supreme Court decree redefined the criteria for determining compliance with the authorization for diversion of 3200 cfs. The running five-year average is increased to a forty-year average. The beginning of the accounting year is changed from March 1 to October 1. The limit on the diversion in any year is set as 3,680 cfs, except for an average of 3,840 cfs in any two years within a 40-year period. The limit on the cumulative algebraic sum of the average annual diversions minus 3,200 cfs during the first 39 years is set as 2,000 cfs-years.

Components of Diversion

The primary components of Lake Michigan diversion consists of (a) water supply taken from the Lake Michigan intake cribs and discharged into the canal system as treated sewage, (b) storm runoff from the diverted watershed of Lake Michigan discharged to the Illinois River system, and (c) water entering the canal system directly from Lake Michigan. From 1961 to 1979 treated sewage, storm runoff, and direct inflow accounted for about 53 percent, 17 percent, and 30 percent of the annual diversion, respectively. A portion of the water supply residual(less than two percent) is discharged to the Des Plaines River and bypasses Lockport.

Measurement of Diversion Flow

Historically the flow diverted from Lake Michigan has been measured at Lockport; mainly because there was no suitable alternative. For the period 1961-79 about seventy-six percent of the diversion flow passed through the two hydraulic turbines, about nine percent through the nine powerhouse sluice gates, about twelve percent through lockage and leakage at the USCE Lock and Dam, and about three percent released through the Controlling Works gates. In addition, the total flow at Lockport contains a portion of flow that is not part of the diversion. The storm drainage and sewer systems of the greater Chicago area extend beyond the limits of the Chicago and Calumet River Basins and for the most part the Sanitary and Ship Canal lies within the Des Plaines

Basin. So the storm runoff and infiltration from five areas of the Des Plaines watershed, totaling 217 square miles, plus domestic pumpage entering the canal above Lockport must be determined and deducted. Direct gaging, records from sewage treatment plants, records from an interim TARP pumping station, and gaging station records from a nearby watershed are used to determine these deductible flows. Similarly records of domestic pumpage and the North Shore sewage treatment plant are used to determine the relatively small portion of the diversion flow that bypasses Lockport.

First Technical Committee: Findings and Recommendations

In 1981 the first technical committee found the measurement and accounting processes to be a summation of complex components synthesized by a variety of hydraulic and hydrologic techniques developed over a long period of time. Some of the techniques had been used for more than three decades and are poorly documented.

The committee found all aspects of the processes, that is, planning, measurements, analysis, and certification to be deficient in some respect. Overall the processes suffered from the absence of a sound quality assurance program.

All components of the Lockport measurement were found to be in need of improvement. Of particular concern was the turbine flow which accounts for three fourths of the total. The calculation of flow through the turbines, installed in 1936, is based on laboratory tests of a scale model observed head and adjusted generator output. Periodic corrections are required to achieve agreement between the kW and kW-hr meters, neither of which are calibrated. More importantly the turbine efficiency is assumed constant with time even though the incomplete maintenance and repair records indicate the runners and liner have undergone several major restorations to correct cavitation damage. Efforts to verify the turbine ratings in the late 1970s were flawed and inconclusive. There is little doubt that the actual flows through the turbines exceed the calculated flows.

In the State of Illinois' petition to the Supreme Court it had requested an exception to the Court's Decree specification for measurement of diversion at Lockport and proposed an assignment of a constant value representing the average runoff from the diverted Lake Michigan Basin and measurements at the lakefront rather than Lockport. A review of the testimony indicated no significant disagreement with the concept. However, the parties could not agree on a numerical value for the runoff constant. The petition which still has considerable merit, failed because the measurement and accounting processes lacked credibility.

The principal recommendations of the technical committee were:

A master plan for diversion accounting which insures the required acceptable accuracy, promotes credibility, operational flexibility, and quality assurance; a feasibility study for an acoustical velocity meter (AVM) installation in the canal above Lockport; and a scheme for the calibration and use of the Lockport facilities for continued diversion measurement use if necessary.

Diversion Activities 1981-87

Illinois DOT and the Chicago District, USCE, undertook an evaluation of the first technical committee report as part of a plan to carry out improvements in the diversion program. Several investigative studies were made. Decisions were taken to develop a new accounting system for diversion using a simulation model to calculate diversion-related flows, and to establish an acoustical velocity meter system in the canal upstream from Lockport as the primary measuring point for diversion flow.

IDOT introduced the new system and reporting format diversion accounting starting with the 1983 WY. The system was developed and is operated by the Northeast Illinois Planning Commission (NIPC) in cooperation with IDOT. In March, 1984 the U.S. Geological Survey, in cooperation with IDOT, installed an AVM system at Romeoville. By 1986, the 1983 and 1984 diversion record were computed by NIPC. The AVM was installed in 1984 and was used to compute the flow records for the 1985 WY. These diversion activities were still in the implementation stage in 1986 and provided the second technical committee a challenging and interesting opportunity to interact with those responsible for the new diversion.elements.

The NIPC model consists of two main programs, LANDS for hydrologic simulation, and SCALP for hydraulic simulation. The LANDS model developed from the Hydrocomp program, is a derivative of the Stanford Watershed Model.

SCALP was originally developed by the City of Chicago to model the Tunnel and Reservoir Plan (TARP).

Under the new system NIPC uses the model to simulate all of the non-diversion flows from the Des Plaines catchments that are deducted from the Lockport flow. In addition, the model is used to simulate the runoff from the diverted watershed, and combined with the water supply and direct inflow at the lakefront structures to provide a supposedly independent calculation of diversion.

The Chicago District, USCE arranged for the Hydrologic Engineering Center (HEC) to review the NIPC model, simulation results for 1983 WY, and make recommendations for future activities (reported in 1986). The HEC review pointed out some of the constraints due to lack of data and need for calibration, the inability to quantify the wastewater and infiltration flow components at the treatment plants, and the uncertainties associated with apparent errors in the Lockport flows. The HEC report stopped short of evaluation of the 1983 simulation results, but points out the differences in measured and simulated flows at two treatment plants.

The AVM system at Romeoville consists of three transducer paths equally distributed in the vertical with a single crossed path at the middle path elevation. Seven current meter measurements made during the first year verified the AVM calibration. On or about March 21, 1985 the submarine cables connecting the transducers were severed by shipping in the canal. This marked the beginning of a period characterized by a variety of operational problems which resulted in changes to the calibration that persisted until September 1986. Nevertheless the AVM record and the current meter measurements by the USGS during the first year of operation proved invaluable to the second technical committee.

A comparison of 1985 discharge record from the AVM with the Lockport flow indicated that flow through the turbines is significantly under reported. This prompted IDOT to initiate a study to assess the impact of a possible AVM-based adjustment to the historical diversion record. The timing proved to be unfortunate because it was determined later that the AVM record was unreliable for a significant part of the time period chosen for analysis.

Second Technical Committee: Findings and Recommendations

The simulation model is a sophisticated continuous hydrologic model and supports IDOT's initiative to develop a better understanding of the hydrologic complexities that are an integral part of the process of accounting for flow diverted from Lake Michigan. While the NIPC model is state of the art and has been used extensively in the Chicago area for planning and design applications, the current use of the model for representation of diversion is based on earlier calibration work. Despite an awareness of the deficiencies in the calibration data, insufficient action has been taken to correct these deficiencies. There is some concern for what seems to be a greater emphasis on the overall water budget analysis than has been placed on the reliability of diversion component values derived by hydrologic modeling. Similarly, there are questions regarding the accuracy of the modeling results for some non-diversion areas because of questionable input data. The degree to which the continued use of the current hydrologic modeling will be acceptable depends on the efforts made to (1) assure input data reliability, (2) improve model calibration and verification as applicable to areas for which simulation is used to estimate unmeasured diversion and non*diversion flows, and (3) to definitively define the goals and objectives of the hydrologic modeling.

The model simulations indicate that MSD Lockport flows during storm periods may be over reported. A similar but independent conclusion was made on the basis of AVM data and field measurements in March 1985. A comparison of the MSD measured flows with simulated flows for 1983 and three months in 1984 indicate the MSD measured turbine flows to be 11 and 0.3 percent higher respectively. However the AVM flow record during the same 1984 period shows the correct flow at Lockport is about 14 percent higher than the simulated flow.

Much of the input data used in the simulation of runoff for the combined sewer area is more than 20 years old and some was out of date even in 1970. During the TARP studies some of the data for the Des Plaines basin was found to be in error. These errors were corrected and updated in 1976. The more recent data indicates the simulated deductible flows may be 70 to 130 percent too high.

The reported imbalances in the 1983 water budgets for the three principal treatment plants seem most likely to be unreported inflow derived from the waterways. If true, unreported inflow from the Des Plaines watershed is not accounted for by simulation, and more importantly is not claimed as a legitimate deduction from the Lockport flow. The calculations representing the so-called sewer induced groundwater inflow should be eliminated from the process.

The reliability of the accounting of diversion, with the level of dependability in the AVM system which has prevailed since September 1986, has been improved significantly over the diversion accounting procedures used five years ago. However, despite the current level of accuracy and reliability of the AVM system, a backup system is necessary. The AVM has demonstrated its viability as an alternative to the Lockport structures for measurement of diversion flow.

References

1. Espey, Dr. William H., Jr., Chairman, Harry H. Barnes, Jr., and Dr. Svein Vigander. October 1981. Lake Michigan Diversion: Findings of the Technical Committee for Review of Diversion Flow Measurements and Accounting Procedures.

2. Espey, Dr. William H., Jr., Chairman, Harry H. Barnes, Jr., and David E. Westfall. November 1987. Lake Michigan Diversion: Findings of the Second Technical Committee for Review of Diversion Flow Measurements and Accounting Procedures.

MEASURING BENEFITS OF WATER SUPPLY PROJECTS

Farhad Farnam[1]

Abstract

Various approaches are used to determine the value of water supply projects. Deterministic methods will lead to biased valuation of additional supplies of water. Calculation of risk premium to avoid adverse water conditions is an indication of farmers' willingness to pay.

Introduction

Due to the stochastic nature of water supply, deterministic or static approaches to water supply planning and management will result in policies that do not reflect the economic value of water accurately. In deterministic studies, "most likely" or "average" conditions are assumed as the appropriate state of the nature and benefits of water projects are derived on the basis of this assumption. This approach tends to underestimate the benefits when the water supplies are below the average (dry or critical years) and overestimate the benefits when they are above the average (wet years). Determination of "willingness to Pay" of beneficiaries of water supply projects is crucial to policy makers since they are expected to bear the full cost of the projects. Traditionally, deterministic approaches have been used by federal and state agencies to ascertain potential users willingness to pay or "payment capacity".

The purpose of this study is to determine California farmers' willingness to pay under uncertain and stochastic

---

[1]Economics Specialist, California Department of Water Resources, P. O. Box 942836, Sacramento, CA 94236-0001.

conditions of supply of water. Various measures will be employed for this purpose; deterministic, expected benefits, and expected utility approach. Results will be compared to determine the extent of divergence among them.

Results of the study have variety of applications which range from determination of economic feasibility of water projects to exploration of potential for water transfer and willingness of farmers for purchase of "certain" sources of supply (insurance) to protect themselves against adverse water conditions.

Study Area

California agriculture is considered one of the most diversified in the world, with over 250 different crops and livestock commodities. It is the number one agricultural state in the United States. The rich Central Valley of California is the heartland of this abundance. Nearly half of the State's farmland, two thirds of the State's cropland and over 75 percent of the irrigated land is found in the Central Valley. The Central Valley is located between the coast ranges and the Sierra Nevada. It extends north to south nearly 450 miles from the Klamath/Cascades to the Tehachapis Mountains. Within the Central Valley, there are three distinct production zones--the Sacramento Valley, the Delta and the San Joaquin Valley. The Sacramento Valley with cooler winters and higher rainfall, is the main water source for the State. Rice is the predominant irrigated crop in this area where water is inexpensive and soils impervious. The area produces small grain crops and has an excellent seasonal grazing on its non-irrigated acreage. A variety of fruit and nut crops are produced on the deeper, better-drained and, more fertile soils, while row crops such as tomatoes, beans, corn, sugar beets, mile sunflowers are grown extensively. Alfalfa and a variety of seed crops are also found.

The Delta formed by the Sacramento River and the San Joaquin river is the focal point of any water distribution system in California.

The San Joaquin Valley is the most extensive and productive of the agricultural regions of California. It is the fruit and nut basked of the nation. Nearly half of the cropland and more than half of the irrigated acreage in California lie in this region. With mild winter and hot dry summers, this area would be little more than a desert without the extensive water distribution system found in this area. 44 percent of its land area is irrigated. Many high valued crops are grown here. Deciduous tree fruits, tree nuts, grapes and citrus are the major cash crops, in addition to cotton, alfalfa and a broad spectrum of vegetables and other field crops.

Central Valley Production Model

In order to analyze the value of an additional 500,000 acre-feet of water in the Central Valley, the Central Valley Production Model (CVPM) which has been developed by the California Department of Water Resources is employed. CVPM is a Positive Quadratic Programming model (PQP) with the following specification:

$$\text{Maximize } Z = c'x_t + 1/2 x'_t D x_t - (K'x + 1/2 \, x \, 'Sx)$$
$$\text{Subject to } Ax \leq b$$

where:
- x_t = a vector of statewide cropping activities;
- x = a vector of regional cropping activities;
- c = a vector of intercepts of statewide linear demand functions;
- D = a diagonal matrix of slopes of the demand functions;
- k = a vector of variable production costs for the regional activities;
- S = a diagonal matrix of regional linear supply functions;
- A = a matrix of linear input-output coefficients for the regional activities;
- b = a vector of physical resource limits.

The objective function is quadratic in revenue and cost and maximizes the area between linear demand and supply curves. The maximum consists of the sum of consumer and producer surplus, a standard measure of net economic welfare. The model implicitly assumes a competitive economic system where individual consumers and producers are price takers.

The regional cost function consists of the linear portion $k'x$ and the nonlinear quadratic form $1/2 x'Sx$. The matrix S presupposes the existence of decreasing returns (or increasing costs) with rising production of a given activity, due to declining yields as operations expand onto less suitable lands as well as to the increasing risks of specialization.

A detailed description of PQP methodology can be find in Hqwitt and Mean [3].

CVPM divides the Central Valley of California into 47 regions growing 50 major crops. Main constraints in CVPM are land and water; the later is accounted for as local surface water, ground water, State Water Project water (SWP), and Central Valley Project water (CVP).

Analysis

Table (1) shows probabilities of different water years which are calculated based on DWR's Four River Index (1872-1988).

Table (1): Probabilities for Water Year

Water Year	Probability
Wet	.47
Above Normal	.15
Below Normal	.14
Dry	.15
Critical	.09

In order to simulate each water year; surface water availability was reduced (or increased) to reflect the historical water availability in each water year. Ground water pumping costs were increased for below normal, dry, and critical water year scenarios to reflect the increase in lift if the surface water deficiency continues. CVPM runs determined the value of the producers' surplus for each scenario.

To determine the value of an additional 500,000 acre-feet of water; 500,000 acre-feet of surface water (at the cost of local surface water) was added to the existing surface water availability in each scenario and producers' surplus were calculated through CVPM.

Table (2) shows the change in the value of producers' surplus as a result of an additional 500,000 acre-feet of water for each water year.

Table (2): Changes in Value of Producers' Surplus

Water Year	Change in Producers' Surplus
Wet	$ 6,452,600
Above Normal	7,704,200
Below Normal	47,817,700
Dry	50,411,200
Critical	53,014,440

As expected, the additional water will contribute more to the producers' surplus when the water becomes more scarce. If we attempt to determine the value of the additional water in a so called "normal" year, we will arrive at a value of approximately $15 per acre-foot (mainly due to substitution of cheaper surface water for ground water in some areas), while the value (average) of additional water in a dry year is $106 per acre-foot.

To arrive at a measure of benefit for all states of the nature, the expected value of the additional water is be calculated by using the probabilities from Table (1). The expected addition to the producers' surplus is $23,215,708 which would imply an average value of $46 per acre-foot.

Expected Utility

Let us assume farmers are risk-averse and posses a negative exponential utility function $U(s)=1-\exp(-\emptyset s)$, where $\emptyset$ is the Pratt's [6] absolute risk aversion coefficient and s is the producers' surplus. The objective of farmers is to maximize expected utility of surplus:

$$\max EU(s) = 1-\exp[-\emptyset(E(s) - \frac{1}{\emptyset} Var(s))] \quad (1)$$

i.e. the mean-variance (MV) model of Markowitz[4] and Freund[2].

Risk-averse farmers operating in an uncertain environment are willing to pay a risk premium to protect themselves against adverse water conditions. Risk premium can be derived based on the following "indifference" equation:

$$EU(s) = U[E(s) - RP] \quad (2)$$

which implies that farmers are willing to pay a risk premium, RP, as large as required for being indifferent between choosing to face input uncertainty, EU(s), and the utility derived from a certain sum of money accepted in order to avoid that uncertainty, U[E(s) - RP]. The term [E(s) - RP] is also called "uncertainty equivalent".

With U(.) strictly monotonic (exponential utility function), risk premium can be derived from (1) and (2) as:

$$RP = E(s) - U^{-1}[EU(s)] = -\frac{\emptyset}{2} Var(s)$$

Assuming collective risk and an absolute risk aversion coefficient (ø) of 10^{-7}, RP was calculated as $22,187,450 or $44 per acre-foot which implies that farmers are willing to pay a risk premium of $44 per acre-foot under any water condition to secure a sure supply of water.

Conclusion

While determining the economic value of additional supply of water, various states of the nature should be taken into account so that an unbiased estimate of benefits is derived. Calculation of risk premium will provide policy makers with additional information on farmers, willingness to pay for the water.

References

G. B. Dantzig, "Linear Programming Under Uncertainty", Management Science 1, 197-206 (1955).

J. Freund, "The Introduction of Risk Into a Programming Model", Econometrica 24, 263-273 (1956).

Howitt, R. F., and Mean, P. Positive Quadratic Programming Models. Working Paper No. 85-10, Department of Agricultural Economics, Davis, California, 1985.

H. M. Markowitz, "Portfolio Selection", J. Finance 7, 77-91 (1952).

Q. Paris, "Revenue and Cost Uncertainty, Generalized Mean-Variance and the Linear Complimentarily Problem", Amer. J. Agric. Economics 61, 286-275 (1979).

J. W. Pratt, "Risk Aversion in The Small and in The Large", Econometrica, 32, 122-136 (1964).

ABILENE, TEXAS, FLOOD CONTROL STUDY - CASE HISTORY

Weldon K. Scrivner, P.E.[1]

ABSTRACT

The Corps of Engineers, Fort Worth District, is currently performing a study of flooding problems of Abilene, Texas. This is the first study under the General Investigations authority to be performed in the Fort Worth District under the new cost sharing rules mandated by Congress in 1986.

This paper will present a discussion of the background of the Water Resources Development Act of 1986 and its implications for changing the way the Corps of Engineers does business. A case history of the flood control study of the Elm Creek watershed, Abilene, Texas, is presented to show how the new procedures are being implemented as well as to demonstrate how intergovernmental cooperation in water resources planning can be favorably accomplished.

WATER RESOURCES DEVELOPMENT ACT OF 1986

The provisions of the Water Resource Development Act of 1986 (Public Law 99-662), approved November 17, 1986, radically changed the way the Corps of Engineers conducts and finances civil works projects. Specifically, changes were made concerning cost sharing requirements for planning studies and project financing which local sponsors must meet for the Federal Government to be involved with water resource projects. Generally, the non-Federal sponsor(s) is responsible for the following:

1. Equal cost sharing of any feasibility studies with no more than 50 percent credited for Work-In-Kind services.

2. Providing all lands, easements, rights-of-way, relocations, and disposal areas (LERR&D) for the project.

3. The Sponsor must provide a minimum of 5 percent of the total project cost in cash during construction.

---
1. Civil Engineer, Fort Worth District, U.S. Army Corps of Engineers, P.O. Box 17300, Ft. Worth, Tx. 76102-0300.

4. The Sponsor's total project cost will be between 25 and 50 percent of the total project cost including the 5 percent cash contribution. If the total percentage is higher or lower than these percentages, the difference in cash is to be contributed or credited. The Sponsor does have the option to pay the percentage of costs above 30 percent over a period of 15 years, with interest.

5. Provide for the operation, maintenance, and replacement needs of the project after completion.

PLANNING STUDIES

Flood control investigations performed under the General Investigations authority are divided into two phases - a Reconnaissance Phase and a Feasibility Phase. The Reconnaissance Phase is fully Federally funded while the Feasibility Phase is cost shared on an equal basis with the Sponsor. These two study phases are summarized in the following paragraphs.

Reconnaissance Phase. The Reconnaissance Phase is normally 12 months in length with a 6-month review period. This study concentrates most of its efforts on problem identification and also identifies at least one potentially viable plan with a Federal interest. The objectives of the reconnaissance study are to:

1. Identify if a viable, economically feasible plan exists,

2. Identify a Federal interest in the implementation of the desired flood control plan, and

3. Identify a non-Federal Sponsor who is willing to cost share in both a feasibility study and a viable flood control project, if such a project exists.

If these requirements are met, a draft Feasibility Cost Sharing Agreement (FCSA) and a letter of intent from the Sponsor are submitted with the draft reconnaissance report. The FCSA details the total estimated study costs, the study completion schedule, and the Sponsor's Work-in-Kind services, if any.

The Reconnaissance Phase ends when funds are released to initiate the Feasibility Phase. To reach this point, Headquarters U.S. Army Corps of Engineers (HQUSACE) has to approve both the reconnaissance report and the FCSA before the Sponsor and District Engineer sign the FCSA document. All reconnaissance studies must compete in Washington for selection as a "New Start." If accepted, there is "seamless funding" through the Preconstruction Engineering and Design (PED) Phase up to the award of the first construction contract.

Feasibility Phase. The Feasibility Phase consists of up to a 36-month feasibility study and a 12-month review at the Washington level. The review period includes Federal/state/local agency review, public meetings, and revisions and printing of the final report. The feasibility study is used to arrive at the best plan to solve the problem(s) identified in the reconnaissance report. The feasibility study is cost shared equally with at least 50 percent of the Sponsor's contribution to be in cash, normally held in an escrow account. The breakout of cash and Work-In-Kind services is determined during the FCSA negotiations.

The Feasibility Phase ends when the final feasibility report is coordinated at the Washington level and approved by HQUSACE to receive PED funds. The project must be authorized by Congressional legislation prior to award of the first construction contract.

ELM CREEK WATERSHED STUDY AREA, ABILENE, TEXAS

Abilene is located in northwest central Texas in Taylor County, about 153 miles west of Fort Worth and 81 miles northeast of the city of San Angelo. Abilene is the county seat of Taylor County and its 1984 population was estimated at 108,000. Abilene is a regional commercial distribution center. Dyess Air Force Base, to the west, is also a major economic influence on the city.

Elm Creek flows east into Lake Abilene, then northeast through the city of Abilene. North of Abilene, Elm Creek flows into Lake Fort Phantom Hill and, eventually, combines with the Clear Fork of the Brazos River in Jones County. The entire Elm Creek watershed has a total drainage area of 485 square miles. The overall basin length is about 52 miles and has an average width of about 10 miles. The major lakes in this watershed are Lake Abilene, Lake Kirby, Lytle Lake, and Lake Fort Phantom Hill. The major tributaries into Elm Creek are Little Elm, Cat Claw, and Cedar Creeks. Figure 1 below shows the features of the Elm Creek watershed in relation to the city limits of Abilene.

Figure 1. Elm Creek Watershed, Abilene, Texas

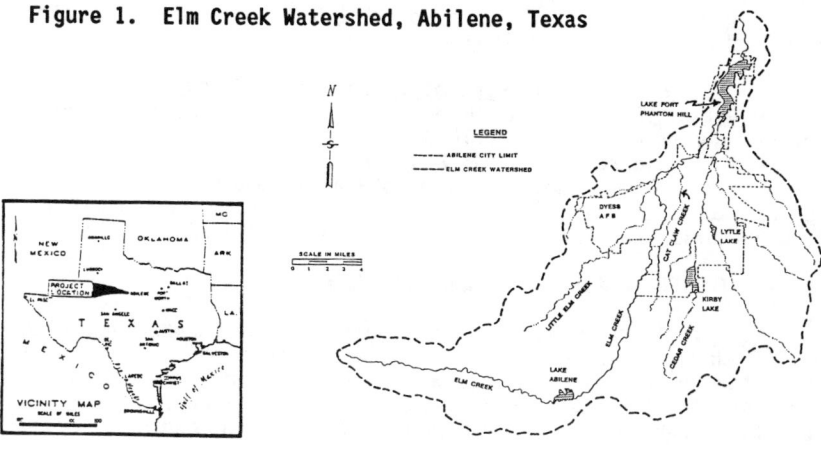

Elm Creek is unusual in that it is a perched stream through the city of Abilene, with the top of the channel being higher than its overbanks. The channel capacity of Elm Creek is inadequate to confine the 20-year flood event and once exceeded, the excess flows spill over into Little Elm and Cat Claw Creek watersheds, further acerbating flooding problems on these streams. Sections of the Cat Claw and Little Elm Creek channels have been improved while Elm Creek remains in its natural state. Residences for about 30,000 people comprise about 90 percent of the 13,200 structures located within the SPF flood plain of Elm Creek. Flooding on October 12-14, 1981, produced from the effects of Hurricane Norma, caused the most flood destruction in Abilene in recent years. The flooding caused losses of $6 million and damaged over 500 homes and businesses. Taylor County was declared an emergency disaster area by the President on October 23, 1981.

PREVIOUS STUDIES OF ABILENE'S FLOOD PROBLEMS

In the 1960's, the U.S. Army Corps of Engineers investigated the flooding problems of the Elm Creek watershed. The following two paragraphs detail the flood protection measures recommended.

1961 Clear Fork of Brazos River Flood Protection - Abilene Area.
An interim review report, dated December 1, 1961, recommended several flood control protection measures which would have provided a 100-year level of protection to the city of Abilene. Briefly, the strategy of this plan was to allow the 2.3-mile diversion dike to divert major flows up to the SPF event from Elm and Cat Claw Creeks into Cedar Creek. Channelization along Little Elm and Cat Claw Creeks was proposed to handle flood inflows downstream of the proposed diversion dike. The total channel improvements along the various creeks within Abilene were about 41.4 miles which includes a 5.4-mile length of clearing and snagging to be performed along the lower portion of Elm Creek. The total estimated cost of these proposed improvements was $38.6 million with a benefit-cost ratio of 1.6 to 1. The estimated Federal share was $31.2 million.

1969 GDM Clear Fork of Brazos River Flood Protection - Abilene Area.
This General Design Memorandum, dated March 1969, further investigated the 1961 Plan's components. The total estimated cost increased to $56.2 million with a benefit-cost ratio of 1.5 to 1. The estimated Federal share was $38.4 million. This project lacked the needed local support to finance this project and was deauthorized by Public Law 93-251, approved November 6, 1977.

CURRENT STUDIES OF ABILENE'S FLOOD PROBLEMS

1987 Problem Identification Report.
A report was completed in 1987 which investigated the water resource problems and needs within the Brazos River Basin, Texas. The city of Abilene was one of fifteen flood prone communities identified as having major flood protection problems and was recommended for further study.

1988 Reconnaissance Report. In 1988, a reconnaissance study was initiated which identified the previously mentioned flooding problems and investigated several nonstructural and structural alternatives. The selected feasible plan was a detention dam located upstream of FM 707 across Elm Creek. The preliminary design features include an earthfill embankment 8,800 feet in length and an overflow spillway, located in the middle portion of this embankment, about 5,800 feet in length. This spillway would have a roller-compacted concrete cover to allow flood flows greater than the 100-year flood event to be passed without erosion of the spillway. Flows up to the minimum channel capacity of Elm Creek, 5,000 cfs, would be passed during non-flooding conditions. This project would control about 55 percent of the drainage area upstream of the city of Abilene and would greatly reduce the amount of damages caused by overspills from Elm Creek into the Little Elm and Cat Claw Creek watersheds.

The project first cost of this detention dam would be about $36.9 million based on May 1988 dollars. About 37 percent, or approximately $13.7 million, would be the responsibility of the non-Federal sponsor, the city of Abilene. This project has a benefit-cost ratio of 2.5 to 1. Since this alternative would only detain floodwaters up to the 100-year flood event, this alternative would help minimize the impacts to the natural setting and would be more environmentally sensitive than a dam which stores water on a permanent basis. Minimal clearing was recommended.

Within the 2,100 acres required for the project, there are about 40 homes south (upstream) of the city limits of Abilene which would need to be purchased and removed. The city of Abilene was aware of this requirement and was in favor of the required public involvement to include these homeowners in a discussion of the alternatives to be evaluated during the Feasibility Study Phase.

The city officials were made fully aware of the mandated cost sharing provisions during the reconnaissance study. During the conduct of this reconnaissance study, it was noted that the principal reason the original 1961 diversion plan had not been endorsed by the city was the impression that "Big Brother," the Federal Government, came in and said, "You have a problem and we're going to construct a project and your share is $17.8 million...... TAKE IT OR LEAVE IT." The city residents felt they were being coerced into paying for this project and decided not to participate in the project. Surprisingly, that same impression was still in the minds of some area residents some 20 years later when the reconnaissance study was initiated. In the new era of cost sharing, the Sponsor is treated as a full and equal partner rather than a payee and the Sponsor's cooperation was greatly enhanced.

1989 Feasibility Study. This study was initiated in February 1989 with a two-year draft report completion schedule. The $600,000 cost was shared equally. During the FCSA negotiations, it became apparent that those persons who would be forced to vacate from the project area were very much opposed to the detention dam project. Accordingly, the Corps, in conjunction with the city, modified the FCSA for alternatives other than the detention dam to be investigated first. Then these alternatives would be compared with the detention dam to determine the most feasible project. Additionally, it was pointed out that if the costs of the Recommended Plan was in excess of the alternative with the greatest net economic benefits, the city would be required to pay this difference in costs. The city officials were supportive of this approach and approved the FCSA on February 15, 1989. The Texas Water Development Board (TWDB) is reimbursing the city of Abilene for half of its required cash payment for the feasibility study.

As of September 1989, ten preliminary alternatives have been selected with input from the city and impacted residents. Some of the alternatives to be considered involved investigation of a new damsite area for the detention dam, modification of the upstream Lake Abilene to provide for flood control storage, and channel modifications and diversion of Elm Creek flood spills into Little Elm or Cedar Creeks. These alternatives are presently being investigated to determine their respective costs, benefits, and impacts to the environment. A presentation to the City Council and area residents will be made in December 1989 of each alternative's features, costs, benefits, and environmental impacts. These alternatives will then be screened with the help of the city and residents and a final alternative will be selected. This alternative would then be optimized to determine the ultimate features, costs, and benefits of this plan. The city staff has been closely involved in every aspect of these investigations and will help decide how the Recommended Plan is to be implemented and at what cost to the city. Presently, monthly study team meetings are held with Corps and city team members to work out the technical issues involved. Executive meetings are held quarterly whereby the Mayor of Abilene and District Engineer are briefed on the progress of the study and decide how to handle important study issues.

Summary. The cost sharing provisions of the Water Resource Development Act of 1986 have significantly increased the financial involvement of the local Sponsor, making them a full and equal partner with the Federal Government in the investigation and construction of civil works projects. Moreover, cost sharing of the Feasibility Phase has increased the involvement of the Sponsor in both the reconnaissance and feasibility study investigations. With their active participation, the most urgent problems and needs are identified and alternatives to meet these needs are quickly and thoroughly investigated. The Sponsor also helps to design the best approach to effectively implement the Recommended Plan. The participation between the Corps of Engineers, city of Abilene, and area residents in these flood control studies has been exemplary. The increased participation in these studies attests to the feasibility of cost shared studies and how the interlocal cooperation between the Federal Government, TWDB, and the Sponsor can help to arrive at feasible/acceptable flood control solutions.

CONFLICT RESOLUTION, REALLOCATION AND MANAGEMENT
OF LAKE TEXOMA RESOURCES

by

Phillip A. Cline *
&
Paul Westbrook

[The views expressed in this paper are those of the authors and do not necessarily reflect official policy of the U.S. Army Corps of Engineers.]

From its inception, Lake Texoma has created conflicts among users of its natural resources. Special interests have become very vocal in their demands for modification of authorized project purposes. In some cases, their demands have hardened into inexorable conflicts among hydropower, water supply, flood control, and recreational users. Conflicts also arise between bordering states regarding water rights.

Although the allocation of resources was delineated in the original authorization for Denison Dam and Lake Texoma, demands from special interests have created problems for the Corps management of lake resources. Some of the more hard-line issues force the Corps to assume a mediative role in its search for acceptable compromises.

Denison Dam, which impounds Lake Texoma, is located on the Red River in Oklahoma and Texas approximately 5 miles northwest of Denison, Texas. Construction of the Denison Dam-Lake Texoma project was authorized by the Flood Control Act of 1938 to control flooding and generate hydroelectric power on the Red River. Subsequent acts of Congress authorized other project purposes and beneficial uses. Beneficial uses include providing fish and wildlife habitat. The currently authorized purposes include flood control, water supply, hydropower, recreation, regulation of Red River flows, and improvement of navigation. No conservation storage is currently allocated to navigation or recreation.

*Red River Planning, U.S. Army Corps of Engieners, Tulsa, OK

RESOURCES FOR WATER MANAGEMENT

Hydropower, water supply, and recreation interests all share usage of the conservation pool storage, which is defined as that portion of the lake lying below the flood control storage and above the inactive storage. Most of the conservation storage is allocated to hydropower which provides water for the operation of two 35 megawatt generating units. Three of the five power penstocks originally installed at Denison Dam are currently unused and provide space to add up to three more generating units without major modifications of the existing dam.

Water supply is normally considered under state law to have a higher beneficial use than hydropower because water is used for human consumption and directly affects quality of life. While hydropower requirements are important, electricity is not necessary to sustain human life; consequently, water supply needs are given priority over those for hydropower. Less than 10 percent of the 1.6 million acre-feet of conservation storage is currently allocated to water supply; however, The Water Resources Development Act of 1986 authorized the Secretary of the Army to reallocate an additional 300,000 acre-feet of hydropower storage to water supply.

Recreational interests are concerned that hydropower discharges and water supply withdrawals will cause excessively low lake levels and result in less recreational usage of Lake Texoma. None of the conservation pool storage is set aside for recreational purposes; however, the existing pool is used for recreational activities such as boating, swimming, and fishing. Recreation has become a very important activity at the lake. Therefore, while recreational users cannot claim rights to the conservation storage, they tend to claim a primary right to usage of the surface area of the lake.

Navigation is also an authorized project purpose of Lake Texoma. Although no storage is allocated in the lake for improving downstream navigational flows, routine releases for hydropower generation have been adequate to meet downstream needs. As use of the Red River for navigation develops, navigation interests may apply pressure on congress to reallocate water for downstream releases. These releases may conflict with the needs of other interests for stable pool levels.

Management of fish and wildlife resources requires a stable or slightly rising pool level during the spring spawning season. Proper management of the fishery also requires a late summer drawdown of the lake to allow revegetation of mud flats and shallow areas that will provide spawning grounds.

Reallocation of conservation storage from hydropower to water supply and subsequent water withdrawals result in less water being available for hydropower production. These reallocations have become the basis for one major conflict. Another results from recreational users demanding higher conservation pool levels, especially during late summer, which conflicts with both hydropower and water supply users as well as with management of fish and wildlife resources.

LAKE RESOURCES CONFLICT RESOLUTION

Several avenues can and have been pursued by special interest groups to resolve conflicts. These include communicating with the Corps of Engineers and other governmental agencies; pursuing resolution through the judicial system by filing pleadings with a court having jurisdiction; and, seeking Congressional legislation to modify the authorized project purposes of Lake Texoma.

The traditional method used by the Corps of Engineers to resolve conflicts among users of resources under its jurisdiction is through the public meeting forum. Through this forum, the public is able to express its views and inform government officials of existing conflicts in resource allocation. Another method is for the Corps to study the problem and recommend solutions. Occasionally, the Office of the Chief of Engineers submits legislative proposals to resolve conflicts.

Congressional legislation also can be initiated by private citizens through their congressional delegates. In response to special interest groups at Lake Texoma, congress passed legislation in July 1987 which mandated that the Corps of Engineers develop a management plan for the conservation pool and establish an advisory committee. According to this law, "The purpose of the Committee shall be advisory only and it shall provide information and recommendations to the Corps of Engineers regarding the operations of Lake Texoma for its congressionally authorized purposes. The Committee shall be composed of representatives equally divided among the project purposes and between the States of Texas and Oklahoma." The Lake Texoma Advisory Committee was subsequently formed and is chaired by Mr. James R. Barnett, Executive Director of the Oklahoma Water Resources Board. This committee acts as a forum whereby conflicts can be resolved and solutions found that are acceptable to all concerned.

The purpose of the conservation pool management plan is to mitigate conflicts among hydropower, water supply, and recreational users. The strategy of this plan is to maintain water surface elevations between 617, the normal pool level, and 612 feet above sea level, except for pool rises due to flood control operations. The plan provides for a normal and relatively stable pool level for recreational use while allowing for water supply withdrawals and hydroelectric power generation. When the water surface is between elevations 612 and 607, the plan provides that hydropower releases should be made to supply only short term peak loads. When the pool level falls below elevation 607, which is ten feet below the normal pool level, the plan specifies that hydropower releases should be made to satisfy only critical power needs, and conservation measures should be implemented by water users to reduce the impact of water withdrawals. These measures help ensure higher conservation pool levels for recreational users.

To moderate conflicts between hydropower and water supply users of the conservation pool, Congress included language in the Water Resources Development Act of 1986 that allowed a system of credits to be established with the hydropower user to compensate for the results of reallocations of storage to water supply. The legislative language states, "If hydropower is lost as a result of the implementation of...[water supply] contracts...the Secretary [Army] ...shall provide credits to the Southwestern Power Administration for costs of the project allocated to hydropower. In each case, the Southwestern Power Administration shall reimburse each preference customer for an amount equal to the customer's actual replacement cost for hydropower lost as a result of such [water supply] contract."

Recreational users and related business interests have become very vocal in demanding stable pool levels. The development of recreational facilities at the lake is extensive. Business establishments have invested millions of dollars in order to service the needs of recreation oriented consumers. Restaurants, marinas, boat sales, motels, retail stores and other businesses service the needs of the Lake Texoma recreational user. Revenues obtained from these services tend to expand the economic base which further increases demands for water supply and hydropower as well as for recreational usage of Lake Texoma.

Other interests also demand stable pool levels. For example, officials of the State of Louisiana seriously object to any proposals to reduce flood control storage at Lake Texoma. They believe reductions in flood control storage would reduce the flood protection afforded areas along the Red River in their state.

Conflicts involving state water rights resulted in the creation of a multistate commission known as the Red River Compact Commission. This commission is composed of representatives of the states of Oklahoma, Texas, Arkansas and Louisiana. According to the Compact, "The principal purposes...[are]...To promote interstate comity and remove causes of controversy between each of the affected states by governing the use, control and distribution of the interstate [waters] of the Red River and its tributaries."

In summary, conflicts generated from resource usage by different interests are a natural occurrence. Conflicts arising among users of hydropower, water supply, recreation, flood control, and navigation create diverse problems for the managers of Lake Texoma's natural resources. Many attempts have been made by the Corps to ameliorate conflict and to find acceptable solutions. Legislative acts occasionally have been required to resolve conflicts. The Red River Compact Commission and the Lake Texoma Advisory Committee are effective in resolving some of the controversies arising from allocation of resources at Lake Texoma. Other disagreements may arise in the future. The U.S. Army Corps of Engineers will continue to manage Lake Texoma resources in a manner that ensures the maximum enjoyment of its resources for the greatest number of people and to find acceptable compromises for any disputes which may arise.

Contracting Provisions to Delay Capital Expenditures
and Extend the Use of Available Water Supplies

J. Tom Ray, P.E.[1]
R. Anne Smith, P.E., Member, ASCE[2]

Abstract

In attempting to schedule construction of future capacity, the problem in a regional water supply system is not only one of insuring that future demands can be met but also of using presently available capacity to its fullest. A contractual means has been established of assuring equitable use of available water supply by the regional participants in the Williamson County Raw Water Line Project. A contract between the Brazos River Authority and each participant provides for optimal use of water supply in the existing Lake Georgetown. The construction of a raw water pipeline to transfer supplies to Lake Georgetown from another reservoir when its available supplies are exhausted is another major feature of the contract. This paper discusses provisions of this contract that allow the joint use of surplus water supply among the participants. This joint use allows pipeline construction to be delayed until absolutely necessary. Construction delays will defer capital expenditures until the customer base has increased, thus decreasing the cost per connection.

The regional participants provide annual projections of their water demands for a five-year period. The Authority compiles the projections and makes an official determination of the Surplus Water available for use by the group. A two year construction period for the 26 mile pipeline will be scheduled whenever the group's annual projections exceed the available supplies in Lake Georgetown.

Introduction

In 1981 a large group of Cities and water districts in Williamson County, Texas came to the Brazos River

---

[1]Planning Division Manager, Brazos River Authority, 4400 Cobbs Drive Waco, Texas 76714-7555

[2]Project Manager, HDR Engineering, Inc., 3000 IH 35, Suite 400, Austin, Texas 78704

Authority to request additional surface water supplies to help meet their future water demands. Williamson County, contiguous to the City of Austin, Texas, was a rapid growing area, particularly in the late 1970's and early 1980's. Existing surface water supplies were limited. Lake Georgetown, located on the North Fork of the San Gabriel River, 3.7 miles northwest of the City of Georgetown, was the only major water supply reservoir in the area. Groundwater supplies were also limited. During drought or high demand periods, water rationing was common occurrence.

In order to provide for the group's future water needs, the Brazos River Authority contracted with each entity for supplies in Lake Stillhouse Hollow. As shown below in Table 1, the Williamson County group contracted for 22,400 acre-ft/yr (2,763 ha-m/yr) of Current Use Water, water available for diversion from Lake Stillhouse Hollow, and for 15,854 acre-ft/yr (1,956 ha-m/yr) of Option Water, supply that will available in the future.

Table 1

Lake Stillhouse Hollow Water Supply
Distribution to Williamson County Group

Participants	Current Water %	Acre-ft/yr	Option Water %	Acre-ft/yr
Cedar Park	0.00%	0	46.90%	7,436
Georgetown	14.24%	1,120	27.30%	4,328
High Gabr.	0.45%	100	0.81%	310
Jonah WSC	3.24%	726	3.24%	513
Leander	15.00%	3,760	2.30%	364
Round Rock	64.57%	16,134	6.80%	1,080
SCB Corp.	2.50%	560	12.13%	1,923
Totals	100.00%	22,400	100.00%	15,854

In September 1984, the Brazos River Authority delivered a report prepared by the engineering firm of HDR Engineering, Inc. to the group that described the most economical method of delivering raw water to Williamson County from Lake Stillhouse Hollow located approximately 30 miles north in Bell County, Texas. A regional project consisting of the following three elements or stages was proposed: (1) a raw water transmission pipeline, (2) a regional water treatment plant on Lake Georgetown, and (3)

CONTRACTING PROVISIONS

an extensive treated water delivery system. Each component of the system would be developed under a separate contract between the Brazos River Authority and those entities electing to participate in that component. The use of Lake Georgetown as an interim storage reservoir allowed the pipeline to be sized to deliver average annual demands rather than maximum day demands.

Raw Water Line Contract

In June 1986, a number of the regional participants including the Cities of Georgetown and Round Rock executed contracts for the construction of the raw water transmission pipeline (Raw Water Line Contract). The water supply of Lake Georgetown is committed to the Cities of Georgetown and Round Rock under a earlier contract with the Brazos River Authority; however, under the Raw Water Line Contract both Cities agreed to allow others to use a portion of their Lake Georgetown water supply that they determined to be in excess of their short-term future water demands. The water would be relinquished when the raw water pipeline was in operation.

The Raw Water Line Contract contains a number of innovative provisions for the use of Surplus Water supply to delay the construction of the raw water pipeline without compromising the final delivery of Lake Stillhouse Hollow water when it is needed. The Contract provides that the Cities of Georgetown and Round Rock will limit their annual water use from Lake Georgetown to an amount that they have previously certified in annual projections submitted
to the Authority. The five-year projections are also submitted by the other participations. These Certified Projections are used by the Authority to determine the amount of Surplus Water available to the group. The participants share the Surplus Water on a pro rata basis. The price of Surplus Water is 150% of the price established in the original contracts for Lake Georgetown water supply between the Cities and the Authority. The City providing the Surplus Water receives the benefit of the fifty percent (50%) price surcharge.

Each year the participants provide the Authority with water supply and projected water demand information for a five-year period. The Authority prepares a five-year projection of the annual average and maximum daily water needs of each participant, determines the availability of Surplus Water in Lake Georgetown, and prepares an associated construction schedule for the pipeline. The

construction schedule will specify when the final design
and construction must begin in order to transfer water
supply from Lake Stillhouse Hollow to meet the projected
water needs that cannot be satisfied with Surplus Water
from Lake Georgetown.

Preliminary Engineering and Right-of-Way Acquisition

In order to complete construction within a two year
period, the Raw Water Line Contract provided that the
preliminary engineering and right-of-way acquisition for
the pipeline be done immediately. A preliminary
engineering report was completed in March 1988. This
report recommended the pipeline route and size as well as
the intake structure type and location. The pump station
was sized and several operational concerns were addressed.
The final stages of right-of-way acquisition are being
completed. For the most part the Authority will obtain
private easement for the 26 mile pipeline.

Certified Projections

The annual update to the five-year projections allows
the Authority to monitor the highly variable water demands
that are characteristic of an area recovering from an
economic decline. Rapid growth could easily resume. The
Certified Projections submitted for calendar years 1987,
1988, and 1989 have shown that the raw water transmission
pipeline should not be needed until after the year 2000.

WATER RESOURCES:
TRANSFER OF DEVELOPMENT RIGHTS

James LeGrotte[1]

This paper addresses the omnipresent perceived conflicts regarding development, land owners rights, accepted land development management practices, and community or public rights. It includes such issues as the mounting pressures for development, density, urban sprawl, the need to conserve open space, community tax base, private land ownership, water resources planning and management, the taking issue, and the role of transfer of development rights as a concept and as it is administered.

The intent of the paper is to explore a system which unlike traditional planning and zoning practices relies on sound planning, and must involve the property owner, the community and the developer in its implementation. It outlines a method through which environmental values can be preserved (including the need to protect water resources); community tax base and revenues can be expanded; property owners can be compensated for lost "taken" development opportunities; and comprehensive land development plans can be implemented; all without an outlay of large amounts of public money.

Examples of transfer of development rights for water resources management are discussed. Problems associated with the implementation of transfer of development rights and resolution of those problems as developed by those directly involved in the early use of transfer of development rights are also included.

Any attempt to assess our direction for the future must be guided by an assessment of our past and an evaluation of our projected goals and objectives. Many years ago Abraham Lincoln expressed this in another way when he said: "If we could first know where we are, and whither we are tending, we could better judge what to do and how to do it."

This is good advice with regard to a discussion of Transfer of Development Rights (TDR). Before we look forward at what could be next, we must first look at where we are; we must have some understanding of how we got here; and we must identify and analyze problems experienced along the way.

---

[1]Community Planner, Federal Emergency Management Agency - Region VI, 800 North Loop 288, Denton, Texas 76201

Since the 1940s the predominant method of managing land use or development has been through what is referred to as 'traditional' zoning.

Traditional land planning and zoning employs a land use classification system with factors ranging from undeveloped land at the lower end and heavy industry at the higher end of the classification range. When used by planners, the phrase "highest and best use" is used to describe the classification best suited for that parcel of land from an academic standpoint. The document generally produced from this approach is referred to as "The Comprehensive Plan" or "The Master Plan" which often contains a series of multi-colored maps and overlays that
prescribe the recommended use for all land within the community. Forcing a pattern of projected land use on a community has all too often resulted in the creation of a series of windfalls and wipeouts with respect to the value of land in private ownership.

Recognizing the need to consider development standards as the primary consideration in the development of comprehensive plans, the planning profession began to use the concept of holding capacities and performance or impact zoning. This concept acknowledged the fact that land can be stressed by improperly planned and unmanaged development. Planners, community administrators and local elected officials also began to accept the fact that what had occurred in the way of development (existing conditions), could also be stressed if future development is not properly planned and implemented.

With performance zoning, communities were advised to develop a set of performance standards to be applied to future development or redevelopment. These standards generally include applied development densities, traffic generation limitations, percent of lot coverage, common open space, setbacks, noise emissions, light emissions, water runoff, erosion, required buffers and screens and other standards which the community identified as important to that particular city, town, county, parish, etc. These standards in some cases included protection of water resources and other environmental concerns, historic preservation and aesthetic values.

Performance zoning is an attempt to integrate development standards and the review process of local governments in order to provide a more sophisticated information base on which to make development decisions. A well developed performance system has four primary characteristics: 1) It relates land use demands to land use capacities or holding capacities; 2) It assesses the consequences of proposed changes in land use; 3) It emphasizes an on-going process rather than a fixed product or an inflexible preconceived land use plan and zoning overlay; and 4) It provides a legislative and administrative framework for land use management and uses minimal land use controls.

DEVELOPMENT RIGHTS TRANSFER

Although performance zoning is a logical step in the evolution of land development management, it has not and will not bring about on a grand scale the formation of Public/Private Partnerships. The missing ingredient is incentive for the private land owner, or "What's in it for me?".

To work well and bring about Public/Private Partnerships, a land development management system must have, as a minimum, the following components: 1) It must increase awareness and knowledge of the interdependent nature of our environment; 2) it must employ planning which is politically impartial, economically equitable, socially reflective of needs and recognizes land holding capabilities or capacities; 3) it must be as non-restrictive as possible; 4) it must contain a systematic educational element; 5) it must be dynamic; (6) it must be guided by policies and criteria; and (7) it must be capable of realistic implementation.

The concept of Transfer of Development Rights (TDR) would appear to provide the only reasonable solution in this regard.

Transfer of Development Rights (TDR) is based on the assumption that all parcels of land within an area have the same development potential. This potential is determined by assigning a percent of all development potential to each parcel of land. The exact percentage would be the same as represented by the percent the parcel of land is to the total land within the area. These development rights are associated with land ownership and would include within the "bundle of rights" such things as water rights, mineral rights, air rights, and the rights to the appropriate percentage of single-family, multi-family, commercial, and industrial development. Since development on all land is not desirable and in some cases not possible, unusable development rights would need to be transferred (assigned) to developable parcels in order for the community to meet its full development potential and designed densities.

Transfer of development credits adds flexibility to zoning by permitting density transfers between non-contiguous parcels. These parcels in most cases would not have common ownership. Landowners desiring to develop at higher intensity than allowed under current zoning (based on the local performance standards) may purchase development rights from land owners who may not, for various reasons, intend to develop their land to the allowable intensity. TDR is a land management device based on the underlying principle that the development potential of privately held land is in part a community asset that government may allocate to enhance general welfare. In effect, TDR severs the development potential from the land and treats it as a marketable item, attempting to mesh the economic forces of the market place with the police power authority of government to protect the general welfare. By meshing economic forces of the market place, the economic interests of the land owner and the police power authority of government, TDR serves the interests of environmental protection, development, and water resources management without running the risk of the ever present challenge of the 'Taking Issue'.

TDR cannot function in the absence of a well conceived land use development plan based on holding capacities, performance standards, and the willingness of the community to implement the concept. This plan must identify specific purposes and areas within which no development or only drastically restricted development will be allowed. The purposes may include such items as historic preservation, open space preservation, preservation of environmentally sensitive areas, flood water detention areas, natural habitat, geologically sensitive areas where development should be prohibited, areas which should remain free from development in order to provide proper drainage and water resources protection and all other areas which should be restricted or remain undeveloped. Within the planning process there would need to be an assessment of the development potential for the community including the identification of the acceptable average density and the allowable high intensity. The average density should be high enough to encourage development and profit to the developer but low enough that the developer will be encouraged to build at a higher intensity in order to maximize return on investment - profit. High intensity development, if fully utilized, should produce the maximum desired density for the community based on the community's ability to provide all of the necessary and desired standards and community services. All of these: habitat, detention, preservation, density, etc. are the performance standards which were discussed earlier and must be agreed upon before the planning process and resultant land development plan will have any validity. Once the planning process has reached this point, certain facts and or factors will be known. We will know where development should be encouraged, where it should be discouraged, what our average density and allowable intensity is, and what performance standards we wish to maintain within the community. In turn, all land within the community will be assigned a proportional share of the development rights based on the average density.

Once these factors have been determined, TDR is ready to be put into practice. For example, a developer wants to develop some land but can make a higher profit if the development could be located somewhere nearer the high intensity limits for the community. The only way the developer can accomplish this is to obtain additional development rights. This can only be accomplished by obtaining additional rights from those whose land has been severely restricted or prohibited for development in order to attain the agreed upon performance standards as outlined in the community's comprehensive plan.

The developer and land owner or owners of the development rights have several options from which to choose. The developer can deal with any number of development rights owners to obtain the best price in order to make the proposed development work. The development rights owner can also work a deal to become a limited investor in the project using the development rights as collateral. The owner of the development rights can also sell the development rights through a development rights bank in the private market or in some cases the community could purchase development rights in order to obtain land for open-space development for preservation or land necessary for public works projects. These development rights could be marketed at a later date. Land has not been taken without compensation once the owner has disposed of the development rights and has been compensated for the unusable or drastically restricted status of their land and the taking issue is no longer an issue. The land having devalued status due to the fact that the development rights representing most of the potential value have been removed through a transfer to other land, or purchased by a third party for future use, should be taxed accordingly at a much lower rate. This is also an incentive for transferring the development rights. With the lower value on the land, the community might be able to purchase appropriate parcels of land for open-space or other municipal uses as long as the intended use did not conflict with the allowable use in the comprehensive plan and the performance standards. Another play on this concept is that land could be purchased by a community or other public entity at a reduced price by leaving the development rights with the original land owner who could then market the development rights at some future date.

TDR is not just a theory or concept, nor is it something which has come about within the last few years. This is evidenced by the following statement by Jared B. Shlaes: "The transfer of development rights , or TDR as it has come to be known, is not wholly new. Liberating but not revolutionary, it has been put to work by the British for more than 40 years. New York City has made use of it to encourage the preservation of landmarks and open space by allowing their owners to transfer development rights to adjacent sites. But it is only since the 1971 publication of the 'Chicago Plan,' which broke away from the adjacency rule to allow transfer of development rights anywhere within a designated zone and which provided a funding mechanism, that TDR began to come of age in America. It is now being widely discussed as a vehicle for the preservation of landmarks, historic districts, and open space (water resources) and as a supplement to, and perhaps replacement for, conventional zoning." Examples of the use of TDR include:

1) The Puerto Rico system which permits the transfer of the development rights from land in "Protected Environmental Zones" (PEZs) to sites in "Transfer Districts" where greater density will not only be unobjectionable in

environmental terms but will actually facilitate the
implementation of the comprehensive planning objectives;

2) The "East Everglades Resources Planning Project" with
the intent to: a) provide a detailed explanation of the
natural systems operating in the East Everglades and the
role these systems play in the overall environment and
economic health of Dade County and the south Florida
region; b) evaluate the impact of existing and potential
land uses on these systems; and c) prepare a plan that
would balance private land development with the needs of
the natural systems. An interesting lawsuit was filed
challenging the ordinances which resulted from the East
Everglades Resources Planning Project. The interesting
point to make with respect to the lawsuit is that it
challenged that the Board had violated the Florida open
meetings law rather than the taking of property without
compensation;

3) The California Coastal Conservancy which may offer
alternative development possibilities through development
rights transfer, cluster development, and flexible financing
to developers if they agree to relocate proposed projects away
from wetlands;

4) The State of New Jersey which studied the TDR concept as
a tool for preservation of open space;

5) The State of Maryland which developed a set of guiding
principles to assist in the implementation of TDR;

6) New York City and its use of TDR as an aid to historic
preservation;

7) Fairfax, Virginia and TDR use as general land use
controls;

8) Marin County, California;

9) Georgetown Waterfront, Washington, D.C.; and

10) Buckingham Township, Pennsylvania.

In conclusion, we in the business of water resources
management must ask: If there is a system which recognizes
planning principles, has well conceived development criteria or
performance standards, will bring about the establishment of
public/private partnerships, affect a reduction in public
expenditures for natural resource preservation, avoid the taking
issue and provide for the protection of water resources; and if
that system is Transfer of Development Rights, why not give it a
try?

References:

Buckingham Township Ordinance
    1975   Buckingham Township zoning ordinance on
    1985   transfer of development rights, 1975 & 1985

Gans, Ellis   "Economic Effects of a TDR System: Marin
                County, California" aspo Planning Advisory
                Service: Report on Transfer of Development
                Rights

LUP Reports
    1973   "NEW JERSEY STUDIES 'TDR' CONCEPTS AS TOOL FOR
                PRESERVING OPEN SPACE"

Marcus, Norman
                "TDR and Historic Preservation: The New York
                City Experience" aspo Planning Advisory
                Service: Report on Transfer of Development
                Rights

Moore, Audrey
                "TDR as the Basic Land Use Control Mechanism:
                TDRs as the Solution to Failings of Existing
                Land-Use Controls: Fairfax County, Virginia"
                aspo Planning Advisory Service: Report on
                Transfer of Development Rights

Pizor, Peter J.
    1978   "New Jersey's TDR Experience" environmental
                comment April 1978

Poole, Sam, Henry Iler, and Charles Siemon
    1982   "Flood, plague, and planning save the East
                Everglades" Planning October 1982

Rahenkamp Sachs Wells and Associates, Inc. and The American
Society of Planning Officials
    1977   "Innovative Zoning: A Digest of the Literature"
                Prepared for The U.S. Department of Housing and
                Urban Development, Office of Policy Development
                and Research

Rody, Martin J.
"Encouraging Redevelopment Through a TDR
System: Georgetown Waterfront, D.C." aspo
Planning Advisory Service: Report on Transfer
of Development Rights

Schnidman, Frank
1978 "TDR: A Tool for More Equitable Land
Management" environmental comment April 1978

Shlaes, Jared B.
1974 "Who pays for Transfer of Development Rights"
Planning July 1974

Willis, Sidney
"TDR and Open Space Preservation"
aspo Planning Advisory Service: Report on
Transfer of development Rights

Some Hydrological Impacts of Climate Change
for the Delaware River Basin

by Gary D. Tasker (1)

Abstract

The Delaware River provides water for approximately 20 million people in New York, New Jersey, Pennsylvania, and Delaware through a system of controlled reservoirs, diversion canals, and ground water wells. Changes in regional climate caused by increases in atmospheric concentrations of carbon dioxide and other gases could impact the availability of water in the Delaware River and thus affect water management practices. To gain insight into possible impacts of climate change on water availability in the Delaware River, two models are linked. The first model is a monthly water balance model that converts the temperature and precipitation values generated by a random number generator to monthly streamflow values. The monthly streamflow values are input to a second model that simulates the operation of reservoirs and diversions within the basin. The output for the two linked models consists of time series of reservoir levels and streamflow at key points in the basin. These time series can be analyzed to evaluate the impact on drought risks of climate change and modified rules of operation.

Model results for a base case, in which monthly temperature and precipitation statistics are unchanged from historical records, are compared to several changed-climate scenarios under a standard set of rules of operation. The comparisons indicate that when average temperature is increased by 2 or 4 degrees C the frequency of declaring drought warnings and drought conditions is significantly increased. Even greater drought risks occur in the model results if a rise in temperature is accompanied by a small decrease in average precipitation.

(1) Hydrologist, U. S. Geological Survey, 430 National Center, Reston, VA 22092

Introduction

The Delaware River flows south from the western slopes of the Catskill Mountains in southern New York past Philadelphia, Pennsylvania and enters the Delaware Bay. Near Trenton, New Jersey it falls about eight feet over a series of rock ledges and enters the tidal estuary. Drainage area above Trenton is about 6780 square miles. Major diversions from the basin are from three reservoirs in the upper part of the basin for water supply for New York City and from the river near Trenton through the Delaware-Raritan Canal for New Jersey. By agreement, the three reservoirs operated by New York City must release an amount of water to maintain a minimum flow at the Montague gage (drainage area 3480 square miles) and are restricted as to how much water may be diverted. The restrictions vary by months and additional restrictions may be imposed in times of drought. In addition to the diversions from the basin, the river is an important source of water for several municipalities in the basin.

Increasing atmospheric concentrations of carbon dioxide and other gases are expected to raise the Earth's average surface temperature by several degrees Celsius in the next few decades. General circulation models indicate that rises of 2 or 4 degrees Celsius in average temperature, accompanied by changes in average precipitation amounts of several percent, are plausible for the Delaware River Basin (McCabe and Ayers, 1989). If such changes occur in the basin they could impact the seasonal distribution and amount of water available. Any change in water availability is of some interest to water resources planners and managers because the Delaware River is a major source of water for approximately 20 million people in New York, New Jersey, Pennsylvania, and Delaware.

To make a quantitative assessment of the impacts of climate change on water available in the basin, computer models are developed to simulate flows in the basin under different climatic conditions. In addition, the models can be used to evaluate the impact of possible mitigation measures such as increasing reservoir capacities and modified operating rules.

Water-Balance Model

A monthly time-step water-balance model was developed and calibrated for the basin. The model, a modification of the one developed by Thornthwaith (1948), is a water budget bookkeeping procedure that accounts for soil moisture, evapotranspiration, water

CLIMATE CHANGE IMPACTS

deficit, snowmelt, and surface runoff. The inputs needed are monthly average temperature and precipitation. General agreement between measured and computed monthly runoff is achieved by adjusting model parameters, such as basin lag and water holding capacity of the basin.

A base for comparison is established by inputing to the water-balance model 100 years of monthly synthetic temperature and precipitation values that statistically match historical records. The time series of temperature and precipitation values are created by randomly generating serially and cross correlated residuals from long-term monthly mean values. The resulting 100 years of monthly runoff are used as input to the basin model described below to establish a base run under present climatic conditions. Similar 100 year runs are made under several changed climate scenarios described below by changing the long-term monthly mean values of temperature and precipitation.

Basin Model

The monthly flows generated by the water-balance model are routed through a basin model that simulates operation of reservoirs, diversion canals, and ground-water wells. The basin model is a mass balance model that accounts for all inflows and outflows at several key nodes in the basin. For example, the flow at the Montague gage in month t would equal the releases from the New York City Reservoirs plus uncontrolled flow for month t minus consumptive uses within the basin above Montague for month t.

Releases from the New York City Reservoirs are made to meet minimum instream flow requirements and to meet a minimum target flow at Montague. When uncontrolled flow at Montague is not adequate to meet the minimum flow requirement the New York City Reservoirs release enough water to make up the difference. Other reservoirs in the basin can be operated in a similar manner during low flows to augment flows to meet minimum flow requirements at Trenton.

Model Results and Conclusions

A quantitative assessment of the impacts of climate change is made by keeping track of how often the basin enters "drought emergency" conditions under both present climate conditions (base run) and changed climate scenarios. The results for a base run and combinations of changes in temperature of 2 and 4 degrees C and changes in precipitation of + or - 10 percent are shown in Table 1.

Table 1. Model results showing percent of months in which the basin was in drought warning or drought conditions for various climate scenarios.

SCENARIOS Temperature	Precipitation no change	-10 percent	+10 percent
no change	12.2	--	--
+2 deg. C	19.0	44.5	8.9
+4 deg. C	29.8	60.2	12.9

Results indicate that when average temperature is increased by 2 or 4 degrees C the probability of entering "drought emergency" conditions in the basin is significantly increased (1.6 to 2.4 times base run). Even greater drought risks occur if the rise in temperature is accompanied by a small decrease in average precipitation (3.6 to 4.9 times base run). If an increase in average temperature of 4 degrees is accompanied by an increase in average precipitation of 10 percent, then the model results indicate little change in drought risks.

References

McCabe, G.J., Jr., and Ayers, M.A., 1989, Effects of global warming on soil moisture and runoff in the Delaware River basin: Water Resources Bulletin (in press).

Thornthwaite, C.W., 1948, An approach toward a rational classification of climate: Geographical Review, vol. 38, pp 55-94.

PREDICTING EFFECTS OF GLOBAL CLIMATE CHANGE ON RESERVOIR WATER QUALITY AND FISH HABITAT

Lisa H. Chang[1] and Steven F. Railsback, A. M. ASCE[2]

Introduction

This paper demonstrates the use of general circulation models (GCMs) for assessing global climate change effects on reservoir water quality and illustrates that general conclusions about the effects of increased carbon dioxide (CO_2) concentrations on water resources can be made by using GCMs. These conclusions are based on GCM predictions of the climatic effects of doubling CO_2 concentrations (the $2 \times CO_2$ scenario). We also point out inadequacies in using information from GCM output alone to simulate reservoir water quality effects of climate change.

Our investigation used Douglas Lake, a large multipurpose reservoir in eastern Tennessee, as an example. We studied water temperature and dissolved oxygen (DO), important water quality parameters that are expected to respond to a changed climate. Finally, we used the temperature and DO requirements of striped bass as an indicator of biological effects of combined changes in temperature and DO.

Methods

Douglas Lake was selected for the study because (1) it is a typical multipurpose headwater reservoir, (2) a calibrated water quality model and input for a typical year were available, and (3) there are no other reservoirs or heat sources such as power plants upstream of the lake. Annual runoff is about 51 cm from a mountainous drainage area of 11,760 km^2, so mean annual flow at the dam is 16 million m^3/day. Lowest dam releases are expected in April to May, when pool levels are raised to summer elevations. Outflow is through a low-level turbine intake 27 m below maximum summer pool elevation. The reservoir stratifies in the summer (Brown et al. 1987).

---

[1]Duke University School of Forestry, Durham, NC 27706.

[2]Oak Ridge National Laboratory, P.O. Box 2008, Oak Ridge, TN 37831-6036. Research sponsored by the Exploratory Studies Program of Oak Ridge National Laboratory, operated for the U.S. Department of Energy by Martin Marietta Energy Systems, Inc., under contract DE-AC05-84OR21400.

The BETTER water quality simulation model has been applied to Douglas Lake (Brown et al. 1987) and was adapted for this study. The model divides the reservoir vertically and longitudinally into an array of volume elements. The model uses daily inflow, outflow, meteorology, and inflow water quality values to predict daily water quality for each volume element. Flow mixing patterns are calculated from the reservoir geometry and thermal density effects.

Predictions of climate change effects are often based on output from GCMs, which provide quantitative estimates of the climatic effects of increased CO_2 concentrations. Climate change analysts often express GCM forecasts as the ratio of the value of a climate parameter under conditions with atmospheric CO_2 doubled to the value under current conditions (the $2xCO_2/1xCO_2$ ratio); these ratios are available for each month. The monthly values of these standardized ratios are obtained from many years of simulated climate. GCMs are grid-based models, and output is produced for each of the large grid cells in each GCM. A discussion of GCM output and its use for impact assessment, and the standardized output for three climate models [the Geophysical Fluid Dynamics Laboratory (GFDL), Goddard Institute for Space Studies (GISS), and Oregon State University (OSU) models] are available from the National Center for Atmospheric Research (Jenne 1989).

We obtained the $2xCO_2/1xCO_2$ ratios for these three GCMs for grid cells that cover our experiment site. We selected more than one grid cell from each GCM, since Douglas Lake is close to the grid cell borders in each model.

We evaluated climate change effects (1) by simulating Douglas Lake water quality and striped bass habitat during a typical year with current CO_2 concentrations and (2) by modifying the input for six parameters by applying the monthly $2xCO_2/1xCO_2$ ratios for the selected GCM grid cells and simulating the resulting water quality and habitat. To simulate water quality and fish habitat conditions for the current climate, we used flow, inflow water quality, and meteorologic records from 1974 (the base scenario). The base year 1974 was fairly typical hydrologically, but had flows higher than average in winter and April.

The reservoir model input parameters that were adjusted with GCM output are wind speed, solar radiation, air (dry bulb) temperature, dew point temperature, inflow water temperature (which was estimated by using a regression relation with air temperature), and flow rate into the reservoir (runoff estimates from the GCMs were used for this parameter). Daily reservoir pool elevations and inflow water quality were not changed between the base and GCM scenarios.

The model was also used to estimate the sensitivity of reservoir water quality to each of these six climate parameters by changing each parameter individually from the base scenario in separate simulations.

Results

We plotted daily simulated lake volumes with optimal, suboptimal, and unacceptable temperatures and DO concentrations for striped bass for the base scenario and the GCM scenarios (Fig. 1 shows examples). These figures show variations between the GCM scenarios. Nevertheless, all the GCM scenarios predict large losses in summer striped bass habitat. All GCM scenarios predict increases in water temperatures to levels higher than those tolerated by striped bass. There is much variability among model scenarios for changes in summer DO concentrations with a changed climate; some predicted large losses of habitat due to low DO concentrations.

Examination of model results and GCM modeling methods led to the following observations concerning the six parameters affected by climate change.

Air and inflow temperature: All GCMs predict air temperature increases throughout the year, with greatest increases in temperature during late winter - early spring and early autumn. Increases in inflow water temperature were estimated from increases in atmospheric temperature. An increase in air and inflow temperatures leads to earlier DO depletion because of earlier algal growth and decay, earlier summer stratification, increases in water temperatures, and increases in respiration rates.

Humidity: The GCMs agree that humidity will increase. The simulated effect of an increase in humidity alone was an increase in surface water temperatures, increased stability of stratification, increased algal biomass, and deteriorated DO conditions. Increased humidity would be expected to offset to some extent any increases in evaporative cooling that would be expected with a rise in surface water temperature alone.

Solar radiation: Most GCMs predict decreased cloudiness; however, model simulation of observed cloudiness is rather poor (Gates 1985). An increase in solar radiation stimulates algal productivity and raises surface water temperatures; these effects would lead to enhanced stratification and DO depletion. Habitat effects observed with a 5% increase in solar radiation were quite small.

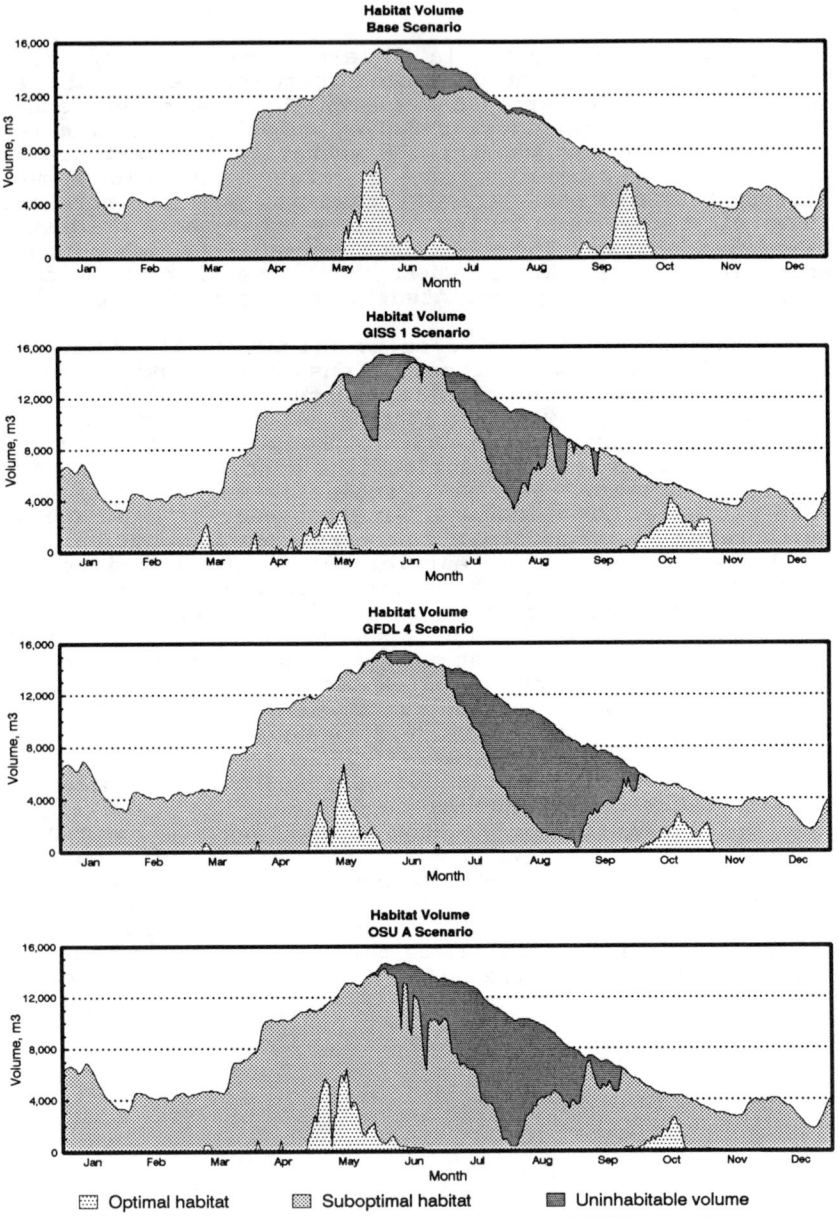

Fig. 1. Striped bass habitat for base and GCM scenarios.

Runoff: In the various GCMs, runoff is generally dependent on precipitation, evaporation, and field capacity. However, among the GCMs, there are differences in precipitation change predictions, field capacity assumptions, and methods for calculating runoff. Climate modelers have suggested that GCM runoff estimates be avoided, in favor of deriving runoff estimates from GCM precipitation estimates (Jenne 1989), but there is no consensus among GCM precipitation change estimates. Large increases in summer runoff, such as those predicted by GISS, will contribute to overall lake warming as warm inflow displaces cool hypolimnetic water and will reduce stratification, residence times, and adverse DO effects. Severe, prolonged low-flow conditions, such as those predicted by the GFDL model, may contribute to a lowering of the thermocline, which would reduce the effects of longer retention of cool hypolimnetic water.

Wind speed: Wind speed and its effects are complex and poorly simulated by GCMs and the reservoir model. Average scalar wind speeds are available with the GISS output; average vector wind speeds are available for other GCMs (average vector wind speed is the average of wind speed with both magnitude and direction considered; average scalar wind speed is the average of wind speed magnitude only). The $2xCO_2/1xCO_2$ ratio of average vector wind speed is meaningful only if it is assumed that the directions of the winds simulated in the $2xCO_2$ climate are the same as those in the $1xCO_2$ simulation, an assumption that is not advised (Jenne 1989). There is a lack of consensus among the GCM predictions of summer wind speed change; a slight majority predict increased wind speeds. Wind speed, with its effect on lake mixing and evaporative cooling, is the most sensitive climate parameter in the BETTER model and is one of the most difficult to model. During summer months, when water temperatures approach the upper bounds of adult striped bass preference range, wind speed effects on evaporative cooling and mixing will be perhaps the factor that determines whether the water remains habitable by striped bass. In general, low wind speed will aggravate adverse climate change effects on striped bass habitat. Increases in wind speed will reduce thermal gradients, lower adverse DO effects, and prevent water temperatures from rising into the uninhabitable range. However, in some late-summer cases, extreme warming extends below the wind-mixed depth of the lake and increased wind speed is ineffective in offsetting other climate change forces.

Discussion

Because of the uncertainties in GCMs, climate modelers suggest that predictions of climate change impacts should be based on a consensus of results obtained from various GCMs, not on the results from any particular model. In addition, when a study site lies close to grid cell boundaries, multiple grid cells for a model should be considered. We simulated water quality and fish habitat changes under climate scenarios predicted by three GCMs and two grid cells for each GCM; all these scenarios predict significant losses in striped bass habitat during summer, mostly due to temperature increases. This consensus of results leads to the conclusion that increased atmospheric CO_2 would make stocks of cool-water species such as striped bass difficult to maintain in Douglas Lake.

Our study pointed out several areas where additional research is needed. Increased atmospheric CO_2 concentrations and resulting climate effects may change watershed-level processes, such as rates of nutrient mineralization and cycling and rates of forest growth and transpiration, which in turn influence runoff and subsurface water quality and quantity. The sensitivity of lake water quality to inflow water quality should be examined to determine if further understanding of the effects of increased atmospheric CO_2 on runoff water quality is needed. Finally, other biological effects such as changes in primary productivity, prey species and competing predator species, could affect game fish populations and need to be considered.

Reservoir simulation modeling was useful in determining what implications climate change may have on water quality and should be useful in addressing the additional considerations that we identified.

Appendix--References

Brown, R. T., et al., 1987. *Douglas Reservoir Water Quality Modeling to Evaluate Mixing Devices*. Center for the Management, Utilization and Protection of Water Resources, Tennessee Technological University, Cookeville, TN.

Gates, W. L., 1985. "Modeling as a Means of Studying the Climate System" in *Projecting the Climatic Effects of Increasing Carbon Dioxide*, MacCracken, M. C. and Luther, F. M., editors, U.S. Department of Energy Publication ER-0237.

Jenne, R. L., 1989. Data from climate models; the CO_2 warming. National Center for Atmospheric Research. Draft revision.

Non-Point Source Contamination of Aquifers

John C. Tracy[1]

Introduction

The contamination of aquifers due to nonpoint sources of pollution has recently become an important topic when discussing environmental problems. Typically, the largest problems occur in agricultural regions, where herbicides, pesticides, and chemical fertilizers used to enhance crop production have been leached from the soil surface and crop root zone down to underlying aquifers. The reason that many aquifers became tainted was due to the underestimation of the effect that chemical application on the soil surface was going to have on the underlying aquifer's water quality. This underestimation is in part due to the inability of existing mathematical models to adequately simulate complex subsurface hydrochemical environments.

The most important problems currently encountered in simulating the movement of a chemical from the soil surface to an aquifer's water table were addressed in Bouwer (1989). These problems can be summarized as the inability to: (1) adequately describe the soil-water pore velocities; (2) determine the decay rate of a contaminant as a function of the properties of different soil layers; and (3) develop adequate descriptions of the adsorption of a contaminant onto the soil medium as a function of soil properties and the degree of water saturation.

Since the movement of a contaminant is primarily a function of the movement of water in a subsurface environment, it is felt that the development of methods to better describe the effect that the soil water velocity distribution has on the contaminant concentration would result in better methods of predicting the arrival of contamination plumes at the water table of an aquifer.

Modeling Deficiencies

Currently, the simulation of contaminant movement in a porous medium is performed using conventional advection-dispersion models.
----
[1]Assistant Professor, Department of Civil Engineering, 119 Seaton Hall, Kansas State University, Manhattan, KS 66506.

These methods have proved useful in studies of point source contamination in a saturated medium, but have encounted difficulties in simulating nonpoint source contamination moving through a variably-saturated medium. The main reason for the difficulty is due to the soil heterogeneities which can create preferential flow paths downward through the soil. When using an averaged pore water velocity in the advection-dispersion equation, the arrival time of a contaminant is significantly underestimated, resulting in an overestimate of the amount of time a contaminant has to decay in the unsaturated zone of a soil before reaching the aquifer. The soil heterogeneities also create difficulties in estimating an effective dispersion coefficient. Many times the dispersion coefficient is assumed to be a function of the average soil water velocity. However, due to the wide range of soil water velocities caused by preferential flow paths, using the average soil water velocity to estimate the dispersion coefficient would not produce an effective average dispersion coefficient.

Thus, a new method for simulating the movement of contaminants from a diffuse source at the soil surface through a variably-saturated porous medium must be developed. The method must be able to account for the effect that the distribution of the soil water velocity and soil properties have on the resulting contaminant concentration in the soil profile, so that an accurate prediction of the arrival time of a contaminant plume at the water table of an aquifer can be determined.

Statistical Approach

This objective can be accomplished by using a statistical approach to simulate the movement of a contaminant through a porous medium. Using such an approach the distribution of a contaminant at any point in the profile at a given time can be computed based on the estimated statistical properties of the parameters which describe the porous medium.

The basis for this approach can be shown for the most simplistic case, where a contaminant is transported downward from a constant surface source, with the soil having an initial constant contaminant concentration of zero. This particular problem can be formulated as a one-dimensional transport problem with the soil properties being treated as having statistical distributions which are assumed to describe the heterogeneities in the soil in the horizontal directions. It is also assumed that effects of molecular diffusion and pore scale dispersion on the movement of the contaminant are small and can be neglected. Furthermore, the statistical distributions which describe the soil properties are assumed to have parameters which do not vary with the depth of the soil profile for this particular demonstration.

For demonstration purposes, it will be assumed that the soil-water content is constant in the vertical and horizontal directions of the soil, as well as constant in time. The soil-water velocities are assumed to be described by some statistical distribution whose parameters are known. Mathematically, this problem can be stated as

$$C(t=0) = 0 \quad z>0, \; A>0 \tag{1}$$

$$C(z=0) = C_0 \quad A>0, \; t>0 \tag{2}$$

$$C(z,t) = g(z,v(A),t) \; ; \quad z>0, \; t>0 \tag{3}$$

in which: C = the contaminant concentration in the soil averaged over the horizontal dimensions; t = time; z = the vertical direction of the soil medium, assumed positive downward; C_0 = the contaminant concentration at the soil surface; A = the horizontal dimensions of the soil; and v(A) = the distribution of the soil water velocities in the horizontal dimensions of the soil with a known probability density function, f(v).

The solution for this particular case is readily obtained by noting that at any time, T, and depth in the soil profile, Z, the probability that the soil water velocity distribution has transported a contaminant past the ratio of the Z to the T is equal to the contaminant concentration at the soil surface multiplied by the cumulative distribution function of the soil water velocity, evaluated at the ratio = Z/T. Mathematically, this can be stated as

$$C(Z,T) = C_0 F(Z/T) \tag{4}$$

in which F() = the cumulative distribution function of soil water velocities.

The effect of the soil water velocity distribution on the contaminant concentration can now be analyzed using the results of Eq. (4) by assuming different probability density functions for the soil water velocity. The effects of the soil water velocity being uniformly and normally distributed will now be examined.

Results

If the soil water velocities are distributed uniformly in the horizontal dimensions of the medium, the resulting horizontally averaged contaminant concentration can be described as a function of depth and time, such that

$$C(z,t) = \begin{cases} 1 & ; \text{ if } tV_{min} \leq z \\ \dfrac{C_0(V_{max} - \frac{z}{t})}{(V_{max} - V_{min})} & ; \text{ if } tV_{min} \leq z \leq tV_{max} \\ 0 & ; \text{ if } tV_{max} \geq z \end{cases} \tag{5}$$

in which: V_{min} and V_{max} = the minimum and maximum soil water velocities, respectively. This result demonstrates that when velocities are distributed uniformly in the horizontal dimensions of the soil, the resulting averaged contamination front is a linear function of space at any particular time, with the slope of the contaminant front being a function of the minimum and maximum soil water velocities as well as time.

If the soil water velocities are distributed normally in the horizontal dimensions of the medium, the resulting horizontally averaged contaminant concentration can be described as a function of depth and time, such that

$$C(z,t) = C_0 \int_{-\infty}^{\frac{z}{t}} f(v) dv \qquad (6)$$

For computational purposes this can be more easily represented as

$$C(z,t) = C_0 \, P(w) \qquad (7)$$

in which: P( ) is the cumulative distribution function for a normally distributed variable with mean zero and unit variance; and

$$w = \frac{v_a t - z}{s_v t} \qquad (8)$$

in which v_a = the average soil water velocity and s_v = the standard deviation of the soil water velocity.

This result demonstrates that the averaged contaminant concentration front is distributed normally as a function of depth in the soil profile with a mean that is equal to the mean soil water velocity multiplied by time and a variance that is equal to the variance of soil water velocity multiplied by time squared.

The results of both Eqs. 5 and 7 are interesting in that the variation in the soil water velocities causes a dispersive type effect on the movement of a contaminant in the soil. However, this dispersive effect in the contaminant concentration over the depth of the soil is entirely a function of both the variance of the soil water velocities and time, as opposed to being a function of the average soil water velocity, which is frequently assumed in many applications of the advective dispersive equations.

References

Bouwer, H. (1989). "Agriculture and groundwater quality." Civil Engineering 59(7), 60-63.

MODELING GROUNDWATER FLOW IN SAN JOAQUIN VALLEY

Alireza S. Taghavi[1], M. ASCE; Nigel W. Quinn[2]; and Lyle B. Everett[3], M. ASCE

Abstract

Water supply, reallocation and conjunctive use options, within the San Joaquin and Tulare basins of the Central Valley of California, are being considered by Federal and State Planning agencies as a means of protecting fish and wildlife resources from adverse impacts associated with agricultural drainage water. These actions will likely be coupled with direct measures aimed at encouraging source control of agricultural drainage, such as the establishment of maximum drainage discharge volumes and/or qualities (i.e., loads, and/or contaminant concentrations), or the establishment of water quality standards for receiving waters. This paper presents a brief account of the groundwater model which has been developed for water supply analysis in the region.

Background

A number of viable options exist for both mitigating current adverse impacts on fish and wildlife resources and enhancing current resources. The first of these is the provision of supplemental water supply for fish and wildlife. Water quality in the San Joaquin River and westside tributaries has been and continues to be degraded by discharge of untreated subsurface agricultural drainage waters. Protection of existing fisheries in the Grasslands water district area could occur through improvement of water quality. This could be affected by :
    a.   Providing replacement water for the agricultural drainage used by Grasslands wetland areas prior to 1985.
    b.   Satisfying full water supply for existing wetlands and possible additional wildlife habitat areas from Delta diversions, Friant releases, and reallocation of agricultural supplies and/or groundwater.

---

[1] Engineer, Boyle Engineering Corporation

[2] Water Resource Engineer, San Joaquin Valley Drainage Program

[3] Principal Engineer, Boyle Engineering Corporation

556   RESOURCES FOR WATER MANAGEMENT

    c.   Replacement of some of Friant-Division, Central Valley Project, deliveries with Delta supplies from the California State Aqueduct and the Cross-Valley Canal in exchange for releases from Friant Dam for fish and wildlife restoration purposes.

The re-allocation of water supply currently being delivered to agriculture could be effected in the following manner.
    a.   Re-allocate existing drainage problem area water deliveries to areas of ground-water overdraft (facilitate reduced pumping).
    b.   Re-allocate existing drainage problem area water deliveries to wetland habitat areas.

These options would likely be coupled with policies of land retirement by which State, Federal and local interests purchases lands underlain my high levels of trace elements or which were known to contribute significantly to drainage loads of trace elements.

The impacts of land-use changes or the retirement of land from irrigated agriculture on firm water supply of the Federal and State water projects will need to be evaluated. Projections of irrigation return flow quantity and quality can be obtained from existing models within the San Joaquin Valley Drainage Program. However analytical tools do not currently exist to integrate combined effects of changes in groundwater and surface water delivery systems.

Development of such a tool would also allow the evaluation of the potential for water transfers between water districts or for the reallocation of water supplies from agricultural use to M&I or fish and wildlife uses. The effects of these transfers on water delivery schedules and capacities, possible groundwater pumping under a conjunctive use system and reservoir operations could also be facilitated. Discharge of drainage to the San Joaquin River is currently the only available means of eliminating salts which otherwise accumulate within the crop root zone and impair agricultural productivity. The value of a combined surface water-groundwater model may allow the most efficient safe use of the river for agricultural drainage discharge while continuing to protect in-stream fisheries and wildlife resources.

A model has been developed to simulate the effect of conjunctive operation of surface water storage and delivery systems and groundwater resources in the San Joaquin Valley. The model consists of a surfacewater and a groundwater module. The surface water module simulates the major reservoir system operations in the Valley in accordance with operational constraints including flood control, recreation, instream flow maintenance, energy, water rights, and consumptive use requirements. These demands include but are not limited to agricultural, M&I, and fisheries. The groundwater module simulates the subsurface flow of water in the layered aquifer system in the Valley. The following discussion is limited to the groundwater model.

Model Development

The San Joaquin Valley is the largest single block of irrigated land in California. A total of about six million acres of irrigable land overlies usable groundwater, 80 percent of which are developed for irrigation. In addition, there are about 300,000 acres of urban land. The main source of irrigation water supply is groundwater, although the irrigation districts on the edge of the valley benefit from the Federal and State surface water delivery systems. Large volumes of pumping has caused overdraft especially in the middle of the valley, while the source of saline irrigation return flows have caused high salinity in the groundwater.

San Joaquin Valley comprises the southern portion of the larger Central Valley which is a large, northwestward trending, asymmetric structural trough that has been filled with as such as 6 vertical miles of sediments in the San Joaquin Valley and as much as 10 miles of sediment in the Sacramento Valley. These sediments range in age from Jurassic to Holocene and include both marine and continental rocks and deposits (Repenning, 1960). The sediments beneath part of the eastern side of the valley are underlain by granitic and metamorphic rocks of pre-tertiary age. Beneath the western side and part of the eastern side, the sediments are thought to be underlain by a mafic and ultramafic complex of pre-Tertiary age (Cady, 1975 and Suppe, 1978). Granitic and metamorphic rocks crop out along most of the eastern and southeastern flank of the Central Valley. Marine rocks of pre-Tertiary age crop out along most of the western flank of the valley, (Page, 1986). The post-Eocine continental rocks and deposits contain most of the fresh groundwater in the Central Valley and crop out over virtually the whole valley. In most places, the Continental rocks and deposits overlie or contain saline water at depth. There are several clay layers impeding the vertical flow of water, the major one is the E clay layer in the San Joaquin Valley. This extensive lacustrine clay of Pleistocene age is known as Corcoran clay layer and covers most of the western portion of the San Joaquin valley. The aquifer above the Corcoran clay layer is known to be semi-confined and below the clay layer it is confined.

A pseudo three-dimensional finite element model is developed to simulate the flow of water in both the unconfined and confined aquifer system in the San Joaquin Valley. The special features of this model include the stream-aquifer interaction to simulate the seepage losses; soil moisture accounting routine to simulate the moisture deficiency in the soil system, as well as the time lag between any recharge water and the aquifer accretions; land use may be specified on an element basis in order to determine the crop water use as well as the M&I use; pumping and surface water diversions are specified on an element basis in order to model the water used by irrigation districts more realistically. The finite element grid is specially tailored to take into account the boundaries of major irrigation districts. (Fig. 1) This feature enables the analysis of water exchange between districts. The model runs on a monthly time step to simulate the effects of monthly changes in pumping and surface water diversions more realistically. The model is calibrated for the period 1961-1977, during which fairly good data is available on pumping, crop use and surface water diversions. The groundwater model will be used as part of the conjunctive use model to analyze different scenarios in water supply and reallocation in the San Joaquin Valley, the results of which will be presented in the conference.

References

Cady, J.W., 1975. Magnetic and gravity anomalies in the Great Valley and western Sierra Nevada metamorphic belt, California. Geological Society of America of America Special Paper 168, 56 P.

Page, R.W., 1986. Geology of the freshwater groundwater basin of the Central Valley, California, with texture maps and sections. U.S. Geological Survey, Professional Paper 1401-C, 54 P.

Repenning, C.A., 1960 Geologic summary of the Central Valley of California, with reference to disposal of liquid radioactive waste. U.S. Geological Survey, Open File Report, 69 P.

Suppe, J., 1978, Cross-section of southern part of northern coast ranges and Sacramento Valley, California. Geological Society of America, MC-28B, 8P.

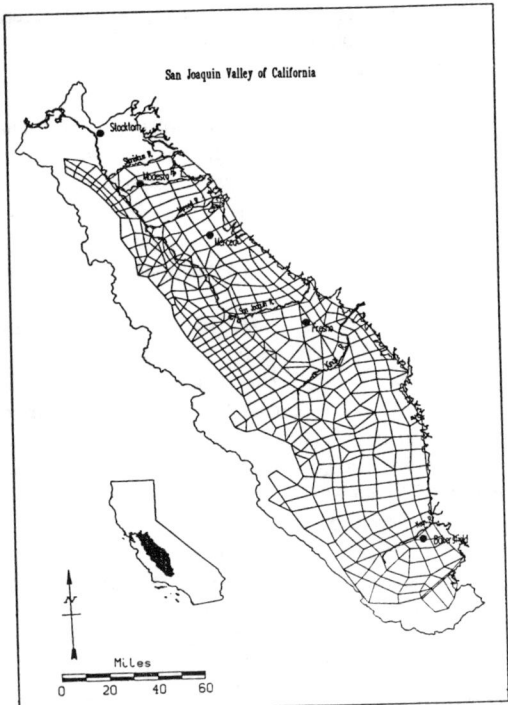

Figure 1. Finite Element Grid for San Joaquin Valley.

GROUNDWATER MODELING OF THE TUSTIN/IRVINE BASIN
Jennifer Goodell[1], M.ASCE, Shih-Huang Chieh[2], M.ASCE, Melih Ozbilgin[3], M.ASCE

Abstract

This paper describes the results of groundwater modeling in the Tustin/Irvine basin situated in the southeastern portion of the Tustin plain, which is the southern extension of the Coastal plain underlying Los Angeles County, CA. The basin has been used primarily for agriculture in the past, but may be used for drinking water in the future, since the area is becoming more urbanized with the rapid growth of Orange County. By utilizing the available field data, the U.S.G.S. Modular 3 - dimensional finite difference code was used to model the groundwater flow field. The study area was horizontally discretized into a mesh of 47 columns and 32 rows. Vertically, the model consisted of 3 layers with controlled vertical leakage between the layers, to simulate semi-confined conditions between water bearing and non-water bearing materials. The model was calibrated against field data available over a five year period, from 1984 through 1988. Results of the modeling showed a fairly good match of simulated monthly piezometric head values compared to actual field measurements at six monitoring wells in the study area. Hydrogeologic parameters, such as transmissivity, recharge and storativity were changed to test the sensitivity of the model. The boundary between the confined and unconfined zones was adjusted according to water levels observed in wells near the boundary. The model was developed as a tool to evaluate groundwater supply, basin management and contamination migration.

Introduction

The groundwater in the Tustin/Irvine basin (Figure 1) has been the attention of local water and irrigation districts, private land owners and other users over the last few decades, as the quality of groundwater has been deteriorating since 1971. In some areas of the basin, concentrations of total dissolved solids (TDS), nitrate, selenium and other organic compounds have exceeded acceptable limits for drinking water, set by the State of California. It is the intent of the local water managers, users and producers to maintain, protect and possibly improve the quality of groundwater, in view of the future high cost and availability of imported water. This study of the Tustin/Irvine

---

[1, 2, 3] Senior Engineer, Supervising Engineer, Principal Engineer, James M. Montgomery, Consulting Engineers, Inc., 501 Lennon Lane, Suite 200 Walnut Creek, CA 94598.

560 RESOURCES FOR WATER MANAGEMENT

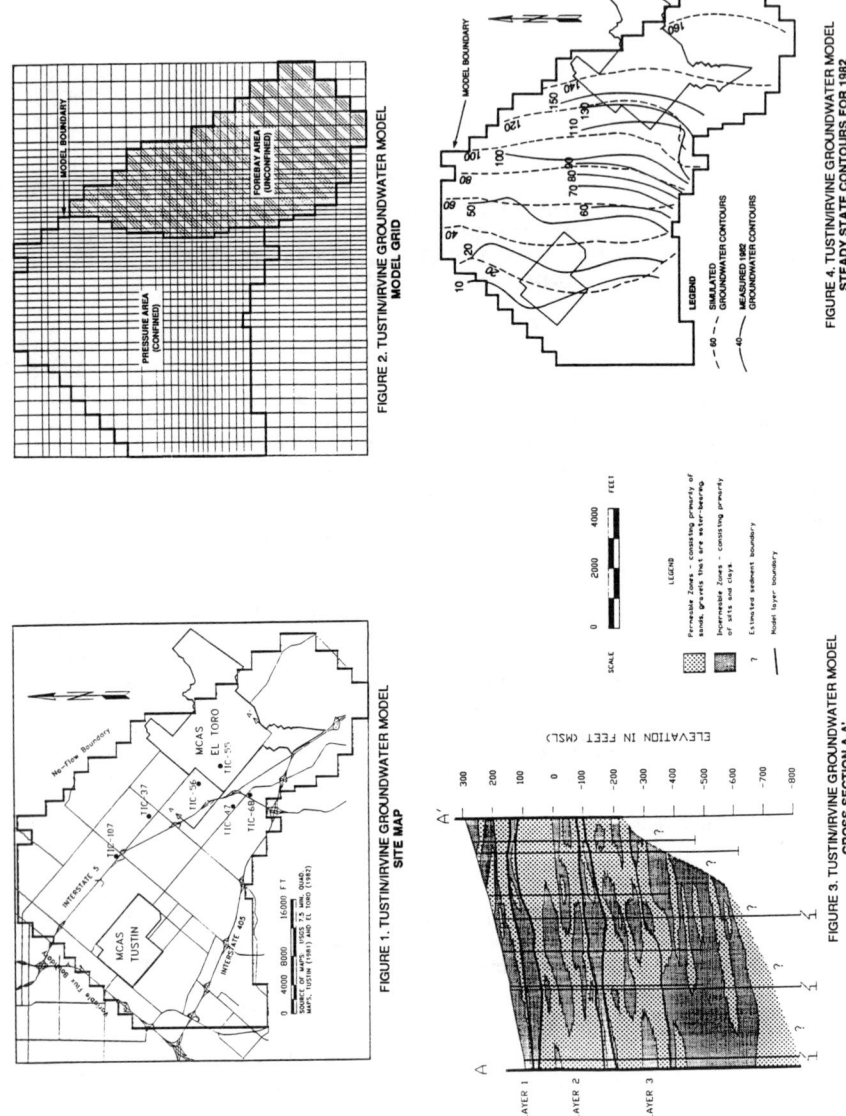

FIGURE 2. TUSTIN/IRVINE GROUNDWATER MODEL MODEL GRID

FIGURE 4. TUSTIN/IRVINE GROUNDWATER MODEL STEADY STATE CONTOURS FOR 1982

FIGURE 1. TUSTIN/IRVINE GROUNDWATER MODEL SITE MAP

FIGURE 3. TUSTIN/IRVINE GROUNDWATER MODEL CROSS-SECTION A-A'

basin was undertaken to better understand the movement of groundwater through confined and unconfined zones within the aquifer, and provide a tool for planning a groundwater management program and predicting contaminant migration within the basin.

Basin Geology

The Tustin/Irvine groundwater basin included in this model consists of a trapezoidal area in the southeastern part of the Tustin Plain. The Tustin Plain is the southern extension of the Coastal Plain of Los Angeles, a topographic basin lying at the northwesterly end of the Peninsula Ranges Province. The major water bearing strata underlying the Tustin Plain are Pleistocene alluvium and late Pliocene semi-consolidated formations. The consolidated rocks below these units, of Miocene age or older, have been classified as non-water bearing due to its poor quality and limited circulation, and therefore were not included in the groundwater model.

The aquifer system under the Tustin/Irvine basin has been divided into a forebay area and a pressure area (Figure 2). The forebay area located adjacent to the hills in the eastern most part of the Plain is unconfined, where recharge to the principal aquifer occurs. The pressure area consists of a confining zone of low permeability silts and clays that overly the producing aquifer zone. The boundary condition between the forebay and pressure areas vary seasonally according to the volume of recharge by rainfall and withdrawal by pumping demands.

Model Development

The study area encompasses approximately 100 square miles, extending from east of MCAS El Toro to west of MCAS Tustin where the Tustin/Irvine sub-basin discharges to the main Orange County groundwater basin (Figure 1). The model area was horizontally discretized into a finite difference grid comprised of 32 rows and 47 columns (Figure 2). The finite difference cell size was varied from 666 ft. by 666 ft. in the area of concern to as large as 2500 ft. by 2200 ft. elsewhere.

The model boundary to the west and northwest was selected as variable flux whereby a head-dependent flux to the main basin was simulated. Model boundaries along Santa Ana Mountains to the northeast and San Joaquin hills to the southwest were simulated as no-flow. The recharge from the base of these mountains and hills were simulated as part of the groundwater recharge applied to the upper layer. The model boundary to the southeast was selected at the edge of the sediment boundary where groundwater is believed to be non-existent, based on lack of well data.

In the vertical direction, the model consists of 3 water bearing layers, varying in thickness in layer 1 from 20 ft. to 100 ft., in layer 2 from 20 ft. to 140 ft. and in layer 3, from 80 ft. to 350 ft. The thickness of each layer was determined by constructing an extensive array of geologic cross-sections from driller's logs throughout the groundwater basin, and identifying layers based on water bearing and non-water bearing characteristics of the sediments. Figure 3 is a typical geologic cross-section along the center of the basin showing the subsurface stratigraphy. The basin bottom was identified in the eastern most part of the basin by the presence of a blue shale.

Hydrostatic pressure and water quality data from single-bore hole multi-port monitoring wells as well as multiple-bore hole cluster wells were compared to further adjust layer thicknesses. The distinct changes in total dissolved solids (TDS) and general mineral concentrations were interpreted to indicate paths of preferential flow where solutioning of the aquifer stratum has occurred. Layer 3, which is considered to be the most prolific aquifer in the area, had TDS concentrations less than 1000 ppm while the lower and upper water bearing zones had concentrations significantly above this value.

Model layer 1 was simulated as confined within the pressure area (low storage coefficient) and unconfined within the forebay area (high storage coefficient). Model layers 2 and 3, were simulated as confined aquifers with vertical conductivity values of 0.0024 and 0.00024 ft/day assigned between the layers, respectively.

Steady-State Calibrations

A relational spatial database was set up that contained information on layers from each geologic log utilized in developing the cross-sections. Contour maps of layer thicknesses were generated, based on layer top and bottom elevations. For each of the three layers, a thickness value was calculated for each nodal cell from these contour maps. Initial groundwater elevation values were obtained from historic groundwater contour maps of the area. These measured elevations were also used to calculate the groundwater flux in and out of the basin along the boundaries.

Initial transmissivity values were estimated for each layer from 29 irrigation wells located throughout the basin where specific capacity tests were performed following installation. These values were adjusted according to the length of screened interval of each well within a given layer. To further adjust and spatially distribute these transmissivity values throughout the basin, a typical permeability value was assigned to each unit observed in geologic logs. Multiplication of these values with unit thicknesses and calculating the harmonic means along layer thicknesses resulted in a transmissivity matrix spatially distributed for each layer.

The 1982 water year was selected for steady-state calibration purposes. This year was selected to represent long-term-average groundwater conditions within the period of available record. The steady-state calibration was accomplished by adjusting permeability (and hence the calculated transmissivity) values as well as the groundwater recharge values. Transmissivity values along the variable flux boundary to the west-northwest were adjusted to control discharge to the main basin. A groundwater recharge matrix was developed to represent (1) infiltration from precipitation throughout the model area, (2) recharge from mountain run-off along southern and northeastern boundaries, (3) irrigation return water in agricultural areas, and (4) infiltration of imported water (i.e., reclaimed water used for landscape irrigation). Figure 4 shows the measured and simulated water levels for 1982 within the main aquifer (layer 3). The calibrated water level elevations are within 10 ft. of the measured water levels over most of the area.

Transient Calibrations

The model was further calibrated against available field data to demonstrate its ability to simulate time-dependent change in piezometric heads and flow conditions of the Tustin/Irvine ground water basin. A variety of available data was used for transient calibrations which included: (1) monthly pumping rates at irrigation wells, (2) monthly and quarterly measurements of water level elevations at irrigation and observation wells, (3) historic groundwater elevation maps prepared by the Orange County Water District, and (4) monthly precipitation records, for estimation of recharge to the aquifer. The availability and quality of the data is uniform throughout the period 1984 to 1988, with the exception of a few errant water level measurements, probably influenced by localized pumping effects. Thus, years 1984 through 1988 were chosen for transient calibrations because of availability of monthly precipitation and pumping data, as well as water level information for comparison purposes.

For transient calibration, the objective was to compare time-varying simulated potentiometric head within the lower layer, to the measured water levels at six wells located throughout the modeled area. Wells TIC-107 and TIC-47 were selected to represent confined conditions within the pressure area, while the other four wells were selected within the unconfined forebay area of the basin. Wells TIC-68 and TIC-37 are observation wells installed to monitor water levels; all other wells are pumped and used for irrigation. The primary screened areas for these irrigation wells are located within layer 3. Since the water level measurements are taken after the well is turned off and water levels are stabilized, the comparison to these values were believed to be representative. Figure 1 shows the locations of all wells used during transient calibrations.

Independent transient calibrations were accomplished by simulating a more detailed model consisting of nine layers over a dense grid covering approximately four square miles near the site of a 72 hour aquifer test. Geologic data was available from wells installed in close proximity to each other. Piezometric data was obtained from a cluster of four wells installed to different depths, at a distance 740 ft. away from the pumping well. The simulated drawdown differed from the measured drawdown by 0.42 ft. to 2.66 ft., and permeabilities ranged from 3.7 to 21.8 ft/day across four model layers representing the wells. The calibrated permeabilities were compared to those simulated during steady state calibrations. Although the values were comparable, the steady state calibration was re-done to assure the integrity of the model results.

For transient calibrations, the groundwater recharge and storage coefficient/specific yield values were adjusted to match measured fluctuations. The potentiometric head matrices from steady-state calibration were used for initial conditions. The model was simulated for a period of 15 to 20 years with varying groundwater recharge and pumping conditions to stabilize transient fluctuations and to adjust storage coefficients.

564 RESOURCES FOR WATER MANAGEMENT

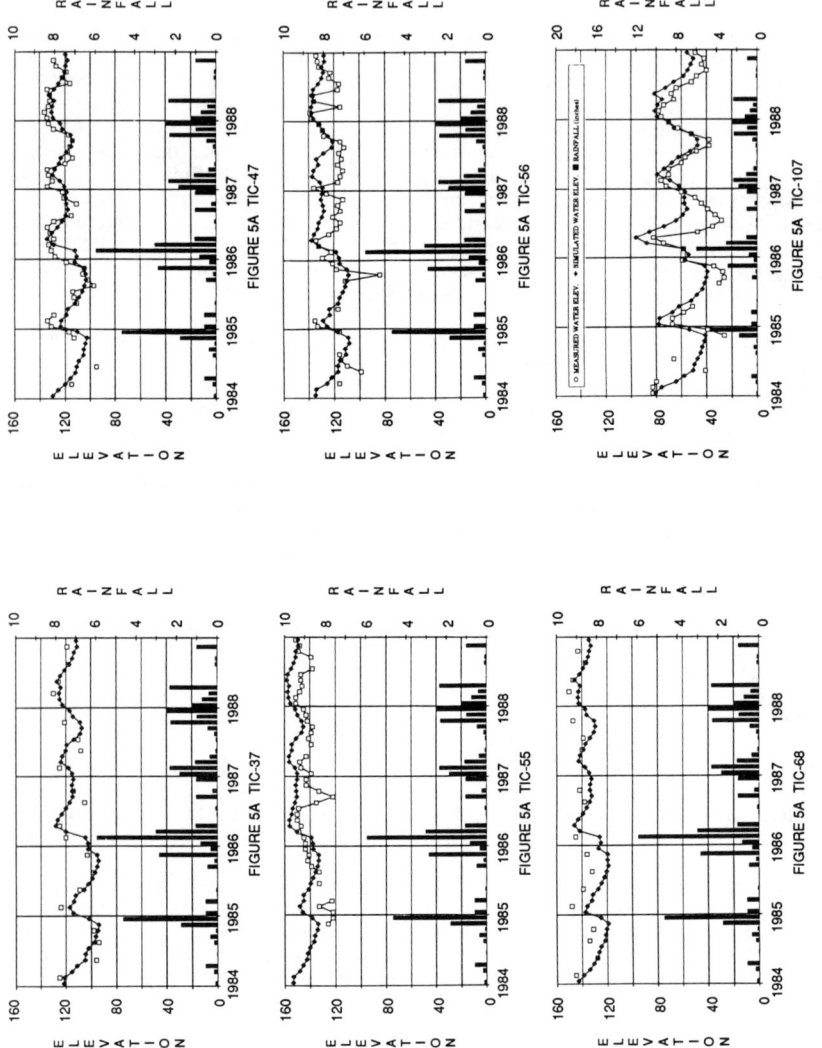

FIGURES 5A-F. MEASURED AND SIMULATED GROUNDWATER HYDROGRAPHS

Figures 5A through 5F show the fluctuations measured within six of the wells. Also shown in figures are the predicted water level fluctuations within the layer 3 and the monthly rainfall data used as part of the groundwater recharge. Comparison of measured and simulated fluctuations suggest that the best fit occurred in wells TIC-37, TIC-47 and TIC-107 shown in Figures 5A, 5B, and 5F, respectively. Both the time and magnitude of fluctuations compared very well in all three of the wells. This is believed to be primarily due to confined nature of the aquifer near wells TIC-47 and TIC-107 where the influences by the applied imported and irrigation return water on layer 3 water levels were minimal to non-existent. The accuracy of the match for TIC-37 was due to the fact that the well monitors only the model layer 3 within the aquifer.

Accuracy of the match in wells TIC-55, TIC-56 and TIC-68, shown in Figures 5C, 5D, and 5E, respectively, was less satisfactory. Although the magnitude of measured and simulated fluctuations were within less than 10 ft. of each other, time of fluctuations were not as well matched as the other wells. This may be due to the fact that the water levels used for comparison in layer 3 are for a specific aquifer zone while the water levels in wells TIC-55, TIC-56 and TIC-68 are for the total thickness of the aquifer due to the aquifer's unconfined nature. Thus the measured and predicted water levels could not be accurately compared, even though the vertical gradients are less than one foot.

Discussion of Results

Test runs showed that the model is sensitive to changes in recharge, storativity and transmissivity. The recharge data was based on a percentage of rainfall assumed to infiltrate into the aquifer. Common values range from 5-25%, depending on evaporation rates, surface runoff rates and land use. A value of 8% was assumed for use in the model, after calibration.

The model showed sensitivity to storativity values. Higher storativity values caused the hydrographs to be less responsive to recharge and pumping. Lower storativity values increased the range in fluctuations, especially in the confined area. The model's sensitivity to changes in transmissivity values were also evaluated over the entire lower layer to keep simulated head values within an acceptable confidence interval.

Conclusion

The model has been calibrated so that it will be useful, both for basin management and contaminant migration and remediation. The accuracy of the model for estimating the basin's safe yield is primarily dependent upon the values of storativity used for each layer. Model layer 3 provides the best confidence for accuracy, because most data available relates to the aquifer represented by this layer. The model will also be valuable in predicting extraction scenarios because parameters such as recharge, transmissivity and storativity are carefully calibrated.

Spatial averaging of statistically anisotropic
point conductivities

J. Jaime Gómez-Hernández[1]
Yoram Rubin[2]

Abstract

This paper presents a new technique to compute the mean, variogram and cross-variograms of the components of block conductivity tensors given the statistical distribution of point conductivities.

Heterogeneity creates anisotropy

One of the major sources of anisotropy is heterogeneity. This study shows how block conductivity values obtained by an averaging technique based on the flow equation become anisotropic due to the heterogeneity of isotropic point values.

For blocks of size of the order of magnitude of the integral scale of the point conductivity variogram, the use of expressions derived for infinite domains will underestimate the expected value of the principal components of the block conductivity tensor and will overestimate the anisotropy ratio. Also, the geometric mean of the point values does not provide information about the block anisotropy and it underestimates the expected value of the block conductivity tensor.

Figure 1 shows the expected values of K_x and K_y for a two-dimensional block of size $0.7I_x$ (I_x being the integral scale of the point conductivity variogram in the x direction) as computed in this study and as

---

[1]Department of Applied Earth Sciences and Stanford Center for Reservoir Forecasting, Stanford, CA 94305.

[2]Department of Civil Engineering, UC Berkeley, CA 94720.

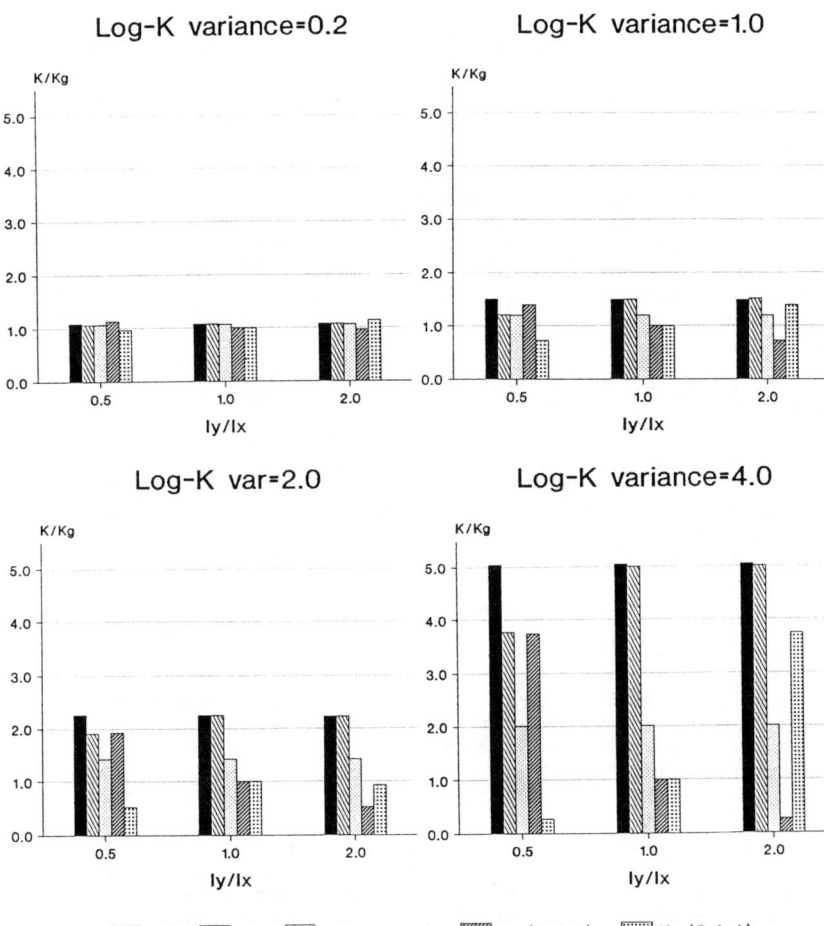

Figure 1. Different results for Kx and Ky. Values for the principal components of the block conductivity tensor for a 2-D square block of size 0.7Ix as predicted by: (1) this study, (2) assuming that the block value is the geometric average of the points within the block, and (3) using the generalized expression of Gelhar and Axness (1983) for blocks of infinite size. In all cases, it was assumed that the point log-conductivity was characterized by a multinormal distribution with an exponential variogram with integral scales I_x and I_y. The results (divided by the geometric mean of the point conductivity K_g) are shown for different values of the point log-K variance and of the ratio I_y/I_x.

computed using the generalized expression given by
Gelhar and Axness (1983) (equation (60) of their paper).
In both cases the log-conductivity is assumed to have a
multinormal distribution with an exponential variogram.
Also shown is the expected value of the geometric mean
of the conductivities within the block.

An important point to notice is that block conductivities remain isotropic ($K_y/K_x=1$) for I_y/I_x larger than or equal to 1.0. Had we used Gelhar and Axness's expression for infinite domains, we could have estimated anisotropy ratios K_y/K_x, of up to 138 (for the case of variance of point log-conductivity of 4.0 and integral scale ratio I_y/I_x of 2.0).

A better characterization of block conductivity distributions

Due to the heterogeneity of the point conductivity, finite-size block conductivities are considered as random functions with a non-negligible variance and spatial correlation. Only when the block size is large with respect to the integral scale of the point conductivity, the variance of the block conductivity will tend towards zero and its expected value towards the effective values reported elsewhere (Dagan, 1979, Gelhar and Axness, 1983).

Using a Monte-Carlo approach we have computed the expected value, variograms and cross-variograms for the components of two-dimensional block conductivity tensors. We used an anisotropic exponential variogram for the point log-conductivity with integral scale ratios (I_y/I_x) of 0.5, 1.0 and 2.0, and variances of 0.2, 1.0, 2.0 and 4.0. The expected value of the point log-conductivities was equal to 0 for all cases. For illustration purposes Figure 2 shows the expected values and variograms of K_x and K_y for a block of size $0.7I_x$, point variance of log-K of 1.0 and point integral scale ratio $I_y/I_x=0.5$.

These variograms are the ones that should be used for conditional simulation of block conductivities. Presently, to overcome the lack of knowledge of these variograms, there are two approaches to the conditional simulation of block conductivities: (1) to generate conditional simulations of point values that later are averaged to obtain the block values; this approach does not require the knowledge of the block variogram but it requires a conditional simulation at a smaller scale plus the average of point values for each block, and (2) to infer the block conductivity variogram by applying standard regularization techniques to the point

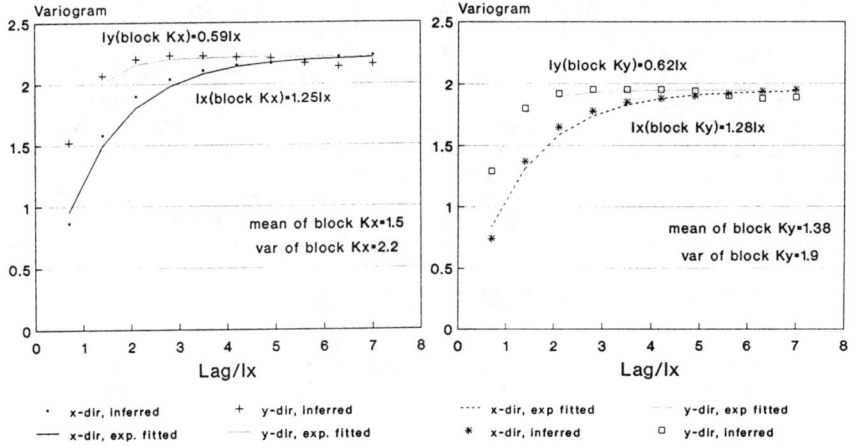

Figure 2. Variograms of the principal components of the block conductivity tensor. Block of size $0.7I_x$, variance of point log-conductivity of 1.0, and exponential variogram of point log-K with integral scales $I_y/I_x=0.5$. For each component K_x and K_y of the conductivity tensor, the variograms in the x and y directions are shown. The figure shows the variogram values inferred numerically and the exponential variograms that fit each direction. Note that the block presents not only conductivity anistropy, i.e., different values for the mean and variance of each of the tensor components, but also statistical anisotropy for each component. All lengths have been divided by the integral scale in the x-direction of the point log-conductivity.

variogram of log-conductivities; this approach cannot account for block anisotropy and it will underestimate both components of the conductivity tensor for blocks of size of the order of magnitude of the integral scale of the point variogram.

Computing the block conductivity statistics

A numerical approach was used to compute the block conductivity statistics. As a preliminary step, a 2-D synthetic field of quasi-point conductivities was generated using the turning band method. The size of the field was $10I_x$ by $10I_x$ and the quasi-point cells were of size $0.1I_x$ by $0.1I_x$. The field was then discretized in larger blocks and a conductivity tensor was obtained using the procedure described below. Finally the variogram and cross-variogram of the components of the block conductivity tensors were inferred numerically from the spatial distribution of block values.

An averaging technique to compute block conductivity tensors

The block values were computed by solving the flow equation for several boundary conditions as follows:

If q_b and $\text{grad}_b(h)$ are the block averages of the point specific discharge q and point head gradient $\text{grad}(h)$, the block conductivity tensor K_b should verify Darcy's law written at the block scale:

$$q_b = K_b \, \text{grad}_b(h)$$

or, rewriting in terms of their x and y components,

$$q_{b,x} = K_{b,xx} \, \text{grad}_{b,x}(h) + K_{b,xy} \, \text{grad}_{b,y}(h)$$
$$q_{b,y} = K_{b,xy} \, \text{grad}_{b,x}(h) + K_{b,yy} \, \text{grad}_{b,y}(h)$$

If the flow equation is solved within a given block for several boundary conditions, several sets of $q_{b,x}$, $q_{b,y}$, $\text{grad}_{b,x}$ and $\text{grad}_{b,y}$ are obtained. These sets define an overdetermined system of linear equations that is solved for the components of the block conductivity tensor using linear least-squares regression. We used constant head on the block boundary A, given by,

$$h(x,y) = J_x \, x + J_y \, y, \quad (x,y) \text{ in } A$$

where J is a vector representing a head gradient.

Differences with previous studies

This study is different from other studies on average conductivities in that (1) it focus on finite size blocks, (2) it regards the block conductivity as a tensor, and (3) each component of the tensor is considered as a random function. Gelhar and Axness (1983) and Dagan (1982) obtained effective conductivities for blocks of infinite extent; Desbarats (1987) computed the expected value of conductivities for finite blocks of sand with shales parallel to the block sides implicitly assuming that the conductivity tensor had principal directions parallel to the shale orientation; Rubin and Gomez-Hernandez (1989) give an analytical solution for a block conductivity variogram valid only for exponential isotropic point variograms with small variance.

Conclusions

For blocks of dimensions of the order of magnitude of the integral scale of the point conductivity, the block conductivity tensors cannot be estimated using the effective conductivity results obtained for infinite domains or by simple geometric average of the point values. We also propose a numerical technique to infer block conductivity tensor and their two-point statistics for later use in the generation of conditional simulations of block values.

Acknowledgments

Financial support for this study was provided by the Stanford Center for Reservoir Forecasting. We are grateful to Andrè Journel for his enlightening discussion in the early stages of the study.

References

Dagan, G, Models of groundwater flow in statistically homogeneous porous formations, Water Resources Research, 15(1), 47-63, 1979.

Desbarats, A. J., Numerical estimation of effective permeability in sand-shale formations, Water Resources Research, 23(2), 273-286, 1987.

Gelhar, L. W. and C. L. Axness, Three-dimensional stochastic analysis of macrodispersion in aquifers, Water Resources Research, 19(1), 161-180, 1983.

Rubin, Y. and J. J. Gomez-Hernandez, A stochastic approach to the problem of upscaling of transmissivity in disordered media, 1, Theory and unconditional simulations, accepted for publication in Water Resources Research, 1989.

DESIGN OF SAMPLING NETWORKS FOR WATER TABLE MONITORING
Donald E. Myers[1]

Abstract

The problem of the design of a sampling network occurs in many contexts in the earth sciences. In the application to the monitoring of water tables the presence of temporal and spatial dependence is of crucial importance. It is this dependence, whether spatial or temporal, that distinguishes the problem from the classical one of determining sample size. Often the network will be used to collect data to estimate or predict the value at an unsampled location where "value" may refer to a very local spatial average, a temporal average, a regional average or even a statistical average. In contrast the objective in designing the network is to maximize the information gained from the network or alternatively to minimize the uncertainty, in some sense, associated with the estimation/prediction process. There are a number of essential steps in the design of such a network, previous literature is reviewed in the context of these steps and a comparison is made of the pertinence of the methods used along with an appraisal of the computing requirements, model assumptions and sensitivity of the selection process to the addition of new information.

Introduction: The monitoring of ground water levels may occur over very large regions such as the Ogallala aquifer in Kansas as described by Olea (1982), Sophocleous (1983) and Rouhani (1986) or for a more limited region such as the Venice lagoon see Gambolati and Volpi (1979) or for an area previously used as a nuclear waste dump at a national lab see Hoeksema et al (1989). In addition to monitoring water levels, water quality may be of concern as in Ahlfield et al (1986) or Carerra et al (1984). Identification of plumes may also be interest as in Loaiciga (1988). While not all of these are directly concerned with the design of a network they do epitomize the kinds of monitoring problems for which network design is important.

Olea is an example where network design was of principal concern, in that instance the problem is that of finding an optimal subset of existing wells in order to reduce monitoring costs while maintaining the same or nearly the same level of information. In other instances new wells must be drilled and then the question is where and how many. In general the network will be used to collect data in order to reduce uncertainty about a characteristic at an unsampled location or time or to estimate a regional characteristic such as an average.

Approaches: Most hydrological data is either spatially located and hence spatially dependent and/or temporally dependent. In turn this dependence introduces some form of redundancy in the data to be collected by a network, in some instances the optimal network is obtained by incorporating interdependencies and in others optimality is the result of minimizing their effect. In order to incorporate or to minimize the effect of these interdependencies they must be quantified and in turn this requires some form of model. The model may be deterministic, stochastic or a combination of both. For example it may be deterministic with respect to temporal dependencies and stochastic with respect to spatial. The model may also pre-suppose the absence of dependencies as for example when using classical statistics. When the model relates hydrological parameters such as permeability, hydraulic conductivity to flow the model is most likely deterministic but the parameters may incorporate a stochastic model. Hussain and Caselton (1980) provide a summary of both deterministic and stochastic models used for network design.

[1]Professor, Department of Mathematics, University of Arizona Tucson, AZ 85721

In the last two decades most of the emphasis has been on the use of geostatistical techniques which incorporate the spatial dependence and which are most applicable for local estimation/prediction problems. Barnes (1989) provides a brief overview of papers using geostatistical methods and lists a substantial bibliography of papers using geostatistical methods. In contrast with more classical methods which focus on sample size alone geostatistical techniques stress the role of the sample location pattern and in some instances the use of auxillary data. By analogy with classical statistics which commonly relates sample size to error variances, geostatistical techniques characterize sampling networks in terms of estimation variances.

Geostatistical Methods:In its simplest form geostatistics uses local weighted averages (kriging) to estimate values at unsampled locations or times, alternatively to estimate spatial or temporal averages. The characteristic that sets it apart from the techniques of more classical methods is that the data is considered to be spatially or temporally correlated (possibly both). The spatial (or temporal) dependence is quantified by a covariance function or variogram, while there are no theoretical difficulties in incorporating both types of dependence, in practice these are difficult to model as noted in Rouhani and Myers (1989). Geostatistics has been viewed most often as an interpolator with an associated estimation variance. This variance is in general not constant and is dependent on the pattern of the sample locations, the variogram model and the particular location to be interpolated or the regional for which an average to be estimated. The kriging estimator is linear in the data and the weights depend only the variogram and the sample location pattern hence one can minimize the estimation variance for a location prior to collecting data at that location. There are mathematical difficulties associated with minimizing this function, it is generally not convex and because the function is defined in 2 or possibly even 3-space local minimums may interferre with the search process. Most early work concentrated on selecting new locations from a pre-selected grid, Myers and Jalkanen (1988) have shown that such a restriction is not necessary. Because the geostatistical model is dependent on the variogram (or covariance) the network design may be static or dynamic. That is, the data collected from the network may be used to update the variogram model or the variogram may be assumed fixed throughout the data collection stage.

Optimal Networks:Optimality may be characterized in several different ways and likewise monitoring networks may be designed in different ways but a number of common features may be identified. While one could set up a network simply to collect data, the design is dependent on three important points (i) the overall objective(s) (ii) how the data collected will be used to meet this objective (iii) how optimality is characterized. Optimality may be characterized by several criteria as in Bogardi et al (1985). In turn the useage of the data places restrictions on the type(s) of data to be collected as well requiring some model assumptions. For example if the objective is to tabulate regional average water table levels over some time span then it would seem obvious that measuring table elevations would be required. But is the data used to estimate multiple averages, one for each time point of interest, is it used to predict future averages from past averages or possibly both? To what extent are the measurements (whether elevations or some other variable of interest) spatially or temporally invariant? Are there auxillary statistical or state-equation assumptions? A network might be optimal with respect to one of two nearly contradictory characteristics; minimum cost or maximal information where the latter could mean minimal uncertainty. Often one of these will be considered as a constraint and optimization is restricted to the other. There may also be other constraints. While in general the data will be numerical it may not be limited to one form of measurement and depending on the model assumptions the network design may encompass decisions concerning the nodes on the network (including their number), the data to be collected at each node and at what time points. If a statistical model is assumed then it may be necessary to determine parameters a priori, this may require the use of a preliminary network. In the geostatistical approach the variogram is a prior which quantifies the spatial/temporal dependence. The design of a network for estimation and modeling of this function is quite different from the subsequent network design problem using a "known" variogram, the distinction between these two problems is discussed in Warrick and Myers (1987).

The Search Process: Whatever the criteria and whatever the data objectives, the network design will incorporate a number of sample locations and/or times. There are several possible approaches in terms of the search algorithm. It may be assumed that all sample locations are to be selected from those on a regular grid or in the case of time, equally spaced time points. In this case the problem is essentially a combinatorial one and it would be possible to simply test all possible selections to find the optimal value of the objective function. Because it is a combinatorial problem one is assured of a solution and if there are multiple (equivalent) solutions they will all be identified. Note that although one may select from a grid the result may not appear as a grid. Even if the final network is gridlike this may have some disadvantages from the perspective of its ultimate use for kriging. It may also be difficult to incorporate necessary physical constraints on the network, i.e., areas or regions where it will be difficult to sample. Alternatively one might allow the grid to have a variable mesh and variable orientation, that is the network design will determine the optimal grid mesh and orientation as well as the locations of sample locations on the grid. The problem is no longer combinatorial but still is assured of a solution. More generally the objective function can be considered to be defined on the two dimensional space and the objective is to find the location or locations where the function is optimal. There are at least two problems that occur in this context that do not occur in the others or that are more difficult. First of all the objective function may not be convex and hence has local optimal values, the search algorithm may stop on one of these and not discover that there is a global optimal value, that is there are mathematical difficulties that arise in solving the problem, nearly all algorithms work best or only for convex functions. Secondly, there is the distinction between finding one more sample location and finding several. The difficulty that occurs is the possible distinction between finding a group of new locations and finding the same number but sequentially. That is, if the objective is to find three new locations will the same optimum be achieved if three searches are made, each time adding one location to the network vs finding a group. As shown in Myers and Jalkanen the answer is no in both cases. If the new sample locations are not restricted to a grid then there may not be a unique optimum and the search technique may stop at a local optimum and not proceed further. Moreover sequential selection is not equivalent to group selection.

Summary: The design of a sampling network requires a number of preliminary decisions including the overall objective for the use of the data, whether data is to be collected only spatially or only temporally or both, whether auxillary data or information is to be used and a determination of the objective function which is to be optimized. If a geostatistical model is used it will be necessary to first estimate and model the variograms, the optimal network for this stage is in general quite different from the network used to collect the data. In geostatistics the network design is connected with some form of interpolation which may not always be the appropriate use of the data. Finally the objective function will either be the estimation variance or in some way dependent on it, the advantage of using the estimation variance is that it does not depend on the data.

Even in the context of a geostatistical model there is no unique way of posing the problem and there are mathematical problems associated with finding the optimal value of the objective function.

NOTICE

Although the research described in this article has been funded wholly or in part by the U.S. Environmental Protection Agency through a Cooperative Research Agreement with the University of Arizona, it has not been subjected to Agency review and therefore does not reflect the views of the Agency and therefore no official endorsement should be inferred.

References

Ahlfeld,D.P., Mulvey, J.M. and Pinder, G.P. (1986) Designing optimal strategies for contaminated groundwater remediation. Adv. Water Resources 9, 77-84

Barnes, R.J. (1989) A Partial History of Spatial Sampling Design. Geostatistics Newsletter, 3, No. 2, 10-12 (includes an extensive list of references)

Ben-zvi,M. and Kesler,S. (1986) Spatial Approach to Estimation of missing data. J. Hydrology, 88, 69-78

Bogardi,I.,Bardossy,A. and Duckstein,L.,(1985) Multicriterion Network Design using Geostatistics. WRR, 21 199-208

Carrera,J.,Usunoff,E. and Szidarovsky,F.,(1984) Optimal Observation Network Design for Groundwater Quality Management:Application to the San Pedro River Basin, Arizona. J. of Hydrology, 73, 143-163

Gambolati,G. and Volpi,C. (1979) Groundwater Contour Mapping in Venice by Stochastic Interpolators I. WRR 15, 281-

Hoeksema,R.J., Clapp, R.B., Thomas, A.L., Hunley, A.E., Farrow, N.D. and Dearstone, K.C. (1989) Cokriging Model for Estimation of Water Table Elevation. WRR 25,429-438

Husain, T. and Caselton, W.F. (1980) Hydrologic Network Design Methods and Shannon's Information Theory. in IFAC, Water and Related Land Resource Systems, Cleveland, Ohio 259-267

Loaiciga, Hugo A. (1988) Groundwater Monitoring Network Design. in Proceedings of the VII International Conference on Computational Methods in Water Resources

Myers,D.E. and Jalkanen,J. (1988) Sampling Strategy for Network Design. Fourth Annual EPA Conference on Statistics, Williamsburg,VA 15-18 March

Olea, Ricardo (1982) Optimization of the High Plains Aquifer Observation Network, Kansas. Groundwater series 7, Kansas Geological Survey

Rouhani,S.,(1985),Variance Reduction Analysis. WRR 21, 837-846

Rouhani,S. (1986) Comparative Study of Ground-Water Mapping Techniques. Groundwater 24, 207-216

Rouhani,S. and Fiering,M.B. (1986) Resilience of Statistical Sampling Schemes. J. Hydrology 89, 1-11

Rouhani,S. and Hall.T.J. (1988) Geostatistical Schemes for Groundwater Sampling. J. Hydrology 103, 85-102

Rouhani,S. and Myers,D.E. (1989) Problems in Space-Time Kriging of Geohydrological Data. to appear in Math. Geology

Sophocleous,M.,(1983),Groundwater Observation Network Design for Kansas Groundwater Management Districts,U.S.A. J.Hydrology 61, 371-389

Warrick,A. and Myers,D.E. (1987) Optimization of Sampling Locations for Variogram Calculations. WRR 23, 496-500

ANALYSIS OF UNCERTAINTY IN GROUND-WATER QUALITY MONITORING NETWORK DESIGN

By

Hugo A. Loaiciga[1]

APPROACHES TO GROUND-WATER QUALITY MONITORING NETWORK DESIGN

This section reviews alternative approaches to ground-water quality monitoring network design. The principles underpinning each approach are evaluated herein. Specific methodologies and applications are examined in detail in paper 2.

There are four general approaches to network design: (1) hydrogeologic, (2) simulation, (3) variance-reduction, and (4) optimization. The relative advantages and disadvantages of each of these approaches to specific ground-water quality network design applications depend on: (1) the *scale* of the monitoring program (i.e., *field-scale* or *regional scale*); (2) the type of data available (hydrogeologic, geologic, etc.); (3) the nature of the investigated subsurface process (vadose zone, saturated-zone contamination); (4) the steady-state vis a vis transient nature of ground-water quality properties; and (5) the objective of the monitoring program and the resources available to accomplish it. Ground-water quality network design is an iterative process. An initial design might be upgraded as more data and resources become available. The approaches discussed in this paper are intended to provide a preliminary design for the layout of sampling sites and selection of sampling frequency. The ultimate selection of a sampling plan is often influenced in many cases by institutional and legal considerations. Environmental monitoring programs are dynamic in nature and phased in their implementation. For example, the U.S. EPA (1986) ground-water monitoring document indicated that "... *surface geophysical* techniques can be effectively used in tandem with the installation of monitoring wells as a first phase in the assessment program to obtain a rough outline of the contaminant plume. Based on these findings, a sampling program may subsequently be undertaken to more clearly define the three-dimensional limits of the contaminant plume. In the third phase, a sampling program to determine the concentrations of hazardous waste constituents in the interior of the plume may be undertaken...". This progressive-approach perspective to ground-water quality monitoring network design is indispensable in order to appreciate the utility and limitations of the approaches and methodologies reviewed in this work.

The hydrogeologic approach

The foundational references for this approach are Everett (1980) and U.S. EPA (1986). In the hydrogeologic approach, the number and locations of sampling sites (i.e., wells) is strictly determined by the hydrogeologic conditions near the source of contamination such as a waste impoundment. This approach is better suited for site specific studies where there is a well-delimited source of contamination. The stratigraphy, structural geologic features and the *local* and *regional ground-water* flow patterns at the site determine the spatial (horizontal and vertical) distribution of sampling points. The main objective of the hydrogeologic approach is to detect contaminant presence as soon as the contaminant plume leaves the confinements of a waste impoundment site. Geologic features such as aquifer layering and the presence of fractures, determine the need for the vertical placement of sampling points. These are in the form of either multiscreened wells or *well-clusters*

Figure 1 shows an application of the hydrogeologic approach to ground-water quality monitoring network design. The aquifer is a *glacial outwash* with two sand layers in hydraulic

---

[1] Assistant Professor, Department of Geography, University of California, Santa Barbara, CA 93106

connection through a low-conductivity, *glacial till aquitard*. Bedrock is highly impermeable granite. The upper sand layer has a relatively high hydraulic conductivity and greater Darcian velocity with a southerly direction. The lower, more compacted, sand layer has a lower hydraulic conductivity, and its resident groundwater is part of a deeper regional flow regime with ground-water velocity having a southeasterly direction as indicated by the arrows. Flow through the glacial till aquitard is downward leakage. There are two lined waste impoundments to be located in the upper sand layer with a depth not exceeding the water table elevation in the upper, unconfined, aquifer. The hydrogeology at the site is well-understood and includes the stratigraphic features of the various *formations* as well as piezometric level contours for the upper (unconfined) and lower (confined) aquifers. Up-gradient monitoring wells are screened in the two sand layers to provide *background water quality* information to be contrasted with the downgradient wells. The southern and eastern perimeters of the impoundments are monitored to determine the ground-water quality downgradinet of the contaminant source. The upper, more permeable sand layer is tapped by five monitoring wells, three of which are well-clusters that penetrate the various formations (upper sand, till, and lower sand). Any *leachate* must pass the upper sand and till layers before reaching the lower sand layer. Therefore, fewer single wells are required along the eastern perimeter as shown in Figure 1.

This example indicates that the hydrogeologic approach is data intensive, tailored for site specific applications such as at Superfund sites, where the primary objective is the immediate detection of contaminant migration beyond the site boundaries. Economic and statistical considerations are secondary to the primary objective. The hydrogeologic approach is also clueless about the temporal sampling frequency of a ground-water quality monitoring plan.

The simulation approach

The simulation approach to ground-water quality monitoring network design is versatile, and it is gaining popularity in the broad fields of ground-water quality management (Wagner and Gorelick, 1987) in general. The simulation approach considers the hydraulic conductivity of a porous medium as a *random field*. Because hydraulic conductivity exerts an important control on ground-water velocity distribution and hence, on the advection and dispersion of chemical compounds in ground-water, both velocity and pollutant distributions are stochastic or random fields as well.

The conceptual backbone of the simulation approach is that by generating multiple *synthetic distributions* of hydraulic conductivity, for each of which there will be a corresponding contaminant distribution, it is possible to assess the statistical properties of mass transport in an aquifer, and hence, the performance of a monitoring network. For any given arrangement of monitoring wells and sampling frequency, the simulation approach yields important quantities such as the probability that a contaminant plume might miss all of the sampling points and be undected (Gilbert, 1987; Massmann and Freeze, 1987 a,b; Meyer and Brill, 1988) i.e., the probability of a *false negative*. By careful experimental design of the computer simulation, various network configurations can be entertained and examined for their adequacy in contaminant detection. Therefore, there is some leverage for optimization in the simulation approach.

The simulation approach is computationally intensive. In addition to the generation of the hydraulic conductivity distributions (e.g., Mantoglou, 1987), ground-water flow models (e.g., McDonald and Harbaugh, 1988) and mass transport models (e.g., Konikow and Bredehoeft, 1984) are needed to generate contaminant distributions. This is, in fact, the weakest link in the simulation approach: the better tested mass transport models are not well-suited for heterogeneous and anisotropic aquifers, i.e., those aquifers of greatest practical interest (Loaiciga, 1988a). In spite of this drawback, the simulation approach to ground-water quality network design offers an appealing flexibility to examine the efficacy of alternative network configurations and samping frequencies specially under relatively simple hydrogeologic settings. It also allows for the considerations of resource constraints (e.g., limited budgets). Some degree of design optimization is possible, although computationally requirements render it too cumbersome to consider but for a few network configurations. Because of the linked nature of hydraulic conductivity and mass transport distribution generation, and the computational requirements, the simulation approach seems better tailored for problems involving contaminant monitoring at the field scale as indicated by previous studies (e.g., Massmann and Freeze, 1987a,b).

All things considered, the increased availability of cheap computational power and advances in mass transport modeling (Dagan, 1988) will most likely make the mass transport approach a more attractive alternative for ground-water quality monitoring network design.

The variance-reduction approach

The variance-reduction approach is of a statistical nature (Rouhani, 1985; Task Committee on Geostastical Techniques in Geohydrology, 1989 a,b). This approach uses a methodical search for the number and locations of sampling sites that would minimize the variance of *estimation error* of the variable of interest, such as the concentration of a pollutant. The search for a ground-water monitoring network configuration starts with a number of existing sampling wells to which additional wells are added, one-at-a-time. Each additional well produces the largest reduction in the variance of estimation error. Sampling sites continue to be added until the variance of estimation error can no longer be (or is only marginally) reduced, or when the marginal gain in statistical accuracy is outweighted by other constraints (such as limited resources). If there are no originally existing wells, a subset of sampling locations must be selected based on hydrogeologic or some other relevant consideration. Thereupon, the monitoring network is expanded according to the primary objective of adding those wells that will contribute most to the reduction of the variance of estimation error.

The variance-reduction approach is based on a convenient feature of spatial statistical interpolation, i.e., that the variance of estimation error does not depend on the measured values of the environmental variable (Loaiciga et al., 1988), but rather, on the relative geometric location of the sampling sites. Based on this convenient feature of spatial interpolation, it is possible to express (in closed form) the drop in the variance of estimation error in terms of (1) the variance obtained prior to the addition of the last sampling site, (2) of the monitoring network's configuration, and (3) in terms of the mean and covariance of the environmental variable of interest (Rouhani, 1985). Therefore, the effect of adding one sampling site can be quantified without any difficulty and independently of the particular measurement value at that point. It is assumed in the variance reduction approach, however, that the *structural analysis* (Journel and Huijbregts, 1978) remains invariant under the addition of new sampling sites. Otherwise, the sequential minimization of the variance of estimation error becomes conceptually flawed and, incidentally, the computational efficiency of the variance-reduction approach is entirely lost.

The statistical nature of the variance-reduction approach limits its capability to incorporate complex hydrogeologic settings, and it is most useful when the environmental variable of interest has a homogeneous and isotropic spatial behavior. Previous applications (Task Committee on Geostatistics in Geohydrology, 1989b) seem to indicate that the variance-reduction approach is best suited for the design of regional ground-water quality monitoring networks. As will be seen below, the variance-reduction approach could be considered as a subcase of the optimization approach, since the minimization of the variance of estimation is a well-established optimization criterion. However, the optimization approach depends on explicit formulations of the network design problem within a *mathematical programming* framework subject to numerical optimization, something that the variance-reduction approach does not strive to achieve. Because of its nurturing within the geostatistical community and its widespread use in geostatistical analysis of network design (Bastin et al., 1984), the variance-reduction approach deserves a separate treatment on its own right.

There are other approaches to network design that are of a statistical nature, noticeably that by Olea (1984), that consider the pattern (e.g., square, triangular, or other geometric arrangements) and the density (the number of sampling points per unit area) of the sampling points. The work by Olea (1984) was primarily concerned with measures of global (i.e., over the entire sampling domain) performance of a monitoring program such as the average or maximum variance of estimation. The choice of such global performance standards does not seem to be the most consistent with ground-water quality monitoring goals, where interest is commonly directed to more localized performance parameters, such as contaminant concentrations near a well or over a subregion of the study area. Nevertheless, the use of global performance criteria for ground-water quality monitoring network design can be justified for preliminary or exploratory layouts in regional-scale programs, since the analysis is expeditious and might provide a sound starting basis for posterior, more detailed, refinements of the monitoring network.

Optimization approach

In the optimization approach ground-water quality monitoring network design is posed as a mathematical programming problem. Therefore, there is a well-defined objective function, such as minimizing the probability of human exposure to toxic substances in ground-water, or maximizing the statistical accuracy associated with estimates of measured ground-water quality properties (Hsueh and Rajagopal, 1988; Knopman and Voss, 1988; and Loaiciga, 1989). In addition, constraints are explicitly considered while optimizing the objective function. Such constraints might include resource constraints, governing equations of physical processes such as hydrodynamic dispersion, statistical constraints (e.g., accuracy of ground-water quality parameter estimates) and areal coverage of the monitoring network (Hsueh and Rajagopal, 1988). The mathematical programming problem represented by the objective function and the constraints is solved by specialized numerical optimization algorithms. Because one of the key outputs of the optimization approach is the location of sampling sites, the corresponding mathematical programming problem usually (but not necessarily) involves the use of *integer*, binary, *variables* that reflect either the placement or the absence of an actual sampling site at each potential sampling location (Loaiciga, 1988b; 1989a; Hsueh and Rajagopal, 1988). The *integer programming* formulation has a long tradition in locational theory applications (Church and Revelle, 1974). Examples in environmental monitoring are the early papers by Fiering (1965) and Darby et al. (1974).

The optimization approach is appealing because, in principle at least, it yields optimal sampling locations and sampling times while considering a variety of restrictions on the sampling plan. However, some of the most advanced applications reported to date (that incorporate the contaminant transport equations as constraints) have obvious limitations. Such limitations concern mainly the complexity of the hydrogeologic setting that can be handled before the network design problem becomes upleasantly cumbersome. For example, an actual case study undertaken in Loaiciga (1989) dealt with a field-scale network design in an (assumed) isotropic and homogenous unconsolidated aquifer. Just as is the case with other network design approaches that use ground-water mathematical models (e.g., simulation) the optimization approach offers a clear tradeoff between the ability to model and optimize a network design problem on one hand, and the hydrogeologyc simplifications that must be introduced on the other hand. Based on the hydrogeologic complexity found at the field-scale in ground-water quality monitoring, the optimization approach seems to be more promising as an analytical tool for regional groundwater quality monitoring network design, where the hydrogeologic resolution and detail required is much coarser and easier to model.

There are a few papers available in the hydrologic literature that address ground-water network design for data collection of aquifer parameters (e.g., hydraulic conductivities or transmissivities). In particular, the reader is referred to the papers by Carrera et al. (1984) and Hsu and Yeh (1989), that bear some degree of resemblance with the integer programming applications to ground-water quality network design of Hsueh and Rajagopal (1988) and Loaiciga (1989).

REFERENCES

Bastin, G., Lorent, B., Duque, C., and M. Gevers. (1984). Optimal estimation of the average areal rainfall and optimal selection of raingauge locations, *Water Resour. Res.*, 20(4), 463-470.

Church, R.L., and C. Revelle, The maximal covering location problem, *Pap. Regional Science Assoc.*, 32, 101-118, 1974.

Dagan, D. (1988). Time-dependent macrodispersion for solute transport in anisotropic heterogeneous aquifers, *Water Resour. Res.* 24(9), 1491-1500.

Darby, W.P., Ossenbruggen, P.J., and Gregory, C.J. (1974). Optimization of urban air monitoring networks, *J. Environmental Engr. Div.*, Am. Soc. Civ. Engrs., 100 (EE3), 577-591.

Everett, L.G. (1980). *Groundwater Monitoring*, General Electric Company, Shenectady, N.Y., 440p.

Fiering, M. (1965). An optimization scheme for gaging, *Water Resour. Res.*, 1(4), 463-470.

Gilbert, R.O. (1987). *Statistical Methods for Environmental Pollution Monitoring*, van Nostrand-Reinhold Co., New York, N.Y.

Hsu, N.S., and W. Yeh. (1989). Optimum experimental design for parameter identification in ground-water hydrology, *Water Resour. Res.*, in press.

Hsueh, Y.W. and R. Rajagopal. (1988). Modeling ground-water qulaity decisions, *Ground-Water Monitoring Review*, 121-134, Fall Issue

Journel, A.G., and C.J. Huijbregts. (1978). *Mining Geostatistics* Academic Press, London, 600p.

Knopman, D.S., and C.I. Voss. (1988). Discrimination among one-dimensional models of solute transport in porous media: implications for sampling design, *Water Resour. Res.*, 24(11), 1859-1876.

Konikow, L.F., and J.D. Bredehoeft. (1984). Computer model of two-dimensional solute transport and dispersion in ground-water, *Techniques of Water-Resources Investigations*, U.S. Geological Survey, Book 7, Chapter 2, U.S. Government Printing Office, Washington, D.C.

Loaiciga, H.A. (1988a). Hydrodynamic dispersion: estimation and prediction, *Hydraulic Engineering, Proceedings of 1988 National Conference Hydraulics Div.*, ASCE, Colorado Springs, Colorado, August 8-12, 1988.

Loaiciga, H.A. (1988b). Ground-water monitoring network design, *Procs. VII Intl. Conf. Computational Methods in Water Resources*, vol. 2., Celia, M.A., Ferrand, L.A., Brebia, C.A., Gray, W.G., and G.F. Pinder, eds., MIT, Cambridge, MA, June 13-17, Computational Mechanics Publications/Elsevier, New York, N.Y., pp. 371-376.

Loaiciga, H.A., Shumway, R.H., and W. Yeh. (1988). Linear spatial interpolation: analysis with an application to the San Joaquin Valley, California, USA, *Stochastic Hydrology and Hydraulics*, 2(2), 113-116.

Loaiciga, H.A. (1989). An optimization approach for ground-water quality monitoring network design, *Water Resour. Res.*, in press.

McDonald, M.G., and A.W. Harbaugh. (1988). *A Modular Three-Dimensional Finite-Difference Ground-Water Flow Model*, U.S. Geological Survey, Reston, VA.

Mantoglou, A. (1987). Digital simulation of multivariate three dimensional stochastic processes with a spectral turning bands method, *Mathematical Geology*, 19(2), 129-149.

Massmann, J. and R.A. Freeze. (1987a). Ground water contamination from waste management sites: the interaction between risk-based engineering design and regulatory policy, 1, methodology, *Water Resources Research*, 23(2), 351-367.

Massmann, J. and R.A. Freeze. (1987b). Ground water contamination from waste management sites: the interaction between risk-based engineering design and regulatory policy, 2, results, *Water Resources Research*, 23(2), 368-380.

Meyer, P.D., and E.D. Brill. (1988). Method for locating wells in a ground water monitoring network under conditions of uncertainty, *Water Resources Research*, 24(8), 1277-1282.

Olea, R. (1984). Sampling design optimization for spatial functions, *Mathematical Geology*, 16(4), 365-391.

Rouhani, S. (1985). Variance reduction analysis, *Water Resources Research*, 21(6), 837-846.

Task Committee on Geostatistical Methods in Geohydrology. (1989a). Review of geostatistics in geohydrology, 1. Basic concepts, *Journal of Hydraulic Engineering*, Am. Soc. Civ. Engrs., in press.

Task Committee on Geostatistical Methods in Geohydrology. (1989b). Review of Geostatistics in Geohydrology, 2. Applications. *Journal of Hydraulic Engineering*, Am. Soc. Civ. Engrs., in press.

United States Environmental Protection Agency. (1986). *RCRA Ground-Water Monitoring Technical Enforcement Guidance Document*, Office of Solid Waste and Emergency Response, September, Washington, D.C.

Wagner, B.J. and S.M. Gorelick. (1987). Optimal ground-water quality management under parameter uncertainty, *Water Resources Research*, 23(7), 1162-1174.

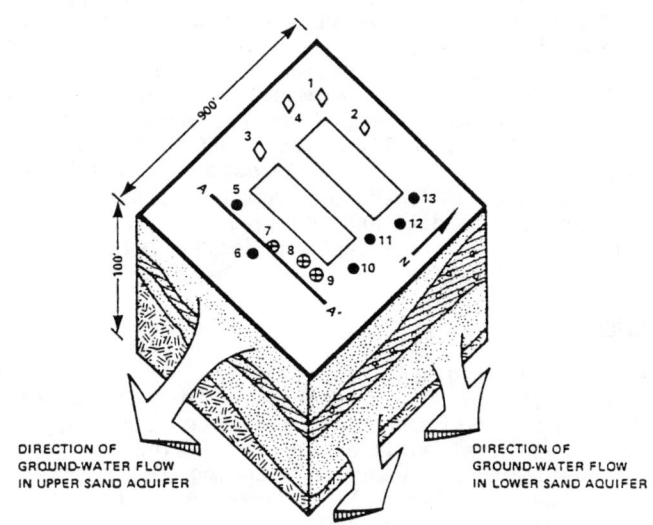

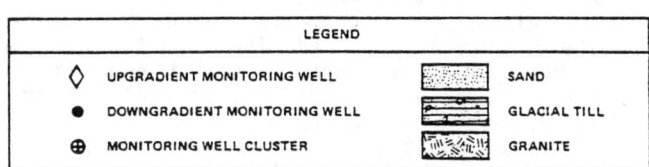

ADVANCES IN HYDRAULIC STREAM MODELING USING HEC-2

Degaldra Gurley, P.E.[1]

ABSTRACT

The Corps of Engineers, Ft. Worth, Texas, Flood Plain Management Services Branch has developed hydraulic stream models for creeks and rivers throughout the state of Texas for the purpose of providing technical information for Flood Insurance Study Reports. These hydraulic stream models were developed using the HEC-2 computer program developed at the Hydrologic Engineering Center (HEC) in Davis, California. HEC has provided updated software packages for the HEC-2 computer program and its supplementary programs. There are computer program modifications that provide additional data and improved computational procedures. These advancements are important in increasing the accuracy of hydraulic stream models.

INTRODUCTION

The Corps of Engineers is authorized by Section 206 of the Flood Control Act of 1960, as amended, to provide information, technical planning assistance and guidance upon request to both Federal and non-Federal entities in identifying the magnitude and extent of the flood hazard and in planning wise use of the flood plains. The Corps' Flood Plain Management Branch administers studies which provide basic hydrologic and hydraulic information to the Federal Emergency Management Agency. To determine the flood magnitude the Corps conducts hydrology and frequency studies using the HEC-2 computer program developed at the Hydrologic Engineering Center in Davis, California. The program calculates water surface profiles for steady gradually varied flow in natural or man-made channels. Both subcritical and supercritical flow profiles can be calculated. The computational procedure, generally known as the Standard Step Method, is based on the solution of the one-dimensional energy equation with energy loss due to friction evaluated with Manning's equation (USACE 1982).

---
1. Civil Engineer, Fort Worth District, U.S. Army Corps of Engineers, P. O. Box 17300, Ft. Worth, Tx. 76102.

HYDRAULIC STREAM MODELING   583

SOFTWARE PACKAGES ON THE PERSONAL COMPUTER

Two versions of HEC-2 have been developed by the Hydrologic Engineering Center. The standard version of HEC-2 may be utilized on most medium to large computers. A microcomputer version of HEC-2 has been developed for use on the IBM PC/XT microcomputer (USACE 1982). Due to the increased usage of personal computers by most engineering firms, this paper will reference software associated with the personal computer.

The HEC-2 supplementary programs for the personal computer consist of a data Edit program (Edit-2) and a graphics program (Plot2). The Edit-2 program will process an entire HEC-2 input data file and provide a list of all the data errors. The Plot2 program will provide a graphical display of cross-section data and computed water surface elevations obtained from the HEC-2 output data.

PROGRAM MODIFICATIONS

Input File. The hydraulic stream model of Cottonwood Branch located in Hays County, Texas was computed using the HEC-2 Water Surface Profiles computer program. The data input file, Figure 1, herein referred to as ICotton, represents the geometric characteristics of the defined channel cross sections. The accuracy of the data output file, Figure 2, herein referred to as OCotton, depends greatly on the accuracy of the data in ICotton.

The title record cards T1 through T4 located at the beginning of ICotton are a source for providing study information. These cards reference the study name and date, discharge frequency, stream name, and study manager, as well as the main stream. The list of title record card identifiers can be expanded to include T1 through T9 records. These cards can be specified in any order and the file can include as many title cards as are needed (USACE 1988).

The messages in the input file list of ICotton reference the source of the raw data, road names, culvert size, as well as other information pertinent to data entry. These messages were inserted in ICotton by placing the record identifier , "*", in field zero of the line containing the information (USACE 1988). The messages were printed in the input listing of OCotton, but was not printed at any other location in this file. This format allows immediate referencing to messages at the cross section location.

The bridge geometry described by the BT card for the Oakwood Lane culvert at section 5385 in ICotton was formatted so that changes to this card during editing are easy and less time consuming. The negative number of points described in the first field of the BT card allows for formatting the station, top of road elevation, and low chord elevation so that they line up vertically in the set (USACE 1982).

The three blank lines preceding the ER, end of run card, formally required for program execution have been omitted from ICotton. These blank lines are no longer needed for program execution (USACE 1988). Although, blank lines have been inserted in ICotton for the purpose of separating sets of cards that represent one cross section location.

```
T1         HAYS COUNTY FLOOD INSURANCE STUDY
T2         100 YEAR FREQUENCY FLOOD
T2         SEPTEMBER 1989
T3         COTTONWOOD BRANCH                  DG
T3         A PORTION OF THE COTTONWOOD BRANCH INPUT DATA
T4         TRIBUTARY OF BARTON CREEK
J1   -1         2                     0.00000                          1056.25
J2    1                       -1
J3   38        43         1       40        41       10       56       59       60       58
QT    1      3100
NC                                  .1        .3
NH    5     .070      1422      .065     1467     .060     1489     .065     1500     .070
NH 2015
*          COTTONWOOD BRANCH AERIAL SURVEYED SECTION #18
X15085.0      10.0    1422.0    1500.0        0        0        0     0.00     0.00     0.00
*          FIELD 10 OF X2 CARD REQUEST FLOW DISTRIBUTION TABLE AT THIS SECTION
X2                                                                                         15
GR1057.5    1348.0    1054.2    1422.0   1048.5   1467.0   1048.5   1489.0   1052.6   1500.0
GR1057.4    1527.0    1059.9    1563.0   1060.0   1564.0   1061.5   1622.0   1064.2   1670.0

NC   .070     .070      .060
QT    1      1920
*          COTTONWOOD BRANCH AERIAL SURVEYED SECTION #19
X15300.0      10.0    1517.0    1601.0    225.0    225.0    215.0     0.00     0.00     0.00
GR1060.7    1488.0    1060.6    1490.0   1058.9   1517.0   1056.9   1538.0   1052.5   1548.0
GR1052.5    1582.0    1057.0    1601.0   1062.0   1634.0   1063.9   1668.0   1067.0   1722.0

NC                                  .3        .5
*          OAKWOOD LANE CULVERT DOWNSTREAM (SIX 5FT. DIA. PIPES)
X15355.0       0.0       0.0       0.0     55.0     55.0     55.0     0.00     0.00     0.00
X3   10                                                                    1055.5   1055.5
SB 1.25       1.56      2.70         0     31.3      7.7    117.8        0   1051.5   1051.5

*          COTTONWOOD BRANCH AERIAL SURVEYED SECTION #20 - OAKWOOD LN. UPSTREAM
X15385.0      15.0    1486.0    1553.0     30.0     30.0     30.0     0.00     0.00     0.00
X2             0                    1   1056.5   1057.5
X3   10                                                                    1057.5   1057.5
BT   -8     1373.0    1067.1       0.0   1429.0   1062.7      0.0   1465.0   1061.3   1056.5
BT          1494.0    1058.5    1056.5   1531.0   1057.5   1056.5   1558.0   1057.7   1056.5
BT          1578.0    1063.8       0.0   1603.0   1066.9      0.0
GR1067.5    1364.0    1065.0    1399.0   1061.5   1439.0   1059.1   1486.0   1059.1   1486.0
GR1059.1    1486.0    1059.1    1486.0   1056.1   1511.0   1051.5   1529.0   1051.5   1534.0
GR1058.8    1553.0    1063.8    1578.0   1066.9   1603.0   1068.8   1646.0   1072.4   1689.0
EJ
ER
```

FIGURE 1 - ICotton (Input Data File)

<u>Output File</u>. The HEC-2 computer program provides the user with a wide variety of data output. This output information is essential in checking the accuracy of water surface profile results. For example, special notes and error messages are printed at several locations in the cross section data output to inform the user of assumptions or options that have been used during computations (USACE 1982).

HYDRAULIC STREAM MODELING   585

The output data for section 5300 located in OCotton has provided a message, WARNING: CONVEYANCE CHANGE OUTSIDE OF ACCEPTABLE RANGE. The term "k" is known as the conveyance of the cross section, it is a measure of the carrying capacity of the cross section, since it is directly proportional to discharge (Chow 1959). The KRATIO is the ratio of the upstream to downstream conveyance. The KRATIO at section 5300 is 0.5 which is outside of the range: 0.7 < KRATIO < 1.4, therefore the warning message appears in the output. In an effort to eliminate this message, cross sections spaced at relatively short intervals should be added to the ICotton file. The conveyance change test is meant to be applied in natural open channel conditions, its significance in the vicinity of bridges is questionable (USACE 1988).

Variable names are used to identify various input and output information for the HEC-2 model. The special bridge method of the program uses the BT card data at section 5385 in ICotton to define the weir profile for the weir flow calculations. Flow over the bridge and the roadway approaching the bridge is calculated using the standard weir equation: $Q = CLH^{3/2}$ where L is the effective length of weir controlling flow (USACE 1982). The variable, WEIRLN, describing the effective length of the weir is listed in the special bridge output data of OCotton (USACE 1988). Thus, comparing the weir described on the BT cards in the input data with the effective weir length (WEIRLN) provided in the output data the program has established another means for checking data accuracy.

Computational Changes. For the special bridge method the program used the maximum upstream low chord elevation (ELLC = 1056.5) located in field four of the X2 card in ICotton to help distinguish between pressure and low flow (USACE 1982). Although the ELLC is 1056.5 at station 1465 on the BT card in ICotton the program will limit the check for the ELLC to the area between the bank stations (1486 and 1553) described on the X1 card (USACE 1988). This allows the program to more accurately determine between pressure and low flow.

Manning's "n" value (channel roughness coefficient) has been inputted on the NH card at section 5085 to separately describe the left and right channel bank and channel bottom. The HEC-2 program tested the applicability of the subdivision of roughness within the channel portion of cross section 5085. A composite roughness "n" has been computed at section 5085. The criteria for this computation is based on either channel side resulting in a slope steeper than 5H:1V. The channel side slope used by HEC-2 is defined as the horizontal distance between adjacent NH stations within the channel over the difference in elevation of these two stations. The third field of the J6 card will give the user the option of selecting a) 0 (test for applicability of subdivision), b) -1 (allow the program to subdivide), c) +value (redefine the side slope criteria) (USACE 1988). The computations using the NH card has been modified to better represent the conveyance for the cross section.

586 RESOURCES FOR WATER MANAGEMENT

The <u>flow distribution option</u> has been requested in field 10 of the X2 card at section 5085 in ICotton and the channel has been subdivided using the NH card. Therefore, flow distribution and an average depth is provided at section 5085 in OCotton for each subsection of the entire cross section including the channel (USACE 1988).

```
        SECNO     DEPTH     CWSEL     CRIWS     WSELK     EG        HV        HL        OLOSS     BANK ELEV
        Q         QLOB      QCH       QROB      ALOB      ACH       AROB      VOL       TWA       LEFT/RIGHT
        TIME      VLOB      VCH       VROB      XNL       XNCH      XNR       WTN       ELMIN     SSTA
        SLOPE     XLOBL     XLCH      XLOBR     ITRIAL    IDC       ICONT     CORAR     TOPWID    ENDST

       *PROF 1
      O

        CCHV=     .100 CEHV=      .300
        1490 NH CARD USED
       *SECNO 5085.000
        1530 MANNINGS N VALUES FOR CHANNEL COMPOSITED
        5085.00    7.75   1056.25        .00   1056.25   1056.86      .61      .00       .00    1054.20
        3100.       87.   2912.         101.       47.     454.       37.       0.        0.    1052.60
          .00      1.85   6.42          2.69      .070     .064      .070     .000    1048.50   1376.03
        .007355      0.     0.            0.        0        0         0       .00     144.50   1520.53
      O
        FLOW DISTRIBUTION FOR SECNO=   5085.00             CWSEL=   1056.25

        STA=      1376.     1422.     1500.     1521.
        PER Q=     2.8       93.9       3.3
        AREA=     47.1      453.7      37.5
        VEL=       1.8        6.4       2.7
        DEPTH=     1.0        5.8       1.8

       *SECNO 5300.000

        3302 WARNING:  CONVEYANCE CHANGE OUTSIDE OF ACCEPTABLE RANGE
        5300.00    5.58   1058.08         .00       .00   1058.73      .66     1.86       .02    1058.90
        1920.       0.    1914.           6.        0.     294.        4.       2.        1.    1057.00
          .01       .00    6.51         1.50      .000     .060      .070     .000    1052.50   1525.65
        .011575    225.    215.         225.         2        0         0       .00      82.46   1608.10
      O
        CCHV=     .300 CEHV=      .500
       *SECNO 5355.000
        5355.00    6.34   1058.84         .00       .00   1059.28      .44      .49       .06    1058.90
        1920.       0.    1901.          19.        0.     355.       11.       2.        1.    1057.00
          .01       .00    5.36         1.67      .000     .060      .070     .000    1052.50   1517.60
        .006966     55.     55.          55.         2        0         0       .00      95.57   1613.17
      O
      1
         9/13/89      17:38:45

        SECNO     DEPTH     CWSEL     CRIWS     WSELK     EG        HV        HL        OLOSS     BANK ELEV
        Q         QLOB      QCH       QROB      ALOB      ACH       AROB      VOL       TWA       LEFT/RIGHT
        TIME      VLOB      VCH       VROB      XNL       XNCH      XNR       WTN       ELMIN     SSTA
        SLOPE     XLOBL     XLCH      XLOBR     ITRIAL    IDC       ICONT     CORAR     TOPWID    ENDST


        SPECIAL BRIDGE
        5227 DOWNSTREAM ELEV IS   1054.82 , NOT   1058.84 HYDRAULIC JUMP OCCURS DOWNSTREAM (IF LOW FLOW CONTRO

        SB   XK      XKOR      COFQ      RDLEN     BWC       BWP       BAREA     SS        ELCHU     ELCHD
             1.25    1.56      2.70        .00     31.30     7.70     117.80       .00    1051.50   1051.50

       *SECNO 5385.000
        PRESSURE AND WEIR FLOW

        EGPRS     EGLWC      H3       QWEIR     QPR       BAREA     TRAPEZOID   ELLC     ELTRD      WEIRLN
                                                                    AREA
        1065.28  1060.78      .00     913.     1008.      118.       118.      1056.50   1057.50      95.

        5385.00    8.52   1060.02         .00       .00   1060.61      .59     1.33       .00    1059.10
        1920.      10.    1905.           5.        8.     308.        4.       3.        1.    1058.80
          .01      1.17    6.19         1.39      .070     .060      .070     .000    1051.50   1467.91
        .008519     30.     30.           30.         3        0         4       .00      91.20   1559.12
```

FIGURE 2 - OCotton (Output Data File)

SUMMARY

The HEC-2 program objective is quite simple - compute water surface elevations at all locations of interest for given flow values. The data needed to perform these computations include: flow regime, starting water surface elevation, discharge, loss coefficients, cross section geometry, and reach lengths (USACE 1982). Among this data, loss coefficients, cross section geometry and reach lengths seem to be the most critical in affecting the accuracy of the model. The cross section data for Cottonwood Branch was computed from bridge plans and aerial spot elevation surveys. The cross section data derived from topographic maps are usually less accurate than data from aerial spot elevation methods. The majority of the cost of aerial mapping and spot elevation data involves flying, photography, ground control and contour mapping. Obtaining additional cross sections is inexpensive. Therefore, more sections can be provided in an effort to increase the accuracy of the water surface profile results.

The Manning's coefficient for Cottonwood Branch were based on field reconnaissance and aerial photographs. Error in Manning's coefficient can have a significant impact on the profile accuracy. The accuracy of Manning's coefficient is usually most critical on steep, confined and extremely flat streams. The sensitivity of Manning's coefficient should be tested individually for each stream studied.

The computation of water surface profiles is not considered an exact science. Nevertheless, the accuracy of these profiles is important and greatly affects development, flood control measures, property owners, and the entire water resources community. The HEC-2 program modifications, veteran engineering experience, and sound engineering judgment continue to contribute to the advancement and accuracy of hydraulic stream modeling.

APPENDIX I. REFERENCES

1. Chow, V.T., <u>Open Channel Hydraulics</u>, McGraw-Hill Book Company, 1959, p. 128.
2. U.S. Army Corps of Engineers, The Hydrologic Engineering Center, "HEC-2 Water Surface Profiles", Users Manual, Davis, CA., September 1982.
3. U.S. Army Corps of Engineers, The Hydrologic Engineering Center, "Computing Water Surface Profiles With HEC-2 on a Personal Computer", Training Document, Davis, CA., September 1988.
4. U.S. Army Corps of Engineers, The Hydrologic Engineering Center, "Supplement to HEC-2 Users Manual", Davis, CA., September 1988.

MONTGOMERY POINT LOCK AND DAM
ENTRANCE TO THE MCCLELLAN-KERR
ARKANSAS RIVER NAVIGATION SYSTEM

R. Chris Hicklin, P.E. [1]

Abstract

Completed in the late sixties and early seventies, the McClellan-Kerr Arkansas River Navigation System has experienced a steady and positive increase in use. Major investments have been made at ports all along the 445 miles of the navigation system.

However, in the last 10 years changing conditions along the Mississippi River have caused a loss in the reliability of the system. The Montgomery Point Lock and Dam study has determined that the only engineering solution to the problem is a lock and dam at the entrance to the system.

The impact of the lock and dam is a vital concern since the geographic area has considerable environmental importance. One of the last remaining major tracts of bottomland hardwoods in the Mississippi River delta is found in the area.

Additional problems dealing with dredged material disposal and the determination of economic feasibility of the proposed project are also significant concerns.

Introduction

The 445-mile long McClellan-Kerr Arkansas River Navigation System was authorized by Congress in the River and Harbor Act of July 24, 1946, for navigation, flood control, hydroelectric power, and other purposes. Construction began in 1957 with navigation reaching the Port of Catoosa in December, 1970 at a cost of $1.2 billion. The tonnage moved on the system averages between 8 and 10 million tons per year.

---
[1] Civil Engineer, Project Manager, Project Reports Branch, Planning Division, U.S. ARMY ENGINEER DISTRICT, P.O. BOX 867, LITTLE ROCK, AR 72203-0867.

The navigation system begins at the confluence of the White River and the Mississippi River in southeast Arkansas, proceeds 10 miles upstream on the White River to the man-made Arkansas Post Canal and then extends 9 miles through the canal to the Arkansas River. It crosses the State of Arkansas into Oklahoma on the Arkansas River to the mouth of the Verdigris River at Muskogee and terminates 51 miles upstream on the Verdigris River at Catoosa, Oklahoma, near Tulsa.

A minimum depth of nine feet is authorized along the navigation system, and the width varies from 300 feet in the White River and Arkansas Post Canal to 250 feet on the Arkansas River and 150 feet on the Verdigris River. There are 17 locks located on the system with a total lift of 420 feet occuring between the Mississippi River and Catoosa. A vicinity map is shown in Figure 1.

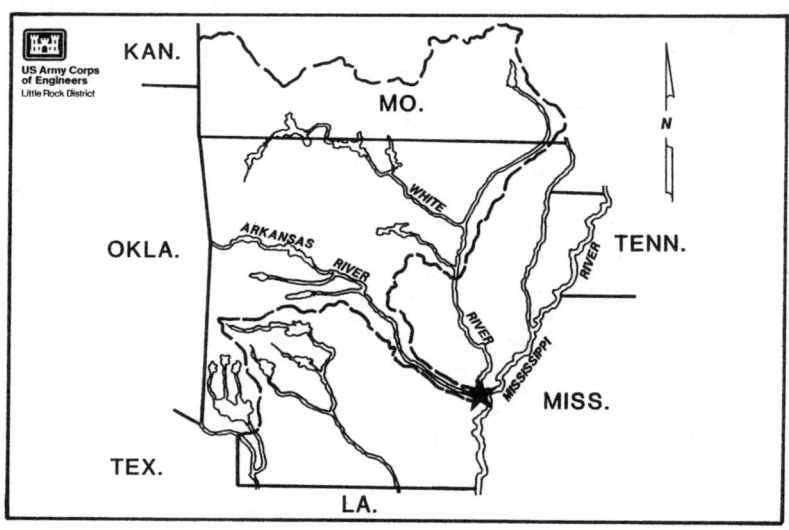

Vicinity Map
Figure 1

Discussion

The White River entrance channel is the only portion of the McClellan-Kerr Arkansas River Navigation System that is not controlled by a lock and dam. This reach of the system is controlled by the Mississippi River. Recently the Mississippi River in the vicinity of the mouth of the White River, has experienced a downward shift in the stage discharge relationship for medium to low flows. That is, stages are decreasing for a given flow. When the McClellan-Kerr system was designed in the early sixties the minimum recorded elevation at the mouth of White River was elevation 110.0, National Geodetic Vertical Datum (N.G.V.D.). This elevation was used as the minimum design elevation expected at the entrance to the system.

Since that time, lower elevations have occurred frequently and with increasing duration. Recent analysis of this phenomena indicates that this trend will continue into the future. The results of this analysis are shown in Figure 2.

The impacts to the system from the lower stages are increased duration of navigation restrictions in the entrance channel. That is, draft is reduced, length and width of tows are reduced, and the available hours of operation are reduced. As a result of these restrictions, commercial navigation is hampered and the reliability of the system is reduced.

To determine a solution to the problem, physical model studies were conducted at the U.S. Army Corps of Engineers Waterways Experimental Station (WES) in Vicksburg, Mississippi. Combinations of contraction works, sediment traps, and diversion of Arkansas River water were modeled, but were unsuccessful in solving the problem. The only solution to the problem was found to be a lock and dam near the mouth of the White River.

This study has presented several unique problems and opportunities. Among them are the remote location of the proposed project, the significant environmental concerns of the area, the method of dredge material disposal without the project and the dredging need that will remain if the proposed project is built.

In the study area is one of the last remaining major bottomland hardwood forests in the Mississippi River delta. This area is environmentally significant and that fact must be considered in the plan formulation and the economic analysis of the project. Of major concern is the impact on the wetlands, disposal of the dredge material without the project, and the amount of dredging that will remain with the project.

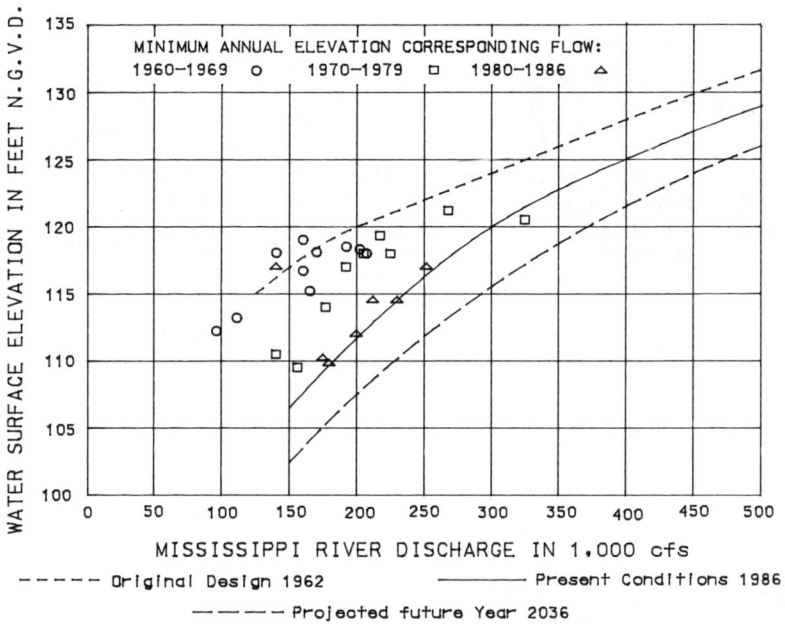

ELEVATION - FLOW RELATIONSHIP
WHITE RIVER ENTRANCE CHANNEL

These concerns are being addressed and evaluated in the design and economic analysis which is identifying costs and benefits associated with the project. Cost estimates are being prepared using computer-assisted technology. This includes CADD (Computer Aided Drafting and Designing) and M-CACES (Micro-Computer Aided Cost Estimating System.)

Upon completion and approval of the study, Congress may choose to finance the project in a number of ways. Since the project is part of the inland navigation system, the cost of the project is 100% Federal. However, Congress may require that 0 to 50% of the total cost be from the Inland Waterways Trust Fund. The Water Resources Development Act of 1986 (PL 99-662) states "the Federal share of the cost of operation and maintenance of any project for navigation on the inland waterways is 100 percent."

Summary

The Montgomery Point Lock and Dam study is examining the complex and challenging problem of attempting to remedy the loss of navigation depths on the McClellan-Kerr Arkansas River Navigation System at the White River entrance channel. Using the latest technology the Corps of Engineers has concluded that the only engineering solution is a lock and dam. Environmental and economic concerns are constantly being weighed as the study progresses toward a September 1990 deadline.

APPENDIX

UNITS OF MEASURE

Feet - Meters

Miles - Kilometers

Cubic Feet per Second - Cubic Meters per Second

INSTREAM HABITAT CONSIDERING HYDRO-PEAKING

Robert T. Milhous[1]

Abstract

The determination of instream flow needs in the tailwater of a hydroelectric project operated in a peaking mode are addressed in this paper. Hydroelectric projects with storage have the characteristic of being able to generate electricity with short notice and to stop generating electricity with equally short notice. This peaking mode of energy generation typically leads to rapid changes in streamflow downstream of the project. Velocities and depths change rapidly with the rapid changes in streamflow; some areas become dry as a result of a rapid decrease, and other areas become wetted so fast as a result of an increased flow that most aquatic organisms have insufficient time to utilize these rapidly changing areas and may be washed from areas that have gone from good habitat to hazardous to the organism. An analytical tool developed to look at the aquatic habitat associated with these rapid changes is based on the minimum habitat associated with the two flows forming the generation cycle. The results of this dual-flow analysis can then be used to select acceptable combinations of base and generation flows.

Introduction

A characteristic of many hydroelectric projects is the daily variation of streamflows caused by the project. In this paper, releases from a reservoir are considered to be dual-flows; a generation flow and a base flow. The components of these dual flows can be very different. For example, the base flow in the Salmon River in upstate New York is 25 cfs with a common generation flow of 1,200 cfs. The analysis of dual-flows requires an aquatic habitat model that accounts for the impact of the dual-flows on the worth of an aquatic habitat below the project.

---

[1]Hydraulic Engineer, National Ecology Research Center, U.S. Fish and Wildlife Service, 4512 McMurray Ave., Fort Collins, CO 80525-3400.

The idea of a dual-flow habitat is best understood when compared to steady-flow habitat. Steady-flow habitat is the habitat that exists when the streamflow is constant (Nestler et al. 1988; Milhous 1984). For steady flow habitat, the statement "there is a weighted useable area of 101 sq ft/ft for smallmouth bass at a flow of 85 cfs" means there is a 101 sq ft/ft of habitat at all times. To use a steady flow habitat relationship in the analysis of a water resource system, the requirement for steady flows is relaxed by making one or both of two assumptions. The first is that if the flows change relatively slowly, the aquatic organisms have time to adjust to the new habitat condition. The second is that the aquatic organisms can tolerate short and relatively infrequent periods of high flows with poor habitat by concentrating in refuges and waiting out the storm.

The rapid changes in streamflow caused by rapid and frequent changes in streamflow are not consistent with the assumptions made for the steady-flow habitat and requires a different approach.

Theory

The different approach must be consistent with the observation that individual locations (cells) in a stream channel have different functional relationships between the worth of the habitat and discharge with some cells decreasing while others increase. For steady flows this does not matter because the habitat is whatever is found, but with a rapid change in flow this is no longer the case because the aquatic organism must be able to move to maintain adequate habitat conditions. If the streamflow change is slow, many aquatic animals can move, but if the changes are fast enough, few aquatic animals can move. The new approach accounts for the fact that aquatic animals may be restricted in the degree they can move when the flows change. In this paper, only the case where the animals cannot move will be considered.

The logic behind the calculation of dual-flow habitats when the aquatic organism cannot move is illustrated in Figure 1. The basic assumption is that the available habitat is the minimum of the habitat available with the dual-flows on a cell-by-cell basis. The habitat with dual-flow will be equal to, or less than, minimum steady-flow habitat calculated for the two flows.

An example of the habitat versus streamflow relationship is given in Figure 2. The steady-flow habitat function is the "traditional" product of the application of PHABSIM (Milhous et al. 1989).

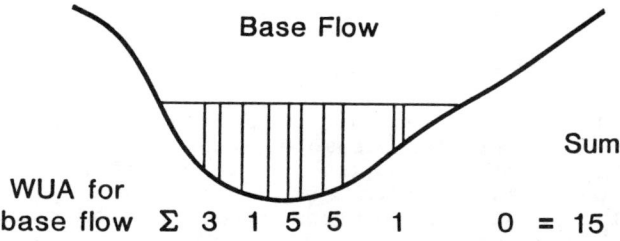
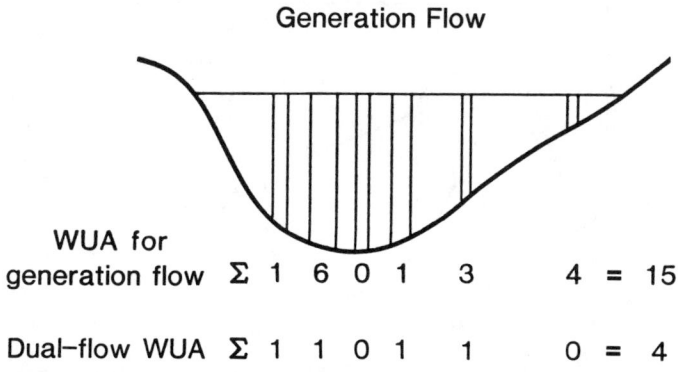

Figure 1. The calculation of dual habitat when the aquatic organism cannot migrate as the flows change.

Associated with rapid changes in streamflow is the possibility of stranding aquatic animals as the flow rapidly decreases and areas either become dry or too shallow to support a specific aquatic animal. Consequently, a stranding index has been developed based on the assumption that the aquatic organisms will be distributed in proportion to the distribution of physical habitat at the generation flow; then, as the flow rapidly decreases to the base flow state, the organism will escape to suitable habitat conditions only if the conditions at the base flow are suitable for escape. The stranding areas (SA), then, are those areas unsuitable for escape at the base flow, but with suitable habitat at the generation flow. The stranding index (SI) is

$$SI = \sum_{i=1}^{n} SA(i)/WUA(Q_G)$$

where $SA(i) = 0$ if conditions are suitable for escape and equals the weighted useable area for the cell if the conditions are not adequate for escape, and $WUA(Q_G)$ is the total weighted useable area at the generation flow (Q_G). The stranding index for one life stage of salmon in the Pineville reach of the Salmon River, NY, is presented in Figure 3 for two generation flows.

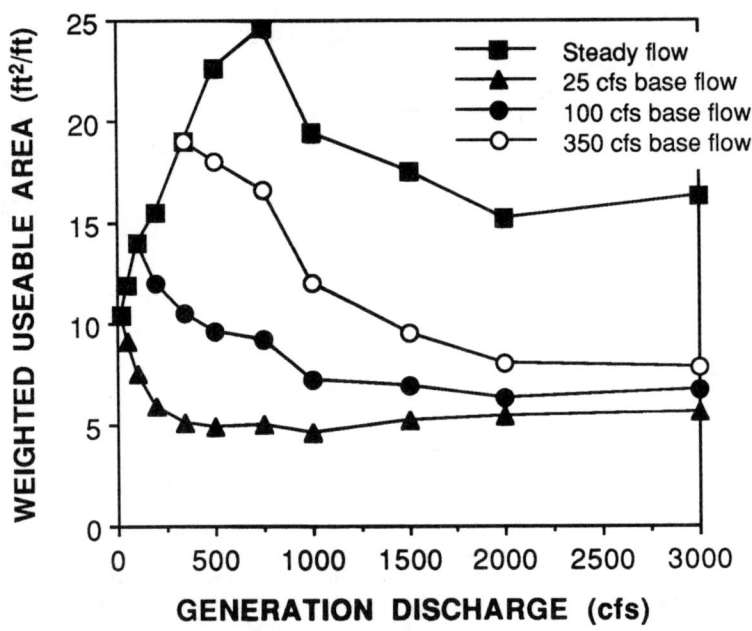

Figure 2. The steady-flow and dual-flow habitat versus streamflow functions for benthic grazers in the Pineville Reach of the Salmon River with the base flow held constant.

Application

One use of Figures 2 and 3 is to establish a minimum (or base) flow for the operation of a hydroelectric project. Figure 2 suggests hydropeaking should not be done because it always causes a loss of habitat, but this would not meet the societal goals of having cheap power and a quality aquatic environment. Consequently, the no hydropeaking option can usually be rejected. Figure 3 suggests stranding is probably not a problem with a base flow of 350 cfs. A base flow of 350 cfs and a generation flow of 1,000 cfs would have about 50% of the habitat for benthic grazers at a constant flow of 350 cfs. In the absences of any other information, it appears that 350 cfs would be at least acceptable as a minimum flow.

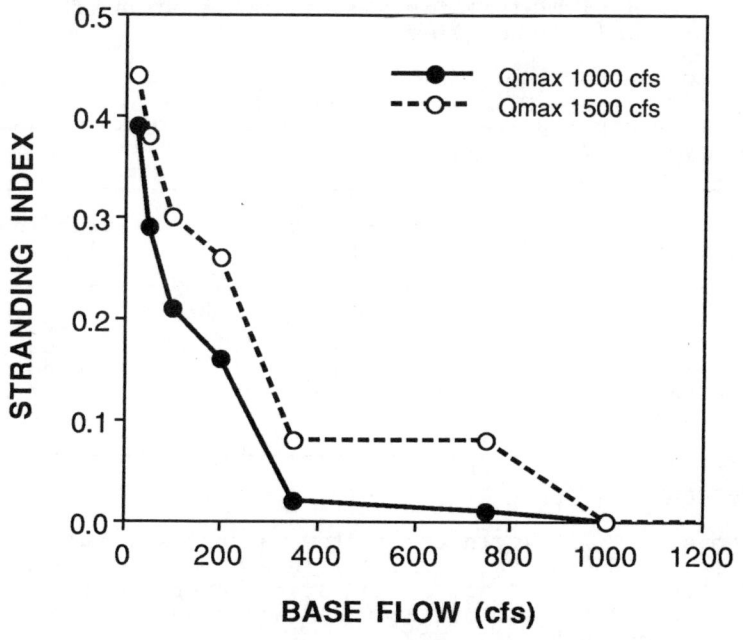

Figure 3. The adult steelhead stranding index for the Pineville Reach of the Salmon River as a function of base flow and for two generation flows.

The average annual flow of the Salmon River is 560 cfs and the June-September average flow is about 150 cfs. If the reservoirs were full on June 1 and empty on September 30, and the average inflow flow was 150 cfs, then the average flow in the river would be 390 cfs, suggesting that the minimum flow of 350 cfs is not very realistic, but is a possibility.

Another logic would be to select 80% of the steady-flow of the aquatic base flow used by the U.S. Fish and

Wildlife Service in New England as the desired habitat, and then use this habitat to select reasonable dual-flow sets. The results of applying this assumption are given in Table 1. The aquatic base flow is 0.5 cfs/sq mi, which is 94 cfs for the hydroelectric project on the Salmon River.

The results in Table 1 are one possible set of base flow/generation flow combination. The final selection of dual flows should be done after simulation studies using water supply data, the characterization of the hydroelectric project, and reasonable dual-flows such as those given in Table 1 for the various species of aquatic animals found in the river.

Table 1. Permissible base and generation flow combination for a target habitat of 50% of the steady-flow habitat at 150 cfs.

Base flow (cfs)	Generation flow (cfs)	Stranding index
35	35	0.00
50	75	0.02
100	270	0.05
200	830	0.12
350	1200	0.08

References

Milhous, R.T. 1984. Instream flow values as a factor in water management. Pages 231-237 in R.J. Charbeneau and B.P. Popkin, eds. Regional and State water resources planning and management. American Water Resources Association, Bethesda, MD.

Milhous, R.T., M.A. Updike, and D.M. Schneider. In press. Reference manual for the Physical Habitat Simulation System (PHABSIM) - Version II. Instream Flow Information Paper No. 26. U.S. Fish Wildl. Serv. Biol. Rep. 89(16).

Nestler, J.M., R.T. Milhous, and J.B. Layzer. In press. Instream habitat modeling techniques. In J. Gore, ed. Alternatives in Regulated River Management.

Application of the GRASS Geographic Information System in a Sensitive Environment of the Arkansas River Navigation System

Manuel Barnes [1]

Abstract

A Geographic Information System (GIS) was used to assist the selection of environmentally sensitive dredge material disposal sites along the Arkansas River Navigation System. Maintenance of the lower navigation system requires dredging about 4,000,000 cubic yards of alluvial material annually. Finding environmentally acceptable disposal sites has become increasingly difficult since wetlands comprise more than 95 percent of the surrounding area. These bottomland hardwood wetlands exhibit some of the highest habitat value in the Lower Mississippi River Valley. The Geographic Resources Analysis Support System (GRASS) software provided state-of-the-art technology for planning an ecologically balanced water resource project. Examples of the digital data layers include: dredge disposal corridor, roads and railroads, hydrology, wetland areas, and oxbow lakes, endangered species habitat, riverine habitat, and elevation.

Introduction

A new means to analyze earth resources has evolved in recent years. This means is referred to as Geographic Information Systems or GIS for short. A GIS is a spatial, overlay technology with superb analytical capabilities. GIS is a very practical tool. The user of a GIS can input, modify, overlay, search, analyze, archive, or simply display maps, and images from sources such as conventional texts, photographs or satellites. Over 90 million dollars was expended last year by the federal government in pursuit of this new technology. GIS has the tremendous ability to

----

[1] GIS and Remote Sensing Manager, Little Rock District, U.S. Army Corps of Engineers, P.O. Box 867, Little Rock, Arkansas 72203

integrate environmental sensitivity in conventional land and water resource planning. Certain features such as special habitat or sensitive areas can be avoided. Other criteria can be given increased weight. A multivariate analysis using GIS reveals otherwise unknown alternatives. The uses of this technology are as infinite as man's imagination. The author believes that the GIS technology will revolutionize land and water resource conservation on a national and global basis.

GIS technology is assisting the selection of environmentally sensitive dredge material disposal sites along the McClellan-Kerr Arkansas River Navigation System. The navigation system provides the infrastructure for the annual transportation of millions of tons of commodities. A significant navigation problem has occurred in recent years due to sedimentation. The problem has been most severe in the lower 10 miles of the system, from the confluence with the White River to the confluence with the Mississippi River. In 1988, 6,000,000 cubic yards of dredged material were removed due to low Mississippi River stages. It is estimated that about 4,000,000 cubic yards will be dredged annually from this reach in the future.

Finding places to discharge the dredged material is complex. Project area population densities of terrestrial species are very high according to the U. S. Fish and Wildlife Service. Over 100,000 wintering ducks rest and feed in the immediate project area wetlands. Plentiful fish and wildlife grow to trophy sizes in area bottomland hardwood, riverine and oxbow habitats. The White River National Wildlife Refuge and the Trusten Holder Wildlife Management Area join the project area. More than 95 percent of the adjacent area is comprised of wetlands. These wetlands exhibit some of the highest habitat value in the Lower Mississippi River Valley. Very healthy populations of sport and commercial fish inhabit the project area.

A GIS digital data base was developed to help solve this complex disposal problem. Digital data layers were developed on a GRASS based GIS. GRASS is an acronym for Geographic Resources Analysis Support System and was produced by the Corps of Engineers, Construction Engineering Research Laboratory. Data layers developed thus far for this Arkansas River evaluation include hydric soils, hydric vegetation, dredge disposal corridor, roads and railroads, hydrology, wetland areas and types, oxbow lake habitat, scenic stream location, endangered species habitat, riverine habitat, and elevation data. Mylar separates are the preferred medium for digitizing. There is a reduced error factor associated with digitizing from mylar as compared to paper maps. Figure 1 illustrates the extent of wetlands using GRASS software.

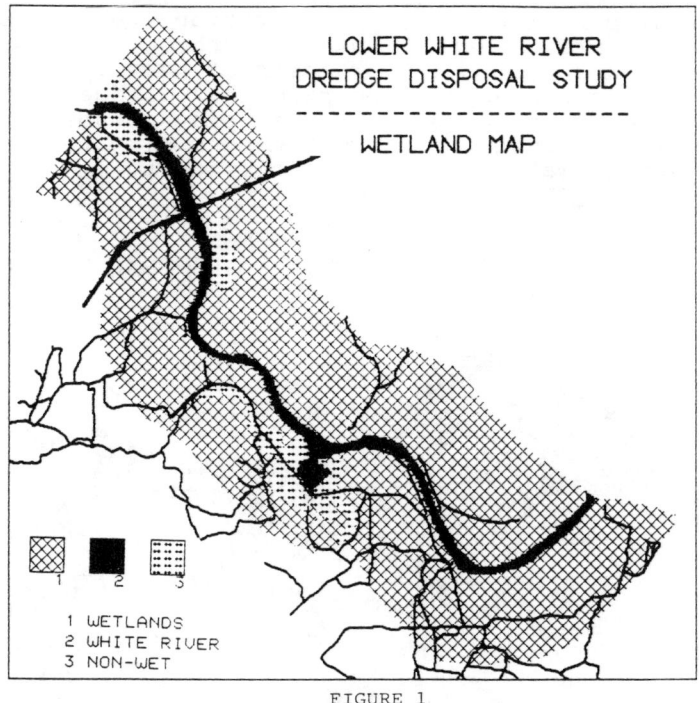

FIGURE 1

Roads and railroad features have been overlaid in this figure. This is a black and white copy of a color product. The color GIS product offers much more detail. It is noted that 256 different colors are possible with the printed product.

Numerous quantifications and a variety of multivariate analyses have been conducted on digital layers to arrive at alternatives for disposal. The selected plan will be one that is both economically and environmentally acceptable. Information from a variety of conservation agencies and groups such as the Arkansas Game and Fish Commission, U. S. Fish and Wildlife Service, Arkansas Natural Heritage Commission, The Nature Conservancy, Arkansas Scenic Rivers Commission and the Arkansas Protection Planning Committee has been utilized in the GIS analyses. Disposal alternatives include 1) open water disposal in the Mississippi River, 2) excavation of existing disposal areas and reuse of these areas, 3) riparian disposal, 4) creation of new conventional disposal areas and 5) pumping the dredge material from the White River to the old Arkansas River channel. Figure 2 shows the possible routes for five dredge material pipeline corridors.

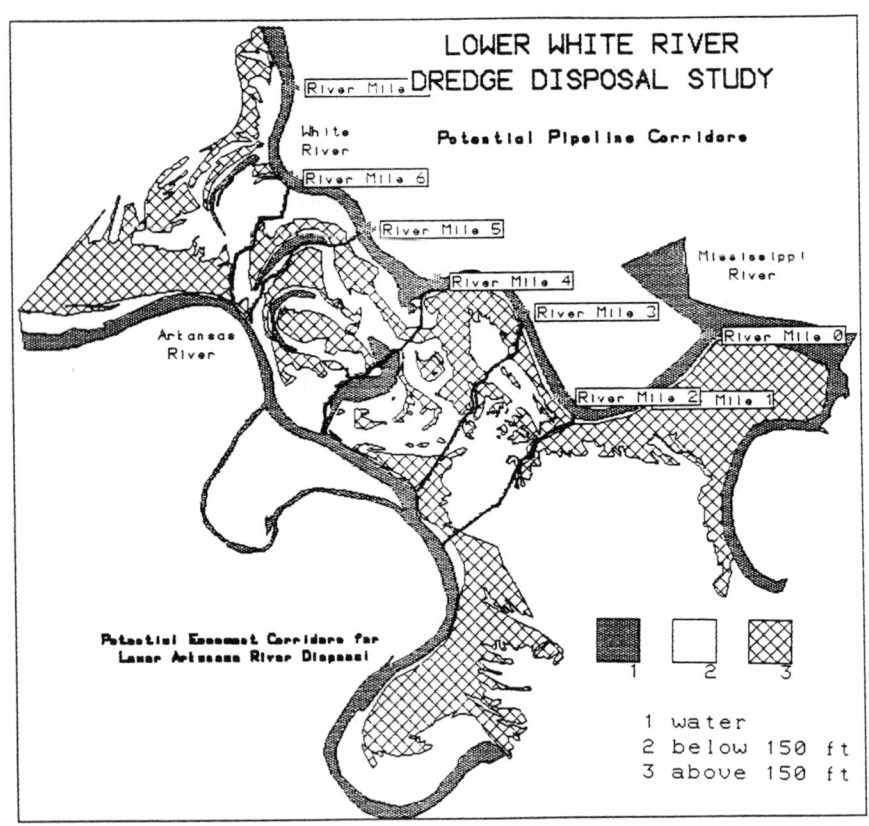

FIGURE 2

GEOGRAPHIC INFORMATION SYSTEM

The potential corridors are the continuous grey lines that span the two waterways at five locations. These locations are River Miles 2, 3, 4, 5, and 6. Spacings are necessary to accommodate economically feasible pumping distances from dredging sites.

The pipelines corridors would result in discharge in or along the old Arkansas River which is considered a scenic river and is starved of sediment. Dredged material could be used to construct beneficial island habitat for the interior least tern, Sterna antillarum athalasso. This bird is listed by the U. S. Fish and Wildlife Service as endangered. It is known to nest and rear in the lower Arkansas River area.

Water resource planning associated with the McClellan-Kerr Arkansas River Navigation System has been significantly enhanced by the GIS technology. Satellite imagery is being analyzed to further refine the selected dredge material disposal plan for the Arkansas River Navigation System.

In conclusion, the development of the GIS digital data base has numerous possibilities beyond this initial GIS project. The data base can be reused for other projects such as real estate easement determinations or habitat manipulations for the North American Waterfowl Management Plan. The data base can be displayed and provided in report form at a variety of scales. Newly digitized information can be merged to a common scale in a matter of minutes. Old land use maps can be updated via remotely sensed data. Digital data sharing with other agencies and institutions to reduce initial data base development cost is very attractive.

The Little Rock District, Corps of Engineers has accomplished sharing the cost of digital data, for example, with the U. S. Soil Conservation Service and the Arkansas Archeological Survey. Data storage space is greatly reduced and data organization enhanced with GIS computers.

Identification of Aquifer Parameters
in Confined Groundwater Flow

Mohamed S. Hantush[1] and Miguel A. Mariño,[2] M. ASCE

Abstract

The problem of identification of the hydraulic properties of a confined aquifer is analyzed in a geostatistical framework. The logarithm of the aquifer properties, log transmissivity (log T) and log storativity (log S), are regarded as realizations of stochastic processes whose estimates are required. The solution to this problem is achieved as follows. First, select a statistical structure that characterizes the average fields of log T and log S and their variabilities at different scales. Second, establish a covariance matrix of point head measurements and cross-covariance matrices among head measurements and log T and log S. This is done by solving a first-order approximation of the governing groundwater equation. Third, given all available head and aquifer properties measurements, the maximum likelihood method is used to identify parameters of the proposed statistical structures of log T and log S. Fourth, cokriging or standard linear estimation is used to predict block-averaged log T and log S fields with their mean square errors of estimates.

Introduction

One of the most useful tools for analyzing groundwater flow and contaminant transport in a porous medium at a regional scale is the numerical solution of partial differential equations. The lack of knowledge

----

[1]Research Assistant, Department of Land, Air and Water Resources, University of California, Davis, CA 95616.

[2]Professor, Department of Land, Air and Water Resources and Department of Civil Engineering, University of California, Davis, CA 95616.

of the spatial distribution of the aquifer parameters and the lack of reliable estimates of these parameters at nodal points render any groundwater management and remediation study, based on the numerical solutions, unrealistic. The problem of identification of unknown aquifer parameters given the model input and output measurements and the input-output model is referred to as parameter identification or the inverse problem.

Historically, aquifer parameters have been determined using either pumping test data and type curves or trial and error procedures. Type curves are based on the assumption of wells tapping homogeneous aquifers which are not influenced by pumping or recharge in their vicinity. They generally yield effective values of the parameters which are not suitable for use in regional groundwater models. Calibration of groundwater models in real-world situations started with manual trial and error procedures. These procedures, in general, are expensive, time-consuming, and may lead to erroneous results.

New approaches have evolved in the last two decades such as the optimization approach, the direct approach, the statistical approach, and the geostatistical approach (Cooley, 1977; Yeh and Yoon, 1981; Vecchia and Cooley, 1987). Both the optimization and direct approaches are computationally burdensome, subject to the problem of overparameterization, and the results are highly sensitive to measurement errors. Also, these approaches avoid the use of available measurements of aquifer properties for identification of property fields. Statistical approaches, on the other hand, account for measurement errors and their spatial distribution (Neuman and Yakowitz, 1979; Yeh et al., 1983; Carrera and Neuman, 1986; Loaiciga and Mariño, 1986). They also provide the reliability of the estimates; however, they usually suffer from the aforementioned difficulties associated with the optimization and direct approaches. In the geostatistical approach, aquifer parameters (e.g., transmissivity and storativity) and head values are considered as random fields. Each unknown parameter field is treated as an unknown realization of a stochastic process whose estimate is required (Kitanidis and Vomvoris, 1983; Aboufirassi and Mariño, 1984; Hoeksema and Kitanidis, 1985; Dagan, 1985, 1987). The approach accounts for the spatial distribution of the property under consideration and its small-scale variability. Overparameterization is avoided since it involves only the parameters which characterize the geostatistical structures of the properties to be estimated. The method requires less computational effort as compared to the preceding methods. Also, sensitivity to measurement error is reduced by including small-scale variability to property and head measurements. To the authors' knowledge, the application of the geostatistical approach in groundwater has been limited to steady-state conditions.

In this paper, the geostatistical approach is extended to the case of transient conditions in which the groundwater system is influenced by vertical recharge and subject to random initial conditions. Point log S values are also incorporated to point log T and point head measurements to simultaneously estimate block-averaged values of log S and log T and, possibly, to identify vertical recharge if it is not known. The method is flexible enough to include measurement errors and uncertainties involved in fixed-head boundary conditions.

Theory

The equation governing two-dimensional confined flow can be written as

$$\nabla \cdot T \nabla \Phi = S \frac{\partial \Phi}{\partial t} - N \qquad (1)$$

in which $\Phi(x,y)$ is the hydraulic head [L], $T(x,y)$ is the aquifer transmissivity [$L^2 T^{-1}$], $S(x,y)$ is the storativity of the aquifer [dimensionless], and $N(x,y)$ is an effective vertical recharge [$L^2 T^{-1}$]. The following decompositions are made

$\Phi(x,y) = \widetilde{\Phi}(x,y) + h(x,y),$ $E(h) = 0$

$\log T(x,y) = \theta_1 + f(x,y),$ $E(f) = 0$

$\log S(x,y) = \theta_2 + \sigma(x,y),$ $E(\sigma) = 0$

in which $\widetilde{\Phi}(x,y)$ is the average (deterministic) head field; $h(x,y)$ is a zero mean head perturbation; θ_1 is the average (assumed constant) log T field; $f(x,y)$ is a zero mean log T perturbation; θ_2 is the average (assumed constant) log S field; and σ is a zero mean log S perturbation. Upon the substitution of these decompositions in Eq. 1, the following deterministic and stochastic dynamic systems (discrete in space via finite elements) can be obtained:

$$A_1 \frac{d\widetilde{\Phi}}{dt} + B_1 \widetilde{\Phi} - u_1 = 0 \qquad \text{(deterministic)} \qquad (2)$$

$$A_2\frac{dh}{dt} + B_2 h - C(\tilde{\Phi})f - \frac{dD}{dt}\sigma = 0 \quad \text{(stochastic)} \quad (3)$$

in which **h** is a vector of nodal head perturbations; **f** and σ are vectors of block-averaged log T and log S perturbations, respectively; u_1 is a vector that accounts for deterministic boundary conditions and recharge; and A_1, B_1, A_2, B_2, C, and D are finite element matrices. Using an eigenvalue technique, the continuous time solutions of the preceding equations are

$$\tilde{\Phi}(t) = e^{-A_1^{-1}B_1 t}\tilde{\Phi}(0) + \int_0^t e^{-A_1^{-1}B_1(t-\tau)} u_1 d\tau$$

$$h(t) = e^{-A_2^{-1}B_2 t}h(0) + \left[\int_0^t e^{-A_2^{-1}B_2(t-\tau)} C(\tau) d\tau\right] f$$
$$+ \left[\int_0^t e^{-A_2^{-1}B_2(t-\tau)} \frac{dD}{d\tau} d\tau\right]\sigma$$

The covariances, autocovariances, and cross covariances among point measurements are obtained using the preceding solutions as

$$Q_\Phi(t,s) = WE[h(t)h'(s)]W'$$

$$Q_{\Phi,\log T}(t) = WE[h(t)f']$$

$$Q_{\Phi,\log S}(t) = WE[h(t)\sigma']$$

in which W is a weighting matrix that relates, approximately, point head measurements to the finite-element nodal (perturbed head) values.

The following models are assumed valid for characterizing the variabilities of log T and log S (i.e., $Q_{\log T}$, $Q_{\log S}$, and $Q_{\log T, \log S}$)

$$\text{Cov}(\log T_i, \log T_j) = \theta_3 \delta_{ij} + \theta_4 d_{ij}$$

$$\text{Cov}(\log S_i, \log S_j) = \theta_5 \delta_{ij}$$

$$\text{Cov}(\log S_i, \log T_j) = \theta_6 \delta_{ij}$$

in which δ_{ij} is the Kronecker delta (1 if i = j and 0 if i ≠ j) and d_{ij} is a parameter which is a function of the separation distance and integral scale. This enables the construction of a point-measurements global covariance matrix for maximum likelihood estimation of the vector of unknown statistical parameters θ

$$\theta' = (\theta_i, i = 1,6)'$$

Once the vector θ is identified, block-averaged estimates of aquifer properties can be obtained with their mean square errors using cokriging or a standard linear estimation procedure.

Acknowledgment

The research leading to this report was supported by the University of California, Water Resources Center, as part of Water Resources Center Project UCAL-WRC-W-697.

References

Aboufirassi, M., and Mariño, M. A. (1984). "Cokriging of aquifer transmissivities from field measurements of transmissivity and specific capacity." Mathematical Geology, 16(1), 19-35.

Carrera, J., and Neuman, S. P. (1986). "Estimation of aquifer parameters under transient and steady state conditions, 1, Maximum likelihood method incorporating prior information." Water Resources Research, 22(2), 199-210.

Cooley, R. L. (1977). "A method of estimating parameters and assessing reliability for models of steady state groundwater flow, 1, Theory and numerical properties." Water Resources Research, 13(2), 318-324.

Dagan., G. (1985). "Stochastic modeling of groundwater flow by unconditional and conditional probabilities: The inverse problem." Water Resources Research, 21(1), 65-72.

Dagan, G. (1987). "Stochastic identification of transmissivity and effective recharge in steady groundwater flow, 1, Theory." Water Resources Research, 23(7), 1185-1192.

Hoeksema, R. J., and Kitanidis, P. K. (1985). "Comparison of Gaussian conditional mean and kriging estimation in the geostatistical solution of the inverse problem." Water Resources Research, 21(6), 825-836.

Kitanidis, P. K., and Vomvoris, E. G. (1983). "A geostatistical approach to the inverse problem in groundwater modeling (steady state) and one-dimensional simulations." Water Resources Research, 19(3), 677-690.

Loaiciga, H. A., and Mariño, M. A. (1986). "On the solution of the inverse problem for confined aquifer flow via maximum likelihood." Mathematical Geology, 18(7), 677-692.

Neuman, S. P., and Yakowitz, S. (1979). "A statistical approach to the inverse problem of aquifer hydrology, 1, Theory." Water Resources Research, 15(4), 845-860.

Vecchia, A. D. and Cooley, R. L. (1987). "Simultaneous confidence and prediction intervals for nonlinear regression models with application to a groundwater flow model." Water Resources Research, 23(7), 1237-1250.

Yeh, W. W-G., and Yoon, Y. S. (1981). "Aquifer parameter identification with optimum dimension in parameterization." Water Resources Research, 17(3), 664-672.

Yeh, W. W-G., Yoon, Y. S., and Lee, K. S. (1983). "Aquifer parameter identification with kriging and optimum parameterization." Water Resources Research, 19(1), 225-233.

Optimization of a Groundwater Well Monitoring Network

Fethi Ben Jemaa[1] and Miguel A. Mariño,[2] M. ASCE

Abstract

An optimization model is presented for the design of a well monitoring network for groundwater quality and quantity parameters. The model utilizes a geostatistical procedure to estimate the optimal sampling locations. Kriging is used in an inverse problem, assuming a minimum variance of estimation to find the monitoring sites. The optimal sampling locations are selected from all possible sites using a tree search procedure.

Introduction

Monitoring the groundwater quality and quantity is a necessary and crucial task in order for a groundwater strategy to be successful. A monitoring network constitutes the baseline for the formulation of short- and long-term strategies which will enforce standards and prevent non-rational measures leading to the degradation of the groundwater quality or quantity. Because a monitoring network is strictly an informational system, its benefits are not immediate and might not be obviously foreseen. Consequently, the cost of monitoring can only be justified by the undesirable consequences resulting from a decision maker's inappropriate measures due to a lack of information about the environment. The amount of data collected will be a function of the network density and the frequency of the observations. Because the variability

----

[1] Research Assistant, Department of Land, Air and Water Resources, University of California, Davis, CA 95616.

[2] Professor, Department of Land, Air and Water Resources and Department of Civil Engineering, University of California, Davis, CA 95616.

of groundwater parameters is not uniformly distributed within the aquifer, the monitoring network has to be layed out according to the fact that some regions have higher variability than others. Thus, minimizing the loss of information means a higher network density in the regions where high variability of parameters is encountered. As the number of measurements increases, more information is provided by the monitoring network, thus better modeling and overall decisions can be made. However, an efficient monitoring strategy needs only a restricted number of sampling locations and a reasonable amount of observations, since in reality one is always confronted by budgetary and economic constraints. In such a situation, econometric methods have to be considered and the monitoring problem will be treated as an optimization problem where, for a given budget, not only a maximum amount of observations is desired, but more importantly, a minimum loss of information is sought by selecting the right locations for data collection. When the variability in the observed data, and therefore its variance increases, the loss of information increases as well. Hence, a method with the objective of optimizing the monitoring network has to consider a variance minimization.

Model Development

The optimal design of a monitoring network has the objective of finding the sampling locations which will give a minimum value of the error of estimates of parameters. While numerous approaches have been used for this purpose, one of the most commonly used criterion is the minimization of the sum of variances of the parameter estimates or the squared error of estimation (Rouhani, 1985; Loaiciga, 1989). Another approach used to improve the sampling design techniques is based on the D-optimal criterion which minimizes the area of 1-α joint confidence region around the parameter estimates (Casman et al., 1988).

The model developed herein is a combination of a geostatistical approach with a feedback method of control (Chow, 1981). A geostatistical approach is first applied to determine the variogram and find the locations with high variance of estimation. As the idea is to achieve a minimum sum of variances in order to extract more information, the points in space having a large variance of estimate will serve as candidate locations for future sampling. If observations $Z(x_i)$ were made at locations $x_1, \ldots, x_n$, then the kriging estimate at a given point x_0 of the variable Z will be (DeMarsily, 1986)

$$\hat{Z}(x_0) = \sum_{i=1}^{n} \lambda_i Z(x_i) \qquad (1)$$

in which λ_i are kriging weights satisfying the condition $\sum_{i=1}^{n} \lambda_i = 1$ (a condition which can be derived from the unbiasedness condition) and $Z(x_i)$ is the observed value at location x_i. The kriging variance or variance of estimate will be

$$V(x_0) = \text{Var}[\hat{Z}(x_0) - Z(x_0)] = \{E[\hat{Z}(x_0) - Z(x_0)]\}^2 \qquad (2)$$

under the condition of unbiasedness of the estimator $\hat{Z}(x_0)$ which can be written as

$$E[\hat{Z}(x_0) - Z(x_0)] = 0 \quad \text{or} \quad E[\hat{Z}(x_0)] = E[Z(x_0)] \qquad (3)$$

where $Z(x_0)$ is the true value of Z at point x_0. By minimizing the variance of estimation (Eq. 2), a kriging system of equations will be obtained which can be solved for the kriging weights λ_i's.

Generalizing the above concept for the case of multiple variables $Z_j(x_i)$, $j = 1,\ldots,N$, in which N is the number of variables, and $i = 1,\ldots,n_j$, in which n_j is the number of observations made for variable Z_j, the cokriging estimate at a given point x_0 of the variable Z_j will be

$$\hat{Z}_J(x_0) = \sum_{j=1}^{N} \sum_{i=1}^{n_j} \lambda_{ij} Z_j(x_i) \qquad (4)$$

in which λ_{ij} is the kriging coefficient of variable Z_j measured at location x_i. Similarly, using the unbiasedness conditions and minimizing the squared error of estimation, the kriging equations can be solved. The minimization of the error of kriging estimates will provide the optimal number and locations of the monitoring wells for a given budget constraint, which can be written as

$$\sum_{j=1}^{N} \sum_{i=1}^{n_j} \beta_{ij} C_{ij} \leq B \qquad (5)$$

in which C_{ij} is the cost of sampling the variable Z_j, B is the available budget, $\beta_{ij} = 1$ if variable Z_j is being sampled at site i, and $\beta_{ij} = 0$ otherwise.

The unbiased condition implies that

$$\sum_{i=1}^{n_j} \lambda_{ij} = \begin{cases} 1 & \text{for } j = J \\ 0 & \text{for } j \neq J \end{cases} \qquad (6)$$

GROUNDWATER WELL MONITORING

Minimizing the variance of estimation error

$$\text{Var}[\hat{Z}_J(x_0) - Z_J(x_0)] = \sum_{j=1}^{N}\sum_{i=1}^{n_j}\lambda_{ij}\gamma_{Jj}(x_0 - x_i) + \mu_J \tag{7}$$

yields the following cokriging system of equations

$$\sum_{j=1}^{N}\sum_{i=1}^{n_j}\lambda_{ij}\gamma_{Kj}(x_\ell - x_i) + \mu_K = \gamma_{JK}(x_0 - x_\ell) \tag{8}$$

$$\sum_{i=1}^{n_j}\lambda_{ij} = \begin{cases} 1 & \text{for } j = J \\ 0 & \text{for } j \neq J \end{cases} \tag{9}$$

in which μ is a Lagrange multiplier; $K = 1,\ldots,N$; $\ell = 1,\ldots,n_J$; $\gamma_{\alpha\beta}(h)$ = the cross-variogram of variables Z_α and Z_β; h = the distance between the measurements of the variables Z_α and Z_β; and $\gamma_{\alpha\alpha}(h)$ = the variogram of variable Z_α. It is evident that cokriging equations (8) and (9) depend only on the locations of sampling but not on the values of the observed data.

The aforementioned variogram is defined for a single variable Z as

$$\gamma(h) = \frac{1}{2}E[Z(x + h) - Z(x)]^2 \tag{10}$$

For two variables, the cross variogram is defined as

$$\gamma_{\alpha\beta}(h) = \frac{1}{2}E\{[Z_\alpha(x + h) - Z_\alpha(x)][Z_\beta(x + h) - Z_\beta(x)]\} \tag{11}$$

The variogram and cross-variograms can be estimated by simply using observed data points (DeMarsily, 1986) and fitting one of the common variogram models (linear, spherical, etc.).

The kriging method as presented above is commonly used to optimize the estimation of a variable at some location, given observed data at a network of points $x_1,\ldots,x_n$. Here, the inverse problem is considered. With the goal of minimizing the variance of estimation, one needs to determine the optimal locations for collecting observations. Determining the optimal locations for sampling before having any observed data is not as difficult as it seems since the variance of estimation depends only on the positions of sampling sites. Knowing a minimum variance of estimation leads to the system of equations (for a single variable):

$$\sum_{i=1}^{n}\lambda_i\gamma(x_j - x_i) + \mu = \gamma(x_j - x_0) \quad j = 1,\ldots,n$$

$$\sum_{i=1}^{n}\lambda_i = 1$$

A way of solving such a system of equations is to

consider that all the observations are of equal importance. This means that all the kriging weights are equal, $\lambda_i = \lambda = 1/n$. However, by having the sampling locations unknown, the system of equations will have more unknowns $\{[n(n+1)/2]+1\}$ than equations $(n+1)$. As an alternative, the domain can be discretized into a grid of locations, and the optimal monitoring locations minimizing the estimation variance can be sought using a tree search procedure (Carrera et al., 1984). Considering all potential locations for the monitoring sites a priori is a more practical procedure since, from a practical point of view, not any location can be a good candidate for installing an observation well. The number of sampling locations is a function of the budget constraint. According to the available budget, only a limited number of locations are to be considered. The additional locations are eliminated from the network in such a way that the network will provide a minimum sum of variances of point estimations over the entire domain. Every time an additional site is eliminated, the kriging system is solved, and the total variance of point estimates is recalculated to find the locations to be eliminated with a minimum increase in the variance.

Acknowledgment

The research leading to this report was supported by the University of California, Water Resources Center, as part of Water Resources Center Project UCAL-WRC-W-697.

References

Carrera, J., Usunoff, E., and Szidarovszky, F. (1984). "A method for optimal observation network design for groundwater management." J. Hydrol., 73, 147-163.

Casman, E. A., Naiman, D. Q., and Chamberlin, C. E. (1988). "Confronting the ironies of optimal design: Nonpoint sampling designs with desirable properties." Water Resour. Res., 24(3), 409-415.

Chow, G. C. (1981). Econometric analysis by control methods. J. Wiley and Sons, Inc., New York, N.Y.

DeMarsily, G. (1986). Quantitative hydrogeology. Academic Press, San Diego, Calif.

Loaiciga, H. A. (1989). "An optimization approach for groundwater quality monitoring network design." Water Resourc. Res., 25(8), 1771-1782.

Rouhani, S. (1985). "Variance reduction analysis." Water Resourc. Res., 21(6), 837-846.

Modeling Volatile Organic Transport with Vapor Sorption

Teresa Culver, Christine A. Shoemaker, and Leonard W. Lion[1]

Abstract

A flexible finite element simulation model is developed to predict the movement of volatile organic compounds in variably saturated subsurface regions. The model incorporates both the saturated and unsaturated regions with a variable water table and can simulate transient or steady-state conditions. In the model, sorption out of the aqueous phase is distinguished from sorption out of the vapor phase. The model incorporates the impact of this additional 'vapor sorption' observed in the unsaturated zone. Example simulations of volatile organic waste discharges in humid and arid regions are described. Vapor sorption may have a significant impact on the transport and volatilization rates of volatile organic compounds in the unsaturated zone under certain conditions and may need to be incorporated into predictions of groundwater quality for restoration and management applications.

Introduction

Understanding the significance of vapor phase transport and reaction may be important for accurately forecasting the movement of volatile contaminants and for evaluating the usefulness of alternative methods for the removal of these pollutants. Recent experimental results indicate that sorption of VOCs under unsaturated conditions may be substantially greater than sorption under saturated conditions (Chiou et al. 1985, Peterson et al. 1988). In this research we develop a numerical transport model for the unsaturated and saturated zones that includes the recent findings on the sorption of VOCs in the unsaturated zone. The numerical model developed in this paper can incorporate heterogeneous soil moisture and soil type, time-varying precipitation

---

[1]Graduate research assistant, Professor and Associate Professor, Civil and Environ. Engineering, Cornell Univ., Ithaca, NY 14853-3501

inputs and water velocities. and variable water table height and hydraulic heads.

Following Shoemaker et al. (in press), we conceptualize a VOC in an unsaturated porous media as existing in a four compartment system:

C_L = aqueous concentration [Mass / Vol of pore water]
C_G = gaseous concentration [Mass / Vol of soil air]
C_{SL} = sorbed concentration due to aqueous sorption
         [Mass contaminant/ Mass of soil]
C_{SG} = sorbed concentration due to vapor sorption
         [Mass contaminant/ Mass of soil]

No immiscible phase is considered.

We assume the phase partitioning of the VOC is at equilibrium and is governed by three equilibria: the aqueous adsorption isotherm, the vapor adsorption isotherm and Henry's law:

$$C_{SL} = K_D C_L \qquad (1)$$
$$C_{SG} = K_{SG}(\theta) C_G \qquad (2)$$
$$C_G = K_H C_L \qquad (3)$$

where K_D is the solid-liquid partitioning coefficient, K_H is Henry's law constant, θ is the volumetric water content and $K_{SG}(\theta)$ is the vapor sorption coefficient, which is a function of the water content.

The two-dimensional finite element model developed here incorporates transport by aqueous advection, aqueous dispersion, aqueous and vapor diffusion, and surface volatilization. Vapor phase advection has not been included in the numerical model. Sorption is divided into aqueous and vapor processes. Degradation has been neglected.

VOC Transport Simulations

<u>Humid region scenario</u>- In this scenario a waste seepage pond is envisioned to be discharging an aqueous solution containing dissolved Trichloroethylene (TCE) through a strongly sorbing organic soil above a shallow water table. The domain simulated was 16 meters deep and 25 meters long, with the ground surface at the top and the water table approximately 9 meters deep. A one-meter deep waste tank had a constant seepage rate of 2.0 cm/day. This scenario could describe a

leaking waste storage tank or a waste seepage pond. The soil type was the same throughout the domain.

For the humid region scenarios, two different water content profiles were generated; one assumed an average net rainfall of 0.25 centimeters/day and the second approximated drought conditions assuming no net rainfall, i.e. rainfall equals evapotranspiration. The profiles are very similar except near the soil surface. Under drought conditions, the predicted water contents near the soil surface are extremely low (less than 10% saturation). Vapor sorption is the strongest in this dry area. Yet, being near the soil surface, soil volatilization will also strongly affect this region of the soil. This scenario will thus demonstrate the moisture-dependent impact of vapor sorption on VOC transport and volatilization in a strongly sorbing soil.

The vapor sorption function is based on laboratory findings of Swanger (1990) who measured vapor sorption of TCE onto a synthetic soil under varying moisture contents. The following empirical formula predicts the vapor sorption coefficient:

$$K_{SG}(\theta) = 0.0268 \left(\frac{\theta}{\phi}\right)^{-3.80} - 0.0268 \qquad r^2 = 0.96 \qquad (4)$$

Vapor sorption increases dramatically as the soil becomes dry.

Under moist conditions, the effect of vapor sorption on volatilization is minimal. Comparing the predicted contaminant plume after two years of transport including vapor sorption to the plume predicted without vapor sorption, the total mass of contaminant remaining in the soil system has increased by 2%. Under drought conditions, the effect is more significant. The amounts of contaminant moving into the saturated zone are similar. The primary differences in the contaminant profiles are in the very dry soil near the surface where vapor sorption is inhibiting volatilization. After two years, there is 25% more contaminant left in the soil matrix that includes vapor sorption. These simulations demonstrate that under dry soil conditions vapor sorption may have a significant impact on the transport of VOCs.

Arid region simulations - Vapor sorption is greatest in very dry soils, and deserts provide the driest naturally occurring conditions. Simulations of an arid region were based on conditions near Los Alamos, New Mexico. In this area, there is essentially no recharge to the water table, which is over 300 meters deep (Abrahams et al. 1961).

The simulations performed here describe a leak of TCE contaminated material from a waste storage shaft. The radially symmetric domain was 70 meters wide and 100 meters deep. The waste storage shaft was assumed to be 2.0 meters wide and 17.0 meters deep, typical of storage shafts in the area. The porous media of the domain was tuff, except for the top 1.5 meters that were modeled as a Hackroy soil, which is a loam-clay material derived from the tuff. Moisture profiles characteristic of the area (Abrahams et al. 1961) were provided as input to the waste transport model.

Laboratory measurements have found that the tuff material has only slight aqueous sorption and no significant sorption of vapors above dissolution into the soil moisture (Ong and Lion 1989 submitted). Only in the surface soils, which tend to be finer and have higher organic matter contents, would one expect to observe strong vapor sorption. The vapor sorption profile applied to the Hackroy soil will be referred to as moderate vapor sorption and is described by equation (5):

$$K_{SG}(\theta) = 4 \exp\left(\frac{0.16 - f}{0.026}\right) \quad \text{where} \quad f = \text{percent saturation}$$
(5)

The initial conditions for the arid simulation assume that a three-meter-deep region directly below the waste shaft has been contaminated with TCE. Simulations were run for 2 years. In each case the domain was described as tuff overlaid by surface soil. The vapor sorption behavior varied between runs. Simulations were made with no vapor sorption, with moderate vapor sorption (described by Equation 5) in the surface soil, and with strong vapor sorption (described by Equation 4) in the surface soil. The resulting volatilization losses over time are shown in Figure (1). Strong vapor sorption has cut in half the mass of contaminant volatilized over two years. Equation (4) is an exceptionally strong sorption profile and is used to here as an indication of the maximum effect vapor sorption might have in this domain. Thus, for some soils vapor sorption may act to significantly reduce surface volatilization.

Conclusions

The numerical model was developed to investigate the potential significance of vapor sorption on the transport of VOCs in variably saturated porous media, including surface volatilization and transport below the water table. Our analysis indicates that vapor sorption can have a large impact on the subsurface transport of volatile materials when low soil moisture is combined with a soil type that has strong vapor sorption characteristics. Under very dry conditions, vapor sorption may significantly retard the transport and volatilization of VOCs. Furthermore, our simulations have shown that the overall impact of vapor sorption is highly sensitive to changes in soil moisture profile.

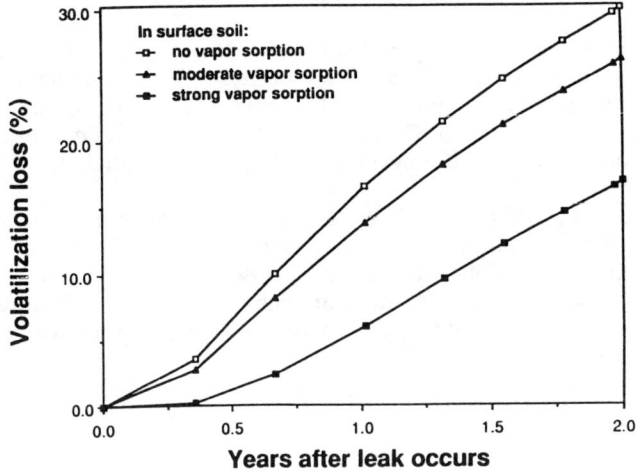

Figure 1. Percent of the initial mass of leak volatilized from the arid domain over time for varying strengths of vapor sorption in the surface soil. Simulations include runs with no vapor sorption, with moderate vapor sorption (equation 5), and strong vapor sorption (equation 4) in the surface soil. No vapor sorption occurs in the tuff.

In regions subject to extended dry periods, vapor sorption may be an important phenomenon to consider to successfully predict VOC transport. At sites where VOCs contaminate the vadose zone, vapor sorption may extend the period of exposure by slowing the dissipation into the atmosphere. In addition the VOC removal efficiency of new reclamation techniques, such as vapor extraction, may be reduced due to the retarding effect of vapor sorption.

Literature Cited

Abrahams, J.H., Jr., J.E. Weir, Jr., and W.D. Purtyman, Distribution of moisture in soil and near-surface tuff on the Pajarito Plateau, Los Alamos County, New Mexico. Short papers in geologic and hydrologic sciences, Articles 283-435. U.S. Geological Survey Prof. Papers 424-D, 1961.

Chiou, C.T., T.D. Shoup, and P.E. Porter, Mechanistic roles of soil humus and minerals in the sorption of nonionic organic compounds from aqueous and organic solutions, Org. Geochem, 8(1), 9-14, 1985.

Ong, S.K. and L.W. Lion, Effects of soil properties and moisture contents on the sorption of TCE vapor, submitted to Water Research, 1989.

Peterson, M.S., L.W. Lion, and C.A. Shoemaker, Influence of vapor-phase sorption and diffusion on the fate of trichloroethylene in an unsaturated aquifer system, Environ. Sci. Technol, 22(5), 571-578, 1988.

Shoemaker, C.A., T.B. Culver, L.W.Lion, and M.S. Peterson, Analytical models of the impact of two-phase sorption on subsurface transport of volatile organics, Wat. Resour. Res., In press.

Swanger, J.L., Vapor-phase sorption of trichloroethylene and toluene on unsaturated soils, M.S. Thesis, Cornell University, Ithaca, N.Y.,1990.

Groundwater Quality Network Design

Donald P. Walker[1] and Miguel A. Mariño,[2] M. ASCE

Abstract

This paper presents a methodology that uses optimization for designing a groundwater monitoring network. The methodology incorporates parameter estimation in conjunction with a numerical model of a groundwater system to develop the objective function and constraints used to determine the optimal location of a monitoring well. A one-dimensional contaminant transport problem is used as an example to illustrate the methodology.

Introduction

As the attention and recognition of groundwater contamination continues to grow, so does the research into various aspects of groundwater and pollution. One such aspect that has been receiving increased attention is the area of groundwater monitoring network design.

Early research on hydrologic network design focused mainly on surface water networks such as stream gauge or rain gauge locations. Later, more attention was given to groundwater networks where designs were based on either qualitative or quantitative methods. A common qualitative approach uses a subjective analysis which reviews cultural and physical information such as geologic, hydrologic, land use, and chemistry data to aid in selecting a well location. A common quantitative method uses systems analysis to choose locations that

----

[1]Geohydrologist, Dames and Moore, 9300 Tech Center Drive, # 100, Sacramento, CA 95826.

[2]Professor, Department of Land, Air and Water Resources and Department of Civil Engineering, University of California, Davis, CA 95616.

minimize the variance of a regionalized variable, such as a chemical concentration, subject to cost constraints. Mixed integer programming is then used to solve the optimization problem.

A quantitative method is used in this work to select the location of a second monitoring well. The mathematical analysis is formulated by first using a numerical model to describe a physical system. A one-dimensional contaminant transport system is used for illustrative purposes. Unknown parameters needed to describe the system are estimated by the method of maximum likelihood. The maximum likelihood method provides a distribution of parameter values which are then used to develop the objective function and constraints of an optimization model which is in turn used to locate a monitoring well.

Problem Description

The transport of a conservative substance in a homogeneous and isotropic confined aquifer is used to illustrate the design procedure. Specifically, a conservative substance is released an unknown distance, x, upgradient from an existing monitoring well. A series of concentration measurements are collected over time at the monitoring well. The goal is to determine the location of a second monitoring well upgradient from a supply well (i.e., between the existing monitoring well and the supply well). The known parameters of the system include the velocity field ($v = 0.1$ m/day), the distance between the existing monitoring well and the supply well ($L = 300$ m), the initial concentration of the contaminant ($C_0 = 100$ units), and a series of concentration measurements taken at the existing monitoring well (C_1, C_2, ..., C_n, measured 30 days apart). The unknown parameters which need to be estimated include the dispersion coefficient, D, and the distance between the source and existing monitoring well, x.

The unknown parameters are estimated using the measurements taken at the monitoring well. Concentration values are generated using the well-known analytical solution to a one-dimensional conservative contaminant transport problem (Ogata and Banks, 1961)

$$C = \frac{C_0}{2} \left\{ \text{erfc} \left[\frac{x - vt}{2(Dt)^{\frac{1}{2}}} \right] + \exp \left[\frac{vx}{D} \right] \text{erfc} \left[\frac{x + vt}{2(Dt)^{\frac{1}{2}}} \right] \right\} \quad (1)$$

Values of $x = 100$ m and $D = 10$ m^2/day along with values given above are used to generate values C_1, C_2, ..., C_n. Random error terms with mean equal to zero and variance equal to σ_e^2 are added to the concentration values C_1, C_2, ..., C_n.

Parameters are estimated using the method of maximum likelihood in which, by standard convention, the negative log-likelihood function is minimized

$$f = \frac{n}{2} \ln(2\pi) + \frac{n}{2} \ln(\sigma^2) + \frac{1}{2\sigma^2} \sum_{t=1}^{n} e_t^2 \qquad (2)$$

where n = the number of concentration measurements; σ^2 = the variance of the errors between calculated and measured values of C; and e_t^2 = the square of the difference between measured and calculated values of C. The calculated values are computed using a finite element numerical model.

The minimization algorithm uses a version of the Gauss-Newton method to minimize Eq. 2. The algorithm is an iterative process which proceeds until changes in the parameters D and x meet a specified criterion. The distribution of the parameter estimates, for a sufficiently large n, are approximately normally distributed, in which the variance can be estimated by the inverse of the sample information matrix. Once the values of $\hat{D}$ and $\hat{x}$, along with their covariance matrix are calculated, then this information is used to help determine a monitoring well location.

The optimization model used to determine a new monitoring location minimizes the variance of concentration, σ_c^2, which is a function of x and t, subject to drilling and penalty costs. The form of the objective function is determined by first running a Monte Carlo simulation and then determining the values of σ_c^2 over x and t. The penalty costs are formulated as chance constraints based on the distribution of the estimated parameters $\hat{D}$ and $\hat{x}$. A penalty cost is derived on the basis of a forewarning time needed before the contaminant reaches the supply well. The forewarning time is based on the probability the contaminant will travel a given distance. The probability distribution is determined by running a second Monte Carlo simulation, in which the distance the front moves over a given time is found using $\hat{D}$, $\hat{x}$, and the covariance matrix of $\hat{D}$ and $\hat{x}$. Drilling costs are based on the limited number of locations available for wells, three in this case, and vary with location.

The optimization problem is formulated as a mixed integer programming model due to the limited number of locations for drilling. Solutions to the problem are

11/750. The solution of the problem is of course dependent on the form of σ_c^2 and the values used for drilling costs, penalty costs, and the total budget. The location chosen for drilling always minimizes the variance allowed by the budgetary constraints. The location chosen could be changed by changing the amount of money available or by changing the costs associated with the various drilling sites.

Summary

This paper illustrates an approach to network design that is used in conjunction with numerical modeling and parameter estimation. The important aspect of this work is the use of the covariance matrix of $\hat{D}$ and $\hat{x}$ to determine the form of the objective function and some of the constraints. The use of a one-dimensional system is simplistic, but illustrates the ideas presented in this work. More complex systems could be used in future work, including parameters that are functions of space and time, expanding the groundwater system to two dimensions, or using algorithms other than linear programming to solve the optimization problem.

Acknowledgment

The research leading to this report was supported by the University of California, Water Resources Center, as part of Water Resources Center Project UCAL-WRC-W-697.

References

Ogata, A., and Banks, R. B. (1961). "A solution of the differential equation of longitudinal dispersion in porous media." USGS Prof. Paper 411-A, U. S. Geological Survey, Reston, Va.

AN ECONOMIC EVALUATION OF PROPERTY RIGHTS TO
GROUNDWATER RESOURCES IN THE STATE OF TEXAS

Duane J. Rosa*, Ph.D., ASCE Member

Introduction

In the State of Texas many serious groundwater
problems have developed in recent years. Along the Gulf
Coast extensive pumping of groundwater has resulted in
saltwater intrusion, threatening water quality in the
area. In the central part of the state heavy withdrawals
of groundwater have threatened to reduce the flow of
rivers, and have resulted in water shortages. In West
Texas and the Texas Panhandle, the most intensively
irrigated area in the state, shortage of groundwater has
affected the agricultural and industrial sectors of the
economy. The gravity of the state's groundwater problems
can be properly understood when one considers that the
majority of the state's water needs are met by
groundwater supplies.

The objective of this paper is to evaluate the
basis for determination of property rights to groundwater
in Texas, and to consider the implications of existing
groundwater legislation for the future of the Texas
economy. This paper will consist of three sections.
First, the legal development of groundwater legislation
will be analyzed. Second, groundwater legislation in
Texas will be examined both in terms of its efficiency
and equity in dealing with potential groundwater
problems. Finally, this paper will conclude with an
economic assessment of property rights to groundwater,
focusing on economic efficiency and incentives for
conservation.

Development of Groundwater Law

The issue of an individual's property rights to
groundwater was first considered in England in 1843[1]. A
plaintiff-landowner sought damages for the impairment of
his underground water supply caused by his neighbor's
pumping of the groundwater. The court denied the
plaintiff any relief and formulated the theory that has
become known as "common law doctrine" or the English
rule. Under this doctrine, underground water is
considered to be the property of the overlying landowner
who may withdraw it regardless of the effect

---

* Assistant Professor of Economics, West Texas
State University; Canyon, Texas.

on other wells or the reasonableness of his use.
In the United States the rationale for the common
law doctrine was first explained in 1861 by the Ohio
Supreme Court[2]. They concluded that the nature of
underground water was such that no one could be certain
that the supply of one underground user was or was not
being affected by the withdrawals of another user. The
first state to reject the English rule was New Hampshire
in 1862[3]. They adopted the "American or Reasonable Use
Rule" which recognized the private ownership of
groundwater by the overlying landowner, but required that
the permissible use of the groundwater be limited to
beneficial uses connected with the overlying land. Here
the court recognized that the rights of groundwater users
are interdependent, and the supply of one user is
affected by the activities of other users.

The next modification to the common law doctrine
was in California in 1903[4]. The California Supreme Court
stated that the common law doctrine did not adequately
protect underground water rights. They adopted the
correlative rights doctrine, which does not recognize
private ownership of groundwater. Each groundwater user
is viewed as having equal right of use and enjoyment in
the available supply. In adjudicating the rights of
groundwater users in times of shortage, the overlying
owners are entitled to no more than their "fair and just
proportion" for all users.

The fourth groundwater doctrine, the restatement
rule, was adopted by Wisconsin[5]. Here a well owner may
withdraw water for use on his own or nonoverlying land
unless other users are unreasonably affected. There are
three criteria for determining unreasonable interference:
(1) causing unreasonable harm by lowering the water table
or reducing artesian pressure; (2) exceeding the owner's
reasonable share of the total annual supply; or (3)
having a direct and substantial effect on surface
supplies and causing unreasonable harm to surface water
users.

A fifth theory is the appropriation doctrine, which
was originally developed to govern surface water. Under
this doctrine groundwater is declared by statute to be
the property of the state subject to existing vested
rights held by landowners. After filing an application
with the state, the landowner is issued a permit to
divert a specific quantity of groundwater from the public
water supply. When water shortages occur, individuals
with vested rights have first priority to the available
water, followed by the appropriators in descending order
of the date of their permit. Hence the phrase, "first in
time is first in right" emerged to describe this theory.

A final theory has developed in certain areas of the United States, and can be referred to as statewide or critical areas management systems. The management systems differ radically from one another: Arizona, Colorado, and New Mexico rely on different forms of state management; Kansas, Nebraska, and Texas utilize varieties of local management; California has a system administered by courts and water districts. Seven other western states have modified the appropriations doctrine by statutes that authorize setting reasonable pumping levels for all or part of the state.

Texas Groundwater Law

In 1904, the Texas Supreme Court set the basis for the state's groundwater law[6]. The court adopted the English rule for groundwater noting that the nature of underground water was so mysterious that its regulation was impossible. Also they stated that the recognition of correlative rights in groundwater would impede the state's economic development. In 1955[7] and again in 1978[8] the Texas Supreme court upheld the common law doctrine. In these later rulings the Supreme Court indicated that the English rule had become an established rule of property in Texas. Any rejection would drastically alter Texas' property law, and that such a change would have to be a legislative function. The only other state that allows absolute ownership of groundwater besides Texas is Indiana.

Even though Texas has not changed its fundamental groundwater approach, it has enacted some additional legislation regarding groundwater use. In 1917 the "Conservation Amendment" to the Texas Constitution was adopted. This amendment stated that the state's public policy was to conserve natural resources, including groundwater, and directed the legislature to enact appropriate legislation to implement this policy. It wasn't until 1949, however, that the legislature passed the Texas Groundwater District Act, which authorized local voters to form underground water conservation districts. Owners of land overlying defined groundwater reservoirs may adopt voluntary well regulation through mutual association in underground water conservation districts (Section 52.001, Texas Water Code), and to date 22 districts have been created. The major problems with these water districts are that they are formed around political rather than aquifer boundaries, and there are no controls over production.

In analyzing the current state of legislation in Texas, there are two major problems. First, there are insufficient regulations to provide for effective conservation, and to ensure an economically efficient allocation of the groundwater stock. Second, the basis for the common law doctrine fails to adequately protect the property owner who is injured by another person's unreasonable use of groundwater. The Texas courts have refused to restrict excessive groundwater use, and generally only consider as actionable negligent pumping that causes subsidence rather than groundwater mining. Thus, given the current legislation, neither an injured neighbor nor the State can effectively exercise control over water-use practices involving groundwater.

Economic Analysis

In order to promote the efficient allocation of water resources property rights must be clearly specified, have exclusive ownership, and be enforceable and transferable. Well defined rights are basically rights that make clear and exclusive assignments to one entity. The other two attributes, enforceability and transferability, follow from an exclusive assignment. Once an individual sphere of control is delineated, it is possible to determine what is an interference and to protect the right holder against it. If all values associated with water are encompassed in property rights, then market prices will reflect social values, and the right holder will be faced with the full opportunity of water use.

Completely specified, enforceable, and transferable property rights are the ideal institutional conditions for efficient market performance. With respect to groundwater, however, it is difficult to assign exclusive rights due to the common property nature of groundwater. Common property resources are defined with respect to the prevailing institutional framework of pricing environmental services. In the common property situation, the actions of each individual user influences the quantity of water available and the cost of pumping water for all others. Each user perceives his withdrawals only in terms of his own costs and benefits. Since externalities, or costs to third parties, are incurred that are not compensated for in the market, the result can be an inefficient allocation of resources due to a greater than optimal current rate of extraction. Groundwater pumping thus becomes a problem of reciprocal externalities. The quantity interrelationship can be solved only by rules that fix a definite quantity for each user, as California did through the doctrine of mutual prescription. The pumping level issue to harder to solve, though, because each groundwater user causes external effects to others. Here a truly efficient solution would be one that charged each user for his share of the reciprocal externalities.

Conclusions

The type of groundwater law in place can affect the economic development of a region depending upon the certainty of acquiring adequate water resources. Texas' heavy reliance on groundwater as its primary source of supply for agricultural, municipal, and industrial needs invests the resource with a significant public interest. The current state of the law, however, does not reflect the economic importance of groundwater to the state.

References

1. Acton versus Blundell, Decision of the Excheguer Chamber (152 Eng. Rep. 1223, 1224), 1843.

2. Frazier versus Brown, Decision of the supreme court of Ohio, (12 Ohio St. 294), 1861.

3. Basset versus Salisbury Manufacturing Co., Decision of the supreme court of New Hampshire, (43 N.H. 569, 573), 1862.

4. Katz v. Walkinshaw, Decision of the supreme court of California, (141 Cal. 116, 70 P. 663), 1903.

5. State of Wisconsin versus Michels Pipeline Construction, Inc., Decision of the supreme court of Wisconsin, (63 Wis. 2d 278, 217 N.W.2d 339, 351), 1974.

6. Houston & T.C. Railway versus East Decision of the supreme court of Texas, (98 Tex. 146, 81 S.W. 279), 1904.

7. City of Corpus Christi versus City of Pleasanton, Decision of the supreme court of Texas, (154 Tex. 289, 276 S.W.2d 798), 1955.

8. Friendswood Development Co. versus Smith-Southwest Industries, Inc., Decision of the supreme court of Texas, (576 S.W.2d 21), 1978.

A Newsboy Approach to Real-Time Reservoir Operation Modelling

Emmanuel U. Nzewi[1], A.M. ASCE

Abstract

Real-time reservoir operations refers to the scheduling of releases or outflows from a reservoir system in daily (at most weekly), hourly or smaller time intervals. The problem of optimally operating a multi-purpose reservoir or reservoir system is complex. It is one of obtaining maximum benefits from the operation of a reservoir system by balancing various counteracting objectives/uses of a reservoir system. This investigation focuses on the use of mathematical programming techniques to develop a model for scheduling, in real-time, the releases from a single reservoir via a probabilistic approach based on the classical Inventory Theory problem called the Newsboy or Christmas-Tree problem. The theoretical development of such a model is presented and the probabilistic objective function is discussed. The objective is to minimize the sum of expected deviations from the statistically ideal operating levels.

Introduction

The problem addressed in this study and similar ones is to formulate a set of rules by which day-to day release decisions may be optimally made with respect to long-term operating goals. The analytical study presented here derives a probabilistic mathematical model for real-time reservoir operations based on a closely related classical Inventory Theory problem - the Newsboy or Christmas Tree problem. A fundamental incentive for the use of a probabilistic mathematical model is to achieve the calibration of the real-time reservoir operations model with relative ease. Calibration has been a significant problem with the other real-time reservoir operations modelling approaches (Houck, 1982). The mathematical model proposed here identifies optimal decisions as those that minimize the sum of the expected values of the deviations, from statistically ideal levels, of the pertinent decision variables. In the model proposed here, the probability distribution functions (PDFs) of the respective decision variables are incorporated into the model usually as marginal cumulative distribution functions (CDFs).

Penalty-based models have a long history of development and discussion in the literature (for example, Yeh, 1985) but probabilistic mathematical models appeared on the scene recently (Houck, 1982; Nzewi and Houck, 1989). The general mathematical program for daily real-time reservoir operations is equations 1 to 9. Equation 1 is the objective function in which the appropriate optimization strategy is to be substituted. Equation 2 is the reservoir continuity condition for the current period

---

[1] Assistant Professor, Department of Civil Engineering, North Carolina A&T State University, Greensboro, NC 27411.

N, and equation 3 is for the remaining days in the forecast horizon. Equation 4 is the transformation for determining the amount of hydroelectric energy generated as a function of the values of S_t and R_t. Equation 5 is an example of a flow routing formula to calculate the flows at a point downstream of the reservoir. Equations 6 to 9 are the bounds on the decision variables.

(1) Optimize $obj(S_{t+1}, F_t, H_t)$
     subject to:
(2) $S_{N+1} + R_N = SB_N + I_N$
(3) $S_{t+1} - S_t + R_t = I_t$ $t \in t^0$
(4) $H_t - \rho(R_t, S_t) = 0$ $t \in t^1$
(5) $F_t - \sigma(R_t) = 0$ $t \in t^1$
(6) $SMIN \leq S_t \leq CAP$ $t \in t^2$
(7) $RMIN \leq R_t \leq RMAX$ $t \in t^1$
(8) $H_t \leq HMAX$ $t \in t^1$
(9) $R_t, F_t, H_t, S_{t+1} \geq 0$ $t \in t^1$

where: $t^0 = N+1, .., N+T-1$, $t^1 = N, N+1, .., N+T-1$ and $t^2 = N+1, .., N+T$.

SB_N is the known reservoir storage volume at the beginning of day N [m^3]; S_t is the anticipated reservoir storage at the beginning of day t [m^3]; R_t is the anticipated volume of water released during day t [m^3]; I_t is the forecast volume of inflow into the reservoir during day t [m^3]; F_t is the volume of water flowing through a downstream control station as calculated by equation 5 [m^3]; H_t is the amount of hydroelectric energy produced on day t [kWH] as determined by equation 4; the limit on H_t is HMAX. The pairs CAP and SMIN, RMAX and RMIN are the lower and upper bounds on S_t and R_t, respectively; T is the forecast horizon [days]; N is the index of the current day [-].

Classical Inventory Theory Newsboy Problem

The Newsboy or Christmas-Tree problem has received a lot of attention in the past (Silver and Peterson, 1985). A single-period one-item Newsboy problem may be posed as follows: a newsboy must decide on the number of copies of a daily newspaper to stock on a given day and intends to place an order in such a way that his expected operations losses for the day are minimized. Assume that ζ is the unit cost for newspapers remaining unsold at the end of the day and η is the unit cost for demand not satisfied. Assume also that f is the defined and stable probability distribution function of demand for the particular newspaper on that day. Let Q be the potential number of newspapers ordered by the newsboy and let q be the random variable of demand for a particular day.

Expected operation costs may be expressed mathematically as:

(10) $E[cost] = \int_Q^\infty \eta (q - Q) f(q) dq + \int_0^Q \zeta (Q - q) f(q) dq$

Assuming a minimum exists for this unconstrained minimization problem :

(11) $\dfrac{\partial E[cost]}{\partial Q} = 0$

Next, consider a one-period multi-item problem where more than one type of newspaper is stocked. Suppose the newsboy may not acquire more than a total of W newspapers and that his objective is to minimize the expected costs of stock-outs or over-stocking. Let q_i, Q_i, f_i, ζ_i and η_i be defined as q, Q, f, ζ, and η, respectively, but now for newspaper type i; and let n be the number of newspaper-types stocked. The demands for the various types of newspapers are assumed independent. The mathematical program solved to determine the optimal stocking strategy is:

(12) $\quad$ Minimize $\quad NB_n = \sum_{i=1}^{n} \left\{ \int_{Q_i}^{\infty} \eta_i(q_i - Q_i) f_i(q_i) dq_i + \int_{0}^{Q_i} \zeta_i(Q_i - q_i) f_i(q_i) dq_i \right\}$

subject to:

(13) $\quad \sum_{i=1}^{n} Q_i \leq W$

Let λ be the Lagrange multiplier associated with equation 13; and assume a strict equality in equation 13. The Lagrange function to be optimized is:

(14) $\quad L = NB_n - \lambda \left\{ \sum_{i=1}^{n} Q_i - W \right\}$

Simplifying leads to:

(15) $\quad P[q_i \leq Q_i] = \dfrac{\eta_i - \lambda}{\eta_i + \zeta_i} \quad \forall_i$

(16) $\quad \sum_{i=1}^{n} Q_i = W$

For n = 2, and the special case where $\eta_1 = \eta_2$ and $\zeta_1 = \zeta_2$; and simplifying:

(17) $\quad P[q_1 \leq Q_1] = P[q_2 \leq Q_2]$
(18) $\quad Q_1 + Q_2 = W$

The following probabilistic mathematical program may be solved to provide the solution to equations 15 and 16.

(19) $\quad$ Minimize $\quad NB_2 = $ Maximum $\{P[q_1 \leq Q_1], P[q_2 \leq Q_2]\}$
Subject to:
(20) $\quad Q_1 + Q_2 = W$

Similarly for n=3, the probabilistic mathematical model is:
(21) $\quad$ Minimize $\quad NB_3 = $ Maximum $\{P[q_1 \leq Q_1], P[q_2 \leq Q_2], P[q_3 \leq Q_3]\}$
Subject to:
(22) $\quad Q_1 + Q_2 + Q_3 = W$

In conclusion, for a multi-item Newsboy problem with n items to consider, a probabilistic mathematical program could be formulated to provide the optimal acquisition strategy under the assumptions stated previously.

Newsboy Approach to Reservoir Operations

Consider a single reservoir and one day of operation. Assume that forecasts are perfectly made and that the forecast horizon is one day and a reservoir used for flow augmentation, water supply and flood damage mitigation -- that is, only storages and releases are the important operating parameters. The objective is to minimize the expected deviations from ideal operations -- the statistically ideal storage (s) and release (r) levels. Storages (S) and releases (R) correspond to "commodities" in the Newsboy context. A similar assumption that, as with the multi-item Newsboy

Problem, S and R are independent and random is made here. During each day, the amount of water available for release or storage is equal to $S_0 + I$, where I is the forecast inflow during the day and S_0 is the storage at the beginning of the day. Here $S_0 + I \equiv W$ in equation 13. Note that by the nature of the objective function, $\zeta_i = \eta_i = 1.0$, automatically. The mathematical model is:

(23) Minimize $\text{NBRES2} = \int_R^\infty (r - R)\phi(r)dr + \int_0^R (R - r)\phi(r)dr$

$$+ \int_S^\infty (s - S)\theta(s)ds + \int_0^S (S - s)\theta(s)ds$$

subject to:
(24) $R + S = I + S_0$
(25) $\text{SMIN} \leq S \leq \text{CAP}$
(26) $\text{RMIN} \leq R \leq \text{RMAX}$

Here the pairs ϕ and Φ, and θ and Θ are respectively the marginal probability distribution functions (PDFs) and marginal cumulative distribution functions (CDFs) of releases (R) and storages (S). Ignoring the bounds, and introducing a Lagrange multiplier, γ, for equation 24, the Lagrange function to be minimized is:

(27) $\text{LFRES2} = \text{NBRES2} - \gamma(S + R - S_0 - I)$

Expanding and solving equation 27 with equation 24 yields:

(28) $P[s \leq S] - (1 - P[s \leq S]) - \gamma = 0$
(29) $P[r \leq R] - (1 - P[r \leq R]) - \gamma = 0$
(30) $R + S - I - S_0 = 0$

Simplifying equations 28, 29 and 30, results in:

(31) $\Theta(S) - \Phi(R) = 0$
(32) $R + S - I - S_0 = 0$

The appropriate probabilistic mathematical model is:

(33)   Minimize $\text{PRES2} = \text{Maximum}\{\Theta(S), \Phi(R)\}$
subject to:
(34) $R + S = I + S_0$

This model is similar in form to equations 1 through 9 for a forecast horizon of one day if a probabilistic objective function is substituted. When hydropower production is also considered, a probabilistic mathematical model derived through the Newsboy problem approach is also appropriate under certain assumptions.

References

1   Houck, M.H., "Real-Time Reservoir Operation by Mathematical Programming", *Water Resources Research*, Volume 18, No. 5, pp. 1345-1351, October, 1982.
2   Nzewi, E.U. and M. H. Houck, "Real-Time Hydrosystem Operations Using Probabilistic Balancing Rule Models", *Proceedings*, Computerized Decision Support Systems for Water Managers, July, 1989.
3   Silver, E. A. and Rein Peterson, *Decision Systems for Inventory Management and Production*, John Wiley, 1985.
4   Yeh, W. W-G., "Reservoir Management and Operations Models: State-of-the-Art Review", *Water Resources Research*, Vol. 21, No. 12, December, 1985.

APPLICATIONS OF PROBABILITY MATRIX METHODS
FOR TEXAS RESERVOIRS

Samuel K. Vaugh, P.E., A.M. ASCE

Introduction

Design and management of surface water resources in Texas has typically been based on critical period methods which assign a firm or dependable yield to a reservoir project on the basis of the most severe drought of historical record. Probability matrix methods, on the other hand, facilitate the definition of a probability distribution of reservoir storage as a function of hydrologic inputs, initial storage conditions, water supply allocations, and operation policy. The probability distribution of storage simply expresses the likelihood of attaining various storage levels at specified times in the future. Probability matrix methods provide managers of surface water supply systems with a means of investigating the risks and ramifications associated with various water supply allocations or management policies.

Critical Period Methods

Critical period methods of storage analysis are generally used to estimate the firm yield or dependable supply available from a reservoir or system of reservoirs. The firm yield is defined to be the maximum amount of water which could have been withdrawn on a consistent annual basis without shortage during the period of historical record. The most commonly used critical period method in Texas is behavior (or simulation) analysis which may be performed using RESOP-II (TDWR, 1978) or one of a number of similar computer programs.

The results of behavior analysis for the computation of firm yield are illustrated in Figure 1 which traces the simulated percentage of active storage in Lost Creek Reservoir (HDR, 1987) near Jacksboro, Texas through the 1945-84 period of record subject to diversion of the firm yield and the reservoir being initially full. It is apparent that the critical drought or most severe depletion of storage occurred during the 1950's, however,

PROBABILITY MATRIX METHODS

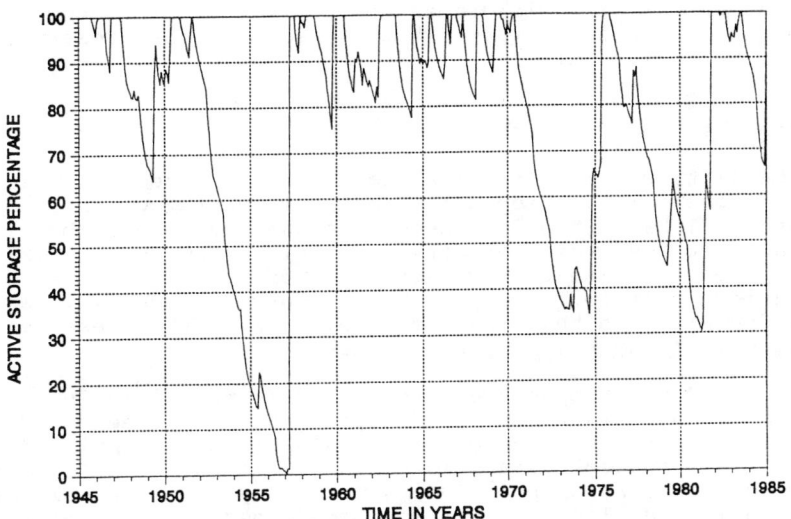

Figure 1 - Firm Yield Trace, Lost Creek Reservoir

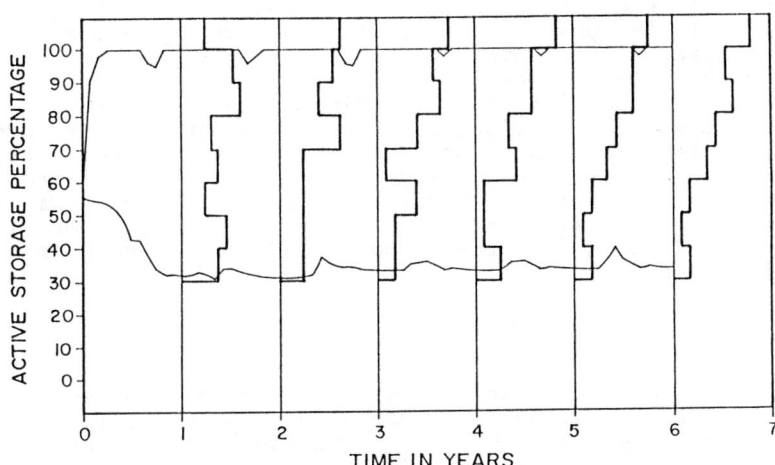

Figure 2 - Projected Probability Distributions of Storage, Highland Lakes System

the numerical firm yield does not reflect the frequency of storage depletion or the effect of assuming the reservoir to be initially full.

Probability Matrix Methods

Probability matrix methods are a class of procedures which were generally developed from Moran's Theory of Storage (Moran, 1959). Many of these procedures are described in detail in Reservoir Capacity and Yield (McMahon, 1978). In essence, probability matrix methods are a means of relating hydrologic inputs to reservoir capacity and withdrawals such that the probable state of the reservoir contents at any time may be estimated.

The method used to generate the examples presented herein is referred to as transient analysis which has been coded into a computer program called PROSTOR (Vaugh & Maidment, 1987). Transient analysis employs a monthly reservoir contents simulation procedure governed by the principle of continuity utilizing historical sequences of hydrologic data. Given initial storage conditions, system operation rules, monthly distribution of annual water demands, and a selected forecast period, a set of possible future storages is computed. Based on this set of projected storages, the probability distribution of future storage may be estimated for each year of the selected forecast period. A graphical presentation of projected probability distributions of storage in the Highland Lakes System near Austin, Texas subject to an initial active storage of 55 percent and fixed water supply releases is provided in Figure 2 as an example. Note that the shapes of the projected probability distributions tend to approach a steady-state distribution with time as system performance becomes less dependent on initial storage conditions. Interpretation of probability distributions of the type presented in Figure 2 can provide valuable insights into water supply reliability and reservoir performance in terms of both short- and long-term management considerations.

Example Applications

As water resources engineers, we are often confronted with certain key questions by managers and developers of surface water supply reservoirs. These typical questions may be formulated as follows:

1. What is the firm yield of this reservoir project?
2. How quickly will this reservoir fill after completion of the dam?

3. How can we manage this reservoir project to maximize water supply?

Unfortunately, these questions do not have simple, reliable answers due to future hydrologic uncertainty. Firm yield can be readily computed on the basis of available historical hydrologic data using critical period methods, however, there is no assurance that a drought of greater severity will not occur in the future. Furthermore, critical period methods typically applied in the computation of firm yield can not readily provide answers to the second and third questions above. Probability matrix methods, however, can be a viable means of addressing these and other questions of concern to managers of water supply systems as illustrated by the following example applications.

The probability of filling a reservoir with respect to time may be assessed on a monthly basis using transient analysis assuming an initial active storage percentage of zero and a projection period extending several years into the future. The probability of filling Lost Creek Reservoir near Jacksboro, Texas assuming dam closure on January 1 is presented in Figure 3. As indicated in the figure, the probability of filling the reservoir increases from only about 3 percent at the end of the first year to about 69 percent after 6 years.

The long-term (steady-state) performance of Lost Creek Reservoir subject to annual diversion of the computed firm yield was evaluated in terms of the probability of exceeding various water surface elevations during two key months of the year as shown in Figure 4. For this reservoir, the long-term expected storage levels in February and May are the lowest and highest during the year, respectively. Reviewing Figure 4, one might observe that the chance that the water surface elevation will exceed 1000 feet-MSL is 58 percent in May and only 40 percent in February. One might also note that the expected (50 percent probability of exceedance) water surface elevation varies between 997 ft-MSL and 1002 ft-MSL for the assumed rate of withdrawal. Information of this type is useful in many aspects of design including vertical location of intake gates, raw water pump phasing, computation of operations and maintenance costs for electrical power to pumps and for vegetation control, and design of recreational facilities such as boat ramps.

Probability matrix methods may also be used as a management tool to assist in the determination of acceptable annual water supply allocations (withdrawals) in excess of the firm yield of a reservoir. This possibility was investigated by the Canadian River

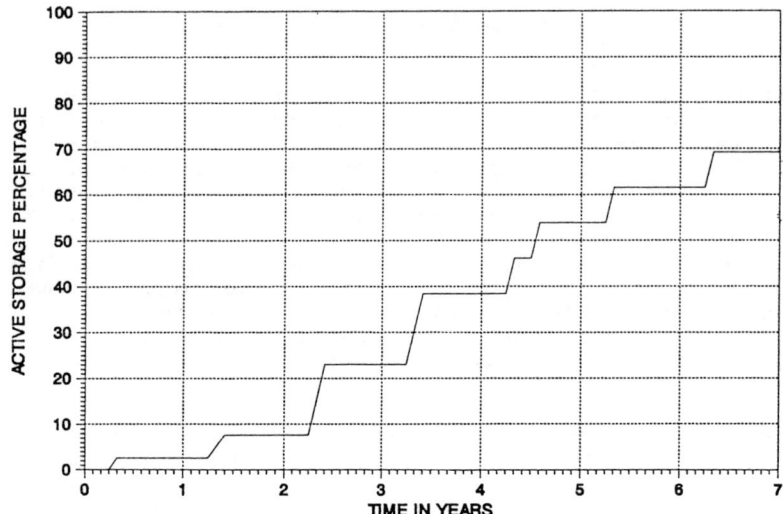

Figure 3 - Probability of Filling, Lost Creek Reservoir

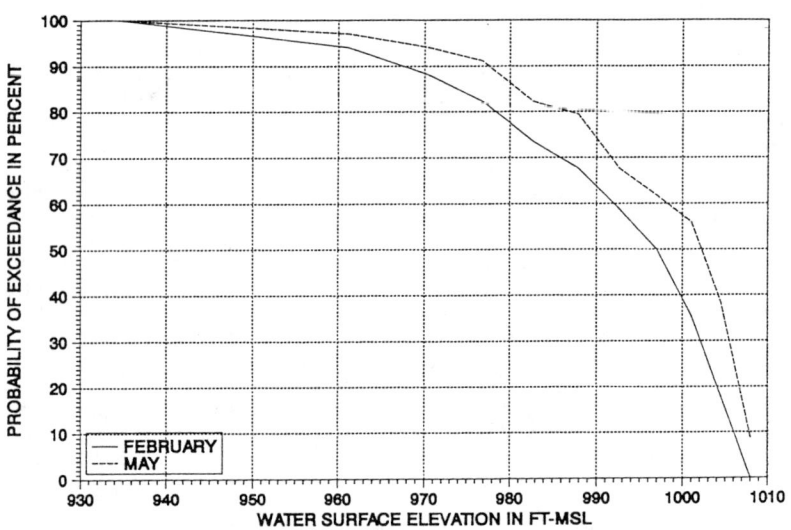

Figure 4 - Probability of Exceedance Versus Water Surface Elevation, Lost Creek Reservoir

Municipal Water Authority (Vaugh, 1987) which manages Lake Meredith near Amarillo, Texas when the firm yield was determined to be some 25 percent less than the originally estimated yield. Rather than limit annual allocations to the firm yield, a variable yield water supply management policy based on probabilistic forecasts of storage and considering the availability of back-up groundwater supplies was evaluated. Annual withdrawals were selected based on an 80 percent chance of exceeding 20 percent of active storage after 3 years at the specified withdrawal rate. Withdrawals were allowed to vary between 65 percent and 133 percent of the firm yield. Adherence to this variable yield management policy could increase average annual yield by 9.8 percent while actually decreasing long-term dependence on groundwater and the risk of supply shortage.

Conclusion

The examples presented herein illustrate how the application of probability matrix methods to reservoir systems may provide valuable information to water supply managers in addition to the basic determination of firm yield. It is hoped that these methods may gain wider acceptance and lead to more efficient development and management of surface water supply sources.

References

HDR Engineering, Inc. (1987). "Preliminary Engineering Report for Alternative Reservoir Sites Within the Lost Creek Watershed." City of Jacksboro, Texas.

McMahon, T.A. and Mein, R.G. (1978). Reservoir Capacity and Yield. Developments in Water Science, 9, Elsevier, Amsterdam, Netherlands.

Moran, P.A.P. (1959). The Theory of Storage. Metheun, London, England.

Texas Department of Water Resources (1978). RESOP-II, Reservoir Operatin and Quality Routing Program. Program Documentation and Users Manual, UM-20.

Vaugh, S.K. and Maidment, D.R. (1987). "Projecting Storage in Highland Lake Reservoir System." J. of WRPMD, ASCE, 113(5), 659-676.

Vaugh, S.K. (1989). "Variable Yield Management of Surface Water Supplies, Lake Meredith Texas." Mid- Year Technical Conference, Texas Water Conservation Association.

MARGINAL COST TECHNIQUES FOR
RESERVOIR OPTIMIZATION
By
Fred Pinkney, Ph.D., Frank L. Shorney (Member ASCE),
and L. Jeffrey Klein (Associate Member)[1]

ABSTRACT
Selection of the optimum water supply reservoir from multiple reservoir sites under consideration in a water resource planning study for the Houston Metroplex evaluated hydrology, engineering, and cost information. Application of this marginal cost analysis technique permitted the determination and selection of the most economical or optimum reservoir from multiple reservoir sites. Thirty-three reservoir sites were investigated as potential water supply sources. Of these sites, the Bedias 10-mile site was selected as the optimum reservoir with a yield 78,500 acre-feet per year at a conservation pool elevation of 210 feet, USGS and a project formulation cost of $0.50/1,000 gallons.

INTRODUCTION
Selection of the optimum water supply reservoir from multiple reservoir sites under consideration in a water resource planning study requires a combination of hydrology, engineering, and cost information. Application of this information in a marginal cost analysis permits the determination and selection of the most economical or optimum reservoir size(s) from multiple reservoir sites.

Marginal cost optimization procedures are being used by the Bureau of Reclamation and Burns & McDonnell Engineering Company (consultant) for the selection of new reservoirs in a regional water supply study for a 27-county area in southeast Texas. The regional water supply study encompasses the City of Houston Metroplex. In this study, a new reservoir, referred to as Bedias Reservoir, is located and sized on the basis of marginal cost economic analysis. The study objective was to select the

---

[1]Fred Pinkney, Manager, Bureau of Reclamation, P.O. Box 25007, Denver, Colorado 80225-0007, Frank L. Shorney, Manager, Burns & McDonnell Engineering Company, P.O. Box 419173, Kansas City, Missouri 64141-0173, L. Jeffrey Klein, Staff Engineer, Burns & McDonnell Engineering Company, P.O. Box 419173, Kansas City, Missouri 64141-0173.

RESERVOIR OPTIMIZATION

optimum reservoir site and size, and to recommend this selection for construction. Procedures used in the selection of Bedias Reservoir are discussed subsequently in this paper.

POTENTIAL DAM SITES

In the regional water supply study, 33 reservoir sites were investigated as potential water supply sources. These reservoir sites were evaluated using conventional techniques of applying construction, operation, maintenance and replacement cost estimates to reservoir firm yield to determine the unit cost of water ($ per 1,000 gallons). Three reservoirs having the lowest and same general magnitude of unit water costs are selected for more detailed analysis. Other reservoirs having greater unit costs in the order of magnitude of 2 times greater or more than the three least costly reservoirs are discarded as viable alternatives. Of the three viable reservoirs analyzed in detail, the Bedias Reservoir is the most economical reservoir based on the marginal cost analyses.

Selection of the optimum reservoir from multiple dam sites for the proposed Bedias Reservoir is used as an example of marginal cost analysis in this paper. These sites are named Bedias 10- and 13-mile to describe respective dam site distances upstream from Farm-to-Market-(FM) Road 247, near the confluence of Bedias Creek and Lake Livingston.

Each of the two potential dam sites is evaluated for several conservation pool levels. The maximum height of each dam is influenced by the height of the drainage valley walls with consideration of possible upstream backwater restrictions. For the purpose of this paper, a surcharge pool of 10 feet and a freeboard allowance of 10 feet is used between the top of dam and the reservoir conservation pool. No flood storage is provided at any of the potential dam sites due to the lack of downstream development.

The maximum top of dam elevation for the 10-mile and 13-mile dam sites are set at 260 feet USGS, also the height of the valley walls. For these two sites, a dam at an elevation of 250 feet USGS would require the construction of dikes at the low points in the drainage valley walls.

FIRM-YIELD COMPUTATIONS

Annual firm yields for each reservoir dam site are shown in Table 1. Firm yields are determined at various conservation pool elevations at each dam site for use in subsequent reservoir optimization analysis.

Stream flow records are developed and utilized as the inflow for the Bedias 10-mile dam site. Inflow at the other three dam sites are developed from this record by applying a ratio of the respective drainage areas.

The total firm net yield is composed of local demands, minimum releases, and direct diversions and is shown in Table 1. Local water demands in the immediate area surrounding the proposed reservoir are assumed to be a maximum of 5,000-acre-feet per year (AFY), based on discussions with the Trinity River Authority. Minimum reservoir releases for fish and wildlife are assumed to vary with total firm net yield from 500, 2,000, 4,000, 6,000 to a maximum of 8,000-acre-feet per year (11 cfs) with the smallest releases associated with the smallest yield. Direct diversions are the difference between the total firm net yield and the sum of the local demands and the minimum releases. The inactive or minimum reservoir pool storage is assumed to be 6,000-acre-feet (AF) or 10 percent of the conservation pool storage, whichever is less.

Area capacity curve data for the firm yield studies of each dam site are developed from 1:24,000 scale USGS topographic maps. Area-capacity curve data is shown in Table 2.

Table 1
POTENTIAL BEDIAS RESERVOIR DAM SITES
FIRM YIELD ANALYSES (acre-feet per year)

Dam Site	Conservation Pool Elevation (Feet USGS)	Local Demands	Minimum Releases	Direct Diversion	Total Firm Net Yield
10 Mile	170	0	500	1,500	2,000
	180	0	2,000	12,500	14,500
	190	5,000	4,000	27,500	36,500
	200	5,000	8,000	48,000	61,000
	210	5,000	8,000	65,500	78,500
	220	5,000	8,000	81,500	94,500
	230	5,000	8,000	92,000	105,000
	240	5,000	8,000	100,500	113,500
13 Mile	190	0	2,000	11,000	13,000
	200	5,000	8,000	24,500	37,500
	210	5,000	8,000	50,000	63,000
	220	5,000	8,000	68,000	81,000
	230	5,000	8,000	83,500	96,500
	240	5,000	8,000	93,000	106,000

Table 2
POTENTIAL BEDIAS RESERVOIR DAM SITES
AREA-CAPACITY DATA[1]

Reservoir Dam Site	Elevation (Feet USGS)	Area (acres)	Storage Capacity (acre-feet)
Bedias	200	7,600	105,500
10 Mile	210	10,000	192,700
	220	18,200	337,000
	230	23,000	541,400
	235	26,800	665,700
	240	30,500	808,100
Bedias	200	5,000	51,500
13 Mile	210	7,300	111,400
	220	14,200	219,000
	230	17,500	377,600
	240	23,900	439,500

Notes:
[1] Values generated from USGS topographic maps using AutoCAD.

Colorado State University's MODSIM reservoir operations model and previously described stream flow records and area-capacity curve data are used to determine reservoir firm yields. With the MODSIM model, the firm yield or maximum water demand which each reservoir can sustain is determined by operating the reservoir through the worst drought of record for various reservoir conservation pool levels by iterative trial and error techniques.

RESERVOIR OPTIMIZATION

A marginal cost analysis is used to determine the optimum reservoir yield (or size) for water supply at each of the two Bedias dam site locations. In this analysis, total annual project costs per unit of yield (annual formulation cost) are compared with annual marginal project costs per unit of yield (marginal formulation cost) and the optimum reservoir is selected for the yield (or size) at which marginal cost equals annual cost. Formulation cost is expressed in $/1,000 gallons.

COST ESTIMATES

Project cost, interest during construction (IDC), total investment cost and annual operation, maintenance, replacement and energy (OMR&E) cost estimates used in the reservoir optimization studies are shown in Table 3. Project costs include dam structure, clearing, relocations, permanent operating facilities, and land and mitigation costs. Total investment costs include project costs plus IDC. IDC is figured at 9.125 percent for a 5-year construction period. Annual OMR&E cost estimates are based on both fixed and variable costs for each reservoir site analyzed elevation.

Table 3
BEDIAS RESERVOIR
COST ESTIMATE SUMMARY[1]

Dam Site	Conservation Pool Elevation (Ft. USGS)	Project Cost ($Mil)	Interest During Construction ($Mil)	Total Investment Cost ($Mil)	Annual OMR&E Cost ($Mil)
Bedias 10 Mile	190	78.6	20.2	98.8	0.53
	200	92.3	23.8	116.1	0.55
	210	106.0	27.3	133.3	0.56
	220	140.7	36.2	176.9	0.58
	230	174.9	45.0	219.9	0.60
	240	235.3	60.5	295.8	0.66
Bedias 13 Mile	190	68.1	17.5	85.6	0.52
	200	80.2	20.6	100.8	0.54
	210	87.9	22.6	110.5	0.54
	220	113.0	29.0	142.0	0.57
	230	176.2	45.3	221.5	0.63
	240	225.8	58.1	283.9	0.67

Note:
[1] Based on 1987 Dollars

MARGINAL COST ANALYSIS

Total project and marginal formulation cost data for each dam site and reservoir at 10-foot conservation pool elevation intervals are used in the marginal cost analysis and are shown in Table 4.

These costs are determined for a 100-year project life at a 9.125 percent discount rate and include project costs, interest during construction, and operation, maintenance, replacement and energy (OMR&E) costs. Formulation costs are expressed as annual costs per 1,000 gallons of reservoir firm yield.

Graphic plots of average annual cost versus reservoir yield for each dam site at various conservation elevations are shown in Figure 1.

The optimum reservoir yield is determined as the point where the marginal cost curve intersects the annual cost curve. At this point, the largest reservoir yield (or size) is available at which the marginal unit cost is equal to the total project unit cost, thus representing the optimum reservoir for the dam site under consideration. Using optimum yield, the corresponding optimum storage capacity is obtained from reservoir yield versus storage capacity curves and the optimum conservation pool elevation is obtained from reservoir elevation-area-capacity curves.

RESERVOIR OPTIMIZATION

TABLE 4
BEDIAS RESERVOIR SITE OPTIMIZATION DATA
MARGINAL COST ANALYSIS

Dam Site	Conservation Pool (Feet USGS)	Annual Yield (AFY)	Project Cost ($)	Annual Formulation Cost ($)	Annual Average Project Cost ($)	Marginal Annual Cost ($)	Marginal Annual Yield (AFY)	Formulation Cost of Marginal Yield ($/1,000 gal)
Bedias 10 Mile	190	36,500	78,635,000	0.80	9,554,000	9,554,000	36,500	0.80
	200	61,000	92,332,000	0.56	11,142,000	1,588,000	24,500	0.20
	210	78,500	106,014,000	0.50	12,721,000	1,579,000	17,500	0.28
	220	94,500	140,665,000	0.54	16,720,000	3,999,000	16,000	0.77
	230	105,000	174,941,000	0.60	20,674,000	3,954,000	10,500	1.16
	240	113,500	235,269,000	0.75	27,650,000	6,976,000	8,500	2.52
Bedias 13 Mile	190	13,000	68,100,000	1.97	8,337,000	8,337,000	13,000	1.97
	200	36,000	80,246,000	0.83	9,744,000	1,407,000	23,000	0.19
	210	60,500	87,915,000	0.54	10,630,000	886,000	24,500	0.11
	220	76,000	112,956,000	0.55	13,530,000	2,900,000	15,500	0.57
	230	92,000	176,166,000	0.70	20,844,000	7,314,000	16,000	1.40

TABLE 5
OPTIMUM BEDIAS RESERVOIR DATA (Water Supply Data)

Dam Site	Yield (AFY)	Conservation Pool Elevation (Feet USGS)	Storage Capacity (AF)	Construction Cost ($)	OMR&E ($)	Total Annual Cost ($)	Formulation Cost ($/1,000 Gal)
Bedias 10 Mile	78,500	210	200,000	106,000,000	557,000	12,720,000	0.50
Bedias 13 Mile	67,500	213	150,000	93,000,000	543,000	11,214,000	0.51

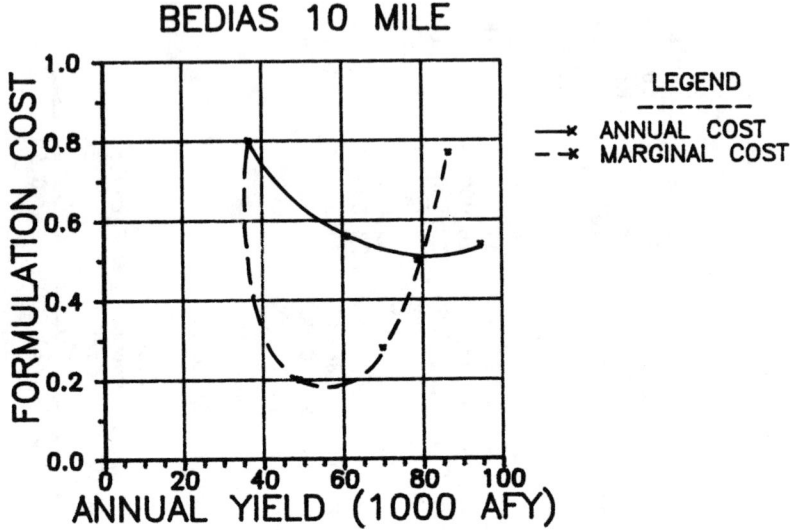

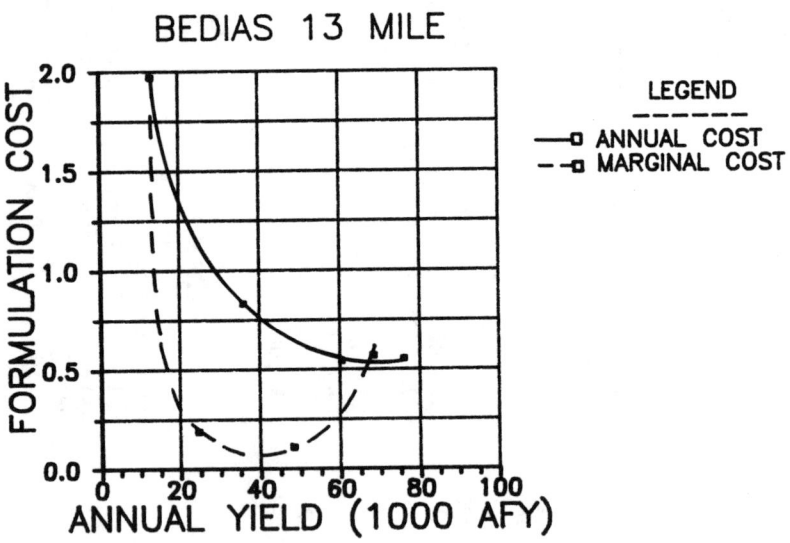

Figure 1 - Formulation Cost vs. Annual Yield

OPTIMUM RESERVOIR

Hydrology and cost data for the optimum reservoir at the Bedias 10- and 13-mile dam sites are shown in Table 5. Each reservoir shown represents the optimum condition based on a marginal cost analysis of alternative reservoir sized (or yields) for each dam site.

Based on the analysis, the Bedias 10-mile dam site has optimum formulation costs of $0.50 per 1,000 gallons. The Bedias 10-mile site has a yield of 78,500 acre-feet per year (AFY) at the optimum conservation pool elevation of 210 feet (USGS). The Bedias 13-mile dam site has a lower yield of 67,500 AFY at the optimum conservation pool elevation of 213 feet (USGS). Because of the higher yield of 78,500 AFY, the Bedias 10-mile site is selected at the optimum reservoir.

ACKNOWLEDGEMENTS

We would like to thank the staffs of the Bureau of Reclamation - Great Plains Region and Burns & McDonnell for all their assistance in this project. Without them, this project would not have been possible.

A Comparison of Two Reservoir Projects
and Associated Fisheries Impacts

Barbara A. Schauer[1] and Alan B. Cooper[2]

Abstract

The evaluation of environmental impacts is a critical component of reservoir project development. Impacts to fisheries are especially significant because of the extensive alteration to habitat that results. Utilizing the habitat value approach to fisheries impact assessment offers a variety of opportunities for avoiding, minimizing, and mitigating impacts; facilitating regulatory acceptance of project development; and cost saving.

Introduction

Impacts to fisheries are especially crucial in public water supply projects involving river intakes, impoundments, dams, and releases and can involve costly mitigative measures. The evaluation and mitigation of environmental impacts is a critical component of reservoir project development.

A number of permit requirements must be satisfied in order to construct an impoundment to provide water supply. The most comprehensive are under Section 404 of the Clean Water Act, which regulates the use of fill material in waterways and wetlands, and the disposal of dredged material. The Section 404 permit application requires the preparation of an Environmental Assessment, which forms the basis for an Environmental Impact Statement (EIS), prepared by the U.S. Army Corps of Engineers. The purpose of the EIS is to assess and document the environmental impacts associated with projects. For reservoir projects, a complete array of environmental issues are assessed including fisheries, wildlife, and wetlands. In particular, adverse impacts to fish include changes in stream flow and water quality, alteration of habitat from a stream to a lake, and loss of wetlands, which function as nursery grounds.

----

[1] Staff Engineer/Scientist, Black & Veatch Engineers-Architects, 18310 Montgomery Village Avenue, Gaithersburg, Maryland 20879.
[2] Project Manager, Black & Veatch Engineers-Architects.

For two reservoir projects, in Carroll County, Maryland and Hanover
County, Virginia, a unique approach was employed to evaluate
impacts to fisheries. This approach was not limited to the
traditional assessment of fish species type and abundance, but was
expanded to include an evaluation of the presence and value of
fishery habitat. The habitat value determination was accepted by
the regulatory community and proved extremely useful for developing methods to avoid and mitigate adverse environmental impacts to
fishes. Environmental and engineering documentation for the two
projects is being prepared to submit to federal and state agencies
for review. The innovative approach that was used to assess
impacts to fisheries and which resulted in greater regulatory
acceptance and reduced costs, is presented.

Hanover County, Virginia

Hanover County is located in east-central Virginia, just north of
Richmond. The proposed 960-acre off-line reservoir would be
created by constructing a cross-stream impoundment on Crump
Creek, a tributary to the Pamunkey River. Additionally, the reservoir would receive raw water pumped from the Pamunkey River to
augment supply.

The Pamunkey River is a well-defined riverine system with steep
banks and a gravel/silt substrate. The mean annual flow in the
river is 1,035 cubic feet per second (cfs), based on U.S. Geological Survey stream gage data. At its confluence with Crump
Creek, the river is nearly 50 feet wide and 9 to 15 feet deep.
Crump Creek is characterized by wide, flat streambeds that
meander in fairly undefined, shallow channels, with average depths
from zero to five feet.

Anadromous fish migrate from the mouth of the Chesapeake Bay up
the York and Pamunkey Rivers to spawn near the intake for the
proposed reservoir. These fish inhabit salt waters but migrate
upriver to freshwater, in the spring, to spawn. A survey was conducted in the Spring of 1987 to establish the utilization of the
Crump Creek system by anadromous fish (Black & Veatch, January,
1988). Hydrologic and water quality conditions were surveyed as
part of the assessment. Water samples were collected from Crump
Creek on monthly basis between August, 1986 and August, 1989
and tested for a range of chemical parameters. Water temperatures
in Crump Creek and the Pamunkey River were also monitored. Three
anadromous species were targeted for sampling based on their
uniqueness, sensitivity, commercial use, and likelihood of
occurrence: alewife (<u>Alos</u> <u>psuedoharengus</u>), blueback herring
(<u>Alosa</u> <u>aestivalis</u>), and American shad (<u>Alosa</u> <u>sapidissima</u>).

Fish collection was conducted during a nine-week period to coincide with the anticipated spawning run for the targeted species.
Six sampling events took place using fyke, gill, and plankton nets

to capture both adult fish and ichthyoplankton (eggs and larvae). Captured adult fish were analyzed, identified by species, sexed, and spawning condition determined (ripe or spent). During the nine weeks of the survey, individuals from all three target species were captured in nets set in the Pamunkey River; however, no adult fish were captured in Crump Creek or Pollard Creek. Ichthyoplankton was sampled at two sites; one in the Pamunkey River and one in Crump Creek, just upstream of its confluence with the river. Samples were sorted and identified in the laboratory. Eggs and larvae were found at both sites although densities in the Pamunkey River were significantly higher than in Crump Creek. From analysis of ichthyoplankton densities it was determined that peak spawning was coincident in the river and the creek.

The findings indicated the relatively low usage of Crump Creek by spawning anadromous fish, as compared to the Pamunkey River. Eggs and larvae found in the downstream portions of Crump Creek are most likely from fish spawning in proximity to the confluence with the river because upstream use of the creek is blocked by a large beaver dam. Only the portion of Crump Creek near its mouth was found to have potential for migratory habitat. The upstream portions, which would be inundated by the proposed reservoir, appear not to be utilized for spawning.

Mitigative measures were incorporated into the engineering design of the reservoir to minimize impacts to migratory fish in the project area. The proposed off-line reservoir has an intake on the Pamunkey River, which would be equipped with screens to minimize egg impingement and fish entrapment. Downstream of the proposed dam, Crump Creek would become a more well-defined riverine system because of reduced stream discharge. This would enhance the habitat for spawning of blueback herring, which prefer swifter and deeper streams. Mitigative measures also include the maintenance of a pooled area near the mouth of Crump Creek to encourage alewife spawning, which prefer slower moving streams and will also spawn in ponds.

A ladder to facilitate fish passage over the dam is no longer required because the survey determined that the project area is not utilized for spawning. This resulted in significant cost saving for the county.

Carroll County, Maryland

Gillis Falls is located in southern Carroll County, Maryland, northwest of the City of Baltimore. The stream flows in a southerly direction before becoming tributary to the South Branch of the Patapsco River. The Patapsco River flows in a southerly and then easterly direction towards its mouth at the Baltimore Harbor of the Chesapeake Bay. Gillis Falls flows in well-defined channels with steep, primarily wooded side slopes. The elevation of the stream drops nearly 300 feet from its headwaters to its mouth. The mean annual flow has been estimated as 20.9 cubic feet per second (cfs).

A proposed 420-acre public water supply reservoir would be created by impounding water on Gillis Falls. Gillis Falls and its tributaries are classified as Class III natural trout waters by the Maryland Department of the Environment. Considerations in describing the existing aquatic habitat largely revolved around trout. The objectives of the aquatic survey were to characterize the existing fish community and assess the quality of the stream as it is related to the support and maintenance of trout populations (EA, April, 1989).

The specific goals of the survey were:

1. to provide a general inventory of water quality, instream and nearstream habitat, and flow regime variables;

2. to determine species composition, relative abundance, and general distribution of fish and benthic macro invertibrates;

3. to characterize the existing lotic habitat and its suitability for trout populations.

The survey took a two phase approach. The first phase analyzed water quality variables that likely to limit trout survival and the second phase involved quantification of the physical habitat and assessment of its quality. Sampling events were conducted during two seasons to coincide fish collection with spawning and summer growth periods. Six sites were selected and representative fish habitats, consisting of riffles, runs, and pools were sampled at each site using nets and electroshocking. Physiochemical parameters, including pH, dissolved oxygen, and conductivity were also measured at each site. Stream water temperatures were continuously monitored for a three month period at four locations on Gillis Falls and Middle Run to assess the thermal regime of the streams. Benthic macroinvertebrates are good indicators of water quality and were sampled at three locations during the survey and analyzed in the laboratory.

The most important general abiotic factors for fluvial fish habitat are temperature, rate of water flow, fluctuation in discharge, and cover availability. Optimal riverine habitat for trout is clean, cool to cold water, silt-free rocky substrates in riffle-run areas, approximately 1:1 riffle-pool ratio with areas of slow, deep water, well-vegetated stream banks, abundant instream cover, and relatively stable water flow, temperatures, and stream banks. Some variables consistently limit trout inhabiting streams. These include maximum summer temperatures, cover, late summer flows or base flow, flow variability substrate composition, and food availability. In order to determine if the criteria for trout habitat were present various habitat variables related to temperature, stream-bank conditions, instream cover, pool depth and quality, depth, substrate, and velocity were selected for analysis.

The results of the aquatic habitat survey indicate that habitat requirements for trout are suitable to optimal in Gillis Falls. This is supported by the presence of a small, naturally reproducing trout population. The actual number of trout captured during the survey was less than two percent.

Mitigative measures to maintain suitable habitat requirements in the portion of Gillis Falls downstream from the dam and upstream of the impoundment, would be implemented. Controlled releases from the reservoir would be used to maintain temperature and dissolved oxygen requirements in the downstream portion of Gillis Falls. Cold water would be released from deeper elevations in the reservoir to maintain temperature requirements for trout and the outlet works would be equipped with turbulence-creating valves to aerate releases and maintain dissolved oxygen levels. Stream shading is an important element in maintaining cool water temperatures in the stream. Vegetation along stream banks, in upstream and downstream portions, would be maintained and protected as part of the mitigation plan. Abundant instream vegetation cover and stable water flow are additional elements that contribute to optimal trout habitat. To prevent damage to instream vegetation through scouring from high velocity discharges and to maintain stable water flow, the outlet works would be equipped with a settling basin and baffles to reduce the energy in reservoir discharges.

Summary

Federal, state, and local regulatory agencies contributed to the design of the aquatic surveys for both projects, which facilitated regulatory acceptance as the project developed. Habitat value assessments enable project engineers and scientists to have greater understanding of the habitat requirements of wildlife. As a result, greater opportunities exist during project development to avoid, minimize, and mitigate impacts to sensitive and important natural resources. Understanding habitat requirements and life processes of trout and anadromous fish have enabled two counties to avoid and minimize impacts, optimize mitigation, and reduce project costs.

References
1. EA Engineering, Science, and Technology, Inc. Gillis Falls Fish, Macroinvertebrate, and Aquatic Habitat Survey, April, 1989.
2. Black & Veatch, Results of an Anadromous Fish Survey Conducted in Crump Creek, Hanover County, Virginia, January, 1988.

STUDY OF DIRECT POTABLE REUSE OF RECLAIMED WASTEWATER: PRELIMINARY RESULTS OF A FIVE YEAR STUDY.

Adam W. Olivieri, Dr.PH[1], Don Eisenberg, Ph.D.[1], Robert C. Cooper, Ph.D.[2], Richard E. Danielson, Ph.D.[3], and Regina Rudnicki, M.S.[4].

Abstract

The City of San Diego, California has received Clean Water Grant funding to build and operate a 0.5 million gallon per day facility to demonstrate a wastewater treatment system, utilizing a unique combination of treatment methods, to treat wastewater to a quality which may be acceptable for human consumption. The demonstration of this water reclamation system includes a substantial research effort to estimate the risk associated with the treated water. The study includes a comprehensive attempt to measure as many as possible of the parameters which may effect the risk associated with potable reuse of municipal wastewater, after treatment to a very high quality in a state-of-the-art advanced wastewater treatment system. The study also includes comparison of the risk relative to that associated with the City's present water supply. The basic elements of the study were outlined and defined in a previous paper (1987). Conduct of the monitoring components of the study have been underway since July 1987. A substantial body of data has been collected on both the reclaimed water system and the raw City water supply. The preliminary results of the screening phase of the study were presented in a previous paper (Olivieri et al., 1989). The purpose of this paper is to present the preliminary results and findings from the monitoring effort. The discussion includes monitoring results

---

[1] Project Manager- Western Consortium for Public Health (WCPH), 2001 Addison St., Suite 200, Berkeley, CA 94704-1103

[2] Professor, School of Public Health, University of California, Berkeley, CA 94704

[3] HES Project Microbiologist- WCPH

[4] HES Laboratory Manager- WCPH

relative to bacterial, viral and parasitic disease agents, routine bacterial indicator organisms, chemical screening, and genetic toxicity testing.

Introduction

Recycling of municipal wastewater has been proposed by the City of San Diego as representing an important supplemental water source given a projected shortfall of drinking water within the next decade. For such water recycling to occur questions regarding the technical feasibility and potential health implications need to be resolved at an early date to the satisfaction of the state and local public health authorities and the people of San Diego.

The Clean Water Act was amended in 1983 to require that funding be made available to assist the City of San Diego in developing a Total Resource Recovery wastewater reclamation system. The City of San Diego received a Clean Water grant in 1983 from the Environmental Protection Agency and the California State Water Resources Control Board (SWRCB) to design, construct, operate, and evaluate an innovative/alternative wastewater treatment system. Based on the State's interpretation of the Clean Water Act wording, the grant funding required incorporation of water hyacinths and advanced wastewater treatment technologies capable of providing a treated wastewater fit to be a raw water source for human consumption. The details and theory of its' operation have been previously described (Tchobanoglous, 1987).

The Western Consortium for Public Health entered into a contract with the City of San Diego in July 1985 to conduct a Five Year Health Effects Study (HES) for the City of San Diego to investigate whether the proposed wastewater treatment scheme can reliably reduce contaminants of concern to levels such that the health risks to the population are no greater than those associated with the present water supply.

The basic elements of the HES are: on-site field coordination and sampling; monitoring for infectious disease and chemical agents as well as disease vectors; assessing plant reliability; an epidemiological study to collect baseline data of the San Diego population; and chemical and biological risk assessments.

The purpose of this paper is to present some preliminary findings following the fourth years work on the HES.

Infectious Disease Agents

The infectious disease element involves three separate subtasks. These are, the monitoring for (1) Enteric Pathogens, (2) Enteric Viruses, and (3) Parasites.

1) Enteric Pathogen Monitoring: A two year enteric pathogen monitoring study was conducted, with laboratory sample analysis conducted by the California Department of Health Services, Microbial Disease Lab. These data are presented in Table 1. Quality assurance studies indicated that the concentration of Salmonella, as detected by the MPN method employed above, occur at an order of magnitude more than what is being measured in the water sample. This means, that as a worst case, the lowest level of detection would be <2.0 MPN/L.

2) Virus Monitoring: The laboratory analysis for enteric viruses is being conducted by the California Department of Health Services, Viral and Rickettsial Diseases Lab. To date, some 45 UCW samples, 40 AWT samples, and 35 RWW samples have been analyzed for enteric viruses. Preliminary results have not identified enteric viruses in either the UCW or AWT waters. The recovery of enteric viruses from the RWW was frequent.

The results of a polio vaccine virus spike experiment indicates that the measured pond effluent virus concentration was reduced by a factor of 100 from the expected theoretical concentration if no removal occurred. Because the virus analysis technique results in virus recoveries ranging from approximately 5 to 20% the virus removal efficiency in the pond system of between 90 to 99%. No virus were observed in the AWT effluent.

3) Parasite Monitoring: The laboratory analysis of water samples for the presence of parasites is being conducted by the University of California at San Francisco (UCSF), Tropical Disease Laboratory. Results of the routine monitoring are shown in Table 1. Two of these organisms, Acanthamoeba, and Naegleria, are being found, at similar levels, in both the AWT and UCW waters. In addition, Toxocara was identified in the UCW water. It should be noted that these tables contain only a summary of the range of organisms found. Specific species have not been identified, and additional data analyses of the frequency of occurrence is necessary before any conclusions on the significance of these results can be made.

Chemical Agents

Table 1
Comparsion of Biological Sampling Between Test Waters

ORGANISM/INDICATOR	METHOD EMPLOYED	VOLUME SAMPLED			SAMPLES COMPLETED TC 9/1/89			GENERAL RESULTS		
		AWT[1]	UCW[1]	RWW[1]	AWT	UCW	RWW	AWT	UCW	RWW
COLIFORMS	MPN	100 ml	100 ml	100ml						
TC					339	339	172	Range: <2- 80 MPN	<2- >1600 MPN	$220 \times 10^5 - 1.6 \times 10^8$
FC					339	328	172	<2 MPN	<2- 30 MPN	$30 \times 10^5 - 1.6 \times 10^8$
FS					339	328	172	<2 MPN	<2- 1600 MPN	$5.6 \times 10^5 - 2.7 \times 10^7$
Salmonella	Filtration	10 L	10 L	1 L	48	48	75	<0.2 MPN/L	<0.2 MPN/L	<0.2-2.5x10^{-4} MPN/L
Shigella	Swab	3 dys	3 dys	3 dys	5	9	14	None Detected (ND)	ND	ND
Campylobacter	Filtration	10 L	10 L	1 L	6	5	6	ND	ND	ND
Enteric Viruses	Filtration	3000 L	3000 L	1 L	39	52	32	ND	ND	0- 3.12x10^2 PFU/L
Protozoans	Filtration	3Q00 L	3000 L	3-5 L	40	37	37	Range: Ciliates: 1-15^2 Flagellates: 1-10 Rotifers: 1-20 Acanthamoeba: 0-1 Naegleria: 1-20 Algae: Giardia: ND	1-100 100-400 10-70 5-250 5-250 (+)-(+++) ND	50-5000 50-5000 100-1500 10-600 100-2000 25-75
Helminths	Filtration	3000 L	3000L	3-5 L	40	37	37	Hookworm-like Egg: 0.01^2 Nematodes: ND Toxocara: ND	ND 1-40 1-50	15-600 400-1000 ND

1. AWT= Advanced Wastewater Treatment; UCW= Untreated City Water; RWW= Raw Wastewater.

2. Numbers for Protozoans and Helminths are in organisms/L.

The chemical agents element of the project is being handled as five separate subtasks that include: 1) Chemical Screening and Monitoring, 2) Bioassay (Genetic Toxicity Testing), 3) Biomonitoring, 4) Toxicological Literature Review, and 5) Chemical Agent Risk Assessment. Only the first three subtasks are discussed in this paper.

Chemical Screening and Monitoring

The chemical screening and monitoring portion of this project is being conducted at UCLA, in the School of Public Health, and the Engineering and Environmental Sciences program. The work in this subtask is planned to be carried out over a three year period with year 1 as the chemical screening phase and years 2 and 3 as the chemical monitoring phase. The results from the screening phase have been presented recently (Olivieri et al., 1989).

The monitoring phase was instituted based on the results of the screening phase, which identified chemicals of public health concern and their concentrations in the three waters (i.e., AWT, UCW, RWW).

The results of the Year 1 monitoring phase are summarized below and presented in Table 2:

o Metals: Inductively Coupled Plasma Atomic Emission Spectrometer was used to conduct the sample analysis for metals. The detection limits ranged from 1 ug/l to 1.26 mg/l, depending on the specific metal. Among the metals of health concern (i.e., Arsenic, Barium, Cadmium, Chromium, Copper, Lead, Mercury, Nickel, Selenium, Silver, and Zinc) only Arsenic, Barium, Cadmium, Lead and Zinc were identified in the raw wastewater and the raw potable water supply above levels of detection. In those cases where the heavy metal concentration in the AWT (Barium, Copper, and Lead) was consistently greater than the detection limits, the values were far below MCL's.

o Purgeable Organics: This analysis was performed by GC-MS, following the EPA method 624 protocol. Using this specific equipment allowed for a level of detection of 0.4 ug/l. The results of the purgeable compounds analysis show that, with the exception of trihalomethanes, there were no purgable compounds found above the detection limit in either the AWT or the UCW.

o Base Neutral acid Extractables: This analysis was performed by GC-MS, following the EPA method 625

TABLE 2.
CHEMICAL ANALYSIS
SUMMARY OF YEAR 1 MONITORING

ANALYSIS	METHOD	ANALYTE	AWT[1]	UCW[2]
Heavy Metals	ICP-AES & AA	Heavy Metals	< UCW & < MCL	<MCL[3]
Purgeables	GC-MS (EPA 624)	THM	< 0.4 ug/L[4]	< 5 ug/L
		non-THM	< 0.4 ug/L	< 0.4 ug/L
Base/Neutral/Acid Extractables	GC-MS (EPA 625)	Benzoic Acid Phthalates	< 1.0 ug/L[4] < 14 ug/L	0.0146 ug/L < 15 ug/L
Pesticides	EPA 608		< 1 ug/L[4]	< 1 ug/L
TOC (average)			0.41 mg/L	3.4 mg/L
TOX (average)			19 ug/L	72 ug/L

1. AWT= Advanced Wastewater Treatment
2. UCW= Untreated City Water
3. MCL= Maximum Contaminant Level
4. DL= Detection Level

protocol. Using this specific equipment allowed for a level of detection of 1.0 ug/l. Only phthalates, were consistently observed in both AWT and UCW. However, phthalate concentrations were generally at or near the level of detection. Benzoic Acid has been detected in the UCW, but at very low concentrations.

o Pesticides and Polychlorinated Biphenyls: This analysis was performed following EPA Method 608. Detection levels for most compounds were less than 1.0 ug/l. No method 608 compounds were detected in any AWT and raw water supply samples in either the screening or the monitoring phases.

o Total Organic Carbon (TOC) and Halogen (TOX): The organic carbon concentration in the UCW and AWT waters are approximately 3 and 0.4 mg/l, respectively. The average organic halogen content of the UCW and the AWT waters are approximately 72 and 19 ug/l, respectively.

Bioassay (Genetic Toxicity Testing)

The bioassay subtask is also being conducted at UCLA. The short term assays being conducted in this program include: the Ames Salmonella Assay; the Micronucleus test; 6-Thioguanine resistance in CHO cells; and, the cellular transformation test in C3H 10T1/2 cells.

Extracts obtained from the AWT effluent and UCW waters using XAD-4 and XAD-8 resins have been tested with the above tier of short-term bioassay. With the exception of a weak positive response to the UCW extracts in the Ames Assay, the results of the bioassay have been negative for both waters. GC-MS analysis of the extracts indicate that a large number of unidentified compounds exist at the ppt range.

Biomonitoring

A biomonitoring component of the HES is being conducted at San Diego State University, School of Public Health.

The objectives of biomonitoring subtask include: monitoring the accumulation of selected compounds within fish for two test waters (AWT and UCW), calculating the respective bioaccumulation of chemicals in fish, calculating BCFs for spike tests, monitoring and comparing observational differences (length, wet weight, behavior) associated with the fish grown in the two test waters, monitoring a surrogate parameter (TOX) for chlorinated hydrocarbons as a method of monitoring for plant releases not picked up by the chemical sampling program. An additional objective, but less achievable, is use of the biomonitoring data for human carcinogenic risk estimates. The maintenance of fish in the AWT effluent also provides Public Relations benefits. The results are presently under review.

Conclusions

The study described here represents a comprehensive attempt to measure as many as possible of the parameters which may effect the risk associated with potable reuse of municipal wastewater, after advanced wastewater treatment. The preliminary monitoring results presented indicate that the Advanced Wastewater Treatment (AWT) water is of similar of better quality than the Untreated City Water (UCW). Two key issues which will be addressed as part of this comparison include identification of the relative public health risk between the AWT and UCW waters, and the evaluation of AWT plant reliability. This work, along with the routine monitoring of both waters is presently underway and will not be completed until late 1990. Completion of the overall study should provide a significant contribution relative to the public health implications of the technical discussions that surround the issue of municipal water reuse.

References

Eisenberg, D.M., et.al., "Evaluation of Potential Health Risk of Direct Potable Reuse of Reclaimed Wastewater," ASCE National Engineering Conf., Orlando, FL. July 1987.

Olivieri, A.W., et al., "Study of Direct Potable Reuse of Reclaimed Wastewater: Preliminary Results," ASCE Annual Environmental Engineering Conference, Austin TX, July, 1989.

Tchobanoglous, G., et al.. "Evolution and Performance of City of San Diego Pilot Scale Aquatic Wastewater Treatment System Using Water Hyacinths," 60th Annual Conference of Water Pollution Control Federation, Philadelphia, PA. October, 1987.

Acknowledgements
This work is being funded by the City of San Diego. As noted, elements of the work are being conducted by the California Department of Health Services, the University of California, Los Angeles School of Public Health, the University of California, San Francisco, Tropical Disease Laboratory, and the School of Public Health at San Diego State University.

Hueco Bolson Recharge Demonstration Project

Bethany Barron/Randy Brock[1]

Abstract

The Hueco Bolson Recharge Project in El Paso, Texas, is a unique recharge system, being a full-scale program in operation for 5 years in which municipal sewage is treated to potable quality at the Fred Hervey Water Reclamation Plant, and injected directly into a major drinking water aquifer, the Hueco Bolson. This paper will discuss the ongoing monitoring plan and the specific goals of the plan to advance the state-of-the-art of groundwater recharge techniques.

Introduction

The recharge system includes a 10 MGD advanced wastewater treatment plant, a pipeline system, and ten injection wells. All sewage collected in the northeast area of El Paso is pumped to the treatment plant and treated to potable quality. The treated water is then pumped to the injection system. Injection occurs across the freshwater section of the Hueco Bolson between existing production wells. Wells are spaced and flow is controlled so that the residence time is at least two years prior to production. Produced water is chlorinated before being discharged into the distribution system. Because the HBRP is designed to augment the drinking water supply, a monitoring plan was developed to meet the goals of the Hueco Bolson Recharge Demonstration Project.

Description of Treatment System

The influent characteristics for the HBRP indicate a moderately weak sewage that is primarily domestic in origin. The treatment process is highly
----

[1] Engineers, Parkhill, Smith & Cooper, Inc., 810 E. Yandell, El Paso, TX 79902.

reliable in the removal of all potential contaminants through multiple, redundant units.

The process train includes screening, degritting, primary settling, equalization, a two-stage powdered activated carbon treatment (PACT) system, lime treatment, sand filtration, ozone disinfection, granular activated carbon (GAC) filtration and storage. The treatment plant has two 5 MGD parallel treatment trains. Flow proceeds through the process to a three compartment 10 MG clear well. A small chlorine residual is added to the water prior to storage to prevent biologic growth in the tanks and recharge system.

The reliability of the process is illustrated by the fact that there are many barriers through which incoming pollutants must pass before reaching the end of the process. For example, suspended solids are removed at three stages. The primary barrier is primary clarification aided by PACT. The second barrier is lime treatment in the secondary clarifiers, and the tertiary barrier is sand filtration. The treated water is stored for a minimum of eight hours during which time analysis are made to verify the water quality.

Description of Injection System

There are 10 injection wells currently in operation with an eleventh well soon to be brought on line. The water bearing strata of the Hueco Bolson aquifer is a fine grained alluvium under water table conditions. Each well is approximately 800 feet deep and is completed to about 450 feet into the water table. Normal static water levels are about 350 feet below the surface.

Currently all wells are operating at an injection rate of approximately 700 gpm. Hydrostatic buildup under injection conditions ranges from 100 feet to 150 feet initially and builds to approximately 250 feet before the well is backwashed with a pump installed in the well. Backwashing consists of pumping the well at a rate of 1000 gpm for several 30 minute periods so the well is surged. This procedure is usually done approximately every 3 months.

There are six observation wells in use. These wells are clustered in groups of two around two of the injection wells and are located 300 and 700 feet downgradient from the injection well. Two more observation wells are located 300 feet upgradient from different injection wells. These wells are monitored quarterly with fluid resistivity logs and samples are taken at points indicated by the logs.

Monitoring Plan

The High Plains States Groundwater Demonstration Program Act of 1983, the U.S. Bureau of Reclamation (USBR), and the El Paso Water Utilities (EPWU) Public Service Board have entered into a cooperative agreement to demonstrate the effectiveness and viability of the Hueco Bolson Recharge Project. The specific objective is to use the study results to enhance the state-of-the-art for groundwater recharge, through development of guidelines, criteria, and protocols to be used in the selection, design, and monitoring of other recharge projects.

The monitoring program began in Fiscal Year 1989 and will continue through Fiscal Year 1992. Primary goals of this monitoring plan include the evaluation of public safety, the effects of recharge on the quality of groundwater, and to determine how well each stage of the treatment process, the recharge process, and the management process works. The monitoring plan will also be used to determine whether the treatment system produces potable water on a reliable and cost-effective basis.

A series of Research Memoranda will be produced as part of the detailed study of the HPRP and are listed below for each fiscal year.

Fiscal Year 1990

1. Analysis of the Existing Monitoring Program. This memo will consist of cataloging and evaluating the existing data on the aquifer from 1967 and on the treatment plant and recharge system from 1985. Recommendations will be made on the validity of the data from the aspects of sample collection, analytical procedures, quality control, and necessity of individual analysis.

2. Priority Pollutants. This memo will evaluate whether any priority pollutants are reaching the public water supply due to this recharge project; where the pollutants are being removed in the treatment plant, and corrective measures to be taken should priority pollutants be detected in the aquifer.

3. Aquifer Impact. This memo will present a thorough analysis including a state-of-the-art transfer model involving retarded transport of constituents. The model will be used to define the impacts of recharge on water quality in the aquifer.

Fiscal Year 1991

4. Pathogens. This memo will evaluate whether any pathogens are reaching the public water supply due to this recharge project; where the pathogens are removed in the treatment plant; the relative kill efficiencies of different components of the system, and corrective measures to be taken should pathogens be detected in the aquifer.

5. Biotoxicity. This memo will evaluate whether any biotoxic compounds are present in the treatment plant or created during the treatment processes. Recommendations to prevent the formation of biotoxic compounds will be presented.

6. Engineering Performance. This memo will evaluate the performance of each unit of the treatment plant, the removal efficiency of conventional pollutants, reliability of the unit, and the treatment costs.

7. Injection Well Analysis. This memo will evaluate the performance of each injection well, and of the field as a unit. The evaluation will consider actual performance, reliability and costs, versus design objectives.

Fiscal Year 1992

8. Collection System Analysis. This memo will evaluate the composition of the sewage entering the plant with regard to flow variations, contaminant concentration, variety of contaminants, relative contribution of industries and commercial businesses, and the effect of the EPWU's industrial pretreatment program.

9. Production Wells. This memo will evaluate the effect of the project on water produced and delivered by EPWU. The primary emphasis will be on determining the extent to which adverse quality aspects of recharge water are diluted in the aquifer and in the distribution system, and quantification of changes in delivered water quality which can be ascribed to the project.

10. Management System. This memo will evaluate the project on the basis of original objectives and criteria as set forth in EPA's 1980 EIS. It will assess whether the project has succeeded in terms of wastewater and water supply management; whether environmental protection has been accomplished; and how the project has performed in terms of the 8 original safety criteria which were used to predict that the project would have acceptable public health effects.

11. Public Acceptance. This memo will evaluate the reaction to the project by people in El Paso. This evaluation will include interviews with selected community leaders and a small-scale survey of the general public and will consider the extent to which there are public concerns or support for the project, and whether the project has added to an overall awareness of water issues and the need for conservation.

12. Final Summary Report. This memo will present an overview of the project, identify significant findings, and make recommendations for future work efforts. It will include site selections criteria, i.e., water resources, site geological criteria, and design criteria.

Each Research Memorandum will be able to "stand alone" with the last memorandum, the Final Summary Report, summarizing all the results of the demonstration project. The Final Summary Report will act as a quick reference, present an overview of work accomplished and provide recommendations for future work on the HBRP.

The presentation of this paper at the ASCE Water Resource Conference in April 1990 will discuss the treatment system, the injection system and the existing monitoring plan. Results of the evaluation of the existing monitoring plan will also be presented as a brief summary of Research Memorandum One.

CONJUNCTIVE MANAGEMENT OF THE EDWARDS AQUIFER
AND CONNECTED SURFACE STREAMS IN SOUTH CENTRAL TEXAS

John H. Specht[1]

The Edwards Aquifer is a long, narrow conduit through which water moves underground across parts of South Central Texas. The conduit receives and dispenses major amounts of water averaging about 600,000 acre feet per year. The Edwards Aquifer supports the two largest springs in Texas, in addition to large municipal, industrial, and irrigation supplies, including the supply for the City of San Antonio. The underground water originates largely from surface sources which enter the Edwards in identified reaches of streams mostly west of San Antonio. This water then moves underground toward the east and northeast to be dispensed via springs in the Guadalupe River Basin or to be captured by wells before reaching the springs.

Increased use of water from the Edwards Aquifer has been substantial as regional population has grown, particularly around the City of San Antonio, and irrigation has increased in Kinney, Uvalde, Medina, and Bexar Counties, in South Central Texas. In 1934, the total diversion from the Edwards Aquifer was 102,000 acre feet. In 1985, 522,500 acre feet were diverted. Based on 1982 data, water from the Edwards is used for municipal use (59 percent), industrial use (35 percent), irrigation (29 percent), and other uses (9 percent).

Current levels of diversion from the Edwards Aquifer can not be sustained if another drought occurs equal to or greater in severity than the drought of record. Inflows to the Aquifer during the drought of record in the Guadalupe River Basin (from 1948 to 1956) averaged only 212,800 acre feet per year. Current annual use is well over twice this amount.

---
[1]Specht, General Manager, Guadalupe-Blanco River Authority, 933 East Court Street, Seguin, Texas, 78155.

Continued population growth is predicted for the region which currently is dependent upon the Edwards as its sole source of water. As a result of the anticipated population growth and the attendant rise in economic activity, average water requirements in the region served by the Edwards are projected to rise to approximately 600,000 acre feet in 2010 and approximately 900,000 acre feet in 2040.

In 1956, the Comal Springs ceased to flow for a five month period, and the San Marcos Springs were reduced to a minimum flow of 46 cubic feet per second. Because of the increased diversions from the Edwards since 1956, spring flows now fluctuate dramatically during less severe drought conditions. It is projected that, if diversions from the Edwards are allowed to increase, the springs will become intermittent and finally cease to flow except during periods of high rainfall.

Over the 1940-1985 period, flows from the Comal and San Marcos Springs comprised 30.6 percent of the total flow in the Guadalupe River on an average annual basis at (just downstream of) the confluence of the Guadalupe and San Marcos Rivers. In the Lower Guadalupe Basin near Victoria, spring flows comprised 25 percent of the total average annual flow of the river.

Over the nine year drought of record in the Basin (from 1948-1956), spring flows were 48 percent of the average annual flow at the Guadalupe/San Marcos confluence. More significantly, spring flows comprised 76.2 percent of the total river flow at the Guadalupe/San Marcos confluence in one of the nine years (1954), over 70 percent in three of the nine years, and over 60 percent in five of the nine years.

The relative contribution of the Edwards to the flow of the Guadalupe River, over any period of time would have been significantly greater had there been no diversions from the Edwards.

If diversions from the Edwards are allowed to increase, flows from the Comal and San Marcos Springs will decrease even further, and flows in the Guadalupe River south of the Balconies Escarpment will cease during periods of extreme drought. The loss of natural river flow, even for brief periods of time will result in severe environmental and economic damage to the Guadalupe River Basin, adjacent coastal basins, and the San Antonio Bay and Estuary which receive freshwater flows from the river system.

Rights to divert water from the Guadalupe River issued by the State of Texas for municipal, industrial, irrigation and other useful purposes are of no benefit when the river ceases to flow.

The State of Texas, through the Texas Water Commission, regulates the use of all water owned by the State through a system of permits issued to water users with priority of use based on the doctrine of "first in time is first in right". Privately owned groundwater currently is not subject to regulation by the State and is available for use by landowners with only minor restrictions imposed through various groundwater districts. The Edwards is significantly different from other water bearing formations in Texas - it is an underground stream. In a lawsuit filed in State District Court, the Guadalupe-Blanco River Authority contends that the waters flowing in the Edwards are owned by the State under current State law and are therefore subject to regulation by the Texas Water Commission under the same regulatory system applicable to State owned surface waters.

It is essential that uses of water from the Edwards be regulated in conjunction with regulation of use of water from the Guadalupe River. The current use of water from the Edwards exceeds the availability of water during critical drought conditions, and has reduced spring flow so as to impair existing surface water rights in the Guadalupe River. Left unregulated, diversions from the Edwards will continue to increase, causing ever-greater water shortages in the region during droughts. Such a shortage will cause severe damage to the environment and the economy of the region.

Regulation of the Edwards should begin with an adjudication of all claims of rights to divert water from the Edwards. To the extent that users may not now have sufficient rights to withdraw water from the Edwards, such rights should be granted by the Texas Water Commission or, perhaps, by the Legislature directly. Rights to use waters from the Edwards should be a property right, as are all rights to use State owned surface waters. Such rights may be sold to other users and, if necessary, amended by the Texas Water Commission.

To the extent that the Edwards can not meet all current or future needs, water users will find it necessary to seek supplemental sources of water. Initially, conservation of water or the reduction of water requirements through efficiency of use may be the most economical means of responding to water shortages. To some extent, water rationing during periods of drought can be used to affect a reduction by major users such as municipalities and certain industries. After water conservation methods and re-use of untreated wastewater have been effectively applied, supplemental sources of water may be necessary to meet future requirements, and promote and sustain a health economy.

In the river basins that are crossed by the Edwards, a potential exists south of the Balconies Escarpment for the development of surface water reservoirs. These potential reservoirs would store flood waters for use during periods of drought to provide additional water supplies to meet regional requirements that exceed the amounts available from the Edwards. These stored waters would also provide supplemental supplies for uses of water from the Guadalupe River and its tributaries during periods of drought.

Managing an Interruptible Water Supply

Gene Richardson[1], Wes Birdwell[2], M. ASCE

Abstract

The Lower Colorado River Authority has developed a plan for the management of an interruptible water supply for demands which do not require a firm commitment of specific amounts of water. The plan utilizes a rule curve for overdrafting of the Highland Lakes during years of ample water supply while assuring the availability of water to meet firm demands during the critical drought of record.

Background

The Lower Colorado River Authority owns and operates a series of dams on the Colorado River in Central Texas known as the Highland Lakes. These reservoirs which are operated for water supply, hydropower generation, flood control, and recreation have a combined total conservation storage capacity of about 2.3 million acre-feet. Water rights authorizing the use of water in these reservoirs were issued by the State of Texas and date back to 1926. During the Texas Water Commission's adjudication of the water rights on the lower Colorado River, the LCRA petitioned for the right to utilize up to 1.5 million acre-feet of water per year which is in excess of the firm yield of the reservoir system. TWC's final determination in the water rights adjudication process authorized this 1.5 million acre-feet per year use contingent upon the LCRA submitting a plan for the management of an interruptible supply. LCRA submitted

---

[1]Director, Water Resources Division, Lower Colorado River Authority, P.O. Box 220, Austin, TX 78767.

[2]Manager, Hydrology Programs, Lower Colorado River Authority, P.O. Box 220, Austin, TX 78767.

the Water Management Plan in July, 1989, and it was approved by the Texas Water Commission in September, 1989.

Combined Firm Yield Determination

The Highland Lakes are a chain of five reservoirs on the Colorado River in central Texas named Lake Buchanan, Inks Lake, Lake LBJ, Lake Marble Falls, and Lake Travis. Lakes Buchanan and Travis have water conservation storage, with the three intermediate reservoirs, Inks, LBJ, and Marble Falls, used strictly for hydro generation, recreation, and power plant cooling. Because the lakes are operated together as a system, the term "Combined Firm Yield" was defined as that portion of the Buchanan and Travis' yield remaining after honoring the full extent of upstream and downstream senior water rights. It was determined to be 445,266 acre-feet per year by a reservoir operation model which LCRA developed to analyze the reservoir system's ability to supply water under numerous scenarios. Demands downstream of the Highland Lakes had to be satisfied to the maximum extent possible by inflows downstream of the lakes on a daily basis. This required identifying the major senior water rights in the lower river and estimating their daily water demands and attempting to fully satisfy them. Those daily water demands that were not satisfied by the unregulated runoff became demands upon the daily inflows into the Highland Lakes. An optimization procedure was used to calculate the minimum required pass through of daily inflows to meet the remaining downstream water demands, to the extent possible. The daily reservoir inflows remaining, after the calculated pass through flows were subtracted, were stored in the Highland Lakes.

Interruptible Water Supply Concept

The Combined Firm Yield determination was controlled by the inflow which occurred during the most severe drought of record, and by the senior water rights diversions to their full authorized extent. In most years, however, significantly greater amounts of inflow occur, and currently, senior water rights diversions are significantly less than their full authorized amount. Endorsing the practice of many western states, LCRA proposed providing water above the "firm" yield of Lakes Buchanan and Travis on an interruptible basis to increase their average water supply potential. Under this concept, LCRA operates Lakes Buchanan and Travis to annually withdraw amounts of water in excess of the Combined Firm Yield, up to 1.5 million acre-feet (MAF).

The minimum annual amount is governed by near term projections of firm demands, or those needs for water which must be supplied year in and year out. When analyzed over the historical period of record, operation by this interruptible principle reduced spills and increased the average usable yield. An annual Operations Rule Curve was developed to insure that minimum demands could be met during a repeat of the record drought.

Annual Operations Rule Curve

Development of the Rule Curve involved simulating the operations of Lakes Buchanan and Travis based on the historical inflow of the Colorado River, to determine the performance and evaluate the increased yield potential. The initial step in the analysis included placing various levels of annual demand on the lakes while allowing for the annual fluctuations of inflow to replenish storage. Reasonable limits of supply for the system were determined by computer simulation of reservoir system operations to determine the percentage of time various annual demands could be met throughout the period of record 1941-1981. Starting with the reservoirs full, various demands ranging up to 1.5 MAF were placed on the system for the period. It was found that 100% of the maximum demand was met in 46% of the years, 75% was met in 63% of the years, and 50% was met in 80% of the years.

The second step performed a number of annual reservoir operations using various annual demands and starting system storages. This defined the minimum system storage attained over the period of record to determine how the system would respond to these various annual demands if the year began with the lakes less than full and established an annual supply commitment based on the beginning-of-year system storage. It was assumed that:

The known period of record includes the worst possible drought.

The chances of the critical year immediately repeating itself are not considered statistically reasonable.

The results of these operations are shown in Figure 1.

Based on this analysis, for the worst case annual system inflow, the system would have to begin its operational year at a storage of no less than 30%.

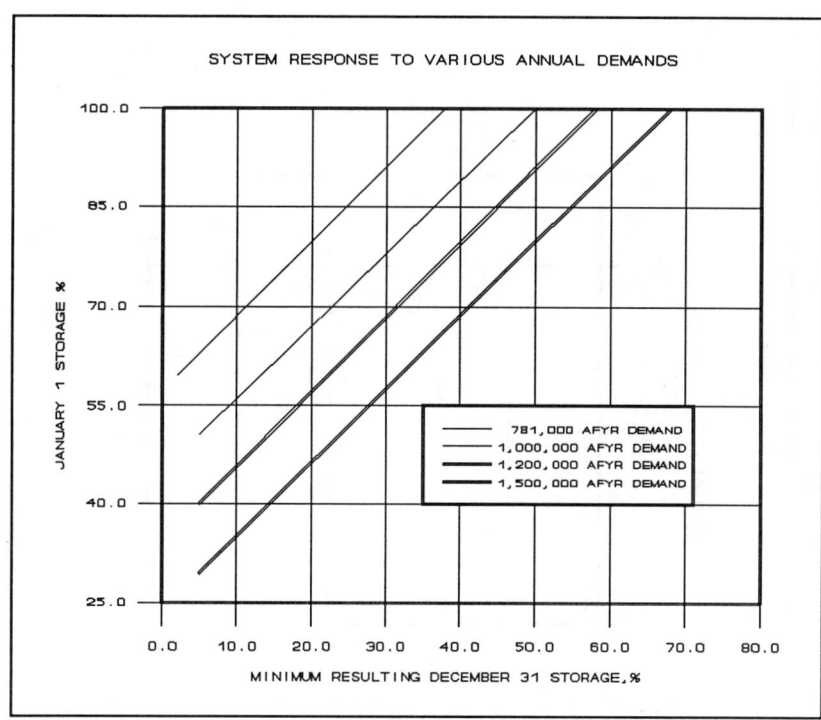

FIGURE 1

In the third step, this 30% amount is kept in reserve at the end of the worst case year as carryover storage under the various range of demands. It can therefore be determined, at the beginning of each calendar year, the amount which may be safely committed that year. The inherent conservatism of this rule curve is based on the facts that only the inflow which occurred in the worst case year is included, and considerable carryover storage is reserved. Figure 2 illustrates the conceptual rule curve for the Highland Lakes.

Conceptual Rule Curve Operations

The results of simulated operations over 41 years of record by a conceptual Annual Rule Curve which required a minimum annual demand of 628,000 acre-feet to be met. Computer runs were made using progressively higher annual demands, from 781,000 acre-feet up to 1.5 million acre-feet. Each successively larger demand put a greater average amount of water to beneficial use over the 41 year period of record, as shown in Table 1.

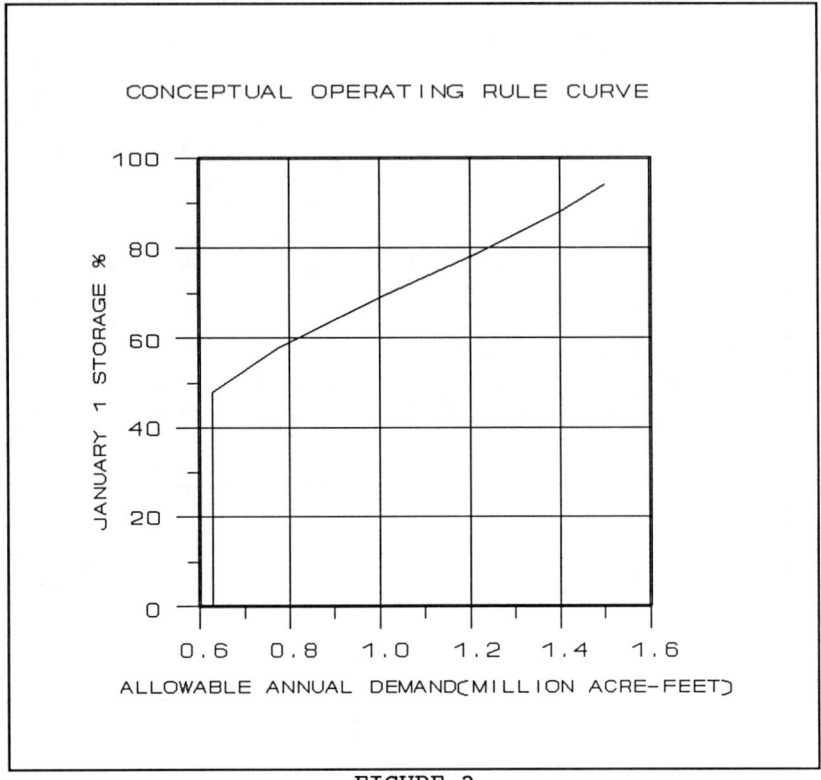

FIGURE 2

TABLE 1
Conceptual Rule Curve Operation Results

Demand ac-ft/yr	Years Demand Met (Years 80% Met)	Average ac-ft/yr	Spill ac-ft/yr
781,000	41 (100%)	781,000	366,000
1,000,000	7 (78%)	881,000	276,000
1,200,000	5 (46%)	937,000	227,000
1,500,000	2 (27%)	993,000	178,000

Even though this analysis does not evaluate the effect of passing inflow for senior downstream rights, it very effectively shows the beneficial impact of over drafting the reservoir yield while operating by a rule curve. The average annual supply was increased by over 200,000 acre-feet by reducing spills, while firm demands up to 628,000 acre-feet were met in all years.

Corps of Engineers
Drought Contingency Plans in Texas

Arnoldo I. Escobar, P.E.

Abstract

The Corps of Engineers, Fort Worth District, is currently preparing Drought Contingency Plans (DCP) for the river basins and its projects. These plans will be incorporated into the master water control manuals. The framework of the plan addresses several basic elements emphasizing actions that are to be taken prior to and during a drought. These elements include drought identification, water uses and users, constraints, drought management plan and public information. A cooperative effort is underway with state and Federal agencies to review the DCP for exchanging information relative to water management decisions and responding to a water shortage. This paper will review the DCP prepared for the Trinity River Basin in the state of Texas.

Introduction

The purpose of the Drought Contingency Plan is to provide a basic reference for water management decisions and responses to a water shortage in the Trinity River Basin induced by a climatological water shortage event. As a water management document, it is limited to those drought concerns relating to water control management actions. Because of the long-term nature of a drought and the uncertainties of the specific problems that may result, this document details only a limited number of specific actions that can be carried out relative to water control. Its primary value is in documenting data needed in decisions and defining the coordination needed to manage the district's water resources to insure that

---

1. Civil Engineer, Fort Worth District, U.S. Army Corps of Engineers, P.O. Box 17300, Fort Worth, Texas 76102-0300

they are used in a manner consistent with the needs by which they were developed. The guidance contained here is related specifically to naturally developed shortages and not to water shortages caused by overuse of the resource while in a normal climatic pattern. Projects included in this plan are Benbrook, Joe Pool, Ray Roberts, Lewisville, Grapevine, Lavon, Navarro Mills and Bardwell in the Trinity River Basin.

Authorities

Authorities that are pertinent to the preparation of drought contingency plans are directed therein. These authorities provide the regulation policies and guidance for the preparation of DCP, special regulations to be conducted during droughts, provisions for drought disaster assistance, contracting of surplus water and agreements for water withdrawals.

Drought Identification

A report on "Drought in the Great Plains and the Southwest" published in October 1958, states that records of precipitation in five southerly states in the Great Plains Area (including Texas) shows several severe droughts that occurred in the previous 100 years: 1865-1875, 1890-1895, 1901-1904, 1910-1914, 1920-1925, 1933-1940 and 1950-1957. The report also states that the severity of the 1950-1957 drought had not been exceeded in most states since the beginning of reliable records. A review of the "Climatalogical Data Annual Summary, Texas 1987" published by the National Oceanic and Atmospheric Administration shows that the 1950-1957 drought has not yet been exceeded in severity in Texas.

The National Weather Service (NWS) utilizes a numerical index to quantify the status of the climatically induced water balance between rainfall and moisture. This index, the Palmer Drought Severity Index (PDSI) is routinely on a statewide basis calculated for Texas and separately for each NWS climatic division within the State. The Palmer Index reflects the cumulative excess or deficiency in moisture relative to seasonal norms and typically ranges from +4 to -4 but may exceed these values in cases of a long duration of abnormal rainfall. Historical droughts which have occurred in the Trinity River Basin are described for severe droughts, noting the magnitude and duration of corresponding PDSI values.

As the district enters a drought period it is impossible to predict its duration or the severity. However, there are sufficient hydrometerological parameters such as stream flows, NWS rainfall and soil moisture indexes, and lake elevation conditions to establish procedures in developing a drought management plan. Four levels of drought conditions have been defined in this plan to determine the severity of the drought and actions needed to respond under each situation. Historical duration of droughts, Palmer Indexes and pool elevations constitute the concept for these severity levels.

Water Uses and Users

Project storage in the eight multipurpose projects within the Trinity River Basin is used primarily for the authorized purposes of flood control and water supply. Secondary uses include recreation, fish and wildlife, water storage for navigation and instream flow.

Current users of the stored water in each of the Corps projects on the Trinity River Basin have contracted storage allocation with the Government to store water for water supply needs. Since these users are under contract, they have exclusive priority to use their share of the stored water.

Available storage in excess of current uses is identified as inactive storage, ie, storage reserved for future sediment accumulation and not contracted out to a user(s).

Constraints

Legal constraints to the availability of water in Texas are governed by water rights. Water law in Texas recognizes four distinct classes of water: (1) diffuse surface water, (2) streamflow, (3) percolating groundwater and (4) underground streams. Only water in a watercourse is subject to state ownership in Texas. Legal rights to the use of streamflow in Texas are based on two alternative doctrines, riparian and prior appropriation.

Water resources in Texas are managed by hundreds of local agencies with the assistance of several State and Federal agencies. The river authorities, water districts and municipalities can enter into contracts with the Federal government for water supply storage in Federal lakes. The amount of water available for additional supply, as needed in a drought, is limited to the amount of water free from contractual obligations.

Surface water found in watercourses is owned by the state. Diffused surface water and groundwater is owned by individual landowners. Water rights are granted by a State license or permit, which grants to the holder the use of a specified amount of water, at a specific location and for a specific purpose.

Drought and other exigencies affecting domestic, municipal and industrial water supplies will likely generate requests for water stored in Corps lakes. When these situations occur, request may require immediate action. Section 6 of the Flood Control Act of 1944 provides an opportunity to be responsive to such requests.

Drought Management Plan

The Drought Management Plan presents a broad outline of actions necessary to effectively manage the district's water resources during time of shortage. The actions of the district will be broadly related to the level of drought severity. While it is recognized that severity of impacts may be widely variant among the various water user groups, the district has established four drought action levels in response to a worsening drought situation. These levels are based on the duration and severity associated with NWS Palmer Index, lake inflows, lake elevations, lake withdrawals and serve as indicators for determining each drought level being experienced. The four level system is used to give district managers a basic framework with which to execute a drought response.

The Corps of Engineers, in recognition of the potential water needs that might develop during severe droughts, has developed a strategy for necessary actions and coordination needed to meet these potentialities. As drought conditions become more severe, a greater demand is placed on the need to predict probably duration and severity. Four parameters provide sufficient information to establish guidelines for developing drought severity indicators. These parameters (PDSI, lake inflows, lake elevations, and dependable yield) define drought levels of varying severity conditions.

The four level system as shown in Table-1 is based on the duration of the drought and the pool elevations at each of the projects which correspond to the four levels.

Table-1 Drought Action Levels Designations

Level	(1) Duration (Months)	Limits	Ben-brook	Joe Pool	Ray Roberts	Lewis-ville
Top of Conservation Pool:			694.0	522.0	632.5	522.0
I	0-15	Lower	686.0	511.0	619.0	512.5
II	15-35	Lower	679.0	501.0	607.0	503.5
III	35-55	Lower	673.5	490.0	586.0	490.5
IV	>55					
Bottom of Conservation Pool:			665.0	456.0	524.0	481.0

Table-1 Drought Action Levels Designations
Continued

Level	(1) Duration (Months)	Limits	Grape-vine	Lavon	Bard-well	Navarro Mills
Top of Conservation Pool:			535.0	492.0	421.0	424.5
I	0-15	Lower	525.5	482.5	414.0	420.0
II	15-35	Lower	517.0	474.5	408.0	415.0
III	35-55	Lower	507.5	463.0	403.0	410.5
IV	>55					
Bottom of Conservation Pool:			500.5	453.0	391.0	375.3

(1) Duration refers to the number of consecutive months that the applicable PDSI value has been below zero.

Level 1 is designated as an alert phase in which the water managers monitor the onset of an apparent mild drought situation. Level II expands actions ongoing on Level I and initiates the need to activate the Corps Drought Management Committee (CDMC). At Level III drought conditions, the District Engineer will activate the Inter-Agency Drought Management Committee (IDMC). Coordination of actions during Level IV will follow similar procedures as presented in Level III. However, if Level IV drought conditions continue to deteriorate, utilization of the inactive storage must be considered.

Public Information

The success of this plan depends largely on its acceptance by the local governments and residents within the basin. Much of the plan has to do with how the Corps will react to their needs and requests. It is paramount that the public perceive that the Corps is acting in a rational and timely manner. Above all, the Corps must be open and informative about its actions and intents. To this end, a prearranged concept of public information dissemination is established to ensure that the public is kept abreast of drought developments and to reduce the likelihood of potentially damaging rumors and misinformation.

All information releases regarding the drought situation will be made through the Public Affairs Office of the Fort Worth District. Specific releases will be made when water levels are anticipated to impact on any of the contract water supply interests on the lakes or when the lake levels are approaching the lower boat ramp elevations. All information releases will be cleared by the committee or the proponet technical office regarding accuracy of the contents before being issued to the public.

Summary

The Corps of Engineers is making a significant contribution towards providing a basic reference for water management decisions during periods of critical water shortages. To anticipate actions necessary to meet declining water resources, data sharing and coordination between agencies is now being developed. Drought impacts on the Trinity River Basin can therefore be minimized, allowing maximum usage of all resources available.

BENEFITS FROM FLOODPLAIN MANAGEMENT ACTIVITIES
IN RELATION TO OPERATING SOUTH HOLSTON DAM

by

Forrest J. Crayford, Jr.
Member, ASCE[1]

Gregory W. Lowe
Associate Member, ASCE[2]

Arland W. Whitlock
Member, ASCE[3]

The benefits derived from effective floodplain management have been recognized through the years in reducing potential flood damage and loss of life. Floodplain management activities have primarily been directed toward (1) avoiding floodplain siting where practical; (2) where siting is unavoidable, elevating structures, facilities, or equipment to minimize flood damage and avoid floodwater contact with people; and (3) implementing structural measures to reduce flood risk to existing development if benefits would exceed costs. However, in many cases where the cost would not justify structural measures, one of the major problems is what can be done to minimize the flood impacts to existing low-lying development and to reduce the threat to life. This paper describes how a floodplain assessment of structures at risk from flooding resulted in TVA and local officials joining together to implement a flood warning and response procedures for residents downstream from South Holston Dam.

---

1. Civil Engineer, Flood Protection, TVA, Knoxville, Tennessee 37902

2. Manager, Flood Protection, TVA, Knoxville, Tennessee 37902

3. Program Manager, Reservoir Regulation, TVA, Knoxville, Tennessee 37902

The Tennessee Valley Authority (TVA) operates an integrated system of 47 dams and reservoirs to provide navigation, flood control, and hydro electric generation to the citizens of the seven-state Tennessee Valley region. TVA purchased fee ownership and/or acquired flood easement rights over those lands which would be impacted by construction of these projects. In the case of South Holston Dam, a tributary dam on South Fork Holston River completed in 1950, property downstream from the dam remained in private ownership because flood risk was significantly reduced below natural flooding as a result of regulation by the dam. For many years this land was primarily agricultural, with development limited to the easily accessible prime lakefront property near the major metropolitan areas. With the prime lakefront property almost all developed, development has moved to the marginally acceptable lakefront property remaining and to riverfront property downstream from the dam. For the last 10 to 20 years, new downstream residential development has taken place in the floodplain without, in many cases, regard for the flood risk which remains after regulation.

South Holston Dam is located on South Fork Holston River at river mile 49.8, approximately 7 miles southeast of Bristol, Tennessee-Virginia. The dam is a rockfill and impervious-rolled earthfill embankment with a length of 1,600 feet and maximum height of 285 feet. The drainage area at the dam is 703 square miles. The outlet works consist of an uncontrolled morning-glory spillway located at the left abutment, sluiceway with 34-foot-diameter tunnel and two 96-inch Howell-Bunger regulatory valves, and a chute-type auxiliary spillway located in a saddle 1.5 miles from the dam. Power facilities at the dam consist of a single Vertical Francis turbine.

Following the May 1984 flood, TVA's Reservoir Operations Section received a few complaints of minor flooding, although releases were only slightly above turbine capacity. During a similar release in 1987, the number of complaints increased dramatically. Calls were received from several new landowners stating that water had entered carports and threatened buildings.

The properties downstream from South Holston are located in Sullivan County, Tennessee. Historically, property owners in upper east Tennessee have been averse to any type of government controls on use of their lands. Attitudes have gradually changed and, in 1977, the county entered the National Flood Insurance Program (NFIP). A Flood Hazard Boundary Map was developed in 1979 and remained in effect until 1982 when an updated Flood Insurance Rate Map was published by the Federal Emergency Management Agency. Both maps showed approximate 100-year floodplain boundaries. Although Sullivan County passed the enabling resolutions to enter the NFIP in 1977, no enforcement took place because Sullivan County did not have county-wide land-use zoning

FLOODPLAIN MANAGEMENT BENEFITS 683

and county residents had an apathetic attitude. Ever since the
county entered the NFIP, TVA (through its Floodplain Management
Program) made an effort to guide development using the county's
floodplain resolutions by working with the Tennessee Department of
Economic and Community Development's Johnson City, Tennessee,
Local Planning Office.

In 1986 TVA received requests for 100-year flood elevations for
two new development sites below South Holston Dam. These
elevations were estimated based on best available 100-year
discharge information and use of marked historic flood profiles.
During a high release in 1987, one of the new residents complained
about flooding of his property. The floor of the house was high
enough but the carport was low and had 2 feet of water over it.
The lack of understanding by county employees and incomplete
floodplain information (lack of accurate flood elevations and
floodway data) led to improper siting of this residence when it
was built in 1986.

In 1988 the Sullivan County commission adopted county-wide
comprehensive land-use zoning, including floodplain regulations,
and began to enforce existing resolutions. A tour of the
floodplain to identify low-lying residences below South Holston
Dam was completed in December 1988 by TVA personnel from Land
Management and Floodplain Management, along with a local planning
office official. This tour identified 56 structures which would
likely be subject to flood damage if a discharge of 100-year
magnitude or less were released from South Holston Dam. Of these
56 structures, 20 appeared to have high risk potential for flood
damage from flooding of significantly less than 100-year magnitude.

Little can be done for the existing development to prevent
substantial property damage if flood conditions develop that
require reservoir operations to discharge releases that would
inundate downstream property. However, a warning procedure could
give residents advance warning of potential damaging releases from
the dam. This would allow for quick action to prevent some
damage, evacuation, and lessen the possibility of loss of life.
It would not, however, provide any warning of flooding caused by
runoff from the 85-square-mile unregulated watershed between South
Holston Dam and the next downstream reservoir.

In January 1989 the county employed a zoning administrator (ZA) to
issue building permits. TVA's Floodplain Management staff
provided training in basic floodplain management concepts and the
NFIP. This training included field evaluation of development
proposals and assistance with the issuance of floodplain permits
for development on several streams in the county. In April 1989 a
TVA Floodplain Management field engineer met with the Sullivan
County executive, a county commissioner, and the ZA to encourage
executive support for floodplain management activities and to

inform the county executive of TVA's concerns about new floodplain development which was taking place downstream from the dam.

TVA's Floodplain Management field engineer and the ZA visited the South Fork Holston River floodplain on several occasions. Using the estimated 100-year flood depths based on historic flood profiles, they confirmed that the 20 structures previously identified would suffer some flood damage in floods of less than 100-year magnitude. They photographed these 20 residences, and the ZA plotted them on a property map and obtained names and addresses of the owners. Some of the residences were vacation/leisure homes rather than full-time residences. All except one or two were very expensive structures. This information was assembled and organized into a usable format in early May for possible use in an early warning if it appeared a release from the dam might jeopardize some of these structures.

On May 9, 1989, TVA's Reservoir Operations Section informed Floodplain Management staff that forecast rainfall in the watershed above South Holston Dam could require a discharge rate similar to that which occurred in 1984 and 1987. The reservoir was near full summer level and 3 to 4 inches of additional rainfall was forecast. They asked the question: Was there a way to notify residents below the dam? TVA's Floodplain Management staff notified the ZA that, if predicted rain developed, outflow from the dam would affect some of the lowest-lying houses. The ZA and the county executive determined that warning these residents was the responsibility of the local civil defense coordinator (CDC). The ZA provided the photographs, a copy of the property map showing the 20 houses, and a telephone/address list of the owners of these properties to the CDC. The CDC had a deputy sheriff drive him to the 20 residences over about a 2-hour period. He had a poster-type notice about the possibility of a release from the dam if forecast rainfall developed, and either told the people in person or attached the notice to the door where no one was home.

Fortunately, the predicted rainfall did not develop. Several of the property owners who were notified indicated that the notice had alarmed them. The citizens asked for a meeting with TVA to explain the warning and operating criteria for the dam. On June 5, 1989, the ZA, CDC, and TVA officials met with 14 residents of the floodplain area who had received the notice. At the meeting TVA officials explained the operation of the dam, the effort which was underway to identify low-lying residences and the proposed study being forwarded to FEMA requesting funding to develop detailed 100-year flood elevations and floodway for the South Fork Holston River. The ZA explained the permitting process for new development or substantial improvement to existing structures. The CDC explained the warning process which was followed in May and would probably be followed in the future.

The floodplain residents believe that TVA should alter its operating procedure and/or reduce full summer pool levels to provide better flood protection for them. They agreed that the downstream floodplain property was mainly "corn field" when the dam was built. However, they thought that, because of the construction of the dam, there was very little if any risk of flooding, making the area attractive for development. There is little likelihood that TVA's operating guides for South Holston Dam will be modified for the sole reason that the floodplain downstream has been inhabited. It is likely, however, that cooperation between Federal, State, and local agencies will need to continue to provide for some degree of advance warning if operation of the dam itself will cause flooding downstream. TVA along with other communities and counties downstream from other projects are currently evaluating the Sullivan County plan to see if it can be modified to meet their needs.

Review of the Design, Construction, and Operation
of the Lake Carolyn Flood Control Pump Station

George E. Gay,[1] P.E, Assoc. M.ASCE, A W. Ernest Clement,[2]
P.E., Life Member, and Stanford W. Lynch,[3] P.E., Assoc Member, ASCE

Abstract

A review of the design, construction, and initial operation of the Lake Carolyn Flood Control Pump Station in Irving, Texas is presented. Staged water resource development design concepts with recommended design modifications resulting from construction difficulties and initial station operations are reviewed.

Introduction

The Dallas County Utility and Reclamation District (DCURD) provides municipal utility services for the Las Colinas development in Irving, Texas, located between Dallas and Fort Worth. As part of these services, the District is responsible for developing the flood control infrastructure which includes the Lake Carolyn Flood Control Pump Station. The service area is located inside a levee adjacent to the Elm Fork of the Trinity River. Initial development of the flood control system in 1973 was reclamation of floodplain land, construction of a flood control levee designed to protect from the Elm Fork's Standard Project Flood, construction of a gravity flow outlet structure capable of passing an interior 100-year flood, and excavation of Lake Carolyn. The 110-acre Lake Carolyn provides a central water based resource to Las Colinas as well as acting as an irrigation source and a collector for storm drainage. However, normal freeboard to the top of the lake's concrete perimeter wall is only 2 feet. Continued development adjacent to the lake, as well as increasing frequency discharges due to development in the Elm Fork watershed resulted in the District's desire to increase the level of flood protection in spite of its being acceptable from a regulatory stance.

[1] Project Manager, Freese & Nichols, Inc. Consulting Engineers, 811 Lamar Street Fort Worth, Texas 76102
[2] Senior Engineer, Freese & Nichols, Inc. Consulting Engineers, 811 Lamar Street Fort Worth, Texas 76012
[3] General Manager, Dallas County Utility and Reclamation District, P.O. Box 160035 Irving, Texas 75016

FLOOD CONTROL PUMP STATION   687

The design and construction of the 555,000 gpm Lake Carolyn Flood Control Pump Station is reviewed here and recommendations for future flood control pump stations provided.

Design

Project Constraints. -The architectural requirements of Las Colinas required the building be unobtrusive and compatible with future development. A Mediterranean style building was selected, using precast exposed aggregate concrete panel walls and a Spanish tile roof, to be compatible with future two story development. A premium demand for real estate adjacent to Lake Carolyn dictated that the pump station be set 80 feet back from the lake, thereby allowing commercial development adjacent to the lake. The site needed to be near the Elm Fork to minimize discharge pipeline lengths and the alignment of the pipeline should parallel one of the existing roads to reduce easement problems. Dual electric feeds, initially installed overhead, would be placed underground in the future in accordance with the architectural requirements of the Development. Provisions for implementation of a central flood control system within the station for existing and future flood control facilities was needed. An existing District raw water irrigation pump station site was selected, located on a bay of Lake Carolyn as shown in Figure 1, and the irrigation pumps were relocated into the building.

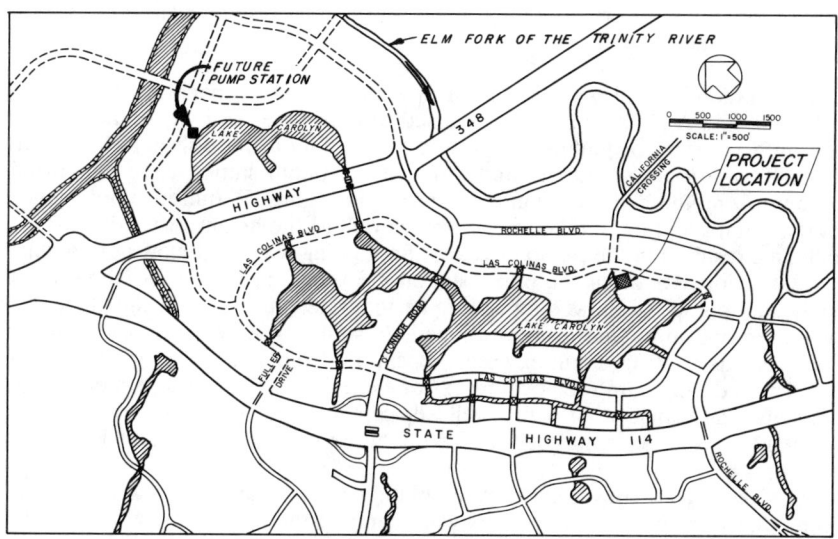

LOCATION MAP

FIGURE I

Hydraulic Design. -The drainage area is 2.2 mi^2, one half of which is adjacent to the lake. This local drainage has an average time to peak of eight minutes. Hydraulic simulations demonstrated a need for two pump stations, the present 555,000 gpm station and a future 105,000 gpm station located on a hydraulically constricted northern arm of the lake to limit the lake's rise to two feet above normal. Simulations of concurrent 100-year floods on the Elm Fork and the project area without the pump stations indicated six feet of rise in Lake Carolyn, four feet more than deemed acceptable, would occur and be capable of flooding the lowest buildings. Staged development of additional flood control facilities was possible since the northern arm could flood and detain local flood waters until development is initiated in the northern area.

Operation. -A manned pump station operation scheme was adopted. This mode of operation was selected because of the short response time required to activate the pump station during periods of flooding on the Elm Fork. The Corps of Engineers operates two major multipurpose reservoirs, including flood control capabilities, upstream of the District allowing accurate forecasting of river stages. The frequency of river stages exceeding the gravity system's capability is sufficiently low so that maintaining a manned system during flood periods is not unreasonable. During flooding periods, the lake level is lowered 0.5 feet below normal. Rainfall forecasting, weather radar, and fifteen years experience in operation of the gravity system are utilized in making judgemental determination by the operators regarding operation of the pump station. During sever weather forecasts and storm events, the lake is maintained at its lowered level until all pumps are operating. This criteria provides the level of protection selected by the District.

Pump Station Design. -Vertical axial flow pumps with capacities of 5-90,000, 1-60,000, and 2-22,500 gpm were selected to maximize flexibility and minimize the different sizes of pumps. The future pump station will utilize 1-60,000 and 2-22,500 gpm pumps. Depth and width of the pump station were minimized by optimizing the hydraulic configuration of the sumps. Required submergence of the pumps and the intake at the lake, as well as the height restriction on the building, resulted in the pump discharge floor being five feet below normal lake level. Sectional views of the pump station are shown in Figure 2. Removal of individual pumps is allowed by closing its separate sluice gate at the sump/wet well area and unbolting from an embedded wall ring which serves as a sump roof seal as well as a pump base. Backflow from the discharge header is prevented during pump removal by use of a check valve. Sufficient sump pump capacity was provided in a dry well adjacent to the wet sumps to allow for drainage of isolated pump cells as well as to cope with other water leakage.

The intake culvert converges from the pump station to the headwall at the lake to minimize concrete requirements while limiting the maximum velocity at the intake to 3 fps. Interior flow splitters were utilized to distribute the flow to the eight sumps as well as providing structural support for the culvert roof and future building construction. Four inch square grid screens were provided at the headwall intake.

FLOOD CONTROL PUMP STATION

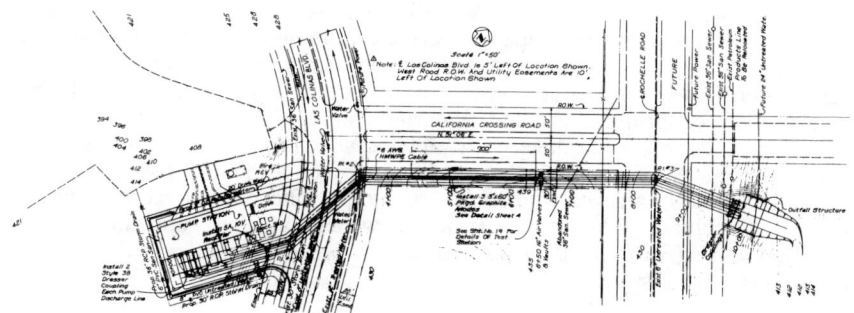

a. Site Plan

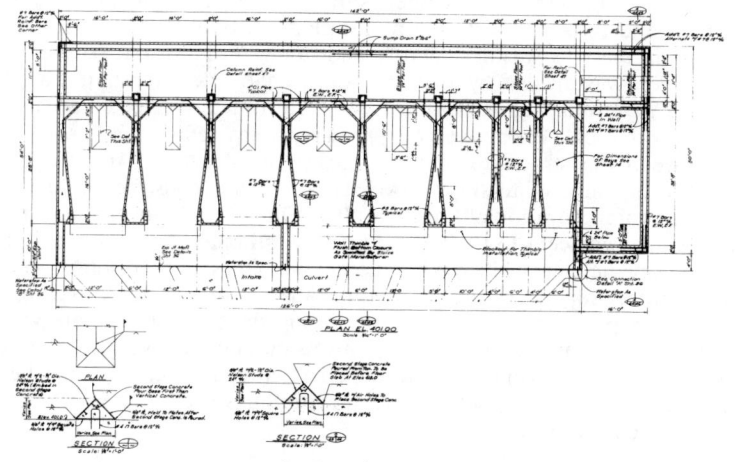

b. Sectional Plan

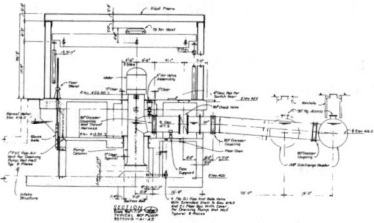

c. Cross Section

FIGURE 2

The discharge piping selected was twin 108-inch diameter steel pipe with epoxy lining and coating. The steel pipe was selected to minimize pipe outer diameter due to existing utility clearances. A cathodic protection system protects the pipe against corrosive soil conditions. Very close utility clearances during construction confirmed the pipe material choice. Access manholes were provided at three points along each pipeline which also function for air and vacuum relief. A high point in the pipeline provided a minimum static head of eight feet which narrowed the range of pumping heads and reduced pump design difficulties. The outfall structure which has flap gates to prevent backflow during river flooding periods and to prevent unauthorized entrance during low flow periods.

Structural Design. -A reinforced concrete substructure and intake culvert with a superimposed steel frame building was selected. These structures were founded on drill shafts 50 feet deep, embedded in shale to limit differential settlement and resist uplift during dewatering. A double wall steel sheet pile cofferdam in the lake was designed to allow dewatering of the excavation. The intake culvert was divided by a central wall to allow dewatering of each half if required. Future building support pads were furnished at selected points on the intake culvert roof. Expansive soil pressures were reduced by use of a sand zone between the structures and the backfill and carton forms were placed under slabs on piers. Waterstops were used at building construction joints below the normal water elevation of Lake Carolyn. Differential movement of the pipe discharge lines adjacent to the pump station was limited by use of sand backfill below the pipe headers while double dresser couplings allowed some movement. The steel frame superstructure allowed installation of a 25 ton traveling bridge crane for pump removal as well as supporting the precast concrete walls and tile roof. Building mechanical equipment was mounted above the crane runway and below the roof to enhance the building's appearance. The lake headwall adjacent to the intake structure and the outfall structure were designed as cantilever retaining walls.

Electrical Design. -Dual electrical service feeders were provided to allow redundancy for power. Temporarily, the power supply is overhead, but it will be placed underground in the future to further reduce risk of power failure. The motor control center bus was split to allow one half of the station to operate on each service with a locked tie breaker to allow connecting the busses if required. The 4,160 volt 3 phase pump motors were protected by phase failure/imbalance protection. Motor and bearing temperature readouts as well as voltage and current meters were provided but were not tied to the controllers to preclude unnecessary tripouts of the motors during emergency conditions. Standard lake level, sump level, and deviant condition alarms were provided as well as provisions for transmitting alarms and signals to the control room from existing and future flood control facilities.

Construction

No major problems occurred during construction. Excessive seepage through the sheet pile cofferdam was a problem until a differential head of four feet was obtained at which time the tightening of the interlocks reduced seepage flow. Installation of the drilled piers was difficult due to a sand and gravel layer overlaying the foundation shales which was hydraulically connected to Lake Carolyn. The piers were installed under 20 feet of artesian head and use of a temporary steel casing to limit flow through the bore holes proved successful. The casings were filled with concrete to 125 percent of the uplift water pressure before extraction began. Carton forms under slabs on piers had to be replaced due to wetting. Two of the pump/sump mounting rings had to be epoxy injected due to excessive shrinkage during second stage grouting of the mounting rings. Additional pea gravel content in the subsequent grouting reduced shrinkage. Temporary construction supports of the cathodically protected discharge piping through the pump station wall and outfall structure wall resulted in grounding the cathodic protection system to the wall reinforcing steel, requiring installation of additional anodes. The thin wall discharge piping proved difficult to maintain in shape for joint engagement prior to welding. Initial station testing and semi annual tests since 1986 have not disclosed any basic problems with the pump station or its operation.

Operation

An approximate flood of 10 to 25-year rainfall frequency on the local drainage area occurred in May 1989 while the Elm Fork was in flood stage requiring use of seven of the eight storm water pumps. Operation of the pump station was satisfactory. Without the pump station, Lake Carolyn would have risen to elevation 422, or two feet above the lake walls, and would have entered the lowest building in the development. Maximum lake elevation of 419.2 was monitored during the flood.

Recommendations For Future Design

The features described above for the Lake Carolyn Flood Control Pump Station generally were constructable and functioned as desired. Hydraulic model testing would be desirable to verify hydraulic design assumptions. The ability to install drilled piers under artesian conditions was confirmed. The foundation area needs to be maintained in a dry state when using carton forms. Installation of plywood sheathing on top of the carton forms was found highly beneficial. A detailed design and sequence for installation of large pump/sump mounting rings is desirable. Cathodic protection insulation kits should be installed on the exterior of structures to minimize the risk of grounding the system.

Conclusion

The concept of constructing flood control facilities in stages was utilized in this project in the evaluation of need, determination of required immediate construction, and planning for future construction. Early development of project constraints and objectives resulted in optimal development of an overall plan and construction of intermediate facilities.

CAUSES AND POSSIBLE CONTROL MEASURES OF FLOOD IN BANGLADESH

Jobaid Kabir, M ASCE [1]
Nadira Kabir, AM ASCE [2]

ABSTRACT

Intensity and frequency of occurrence of devastating floods in Bangladesh have increased significantly over the past two decades. Large scale deforestation in the upstream reaches of Ganges, Brahmaputra, and Meghna Rivers in India, Nepal, China, and Bhutan are causing increased flows of water and sediment to these rivers. Barrages constructed at the upstream reaches in India are being operated without sufficient coordination with the downstream conditions at Bangladesh. As a result, flood flows are more severe than they would have been without their existence. Regional and local flood control measures are essential for alleviating this annual tragedy.

INTRODUCTION

Bangladesh is the largest delta of the world formed by three mighty rivers - Ganges, Brahmaputra, and Meghna with their origins in the Himalayan mountains. Combined flow of these rivers is in excess of six million cubic feet per second during monsoon season. Approximately 80 percent of all the flood flows originates at the upstream reaches in India, Nepal, China, and Bhutan. About 8 percent of the total drainage area of these three rivers is located inside Bangladesh.

---

1. Engineer, Lower Colorado River Authority, P.O. Box 220, Austin, Texas.
2. Hydrologist, Texas Water Commission, P.O Box 13087, Capitol Station, Austin, Texas.

Frequency of occurrence of these devastating floods in the recent years have increased due to the increased human interference with natural processes at the upstream reaches of the rivers. This situation may have deteriorated further due to the global warming of the earth's atmosphere.

CAUSES OF FLOOD IN BANGLADESH

Most of Bangladesh is located in an active delta formed by the deposits carried by three mighty rivers - Ganges, Brahmaputra, and Meghna. Ground surface elevations of the majority of the land mass of the country varies from two to thirty feet above the sea level. As a result, historically flooding of the river banks were routine phenomenon. These floods were considered as blessings by the farmers because of the fertile soil and moisture left behind by the receding water. But, due to uncontrolled human interferences with natural processes at the upstream reaches, flooding in Bangladesh has turned from blessing to annual misery in the past two decades.

Total drainage area of Ganges, Brahmaputra, and Meghna Rivers is approximately 600,000 square miles, more than ninety percent of which is located outside Bangladesh, at their upstream reaches in India, Nepal, China, and Bhutan. Precipitation in the watersheds are generally very high. 80 percent of all rainfall occur between May and September. Combined flows of these three rivers during monsoon is approximately 6,000,000 cubic feet per second. Total volume of water being discharged to the Bay of Bengal through Bangladesh is 953 million acre-feet per year.

Recent increase in the intensity and frequency of flooding in Bangladesh is caused by human interferences. These causes may be divided into four groups. Such as (a) Uncontrolled deforestation; (b) Upstream flood control measures; (c) Unplanned developments; and (d) Other Causes.

UNCONTROLLED DEFORESTATION: Due to the increased population and high demand of lumber and fire wood in India and Nepal, range land with dense forest and natural vegetation are being cleared at an unprecedented rate. In 1961, out of the total 57,000 square miles of land in Nepal, 32,000 square miles were forest. In 1982, range land in Nepal has reduced to only 12,000 square miles. Similar conditions exists in India, China and Bhutan.

There are two negative impacts of these large scale deforestation. These are increased flows due to reduced soil infiltration, and increased sediment loads to the rivers as a result of accelerated erosion of top soil. Total sediment load carried by Ganges, Brahmaputra, and Meghna is approximately 2.5 billion tons per year.

Due to the increase in sediment loads in the rivers beyond their carrying capacities, sand bars are forming at an unprecedented rate. Recent studies show that river bottoms of several major rivers within Bangladesh are on the rise at a rate of more than two inches per year as result of the accumulation of sediments. These sand bars and elevated river beds are creating additional obstructions to the flow passage.

UPSTREAM FLOOD CONTROL MEASURES: Flood control measures adopted by India at the upstream reaches have significantly deteriorated flood situation in Bangladesh in the recent years. Due to the construction of barrages and embankments at the upstream reaches, area of flood flow passage for these rivers have decreased dramatically. Consequently, flood flows are rushing towards the flat lands of Bangladesh at a much higher velocities. Effect of this was particularly felt in the 1988 flood when more than 75 percent of the country was inundated within a very short time.

It has been observed during the past few years that flood situation in Bangladesh has significantly deteriorated due to the construction of barrages and embankments in India. Most devastating effect was felt from the operation of Farakka Barrage. This barrage has been operated with very little or no considerations to the downstream conditions at Bangladesh.

UNPLANNED DEVELOPMENTS: In the past two decades population of Bangladesh has increased dramatically. Consequently, rural roads were built to provide communication to the newly developed communities. Due to limited available financial resources, a large portion of these roads were built with inadequate culverts and bridges. Consequently it is taking much longer time for the flood water to recede and also causing severe damage to these roadways.

OTHER CAUSES: In addition to the three major causes for flood in Bangladesh, there may be few more reasons for the increase in the frequency of devastating flood.

FLOOD CAUSES AND CONTROL 695

These are (a) rise in global temperature due to the so called greenhouse effect; (b) coal dust sprinkling by India over the glaciers of the Himalayas; and (c) Earthquake in the Himalayan mountain range.

POSSIBLE FLOOD CONTROL MEASURES

For the implementation of a successful flood control program, both local and regional measures are necessary. Regional measures will require extensive cooperation with India, Nepal, China, and Bhutan. Regional measures will require a long period for implementation and massive capital investment.

To avoid total dependance on India and to secure some short term relief, local flood control measures within the country also has to be implemented simultaneously. These measures will be relatively less time consuming but will also require massive international assistance. Both regional and local flood control measures could be divided into structural and non-structural categories.

REGIONAL STRUCTURAL MEASURES: Regional structural measures may include construction of dams to create reservoirs at the upstream reaches of the rivers. Several ideal locations for constructing such reservoirs are available in Nepal, India, and China.

Construction of these reservoirs will not only help control flood in Bangladesh, these reservoirs will be able to produce large amount of hydroelectricity. For example, if China decides to build a reservoir on Zangbo River at the great bend area where the river drops a whooping 7,000 feet in only 150 miles, it could become the largest producer of hydro-electricity in the world.

REGIONAL NON-STRUCTURAL MEASURES: Devastating effect of these floods could be decreased by creating new forests. Considering the population growth and consequent pressure on the agricultural land, it is quite obvious that such large scale afforestation will not be feasible. But schemes could be implemented for systematic development of agricultural lands with the aim of increasing soil infiltration and reduced erosion by developing successful erosion control and soil conservation programs.

Non-structural measures that can be taken at

regional level in cooperation with India, Nepal, and China could also include the development of a flood forecasting system. This flood forecasting system will require up to date information on flow rates at the upstream locations. These information may be shared between the participating countries.

LOCAL STRUCTURAL MEASURES: Local structural measures may include construction of embankments along the length of the rivers, construction of barrages on major rivers, and routine dredging of the rivers beds. Construction of Ganges, Brahmaputra, and Tista Barrages are essential for successful flood control within Bangladesh. These barrages will retard the flood flows by storing a part of the inflows.

Construction of embankments along the length of the rivers is essential for flood control in Bangladesh. Flood flows will be contained within the embankments for protecting populated areas and agricultural land from flooding by the rushing water from the upstream reaches.

An annual dredging of the river bottom is essential for proper maintenance of these rivers. Although expensive, mechanical means will be necessary for dredging some sections of the river. But due to the availability of inexpensive labor, majority of the digging at the channel bottom can be accomplished using human labor.

Due to the accumulation of sediments over the years at the river beds, several major rivers within Bangladesh are unable to carry flood flows to their full potential. For example, Old Brahmaputra, Dhaleshwari, Gorai, and Arial Kha Rivers could be reclaimed by excavation and dredging.

Roadways with inadequate culverts and bridges should be improved by adding new culverts and bridges. Resistance to the flood flows may also be reduced by increasing capacities of the existing culverts and bridges. More emphasis should be given to the development of river based communications over building new roads. Any additional road will add resistance to the flood flows and will take longer time for flood water to recede.

Automatic gates should be built on the coastal rivers for stopping saline tidal waves from entering inland. These gates will allow river water to flow freely to the Bay of Bengal but will not allow tidal waves to enter inland. Also polders with adequate pumping facilities should be built in the water logged lands in the coastal areas.

LOCAL NON-STRUCTURAL MEASURES: Non-structural measures within the country could include establishment of zoning and flood forecasting program. Implementation of these measures will require coordination with various sections of the government. Engineering and technical expertise will be necessary for the development of these schemes but administrative wings of the government should be responsible for the implementation of these scheme.

Using topographic information, zones of various flood potentials should be identified. Policies should be implemented identifying various activities allowed within each zone. Flood warning and evacuation system could be developed for informing public of any forthcoming flood. This program may also include developing an organized relief effort even before flood season starts.

CONCLUSIONS

Recent increase in the intensity and frequency of flooding in Bangladesh is caused by human interferences in the upstream reaches of the rivers and also within Bangladesh. Flooding in Bangladesh can be controlled by implementing regional and local measures. Both regional and local flood control measures will require massive capital investments. Economic conditions of Bangladesh and neighboring countries have prohibited seeking such flood control measures in the past. Implementation of a comprehensive flood control program will require extensive international support in the form of both technical and financial assistance.

In the 1989 summit meeting of the industrialized nations, four proposals were discussed for the flood control measures. These proposals came from the Unites States, France, Japan, and the United Nations. Although these proposals are different from each other, it is expected that a reasonable compromise will be reached between the donor nations to come up with a sound flood control program for Bangladesh.

GOVERNMENT COOPERATION IN WATER RESOURCES PLANNING AND MANAGEMENT

John W. Brown and Neil W. Schild

In 1985 California had a population of 26.1 million and used 34.2 million acre-feet for all consumptive water uses. Population is projected to grow to 36.3 million and water use to 35.6 million acre-feet by the year 2010. The State's current developed water supply is approximately 32 million acre-feet per year. This leaves an annual 2 million acre-foot shortfall which is made up by mining ground-water basins, mostly in the San Joaquin Valley.

Several new projects are being considered to eliminate the shortage and help meet projections. The State is pursuing offstream storage for the State Water Project in the west side of the San Joaquin Valley along with expanded ground-water storage and conjunctive use programs particularly in Kern County. The U. S. Bureau of Reclamation (USBR) for 25 years has been trying to build Auburn Dam and Reservoir. Major projects like Auburn Dam are getting very difficult to construct in California. The outlook of being able to construct new major projects particularly dams is not very bright. Such projects meet heavy opposition from environmental groups and groups which may have self serving interest. To this end mitigating between interests causes delays with resulting high-benefit costs.

John W. Brown
Regional Director, Boyle Engineering Corporation
100 Howe Avenue, Suite 250 North
Sacramento, California 95825

Neil W. Schild
Assistant Regional Director, U. S. Bureau of
   Reclamation, Mid-Pacific Region
2800 Cottage Way, Room W-1105
Sacramento, California 95825

California has ample precipitation to meet current and
most projected needs. The 1300 reservoirs and
thousands of miles of conveyance facilities deliver
conserved surface water to irrigate 10 million acres of
land growing about 250 different field crops, fresh
vegetables and permanent crops. In 1985, approximately
84 percent of all fresh water developed went to
agriculture with the remaining 16 percent to urban use.
The urban use is projected to approach 20 percent by
the year 2010 due to the influx of approximately
500,000 people annually.

This background can help understand the problems with
Plan 1 "of building new major water development
facilities" and why a Plan 2 is being considered, along
with Plan 1. Plan 2 takes into consideration making
more efficient use of the existing developed water.
Federal and State Government programs and State
Legislature provide incentives and legislation to
encourage regional and local water conservation. Major
pending and existing legislation includes:

o   Water Reclamation Loan Program: The Bond Law of
    1984 established a   revolving fund of low interest
    loans to public agencies for the design   and
    construction of water reclamation projects. Loans
    may be for a   period up to 20 years with an
    interest rate of approximately 4 percent. No
    single program may receive more than $5 million.
    The current program $33 million is funded by bond
    laws passed in 1988.

   o The Water Conservation and Water Quality Bond Law
     of 1986 provided up to $75 million in low interest
     loans for the construction of agricultural drainage
     water facilities which is administered by the
     California State Water Resources Control Board. A
     similar program is administered by the California
     Department of Water Resources for water
     conservation projects.

   o The Safe Drinking Water Bond Law of 1986 provided
     $100 million for low interest loans and grants for
     improvements to domestic water systems. This fund
     is administered by the California Department of
     Health Services.

   o Assembly Bill 1029 by California Assemblyman Dave
     Kelley provides incentives to the areas of origin
     for water conserved and exported. This Bill was
     approved by the Governor in September 1985.

o Water Transfers/Marketing: California A.B. 3491
(Katz 1982) directs State agencies to encourage
water transfers, sales and exchange from a water
surplus area to water short areas. Such
transactions may occur directly between two or more
such agencies but are limited to a period of seven
years. A subsequent bill by Assemblyman Dave
Kelley (A.B. 3427) removed the seven year
limitation.

o Water Conveyance: California A.B. 2146 (Katz 1986)
provides for conveyance capacity in unused public
facilities to others implementing water transfers.

o A.B. 1312 co-authored California State Assembly
Members William Filante and the late Bill Bradley,
if adopted would authorize the issuance of $200
million in State Bond Funds to finance low interest
loans for Water Reclamation projects.

Major conservation projects and some innovative ideas
include:

o Imperial Irrigation District (IID) and
Metropolitan Water District (MWD) - The program
under consideration provides for MWD to pay for
conservation practices in the IID in order to
divert the quantity of conserved water to MWD. The
conservation practice under consideration includes
the lining of several miles of canal and may be
expanded to include other conservation practices.
The anticipated quantity of water to be saved is
approximately 250,000 acre-feet annually.

o Improved Irrigation Efficiencies - Irrigation
efficiency has increased in the past due to
increasing cost of energy, water and crop
production. It is expected that irrigation methods
will be converted to more efficient systems as
economics demand. However this might be
accelerated if it can be justified on a statewide
basis. For instance if the value of water
conserved through improved irrigation systems can
compete with the Department of Water Resources
(State) best water development program, then the
State would likely be interested in developing a
program with financial incentives to accomplish
the improved irrigation systems project.

Reclaimed Waste Water: In 1985 approximately 3.4
million acre-feet of urban waste water was

generated. Of this approximately 300,000 acre-feet were reused mainly for irrigation. The reuse is projected to increase to 500,000 acre-feet by the year 2010. The total projected water use by 2010 is 35.6 million acre-feet. Urban use is projected to be approximately 20 percent of the total which equals approximately 7 million acre-feet annually, generating approximately 4.5 million acre-feet annually for potential reuse. The projected 500,000 acre-feet is only 11 percent of the total effluent generated. This percentage figure seems low and it is believed greater reuse potential exists in the larger metropolitan areas of Southern California and San Francisco Bay areas.

o Revised Cropping Patterns - There are approximately 2 million acres of irrigated pasture and alfalfa. It may be possible to convert some of the flood or furrow irrigation crops requiring 4 to 5 acre-feet/acre/year over to permanent crops requiring 2 to 3 acre-feet/acre/year with drip, spitter or sprinkler irrigation.

o Water Meters - Through the use of water meters there may be some conservation of water on an individual basis. The advantage(s) of metering is that each user accountable for use, reduced water use and quantities to treat and the fact that water quality would not be deteriorated by being transported through an urban area (streets, open channels or ground water).

o Conjunctive Use - California has approximately 850 million acre-feet of ground-water basin storage. Collectively there are approximately 43 million acre-feet of surface water storage. Local and State agencies are pursuing greater use of surface water supplies during water surplus years and for greater reliance on ground water during drought years to increase State yields. California Senate Bill 187 was signed into law in 1985. It authorizes for ground-water storage extraction projects south of the Delta to be included into the State Water Project.

There are a number of examples that can be given with governmental cooperation in planning and developing water resources. Some examples are the State Water Project and Central Valley Project, San Luis Unit in California; the Coordinated Operations Agreement - 1986 - California; and Los Vaqueros Dam and Reservoir in Contra Costa County with a number of cooperators. The examples will be discussed in the presentation of the paper.

In summary, the California State Legislators have shown real concern in trying to do something about the clearly identified water shortage. Many bills and funding programs have been proposed to encourage conservation. The State Agriculturalists have taken advantage of these programs and progress is being made. However, it is the authors opinions that conservation alone will not solve the problem and that Federal, State and local support must come forth together for major projects if we are to discontinue mining supplies from future generations. The time and economy are good now and we should at least pay our own way or better yet help to build up the ground water basin for others to use in the future.

References:
California Water - Looking to the Future - Bulletin 160.87, State of California, June 1988

Agricultural Water Conservation in Relation to Projected Water Demands and Supplies - By David C. Davenport and Robert M. Hagan, August 1985

STREAMFLOW PREDICTION AND ALLOCATION MODEL IN TEXAS

Richard E. Brown[1], A.M. ASCE and Norman D. Johns[2]

Abstract

The State of Texas' Water Rights Adjudication Act of 1967 provided for the creation of regional watermasters to divide the water of state streams in accordance with the adjudicated water rights. A computer model has been developed to assist in the efficient allocation of this water. The first step is to predict the daily streamflows expected at all diversion points in a river basin for the next 7 to 10 days. These forecasts are made by applying autoregressive time-series equations to daily streamflow values retrieved via satellite from USGS streamflow gages. Next, the model performs an allocation of these streamflows to the valid water right holders which have declared an intent to divert during the forecast period. This allocation is done on a seniority basis, as prescribed by the Texas Water Code. A watermaster can approve only diversions which do not impair the ability of any senior water right to meet their requested diversion. An evaluation of potential adverse impacts on senior diverters, with respect to location and travel times, must be made for each proposed diversion. This paper presents an outline of the computer model and how it will be used by the watermasters.

Introduction

In September 1988, the Texas Water Commission (TWC) created the South Texas Watermaster, which includes the basins of the Guadalupe River, San Antonio River, Nueces

---

1. Engineer, Texas Water Commission, P.O. Box 13087 Austin, Texas 78711

2. Hydrologist, Texas Water Commission, P.O. Box 13087 Austin, Texas 78711

River, and associated coastal areas. The TWC has developed a computer model to help the Watermaster perform the important function of dividing water among water right holders, especially during low-flow periods. This model has two phases: an autoregressive streamflow prediction phase, and a streamflow allocation phase. The model must be calibrated to each river basin in which it will be used.

Autoregressive Equation Analysis

The primary objective of the first phase of the model is to accurately predict streamflows during low-flow conditions. A time-series approach was selected to develop an equation to predict the daily streamflows at U.S. Geological Survey gages. A series of daily streamflow data often contains components of a trend, periodic cycles, and random fluctuations (Salas, 1980). This analysis of historical records is intended to identify and quantify the first two components. Then an equation is fit to this conditioned data to explain the autoregressive character of the series. The remaining series, or residuals, should be random variations (white noise). This model will be used to forecast streamflows on a real-time basis.

The region of the South Texas Watermaster, the first in which this model is being applied, is semi-arid. Most of the rivers here have minimal baseflow with a substantial portion of the total annual flow occurring during a few flash floods throughout the year. In order to limit the effect of these peaks on the autoregression coefficients to predict low flows, the first step in the analysis is to identify those flash flood outliers. Since discarding these data would result in a discontinuous series, these values are converted to a maximum limit. The form of the equation used is:

$$x_t \leq \mu + i\sigma \qquad \text{(Eq. 1)}$$

where x_t is the t-th value in the daily streamflow series, μ is the overall mean of the x_t series, i is a coefficient, and σ is the overall standard deviation of the x_t series. Preliminary examinations have indicated that using i=2 is appropriate.

Trend in a series may be tested for in a number of ways. The selected method is using Student's t test (Kennedy and Neville, 1976). The period of record is broken into two parts and a t statistic is calculated to compare the means of the two parts. If it is found that the two means are statistically different, indicating trend, then a linear regression equation is fitted to the overall data set. Then the data are adjusted so the slope of the regression is equal to zero.

Most statistical techniques assume that the data are normally distributed. A histogram of daily streamflow data clearly shows that even after an upper limit is set, the distribution is heavily skewed toward high values. A transformation is required to result in a more normally distributed data set. A one-parameter log transformation was selected:

$$y_t = \log_e (x_t - x_{min} + 1) \qquad \text{(Eq. 2)}$$

where y_t is the t-th value in the log transformed series and x_{min} is the minimum value of the x_t series. To avoid taking the log of 0, the value 1 is added to the difference.

A periodic cycle throughout the year is characterized by considering the values for the τ-th day of each year of record, so τ ranges from 1 to 365 (leap days are ignored). In order to remove effects of the periodic cycles the data is periodically standardized. For each value in the y_t series, this is done by subtracting the appropriate value of μ_τ, the periodic mean series, and dividing by the appropriate value of σ_τ, the periodic standard deviation series. These periodic means and standard deviations may be calculated and the actual values used, or a Fourier series may be fitted to each set and approximate values generated. The advantage of the Fourier series is that fewer parameters will be carried forward. The standardization equation is:

$$z_t = \frac{y_t - \mu_\tau}{\sigma_\tau} \qquad \text{(Eq. 3)}$$

where z_t is the t-th value in the periodically standardized series.

After the streamflow data have been conditioned to minimize the effects of flash flood events, trend, non-normal distribution, and periodic cycles, the final step is to solve for the autoregression coefficients. This analysis, explained in detail by Salas (1980), yields the order p autoregression equation:

$$z_t = \bar{z} + \left\{ \sum_{j=1}^{j=p} \phi_j (z_{t-j} - \bar{z}) \right\} + \epsilon_t \qquad \text{(Eq. 4)}$$

where $\bar{z}$ is the overall mean of the z_t series, p is the maximum lag considered in days, ϕ_j are autoregression coefficients, and ϵ_t is a random variation series. This equation, with ϵ_t set to zero, can be used for forecasting.

The historical data is then used to generate the series of one-step ahead forecasts. To generate this series, the first p days of the historical data are used in Eq. 4, with ϵ set to zero, to forecast the value for day p+1. Then to forecast for day p+2, the historical values for days 2 through p+1 are used in the equation. Repeating this process through the period of record yields the series of one-step ahead forecasts. The differences of the historical value and the corresponding one-step ahead forecast is the model residual series. This series has all the autoregressive characteristic removed.

In the next step, a multivariate analysis is performed, where the residual series of two or more gages of a stream are analyzed for significant cross-correlation. This allows information from upstream gages to be used in the forecasts at a downstream gage. The arrangement of gages along a river network will determine the usefulness of such an approach within a particular basin. Multivariate analyses will be evaluated as the model is calibrated to each river basin.

Forecasting Streamflow

The prediction of daily streamflows must be based on the most recent data available. The U.S. Geological Survey maintains some streamflow gages that are equipped with satellite telemeters to transmit hourly gage values. This data is available via computer with a connection to the U.S.G.S. ADAPS system. Within the river basins of the South Texas Watermaster there are 28 telemetric gages. This system allows real-time discharge values to be retrieved.

Data from these gages will be obtained on a daily basis and entered into the first phase of the model. The autoregression equations are used to predict streamflows at the gages for a 7 to 10 day horizon. Each river basin is broken into subareas, typically 10 to 20 square miles per subarea. Streamflows at the gages are disaggregated into contributions from each subarea based on drainage area ratios. The predicted streamflows at any diversion point in the basin are found by summing all contributing streamflows.

Streamflow Allocation

The second phase of the model is allocation of the streamflows. In this allocation, each day for the forecast horizon must be considered. Travel times are estimated for the diversions and their subsequent effects on downstream diverters.

Prior to actually pumping water from a state stream, all water right holders must declare to the watermaster an intent to divert. All such requests are examined for validity, i.e., is the request from the proper owner (or an authorized agent), is the type of use authorized, and is the volume to be diverted within the annual limit. Valid requests are forwarded to the model. Since seniority of the right must be honored in allocating water, the requests are considered starting with the most senior right. As each request is considered, two conditions must be satisfied before approval can be given by the watermaster. First, sufficient flows must be predicted for the requested days at the point of diversion. If this condition is met, then the request is tentatively approved. For the second test, a downstream checking routine is activated to insure that this tentatively approved diversion is not depleting streamflows needed by a more-senior right (which would have already received approval). If such a conflict is found, the tentatively approved request must be curtailed and the water right holder so informed.

Summary

The Texas Water Commission has developed a streamflow prediction and allocation computer model for the area of the South Texas Watermaster. This two phase model aids the Watermaster in the efficient allocation of this limited resource among the valid requests for diversion made by water right holders. The first phase of the model uses an autoregression approach to forecast streamflows. The second phase of the model allocates the predicted flows among requested diverters with an algorithm using seniority order and travel times.

References

Kennedy, J.B. and A.M. Neville. 1976. Basic Statistical Methods for Engineers and Scientists, IEP.

Salas, J.D., et al. 1980. Applied Modeling of Hydrologic Time Series, Water Resources Publications.

WATERMASTER ADMINISTRATION OF TEXAS STATE WATERS

Norman D. Johns[1] and Richard E. Brown[2], A.M. ASCE

Abstract

The State of Texas is developing a watermaster program which will enable the State to administer water right issues on a regional basis. A primary role of a watermaster operation is to provide for the lawful distribution of state water during periods of low-flow. Presented in this paper is a comprehensive overview of the historical events leading to this program and the efforts to implement it.

Introduction

The State of Texas is currently implementing a watermaster program, under the auspices of the Texas Water Commission. This program, consisting of a series of regional offices, will allow the State to properly administer use of state water and to respond to low-flow situations quickly.

In addition to frequent droughts in Texas, other nonclimatic factors have had a major influence on the creation of this program. Foremost is the State's complex water rights history, arising from being first a territory of Spain, then Mexico, then an independent Republic, and finally a State. This history led to an essentially dual system of water rights (Freeman and Akers, 1979). Since the late 1800's a water right could be acquired by obtaining authorization from the State to use water under the doctrine of "prior appropriations." However, depending on the time frame of the land grant in question, the State had also recognized various other water rights, including those of Mexican and Spanish land grants and some riparian rights. Only those water rights formally granted from the State (about 50%) were well defined,

---

1. Hydrologist, Texas Water Commission, P.O. Box 13087, Austin, Texas 78711
2. Engineer, Texas Water Commission, P.O. Box 13087, Austin, Texas 78711

STATE WATERS ADMINISTRATION 709

quantifiable, and subject to regulation.

With this mixed water right system, recurring droughts, and a growing population, it became increasingly difficult for the State to handle water right disputes. In the 1960's, a fifteen year legal battle over water rights in the Lower Rio Grande Valley culminated with the court determination of water rights and a court-appointed watermaster for the Lower Rio Grande.

In 1967, largely in response to this court battle, the Texas Legislature passed the Water Rights Adjudication Act. This Act established a mechanism to make a comprehensive adjudication (determination) of water rights as to quantity, priority date, and conditions of use. Also authorized was the creation of watermaster offices to oversee those water rights. Now, after final determinations of water rights for the Nueces River, San Antonio River, Guadalupe River, and associated coastal basins, the Texas Water Commission has begun a watermaster operation for this region, as shown in Figure 1. This office, the first outside of the Rio Grande, is known as the South Texas Watermaster. It is the first in a series of regional offices which will eventually cover most of the state.

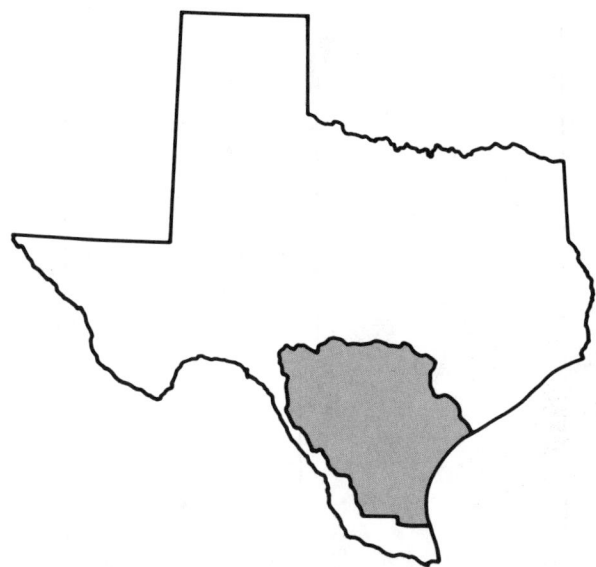

Figure 1 - Jurisdiction of the South Texas Watermaster

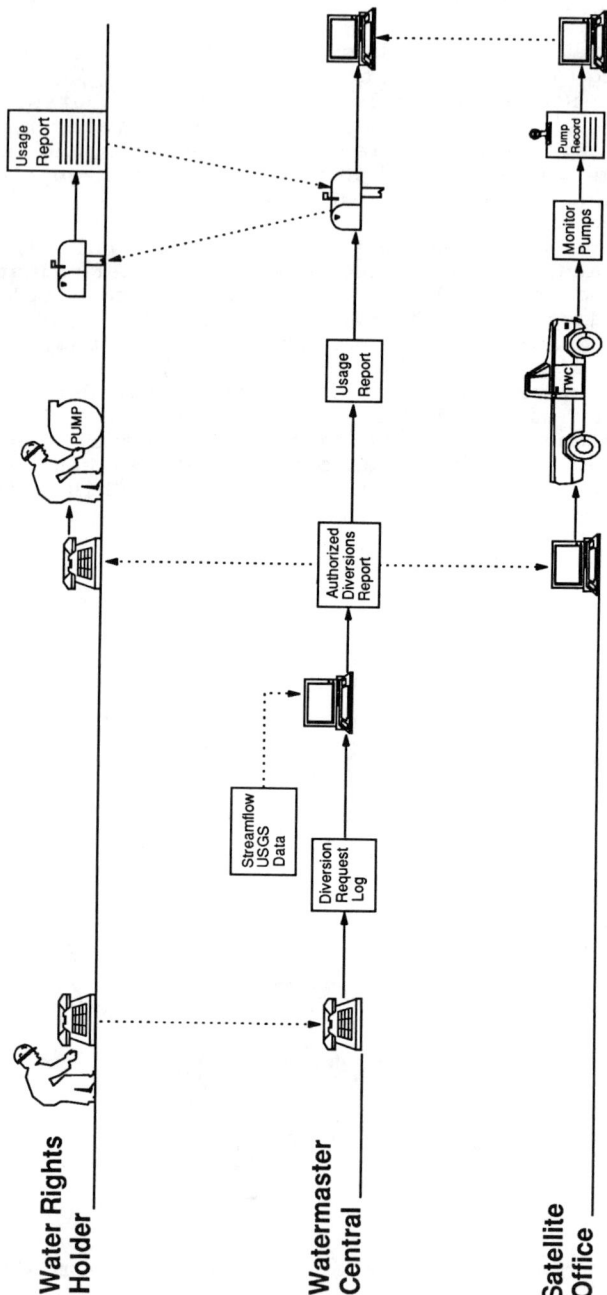

Figure 2 - Flow of information for the watermaster operation

Operations of the Watermaster

The basic task of the South Texas Watermaster is to "divide the [State] water of streams or other sources of supply in his division in accordance with the adjudicated water rights (Vernon's, 1988)." Due to the great size of the river basins involved, and in order to provide for a timely response to water right issues this operation is headquartered in San Antonio, with three field satellite offices.

One of the most important functions of the watermaster is to provide for the lawful allocation of water during drought conditions. To this end, a set of administrative rules has been developed which outlines the role of the watermaster and requirements of the water right holders. Much of the design of the watermaster program has been done with the primacy of this function in mind.

The watermaster rules require that any water right holder file an intent (request) to divert before beginning diversion. The watermaster will then make a collective evaluation, on a daily basis, of all such requests to decide which water right holders may divert water. A central element in this decision process will be a computer model, now under development, to evaluate the ability of predicted streamflow to satisfy the outstanding requests. The central office will serve as a control center for water allocation, with the field offices serving a monitoring role. The actions and communications linkages between the water right holders, the central office, and the field satellites are depicted in Figure 2.

Future Plans

The Texas Water Commission has taken a large step toward the goal of thorough administration of water rights by developing the South Texas Watermaster office. This office opened in San Antonio early in 1988. The Commission plans to begin watermaster operations for the Colorado River in late 1990, and for other Texas river basins in the near future.

References

Freeman, R.J. and M.E. Akers. 1979. Water Rights Adjudication Introduction and Background. Interoffice report, Texas Department of Water Resources. Feb. 1979.

Vernon's Texas Codes Annotated. 1988. Water Code. West Publishing Co., St. Paul, Minn.

WATER FOR TEXANS
Using the Water Development Fund
Bobbie Ray Critendon[1]

This paper is presented to provide information on the Texas Water Development Fund. The Fund is available as a source that can provide financial assistance to political subdivisions of Texas for water, wastewater and flood control projects.

The Texas Water Development Fund was created in 1957 following the severe drought of the early 1950's. With voter approval the Texas Constitution was amended in that year by adding Section 49-c to Article III. This Section authorized the creation of the Texas Water Development Board and empowered the Board to issue $200,000,000 of Texas Water Development bonds, establishing a general obligation of the State under the Texas Constitution. This revolving fund receives all monies from the sale of bonds issued by the Board. With the initial bond proceeds, loans were provided to political subdivisions for the construction of dams, reservoirs, and other water storage projects, including systems necessary for the conveyance of water from storage to treatment and distribution facilities for wholesale purchasers of water. This basic program has been amended in 1962, 1966, 1971, 1982, 1985, 1987, and changes are proposed for 1989.

In the past, funding eligibility was based solely on a hardship criteria. The Fund was available only to political subdivisions that were unable to access the commercial bond market at a reasonable interest rate. Over the years the Legislature, with voter approval, has relaxed the eligibility requirement to include projects for construction of regional water and wastewater facilities, conversion from a ground water supply to a surface water supply, and flood control.

The program has evolved into four financing funds in order to facilitate administrative requirements.

---
[1]Chief, Engineering Section, Texas Water Development Board, P.O. Box 13231, Austin, Texas 78711-3231

These funds are as follows:
Texas Water Development Fund for financing projects related to water supply, wastewater, flood control, and state participation;
Water Assistance Fund for water loan assistance, research and planning, reservoir storage acquisition, irrigation improvements, and agricultural assistance;
State Revolving Fund for construction of wastewater treatment projects; and
Texas Water Resources Fund for the revenue bond program.

Funds for construction are provided predominantly by the Texas Water Development Fund using five separate accounts. These accounts and current available funds are as follows:
1. The water supply account for making loans to construct water projects has approximately $202 million in authorized but unissued bonds remaining;
2. The water quality enhancement account for making loans to construct sewer projects has approximately $289 million in authorized but unissued bonds remaining;
3. The flood control account for making loans to construct flood control projects has approximately $199 million in authorized but unused bonds remaining; and
4. The state participation account for state acquisition of parts of regional water and wastewater facilities and flood retention basins has all $400 million of the authorized amount remaining.

In addition to these accounts construction funds are available in the State Revolving Fund for construction of wastewater treatment facilities.

The procedures by which political subdivisions may receive these funds are generally the same for each account. They include:

Pre-Application Phase
(a) A pre-application conference between Board staff and applicant in which the applicant is represented by an authority of the applicant, a financial advisor, and engineer;
(b) Application preparation by financial advisor and engineer;

Application Phase
(c) Staff review of the application which addresses projected population growth for the area to be served, water availability

to the project area, evaluation of project alternatives and costs estimates, evaluation of environmental impacts and a financial review of the total project;
(d) Development Fund Manager's recommendation to Texas Water Development Board for disposition of the application;
(e) Board consideration of and action on the application;

Pre-Construction Phase

(f) Project design, preparation of plans and specifications for Board approval, and bidding;
(g) Execution of construction contracts and legal review by Board;
(h) Bond purchase and release of funds for construction;

Construction Phase

(i) Construction of project with construction monitoring by Board staff;
(j) Financial monitoring by Board staff;

Post Construction Phase

(k) Final accounting at completion of construction and financial monitoring throughout repayment period of the loan; and
(l) Periodic inspection of project facilities throughout repayment period.

Through September, 1989, 739 loans have been closed of which 353 have been for water supply, 384 for wastewater, and two for flood control. There has never been a default on a Water Development Fund loan.

Changes and additions to the Texas Water Development Fund programs are pending based on legislative action of Texas' 71st Legislature, Regular Session. Some of the changes are administrative in nature but $500 million in additional bond authorization will be added if a constitutional amendment is approved by the voters at the November 1989 election. The $500 million is divided as follows: $250 million for financial assistance on water supply projects; $200 million for wastewater projects; and $50 million for flood control projects. The amendment also would remove the current prohibition against funding retail distribution improvements.

Another aspect of the $500 million authorization will provide financial assistance to economically distressed areas through both loans and grants from the Economically Distressed Areas Fund of the Water Development Fund. Twenty percent of the proposed amount would be dedicated for these areas. Counties

WATER DEVELOPMENT FUND

with unemployment greater than 25 percent above the state average and per capita income 25 percent below the state average as well as all counties adjacent to Mexico would qualify. Legislation has placed a limitation of $25 million on the amount of bonds that could be issued per calendar year.

With passage of this amendment, the Board would have the ability to pay up to fifty percent of a loan unless the Texas Department of Health determines a danger to public health and safety exists from water or sewer problems in the area in which case it could pay more. However, no more than 75 percent of the total principal and interest of bonds authorized can be paid by the state.

An eligible county must either guarantee repayment of debt service on the bonds or provide a minimum of 2.5 percent of the project cost or $500,000. Counties will be given new authorization to issue revenue bonds for water and sewer service under this program. Repayment of the bonds will be determined by the Board based on the use of ability to pay considerations determined by what is paid by other families of similar income for comparable service.

The Board would also be able to provide grants for project engineering under the Research and Planning Fund using $10 million in appropriated funds.

The Board, the Texas Water Commission, and the Texas Department of Health will be required to develop model rules to establish minimum standards for water and sewer service for depressed areas. These rules will have to be adopted by both the county and a municipality containing the proposed service area before an application can be made to the Board for financial assistance. The purpose of the rules will be to prohibit the proliferation of development without adequate water or sewer services.

The Water Development Fund is a financing alternative for providing WATER FOR TEXANS.

THE COMING DROUGHT: ARE YOU READY?

Michael D. Day, P.E.[1]

Abstract

Drought planning is necessary for the orderly development of a water supply system. Long range planning, risk analysis, multi-discipline cooperation, and public awareness are critical to efficiently meet water demands.

Introduction

During the 1950's, North Central Texas experienced the worst drought on record. Drastic emergency measures were necessary to avoid running out of water in Dallas. This experience focused public attention on the importance of water and the necessity for long range water planning.

Dallas is completing its third Long Range Water Supply Study (1957, 1975, and 1989). These studies look 50 years or more into the future to assure an adequate water supply for the 1.5 million people served by the City of Dallas Water Utilities Department. Long range supply studies are supported by operational plans to assure water will be available to each treatment facility and to each customer throughout a drought.

Drought Planning

Orderly development of a water system requires looking at the drought of record under multiple conditions. Annual, monthly, daily, and even hourly conditions must be analyzed. Utilities with multiple supplies have benefited from the use of computer modeling for many years. Dallas has found it possible

---

[1]Deputy Director, City of Dallas, Water Utilities Department, 1500 Marilla, Room 5 A S, Dallas, Texas 75201.

to increase the yield available during a drought through changes in reservoir operations guidelines. Additionally, operating costs can be reduced through maximizing the use of less costly supply sources during wet years.

Microcomputers have made computer modeling available to smaller utilities. To take advantage of this resource, hydrologic data must be developed to determine inflow during a critical drought. Historical data must be adjusted for changes that affect inflow. These changes include additional Soil Conservation Service (SCS) structures, land development, and wastewater treatment plant discharges in the watershed. Historical demand data must be analyzed to derive an estimate of the increase in demand over normal weather likely to occur during an extended drought. Finally, future population and per capita water demand must be projected. This data provides the basis for determining the utility's supply needs during a future drought.

During the drought of the 1950's, water demand jumped by as much as 17% over projected normal weather demand. Ability to meet normal weather demand is no assurance that drought demands can be met. Dallas has invested hundreds of millions of dollars to acquire surface water supplies capable of meeting anticipated drought demands almost twenty years into the future.

Peak day and peak hour demands must be considered in planning water treatment and transmission facilities. Peak day, drought weather conditions are used to size raw water transmission and water treatment facilities. Engineers use peak hour demands to size treated water transmission, storage, and pumping facilities. Dallas has also invested hundreds of millions of dollars to construct facilities capable of meeting peak day drought demands. Dallas' treatment and distribution capability of 700 million gallons (2,650,000 m^3) is now being expanded to 815 million gallons (3,090,000 m^3) per day in agreement with its long range plan. Adequate treatment and delivery capacity is necessary to assure fire protection during these peak demand periods.

Water Conservation

Water conservation planning should be an integral part of any long range water supply plan. Conservation is essential during a drought. Inclining block rate structures, water leak detection and correction programs, metering of all customers, plumbing codes, public education, use of drought tolerant landscape, and retrofit of water conserving plumbing fixtures are methods commonly used to achieve water usage reductions. Public awareness of the importance of water and the need to use it wisely is the cornerstone of a good conservation program. Customers should be informed of the cost benefits they receive from reducing their peak demands on the water system. Facilities used only a few days each year are typically amortized over water purchased throughout the year. Dallas uses a rate structure designed to recover as much of these additional costs as practical during the summer months. This serves as a direct incentive for the customer to reduce high summer demands.

Drought conditions increase the summer demands as citizens attempt of keep their investment in their landscaping from drying up and blowing away. Foundations can be seriously damaged by significant changes in soil moisture. Public information can play an important role in reducing this damage through proper watering techniques. However, the education process must begin long before the drought to be effective.

Emergency Water Management Planning

Drought policies should be developed to deal effectively with a drought even more severe than the historical drought of record. The use of frequency distributions, risk analysis and, again, computer simulations allow the formulation of orderly steps to prevent water shortages. These tools form the basis for decisions affecting day to day operations as well as long range planning. Progressive steps of increased public information, increased efforts to locate additional sources, curtailment of water use by local governmental agencies, and mandatory water rationing may be used to avoid a water crisis.

Coordination between the engineering staff, engineering consultants, the planning and rate making staff, and the operations staff is critical. No single function within the organization can successfully address the myriad of details necessary to plan, design, and construct a water system capable of handling a severe drought. Involvement and coordination of disciplines throughout the department have allowed Dallas to develop a system capable of surviving weather as severe as the drought of the 1950's without resorting to the emergency measures necessary over thirty years ago.

Is Planning Worth The Effort?

The expense and effort required to plan for drought

conditions may not appear justified considering the infrequency with which a severe drought occurs. Citizens and elected officials can be lulled into complacency by ten to twenty years without an extended drought. One of the greatest challenges facing the water utility manager today is keeping this issue in front of those controlling the purse strings. This is difficult to accomplish without appearing as an alarmist. However, the economic loss to a community during an extended drought can be enormous. It is critical that the citizens and elected officials be kept informed of your planning efforts. Without their support, funding will not be available to carry out your plan.

A water utility must be forward looking. The development of a new surface supply can take twenty years. This can be extended almost indefinitely by litigation over environmental concerns. Waiting for the arrival of a drought to begin planning is a prescription for economic disaster. A formal long range water supply plan can bring business leaders, elected officials, and citizens together in recognizing the importance of water to the economic development of the area.

Long range planning is necessary but not sufficient. Each year should be treated as if the drought of record has begun. If surface supplies do not fill during the winter and spring rains, operating plans for the following year should reflect that the second year of the drought of record has begun. In this way, the utility can meet the demands for water when an extended drought does occur. In this way, short term operating efficiencies do not override extended drought needs. There have been two major droughts in the North Central Texas area during the past seventy years. Each of these droughts lasted over six years. When will the drought come? Dallas operates on the assumption that the next drought arrived this year.

With its drought planning in place, Dallas is ready to face a drought with confidence that the economic viability of the North Central Texas area does not suffer. Implementation of the recommendations of the Long Range Water Supply Study will assure that this will continue to be the case fifty (50) years from now.

DROUGHT INDICATION AND RESPONSE

A Model for the South Central Connecticut Regional Water Authority Reservoir System

Ronald J. Nault[1], M. ASCE

Peter Gaewski[2]

David J. Wall[3], M. ASCE

Abstract

A study of rainfall and reservoir level data was conducted on the water supply system of South Central Connecticut to investigate the possibility of developing reliable, easy to use drought indicators. Frequency analysis techniques were employed to formulate a model to determine the stage and severity of a drought occurrence on a real time basis. Threshold triggering levels for below average rainfall and reservoir volume were established to identify five stages of a water supply emergency. Water conservation measures corresponding to the identified drought stage were proposed to extend the use of available water until replenishment.

Introduction

The South Central Connecticut Regional Water Authority (RWA) supplies drinking water to 380,000 people in the City of New Haven and 12 surrounding towns. The RWA relies on surface water to supply more than 85 percent of water used in the system with a series of river diversions and reservoir impoundments.

---
[1]Senior Engineer, Goodkind & O'Dea, Inc., Consulting Engineers, Hamden, Connecticut

[2]Senior Project Engineer, South Central Connecticut Regional Water Authority, New Haven, Connecticut

[3]Professor of Civil and Environmental Engineering, University of New Haven, West Haven, Connecticut

Rainfall in New England is fortunately plentiful and generally uniform. (For the RWA station at North Branford - average precipitation = 48.4 inches/year; the minimum annual recorded rainfall in 137 years of record = 33.1 inches). Therefore, for the RWA system, drought is defined as an extended period of below average rainfall at levels potentially harmful to the safe supply of potable water.

A frequency based model was developed to establish triggering threshold levels to signal drought stage and establish operating rules for water supply emergency conditions. This is in response to a mandatory Drought Contingency Plan required of all water companies by the State of Connecticut Department of Health Services (DOHS). Through the use of drought indicating parameters (rainfall and reservoir level) and the corresponding set of operating rules based on the drought magnitude triggered, critical decisions will not have to be made during the drought under stressed conditions. The predetermined operating rules will leave RWA managers free to focus on other important drought management tasks comfortable in the knowledge that the system is operating under a set of guidelines based on site-specific data and not an arbitrary or reactionary approach. The triggering levels have been set so as not to signal a drought response prematurely and risk losing public confidence, or too late when there is little water left to save.

Methods
Data Analysis:

The foundation of this study was the observed data from a 40 year period of record. This data contains the drought event of the greatest magnitude in 137 years of record (the mid 1960's drought in the Eastern U.S.), which was used to calibrate the model.

Rainfall:

Frequency analysis techniques were used on local rainfall data to establish historically significant drought levels with recurrence intervals varying from 10 to 500 years. This analysis was performed for 12, 24, 36, 48 and 60 month periods because of the RWA's large reservoir system storage (320 days demand capacity when full) which suggests that a critical drought will likely occur from a sustained period of below average rainfall. Table 1 contains the results of this analysis:

Table 1. - Rainfall Statistical Summary

	12 mos.	24 mos.	36 mos.	48 mos.	60 mos.
Mean, $\bar{X}$	48.44"	96.47"	144.36"	192.66"	241.01"
Standard deviation, S	7.38"	12.02"	15.56"	19.13"	23.10"
10 yr.	39.2"	80.6"	123.3"	168.5"	210.8"
20 yr.	37.0"	76.7"	118.8"	161.2"	203.0"
30 yr.	35.8"	73.9"	115.2"	157.8"	199.5"
50 yr.	34.6"	71.8"	111.3"	153.0"	193.0"
75 yr.	33.6"	69.9"	109.5"	150.0"	189.8"
100 yr.	32.9"	68.5"	108.2"	148.2"	187.3"
500 yr.	31.8"	65.5"	104.3"	143.4"	181.5"
Lowest Recorded Value	33.1"	68.0"	106.7"	146.7"	188.9"

Effective Rainfall:

Stormwater runoff that occurs from excess rainfall exists as potential input to the RWA's reservoir system. Quantity and capture efficiency of this runoff is a function of seasonal effects (evapotranspiration, etc.) and reservoir capacity. To model system response to rainfall, research was conducted to determine average monthly reservoir percent capture factors of total rainfall. This factor represents the actual reservoir storage increase divided by the potential input from rainfall events. Table 2 contains the results of this analysis:

Table 2. - Rainfall Percent Capture Factors

JAN	FEB	MAR	APR	MAY	JUN	JUL	AUG	SEP	OCT	NOV	DEC
44	48	58	34	27	22	14	8	11	14	24	29

The Percent Capture Factor was then used itself as a drought indicator to give importance to the timing of rainfall in the water year. Rainfall values alone do not provide an adequate indication of a potential drought. For example, a hypothetical scenario could occur where normal rainfall occurs in the high runoff months of January, February and March filling the reservoirs to normal levels. However, a rainfall deficit in July, August and September could cause the rainfall indicator to trigger a drought response though it probably would not represent a threat to the RWA system. Therefore, rainfall was multiplied by the Percent Capture Factor and a similar statistical analysis was performed to serve as another drought indicator called Effective Rainfall.

Reservoir Storage:

The Rainfall Percent Capture Factors were also used to model reservoir system response to the various drought level rainfalls determined earlier. A reservoir mass balance approach was used whereby monthly input (rainfall multiplied by Percent Capture Factor) was compared to outflow (RWA system demand - projected for the year 1995 with monthly use factors) to determine the change in storage. In this way a drought could be routed through the system to model reservoir drawdown. This technique was carried out for each separate recurrence interval drought rainfall level and duration (12, 34, 36, 48 and 60 months) to determine the critical period. The result of this analysis is the Reservoir Rule Curve to trigger drought stage based on reservoir storage (percent full) as shown in Figure 1.

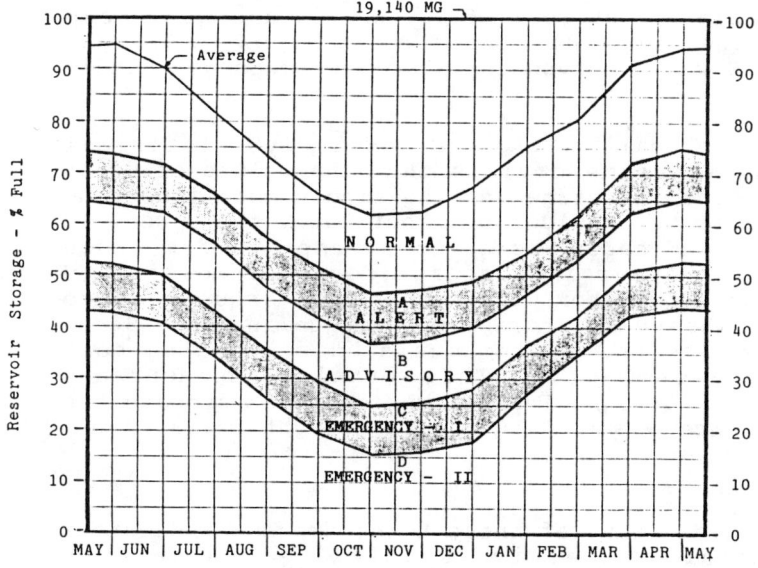

Figure 1. - RWA Reservoir Rule Curve

Results

The three drought indicators - Rainfall, Effective Rainfall and Reservoir Storage were used to form a final Drought Indicator Model and set of corresponding operating rules.

Initial triggering levels were run through the actual system data to determine the frequency and magnitude that each indicator triggered a drought condition. The triggering levels were then adjusted slightly based on desired response to droughts in the past of known significance and effects.

Five drought triggering levels were chosen to conform to the DOHS mandatory drought management plan - A) Drought Alert, B) Drought Advisory, C), D) and E) Drought Emergency Phase I, II and III, respectively. Under this DOHS program, management rules are proposed for each drought stage (under Drought Emergency Phase I-mandatory conservation of 15 percent is dictated through sprinkler bans and other measures, for example) (DOHS, 1986). It is up to the individual water companies to determine the triggering criteria and levels. From this study it was determined to use droughts with a recurrence interval of 20, 30, 50 and 100 years to signal Drought Stages A through D. Drought Stage E was reserved for absolute emergency conditions.

After calibrating the model with historical data, it became obvious that the volume of water in reservoir storage was the single most important factor to be considered. Therefore, the Reservoir Storage indicator was given preemptive dominance over the other indicators (for example, if the Rainfall Indicator was triggering a Drought Stage D but Reservoir Storage was triggering only Stage B, then the RWA system would be responding to a Stage B drought). This final adjustment has yielded a Drought Indicator Model that signals the occurrence and magnitude of a drought reliably.

Conclusions

Development of these three drought indicators - Rainfall, Effective Rainfall and Reservoir Storage, with triggering levels based on site-specific data can be an effective tool in drought management. The methods used will help to separate normal system variations from potentially harmful drought events. The adoption of operating rules based on these indicators removes the burden of decision making on water company managers in times of crisis. The result may be to extend the use of available water in a real drought or prevent the unnecessary loss of revenue and public confidence from a premature call for mandatory water restrictions.

Appendix I. References

Connecticut Department of Health Services (1986) Individual Water Supply Plan Guidance Handbook

Appendix II. S. I. Conversions

1 inch = 2.54 centimeters
1 gallon = 3.79 liters

TRANSFERABLE RATIONS FOR DROUGHT MANAGEMENT?

Robert U. Reed, A.M. ASCE and Jay R. Lund, A.M. ASCE[1]

INTRODUCTION

A common water rationing approach for drought management restricts each household or enterprise to water use below a given level. Water use below the allotment level is charged at some "normal" or "base" rate while water use above the allotment is charged at a significantly higher rate often called an "excess use charge" (DWR 1988a). Where households and commercial enterprises are heterogeneous in terms of how they value water, such rationing programs can cause controversy between those high-demand and low water demand users. This controversy detracts from the overall conservation intent of rationing programs. Moreover, such simple rationing is economically inefficient in that water is not targeted to the highest valued uses.

This paper examines the concept of transferable water rations from an economic perspective. Transferable water rations may improve efficiency in the distribution of water by allowing customers to reallocate rations after being initially distributed by the water district. While transferable water rations may improve economic efficiency, its benefits may be limited and outweighed by transaction costs and wealth redistributional affects which benefit program participants at the expense on non-participants.

WATER RATIONING

Economists suggest that price can be used to efficiently allocate scarce water supplies (Moncur 1989). Several practical problems limit the use of price to allocate water during droughts. Demand for water is relatively inelastic, ranging from -0.1 to -0.4 for urban water districts (Mercer & Morgan 1989, DWR 1988). Price increases of 25 to 100 percent would be required to decrease demand by 10 percent causing excess revenue problems for public water districts. Public policy considerations require some minimum quantity of water be available at low cost to satisfy basic needs. Furthermore, customers seem willing to voluntarily reduce their demand for water when serious water conditions are perceived. Therefore, voluntary and mandatory use restrictions (DWR 1988a, DWR 1989) are effective drought response measures.

Absolute physical rationing is the other extreme of the rationing spectrum. Under absolute physical rationing a maximum quantity of water is fixed for each customer, and customers are prohibited from exceeding the limit (Mercer & Morgan 1989). Absolute rationing is economically inefficient and inflexible. The

---

[1] Post-Graduate Research Engineer and Assistant Professor, respectively, Department of Civil Engineering, University of California, Davis, CA 95616.

allocation of water rations to customers is a critical and often controversial decision; the inflexibility of absolute rationing exacerbates this problem.

A more common approach to water rationing consists of establishing water reduction goals with specific customer allotments to meet the goals, and the encouraging customers to achieve water reduction goals through a steeply increasing block rate structure (DWR 1988b).

A simple model of water rationing using a fixed allotment appears in Figure 1. An allotment is established at 12 units (CCF) per month per customer (about 300 gpd), based on supply forecasts and anticipated duration of the drought. The initial price for water is $1/unit (assumed to be the same as the normal water rate), and is operative below the allotment. Above the allotment a higher price, $3.00, is used to discourage excessive water use.

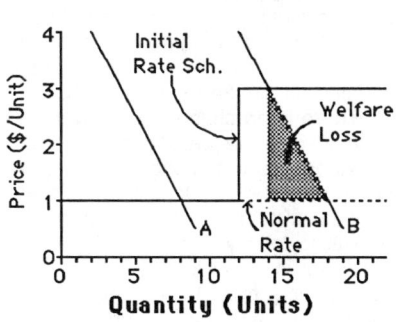

FIGURE 1
WATER RATIONING
Initial Condition

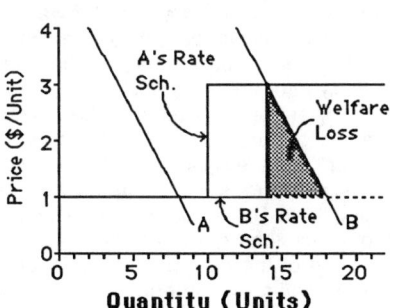

FIGURE 2
TRANSFERABLE WATER RATIONS
First Phase

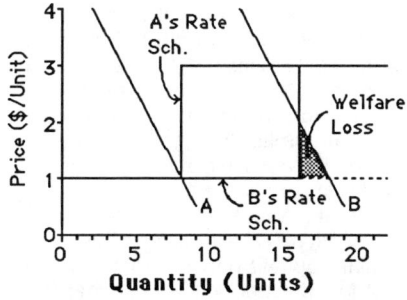

FIGURE 3
TRANSFERABLE WATER RATIONS
Second Phase

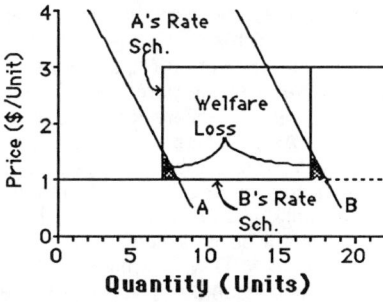

FIGURE 4
TRANSFERABLE WATER RATIONS
Third Phase

Demand functions for two customers, A and B, are shown in Figure 1. Differences in demand could result from many factors including income, household size, lot size, geographic location, etc. Customer A is unaffected by the rationing program since his demand, at 8 units, falls below the allotment. However, customer B is affected by the fixed allotment. Under water rationing, B would choose to use 14 units, the welfare loss associated with this restricted use is represented by the shaded area and has a value of $4. The efficiency of any rationing program can be measured by the total welfare losses which occur. All rationing programs result in welfare losses since supplies are limited. However, economic efficiency is maximized when the welfare loss in minimized.

TRANSFERABLE WATER RATIONS

Transferable water rations have been studied by the authors as a possible means of improving the efficiency of water allocations during droughts. The concept is similar to rationing with resale suggested by Mercer & Morgan (1989). Transferable water rations would allow customers using less than their allotments to sell unused rations (the right to buy water at the normal or base rate) to customers with higher demands having to pay the higher (excess use) rate. A numerical example using the rationing situation depicted in Figure 1 illustrates the concept and highlights its strengths and weaknesses. For clarity, three phases of the transfer are illustrated.

In the first phase (Figure 2), customer B would be willing to pay customer A up to $4 for two units of unused water rations. The exact price would be between $0 and $4 (assuming no transaction costs) and would depend on agreement between A and B. The practical effect of the transaction is to reallocate water rations from A to B, in effect altering each of their rate schedules as illustrated in Figure 2.

What are the effects of this transaction? There is no change in the welfare loss and therefore no increase in economic efficiency since the water use by each customer (and the price to be paid for additional water) has not changed. However, there is a $4 transfer of surplus from producer (the water district) to consumer resulting from B's ability to purchase two additional units of water at the normal rate of $1 instead of the $3 rate he is otherwise willing to pay. The actual distribution of the consumer surplus depends on the price paid for the rations. This observation is important since public water districts must be revenue neutral in the long-term, and therefore producer surplus must net to zero. Since the transfer of water rations results in a drain of producer surplus the water district would have to raise water rates to cover the loss. Therefore participants in the transferable water ration program would benefit at the expense of non-participating customers.

Water ration transfers would continue in a second phase illustrated in Figure 3. Customer A still has two unused water rations which could be sold without affecting his own consumption. Customer B would be willing to buy them at a maximum cost of $3 (equal to the value of the cost savings of purchasing additional water at the normal rate). In this situation there is a decrease in welfare loss (total welfare loss is only $1) and therefore an increase in economic efficiency. At the same time there is no transfer of surplus from producer to consumer. A's consumption is again unchanged and B's consumption rises because he is now able to purchase additional water at the lower "normal" rate.

Finally, in the third phase (Figure 4) customer A can continue to sell water rations if he is willing to reduce his consumption. The transfer of water rations from A to B will continue until the marginal benefit derived from the last unit of water consumed by A is the same as that for B. Specifically, customer B would be willing to pay up to $0.75 for one additional unit. Customer A would require payment of at least $0.25 to compensate for his restricted use. A net reduction in welfare loss of $0.50 occurs, and again there is no loss of producer surplus.

The total result of the transfer of water rations from customer A to B is an increase in economic efficiency (total welfare loss is only $0.50) and a transfer of producer surplus to consumers (A and B) of $4 which is ultimately paid for by customers. This numerical example illustrates several ramifications of transferable water rations. The outcome of any actual transferable water ration program would depend on many factors. For example if the initial allocation were an absolute physical limit to a customer's use and subsequent trading of rations were permitted, then the program would result in increased efficiency without the transfer of surplus from producer to consumer.

EQUITY OF WATER RATIONING

Issues of equity, or fairness, arise in any discussion of rationing and because equity is a highly subjective criterion, the issue is often controversial. Efficient allocation of water is not necessarily equitable. Equity is determined primarily by the initial allocation of water rations and is affected little by subsequent trading. As noted above however, the transferable water rations may result in additional costs being borne by the water district (loss of producer surplus). To the extent that these costs are ultimately borne by all water users the transferable water ration program would tend to benefit participants at the expense of non-participants.

Since the initial allocation of water rations affects customers differently, it often becomes a critical, and political, decision by the governing body of the water district. Transferable water rations may offer insights but do not solve the equity problem.

WATER CONSERVATION BENEFITS

What are the water conservation benefits of transferable water rations? By selling water rations, customers benefit from lower water use, thus it seems that conservation is encouraged. More important is that a transferable rationing program would encourage customers to ponder how much water they use, how much water they can save, and the value of that water to them. Therefore, the mere existence of a transfer program may have the benefits of encouraging customers to be more informed about their water use.

Malueg (1989) evaluates the claim that pollutant emission credit trading programs increase a firm's incentive to invest in more effective pollution abatement technology. A similar analysis of transferable water rations shows that transferable rations do not necessarily increase a customer's incentive to adopt new water conservation measures during rationing; rather the incentive may increase or decrease depending on the position in the market (as buyer or seller of rations). Where a customer is a buyer of water rations, his incentive to adopt new conservation methods is reduced by the transferable ration program.

MARKET MECHANISMS

Several mechanisms are possible for a market in transferable water rations. Markets in transferable property rights have been suggested or implemented in other areas including pollution permits, shares in a mutual water company, gasoline rationing, and others. Possible market mechanisms for transferable water rations include:
- Single price auction as described by Lyon (1982) and Hahn (1988),
- Bid/ask price system similar to stock markets,
- Water district acting as broker, and
- Coupons as proposed for gasoline rationing in the 1970s.

Design of any market mechanism would depend on specific conditions of the situation. Howe, et al.(1986) identified several desirable characteristics for resource allocation mechanisms, these included: flexibility in the allocation, security of tenure, simplicity/predictability of outcome, equity, and efficiency. Other factors to consider in designing a program in transferable water rations are: information and transaction costs, opportunity costs, legal and institutional constraints, temporal aspects of droughts and rationing, and the initial allocation of rations.

CONCLUSIONS

The preceding example illustrates how a program of transferable water rations may lead to some efficiency gains in the allocation of limited water supplies during droughts. It also highlights some of the problems associated with transferable water rations such as equity and implementation. Indeed, in some situations transferable water rations may result in only a redistribution of wealth to program participants from other customers. This is certainly counter to the intent of a rationing program.

Transferable water rations would be effective if implemented in an environment of absolute water rationing. In this case, the ability to transfer rations provides the flexibility to reach a more efficient allocation of water. All transfers would result in reduced welfare loss.

REFERENCES

Browning, E. K. and J. M. Browning (1986), Microeconomic Theory and Practice, Second Edition, Little, Brown and Co., Boston, Massachusetts.

California, Department of Water Resources (1988a), Water Conservation Guidebook No. 7: Urban Drought Guidebook, March 1988.

California, Department of Water Resources (1988b), Water Conservation Guidebook No. 9: Guidebook on Conservation-Oriented Water Rates, Oct. 1988.

Dziegielewski, B. (1986), "Drought Management Options" in Drought Management and Its Impact on Public Water Systems, National Academy Press, Wash. D. C.

Hahn, R. W. (1988), "Promoting Efficiency and Equity Through Institutional Design", Policy Sciences, Vol. 21, pp. 41-66.

Howe, C. W., D. R. Schurmeier, and W. D. Shaw, Jr. (1986), "Innovative Approaches to Water Allocation: The Potential for Water Markets", Water Resources Research, Vol. 22, No.4, pp. 439-445, April 1986.

Lyon, R. M. (1982), "Auctions and Alternative Procedures for Allocating Pollution Rights", Land Economics, Vol. 58, No. 1, pp. 16-31, February 1982.

Malueg, D. A. (1989), "Emission Credit Trading and the Incentive to Adopt New Pollution Abatement Technology", Journal of Environmental Economics and Management, 16, pp. 52-57.

Mercer, L. J. and W. D. Morgan (1989), "Welfare Effects of Alternative Water Rationing Schemes: A Case Study", Water Resources Bulletin, Vol. 25, No. 1, pp. 203-210.

Moncur, J. E. T. (1989), "Drought Episodes Management: The Role of Price", Water Resources Bulletin, Vol. 25, No. 3, pp. 499-505.

Reed, R. U. (1990), Transferable Allocations in Water Management: Short- and Long-Term, M.S. Thesis, Department of Civil Engineering, University of California, Davis, California.

Saliba, B. C. and D. B. Bush (1987), Water Markets in Theory and Practice: Market Transfers, Water Values, and Public Policy, Studies in Water Policy and Management, No. 12, Westview Press, Boulder, Colorado.

FLOWNETS BY COMPUTER GRAPHICS

Sarma V. Seemanapalli[1] and Vijay P. Singh[2], M.ASCE

Abstract

A new method of drawing flownets for determining seepage losses in earth dams is developed. The flow and equipotential lines are drawn by modifying Kinzelbagh's method. The modification allows adjustable spacing between the grid lines and attains greater accuracy. Even a part of the flow domain can be analyzed to obtain the grid that further simplifies the analysis.

Introduction

A flow net consists of a family of interrelated equipotential and flow lines. These lines are usually drawn using the artifice of Forchheimer (1924). The family of curves forming squares can be drawn by trial and error procedure, based on the condition of orthogonal intersection of lines in isotropic media. Due to unrealistic assumptions, the results by Forchheimer's method may, however, be erroneous for general cases. Hence, another method is developed for constructing flownets under more realistic conditions.

Construction of Flownets

It is customary to draw the ϕ-ψ flownet, as shown in Fig. 1, with constant increments between any two adjacent equipotentials, such that stream tubes carry equal discharge as governed by Darcy's law. For

---

[1]Visiting Faculty and Post-Doctoral Researcher, Department of Civil Engineering, Louisiana State University, Baton Rouge, LA 70803-6405
[2]Professor of Civil Engineering and Coordinator, Water Resources Program, Louisiana State University, Baton Rouge, LA 70803-6405

each stream tube, the elemental discharge, ΔQ is given by

$$\Delta Q = T\Delta n_1 \frac{\Delta \phi}{\Delta s_1} = T\Delta_2 \frac{\Delta \phi}{\Delta s_2} \quad (1)$$

or

$$= K\Delta n_1 \frac{\Delta \phi}{\Delta s_1} = K\Delta_2 \frac{\Delta \phi}{\Delta s_2}$$

where T = transmissivity for aquifers, with $T = K$, the permeability coefficient for the case of earth dams, n_1, n_2, s_1, s_2 = dimensions as shown in Fig. 1.

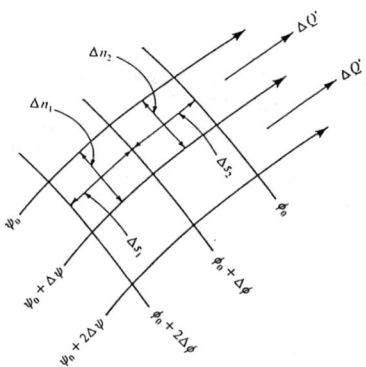

Figure 1. Flownet Showing Grid of Equipotential and Flow Lines.

From Eq. (1), one obtains that

$$\frac{\Delta n_1}{\Delta s_1} = \frac{\Delta n_2}{\Delta s_1} \quad (2)$$

The ratio of $\Delta n/\Delta s$ is constant for homogeneous media and is not constant for non-homogeneous media. Furthermore, the transmissivity is seen to be inversely proportional to the hydraulic gradient. The spacing of equipotentials will be closer in the low transmissivity region and farther in high transmissivity region.

Flow lines are so chosen that the flow tubes carry equal discharge or seepage flow. To that end, the potential head difference should be in equal intervals. Consequently, the flownet can be approximated graphically.

It is difficult to draw flownets under anisotropy or stratification. A new method is developed to draw flownets under sufficiently general conditions. The method consists of two parts. In the first part, the potential heads at the corners of a grid are determined either by a sand-box experiment or more accurately through a resistance-capacitance (R-C) network. The R-C network uses a panel for simulating the conditions in field. The panel consists of a 2m x 3m board, on which resistors (varying from 5 ohms to 5 x 10^6 ohms) and capacitors (10 to 100 micro-farads) are mounted. A variety of resistors and capacitors are available to simulate any situation, with varying permeabilities and storage coefficients. The hydraulic heads can also be determined through numerical techniques for steady or unsteady cases (Wang and Anderson, 1982).

The second part consists of implanting the hydraulic heads to the nodal points of the grid, say 10H x 5V or 20H x 10V, depending on the precision desired. With initial and boundary conditions known, the flownet can be drawn by computer, following the method suggested by Kinzelbagh (1986).

Three computer programs developed by Wolfgang (1986) were used: the Data Input program for the General Flow Model, the General Flow Model program, and the Isolines program. The first two programs were modified for earth dams. The isolines program is changed to suit the nodal points of both the potential and flow lines.

The novel features of this method include:
(1) The method is applicable to simulate the whole or part of the flow domain, while still computing the seepage losses within the embankment of given permeability or storage characteristics. (2) A flexible scale factor can be adopted to enlarge or reduce the size of the figure. (3) Keeping the number of equipotential steps constant (say 10 or 20), the number of stream tubes remains the only variable to be found.

Other parameters such as total hydraulic head, H, in meters, and overall permeability of the medium, K, in m/day, are treated as constant in a steady state situation.

An Example of a Homogeneous
Earthen Dam with Filters

An analogy between flow of water through soils and flow of electricity is used. Accordingly, the seepage discharge is analogous to electric current, pressure-head to voltage and hydraulic conductivity to electrical conductivity.

The earth dam model, as mounted on a resistance-capacitance (R-C) network panel that is 5m long and 2m deep, is as shown below:

U/S W/L 10m————.01.02
Upstream Side   .03.04.05.06.07.08   Downstream Side
.09.10.11.12.13.14.15.16.17.18
.19.20.21.22.23.24.25.26.27.28.29.30.31.32
33.34.35.36.37.38.39.40.41.42.43.44.45.46.47.48.49————0m D/S W/L

The positions of points 1 to 49 represent the corresponding terminals of the resistors where the resistances are measured. Each resistor looks like a plug, with two terminals, separated by a distance of 5cm. Between two such resistors is given space for co-axial capacitors to be plugged in the "nodes." At these nodal points, capacitors of value, either 10 or 100 micro-farads, may be plugged into. These capacitors will act as storage cells to represent stored water in an earth dam that can be released with time. Thus, the capacitors can simulate time-variant phenomena.

The mass of the earthen embankment is represented by 250 k-ohm resistors, signifying soil permeability of 0.001 m/day. As filter material, 50-kohms resistors were used to simulate the material of the filter, five times more porous than the material of the earth dam.

A constant upstream water level of 10m, equal to 10 Volts was kept throughout the study, while the downstream water was at zero level. Hydraulic heads measured in meters by direct and inverse circuits at these points are shown below:

1-10/7.47	2-7.98/10	3-10/2.0	4-10/3.67
5-10/5.7	6-5.94/7.72	7-3.91/10	8-2.91/10
9-10/0.715	10-10/1.07	11-7.67/1.89	12-6.59/2.69
13-5.28/3.77	14-4.04/5.2	15-2.86/6.47	16-1.99/7.57
17-1.13/10	18-0.77/10	19-10/0.085	20-10/0.16
21-6.29/0.38	22-5.12/0.61	23-4.05/0.9	24-3.34/1.41
25-2.67/1.92	26-2.06/2.63	27-1.60/3.27	28-1.03/3.98
29-0.65/5.02	30-0.40/6.19	31-0.17/10	32-0.11/10

33 to 49 - 0/10

Numbers 1 to 49 are nodal points, each of which is given two voltage values. The first number 10, say for node 01 represents the 10m head or 10 volts of potential difference. The second number at node 01, namely 7.47, signifies that a voltage of 7.47 V was registered at node 01 for the inverse case, when the circuit was reversed, changing the boundary conditions in the ϕ-ψ network. Similarly, for the remaining nodes, the first number indicates the value as recorded by direct measurement and the second one the required head/voltage needed for drawing the flow lines.

For analysis of voltages/heads, not all the values at the 49 nodes are essential. A grid, rectangular or square, consisting of the upper and lower boundaries and any of the internal (interior) or external (boundary) nodes would suffice for the sake of analysis. Thus, the grid chosen for the homogeneous case consists of points: 3 to 8, 11 to 16, 23 to 28, and 39 to 44. The corresponding voltages/heads for the homogeneous case, for the 6 x 4 = 24 points, representing 24 values of hydraulic head, as well as equal number of inverse heads to graphically obtain equipotential and flow lines are taken from the readings given above.

Impregnation of filters in earth dams increases their stability. The L-shaped filter was implanted in the earth dam model. This is comprised of nodes 5-6 to 41-42 and 25-32 to 41-49.

Discussion of Results

The results of graphical output shown in Fig. 2a-b are furnished in Table 1. The upstream head applied, the number of stream tubes, equipotential drops and seepage losses, as calculated on the basis of permeability coefficient, K = 0.001 m/day, are given therein. For the homogeneous embankment, Fig. 2a shows the flownet. With the number of steps, N_ϕ chosen as 10/.65 = 15.38, number of stream tubes, N_ψ was calculated as 10/0.50 = 20. Using this data, Eq. (1) gives seepage loss per meter length of the dam as Q_1 = 0.013 cm.m/day.

Fig. 2b and Table 1 show the results of the case when an L-shaped filter was implanted. The effect of the filter is to have more number of stream tubes in the flow domain, which consequently increases the seepage discharge. This results in increased stability of the embankment.

In the present case, a 120% increase is recorded in earth dam filter as compared to that of homogeneous embankment.

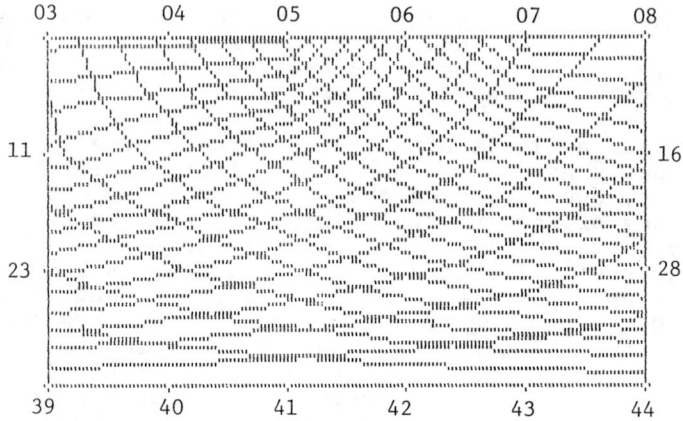

a. Homogeneous earthen embankment;
   Nodes 3-8-44-39-3 for the grid;
   $Q_{homogeneous} = 0.0130$ m^3/s/m.

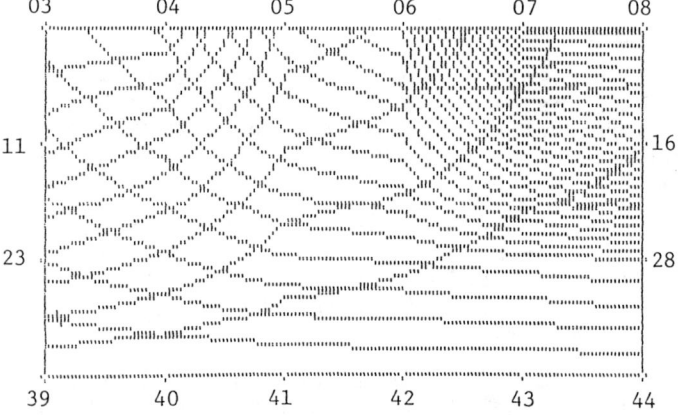

b. Earth dam with L-shaped filter;
   Nodes 5-6-26-32-49-41-5 form the
   grid; $Q_{L-filter} = 0.0286$ m^3/s/m.

Figure 2. Flownets for Homogeneous Embankment
          and Dam with L-shaped Filter

Table 1. Seepage in Homogeneous Earth Dam with Filter

Case Under Study	No. of Eqi-potentials	No. of Stream-tubes	Seepage (m^3/day/m)	Percent Increase
Homogeneous Embankment	15.38	20.00	0.0130	---
With L-shaped Filter	10.00	28.57	0.0286	120

U/S Head = 10m; Permeability Coeff., K = 0.001 m/day; K_{filter} = 5K.

Conclusions

The computer method of drawing flownets is a useful tool in solving seepage problems in earth dams. For attaining greater precision in the flownets, tolerance of the resistors should be such that the variation within the numerous resistors is minimal. Also, the network adopted for the earth dam model could be much larger so as to accommodate 10 to 15 vertical nodes, instead of only 5 rows, in which case the intersections in the network would be near-orthogonal.

Acknowledgments

The authors acknowledge the help rendered by Messrs. M. Wolfgang, G. Sergio, C. Galvao, S. Sastry and P. Everaldo for the suggestions given during modification of the programs. The visiting faculty is grateful for the help rendered through CNPq, a Federal Research Organ in Brasilia, DF.

References

1. Forchheimer, P., 1924, "Hydraulik (Hydraulics)," Dritte Auflage, Verlag and Druck von B. G. Teubner, Leipzig and Berlin, pp. 1-448.
2. Kinzelbagh, W., 1986, "Groundwater Modelling," in Developments in Water Science, Elsevier, New York, Vol. 26, pp. 1-336.
3. Leliavsky, S., 1955, Irrigation and Hydraulic Design, Chapman & Hall, London, Vol. 1.
4. Wang, H. F. and Anderson, M. P., 1982, Introduction to Groundwater Modeling, W. H. Freeman and Co., San Francisco, pp. 1-237.

A TWO-DIMENSIONAL MODEL FOR ESTIMATING
LEACHATE FLOW IN LANDFILLS

By

Shabbir Ahmed[1], R. M. Khanbilvardi[2],

John Fillos[3], and Philip Gleason[4].

ABSTRACT

A numerical model has been developed to compute the leachate flow from solid waste landfills in an unsteady state condition. The two-dimensional moisture flow equation along with the boundary conditions has been solved by using an implicit finite-difference scheme in a vertical plane. The boundary conditions include computation for evapotranspiration, runoff from landfill surface, and infiltration from precipitation into the solid waste inside the landfill. The leachate accretion rate is obtained from the time-history of moisture content. The leachate accretion rate onto the bottom of the landfill helps develop the leachate mound. Solution of the saturated leachate flow equation at the bottom of the landfill gives lateral flow towards the perimeter or the collection system in the landfill. Also, vertical flow through the bottom clay layer is computed by using the concept of Darcy's law. The model was applied to a sample section of a landfill in order to demonstrate the prediction of runoff, evapotranspiration, net infiltration, and leachate flow components in a landfill.

1. Ph.D. Candidate, Department of Civil Engineering, The City University of New York, The City College, N. Y. 10031.
2. Associate Professor; Department of Civil Engineering, The City University of New York, The City College. N. Y. 10031.
3. Associate Professor; Department of Civil Engineering, The City University of New York, The City College, N. Y. 10031.
4. Director of Landfill Engineering, New York City Department of Sanitation.

INTRODUCTION

Leachate is formed from the portion of precipitation that remains after runoff and evapotranspiration and infiltrates through the solid waste landfill. The flow extracts dissolved or suspended materials from the solid waste causing potential contamination of groundwater. The magnitude and timing of the discharged leachate can be determined by solution of the governing equations for the unsaturated and saturated zones of the landfill. The governing equations associated with the boundary and initial conditions and their solution lead to the development of mathematical models. The models formulated to predict leachate flow discharge by Fenn et al. (1975), Dass et al. (1977), Perrier and Gibson (1980), and Gee (1981) are based on hydrologic water balance technique which considers the relationship among precipitation, runoff, evapotranspiration, and change in soil moisture in the cover soil. The Hydrologic Evaluation of Landfill Performance (HELP) model developed by Schroeder et al. (1984) is a quasi two-dimensional deterministic model to compute leachate flow in a quasi-steady state flow condition. Application of unsteady unsaturated flow models in the field of solid waste landfills for leachate flow estimation is still at a very early stage. A time-variation one-dimensional leachate flow model was developed by Korfiatis et al. (1984). None of the afore-mentioned models consider strictly the two-dimensional leachate flow and computation for surface runoff for different slopes of the landfill upper boundary. It is necessary to study adequately the complex moisture flow process through the wastes including evapotranspiration process and runoff considering the effect of side slope in order to obtain an accurate spatial variation and time-history of the leachate flow components.

The objective of this paper is to develop a two-dimensional leachate flow model considering computation for runoff, evapotranspiration, and infiltration at the upper boundary of the landfill. The model was applied to an example of landfill section to predict these flow components using the rainfall data from New York City Department of Environmental Protection and default soil and climatologic data from the HELP model (Schroeder et al., 1984).

UNSATURATED MOISTURE FLOW

The governing equation in the unsaturated zone is obtained by combining Darcy's law with the hydraulic conductivity as a function of moisture content and equation of continuity in two-dimensional unsteady state condition. The two-dimensinal unsaturated moisture flow equation can be expressed as (Jensen, 1983 and Korfiatis et al., 1984) :

$$\partial/\partial x (D(\theta) \partial\theta/\partial x) + \partial/\partial z (D(\theta) \partial\theta/\partial z) - \partial K(\theta)/\partial z = \partial\theta/\partial t \quad (1)$$

where,

θ = volumetric moisture content (vol/vol),
$K(\theta)$ = unsaturated hydraulic conductivity (L/T), and
$D(\theta)$ = diffusivity coefficient (L^2/T)

The boundary condition at the upper surface of the landfill is defined by the input as precipitation less evapotranspiration and runoff. The modified Penman method developed by Ritchie (1972) is used to compute the potential evapotranspiration. The kinematic wave equation (Bras, 1990) is used to compute runoff which is described later.

The lower boundary condition is defined as follows (Korfiatis et al., 1984):

$$z = d, \quad \partial\theta/\partial z = 0 \quad (2)$$

where, d = total depth of landfill (L).

An implicit finite-difference expression of equation (1) for a general internal node (i,j) can be written as :

$$[D_{i+1/2,j}^{k+1}(\theta_{i+1,j}^{k+1} - \theta_{i,j}^{k+1}) - D_{i-1/2,j}^{k+1}(\theta_{i,j}^{k+1} - \theta_{i-1,j}^{k+1})]/(\Delta x)^2 + [D_{i,j+1/2}^{k+1}(\theta_{i,j+1}^{k+1} - \theta_{i,j}^{k+1}) - D_{i,j-1/2}^{k+1}(\theta_{i,j}^{k+1} - \theta_{i,j-1}^{k+1})]/(\Delta z)^2 - (K_{i,j+1/2}^{k+1} - K_{i,j-1/2}^{k+1})/\Delta z = (\theta_{i,j}^{k+1} - \theta_{i,j}^{k})/\Delta t \quad (3)$$

This system of algebraic equations is solved by the successive application of the Gauss-Seidel iteration method.

SURFACE RUNOFF

Overland flow of water on an inclined rough surface is governed by the equation as follows (Bras, 1990):

$$\partial h/\partial t + \alpha \, \partial h^m/\partial x = \bar{q} \qquad (4)$$

where,

h = depth of runoff (L),
$\alpha = 1.49 \, S^{1/2}/n$,
S = slope,
n = roughness coefficient,
$\bar{q} = p - f$,
p = rainfall rate (L/T),
f = infiltration rate (L/T), and
$m = 1.67$.

Infiltration is a function of moisture content, hydraulic conductivity, and depth of water at the soil surface. The infiltration equation developed by Philip (1969) takes into consideration the effect of the afore-mentioned parameters and is expressed as follows:

$$f = 0.5 \ast \{2K_s(\Theta_s - \Theta_i)(h + h_c)\}^{1/2}/\sqrt{t} \qquad (5)$$

where,

K_s = hydraulic conductivity at saturation (L/T),
Θ_s = moisture content at saturation (vol/vol),
Θ_i = initial moisture content (vol/vol),
h = depth of water at the soil surface (L),
h_c = capillary head (L), and
t = time.

The explicit expression for equation (4) for a general node (i+1) was defined by Bras (1990) with the stability criterion as follows :

$$h_{i+1}{}^{k+1} = \bar{q}\,\Delta t + h_{i+1}{}^{k}[1 - \alpha(\Delta t/\Delta x)(h_{i+1}{}^{k})^{m-1}]$$
$$+ \alpha(\Delta t/\Delta x)(h_i{}^k)^m \qquad (6)$$

The stability criterion for the convergence of this scheme is :

$$\alpha\,mh^{m-1}(\Delta t/\Delta x) \leq 1 \qquad (7)$$

The solution procedure at each segment consists of solving for the depth of flow (h) at time $t = k$ and then advancing solution forward to time level $t = k+1$ considering the values of h at the previous time level t as the initial condition.

SATURATED LEACHATE FLOW

The saturated leachate flow submodel describes the unsteady state variation of the leachate mound head due to leachate accretion rate onto the leachate mound and is expressed as (Demetracopoulos, 1988):

$$[K_s h(\partial h/\partial x + \tan\beta)] + N_1 - K_c(h + d)/d = n_e \partial h/\partial t$$

$$(8)$$

where,

$N_1 = K(\theta) - D(\theta)\partial\theta/\partial z$
N_1 = leachate accretion rate onto the leachate mound (L/T),
$T = K_s h$,
T = coefficient of transmissivity (L^2/T),
K_s = saturated hydraulic conductivity of the waste (L/T),
h = head of leachate mound (L),
β = angle of inclination of the bottom clay (degree),
K_c = saturated hydraulic conductivity of the bottom clay (L/T),
d = thickness of clay at the bottom of the landfill (L), and
n_e = effective porosity of the waste in the leachate mound (dimensionless).

The implicit finite-difference expression for

equation (8) for a general node (i) can be written as :

$$[T_{i+1/2}^{k+1}(h_{i+1}^{k+1} - h_i^{k+1}) - T_{i-1/2}^{k+1}(h_i^{k+1} - h_{i-1}^{k+1})]/(\Delta x)^2 - K_{si}\tan\beta_i(h_{i+1}^{k+1} - h_{i-1}^{k+1})/(2\Delta x) + N_{li} - K_{ci}(h_i^{k+1} + d_i)/d_i$$

$$= n_{ei}(h_i^{k+1} - h_i^k)/\Delta t \qquad (9)$$

The values of leachate mound head at all grid points are the only unknowns in equation (9) and are solved simultaneously at each time step by using the Gauss-Seidel iteration method.

APPLICATION

The model was applied to an example of landfill area as shown in Figure 1. An average section of this landfill area is shown in Figure 2 which is schematized into a network of 77 nodal areas. The information of hydraulic conductivity, initial moisture content, and lengths of intervals in x (horizontal) and z (vertical) directions for these nodal areas are given as input into the model. The information necessary to run the model for this example of landfill section is summarized in Table 1.

The climatological data (temperature and solar radiation) for one year and soil data (porosity, field capacity, and wilting point) are used from the default values of the HELP model (Schroeder et al., 1984). Rainfall data from New York City Department of Environmental Protection was analysed for the period 1949-1955 and the rainfall data for the year (1954) closest to the average was selected to run the model. Wehran (1983) determined hydraulic conductivity for solid wastes in Section 6/7 of Fresh Kills landfill to be 0.02 cm/sec. This value of hydraulic conductivity is used for the purpose of leachate flow computation in the present example of landfill section.

The monthly variations of precipitation, evapotranspiration, runoff, and net infiltration are shown in Figure 3. It is observed that the total loss due to runoff and evapotranspiration reduces the net infiltration into the solid waste landfill. The

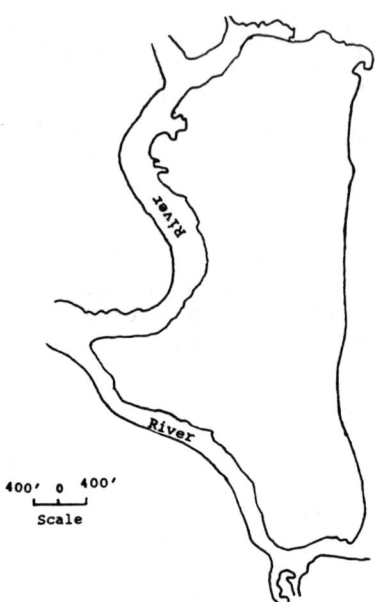

Figure 1. An example of landfill area.

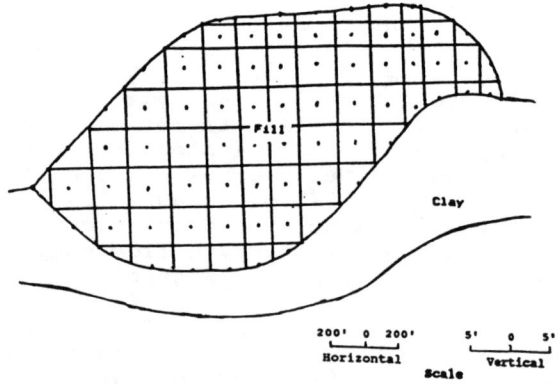

Figure 2. Average vertical section.

ESTIMATING LEACHATE FLOW

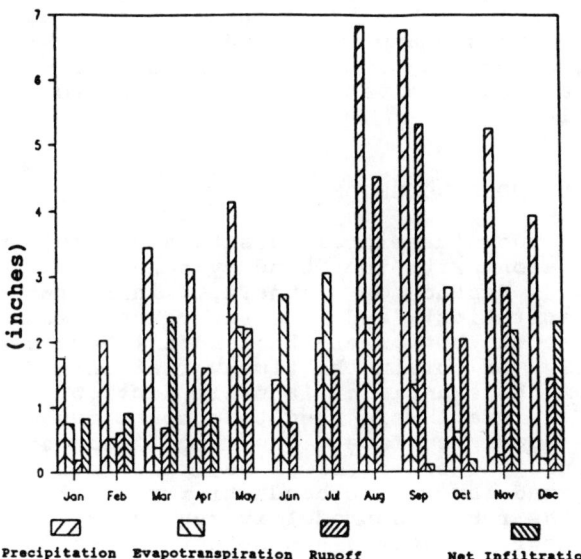

Figure 3. Model output for boundary conditions.

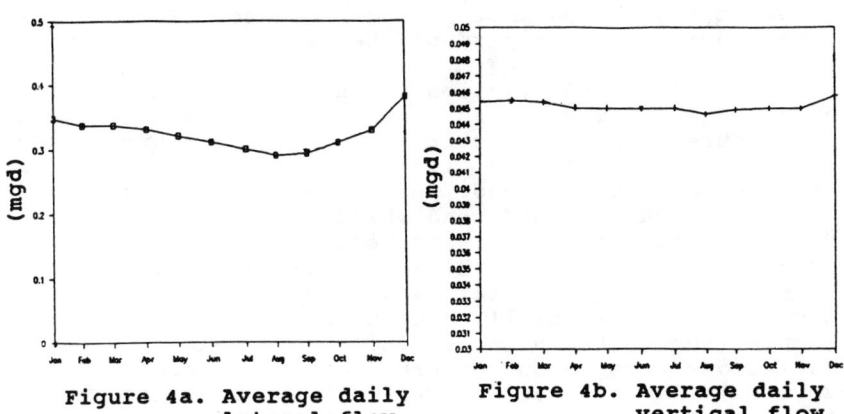

Figure 4a. Average daily lateral flow.

Figure 4b. Average daily vertical flow.

variation of the lateral and vertical flow of leachate from the landfill is shown in Figure 4. The lateral flow component is found to vary between 0.3 to 0.4 mgd. The vertical flow component is found to be very small in comparison with the lateral flow component of leachate in this example of landfill area which is due to the clay at the bottom of the landfill having 10^{-7} cm/sec as the value of the saturated hydraulic conductivity.

DISCUSSION AND CONCLUSION

The two-dimensional unsaturated moisture flow equation along with the boundary conditions (boundary conditions depend on runoff, infiltration, and evapotranspiration) and the saturated leachate flow equation at the bottom of the landfill have been solved numerically to obtain the time-variation of leachate flow from the example of landfill section. The hourly values of rainfall were used to compute runoff from the landfill upper surface. The runoff is computed by considering the effect of slope, roughness, moisture content, and hydraulic conductivity of the landfill surface. The runoff submodel is run for a time interval of one hour. Figure 3 shows that the maximum runoff value of 4.53 inches occurs during August for a total precipitation of 6.83 inches in that month. A total annual runoff of 23.76 inches occurs which is about 54.5% of total annual precipitation. High values of evapotranspiration are found to occur during May to August. This occurs because the potential evapotranspiration values depend on temperature and the temperature during that period is higher (70 to 75°F) than the remaining period of the year.

The net infiltration is the precipitation less evapotranspiration and runoff which actually contributes to the moisture content in the unsaturated zone to produce the leachate accretion onto the saturated leachate mound. The leachate accretion builds up the leachate mound head which causes the leachate flow in both the lateral and vertical directions. It is observed that the lateral and vertical flows vary with time. An average lateral flow of 0.325 mgd is found to occur from the landfill. A peak daily flow of 0.419 mgd occurs due to the high precipitation values. Similar variations are also observed in the case of the vertical flow of leachate. Thus, by using the model, the variation of leachate flow rate can be obtained for changing boundary conditions, and the model results can be used to design the leachate collection system most effectively.

REFERENCES

Bras, Rafael L., 1990. Hydrology : An Introduction to Hydrologic Science. Addison-Wesley Publishing Company, USA. p. 485-488.

Dass, P., G. R. Tamke, and C. M. Stoffel, 1977. "Leachate Production at Sanitary Landfill Sites". Journal of the Environmental Engineering Division. ASCE, Vol. 103. No. EE6. pp 981-988.

Demetracopoulos, Alexander C., 1988. "Overview of Landfill Bottom Liner Hydraulics". Water Resources Bulletin. American Water Resources Association. Vol. 24. No. 1. pp 49-56.

Fenn Dennis G., Keith J. Henley, and Truett V. Degere, 1975. "Use of the Water Balance for Predicting Leachate Generation from Solid Waste Disposal Sites". Report SW-168. U. S. Environmental Protection Agency. pp 8-11.

Gee, J. R., 1981. "Prediction of Leachate Accumulation in Sanitary Landfills". Proceedings, 4th Annual Madison Conferences of Applied Research and Practice on Municipal and Industrial Waste.

Jensen Karsten Hogh, 1983. Simulation of Water Flow in the Unsaturated Zone Including the Root Zone. Technical University of Denmark. Series paper No. 33. pp 13-24.

Korfiatis, George P., Alexander C. Demetracopoulos, Efstathios L. Bourodimos, and Edward G. Naway, 1984. "Moisture Transport in a Solid Waste Column". Journal of Environmental Engineering, Vol. 110. No. 4. pp 780-795.

Perrier, E. R. and Gibson A. C.,1980. Hydrogeologic Simulation on Solid Waste Disposal Sites. EPA - WS-868, US EPA, Cncinnati, Ohio.

Philip, J. R., 1969. "Theory of Infiltration". In: Advances in Hydroscience, Editor : V. T. Chow. Academi Press, New York. pp 215-296.

Ritchie, J. T., 1972. "A Model for Predicting Evaporation from Row Crop with Incomplete Cover". Water Resources Research. Vol. 8. No. 5. pp 1204-1213.

Schroeder, P. R., A. C. Gibson, and M. D. Slomen, 1984. The Hydrologic Evaluation of Landfill Performance (HELP) Model. Volume II. Documentation for Version 1. U. S. Army Engineer Water Ways Experiment Station, Vicksburg, M.S.. Produced by National Technical Information Service, U. S. Department of Commerce, Springfield, VA 22161. pp 14-20.

Wehran, Engineering Co., 1983. Hydrologic Investigation, Fresh Kills Landfill Solid Waste Disposal Operation Plan, Vol. 1. p. 4-22, 4-31 to 4-35.

Table 1. Data required for the model in the example of landfill area.

Area	376 acres
Saturated hydraulic conductivity :	
Wastes inside the landfill	0.02 cm/sec
bottom clay	0.0000001 cm/sec
Porosity :	
Waste	0.417
Bottom clay	0.430
Field capacity :	
Waste	0.0457
Bottom clay	0.2804
Wilting point :	
Waste	0.02
Bottom clay	0.2804

Analysis of Groundwater Quality:
A Database Application for the Nassau County, NY,
Water Management Plan

Laurens D. van der Tak[1] and Mark Maimone P.E.[2]

Abstract

Nassau County, Long Island, New York is presently developing a Comprehensive Water Management Plan. To determine the extent and trends in nitrate contamination of the groundwater, a preliminary analysis of nitrate concentrations was performed using the County's computerized water resource database. Findings confirm the effectiveness of sewering in lowering nitrate concentrations. The study also illustrates the flexibility of the database design in analyzing and presenting data for water management purposes.

Introduction

Nassau County, New York, is the western-most of two suburban counties on Long Island. The county obtains all of its water supply for its 1.3 million inhabitants from three principal aquifers underlying Long Island: the Upper Glacial, the Magothy and the Lloyd (see Figure 1).

Because groundwater is the sole source of drinking water for the County, the Nassau Department of Public Works (NCDPW) is developing a Comprehensive Water Management Plan to safeguard its supply into the future. To collect the necessary data to manage its groundwater resources effectively, Nassau County has established a network of over 400 monitoring wells throughout the County. NCDPW

---

[1]Associate Member; Water Resources Engineer, CH2M HILL, P.O. Box 4400, Reston, VA 22090.

[2]Asst. Superintendent of Water Supply, Nassau County Department of Public Works, Water Management Unit, 170 Cantiague Rock Rd., Hicksville, NY 11801.

records water levels quarterly and assesses the quality from groundwater samples taken annually. In addition, the Nassau County Department of Health (NCDH) assesses the quality of groundwater from public supply wells. In order to make best use of the data being collected, NCDPW has developed a computerized database to support the groundwater management program.

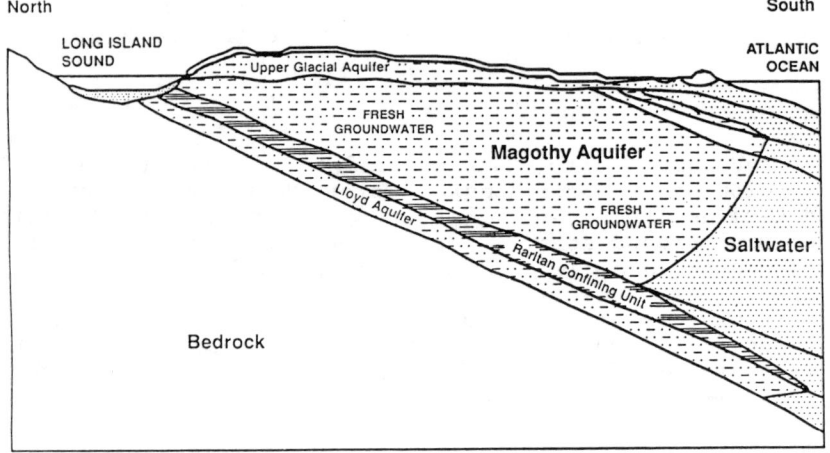

FIGURE 1 – MAJOR GEOLOGIC UNITS IN NASSAU COUNTY

The initial phases of any comprehensive planning effort must concentrate on data collection, problem definition and problem analysis. This paper presents a preliminary analysis of spatial and temporal trends of nitrates in the two uppermost aquifers of Nassau County: the Upper Glacial and the Magothy. A similar analysis for total volatile organic chemicals was also carried out, however inclusion of those results goes beyond the scope of this paper.

This preliminary nitrate contamination analysis is one small part of the overall assessment of the quality and quantity of the groundwater in the aquifer system, and is designed to help decide if any nitrate contamination problems still remain. It also provides information on the effectiveness of sewering in eliminating nitrates as a water quality concern.

Sanitary sewers were installed in Nassau County in two phases. The southwestern portion of the County was sewered between 1953 and 1964. The southeastern portion of

GROUNDWATER QUALITY ANALYSIS   751

the County was sewered between 1974 and 1986. Because sewers were installed primarily to alleviate a nitrate contamination problem, trend analysis of nitrate concentrations is very important in evaluating the effectiveness of sewers in meeting this primary objective.

The paper is divided into three major sections. The first summarizes the methodology used for extracting and analyzing the data in the database. The second summarizes the results, and the third draws conclusions about the usefulness of the database for groundwater quality management.

Methodology

The NCDPW computerized database contains numerous files relating to all aspects of water management in Nassau County. A full description goes beyond the scope of this paper (see Maimone, 1989). The particular part of the database which was used for this study is organized into two dBase IV computer files. Data concerning well location, use, current status, depth, screened interval, and state and county well identification numbers are contained in a file, which is generically referred to as the "Well" file. Well location information used in this study was expressed in (X,Y) coordinates of the New York state plane coordinate system, Long Island zone. The sampling history of inorganic groundwater constituents for each well in the Well file is contained in a separate file, which is referred to generically as the "Nitrate" file.

The nitrate file contains data collected by the two major agencies in the County responsible for groundwater sampling, the Nassau County Department of Public Works (NCDPW) and the Nassau County Department of Health (NCDH). The NCDPW samples a network of shallow and deep monitoring wells, while the NCDH concentrates on sampling public supply wells. The length of the period of record available for nitrate data at the time of this study was 1953 to 1986 for public supply wells, and 1987 to 1988 for monitoring wells.

The first step in processing both the public supply well and the monitoring well data was to sort the wells according to the aquifer where each well is screened. Three aquifer layers were considered. The first is the shallowest aquifer, the Upper Glacial. Although little public supply pumpage occurs in the Upper Glacial, it is important as a guide to water quality trends which will impact the public supply wells at a later time. It is also the aquifer which reacts first to surface contamination as well as to contamination source elimination such as sewering.

The second layer is the upper part of the Magothy aquifer, where a number of monitoring wells are available. The Magothy is generally in direct hydraulic connection with the overlying Upper Glacial and is eventually impacted by the same contaminants. The third layer is the basal Magothy, where most of the public supply wells are screened.

The next data processing step was to compute the average nitrate concentrations measured in each well in a given year. This was required to avoid giving more weight to wells that were sampled several times in a year compared to wells that were sampled only once. With all the data computerized and contained in Dbase IV files, a preliminary statistical analysis such as this is readily carried out within the dBase program itself.

With mean nitrate concentrations determined per well and year, the next step in the data processing procedure was to determine the overall statistics for all wells in Nassau County in each of the three aquifers in each year of available data. The arithmetic mean and standard deviation of concentration of all wells sampled, and the number of wells sampled were determined for the available periods of record. Doing this statistical analysis before sorting wells into concentration categories was essential for choosing the years which were most appropriate for mapping. The results of this analysis are presented in the next section.

The public supply well data from 1954, 1970, and 1986 were selected to produce color coded dot maps of nitrate concentration levels in each of the three aquifer layers. These years bracket the two phases of installation of sanitary sewers and have approximately the highest number of wells sampled at the beginning, middle, and end of the public supply well record for nitrates. Nitrate maps from the monitoring well data were produced only for the 1988 record, which has the higher number of wells sampled in the two years of data available. Therefore, in total, nine nitrate maps were produced from the public supply well data (3 years x 3 aquifer layers) and three were made from the monitoring well data (1 year x 3 aquifer layers).

The map of nitrates reproduced for this paper shows three different symbols which represent different levels of contamination. The concentration categories for nitrates, as used in the map, are as follows:

Category	Nitrate Concentration Range
1	Below Detection Limit to 6 ppm
2	6 ppm to 10 ppm
3	Greater than 10 ppm

Category 1 represents pristine conditions, levels expected from atmospheric pollution and storm water recharge, or low level contamination which is not of concern for drinking water supply. Category 2 is a warning level, below the drinking water standard but indicating that the standard can be exceeded periodically. Category 3 does not meet the drinking water standard.

The maps were produced by writing a dBase program to sort the average nitrate concentration for each well in a given year and aquifer into its appropriate concentration category. All well location and concentration category data for a given year and aquifer were then copied to an ASCII file. This file served as input to an AUTOCAD program developed by CH2M HILL which automatically placed a symbol of the appropriate color code at the exact well location on a digital outline of Nassau County on the AUTOCAD computer graphics system.

Results

A statistical analysis was performed to assess temporal trends in the nitrate data. The county-wide mean nitrate concentration was found to decrease from the Upper Glacial aquifer to the lower Magothy aquifer layer (see Figure 2). Nitrate contamination comes primarily from wastewater (sewage) that reaches the groundwater through cesspools and, to a lesser degree, from lawn fertilizers. The lower Magothy aquifer layer, which is the primary source of drinking water in Nassau County, has very low average nitrate levels throughout the period of record (less than 2 mg/l in every year, except in 1959 when it was 2.26 mg/l). On a county-wide basis, mean nitrate levels did not decrease over the period of record in any of the aquifer layers (see Figure 2). This is due to the fact that there are both sewered areas with declining nitrate levels and unsewered areas with rising nitrate levels. In the upper Magothy aquifer, the mean nitrate concentration was found to increase a small but statistically significant amount. This represents the slow downward movement of Upper Glacial water into the Magothy.

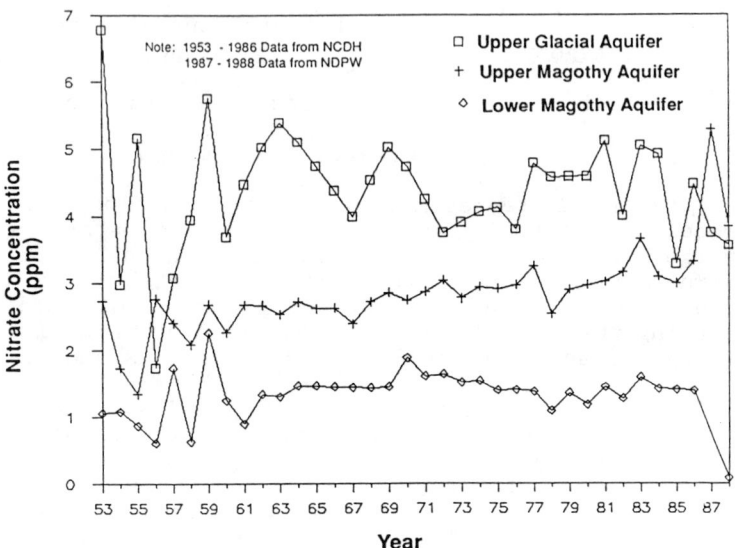

FIGURE 2 – MEAN NITRATE CONCENTRATIONS IN AQUIFERS

Statistical evaluations of the significance of the trends were limited for this study to simple pairwise comparisons using one-tailed tests of the difference between mean concentrations in two selected years, with a 5 percent level of significance. In each case, several pair of years were evaluated. More rigorous trend analyses are planned for future studies.

When the average nitrate concentration is computed for just those wells in Nassau County Sewer Districts No. 2 (southwestern Nassau) or No. 3 (southeastern Nassau), a statistically significant decrease was found between the early 1970s and the mid-1980s in the Upper Glacial aquifer, where the highest concentrations are found (see Figure 3). This seems to indicate that the sewering is proving effective in lowering nitrate concentrations. The nitrate concentrations in the late 1980s are higher in Sewer District No. 3, where sanitary sewers were installed more recently, than they are in Sewer District No. 2. According to the nitrate maps produced in this study, the areas with highest nitrate

GROUNDWATER QUALITY ANALYSIS

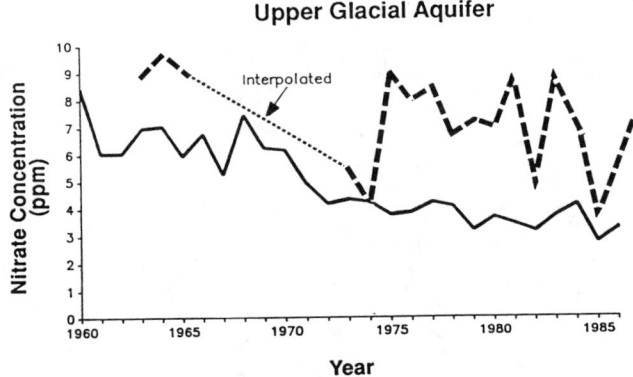

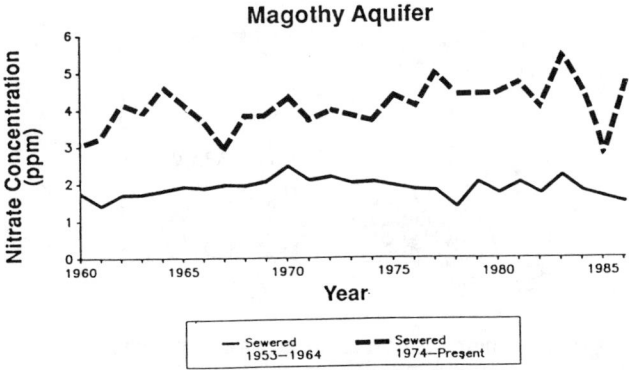

FIGURE 3 – NITRATE TREND IN UPPER GLACIAL AND MAGOTHY AQUIFERS

concentration levels (over 10 mg/l) are primarily in the far northwestern part of the county, and to a lesser degree in the northern third of Sewer District No. 3 (see Figure 4). These are either unsewered areas of relatively high density housing, or have only been sewered in the past few years. The extent of nitrate contamination in the northeast is uncertain because the monitoring network is sparse, especially in the Upper Glacial aquifer. Between 5 and 7 percent of all wells sampled in 1986 and in 1988, in either the Upper Glacial or the upper Magothy aquifers, had nitrate concentrations over the 10 mg/l nitrate drinking water standard (see Tables 1 and 2). However, none of the deep wells in the lower Magothy aquifer showed concentrations over 10 mg/l in 1986 and in 1988.

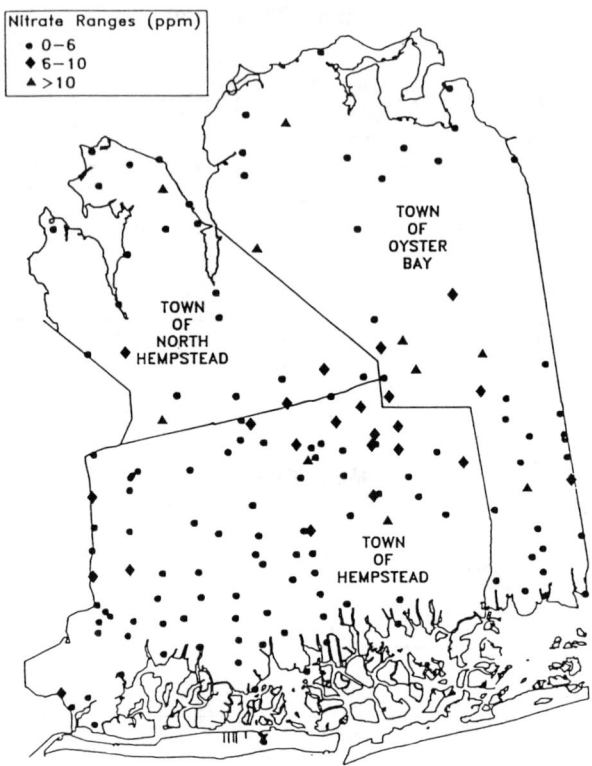

FIGURE 4 – DISTRIBUTION OF NITRATES IN THE UPPER GLACIAL AQUIFER MONITORING WELLS

TABLE 1

FREQUENCY OF OCCURRENCE OF EACH CONCENTRATION CATEGORY IN THE 1986 PUBLIC SUPPLY WELL NITRATE DATA IN THE THREE MAPS CORRESPONDING TO THE UPPER GLACIAL, THE UPPER MAGOTHY, AND THE LOWER MAGOTHY AQUIFER LAYERS

Nitrate Concentration (PPM)	Upper Glacial Aquifer Frequency	(%)	Upper Magothy Aquifer Frequency	(%)	Lower Magothy Aquifer Frequency	(%)
BDL - 6	89	77.3	95	83.3	157	98.1
6 - 10	18	15.7	13	11.4	3	1.9
> 10	8	7.0	6	5.3	0	0.0
TOTAL:	115		114		160	

TABLE 2
FREQUENCY OF OCCURRENCE OF EACH CONCENTRATION CATEGORY IN THE 1988 MONITORING WELL NITRATE DATA IN THE THREE MAPS CORRESPONDING TO THE UPPER GLACIAL, THE UPPER MAGOTHY AND THE LOWER MAGOTHY AQUIFER LAYERS

Nitrate Concentration (PPM)	Upper Glacial Aquifer Frequency	(%)	Upper Magothy Aquifer Frequency	(%)	Lower Magothy Aquifer Frequency	(%)
BDL - 6	127	79.4	34	81.0	11	100
6 - 10	24	15.0	5	11.9	0	0.0
> 10	9	5.6	3	7.1	0	0.0
TOTAL:	160		42		11	

Conclusion

A number of general conclusions can be drawn from this brief study on nitrates about the usefulness of the database in supporting water management activities. It is becoming clear that the effort involved in collecting and computerizing water resource data is well worth it when the actual planning phase of the water management program begins. A preliminary analysis such as the above can be carried out in about a week. This quick turnaround allows the County to focus management efforts on real quality problems and to localize these problems, eliminating wasted time and funds on issues which are not pressing or threatening. In addition, although only rudimentary statistical analysis was performed in the first planning phase, the same techniques and ease of application are available for more sophisticated approaches. For example, the same dBase data can be transferred to a statistics program without any further manipulation for further analysis. Finally, the data which was used for basic or more sophisticated statistical analysis is also readily available for graphic representation using commercial graphics software or AutoCad. This has enabled County water managers to present their findings almost immediately, in a form which is easily understood by decision makers.

Aside from the above, general remarks about the usefulness of the database in water management activities, it is also possible to draw some more specific conclusions about nitrate trends in Nassau County based upon our preliminary findings. The data clearly supports the idea that sewering has eliminated the single, largest source of nitrate contamination in Nassau County. Sewered areas show declining concentrations, while unsewered areas are either reaching an equilibrium at a higher level of nitrate contamination, or are still rising. More detailed examinations of nitrate contamination in unsewered areas of the County are now being carried out to further investigate these preliminary findings. Finally, the data seems to support the results of groundwater modeling carried out by the NCDPW, which shows that vertical movement of Upper Glacial water into the Magothy aquifer occurs very slowly. The long time lag between the urbanization of Nassau County and rising levels of nitrates in the Magothy, as well as between sewering and the decline in nitrate concentrations, is apparent from the above results.

References

Maimone, M. 1989. Developing a Database for Use in Groundwater Management. ASCE. Journal of Water Resources Planing and Management. Vol. 115(1). pp. 75-93.

Acknowledgements

The authors would like to acknowledge the help of Gary Martens of NCDPW and Jeff Hart and John Manzer of CH2M HILL for the processing of data on dBase III Plus and the production of maps on AUTOCAD and on INTERGRAPH's Microstation Software.

WDCR451/034.50

NUMERICAL MODEL STUDY OF GROUNDWATER MOVEMENT IN AN AQUIFER OF BANGLADESH

Shabbir Ahmed (1)
and
Jahir Uddin Chowdhury (2)

ABSTRACT

Annual groundwater level variation in the aquifer of the Mymensingh-Tangail area of Bangladesh was simulated by applying an implicit finite-difference model of groundwater flow. The groundwater level variation in the aquifer was investigated for time-varying withdrawal by pumping wells in the study area for the period 1979-'80 and 1982-'83. The recharge to the aquifer was determined by the calibration process. Total recharge in the model area was found to be less than the total actual withdrawal in 1982-'83. The groundwater levels during 1982-'83 were found to decrease from the groundwater levels during 1979-'80. This was due to the higher withdrawal volume of 1405.7 million m^3 in 1982-'83 than that of 575 million m^3 in 1979-'80.

INTRODUCTION

Groundwater is an important source of irrigation during dry season in many areas of Bangladesh. Extensive exploitation of this resource through pumping wells started in 1972 (Master Plan Organization, 1984). Unplanned rapid increase of irrigation wells caused decline in groundwater level in the northwest and northeast regions of Bangladesh (Figure 1; Master Plan Organization, 1984). As a result, several shallow

---

(1) Ph.D. Candidate, Department of Civil Engineering, The City University of New York, The City College, N. Y. 10031. Formerly Graduate Student, Department of Water Resources Engineering, Bangladesh University of Engineering and Technology, Dhaka, Bangladesh.
(2) Professor, Institute of Flood Control and Drainage Research, Bangladesh University of Engineering and Technology, Dhaka, Bangladesh.

tubewells and hand pump tubewells became incapable of pumping water in those regions. A lowering trend of the groundwater table in the central part of the country has also been reported by Bangladesh Water Development Board (1984).

Seven applications of groundwater models in different parts of Bangladesh since 1976 have been summarized by Master Plan Organization (1984). Effect of withdrawal upon groundwater level variation in Dhaka Metropolitan area of the country was studied by a single layer finite-difference model in 1980 (Ahmed, 1986). Groundwater models were applied to develop strategy for groundwater withdrawal by deep tubewells in the groundwater basin surrounded by the rivers Ganga and Atrai (Master Plan Organization, 1984). None of the model studies in Bangladesh has included the Mymensingh-Tangail area which has a very high groundwater potential. Groundwater exploitation in this area is increasing at a rapid rate due to the increased installation of pumping wells. The effect of withdrawal upon groundwater level variation in this region was investigated by applying a two-dimensional groundwater flow model.

The water years 1979-'80 and 1982-'83 were selected as simulation period for the present study since amount of data available in these periods was better. The simulation was made for these two years to investigate the decline of groundwater level due to unplanned installation of pumping wells. Investigation was also made to determine groundwater recharge and to compare it with the withdrawal occurred in the model area.

MODEL FORMULATION

Groundwater movement in an aquifer can be described mathematically by the following equation :

$$\frac{\partial}{\partial x}(T_x \frac{\partial h}{\partial x}) + \frac{\partial}{\partial y}(T_y \frac{\partial h}{\partial y}) = S\frac{\partial h}{\partial t} \pm Q \qquad (1)$$

where,

h = groundwater level (L),
T_x and T_y = coefficient of transmissivity along x

and y directions respectively (L^2/T),
S = storage coefficient (dimensionless),
Q = withdrawal and recharge (L/T), and
t = time (T).

The model area is discretized into an asymmetric network of polygons. Figure 2 shows a typical polygon. Equation (1) is integrated at the centroid of a polygon by an implicit finite-difference method. The finite-difference equation at a node is given by (Ridder and Erez, 1977) :

$$\sum_i (h_i^{j+1} - h_s^{j+1}) Y_{i,s} + A_s Q_s^{j+1} = A_s S_s (h_s^{j+1} - h_s^j)/\Delta t \qquad (2)$$

where,

$Y_{i,s} = (W_{i,s} * T_{i,s})/L_{i,s}$
       = conductance of path between nodes i and s (L^2/T)
$T_{i,s}$ = coefficient of transmissivity of the path between nodes i and s (L^2/T),
$W_{i,s}$ = width of the side between nodes i and s (L),
$L_{i,s}$ = distance between nodes i and s (L),
h_i = groundwater level at node i (L),
h_s = groundwater level at node s (L),
A_s = area of node s (L^2),
Q_s = net vertical flow at node s (L/T), and
S_s = storage coefficient at node s (dimensionless).

Simultaneous solution of the finite-difference equations using Gauss-Jordan elimination method gives water level at the centroids of the polygons at the end of each time interval of the order of 15 days.

FIELD APPLICATION

The model was applied to the aquifer of the Mymensingh-Tangail area of Bangladesh as shown in Figure 1. The total area of 5056 sq. km. lies between the rivers Jamuna flowing in a braided course in the western side and Old Brahmaputra in the eastern side

(Figure 1). The model area was schematized by a network of 63 polygons and is shown in Figure 3. The model area is composed of alluvial flood plain sediments deposited by Brahmaputra-Jamuna river system. Study of 54 groundwater observation wells in the model area reveals that the groundwater level starts rising in May and reaches to maximum in August at the rate of approximately 0.56 m per month (Ahmed, 1986). The water table begins to recede from October at the rate of approximately 0.33 m per month and reaches to minimum in April. The study of the physiographic units of Bangladesh reveals that the part of the model area remains deeply flooded at a depth of flooding greater than 2 m (Karim, 1984). This indicates that the aquifer is recharged partly by the percolation of flood water.

The input data required for the model are geometric elements of the schematization, initial condition (groundwater level at the start of computation as on April 1, 1979 and 1982), boundary conditions, withdrawal, recharge, storage coefficient, and coefficient of transmissivity. Two types of boundaries have been considered in the study area. River water levels were allocated to external boundary nodes along the sides defined by the rivers Jamuna and Brahmaputra. The north and south borders of the model area were considered gradient specified boundaries and were defined by the slope of the flow lines of the groundwater table associated with the boundary nodes. Initial estimates of storage coefficient and transmissivity were made from the results of pump test data analysis, summarized by Karim (1984) and United Nations Development Program (1982).

Node-wise values of withdrawal was estimated from the actual abstraction by the pumping wells in different parts of the study area for the years 1979-'80 and 1982-'83. Initial estimate of recharge was made from the values determined by analysing long-term records of groundwater level fluctuation (Karim, 1984). The final values of storage coefficient, transmissivity, and recharge were obtained by adjusting the observed and computed groundwater levels through the process of calibration. Adjustment in storage coefficient and transmissivity was made to obtain agreement between observed and computed groundwater levels during October to March (no recharge season) in 1979-'80. Then the recharge was adjusted at every time step at every polygon to obtain agreement during the period April to September (recharge season). The observed and computed groundwater level contours are shown in Figure 4.

EFFECTS OF WITHDRAWAL

The appliances for withdrawal from the aquifer comprise deep tubewells, shallow tubewells, hand pump tubewells, and manually operated shallow tubewells for irrigation. From the discharge characteristics of these tubewells, total extraction in the study area has been computed and are given in Table 1.

Study of groundwater withdrawal in the model area reveals that the extraction of groundwater by pumping wells was increased rapidly over the period 1979-'80 to 1982-'83. Table 1 shows that the withdrawal by shallow tubewells was increased by more than 5 times in 1982-'83 than in 1979-'80. This was due to the installation of more shallow tubewells in the study area for the purpose of irrgation. It is also observed from Table 1 that the increase in withdrawal has occurred in 1982-'83 due to the increase in the installation of deep tubewells, hand pump tubewells, and manually operated shallow tubewells for irrigation. Table 2 shows the monthly variation of rainfall, recharge, and withdrawal in the model area in 1979-'80 and 1982-'83. Total rainfall in 1982-'83 is 158.0 cm which is less than the rainfall 174.6 cm in 1979-'80. This has caused a less recharge of 182 mm in 1982-'83 than the recharge of 211 mm in 1979-'80. Thus increase in withdrawal and decrease in recharge have resulted in rapid decline of groundwater table which is shown in Figure 5.

DISCUSSION AND CONCLUSION

The main objective of the present study was to simulate the groundwater level variation in the Mymensingh-Tangail area due to withdrawal in 1979-'80 and 1982-'83. In order to achieve that goal, calibration was done to estimate storage coefficient, transmissivity, and recharge until close agreement between observed and computed groundwater level was obtained. Sensitivity analysis was also done for these parameters. It was found that the groundwater table was most sensitive to recharge and least sensitive to the coefficient of transmissivity. Figure 4 shows that the close agreement between computed and observed groundwater level contours are obtained. This comparison shows that the simulations are acceptable for all practical purpose.

Total withdrawal volume in the study area has been increased from 575 million m^3 to 1405.7 million m^3 due to the increase in the number of pumping shallow tubewells, deep tubewells, handpump tubewells, and manually operated shallow tubewells for irrigation. Table 2 shows that the withdrawal in 1982-'83 is higher by an amount of 96 mm than the actual recharge to the grundwater table in that period. Due to the high values of withdrawal, the groundwater table has declined on the average by 1.7 m from 1979-'80 to 1982-'83 at node no. 4 and is shown in Figure 5a. The average decline shown in Figure 5b is very high and is 3.2 m at node no. 21. Similar results are also observed in other parts of the study area. At the end of the irrigation period, groundwater table has been found to decline from 10.46 m in March 1980 to 7.22 m in March 1983 at node no. 14. This trend of rapid lowering of groundwater table is evidently due to the unplanned exploitation of groundwater in this area. In order to prevent gradual decline of groundwater table, simulation of groundwater table should be done for future with different withdrawal values. This would help to arrive at the withdrawal strategy by maintaining groundwater table to the desired elevation.

REFERENCES

Ahmed, Shabbir, 1986. Study of Groundwater System in the Mymensingh-Tangail Area Using Numerical Models. M. Sc. Engineering (Water Resources) thesis. Bangladesh University of Engineering and Technology, Dhaka.

Bangladeh Water Development Board, 1984. Trend of Groundwater Level in Bangladesh. Water Supply Paper - 455. Groundwater Circle - II, Dhaka.

Karim M. A., 1984. Upazilla-wise Groundwater Recharge Conditions of Bangladesh. Groundwater Investigation Circle, Dhaka.

Master Plan Organization, 1984. Groundwater Availability. Second Interim Report. Vol. III. National Water Plan Project. Ministry of Irrigation, Water Development, and Flood Control, Bangladesh.

Ridder de N. A. and Erez A., 1977. Optimum Use of

Water Resources. International Institute for Land Reclamation and Improvement/ILRI, P. O. Box 45 Wageningen, The Netherlands.

United Nations Development Program, 1982. Groundwater Survey, The Hydrogeologic Conditions of Bangladesh. United Nations.

Table 1. Total withdrawal by different pumping wells.

	Total withdrawal (in million m^3)	
	1979-'80	1982-'83
Deep tubewells	375.20	566.40
Shallow tubewells	151.80	780.70
Hand pump tubewells	27.00	35.20
Manually operated shallow tubewells for irrigation	21.04	23.40
Total	575.00	1405.70

Table 2. Rainfall, recharge, and extraction in 1979-'80 and 1982-'83.

	Rainfall (mm)		Recharge (mm)		Extraction (mm)	
Month	79-'80	82-'83	79-'80	82-'83	79-'80	82-'83
Apr	72.80	111.28	3.03	3.64	27.10	61.20
May	92.90	141.66	13.86	18.81	6.24	10.04
Jun	341.50	488.62	72.55	94.87	0.60	0.54
Jul	445.80	281.46	73.55	40.12	0.40	0.56
Aug	364.40	245.63	47.79	23.90	0.38	0.53
Sep	269.80	155.88	0.42	0.08	0.38	0.51
Oct	77.42	32.91	0.25	0.05	0.38	0.53
Nov	17.16	16.83	0.00	0.00	0.98	1.32
Dec	28.45	0.15	0.00	0.00	5.14	17.41
Jan	3.72	6.78	0.00	0.00	16.96	49.31
Feb	20.83	16.52	0.00	0.00	22.74	53.50
Mar	10.46	81.88	0.00	0.00	32.19	82.62

766 RESOURCES FOR WATER MANAGEMENT

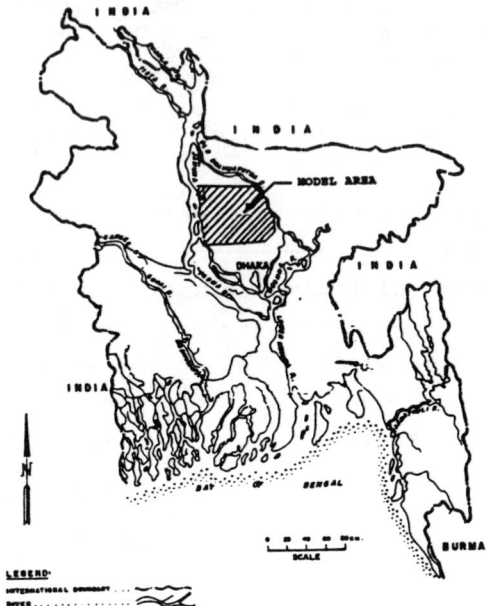

Figure 1. Location of the Model Area.

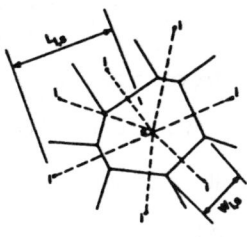

Figure 2. A typical node.

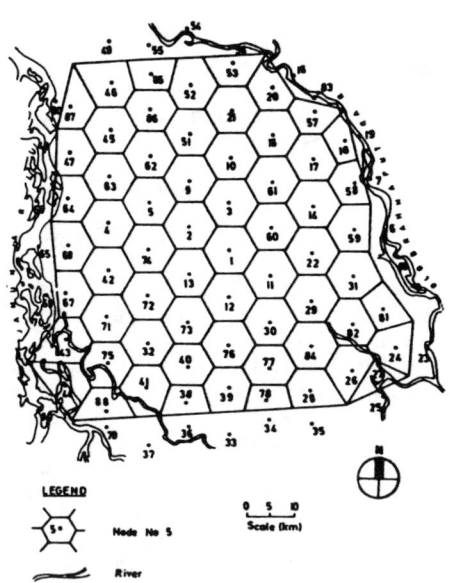

FIG. 3. HEXAGONAL GRID SCHEMATIZATION

GROUNDWATER MOVEMENT STUDY

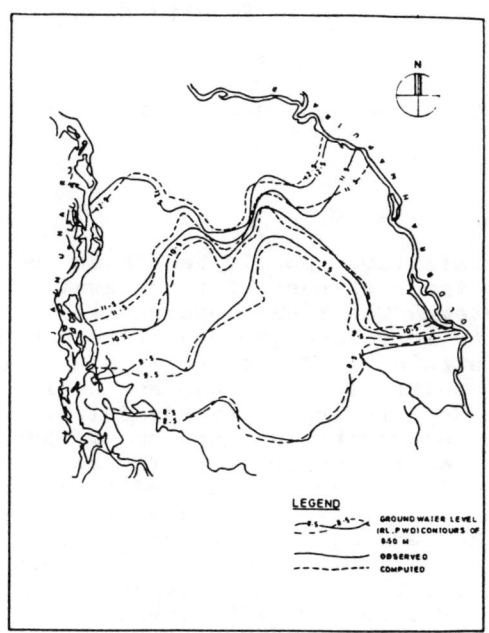

FIG. 4. COMPARISON OF COMPUTED AND OBSERVED GROUND WATER LEVEL CONTOURS ON 12-11-79

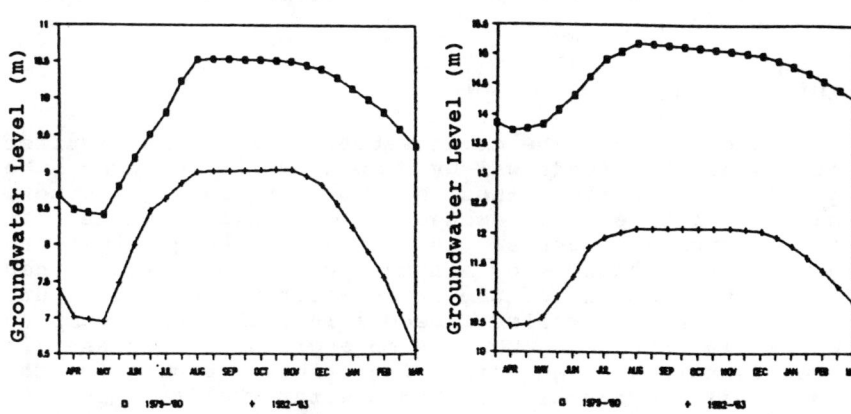

Figure 5a. Groundwater level variation at node no. 2.

Figure 5b. Groundwater level variation at node no. 21.

DEVELOPMENT OF AN OPTIMIZATION MODEL FOR GROUNDWATER WITHDRAWAL

By

Shabbir Ahmed and Reza M. Khanbilvardi[*]

ABSTRACT

An optimization model has been developed to simulate optimal values of withdrawal from a given aquifer system. The linear programming technique has been used to formulate the objective function along with the constraints. The constraints are defined such that the groundwater table does not decline beyond a limit in order to avoid overdrafting. The Simplex method has been used to maximize the withdrawal volume based on the above constraint. The constraint ensures that the model results can be used to design for the sustained availability of groundwater by pumping wells throughout the pumping period. The use of the model was demonstrated by applying it to an example of an unconfined aquifer. The model generated a time-history of optimal groundwater withdrawal for the pumping period. The model results were investigated for time-varying recharge and boundary conditions ensuring the sustained availability of groundwater by the pumping wells.

INTRODUCTION

Decline of the groundwater table in an aquifer occurs due to withdrawal by pumping wells. However, the groundwater table rises due to percolating water, called recharge that reaches the groundwater table. If the pumping exceeds the actual recharge to the groundwater table for a long period of time, then permanent decline of the groundwater table will occur, causing the tubewells to become incapable of pumping water in the long run. Also a gradual decrease in groundwater storage will inevitably result in the continual degradation of groundwater quality due to the increase in the contaminant concentration.

---

[*] Ph.D. Candidate and Associate Professor; Department of Civil Engineering, The City University of New York, The City College. N. Y. 10031.

Permanent decline of groundwater table can be avoided by adopting a pumping strategy which can be obtained by optimizing groundwater withdrawal, subject to the restriction on the decline of the groundwater table beyond a certain limit. The objective of many studies of groundwater systems is to determine the maximum possible withdrawal that ensures sustained availability of groundwater by pumping wells without diminishing groundwater quality. It has been reported by Hamilton (1988) that steadily increasing pumping since 1900's has caused declines in groundwater levels, well interference, and degradation of groundwater quality in southern Virginia. In order to limit the lowering of the potentiometric surface and degradation of groundwater quality by the contaminants, optimal recharge and pumping schedules had been proposed for the Chino groundwater basin in southern California (Taghavi and Miguel, 1988). An Optimization model was applied by Khan and Mawdsley (1984) to estimate the maximum possible yield from the unconfined Chalk aquifer in Hampshire, U. K. Potentimetric surfaces, conjunctive water use and sustained yield strategies were optimized for the aquifer of the Arkansas Grand Prairie by considering a finite-difference form of the Boussinesq equation (Richard, 1985).

In the present model, a two-dimensional unsteady state flow condition has been considered to formulate the objective function represented by groundwater withdrawal. The linear programming model is developed to maximize groundwater withdrawal based on the constraint defined by the groundwater table, restricted to a spcified limit. The model will help to obtain optimal pumping schemes that will avoid overdrafting from the aquifer.

MODEL FORMULATION

The present optimization model for groundwater withdrawal is based on the formulation developed by combining Darcy's law with a continuity equation. Darcy's law and the continuity equation describe the movement of groundwater in the aquifer in an unsteady state flow condition. Study of a groundwater system can be done by schematization of the aquifer area into a network of nodes in the shape of polygons. Figure 1 illustrates a typical node and the model region is discretized into a network of these nodal points. The groundwater movement in the typical node s (Figure 1)

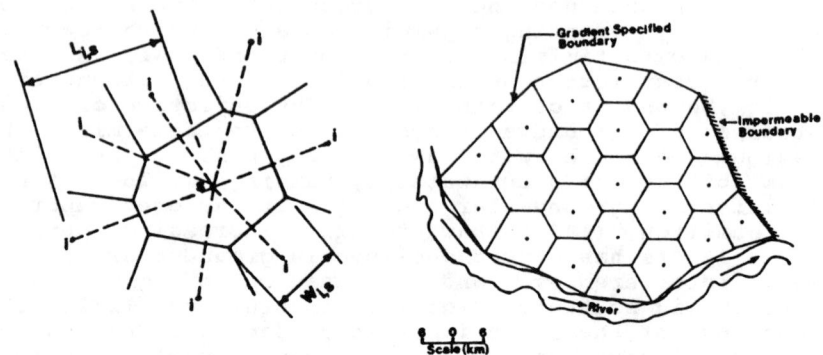

Figure 1. A typical node. Figure 2. Model area.

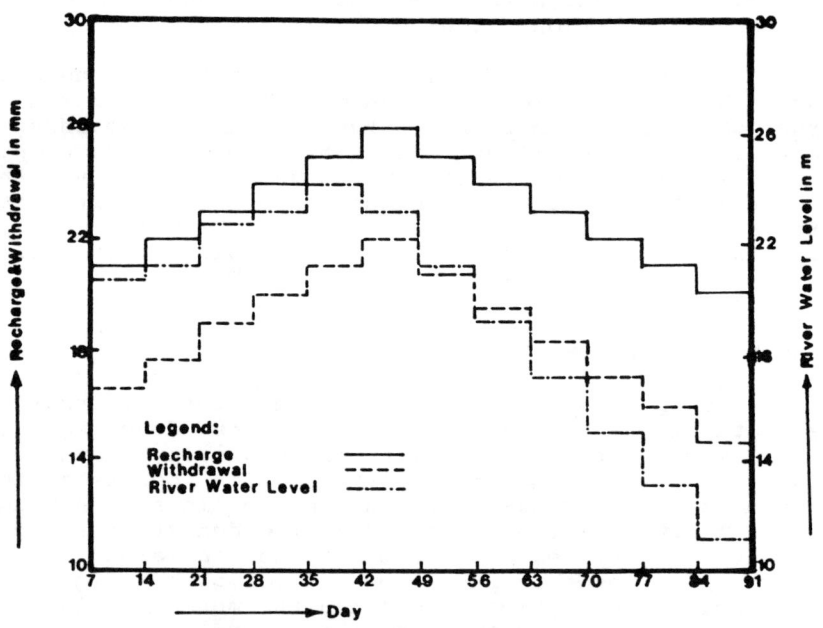

Figure 3. Variation of Optimum Values of Withdrawal for Different Recharge, River Water Level, and Constant Outflow Boundary Condition

can be expressed as (Thomas, 1973) :

$$\sum_i Y_{i,s}(h_i - h_s) + A_s(R - E)/\Delta t = A_s S_s (dh_s/dt) \qquad (1)$$

where,

$Y_{i,s} = W_{i,s} T_{i,s}/L_{i,s}$
       = conductance of path between nodes i and s (L^2/T),
$W_{i,s}$ = width of the side between nodes i and s (L),
$L_{i,s}$ = distance between nodes i and s (L),
h_i = groundwater level at node i (L),
h_s = groundwater level at node s (L),
A_s = area of node s (L^2),
R = recharge during Δt (L),
E = withdrawal during Δt (L), and
S_s = storage coefficient (dimensionless).

Applying finite-difference technique to dh_s/dt, the implicit expresssion for equation (1) can be written as (Thomas, 1973):

$$\sum_i Y_{i,s}(h_i^{j+1} - h_s^{j+1}) + A_s(R - E)/\Delta t = (A_s S_s/\Delta t)(h_s^{j+1} - h_s^j) \qquad (2)$$

where,
   j = previous time level, and
   j+1 = forward time level.

Rearranging equation (2) :

$$W_s^{j+1} = -h_s^{j+1}(\sum_i Y_{i,s} + A_s S_s/\Delta t)\Delta t + \Delta t \sum_i h_i^{j+1} Y_{i,s} + A_s R^{j+1} + A_s S_s h_s^j \qquad (3)$$

where,

$$W_s^{j+1} = A_s E^{j+1}$$

Here W_s^{j+1} is the objective function and h_i and h_s are considered as the decision variables.

In order to maintain the water level at a depth of d_s and d_i below the ground level (GL) in nodes s and i respectively, the constraints can be written as :

$$h_s^{j+1} \geq GL_s - d_s$$
$$h_i^{j+1} \geq GL_i - d_i \qquad (4)$$

The system of equations in (3) and (4) develop a linear programming model which is solved to obtain the maximum value of withdrawal (W_s^{j+1}) by using the Simplex method.

APPLICATION

In order to demonstrate the application of the model, an example unconfined aquifer was selected. The model area covering the aquifer was schematized into a network of polygons as shown in Figure 2. The data required for the example of aquifer is shown in Table 1. The boundary conditions are river water levels along the river boundary, zero flow along the impermeable boundary, and slope of flow lines of the groundwater table along the gradient-specified boundary as shown in Figure 2.

The model run was made to demonstrate the prediction of optimal values of groundwater withdrawal for a period of 13 weeks (3 months) in the example study area. The decline of the groundwater table was restricted up to a point of 10 m below ground level. The slope of flow lines of the groundwater table along the gradient-specified boundary was considered -10^{-6} m/m. Maximization of the withdrawal volume was done for historic recharge inputs. The simulation results for different recharge and boundary condition are shown in Figure 3. It was observed during model run that the slope of flow lines defining the gradient-specified boundary conditions effects the optimal values of withdrawal in the model area. The effect of the gradient-specified boundary condition has been investigated by computing optimal withdrawal for different slope of flow lines (10^{-6} m/m to 10^{-3} m/m) along this boundary, which is shown in Figure 4.

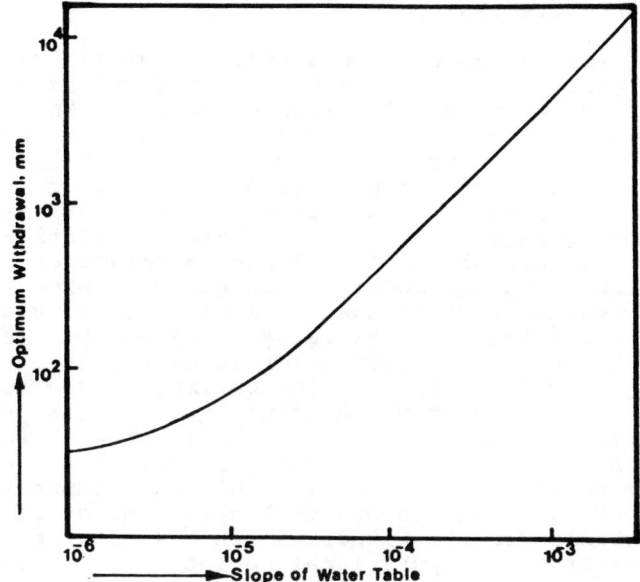

Figure 4. Effect of the Slope of Water Table at the Gradient Specified Boundary on Optimum Withdrawal

Table 1. Data required for the model input.

Total area	1827 sq. km.
Total number of polygons	22
Storage coefficient	0.1
Coefficient of transmissivity	2500 m^2/day
Ground elevation	30 m
Initial groundwater elevation	25 m
Maximum decline of groundwater table from the ground surface	10 m

RESULTS AND DISCUSSION

Optimal values of groundwater withdrawal from the example unconfined aquifer have been obtained for the unsteady stae groundwater flow condition. The optimal values of withdrawal is dependent on the historic recharge inputs and the boundary conditions. The recharge values have been assumed to vary from 20 mm to 26 mm in the present computational period of 3 months (Figure 3). For this recharge variation, the optimal withdrawal value is found to vary from 14.6 mm to 22.0 mm in the model area. Figure 3 shows that a minimum value of withdrawal of 14.6 mm (per week) is obtained for the recharge value of 20 mm (per week) in the last week when river water level reaches to the minimum value of 11.0 m. The optimal value for the first week was higher which is not shown in the Figure. The optimal volume computed for the first week is 2242 million m^3 which is significantly higher than the total recharge volume of 36.5 million m^3. The computation of high optimal volume is due to the initial storage that is available for the withdrawal in the aquifer. For the rest of the computational period, an average of 80.2% of total recharge volume can be withdrawn for the given river water level variation as shown in Figure 3.

The slope of the flow lines along the gradient specified boundary has a significant effect upon the model results. The model results show that the withdrawal values in the model area increase with the increase in the slope of groundwater table along the gradient specified boundary. An increase in the slope of 10 times from 10^{-5} m/m to 10^{-4} increases the withdrawal value from 70.6 mm to 463.8 mm in a week as shown in Figure 4. This is evident from the fact that the increase in the slope significantly increases the inflow to the aquifer, which allows more groudwater to be withdrawn.

SUMMARY

The linear programming technique can be used to compute maximum groundwater withdrawal based on the restriction upon groundwater table not to be lowered below a certain point. This restriction helps avoid overdrafting and decline of the groundwater table beyond a tolerable limit in a groundwater basin. Preliminary assessment of the number of pumping wells and the time-varying pumping strategy can be established for an aquifer system by using such an optimization model.

The demonstration of the model application for an example of unconfined aquifer reveals that the time-varying optimal withdrawal values depend on the historic recharge inputs and the boundary conditions associated with the aquifer system. The results indicate that the maximum withdrawal from the aquifer can be made only for high recharge inputs into the aquifer and high river water level along the river boundary. Also high gradient of flowlines associated with the groundwater table along the gradient-specified boundary increases the lateral inflow into the aquifer causing more water to be available for withdrawal.

REFERENCES

Hamilton, Pixie A., 1988. "Regional Assessment of Pumpage in Southern Virginia". In Proceedings of the 15th Annual ASCE Water Resources Planning and Management Conference; Critical Water Issues And Computer Applications. Edited by : Mike Stretch. ASCE. New York. pp 168-170.

Khan, L. R. and Mawdsley, J. A., 1984. "Estimation of Aquifer Yield Using Linear Programming Technique". Journal of the Institution of Engineers, Bangladesh. Vol. 12. No. 3. pp 9-16.

Richard, C. Peralta, 1985. "Conjunctive Use/Sustained Groundwater Yield Design". In Proceedings of the ASCE Water Resources Planning and Management Division Specialty Conference; Computer Applications in Water Resources. Edited by : Harry C. Torno. ASCE. pp 1391-1400.

Thomas, R. J., 1973. Groundwater Models. Food and Agricultural Organization Irrigation and Drainage Paper. United Nations. Rome.

Taghavi, S. Alireza and Miguel A. Marino, 1988. "Conjunctive Use Study of Groundwater and Surface Water in Chino Basin, California". In Proceedings of the 15th Annual ASCE Water Resources Planning and Management Conference; Critical Water Issues And Computer Applications. Edited by : Mike Stretch. ASCE. New York. pp 112-115.

Spills: The Human-Machine Interface
State of Our Knowledge

Leo Weaver, Fellow ASCE[1]

The International Joint Commission on the Great Lakes, an organization established by the governments of Canada and the United States, has entered into agreements on Great Lakes water quality. Many of the 3000 significant spills that occur in the Great Lakes Basin annually contribute significantly to the basin's toxic burden. A breakdown in the complex relationships between humans and machines often contribute to spills. The Joint Commission has sponsored several workshops on Spills and the Human-Machine Interface and is presently considering a workshop on Reasearch Needs on this topic. A special study was contracted by the Joint Commission to, among other objectives, determine the State of the Art.
A search of data bases through DIOLOG Information Services, Inc. and MARIBASE, the Maritime data base and various accident reports was conducted. The data base search was complimented by contact with more than fifty (50) individuals, industries, universities and agencies in Canada and the United States. These contacts were initiated in large part through participants in the several Joint Commission Workshops.
The study results confirmed that there is now available a large body of information on human factors or behavioral technology as it has been termed. This body of information has largely resulted from the recognition of the importance of the science to the safe accomplishment of assigned responsibilities in the energy and transportation sectors of the economy and the Departments of Defense in both Canada and the United States.
While there is little evidence that this body of knowledge is being directly applied to the control and prevention of spills there is good reason to conclude that in the energy, marine transport, and chemical process fields, at least, there is indirectly significant pollution control and prevention resulting from the consideration of human factors and the machine interface.

---
[1] Environmental Engineering Consultant
6978 Presidio Court, Cincinnati, Ohio 45244

There are now centers at universities in Canada and the United States where inter disciplinary knowhow is being applied to promote studies of the transforming role of technology and from the perspective of its creators and doers.

The descriptive material for the Centre for Technology and Social Development established in 1987 at the University of Toronto states: "The situations and problems modern engineers deal with range from those where a focus on the internal functioning of materials, structures, processes and systems of machines is adequate, to those where a much broader focus is required. To know how a particular technology or engineering undertaking fits into the larger fabric of society and that of the ecosystem... the methods and approaches of the social sciences and humanities must be applied to a variety of problems of concern to modern engineering".

The Center established at the Massachussets Institute of Technology is reportedly looking toward restructuring engineering education to shift emphasis to the social and systemic picture, particularly for those involved in the chemical and nuclear area. The goal has been described as establishing an "ecology of technology" as a transdisciplinary frontier.

The present challenge clearly is to develop the applications of the presently available Human-Machine Interface body of knowledge directly to the prevention and control of spills.

APPENDIX

References:
Workshops: The Human-Machine Interface I, April 14, 1986; II, March 17,18, 1987; Spills Data Base Management in the Great Lakes Basin, February 27,28, 1989. Study Report, The Case for a "Spills: The Human-Machine Interface, Research Needs Workshop", May 1989. International Joint Commission, Great Lakes Regional Office, Windsor, Ontario, Canada.

HUMAN ERROR: A MAJOR CAUSE OF SPILLS

Harold E. Price[1]

Abstract

Accidental spills and releases of toxic and hazardous releases is a much greater problem than realized. While data reporting systems do not adequately account for human error as a causal factor in spills and releases, enough evidence is available to suggest that human error or poor human performance is a major contributor. Most human error is induced by design of the workplace or some other controllable factor and can therefore be reduced. An integrated industry/government human factors program should be established to identify and reduce sources of human error in accidental spills and releases.

Introduction

In 1987, the first year of reporting under the Toxic Release Inventory (TRI) requirement of EPA, manufacturing facilities reported the release of 18 billion pounds of TRI chemicals directly into the air, water, land, or underground wells (USEPA, 1989). Given that approximately half of the TRI consisted of a single chemical -- sodium sulfate and given that the quality of the data is not statistically sound and must be viewed cautiously -- there is, nevertheless, an incredible amount of toxic releases every year. How much of this is human error? No one knows, but the high rate of human error in other system malfunctions (e.g., aviation and nuclear power) is well documented and the evidence is beginning to suggest that human error is a significant contributor to accidental spills and releases.

---

[1]Vice President and Director, Human Factors and Training Group, Essex Corporation, 333 North Fairfax Street, Alexandria, Virginia, 22314.

Is Human Error a Significant Factor in Spills?

A study of accidents at Japanese chemical industry complexes -- especially those caused by human errors -- was reported by Hayashi (1985). He found that the ratio of hard errors (failure of machines and facilities) to soft errors (human errors) was 2:3. Of 284 accidents studied, about two-thirds involved human error. Hayashi also looked at what percentage of the human errors were system errors or "induced" and found this to be 65%. The induced errors were attributable to ergonomic design, operational and environmental conditions, managerial factors, and the operator's individual character.

A report issued by the Great Lakes Science Advisory Board's Technological Committee (1988) to the International Joint Commission on the results of a human-machine interface workshop on the effects of spills in the Great Lakes Basin concluded that accidental releases may significantly exceed the impact of regulated point source discharges. The workshop, composed of specialists in both the environment and human factors, further concluded that in the Great Lakes Basin:

o   There are an estimated 3,000 significant accidental releases of hazardous substances annually;
o   Spills are often caused by the complex relationships between humans and machines;
o   Programs designed to prevent spills are inadequate or non-existent;
o   Accidents or incidents arising from human errors are not adequately addressed.

The U.S. Congress, Office of Technology Assessment (1986) performed an excellent review of hazardous materials transportation accidents. The report looked at general causes of spills by transportation mode and found that human error was a significant factor in all modes. When looking at all modes taken together, it was found that human error is the primary cause of 62% of the incidents.

Perhaps the most revealing data concerning operator error comes from the EPA's Acute Hazardous Events Database (Industrial Ergonomics, Inc., 1988). These data reveal that for "in-plant events" operator error is the attributed cause in 18.2% of the events -- but, accounted for 45.7% of the quantity released. Admittedly, one must be careful about making generalizations from such databases, but the suggestion that human error is a major player is too obvious to ignore.

Has the Significance of Human Factors Been Recognized?

This author has not had the opportunity to thoroughly research or review industry or government programs to determine if the significance of human error or poor human performance as a contributor to spills has been recognized. In general, I think not. Yet, some industry papers have supported human factors, and the EPA clearly has the requirement to support human factors (in this author's opinion).

On the industry side, an <u>International Symposium on Preventing Major Chemical Accidents</u> held in 1987 had a session devoted to human factors with several industry presenters. One paper in this session by Kletz (1987) noted that, "Many accidents in chemical plants are ascribed to human error. This is not an adequate explanation for most such accidents because the design of the work situation often makes errors likely, even inevitable." Kletz further suggested that, "An accident can be prevented by better design, better instructions, etc. ...". Another author in that session (Gibson, 1987) summarizes his paper as follows:

> "This paper records several incidents, which have occurred in the process industries, that could have been prevented by proper consideration of human factors. The paper demonstrates that there is a pressing need for education to alert the process industries to the high rates of return available for investing in basic human factors expertise in design and operation of processes."

The EPA, until recently, seemed concerned more with cleanup than prevention. However, out of concern for serious accidental releases of hazardous chemicals (Bhopal and West Virginia) at least two important initiatives have occurred:

1. The EPA Chemical Emergency Preparedness Program was launched in 1985, and
2. In 1988, Congress passed Title III of the Super Fund Amendments and Reauthorization Act (SARA) in which Section 305(b) required EPA to conduct a "review of emergency systems for monitoring, detecting, and preventing releases of extremely hazardous substances ...".

The review report (EPA, 1988) required by Section 305(b) had the following relevant findings:

o Prevention of accidental releases requires a holistic approach:
- Prevention must take into account capabilities of facility personnel;
- Management must have a commitment to operator training;
o Prevention technologies and techniques must be disseminated to smaller companies;
o Some technologies need further research and development:
- Data on equipment failure and human error rates.

The report also recommended further studies on the causes of chemical accidents and ways to prevent them.

An outgrowth of the Chemical Emergency Preparedness Program (CEPP) has been the establishment of the Chemical Accident Prevention (CAP) program. In a strategy paper for that program (Environmental Protection Agency, 1989), they state, "Reviews of a range of chemical accidents have revealed deficiencies, that if remedied, could reduce the likelihood of such accidents --

o Inadequate worker safety training;
o Lack of coordination between public and private officials on response roles;
o Aging or inappropriate equipment;
o Poor maintenance practices."

I conclude from the SARA legislation and the CAP program strategy paper that EPA has a firm responsibility to include human factors and the reduction of human errors as a part of its prevention program.

Is Human Error Controllable?

Hardly a day goes by that one does not read news articles about some environmental incident causing a spill or release of hazardous materials that has been attributed to human error. Accident reports are full of "causes" such as carelessness, faulty attitude, and inattention. Although labels such as these appear to tell us something, they really don't. Everyone is inattentive at some time or another, and to say that an accident was caused by inattentiveness gives us no clue whatsoever about how we could have prevented it. Yet, in examining reports such as these, it is easy to conclude that the human is a highly unreliable component; in fact, the notion of human unreliability has long been a part of popular wisdom, possibly from the notion that "to err is human" as coined by the poet Alexander Pope.

The facts are that human errors are not a random phenomenon, nor are they usually caused by the perversity of the individual involved. Rather, in the majority of cases, the errors are attributable to factors external to the individual that can be identified and controlled. The majority of human error is "induced" by such controllable factors as the work environment, human-machine interface design, procedures, labeling, communications, supervision, workstation design, and -- more recently -- inappropriate use of automation and high technology. These "performance shaping factors" as they are sometimes known, are controllable.

The high frequency of human errors in system breakdown is well documented and varies from about 85% in transportation systems accidents and incidents to 20% in the much simpler consumer product area. What we must recognize and deal with is that the root causes of human error in most systems is induced and can be controlled; although, some factors (e.g., work environment, equipment design, training and procedures) are more controllable than others (management attitude, personal health or well-being, and spontaneous "random error"). Human factors practitioners recognize that the same factors which cause human error can be redesigned (or designed properly in the first place) to avoid or minimize human error. Recognizing that human error will not be entirely eliminated, a parallel thrust is to design "error tolerant" systems.

To conclude the discussion of human error, I would simply reiterate that "prevention and treatment" exists for the human error "illness", and the earlier applied, the better.

Conclusions

In summary, I would like to present the following conclusions:

- o   Human error is a significant factor in spills.
- o   The significance of human error and human factors has not been adequately recognized by industry and the government.
- o   Root causes of human error are identifiable and controllable.
- o   An integrated program for dealing with the human error issues should be developed by industry and the government, and some early initiatives should be started now.

References

Gibson, S.B. (1987). Investment in Human Factors Pays Dividends. International Symposium on Preventing Major Chemical Accidents. Washington, D.C.

Great Lakes Science Advisory Board's Technological Committee (1988). Spills: The Human-Machine Interface, Proceedings of the Workshops on Human-Machine Interface. Windsor, Ontario: Great Lakes Regional Office, 1988.

Hayashi, Y. (1985). Hazard analysis in chemical complexes in Japan -- especially those caused by human errors. Ergonomics, Vol. 28, No. 6, 835-841.

Industrial Economics, Inc. (1988). Acute Hazardous Events Data Base. Cambridge, MA for USEPA.

Kletz, T.A. (1987). An Engineer's View of Human Error. International Symposium on Preventing Major Chemical Accidents.

U.S. Congress (1986). Office of Technology Assessment, Transportation of Hazardous Materials, OTA-SET-304. Washington, DC: U.S. Government Printing Office.

U.S. Environmental Protection Agency (1988). Review of Emergency Systems, Report to Congress (Final Report). Washington, DC: Office of Solid Waste and Emergency Response.

U.S. Environmental Protection Agency (1989a). The Toxics-Release Inventory, Executive Summary, Pesticides and Toxic Substances (TS-779).

U.S. Environmental Protection Agency (1989b). Chemical Accident Prevention Strategy (unpublished paper).

Oil Spill Impacts on Aquifers

Otto J. Helweg,[1] Fellow, ASCE and Howard Hwang,[2] Member ASCE

Abstract

This study attempts to evaluate the seismic hazards along a forty inch pipeline and the impact of a pipeline rupture in the recharge area of the aquifer serving most of West Tennessee. Two potential break locations were chosen in the alluvial valley of a main river where the probability of a rupture is greatest. The volume and fate of the hydrocarbons are being modeled and remediation strategies are being studied.

Introduction

Three different national concerns have coalesced to provide the impetus for this study. First, the earthquake in California reminded residents of the Mid South that they live in the vicinity of the second most earthquake hazardous zone in the U.S. Second, a national interest in aquifer contamination by hydrocarbons, sometimes called nonaqueous phase liquids (NAPL), has resulted from numerous leaking underground storage tanks (UST). Third, ruptures of several petroleum and other lines have alerted people to the spill potential they present.

Fig. 1 shows the crude oil pipeline routes overlaid on the earthquake zones of the central U.S. (Beavers, et.al., 1986). Estimating the earthquake hazard to these pipelines has been covered by Beavers, et.al. (1986). Also, Hwang, et.al. (1990) have dealt with the earthquake hazard to municipal water distribution systems along a similar line. Consequently, risk or hazard analysis, though part of this study, will not be covered in this paper.

The interest in NAPL contamination is illustrated by the increasing number of books and papers published on the subject. Several examples of books are Canter and Knox (1986) and Calabrese and Kostecki (1988). Another indication of interest is the attendance at the "Petroleum Hydrocarbons and Organic Chemicals in Ground Water" conference. The concern for ground water protection is illustrated by the Conservation Foundations report (1987).

---

[1]Chair and Prof., Dept. of Civ. Engrg. Memphis State Univ., Memphis, TN 38152

[2]Assoc. Research Prof., Centr. for Earthquake Research and Infor., Memphis State Univ., Memphis, TN 38152

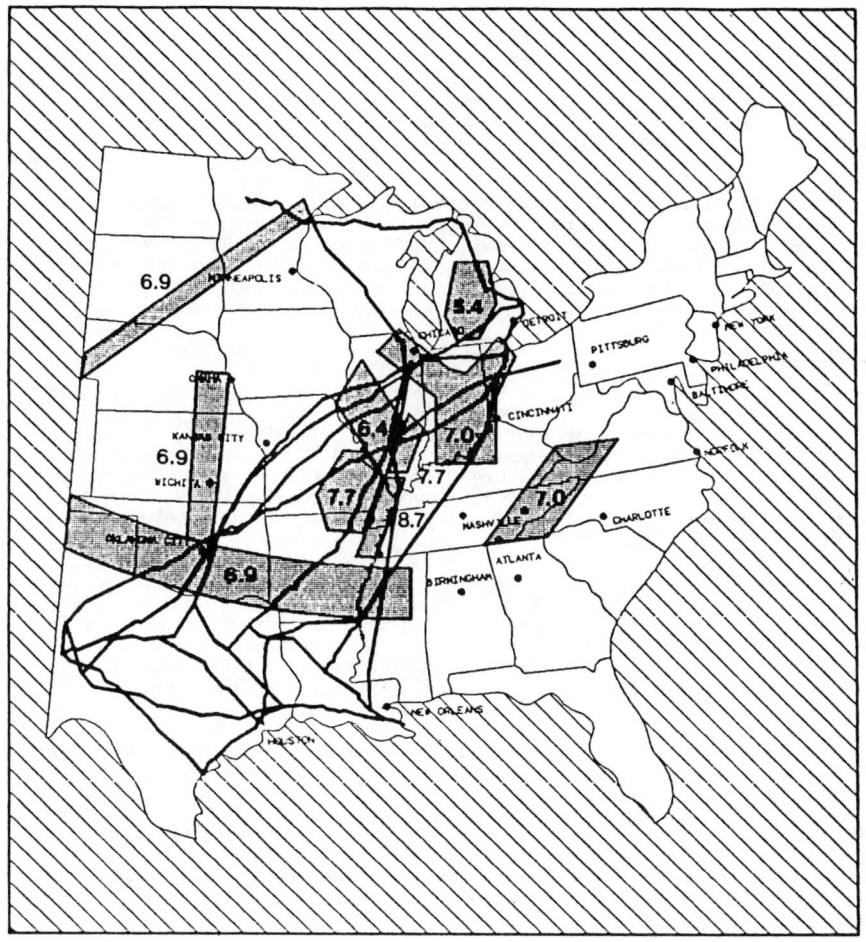

FIG. 1. Central U.S. Earthquake Zones and Crude Oil Pipelines
(Beavers, et.al., 1986)

Study Site

The proposed rupture zone is where the forth inch crude oil pipeline crosses the Wolf River at the Shelby/Fayette County line which is south east of Memphis, Tennessee. Here the pipeline not only crosses a stream channel, but almost one mile of wetlands before the land elevation rises out of the flood plain. The pipe is buried about four feet under ground and this area, as any of the fluvial valleys, is the most susceptible to liquefaction and loss of support.

In the past, engineers felt the Memphis Sands, the confined aquifer from which Memphis Light, Gas, and Water (MLGW) obtain the water supply for the area, was protected by a continuous layer of thick clay, called the Jackson formation. This Jackson formation starts anywhere from ground surface to several hundred feet and has a thickness that varies from zero to 370 feet. Where the layer pinches out provides "windows" for pollutants to enter the Memphis Sands.

The Memphis Sands yields about 200 mgd (757,400 m^3/day). The formation starts from zero to 500 feet and ranges from 500 to 890 feet thick (Gram and Parks, 1986). MLGW obtains about 98% of their water from this aquifer. The water is excellent for consumption and industrial use. Were this aquifer to become contaminated, it would obviously cause sever problems to the greater Memphis area.

Procedure

Two breaks in the forty-inch pipeline will be modeled, one occurring underneath the Wolf River and the other at the edge of the fluvial valley. The first will entail both ground water and surface water contamination; the latter only ground water. The volume of hydrocarbons released after a break is estimated by calculating the volume in the pipeline between the two surrounding shut-off valves plus the amount pumped through the pipeline during the response time.

The fate of the released hydrocarbons are being modeled by the ARMOS and MOFAT models (Kaluarachchi and Parker, 1989). These finite element models are capable of simulating multiphase flow in two dimensions. They will not only define the probable contaminate flume, but assist in predicting the effectiveness of the remediation activities. From these results, emergency procedures and preventative measures will be suggested to MLGW.

Timely response to any spill emergency should facilitate an adequate recovery of the pollutants, especially hydrocarbons since they will remain, initially, on top of the water table. However, since water table elevation of the unconfined aquifer is at a higher elevation than the piezometric surface of the confined aquifer, the Memphis Sands, the downward flux of dissolved pollutants has been calculated. A geographical information system (GIS) has been set up utilizing ARC/INFO software to evaluate and process the research results. Fig. 2 illustrates one aspect of this.

Summary and Conclusions

It is important to be prepared for disasters that **will** happen. Many people think in terms of "**IF** a disaster happens," rather than "when it happens." This study will provide information concerning possible contamination to the Memphis Sands aquifer, extent of surface contamination, and a remediation strategy. Moreover, it will determine what, if any, preventative measures should be taken in light of risk analysis which will consider not only the probability of pipeline rupture, but expected cost.

References

Beavers, J. E., et. al. (1986). "Vulnerability of Energy Distribution Systems to an Earthquake in the Eastern United States: an Overview." Amer. Assoc. of Engrg. Soc.

Calabrese, E. J. and Kostecki, P. T. (1988). **Petroleum Contaminated Soils.** Lewis Publishers, Inc., Chelsia, MI.

Canter, L. W. and Knox, R. C. (1986). **Ground Water Pollution Control.** Lewis Publishers, Inc., Chelsia, MI.

Conservation Foundation (1978). **Groundwater Protection,** The Conservation Foundation, Washington, D.C.

Graham, D. D. and Parks, W. S. (1986). "Potential for Leakage Among Principal Aquifers in the Memphis Area, Tennessee." U. S. Geological Survey, Water Resources Investigations Report 85-4295

Hwang, H., Helweg, O. J., and Smith, J. W. (1990). "Estimating the Earthquake Hazard of Municipal Water Systems." this publication.

Kaluarachchi, J. J. and Parker, J. C. (1989). "An Efficient Finite Element Method for Modeling Multiphase Flow." **Water Resources Research,** Vol. 25, No. 1, Jan.

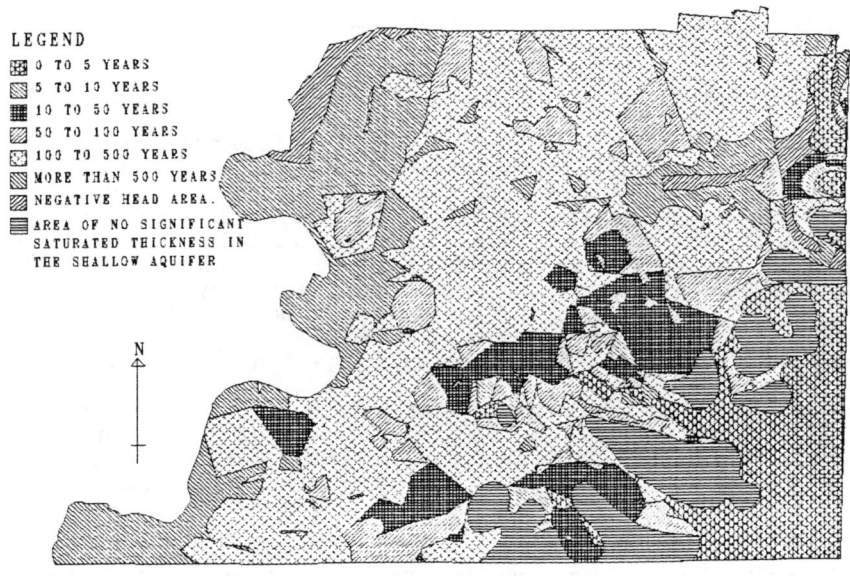

FIG. 2, Vertical Travel Time Through the Jackson Formation

APPLICATION OF A WATER BUDGET FOR INSTREAM FLOWS

Terry Waddle, AM ASCE[1]

Abstract: A portion of a water supply reservoir can be dedicated to supplying instream flows. This sub-reservoir is operated to provide instream fish habitat below the reservoir when releases to the stream channel for other purposes do not provide adequate habitat. A limiting event model, the effective habitat time series, is used to determine when releases to augment streamflow will produce the greatest habitat benefits. Operation rules for the sub-reservoir must consider water rights and past habitat events. An example developed for a proposed water supply reservoir in Colorado shows that use of storage to provide instream flows improves deliveries to other water rights that would potentially sacrifice water to satisfy fixed instream flow requirements.

Introduction

Water supply reservoirs are managed to alter the timing of runoff. Typical hydrograph modifications include within-year time shifts (spring runoff held for summer irrigation) and between year shifts (water banking for drought). Requirements for instream flows below water resource projects have increased in recent years. Such requirements are often presented by regulatory agencies in the form of minimum instream flows. Depending on the system configuration, minimum flow requirements can reduce the firm yield available to water project diversions.

Instream flow requirements present several administrative challenges depending on their method of implementation. One possible approach to providing instream flows is to recognize instream values as a beneficial use and

---

[1]Hydrologist, Nat. Ecology Research Cntr., U.S. Fish and Wildl. Serv., 2627 Redwing Rd., Ft. Collins. CO 80526

allow storage to support instream flows in a similar manner to current storage for irrigation and municipal and industrial (M and I) uses.

The Northwest Power Planning Council (Northwest Power Planning Council, 1982), defined a volume of storage and runoff dedicated to flushing flows for moving small salmon down the Columbia River system as a "water budget". Here, the term "water budget" defines a portion of reservoir storage dedicated to providing instream flows and its operation under the appropriative doctrine to provide long term habitat benefits. This paper presents an example model study of this concept and contrasts the results with a fixed minimum flow requirement.

Reservoir Operations to Provide Habitat

Operation of water budget storage requires some means of estimating benefits. Instantaneous instream benefits can be described in terms of habitat values using the Physical Habitat Simulation System of the U.S. Fish and Wildlife Service (Milhous, 1979). However, discharge events in one year may affect the population for several subsequent years. The effective habitat time series concept (Bovee, 1982) relates habitat events to this memory effect.

The water supply system configuration below a storage reservoir has a significant influence on the amount of water needed to maintain year-round habitat values. If instream flows are needed below major diversion locations, fewer synergistic uses of instream flow can be obtained. If instream flow areas are located upstream from diversions, complementary uses of the water are possible and less stored water need be dedicated to instream flows.

The water budget concept proposed here uses the effective habitat time series to determine when to release water from dedicated sub-reservoir storage to satisfy instream flows. The release is determined by the effective habitat history prior to release decisions, the water budget storage volume and the habitat produced by releases for other purposes. That is, releases from storage for instream flow are used to augment flows from releases for other purposes to achieve instream flow targets derived from the effective habitat time series..

The Effective Habitat Time Series

The effective habitat time series behaves much like the logistic growth function:

$$\frac{dN}{dt} = r(N - \frac{N}{K})$$

where: r = growth rate,

K = upper asymptotic limit of growth.

The major difference in the two models is the manner in which the upper limit is defined. The logistic growth model incorporates an asymptote as part of the differential equation while the effective habitat model uses measured or modeled available habitat values developed outside of the model. The effective habitat model relates potentially usable habitat between life stages by considering average density and mortality factors. The habitat that can be used (effectively used habitat) is determined as the minimum of the potentially usable or available habitat for each life stage in each life year. That is,

EFFHAB = Min(potential habitat, available habitat)

where EFFHAB is the adult effective habitat value, potential habitat is the habitat area that could potentially be used by the number of preceding life stage fish produced in the previous year, and available habitat is the habitat area that flow conditions produce during the current year.

Because it sequentially relates sub-adult life stages, the effective habitat time series exhibits a "memory" effect. This memory is illustrated in the following example (Fig. 1) where severe events for fry and juvenile

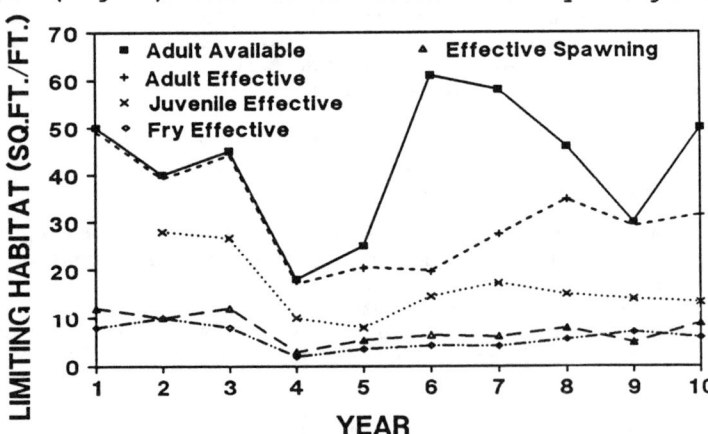

Figure 1.. Effective Habitat Time Series

life stages in year 4 prevent the adult effective habitat from reaching available levels in years 5 through 8.

Application Example

The water budget concept was applied to a proposed reservoir on the Cache la Poudre River, Colorado (Waddle, 1988). To simplify this illustration, water rights were lumped into four diversions and one instream flow right (water right 5 in Fig. 2). The instream flow and its associated storage were assumed to be the most junior right under the appropriative doctrine. Reservoir and instream flow characteristics are summarized in Table 1.

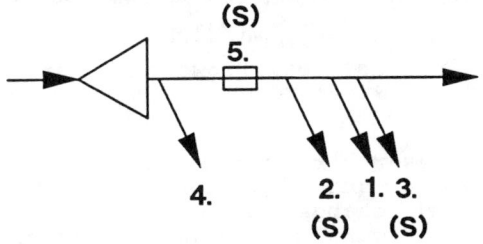

Figure 2. System Configuration, (S) Indicates Water is Supplied by Storage Right, Rights 1 and 4 are Direct Diversion Rights

Table 1. Reservoir and Instream Flow Characteristics

	Fixed minimum Flow	Water Budget
Total Storage	132,000 AF	156,000 AF
Water Budget Storage	n/a	24,000 AF
Total Instream Target	36,000 AF	47,200 AF
Limiting Habitat	n/a	2.17 sq.ft./ft.

The effective habitat time series indicated that for water year 1981 flows producing average habitat conditions were needed. Figure 3 shows the desired instream flow pattern for 1981 and instream flows produced by operating the reservoir to supply diversion rights 1 through 4 with no water budget storage.

To implement the water budget, storage capacity was

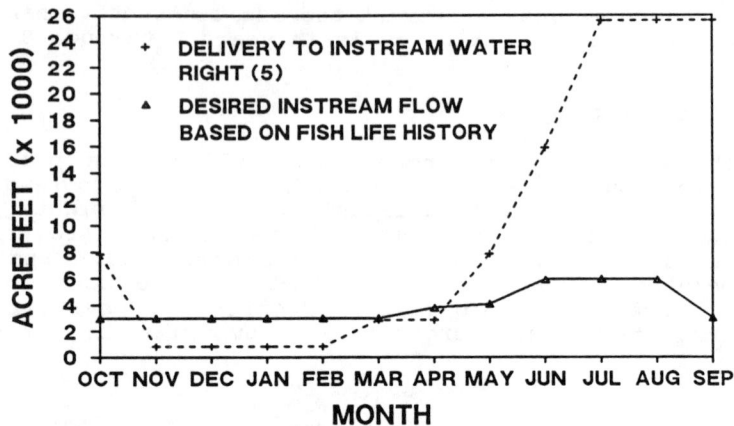

Figure 3. Desired Instream Flows and Instream Flows Without Water Budget Storage

added to the reservoir to provide instream flows when releases for higher priority rights did not meet instream needs. The net changes in water budget storage are illustrated in Figure 4. Storage withdrawals exceed additions; however, 1981 was a dry water year and carry over storage was sufficient to maintain the instream flows. With water budget storage in place, instream flows were maintained at or above target levels in all months.

To contrast the water budget approach with constant

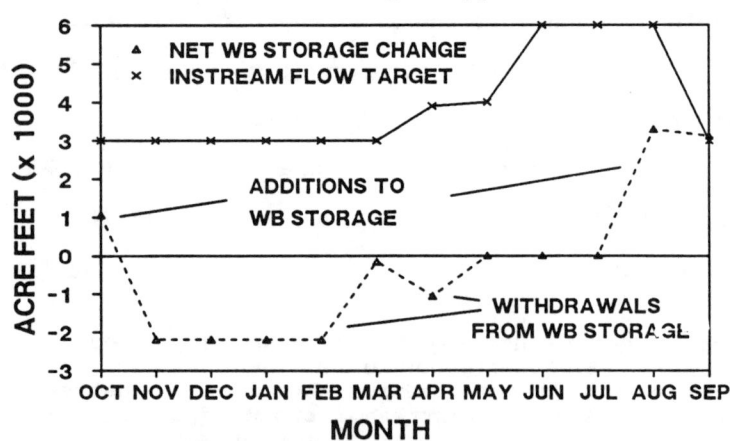

Figure 4. Net Water Budget (WB) Storage Change and Target Instream Flow

instream flow requirements, the reservoir was forced to meet constant instream flows of 50 cfs (about 3000 AF per month) without the additional storage volume used for the water budget. The result was reduced deliveries to the low priority water rights. The third priority right was strongly affected (See Table 2.) due to depletion of its carry over storage.

Table 2. Total Diversion Delivery Shortages (1981)

	Fixed minimum Flow	Water Budget
Water Right 3	48377 AF	0 AF
Water Right 4	19139 AF	13929 AF

Conclusions

Reservoir storage devoted to supplying water for instream flows was shown to be a possible means of allowing water diversions and instream uses to coexist. By providing water to be managed for instream purposes, this concept can lead to reduction of conflicts between instream flow advocates and holders of traditional water rights.

Two issues not addressed here are: legal recognition of storage for instream flows on an equal footing with storage for traditional beneficial uses and responsibility for the cost of additional storage. Resolution of the legal and administrative issues would put the onus on individuals and agencies interested in maintaining instream flows to purchase their share of storage.

Appendix 1. References

Bovee, K. D. 1982. A Guide to Stream Habitat Analysis Using the Instream Flow Incremental Methodology. Instream Flow Information Paper 12, U.S. Fish Wildl. Serv. Biol. Rep. FWS/OBS-82/26, 248 pp.

Milhous, R. T. 1979. "The Physical Habitat Simulation System for Instream Flow Studies" Proceedings 1979 Summer Computer Simulation Conference, Toronto, Canada, July 1979. pp. 440 - 446.

Northwest Power Planning Council. 1982. Columbia River Basin Fish and Wildlife Program. Nov. 15. 225 pp.

Waddle, T. 1988. "Development of Feasible Instream Flow Requirements". Proceedings 6th National Conference on Microcomputers in Civil Eng. Nov. 9-11. pp. 193-198.

Application Of Risk Management And Value Engineering

Techniques To Evaluation Of Water Resources

Projects With Special Emphasis On Geological Hazards

By

David W. Eckhoff[1], M. ASCE and Jeffrey R. Keaton, [2] M. ASCE

INTRODUCTION

The purpose of this paper is to provide: 1) a perspective for identifying and evaluating in comparable terms all hazards at a site; and 2) a means for intelligent decision-making based on these evaluations. Value engineering (VE) is an objective, systematic method for minimizing the total cost of a facility or system for a specific number of years, and therefore is an appropriate hazard management approach. Total cost means ultimate costs to construct, operate, maintain, and replace a facility or system during its design life. The VE approach is a creative effort directed toward the analysis of functions; it is concerned with eliminating or modifying those aspects which <u>add cost</u> without adding function -- or, in the case of hazards, <u>without reducing risk</u>. In this context, a <u>hazard</u> is a naturally occurring or man-induced process which has the potential to cause damage to property or injury to people. <u>Risk</u> is exposure of something of value to a hazard.

Decision-makers and engineers often need answers to four basic questions in order to deal responsibly with geologic and other hazards: (1) When will the hazard occur?; (2) What will happen when the hazard occurs?; (3) What area will be affected?; (4) What can be done to reduce the risk?

Systematic evaluation of hazards and risks permits assessment of the costs associated with alternative responses which provide an acceptable level of risk of damage. Figure 1 is a Hazard and Risk Evaluation Worksheet for geologic hazard management. The initial phase in the assessment is recognition of the hazard; failing to recognize or ignoring hazards may lead to liability for damage caused by the hazards. They may be evaluated in terms of the extent of exposure and consequence of damage. Selection of an acceptable level of risk can be very difficult and often is a public policy issue.

Five alternative responses exist and should be assessed sequentially. A segment of a power plant aqueduct subjected to rockfall, landslide and earthquake damage provides a useful example of the five alternative responses. The <u>first</u> possible response is to continue current practices; this is the so-called "do nothing" alternative. In the context of the aqueduct example, continuing current practices

---

[1] Chairman, Eckhoff, Watson & Preator Engineering, 1121 East 3900 South, Building C-100, Salt Lake City, Utah 84124.
[2] Senior Engineering Geologist, Sergent, Hauskins & Beckwith Engineers, 4030 South 500 West, Suite 90, Salt Lake City, Utah 84123.

would consist of repairing rockfall damage, and relocating the conduit in the landslide area on an as-needed basis. If continuing current practices meets the risk acceptability criteria, then present worth costs are estimated and stored for comparative purposes; if the risk acceptability criteria are not met, then the costs need not be estimated.

The second response is to modify the hazard. In the context of the rockfall example, modifying the hazard could include measures to prevent rocks from falling from the slope. Engineering measures to accomplish such prevention could consist of bolting or strapping rocks on the slope, or draping wire mesh on the slope. Stabilizing landslides is also a hazard modification measure. The third response is to modify the system at risk. For the rockfall example, modifying the system at risk could include constructing a rock deflection shed to protect the aqueduct from falling rocks, and constructing a tunnel/siphon around or under active slide masses. The fourth response is to modify system operation. Modifying the system operation may not constitute an acceptable alternative in terms of reducing risk to the aqueduct. However, considering that the consequent damages of an aqueduct rupture can be disastrous, reducing the risk associated with consequent damages could be a legitimate objective. For example, shutting down the aqueduct during periods of high risk might be considered, so that aqueduct rupture would not result in environmental damage from released water. Alternatively, landslide movement detectors could be installed to provide warning of imminent danger so that immediate aqueduct shut-down could be implemented.

If the risk acceptability criteria are not met by any of the four responses described above, then the acceptable level of risk may be so small that it is approaching absolute safety. The fifth alternative response is to avoid the hazard regardless of the cost. In our example, avoiding the hazard would require relocating the existing aqueduct or abandoning a possible alignment of a proposed aqueduct. Deciding to avoid a hazard can be particularly difficult for existing facilities which may have to be abandoned. Risk management should be an iterative process with continuous checking for changes in the hazards, the risks, or risk acceptability.

DECISION-MAKER'S QUESTIONS

When Will The Hazard Occur?

This is a difficult question for two reasons. First, by definition, hazards are processes or events which occur at potentially damaging intensities. Micro earthquakes and runoff from gentle rains occur frequently with no resulting damage. Major earthquakes and flooding from very heavy rains occur less frequently, often with some consequent damage. Intensities ranging from "no damage" to "total damage" are possible depending on the quality of construction and the character of the hazard. Second, precisely predicting the moment of occurrence of a hazard is generally not possible. Weather forecasting provides a good example of the predictability of natural processes. Weather forecasts are put in terms of probabilities; a 20-percent chance of rain tomorrow in the forecast area. Forecasting earthquakes is much more troublesome. The real question to be answered is, "When will damage occur in St. Louis, Missouri, due to earthquake shaking?" This question is directed at the issue of local moderate earthquakes as well as distant major earthquakes. An adequate analysis of earthquake hazards in St. Louis needs to focus on earthquake sources within about 200 miles of the city.

Earthquake hazards are evaluated by: 1) assessing historical earthquake patterns (historical seismicity); and 2) evaluating geologic features (faults) capable of generating earthquakes (paleoseismicity).

The engineering geology corollary to the Law of Uniformitarianism is, "The recent past is the key to the near future." Thus, for hazards like earthquakes and landslides, the geologic record must be examined for evidence that such processes occurred in the recent past (the most recent 10,000 years or more, depending on the nature of the facility). If such evidence exists, then the magnitude and frequency of such occurrences must be estimated to predict the probability that future events will occur. These probabilities can be annualized or averaged over project lifetimes.

PROJECT ELEMENT	
SUBELEMENT	
NATURE OF HAZARD(S)	
RISK: CONSEQUENCE(S)	
EXPOSURE(S) (Narrative)	
(Statistical)	
ACCEPTABLE RISK LEVEL(S)	

RESPONSE ALTERNATIVES

Response	Accept Risk?	Capital Cost	Annual Exposure X Probability	Annual Expected = Value
(1) Continue Current Practices				
(2) Modify Hazard				
(3) Modify System				
(4) Modify Operations				

COMMENTS

REFERENCES

Figure 1
Hazard And Risk Evaluation Worksheet

What Will Happen When The Hazard Occurs?

The assessment of the effects of a hazard usually is based on two other questions: 1) What has happened in similar events in the immediate area and elsewhere?; and 2) How fragile is the feature or structure at risk? An important issue associated with these questions is the contrast between planned new facilities and existing old facilities. Planned facilities can be designed to accommodate the forces of infrequent hazards, but significant uncertainty commonly is associated with many design details of existing facilities. Structural damage and damage to building components and contents are easy to visualize and understand. An issue commonly overlooked is that of business interruption or loss of function or revenue. Critical facilities -- those needed during and immediately following natural disasters -- clearly have a smaller tolerance for interruption than non-critical facilities. Some critical facilities are municipal water supplies, hospitals, fire stations, police stations and arterial roads. For water resources projects, a significant difference exists between the criticality of a municipal water supply and projects used for other purposes, such as irrigation or hydropower.

What Area Will Be Affected?

Damage usually is greatest close to the "center" of a hazard and diminishes with increasing distance. Flood damage usually is concentrated along the margins of stream channels. Landslide damage usually is confined to the landslide area itself. A notable exception to this generalization is the Thistle Landslide which

RISK MANAGEMENT APPLICATION 797

occurred in central Utah in 1983. The landslide disrupted the routes of a major highway and a major railroad. No facilities were built on the slide mass itself. Thus, immediate damage due to the moving earth of the landslide was restricted to a highway and a railroad. Secondary damage was caused by a lake which formed behind the landslide which dammed the Spanish Fork river. The lake inundated the small community of Thistle, for which the landslide was named. The threat of tertiary damage due to catastrophic release of water in the event the landslide dam failed was sufficiently great that much money and effort were used to reinforce the landslide dam and to drain the lake. The Denver and Rio Grande Western Railroad was losing approximately $1 million each day that they could not use their tracks past the landslide. Coal miners in central Utah were furloughed until coal could be shipped by rail to Wasatch Front markets. Travelers were forced to go hundreds of miles out of their way because the landslide blocked the only transportation route across the northern Wasatch Plateau to central Utah. Thus, although the damage due to primary and secondary hazards was significant, losses due to business interruption and travel extension were at least of equal magnitude.

What Can Be Done To Reduce Risk?

The answer to this question depends on the specific characteristics of the hazard. For relatively little additional cost, proposed facilities can often be designed to resist the forces of infrequent hazards or located to avoid them. Existing facilities, on the other hand, require significant additional cost to be upgraded and strengthened to resist larger forces than originally anticipated. Furthermore, business interruption costs can be substantial while upgrading is done. The costs of alternative responses must be compared to the probability of occurrence of hazards and the potential losses (dollar-value damage, personal injury, and business interruption). An innovative method of addressing this complicated issue is Value Engineering in a risk-based framework.

RISK-BASED FRAMEWORK

A risk-based method for assessing possible improvements for dam safety was developed by Bowles and others (1987). This method consists of four elements: risk identification, risk estimation, risk aversion, and risk acceptance. The risk identification element involves listing the various factors which could contribute to potential losses and organizing these into logical event sequences which cover all expected events and responses. Such event sequences commonly are configured into event trees which serve as risk models for evaluating existing conditions and the effectiveness of proposed mitigation or aversion alternatives. The risk estimation element involves assigning probabilities to each branch of the event tree model and assessing the consequences of each event and response along separate pathways in the event tree. If the expected losses (damage and/or injury) are unacceptable under existing conditions, then some form of risk aversion may be desirable to reduce the probability associated with an initiating event, a system response, or an outcome, or to reduce the exposure to the hazard. Alternative responses for dealing with hazards were described earlier. The risk acceptance element deals with deciding what degree of safety is appropriate or what residual risk will be accepted. This issue commonly is not addressed uniformly with respect to a variety of hazards. Usually only those hazards which are regulated (e.g., floods and earthquakes) are considered. Consequently, a de facto acceptance of risk, even if the risk is unacceptable, results for those hazards which are not considered specifically. Therefore, systematic assessment of all hazards and alternative responses promotes intelligent decision-making.

VALUE ENGINEERING APPROACH

The Value Engineering approach to geologic hazard risk management described by Keaton and Eckhoff (1988) is a creative effort concerned with eliminating or modifying those aspects of a system which add cost without reducing risk. Alternate solutions are developed for the specific function. VE analyzes function or method by asking such questions as: What is it?; What does it do?; What must it do?; What does it cost?; What other material or method could be used to do the same job?; What would the alternate material or method cost?

The VE approach is ideally suited to risk management associated with geologic hazards.

The Team Concept

The use of an analytical team is an important concept in Value Engineering, because of the improvements experienced in both the quality and quantity of the product. Alphonse J. Dell'Isola (1978) discussed the team approach in his manual entitled Value Engineering in the Construction Industry.

The first step is to form a multi-disciplinary team representing a cross-section of technical fields related to the needs of the project. This multi-disciplinary approach is one of the keys to a successful study. The reason for its importance is that more and better ideas tend to be generated, greater consideration is given to the total impact of decisions on both the facility and costs, and improved communications are developed among disciplines. The principal phases of the job plan are information, speculative, analytical, and proposal. During the speculative phase, the principal question to be answered is: In what alternate ways can the necessary function be performed? The foremost approach to creativity in answering this question in VE is the brainstorming technique. A brainstorming session is a problem-solving conference wherein each participant's thinking is stimulated by others in the group.

The quantitative result of a multi-disciplinary group in generating ideas has no parallel. The team concept not only results in a large number of ideas but also improves the creative ability of the participants. There are many reasons for the high quantity of group ideas generated, but perhaps the most important one is the aspect of interdisciplinary communication. Many times, one member's idea motivates the associative processes of the other members. This phenomenon produces a chain reaction, triggering many ideas; and the cycle repeats itself.

In the analytical phase, sometimes called the evaluation and investigation phase, the team examines, and then develops the alternatives generated during the preceding phase into lower-cost alternate solutions. The principal tasks are to evaluate, refine, and cost analyze the ideas and to list feasible alternates in order of descending savings potential. During this phase, the ideas must be refined to meet the necessary environmental and operating conditions of the particular situation. Ideas which obviously do not meet these requirements are dropped for further consideration.

The proposal phase, sometimes called the program planning and reporting phase, is the final step in the VE job plan. During this phase three things must be accomplished: (1) The group must thoroughly review all alternate solutions being proposed to assure that the maximum acceptable risks and significant savings are really being offered; (2) A sound proposal must be made to management. The group must consider not only to whom it must propose, but also how to propose the solutions most effectively; (3) The group must present a plan for implementing the proposal.

Methods

The authors recently directed a Value Engineering/Risk Analysis effort for the appraisal of an existing hydropower aqueduct. The composition of the team was: General Civil Engineer (team leader), Engineering Geologist, Structural Engineer, Metallurgist, and a Tunneling Specialist. Based on observations made during an inspection tour of the aqueduct, the team mutually made determinations of the major elements and subelements of the system. As the analysis continued, revisions and deletions were made. The primary criterion was appropriate isolation of elements and subelements so that unique and independent hazards and risks could be delineated.

Hazard identification was the responsibility of each of the technical specialists on the team. The broad categories of hazard were: (1) Deterioration - structural and mechanical elements; (2) Erosion - undercutting and collapse; (3) Safety - protection and/or exclusion of the public; (4) Malfunctioning Elements; (5) Rockfall; (6) Talus Accumulations; (7) Headscarp Encroachment; (8) Landslide; (9) Earthquake; (10) Thermal Strain. After identification by individuals was completed, the team reviewed the composite list and jointly prepared a matrix (Figure 1) with the following components: (1) Element/Subelement; (2) (Nature of) Hazard(s); (3) Risk: Consequence(s) and Exposure(s); (4) Accelerated Risk Level(s); and (5) Response Alternatives.

This facilitated the grouping of similar hazard-risk scenarios, so that categories of response could be developed and reviewed.

Risk exposures were then suggested by appropriate technical specialists, and the team reviewed the number(s) and the rationale for each. Final selection was made by the team. Subsequently, residual risks (after presumed implementation of corrective measures) were estimated in a similar fashion.

In most cases, recommended response action alternatives were developed by the appropriate technical specialist. However, these individuals represented a broad range and considerable depth of experience. So, the response actions considered were frequently the consensus result of team discussion and analysis. The team concept is very valuable for projects like this. It can be economical, efficient, thorough, and frequently more insightful than the traditionally structured investigative approach.

REFERENCES

BOWLES, D.S., Anderson, L.R., and Glover, T.R., "Design Level Risk Assessment For Dams," in Roesset, J. M., ed., Dynamics of Structures, American Society of Civil Engineers, 1987, p. 210-225.

DELL'ISOLA A.J., Value Engineering In The Construction Industry: New York, Construction Publishing Company, 1975, 181 p.

KEATON, J.R., And Eckhoff, D.W., "A Value Engineering Approach To Geologic Hazard Risk Management", Association of Engineering Geologists, Abstracts and Program, Kansas City, 1988, p. 49.

OPTIMIZATION OF FRESHWATER INFLOW TO ESTUARIES
by

Yeou-Koung Tung[1], A.M. ASCE, Yixing Bao[2], and Larry W. Mays[3], M. ASCE

INTRODUCTION
In many areas of the U.S., particularly the Gulf Coast states and California, the freshwater discharge of rivers has become a limited commodity. The need for freshwater inflow to maintain the productivity of downstream estuaries must compete with the demands of upstream users, viz. municipal and industrial uses, and agriculture. The desired approach to water resources management is to optimize flow into the estuary (by minimizing the total volume of flow, or by maximizing the diversions and storage within limits of water rights and capacity, or both) while preserving an acceptable habitat in specific regions of the estuary to accommodate the requirements of key organisms. This paper presents a methodology that can be used for determining the optimal freshwater inflows into bays and estuaries for the purpose of balancing freshwater demands with the harvest of various types of estuarine resources (e.g., finfish and shrimp). Salinity is expressed as a function of freshwater inflow in a nonlinear regression equation and used as a constraint. Additional nonlinear constraints are the harvest regression equations for the various species which express harvest as a function of the quantity of freshwater inflow. Because of the uncertainty associated with the regression equations for salinity and harvest these constraints are expressed in a chance-constrained formulation. The methodology has been applied to the Lavaca-Tres Palacios Estuary in Texas. The results indicate that the minimum freshwater inflow requirement increases as the required reliability of chance-constraints increases.

---

[1] Associate Professor of Statistics and Research Hydrologist, Department of Statistics and Wyoming Water Research Center, The University of Wyoming, Laramie, Wyoming 82071.
[2] Graduate Research Assistant, Department of Civil Engineering, The University of Texas, Austin, Texas 78712.
[3] Chairman and Professor, Department of Civil Engineering, Arizona State University, Tempe, Arizona 85287.

OPTIMIZATION MODEL

The mathematical programming model can have the objective of minimizing the sum of freshwater inflows, Q_{ij}, for month i and river j,

$$\text{Min} \sum_j \sum_i Q_{ij} \tag{1}$$

subject to
(1) the nonlinear relationship of estuary salinity and freshwater inflow

$$s_{ij} = \phi_{ij}(Q_{ij}) \tag{2}$$

(2) upper ($\bar{s}$) and lower ($\underline{s}$) bounds on the monthly average salinity at a specified location in the estuary, for each river j

$$\underline{s}_{ij} \leq s_{ij} \leq \bar{s}_{ij} \tag{3}$$

(3) lower limits on the i-th monthly inflows for the j-th river, QI_{ij}, to express seasonal biological requirements, such as estuarine marshes inundation

$$Q_{ij} \geq QI_{ij} \tag{4}$$

(4) the sum of monthly flows must be less than or equal to the upper limit of the total annual inflow, QT_j, from each river j,

$$\sum Q_{ij} \leq QT_j \tag{5}$$

(5) upper and lower limits on mean monthly flows in seasons for each river

$$\underline{QS}_{jm} \leq QS_{jm} = \frac{1}{N_m} \sum_{i \in M_m} Q_{ij} \leq \overline{QS}_{jm} \tag{6}$$

where M_m is the set of months in season m and N_m is the number of months in season m;
(6) the nonlinear regression relationship between the harvest of organism k and the seasonal inflow in river j,

$$H_k = \psi_k(QS_{jm}) \tag{7}$$

(7) lower limits on annual fish harvest, $\underline{H}_k$, by species k,

$$H_k \geq \underline{H}_k \tag{8}$$

(8) upper and lower limits on monthly inflows ($\overline{Q}_{ij}$ and $\underline{Q}_{ij}$) from each river

$$\underline{Q}_{ij} \leq Q_{ij} \leq \overline{Q}_{ij} \tag{9}$$

Alternative I The most fundamental formulation of the problem for estuarine management is to minimize the total annual freshwater inflow subject to constraints (2), (3), (4) and (9).

Alternative II A second formulation is to maintain the fisheries harvest at a certain level by minimizing the total annual freshwater inflow. The constraints for Alternative II are equations (2), (3), (4), (6), (7), (8) and (9).

Alternative III Enhance the commercial harvest of fisheries by maximizing the total annual commercial harvest of a given organism k (say shellfish) Max $QS^T \hat{\beta}_{H_K}$ subject to equations (2), (3), (4), (5), (6) and (9), where QS^T is the transpose of vector of the seasonal freshwater inflow, QS, and $\hat{\beta}_{H_K}$ is the vector of estimated coefficients of the harvest regression equation for species k.

Alternative IV This alternative is similar to Alternative I except the minimum seasonal flow (marsh inundation) requirement, constraint (4), is removed.

CHANCE-CONSTRAINT FORMULATION

The regression constraints in the optimization model for salinity and harvest are subject to uncertainty. The basic application of chance-constraints is to account for the uncertainty of random variables in the right-hand side coefficients by formulating the corresponding constraints into probabilistic form and then transforming them into their deterministic equivalents. In the constrained formulation, these stochastic constraints are transformed into probabilistic statements so that each chance-constraint states the probability that the constraint will be satisfied with a specified reliability level. The salinity constraint (3) and harvest constraint (8) can be written in chance-constrainted form as

$$P_r \{\underline{s}_{ij} \leq s_{ij} \leq \bar{s}_{ij}\} \geq p_{ij} \tag{10}$$

and

$$P_r \{H_k \geq \underline{H}_k\} \geq p_k \tag{11}$$

where the salinity s_{ij} and the harvest H_k are random variables due to the uncertainty induced by regression equations (2) and (7); p_{ij} and p_k are desired or required reliabilities. The chance-constraints (10) and (11) can then be expressed respectively as

$$Pr\left\{\ln(\underline{s}_{ij}) \leq \left[\ln(Q_{ij})\right]^T \cdot \beta_{S_{ij}} \leq \ln(\bar{s}_{ij})\right\} \geq p_{ij} \tag{12}$$

and

$$Pr\left\{\left[\ln(QS)_j\right]^T \cdot \beta_{H_{kj}} \geq \ln(\underline{H}_k)\right\} \geq p_k \tag{13}$$

804 RESOURCES FOR WATER MANAGEMENT

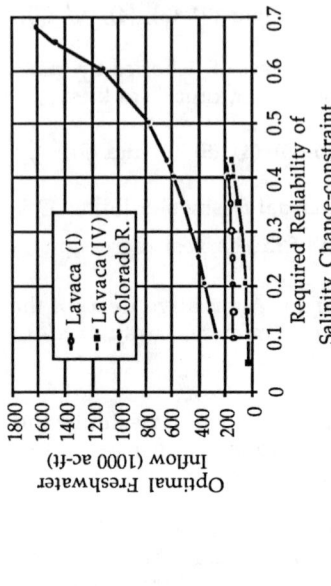

Figure 1 Reliability of Salinity Chance-Constraint for Colorado River Monthly Flow for Alternatives I & IV

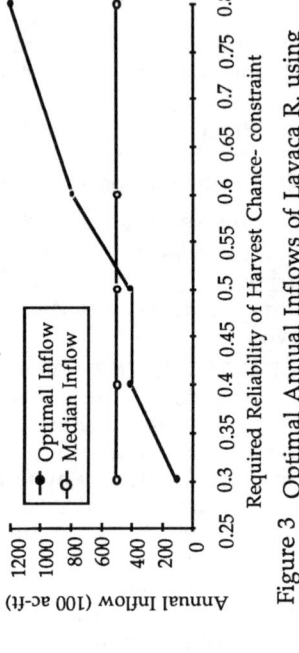

Figure 2 Comparison of Optimal Annual Inflows for Alternatives I & IV

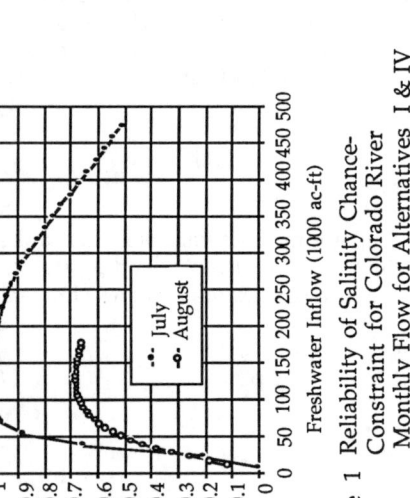

Figure 3 Optimal Annual Inflows of Lavaca R. using 12 Monthly Salinity Eqs. under Alternative II

The nonlinear chance-constrained models described above have both linear and nonlinear constraints requiring a nonlinear programming algorithm. The solution algorithm used in this study is a generalized reduced gradient technique, GRG2, by Leon Lasdon of the University of Texas at Austin.

APPLICATION TO LAVACA-TRES PALACIOS ESTUARY

The nonlinear, chance-constrained models have been applied to the Lavaca-Tres Palacios estuary in Texas, i.e. Matagorda Bay and its associated secondary (e.g. Lavaca Bay), and tertiary (e.g. Cox Bay) systems. The major freshwater inflow sources considered are the Colorado River, Matagorda Bay, and the Lavaca River which principally influences Lavaca Bay. Five species of fish are considered in this application. Figure 1 is one of the examples of optimal monthly freshwater inflow from the Lavaca River in the Alternative IV problem. In general, the reliabilities of salinity chance-constraints increase as the inflow needs increase. As shown in the figure, there exists a maximum reachable reliability in the feasible inflow range considered. The value of the maximum achievable reliability of salinity constraints depends on the variance of the regression models and the salinity limits. Once the reliability reaches its maximum achievable value, additional water releases from rivers into bays will result in a decrease in the probability of the salinity constraints being satisfied.

Figure 2 is an example of results for Alternatives I and IV for the optimal annual freshwater inflow. The maximum achievable reliability for salinity constraints for the Lavaca River is as low as 0.12. As expected, the optimal freshwater inflow increases as the desired reliability, p_j, increases. Although the maximum achievable reliability for salinity constraints for the Lavaca Bay is low, the achieved salinity reliability will increase from 0.10 to 0.43 for a 33% increase in freshwater inflow (46.85 thousand acre/feet). For the Colorado River, the same increase in achieved salinity reliability requires a much higher freshwater inflow.

Figure 3 shows for Alternative II, in which the required reliability of salinity constraints is fixed while the required harvest reliability varies for each computer run. For a given reliability of salinity constraints, the minimum annual freshwater inflow increases almost linearly with the required reliability of harvest constraint. Note that the optimal annual inflow is much higher than that of Alternative I, due to the further restriction of harvest constraints.

KEY ENVIRONMENTAL DEVELOPMENT ISSUES

By Jeff Civins
Vinson & Elkins
Austin, Texas

I. Introduction

Properties should not be acquired or developed without paying attention to environmental considerations. The breadth of environmental regulation is sweeping, the applicability of environmental programs sometimes surprising, and the ramifications of environmental factors often significant.

In general, environmental laws -- those regulating activities because of their actual or potential effect on the environment -- affect real estate in two significant ways. First, they affect the intended use of property: whether a use is possible and, if so, the timing, costs, and conditions of that use. Second, they affect the value of that property. For a prospective developer of property to understand and appreciate these effects and to manage them, it is useful to have some basic understanding of how environmental laws are implemented and the types of activities that are subject to regulation.

Environmental laws exist on the federal, state, and local levels. Many federal programs provide for state assumption of responsibility, with federal oversight. State assumption is encouraged by incentives, e.g., funding, and disincentives, e.g., loss of funding, bans on construction. In some states, independent state programs exist, sometimes paralleling federal programs, e.g., the Texas wastewater discharge program, and sometimes supplementing them, e.g., the Texas industrial solid waste management program.

Environmental statutes dealing with the control of pollutants generally regulate prescriptively, establishing both technical standards, relating to discharges and their effect on the environment, and administrative requirements. Technical requirements especially may affect the feasibility and conditions of an intended use.

Environmental statutes often provide for pre-construction or pre-operation environmental review. Pollution statutes generally establish permitting programs that require pre-activity environmental review, including public notice and the opportunity for an adjudicatory hearing. Other environmental programs provide for pre-activity environmental review not through permits authorizing the activity, but through the imposition of an environmental review requirement as a prerequisite to other, perhaps unrelated, governmental activities, including the issuance of permits under other statutes.

ENVIRONMENTAL DEVELOPMENT ISSUES 807

Environmental review may be narrow, with the focus being on a particular segment of the environment, e.g., air, water, historic sites, the flood plain, or it may be broad, e.g., under the National Environmental Policy Act, which requires that environmental factors generally be considered as a prerequisite to most federal activities. The process of pre-activity review directly affects not only the feasibility and conditions of an intended use, but the amount of time necessary to implement that use.

A number of other federal and state programs, instead of prescribing regulatory requirements, seek to impose liability on prior uses and activities on real property, significantly affecting the value of that property and its intended use. The objective of these programs is to remediate existing sites posing threats to human health or the environment rather than to prospectively control activities emitting pollutants or otherwise affecting the environment.

To establish an analytical framework for use by a prospective acquirer or developer of property, environmental programs may be classed based on their impacts. These classes of environmental laws include: (1) those imposing land use restrictions, directly and indirectly; (2) those requiring permits prior to construction or operation, with associated conditions and the concomitant potential for delay; (3) those imposing restrictions in conjunction with federal permitting or other federal action; and (4) those affecting value and use of property that are triggered by on-site conditions.

II. Applicable Environmental Laws

A. Those Imposing Land Use Restrictions

A number of environmental programs directly regulate land use to implement a specific regulatory objective. Examples include: the Dredge and Fill Program of Section 404 of the Clean Water Act, which has been interpreted to apply to the use of bulldozers to clear bottomland hardwoods, and the National Flood Insurance Program, pursuant to which building permits are required and a building proposed for construction in the flood plain must be flood-proofed or have a slab elevation above the base flood level. 44 C.F.R. § 60.3 (1987). Others indirectly affect land use incidental to the implementation of their regulatory objectives. Examples include the federal Clean Air Act, which provides for the imposition of restrictions on new sources of air contaminants based on their air quality impact, and the federal Clean Water Act, which restricts discharges into waters not meeting water quality standards.

B. Those Requiring Permits Prior to Construction or Operation

As discussed, many of the pollution statutes require permits as a precondition to either construction or operation of sources of pollutants, which may trigger the applicability of other environmental programs as part of the review process. Environmental permit programs include those relating to wastewater discharges, air emissions, and hazardous waste treatment, storage and disposal. The permitting process itself entails a significant potential for delay, especially if the project is opposed. In Texas, the relevant procedures are contained in the Administrative Procedure and Texas Register Act ("APTRA"), TEX. REV. CIV. STAT. ANN. art. 6252-13.

    C.   Those Imposing Restrictions in Conjunction with Federal Action

Among the environmental statutes imposing restrictions in conjunction with federal action, the most famous is the National Environmental Policy Act ("NEPA") pursuant to which federal agencies are required to prepare an environmental impact statement ("EIS") on major federal actions significantly affecting the quality of the human environment. Other statutes providing for more limited environmental review include: the Endangered Species Act, which imposes a duty on all federal departments and agencies to ensure that agency activities do not jeopardize the continued existence of an endangered or threatened specifies or modify or destroy habitat determined to be critical to their survival; the Historic Preservation Act of 1966, pursuant to which all federal agencies are required to give the Advisory Council an opportunity to comment on the agency's "undertakings" and their potential impacts on landmarks listed or eligible for listing; and the Fish and Wildlife Coordination Act, which subjects to review major federal water development projects and other water-related activities for which federal permits are required.

    D.   Those Affecting Value and Use of Property
          That are Triggered By On-Site Conditions

Numerous environmental programs affect property value and may affect the ability to develop a property. Examples include the Superfund Program and the Clean Air Act program for asbestos. Under the federal Superfund statute and analogous statutes, the presence of pollutants on-site that pose a threat to human health or the environment may create not only liabilities for, among others, the owner of that property, but also may prevent those portions of the property that have been contaminated from being developed until remediation has been undertaken. Under the National Emission Standards for Hazardous Air Pollutants ("NESHAPs") program for asbestos, the renovation or demolition of structures containing friable asbestos is subject to regulation. Other on-site conditions of concern to development include radon, which may affect the marketability of property, indoor air pollution, and PCBs and underground storage tanks, which trigger regulatory programs.

III. Dealing With Environmental Considerations

Because of the various ways in which environmental programs may affect the use and value of property, pertinent environmental programs must be identified and an investigation made to determine their applicability to a particular tract of property. The likelihood of a particular program being applicable depends upon the existing and prior uses of the property. An entire industry has arisen to perform so-called environmental audits to identify these environmental concerns.

Once these liabilities and concerns have been identified, they must be factored into the decisionmaking of the prospective purchaser or developer. For example, on-site conditions may directly affect value, regardless of the intended use. The effect of other regulatory programs will depend on the intended use. Applicable regulatory programs will determine whether the potential use is feasible and what conditions might apply. These conditions may apply independently of any permit program. For uses requiring permits, the acceptability of the project to the local residents is a significant concern because of the potential for delay associated with administrative hearings.

Initially, applicable environmental programs should be identified to determine if any render the intended use of the property infeasible; for example, the presence of unique wetlands or the existence of a non-attainment area for a site on which a major source of the non-attainment pollutant is to be constructed. The existence of such a requirement may render the site unsuitable without the need for further analysis.

Assuming no fatal flaw exists, the effects of applicable environmental programs should be quantified and factored into the decisionmaking process, together with pertinent non-environmental considerations, e.g., availability of utilities, transportation, and a work force. The applicability of an environmental program which provides an opportunity for a public hearing may be a key consideration, especially if local opposition exists and may result in the potential for considerable delay. The cost of this delay may be estimated and handled with other relevant costs.

In today's regulatory climate, a failure to consider environmental factors in site selection may be costly or fatal. A systematic analytical approach for the identification and quantification of environmental concerns is recommended.

THE USE OF THE IWR-MAIN SYSTEM AS A PLANNING TOOL
IN PHOENIX, ARIZONA

Jeffrey S. DeWitt[1]

Abstract

The IWR-MAIN water demand forecasting model is used
extensively as a long-range planning tool by the Phoenix
Water and Wastewater Department. Its specific
applications include: conservation program evaluation,
timing of new supplies, drought management, and the
calibration of other models in the Department.

Introduction

The water industry often requires large capital
investments in the form of treatment works, distribution
systems and supply systems. The investment for these
systems may often precede their use by up to twenty
years. To allow for the proper timing of these investments a great deal of emphasis must be placed on long
range demand forecasts. These forecasts can help determine the timing and future capacity requirement of additional supplies. This is no less true in Phoenix,
Arizona which is predicted to require a substantial
quantity of increasingly expensive water supply options
in the next 50 years. To properly time the investments
for these supplies and to ensure that all future demands
are met, a reliable long-term water demand forecast is
needed. This paper details the use of a long range
forecasting model--the IWR-MAIN system--in Phoenix's
long range planning process.

According to Boland (1), the accuracy of water
demand forecasts are of great concern since as much as
50 percent of the operating budget of water or wastewater utility may be allocated to servicing debt
incurred as a direct consequence of a long-range forecast. The consequences of overestimating demand are an

---

1. Water Resource Analyst, Phoenix Water and Wastewater
Department, 455 N. 5th St. 3rd Fl., Phoenix, AZ 85004

overinvestment in unused capacity while any underestimation of future demands will result in inadequate service, or supply shortages. Osborn et al. (4), in their evaluation of the accuracy of water use forecasts across the country, found that the underlying cause of the errors was that the forecasts relied predominately on trend extrapolation methods such as the per capita method rather than addressing the factors influencing the trends. In addition, Boland (1) argues that demand forecasts should be disaggregated by user class, e.g. residential, commercial, and industrial, because of the different water using characteristics of each class. This would suggest that any forecast should, at a minimum, be disaggregated by user groups and be sensitive to the determinants of demand for that specific group. These criteria are met by the IWR-MAIN system.

The IWR-MAIN Water Use Forecasting System

According to Davis et al. (2), the IWR-MAIN water use forecasting system is a sophisticated computer program designed to estimate municipal water demands. It provides water use forecasts that are sectorally, seasonally and spatially disaggregate. Separate forecasts are generated for the residential, commercial, industrial, and public/unaccounted sectors. The residential sector is further divided into several categories such as metered sewered households, apartments and others, while the commercial and industrial sectors provide forecasts down to the three digit Standard Industrial Classification Code. Seasonal water use requirements for each sector are provided in the form of average and maximum day demand. In addition, this highly disaggregated forecast allows the system to take into account the long-term effects of any demand management or conservation practices that the planner wishes to evaluate or implement. In its application to the Phoenix area, slight modifications were made to the system to allow for the water use characteristic particular to Phoenix. The modifications consisted of a residential winter irrigation model and the development of an additional user class for large turf irrigators such as golf courses and parks. These modifications resulted in the renaming of the system to PHXMAIN which will be used throughout the remainder of this paper.

The Phoenix, Arizona Water and Wastewater System

The Phoenix water and wastewater system is divided into two distinct supply and planning areas known as On-Project and Off-Project Areas. On-Project areas are entitled to receive water from the Salt River Project because of lands pledged in 1902 as collateral for a federal loan to finance the construction of Roosevelt Dam (Phoenix Water and Wastewater Dept., 4). Areas inside of the member lands not pledging their land, Nonmember lands, and those outside of the Salt River Project Area, Off-project, are not entitled to Salt River Project water supplies. The Off-Project and Nonmember lands depend mostly on the Central Arizona Project and groundwater supplies for their water needs. The On-project area is located in the slower growing urban core of the city while the Off-project area is located in the rapidly growing outer portion of the service area.

Water supply planning in Arizona must also recognize legislation passed in 1980 known as the Groundwater Management Act. This act requires water providers to significantly reduce their per capita usage and to decrease their dependency on groundwater supplies. This requires new supplies in the Off-project area and an extensive conservation program throughout the service area. The PHXMAIN system was used to evaluate the effectiveness of conservation measures, to determine the timing and quantity of new supplies for normal and drought years, and to calibrate other models used in the Phoenix Water and Wastewater Department.

Applications of the IWR-MAIN System

Evaluation of Conservation Measures

Because of the legal requirements to reduce per capita usage, several conservation programs are planned to meet the requirements of the Groundwater Management Act and to reduce the amount of additional supplies needed. The PHXMAIN system allows the determination of the water savings or the "effectiveness" of a conservation measure. The program can then be evaluated on a benefit-cost basis. If the benefit-cost ratio is greater than one and the program in technologically, socially, and politically acceptable, it is scheduled for implementation and used to produce a restricted water demand forecast. The following are the programs currently in place or planned for implementation.

1. Low flow plumbing code instituted in 1980

2. Ultra low flow plumbing code

3. Ordinance to limit turf area or lawn size

4. Plumbing fixture retrofit of older homes

IWR-MAIN SYSTEM USE 813

5. Primary and secondary education program

6. Implementation of the Best Available Technology (BAT) for commercial and industrial water users.

7. Ongoing Public education program.

8. Annual direct mail campaign of conservation tips and devices to all homes

9. Large turf management program to encourage efficient irrigation practices and a Xeriscape or desert landscaping program for all users.

10. Development of a rate structure to encourage efficient use of water supplies (Possibly based on marginal cost pricing).

The total water savings from this program is expected to reach   Af/YR by 2040.

Timing of Supplies

Based on the PHXMAIN forecast, Salt River Project water supplies should be adequate to meet projected demands in the On-project area. However, in the Off-Project and Nonmember area a shortage, with all of the conservation programs implemented and using current supplies, is projected to occur before the year 2010. This projected deficit will required the development of new alternatives such as groundwater recharge, wastewater reuse for irrigation and potable use, and the purchase of water ranches to bring water from outside of the planning area. All of these supplies are expensive and must be timed to prevent an overinvestment in unused capacity. The PHXMAIN demand forecast was used as a basis to time the application of the several supply alternatives to meet   demands. The supplies were timed based projected demands assuming current conservation program effectiveness. As the effectiveness of the future conservation measures is established, the quantity of future water supply acquisitions can be lowered.

Drought Management

Utilizing work by Dr. David Maidment of the University of Texas on the response of Phoenix water demands to weather events, the PHXMAIN demand forecast was adjusted upward to simulate drought demands. These demands were used in conjunction with estimates of our drought supplies to determine any supply deficits. Water savings from emergency conservation measures were evaluated with the PHXMAIN conservation algorithm. The emergency conservation costs, the cost of emergency supplies and additional supply acquisition were weighted against each other and the potential cost of any deficit to determine an optimal drought plan. This procedure is known as the Drought Optimization Procedure (DROPS) developed by Dr. Benedykt Dziegielewski of Southern Illinois University at Carbondale.

Other Applications

In addition to the previous uses, the PHXMAIN system has been used to calibrate other water supply and wastewater models used by the Phoenix Water Department. The indoor water demand projections and the conservation algorithm of PHXMAIN have been used to determine the effects of planned conservation measures on future sewer flows and wastewater reuse projects. In addition, short-range forecasting models used for revenue forecasting have been calibrated with the PHXMAIN forecasts.

Conclusions

The IWR-MAIN system updated to PHXMAIN by the Phoenix Water and Wastewater Department has proven to be a great asset as a long-range planning tool. The models highly disaggregated water demand projections, its response to the major demand determinants, and the conservation routine, allows sensitivity analysis to be performed to test the effect of changes in any of the determinants of demand or in the implementation of a conservation program. Its complexity does require extensive data preparation and a trained user, however, considering the potential costs of forecasting errors, the Phoenix Water and Wastewater Department has decided to invest in what is considered by many to be the state-of-the-art in water demand forecasting.

IWR-MAIN SYSTEM USE 815

APPENDIX I.-REFERENCES

1. Boland J.J., "Forecasting the Demand for Urban Water," In Municipal Water Systems: The Challenge for Urban Resource Management, edited by Holtz D., and Sebastian, S., pp 91-114. Bloomington, IN, University Press, 1978.

2. Davis, W. Y., Rodrogo, D. M., Opitz, E. M., Dziegielewski, B., Baumann, D. D., and Boland, J. J., "IWR-MAIN Water Use Forecasting System Version 5.1-User's Manual and System Description, Contract Report 88-R-6, U.S. Army Corps of Engineers, Institute for Water Resources. Dec., 1987.

3. Osborn, T. C., Schefter, J. E., and Shabman, L., "The Accuracy of Water Use Forecasts: Evaluation and Implications" Water Resources Bulletin, Vol. 22, No.1, Feb., 1986, pp.101-109.

4. "Phoenix Water Resources Plan 1987", City of Phoenix Water and Wastewater Department, 1987.

The Center for Advanced Decision Support for Water and Environmental Systems

Kenneth M. Strzepek[1]

ABSTRACT

In July of 1988, the US Bureau of Reclamation awarded the University of Colorado a 4 year, 4 million dollar Cooperative Agreement for the development of a Center of Excellence in the *Application of Advanced Computer Technology to Decision Making in water management*. The result of this award is the Center for Advanced Decision Support for Water and Environmental Systems (CADSWES) housed in the Department of Civil, Environmental and Architectural Engineering. Joining the University of Colorado as member of CADSWES was the Ralph M. Parson Laboratory at MIT and the Advanced Computer Applications Group at the International Institute for Applied Systems Analysis (IIASA).

INTRODUCTION

"The purpose of this cooperative agreement is to research and develop advanced technology in decision support for operation and maintenance of river systems. The agreement will result in creation of a center for application of artificial intelligence to operations and maintenance systems related to power, irrigation, municipal and industrial supplies and ground-water use."

"The objective of this cooperative agreement is to develop artificial intelligence technology applicable to planning, operation, and maintenance of river and irrigation systems."

Four key phrases stand out in the purpose and objective of this program:

- Cooperative Agreement
- Research and Development
- Creation of a center for application
- Development of artificial intelligence technology

The implication of these phrases is that this program is not a traditional contract or grant with a very clear deliverable, but rather the whole intent of the program is the establishment of an institutional framework (a center) to assist the Bureau of Reclamation in "Applying Advanced Decision Support Technology" in order to better manage the water and land resources under its jurisdiction.

One of the key elements in any management decision is expertise. Expertise is needed to make any set of tools accomplish its task: expertise to supply factual information (engineers, applied scientists,

---

1. Director, Center for Advanced Decision Support for Water and Environmental Systems, Campus Box 428, University of Colorado, Boulder, CO 80309-0428

technicians), expertise to propose alternatives (system operators and managers), expertise to plan and assess policy (planners, administrators, lawyers) and expertise to evaluate the overall system.

The Bureau of Reclamation is recognized worldwide as the leader in expertise in Water and Land Resource Management. Many countries come to the Bureau for training, and Bureau personnel are constantly on loan to many international organizations and directly to foreign governments.

Due to historical trends in government funding the Bureau's expertise is dwindling. In the last 10 years expertise in drainage alone has been halfed. In cases where replacements are found, seldom do the old and new staff overlap in the position, resulting in no transfer of expertise. It is imperative that some of this expertise be captured so that it can continue to contribute to water and land resource management worldwide.

The CADSWES team has significant expertise in artificial intelligence technology, expert systems, water and environmental resource management and the development of Advanced Decision Support Systems. However, with the stated purpose and objective of the program, the application of artificial intelligence technology to river basin systems, it is clear that this is an enormous task that cannot be completed alone by any "Center". It can be done only by a close cooperation between the Bureau of Reclamation and the program team.

Secondly, given the nature of the program, there is a great need in the initial stages of the project for the center to become familiar with the workings, needs, and priorities of the Bureau in the area of River Operations. There is a need for the Bureau personnel to get familiar with the concepts, strengths, weaknesses, costs, and theory of Advanced Decision Support Systems, Artificial Intelligence, Graphics Workstations, and Interactive Graphics.

This relationship building between the Bureau and the Center dominates the philosophy of this proposal and the work plan for year 1 and beyond.

We have learned over the past years in building ADSS that it is a two-dimensional process to move from an *Ill-Defined and Ill-structured Problem* phase to an **ADSS** that can assist analysts and managers to make more informed decisions.

This process of going from an ill-defined, ill-structured problems phase, to ADSS solutions to these problems, is called *Knowledge Engineering*. The two dimensions in which Knowledge Engineering takes place are:

- Problem Definition
- Problem Structure

Knowledge Engineering is the interaction between two entities:

- Domain Experts: Individuals or groups that, through experience, have become proficient at solving a specific problem or group of engineering-related problems; thus have developed expertise in these areas, and normally are considered *Experts*.

- Knowledge Engineers: Individuals or groups with skills to acquire the knowledge possessed by the domain experts and codify this knowledge primarily in computer-based form.

Other important lessons we have learned are related to:

Domain Expert/Knowledge Engineer interactions.

In the course of the project, each of the six knowledge engineers kept a log of interactions with the Domain Experts. On expert systems that were primarily based on human expertise, we found a ratio of effort of four to five days of Knowledge Engineer Effort to every day of Domain Expert Effort. This seems to fit with other informal data from colleagues. We also found the ratio of effort of the Domain Expert for rule generation and rule verification to be approximately three to one.

Knowledge Engineer's Credentials.

RESOURCES FOR WATER MANAGEMENT

After dealing with a host of Domain Experts on the Bureau project as well as other projects of the center we strongly believe that:

The Knowledge Engineer must have a working knowledge of the domain in which he/she is working, and in addition, it is helpful if that knowledge is of an advanced nature.

We feel that this is true for three reasons:

1. The Domain Expert's initial impression of the Knowledge Engineer is crucial for effective knowledge acquisition. Most "mature engineers" prefer to work with one of "like kind."

2. The time for a non-expert to acquire the jargon and a general understanding of the problem domain may be too long to assure a successful project. This is due to lack of interest or slow productivity which results in management reducing the priority of the effort given by the Domain Expert.

3. We have found that most "crucial" domain experts are extremely busy. Because of this, if the knowledge engineer can postulate rules and knowledge based on skeletal data from the expert, it hastens the Knowledge Acquisition process. Also, most engineers can critique a "concrete proposal" much better than postulate an abstract rule. In some cases, the basics of the domain exist in handbooks, many written by the Domain Expert, and a Knowledge Engineer with a good background in the domain can go far in developing the knowledge base without the Domain Expert.

The Non-Technical.

We have found that the non-technical, interpersonal, and managerial issues are extremely important in successful knowledge acquisition. We feel that if one can identify the type of Domain Expert assigned to the project at an early stage, a lot of heartache can be avoided and the knowledge acquisition process can be tailored to meet the individual needs. Listed below are types of domain experts that we have encountered in the past.

1. The expert who is extremely skilled and full of expertise, but he/she is so good that he/she is constantly out of the office traveling to the field to be an expert. This makes interaction between the Knowledge Engineer and the Domain Expert almost impossible.

2. The expert who does an excellent job, but cannot relate to the Knowledge Engineer how he/she does it. It is more or less a mystical process that is difficult to document.

3. The expert who refuses to cooperate or, even worse, tries to poison other experts from cooperating.

4. The expert who has been assigned by management against his/her wishes, and will do just the minimum required, resulting in a bland product.

5. The expert who will tell all of the obvious things, but refuses to divulge the true expertise.

6. Multiple Experts-This is the approach in which it is assumed that many experts are better than one. Many times, experts have different approaches that work equally well. If you try to mix them the knowledge can be conflicting and disaster occurs.

7. The ultimate Domain Expert. He/she is not only willing to work hard, but has already codified his/her heuristics and procedure in notes, and is thrilled that others will benefit from his/her years of expertise.

APPRENTICE PROGRAM

A key element of the CADSWES approach is the development of an Apprentice Program for USBR personnel to be trained in the tools of ADSS. USBR personnel will spend 3 months to 2 years at CADSWES working "Side-by-Side" with CADSWES staff on joint project. This way CADSWES staff will gain insights to the real problems facing the USBR and USBR will have a manpower infrastructure developed "in-house" to continue the work.

THE LONG-RANGE OUTLOOK

All the efforts in the *Development and Implementation of ADSS for River Operations in the West* will lead to a better **Problem Structure or Problem Definition**, sometimes both. The progress is as follows:

- Year 1 - Primarily Problem Definition. Very little can be said about the exact form that the program will take until after the all important design and problem definition stage of year 1. The Apprenticeship program will help Bureau personnel contribute to the Problem Structure components in future years. A skeletal prototype of an integrated river operation ADSS will be produced as a point of reference. This prototype will be used to examine some generic hardware and software issues. As seen, year 1 will primarily focus on Problem Definition; definition of the scope of the problem and priorities for development, given the funding limitations.

- Year 2 - Additional Problem Definition and Initial Structural Definition. Based on the Problem Definition from year 1 and additional refinement from year 2, work will begin on the construction of software modules for the overall river ADSS. The Apprenticeship component will continue.

- Year 3 - Detailed Testing of the system modules will take place and the design and initial implementation of an integrated system will take place. Existing databases will be more generically linked to the system. The Apprenticeship component will continue.

- Year 4 - Refinement of system modules and linkage of the modules into an integrated system. Detailed testing of the system and identification of future development and database needs. The Apprenticeship component will continue.

CONDUCTIVITY AND TRANSIT TIME ESTIMATES OF A SOIL LINER

I.G. Krapac[1], K. Cartwright[1], S.V. Panno[1], B.R. Hensel[1],
K.H. Rehfeldt[2], and B.L. Herzog[1]

Abstract

A field-scale soil liner was built to assess the feasibility of constructing a liner to meet the saturated hydraulic conductivity requirement of the U.S. EPA (i.e., less than 1×10^{-7} cm/s), and to determine the breakthrough and transit times of water and tracers through the liner. The liner, 8 x 15 x 0.9 m, was constructed in 15-cm compacted lifts using a 20,037-kg pad-foot compactor and standard engineering practices.
Estimated saturated hydraulic conductivities were 2.4×10^{-9} cm/s, based on data from large-ring infiltrometers; 4.0×10^{-8} cm/s from small-ring infiltrometers; and 5.0×10^{-8} cm/s from a water-balance analysis. These estimates were derived from 1 year of monitoring water infiltration into the liner.
Breakthrough of tracers at the base of the liner was estimated to be between 2 and 13 years, depending on the method of calculation and the assumptions used in the calculation.

Introduction

Although there has been increased emphasis on recycling, waste reduction, and incineration to alleviate the waste disposal crisis, the disposal of solid wastes by land burial will continue to be an integral part of any waste-management plan. Compacted-soil liners at waste disposal sites are commonly used to minimize groundwater contamination by leachate. Little research has been done on field-scale liners to evaluate their effectiveness in retarding the movement of leachate.
This study was initiated to provide data on the performance of a field-scale soil liner, using *in-situ* measurements of construction and hydrogeologic parameters. This paper summarizes the hydrologic findings based on monitoring data collected during the first year of a long-term project involving an experimental, field-scale soil liner.

----
[1] Illinois State Geological Survey, 615 East Peabody Drive, Champaign, IL 61820
[2] Illinois State Water Survey, 2204 Griffith Drive, Champaign, IL 61820

Experimental Design and Methods

The Batestown Till Member of the Wedron Formation, an illitic, glacial till, was the material selected for construction of the experimental field-scale liner. The selection was based on the physical properties of the till (Krapac et al., 1989) and on preliminary field studies that indicated the till could be compacted such that the saturated hydraulic conductivity was less than 1×10^{-7} cm/s (Albrecht and Cartwright, 1989). The liner measures 8 x 15 x 0.9 m, and was constructed in 15-cm compacted lifts, using a 20,037-kg pad-foot compactor and standard engineering practices. A shelter was built over the liner to maintain a controlled environment. The liner was compacted at an average moisture content of 11.5%, 1.5% wet of optimum determined by the Standard Proctor test. The mean dry density of the liner was 1.84 g/cm^3, 93% of the maximum Standard Proctor density.

A pond above the liner was filled in April 1988 and is maintained at a depth of 29.5 ± 0.2 cm. Evaporation pans in the pond are used to determine evaporative water losses for mass water balance calculations. When breakthrough occurs, drainage can be collected by an underdrain system and pan lysimeters installed beneath each liner quadrant.

Four large-ring (1.5-m diameter) and 32 small-ring (28-cm diameter) infiltrometers monitor water infiltration into the liner. In addition, tracers (bromide, *o*-trifluoromethylbenzoic acid, *m*-trifluoromethylbenzoic acid, and pentafluorobenzoic acid) were added to each of the large-ring infiltrometers. The moisture content is monitored using tensiometers installed in ten nests of six instruments per nest. Each instrument within a nest is located at a different depth in the liner. Samples of soil water are collected using suction lysimeters located in ten nests of six lysimeters. Further details on liner construction and instrumentation can be found in Krapac et al. (1989).

Cumulative infiltration curves for each infiltration ring were used to determine steady-state infiltrability; cumulative infiltration volume was plotted and regressed with respect to time since filling of the liner pond. The slope of the linear regression divided by the cross-sectional area of the infiltrometer represented the "average" steady infiltration flux for the 1-year period. The saturated hydraulic conductivity was then calculated using the infiltration flux and measured gradient.

A vertical hydraulic gradient for each month since ponding was calculated from the tension data. Monthly gradients were calculated by plotting head at six depths in the liner against elevation. The data were then analyzed using linear regression; the slope of the regression line represented the hydraulic gradient for the entire liner.

Results and Discussion

Gradients and Infiltration
The monthly hydraulic gradients ranged from a low of 1.1 in

August 1988 to a high of 1.72 in April 1989 with a mean of 1.5. The variation in gradient was related to head changes at various depths in the liner. These head changes were a reflection of soil tension deviations in the liner resulting from long-term atmospheric pressure and temperature fluctuations.

Average infiltration fluxes were 7.9×10^{-8} cm/s and 4.9×10^{-9} cm/s for the small and large-ring infiltrometers, respectively. The infiltration fluxes of the 32 small-ring infiltrometers exhibited a low variance (coefficient of variation = 2%), suggesting a relatively homogeneous distribution of the infiltration fluxes throughout the liner. A water-balance approach for the 1-year period determined the overall flux of the liner to be 1.0×10^{-7} cm/s.

Hydraulic Conductivity Estimates

Darcy's Law, the Green-Ampt infiltration model (Green and Ampt, 1911) and the SOILINER model (Johnson et al., 1986) were used to estimate the hydraulic conductivity for the liner calculated from the three sets of infiltration data (Table 1). Conductivities ranged from 2.4×10^{-9} to 7.2×10^{-8} cm/s.

Transit Time Predictions

Water breakthrough at the bottom of the liner has not occurred. Sometime in the future, however, water and tracers will exit the liner. Two analytical solutions (Simple and Modified transit-time equations) were used to estimate the earliest breakthrough of tracers at the bottom of the experimental soil liner (U.S. EPA, 1988). The conductivity value (7.2×10^{-8} cm/s) used in the predictions was the highest value estimated from the infiltration data sets. As suggested by the U.S. EPA (U.S. EPA, 1988), the effective porosity was assumed to equal the total porosity. The Simple transit model predicted breakthrough of tracers would occur in 6.7 years; the Modified transit model estimated 9.9 years.

SOILINER was used to predict numerically the transit time of a non-adsorbed, non-diffused, non-dispersed particle moving from the top of the liner to the base. Using input data representative of the field-scale liner, a transit time of 12.6 years was derived. As with the preceding transit-time equations, total, rather than effective, porosity was used in the calculations. A second numerical model, CHEMFLO (Nofziger et al., 1989) was used to simulate the effects of dispersion and diffusion on the movement of a particle through the liner. Using dispersion values of 9.0 to 0.2 cm and typical diffusion values for clayey materials (10^{-6} to 10^{-7} cm^2/s), transit times of 2.5 to 4.6 years were calculated.

Summary

Based on 1 year of monitoring data, it appears feasible to construct soil liners that meet the saturated hydraulic conductivity requirement established by the U.S. EPA. Estimates of the liners' hydraulic conductivity using either Darcy's law or the Green-Ampt infiltration model ranged from 6.8×10^{-8} to 2.4×10^{-9} cm/s. The numerical model SOILINER estimated a saturated hydraulic conductivity between 3.5×10^{-9} and 7.2×10^{-8} cm/s, based on measured fluxes. Transit-time predictions indicated the range when tracers will exit the bottom of the soil liner to be between 2.5 and 12.6 years.

TABLE 1. Hydraulic Conductivity Values (cm/s) Determined From Infiltration Data

Data Set	Infiltration Flux	Darcy's Law	Method Green-Ampt	SOILINER
Small Rings	7.9×10^{-8}	5.3×10^{-8}	4.0×10^{-8}	5.7×10^{-8}
Large Rings	4.9×10^{-9}	3.3×10^{-9}	2.5×10^{-9}	3.5×10^{-9}
Water Balance	1.0×10^{-7}	6.7×10^{-8}	5.0×10^{-8}	7.2×10^{-8}

Acknowledgment

The authors wish to acknowledge the partial support of this study by the U.S. Environmental Protection Agency and the Illinois Hazardous Waste Research and Information Center.

Appendix - References

1. Albrecht, K.A., and Cartwright, K., "Infiltration and Hydraulic Conductivity of a Compacted Earthen Liner," *Groundwater*, Vol. 27, No. 4, 1989, pp. 14-19.
2. Green, W.H., and Ampt, G.A., "Studies on soil physics: I. Flow of air and water through soils," *Journal of Agricultural Science*, Vol. 4, 1911, pp. 1-24.
3. Johnson, R.A., Wood, E.S., Wood, R.J., and Wozmak, J., "SOILINER model-documentation and user's guide (version 1)," *EPA/530-SW-86-006* U.S.Environmental Protection Agency, Draft Report, 1986.
4. Krapac, I.G., Cartwright K., Albrecht K., Brutcher D.F., DuMontelle, P.B., Follmer, L.R., Griffin, R.A., Hensel, B.R., Herzog, B.L., Larson, T.H., Miller, K.W., Panno, S.V., Rehfeldt, K.H., Risatti, J.B., Su, W., "Field study of transit time through compacted clays," Draft Final Report, U.S. Environmental Protection Agency, Cincinnati, OH, November, 1989.
5. Nofziger, D.L., Rajender, K., Nayudu, S.K., and Su, P.Y., "CHEMFLO: One-dimensional water and chemical movement in unsaturated soils," U.S. Environmental Protection Agency *USEPA/600/8-89/076*, Cincinnati, OH, 1989.
6. U.S. Environmental Protection Agency, "Design, Construction, and Evaluation of Clay Liners for Waste Management Facilities," *EPA/530-SW-86-007F*, U.S. EPA Risk Reduction Engineering Laboratory, Cincinnati, OH, 1988.

WATER REALLOCATION ON THE CARSON RIVER

John W. Bird[1], Fellow, ASCE

Background

The Carson, Truckee, and Walker Rivers all arise in the Sierra Nevada Mountains and flow in California before entering Nevada where they finally come to an end (see Fig. 1). The Walker River is the most southern and flows into Walker Lake, a dead-end lake. The Carson River flows through Carson City and naturally flowed to its terminus in the Carson Sink. The Truckee River flows from Lake Tahoe through Reno to its terminus in Pyramid Lake. The Truckee River is the largest of the three rivers and has the most development related to municipal growth. Up until 1902, the Truckee and Carson Rivers were completely separate in their flows, demands for water, and allocations. The formation of the Department of Reclamation in 1902 (3) and its first reclamation project - the Newlands Project near Fallon, Nevada - changed allocations of water and tied the Carson River and Truckee River together with a priority date of 1902. Nevada applies the Doctrine of Prior Appropriation for water rights within the State.

Withdrawals of water from the Truckee River at Derby Dam, via the Truckee-Carson Irrigation Canal to the Newlands Project, has resulted in reduced flow to Pyramid Lake and a gradual lowering of the lake surface (down about 80 feet). Pyramid Lake is enclosed in the Pyramid Lake Indian Reservation, and the Indians have brought a series of suits (some still ongoing) regarding the flows of the Truckee River.

The waters of the Carson and Truckee Rivers were allocated primarily to agricultural uses with some municipal uses before 1902. From 1902 until 1913, there was construction of the Derby Dam, the Truckee-Carson canal, and the Newlands Project (Project). Ex-

---

1. Professor, Civil Engineering Department, University of Nevada, Reno, Nevada   89557

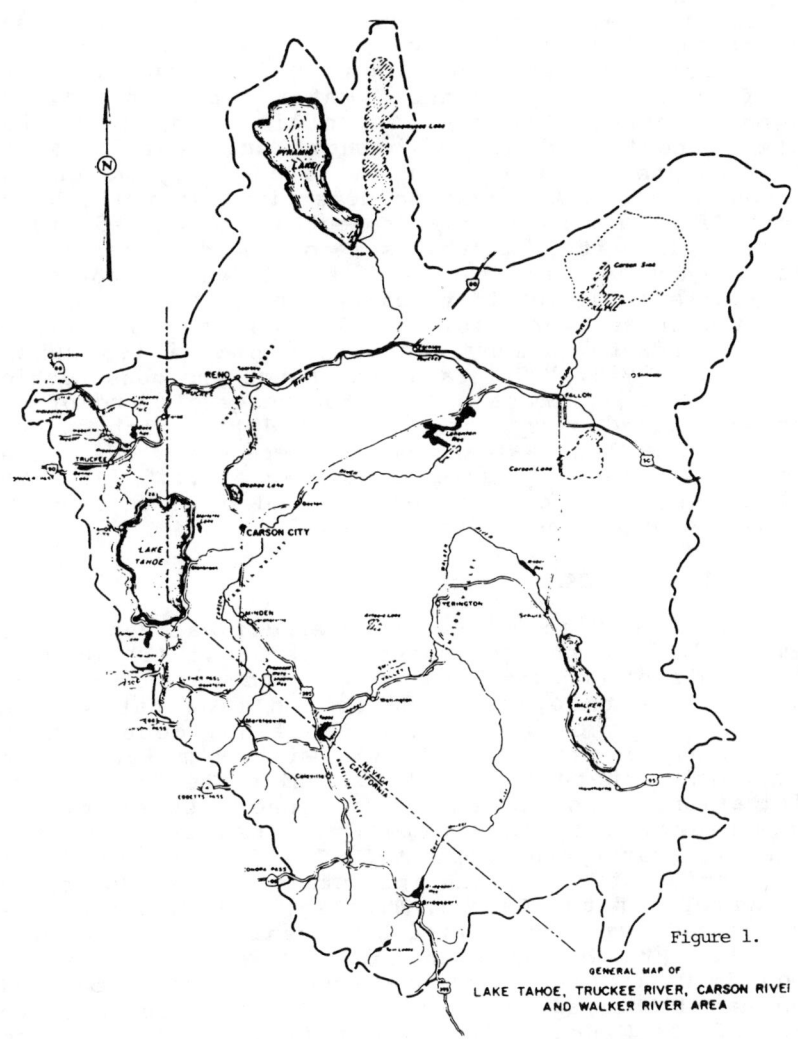

Figure 1.

GENERAL MAP OF
LAKE TAHOE, TRUCKEE RIVER, CARSON RIVER
AND WALKER RIVER AREA

perience in the early days of the Project indicated the necessity of a storage reservoir on the Carson River (now Lahonton Reservoir) and desirable upstream storage reservoirs in California on the Carson River. Before the works contemplated by the Project went into operation, a number of private landowners had established rights to water in the Carson and Truckee Rivers under Nevada and California law. Some ranchers had built small private reservoirs on the Carson River in California to improve their water supply during the summer months. Because of conflicts in claims for water, the United States brought suit against water users on the Truckee River in March 1913 and on the Carson River in May 1925 to determine, in part, water rights for farmers on the Project. The United States alleged, in part, ... "that some of the defendants, although they had, and have had, knowledge and notice of the rights of plaintiff to carry, convey, and transport such waters as aforesaid, and although the lands of the said defendants in many cases have priorities subsequent to July 2, 1902, each year since the construction and completion of said Lahonton Reservoir and of the Irrigation and other works connected therewith, wrongfully and without warrant of law here diverted, store, and use ... large amounts of said water ..." (4). The water users, of course, did indeed plan to continue using the waters as the law allowed.

Interstate Compact

The U.S. District Court entered final decree September 8, 1944 on the Truckee River case (5) in which the rights of Indians, industries, and individuals were determined with priority dates and flow rates. The U.S. District Court entered the final decree on the Carson River suit in 1977 (4) with similar rights determined therein. In 1955, while the Carson River litigation was still under way (one problem was the determination of many priority dates that predated Nevada statutory requirements), California and Nevada began negotiations for an interstate compact concerning the waters of the Carson, Truckee, and Walker Rivers. The compact was promulgated by Nevada and was far more important to Nevada than to California. The eastern edge of California is mountainous, sparsely populated, and has little agriculture or industry. Further, the flow of the Truckee River, the largest of the three rivers, is about 520,000 acre-feet per year, which is about ten percent of the flow to which California has a right from the Colorado River (1). In Nevada, however, the three rivers provide water for Reno, Carson City, a number of smaller communities, and the Project and, as such, is essential for the well-being of Nevada. Opposition to the compact arose from groups wanting to maintain and stabilize Pyramid Lake - not a consideration in the compact. This was lead by the Pyramid Lake Paiutes. When agreement on the compact was reached in 1968, the Indians brought suit (2) relating, in part, to allocation of Carson and Truckee River water to the Project. The Indians claimed that sufficient excess waters had been delivered to the Project over the years to build up adjacent marshlands which, in turn, were designated as the Stillwater Wildlife Refuge and that no controls had been placed on the allocation and/or distribution of water from the two rivers. Meanwhile, the Compact was approved by the two states and forwarded to the U.S. Senate for approval. The purpose of the Compact was to solve water disputes between the two states, and it was designed to protect the existing water rights of all users in both states (the Indians were not considered to be users since they wanted the water to protect a lake). The Compact was not approved by the U.S. Senate; and, in 1987, it was withdrawn from further consideration.

Carson River Decision

One of the results of the suit on the Carson River is that the Court determined water duty to be 3.5 acre-feet per acre for bottom land, 4.5 acre-feet per acre for bench land, 6 acre-feet per acre for alluvial fans, and 9 acre-feet per acre for canal diversion for bench lands in Nevada. The State Engineer estimates net consumptive use to be 2.99 acre-feet per acre. California water users have riparian rights that were not modified; they remain as fully protected riparian rights. The Court held that water rights on the Project are appurtenant to the land irrigated and are owned by individual landowners with a priority of 1902. The Federal Watermaster is to determine the irrigation season and the water right to each piece of land using historic practices. If a municipal or quasi municipal use acquires water from an irrigation user, it is limited to transfer 2.5 acre-feet per acre from irrigation to municipal use. Rights predating 1902 are superior to Project rights.

Present Negotiations

Continuing expensive suits for Truckee River water have lead to a negotiation attempt to settle the disputes between the Indians, the Bureau of Reclamation, the City of Reno, the Project, and others. There is room for negotiation since the Indians are interested in late spring flows for spawning fish and for lake maintenance and since Reno wants more water for future growth needs. The Tribe has water storage available at Stampede Reservoir which is upstream from Reno in California, but the Indians have no water rights for storage; the users in Nevada have water rights but no storage. The points of negotiation are to: 1) trade water storage for water rights, 2) release water for the spawning runs after storage, 3) require water conservation programs in the Reno area, 4) legislate in Congress to change the operation of the river, 5) change the operating criteria and procedures for the Project, 6) substantially reduce water delivery to the Project, and 7) trade water rights between different users. The negotiations are complex, and many people are not happy with some of the trades; but these trades promise to end the expense and uncertainty that have haunted the two rivers since 1913 and could continue to do so for another fifty years. The negotiations, while limited to Truckee River water and water rights, will have an effect on Carson River users and may modify present allocations under the Court decree (4). As more hydrologic information is acquired, the State of Nevada is viewing all present water allocations on the Carson River strictly since the river appears to be over appropriated during average flows. There has been consideration of a major storage reservoir on the Carson River in California, but that has been talk since 1925 and does not appear to be likely in the near future. Such a project would lead to further reallocations on the Carson River.

Conclusions

The federal courts have not been able to allocate the waters of the Carson or Truckee Rivers in such a manner as to satisfy all the users. As a result, there have been a number of suits for reallocation of the waters; some of these were based on reserved rights and were in conflict with other federal project claims. The negotiation process is the only real hope available to water users on the two streams. It may be successfully since each party is involved in the process and has a say in the negotiations. The process won't be finished until all parties agree to all the terms. Then final reallocations of the waters of the two rivers may be completed.

References

1. Arizona v California, 373 U.S. 546 (1963).

2. Pyramid Lake Paiute Tribe of Indians v. Roger B. Morton et al., 354 F. Supp. 252 (D D.C. 1973).

3. Reclamation Act of 1902, 32 Stat. 388.
4. U.S. v Alpine Land and Reservoir Co. et al., U.S. District Court of Nevada, Equity No. D-183 (1977).
5. U.S. v. Orr Water Ditch Co. et al., U.S. District Court of Nevada, Equity No. A-3 (1944).

SUBJECT INDEX
Page number refers to first page of paper.

Acceleration, 494
Accidents, 778
Accuracy, 731
Administration, 120
Agricultural watersheds, 555
Air pollution, 541
Algorithms, 424
Allocations, 86
Alluvial streams, 326
Anisotropy, 566
Aquatic habitats, 593
Aquifers, 226, 232, 326, 377, 402, 551, 604, 621, 661, 666, 759, 768, 784
Architects, 298
Arizona, 180, 810
Army, 71
Artificial intelligence, 288, 816

Bayesian analysis, 449, 454
Benefit cost analysis, 360
Benefits, 513, 681, 726
Bioassay, 499
Budgeting, 34
Bulk density, 476
Bureau of Reclamation, 115, 192, 816

Calibration, 208, 302, 559
California, 1, 124, 242, 513, 559
Canals, 19
Cancer, 442
Capitalized costs, 529
Case reports, 1, 192, 519
Certification, 377
Channel stabilization, 24
Civil engineering, 430
Civil engineers, 298
Claims, 115
Clay liners, 476, 482
Clay soils, 482
Clean Water Act, 171
Climatic changes, 1, 392, 541, 545
Colorado, 816
Colorado River, 13, 413, 468, 670
Compaction, 482
Comparative studies, 648
Computation, 582
Computer aided drafting (CAD), 106
Computer applications, 39, 100, 816
Computer graphics, 731
Computer models, 28, 353
Computer programming languages, 308
Computer programs, 34, 48, 257, 582
Computer software, 28, 308, 599
Computerized control systems, 248

Computerized design, 106, 219
Computerized simulation, 95
Concentration, 555
Concrete deterioration, 265
Conflict, 525, 533
Constraints, 768
Construction, 24, 418, 529
Containment, 482, 489, 621
Contaminants, 499, 551, 555, 604
Contamination, 551, 559
Contingency, 675
Contracts, 529
Control, 294
Coordination, 321
Cost analysis, 640
Cost effectiveness, 149
Cost minimization, 248
Cost savings, 353
Costs, 44, 48, 338, 572, 726
Court decisions, 120
Crop response, 222

Dam safety, 265
Dam stability, 265, 277
Dams, 282, 473, 525, 588, 698
Dams, buttress, 265, 271, 277
Dams, concrete, 265
Dams, earth, 731
Dams, gravity, 265
Data analysis, 106
Data collection, 252, 610
Data handling, 252
Database management systems, 106, 308
Databases, 288, 559, 749
Decision making, 242, 261, 288, 413, 442, 462, 794, 816
Decision theory, 449, 454
Delaware basin, 541
Deltas, 692
Design, 52, 489
Design criteria, 277
Detention basins, 237, 360, 369
Development, 288
Discharge, 149, 171
Dissolved oxygen, 302, 473, 545
Diversion, 505, 666, 703
Drainage, 226, 555
Drainage basins, 153
Dredge spoil, 599
Droughts, 124, 294, 332, 666, 670, 675, 716, 720, 726
Dynamic programming, 39

Earthquakes, 494, 784, 794

Ecology, 599
Economic analysis, 28, 213
Economic factors, 353, 360
Economic feasibility, 588
Economic impact, 402, 454
Economic models, 192
Education, 298
Effluent reuse, 232
Elevation, 588
Embankments, 369
Engineering education, 430, 434
Environmental impacts, 144, 164, 242, 648
Environmental issues, 806, xvii
Environmental planning, 816
Environmental Protection Agency, 171, 418, 778
Environmental quality regulations, 149, 806
Error analysis, 778
Estimating, 738
Estimation, 312
Estuaries, 801
Evaluation, 265, 392, 407
Evapotranspiration, 738
Expert systems, 34, 294

Failures, 44, 434
Farms, 513
Feasibility studies, 19, 294
Federal agencies, 65, 265, 271
Federal control, 806
Field tests, 476
Financing, 62
Finite difference method, 559
Finite differences, 738
Fire protection, 373
Fish habitats, 788
Fish management, 91
Fish protection, 282
Fisheries, 91, 648
Flood control, 62, 144, 158, 298, 321, 347, 373, 381, 454, 519, 686, 692, 712
Flood damage, 213, 681
Flood forecasting, 208, 353, 454
Flood plain planning, 164, 681
Flood plain regulation, 686
Flood plains, 582
Flood routing, 312
Flooding, 519
Floods, 692
Floodwater, 369, 681
Floodways, 381
Florida, 158
Flow, 353, 738
Flow nets, 731
Forecasting, 7, 13, 39, 810

Frequency analysis, 720
Fresh water, 801
Funding allocations, 712
Fuzzy sets, 430, 434, 442, 449, 456

Geography, 100, 106, 111, 176, 213, 219, 599
Goals, 456
Great Britain, 294
Great Lakes, 776
Groundwater, 111, 326, 377
Groundwater chemistry, 226, 489
Groundwater flow, 555, 559, 604, 759
Groundwater management, 180, 222, 424, 572, 625
Groundwater pollution, 396, 442, 749, 784
Groundwater quality, 222, 424, 489, 576, 610, 615, 621, 749, 784
Groundwater recharge, 759
Groundwater supply, 698, 768
Grouting, 271, 277

Hazardous materials, 778
Hazardous waste sites, 476
Health hazards, 442
Highway construction, 144
Human factors, 778
Hydraulic conductivity, 476, 482, 566, 820
Hydraulic loading, 80
Hydraulic models, 582
Hydraulic properties, 489, 604
Hydraulic structures, 369
Hydraulics, 164, 257, 308, 396
Hydrocarbons, 784
Hydroelectric power, 34, 91
Hydroelectric power generation, 48, 282, 342, 413, 593
Hydrogeology, 576
Hydrologic models, 111, 312, 407
Hydrology, 144, 164, 232, 541, 708, 716
Hydrometeorology, 454

In situ tests, 820
Indexing, 462
Indian reservations, 115
Industrial water, 138, 282
Infiltration, 820
Infiltration rate, 820
Inflow, 39, 222, 342, 468, 801
Information systems, 100, 106, 111, 176, 213, 219, 407, 599, 708
Infrastructure, xvii
Inspection, 271
Instream flow, 462, 593, 788
Interagency cooperation, 65

SUBJECT INDEX

Interfaces, 776
Irrigation, 226, 257, 282, 326, 402, 759
Irrigation systems, 816

Jurisdiction, 265

Kentucky, 456
Knowledge-based systems, 288, 430

Laboratory tests, 476
Lakes, 91, 232, 282, 505, 525
Land development, 533
Land management, 321
Land treatment, 80
Land usage, 164, 208, 213, 242, 321, 326
Land usage planning, 237
Landfills, 396, 482, 738
Landsat, 407
Landslides, 794
Laws, 86
Leachate production, 396
Leachates, 738
Legislation, 138, 519, 625, 806
Linear programming, 48, 468, 768
Liners, 489, 820
Litigation, 115, 120, 124, 326
Locks, 24, 588
Louisiana, 19
Low flow, 588

Maintenance, 48
Marketing, 28
Master plans, 257, 387
Mathematical models, 332
Mathematical programming, 630
Maximum probable flood, 219
Measurement, 505, 731
Methodology, 86, 442, 576, 621, 801
Microcomputers, 338
Middle East, 130
Mississippi River, 505
Model studies, 759
Model verification, 74, 257
Modeling, 192, 226, 308, 347, 551, 555, 559, 615, 630, 784
Models, 1, 13, 28, 261, 364, 708, 720, 788, 810
Monitoring, 176, 302, 572, 576, 610, 621
Monte Carlo method, 302
Multiple purpose projects, 473
Multiple use, 369, 525, 670
Municipal engineering, 257
Municipal wastes, 80, 661
Municipal water, 261, 282, 494, 653

Native Americans, 824

Navigation, 24, 588, 599
Navy, 353
Network analysis, 257
Network design, 572, 576, 621
Network reliability, 44
Nevada, 824
New Mexico, 120, 402
Nile River, 130
Nitrates, 442, 749
Nonlinear programming, 261, 342
Nonlinear systems, 424
Nonpoint pollution, 167, 237, 360, 364, 551
Numerical models, 759

Oil pipelines, 784
Oil spills, 784
Oklahoma, 402
Operation, 52, 418
Optimization, 34, 48, 199, 222, 226, 248, 261, 302, 332, 342, 456, 468, 621, 630, 640, 801
Optimization models, 39, 424, 610, 768
Outfall sewers, 176
Outflows, 312

Peak runoff, 360
Peaking capacities, 593
Performance, 381
Permits, 144, 158, 164, 171, 377, 648
Piezometers, 277
Pipelines, 686
Planning, 1, 34, 48, 52, 57, 65, 71, 100, 111, 153, 158, 180, 288, 308, 321, 392, 513, 640, 675, 698, 716, 810, 816
Plumes, 551
Political factors, 130
Pollutants, 149, 167
Ponds, 80, 312, 482
Potable water, 364, 387, 653, 661
Precipitation, atmospheric, 208
Predictions, 499, 545, 551, 615, 615
Pressure responses, 418
Privatization, 134
Probabilistic models, 630
Probability distribution, 392, 634
Professional role, xvii
Programming, 456
Programs, 153
Project evaluation, 794
Projects, 7, 513, 648, 712
Properties, 625
Prototypes, 294
Public land, 533
Public opinion, 454
Public works, xvii

Pumping, 28, 180, 338, 396, 768
Pumping stations, 686
Pumps, 248

Radar, 208
Rainfall, 144, 158, 720
Rainfall intensity, 381
Rainfall-runoff relationships, 219
Recharge wells, 661
Reclaimed water, 653
Regional development, 7, 52
Regional planning, 708
Regression analysis, 13, 48, 801
Regulations, 144, 171, 326
Reliability, 13, 588
Remote sensing, 208, 213
Renovation, 271
Research, 71
Reservoir operation, 39, 192, 282, 294, 332, 342, 392, 456, 468, 630
Reservoir storage, 338, 347, 413, 456, 634
Reservoir system regulation, 48, 342, 720
Reservoirs, 86, 377, 473, 545, 640, 648, 670, 716, 788
Reviews, 164
Risk analysis, 494, 499, 716, 784
Risk management, 442, 794
Risks, 634, 653, 681
River basins, 130, 326, 347, 456, 462, 541, 675, 703
River flow, 824
Rivers, 24, 134, 373, 381, 588, 599, 692, 824
Runoff, 144, 199, 219, 237, 312, 392, 738

Safety analysis, 489
Salinity, 801
Salt water intrusion, 625
Sampling, 302, 572, 610
Sanitary landfills, 476
Satellite mapping, 407
Satellite photography, 213
Satellites, 208
Scheduling, 248, 630
Seasonal variations, 1
Sediment control, 24
Sediment transport, 692
Seepage, 731
Seismic hazard, 494
Selenium, 226
Sensitivity analysis, 424, 559
Sewage disposal, 418, 661
Sewage treatment, 661
Simulation, 74, 332, 347, 716, 759

Simulation models, 95, 302, 413, 424, 615
Site evaluation, 242
Site selection, 242, 610
Snowmelt, 219
Soil conservation, 312
Soil liquefaction, 494
Soil strength, 277
Soil water, 392
Soil water movement, 551
Sorption, 615
Spatial analysis, 100
Spatial data, 106, 566
Spills, 776, 778
Spreadsheets, 7, 74, 192
State government, 62
Statistical distributions, 566
Stochastic models, 222
Stochastic processes, 604
Storage, 80
Storm drains, 369
Storm sewers, 171
Storms, 312
Stormwater, 176
Stormwater management, 153, 158, 171, 360, 369
Stream channels, 582
Streamflow, 34, 39, 462
Streamflow forecasting, 703
Streamflow generation models, 541
Streams, 462
Sumps, 686
Surface runoff, 392
Surface waters, 52, 95, 111, 130, 180, 222, 377, 396, 634, 666
Surveys, 74, 373
System analysis, 298, 332
System reliability, 44
Systems management, 252, 449

Tailwater, 91, 593
Taiwan, 39
Teaching methods, 430
Technology, 100, 111, 776
Telemetry, 252
Tennessee, 494
Tennessee Valley Authority, 473, 681
Tensiometers, 820
Texas, 19, 57, 65, 120, 134, 138, 153, 271, 373, 381, 387, 519, 625, 634, 640, 661, 675, 686, 703, 712
Theories, 434
Time factors, 499
Time series analysis, 788
Toxic wastes, 776, 778
Transport phenomena, 604, 615, 621
Travel time, 74
Two-dimensional models, 738

SUBJECT INDEX

Uncertainty analysis, 449, 576
Uncertainty principles, 434, 442
Uplift pressure, 271, 277
Urban development, 364, 373
Urban runoff, 167, 171, 176
Urbanization, 57
U.S. Army Corps of Engineers, 24, 65, 86, 134, 138, 164, 377, 381, 519, 582, 675, xvii
U.S. Geological Survey, 407
Utilities, 7, 34

Vacuum sewers, 418
Value engineering, 794
Variance analysis, 13
Volatile organic chemicals, 615

Waste disposal, 237, 489, 820
Waste management, 74
Wastewater disposal, 57
Wastewater management, 7, 57, 62, 80, 712, 806
Wastewater treatment, 57, 232, 387, 653
Water allocation policy, 95, 120, 199, 505, 525, 703, 824
Water analysis, 749
Water balance, 80, 541
Water conservation, 71, 124, 716, 720, 726, 810
Water consumption, 13
Water demand, 1, 7, 13, 199, 248, 462, 529, 670, 810
Water distribution, 44, 62, 242, 248, 252, 257, 298, 308, 703, 708
Water flow, 566, 692
Water levels, 232
Water management, 7, 19, 28, 44, 71, 74, 95, 149, 167, 192, 226, 288, 294, 308, 321, 338, 387, 468, 505, 541, 670, 675, 681, 726, 749, 816
Water pipelines, 242, 529
Water policy, 130
Water pollution, 144, 396, 499, 545, 551

Water pollution control, 149, 167, 171, 237, 364, 776
Water pricing, 28, 86, 402
Water quality, 130, 167, 302, 338, 360, 377, 473, 545, 625, 653, 776
Water quality control, 74, 149, 176, 237
Water quality standards, 364
Water reclamation, 387
Water resources, 248, 545, 640, xvii
Water resources development, 124, 134, 138, 199, 519, 533, 712, 794, xvii
Water resources management, 65, 71, 91, 100, 106, 111, 120, 130, 180, 199, 232, 298, 407, 413, 430, 434, 449, 473, 499, 505, 513, 525, 533, 566, 593, 634, 666, 698, 708, 749, 806
Water reuse, 261, 387, 653
Water rights, 95, 115, 120, 124, 326, 377, 468, 525, 533, 703, 708, 824
Water shortage, 130
Water storage, 62, 86, 402, 698, 788
Water supply, 1, 28, 52, 71, 86, 91, 115, 124, 134, 138, 138, 180, 180, 282, 332, 353, 364, 373, 387, 468, 513, 525, 555, 634, 640, 666, 670, 698, 720, 788
Water supply systems, 44, 62, 252, 257, 338, 347, 434, 494, 529, 716
Water surface profiles, 582
Water table, 572
Water transfer, 19, 726
Water transportation, 19
Water treatment, 52, 298
Water use, 13, 222, 226, 261, 321, 529, 555, 666, 675, 698, 726, 801, 824
Watershed management, 364, 519
Watersheds, 153, 176, 208, 232, 312, 407
Waterways, 24
Weather, 1
Weighting functions, 149
Wetlands, 158, 599
Wildlife, 282

AUTHOR INDEX
Page number refers to first page of paper.

Adderley, Virgil C., 13
Ahmed, Shabbir, 738, 759, 768
Allanach, William C., Jr., 377
Al-Omari, Khamis A., 80
Altman, Duke G., 153
Anderson, Ronald E., 28
Andreyev, Nicolas E., 232

Bao, Yixing, 801
Bardossy, Andras, 434, 442
Barnes, Harry H., Jr., 505
Barnes, Manuel, 599
Barron, Bethany, 661
Begel, Nancy E., 381
Bhattacharya, D., 456
Binney, Peter D., 199
Bird, John W., 824
Birdwell, Wes, 670
Blatner, William, 312
Bogardi, Istvan, 434, 442
Bottorff, Loren, 192
Boyd, Mark K., 167
Brazelton, Norm, 180
Brock, Randy, 661
Brooks, Peter F., 462
Brown, D. Clayton, 134
Brown, John W., 698
Brown, Richard E., 703, 708
Buchberger, Steven G., 80

Carper, Kenneth A., 144
Carriere, Patrick, 347
Cartwright, K., 820
Cave, Kelly A., 364
Chameau, Jean-Lou, 430
Chang, Lisa H., 545
Chieh, Shih-Huang, 559
Chowdhury, Jahir Uddin, 759
Chu, Wen-Sen, 39
Civins, Jeff, 806
Clarkson, Christopher C., 338
Clement, W. Ernest, 686
Cline, Phillip A., 525
Collins, Michael A., 167
Combs, Phil, 24
Comiskey, James, 71
Cooper, Alan B., 648
Cooper, Robert C., 653
Coulbeck, Bryan, 248, 252
Crayford, Forrest J., Jr., 681
Critendon, Bobbie Ray, 712
Culver, Teresa, 615

Daniel, David E., 489

Danielson, Richard E., 653
Davis, Jack L., 473
Day, Michael D., 716
DeWitt, Jeffrey S., 810
Dickey, Roger O., 167, 176
Djokic, Dean, 106
Dotson, Karen, 180
Duckstein, Lucien, 434, 442

Eckhoff, David W., 794
Eisenberg, Don, 653
Ernst, Mark R., 387
Escobar, Arnoldo I., 675
Espey, W. H., Jr., 24, 505
Espey, William H., Jr., 153
Everett, Lyle B., 555
Ewen, Jerome F., 153

Farnam, Farhad, 513
Fillos, John, 738
Floris, Vinio, 288
Focht, John A., Jr., 277
Foster, Jerry L., 265
Frick, David M., 199
Fujita, Hideo, 396

Gaewski, Peter, 720
Gay, George E., 686
Gieber, David D., 153
Glass, Peggy W., 499
Gleason, Philip, 738
Goforth, Gary F., 288
Gómez-Hernández, J. Jaime, 566
Gonzalez, Alejandro J., 396
Gooch, Thomas C., 282
Goodell, Jennifer, 559
Goulter, I., 44
Graham, L. Philip, 199
Grahovac, Jovan, 34
Gray, Donald D., 418
Grayman, Walter M., 111
Grigg, Neil S., 120
Grube, Walter E., Jr., 482
Gurley, Degaldra, 582

Hall, Ken C., 1
Haness, Steven J., 176
Hantush, Mohamed S., 604
Harrington, R. A., 208
Harris, Steven C., 115
Hartigan, John P., 364
Harvey, Daniel R., 462
Haydon, Michael J., 74
Helweg, Otto, 494

Helweg, Otto J., 784
Hensel, B. R., 820
Herzog, B. L., 820
Hicklin, R. Chris, 588
Hsu, Nien-Sheng, 39
Huckabee, Adrian J., 57
Hwang, Howard, 494, 784

Jacobs, P., 44
Jemaa, Fethi Ben, 610
Johns, Eldon, 192
Johns, Norman D., 703, 708

Kabir, Jobaid, 7, 692
Kabir, Nadira, 692
Karamouz, Mohammad, 298, 449
Keaton, Jeffrey R., 794
Kelly, Patrick J., xvii
Khanbilvardi, R. M., 738
Khanbilvardi, Reza M., 768
Khanblivardi, Reza, 312
Killgore, Mark W., 219
Klein, L. Jeffrey, 640
Kouwen, N., 208
Krapac, I. G., 820
Kretzschmar, G. E. "Sonny", 62
Krzysztofowicz, Roman, 454
Kuo, Jan-Tai, 39

Lansey, Kevin E., 342
Lansford, Robert R., 402
Larsen, Brent, 171
Law, Daniel L., 199
LeGrotte, James, 533
Leighton, Daniel H., 308
Lemons, Ronnie M., 19
Lence, Barbara J., 149
Lewis, Gary L., 326
Libbin, James D., 402
Lion, Leonard W., 615
Loaiciga, Hugo A., 576

Logan, Carolyn J., 222
Loganathan, G. V., 456
Lowe, Gregory W., 681
Lund, Jay R., 726
Lynch, Stanford W., 387, 686

McCarthy, Robert M., 332
McCuen, Richard H., 360
Maidment, David R., 1, 13, 106
Maimone, Mark, 749
Males, Richard M., 100
Mancini, John L., 499
Mariño, Miguel A., 604, 610, 621
Martin, Quentin W., 468
Mathis, William P., 91
Mays, Larry W., 801
Meiling, Barend W., 369

Memon, Altaf A., 74
Milhous, Robert T., 593
Miller, C. Lynn, 158
Moglen, Glenn E., 360
Moore, Charles I., 338
Muñoz, 242
Myers, Donald E., 572

Nailor, David A., 364
Nault, Ronald J., 720
Nickerson, Barbara A., 377
Nishida, Shinji, 294
Noack, Roger K., 52
Noe, Stephen R., 158
North, Gerald R., 392
Nzewi, Emmanuel U., 630

Oamek, George, 192
Odom, Ed P., Jr., 257
Olivieri, Adam W., 653
Orr, Chun-Hou, 248, 252
Oslin, Aubie J., 407
Ozbilgin, Melih, 559

Padmanabhan, G., 261
Palmer, Richard, 294
Panno, S. V., 820
Parkar, Masud, 252
Pendergrass, Bonnie B., 138
Pettit, Gary M., 381
Pietroniro, A., 208
Pillar, Roxanne L., 373
Pinkney, Fred, 640
Price, Harold E., 778

Quasebarth, Thomas F., 364
Quinn, Nigel W., 555
Quinn, Nigel W. T., 226

Railsback, Steven F., 545
Raines, Timothy, 392
Randall, Dean, 413
Ray, J. Tom, 52, 529
Reed, Robert U., 726
Rehfeldt, K. H., 820
Reznicek, Karoli K., 48
Richardson, Gene, 670
Ringholz, Robert P., 277
Rodman, Paul K., 164
Rogowski, Andrew S., 476
Rosa, Duane J., 625
Rought, Barry G., 65
Rubin, Yoram, 566
Rudnicki, Regina, 653
Rutledge, John Lee, 19

Schauer, Barbara A., 648
Schild, Neil W., 698

Schluntz, Larry, 192
Scrivner, Weldon K., 519
Sear, Thomas R., 232
Seemanapalli, Sarma V., 731
Shaw, Peter H., 213
Sheer, Daniel P., 413
Shoemaker, Christine A., 222, 615
Shorney, Frank L., 640
Silverston, Elliot, 158
Simonovic, Slobodan P., 34, 48
Sims, Kenneth R., 86
Singh, Vijay P., 731
Slaughterbeck, Carol, 294
Smith, David P., 369
Smith, R. Anne, 52, 529
Soulis, E. D., 208
Specht, John H., 666
Stenger, Wren, 171
Strzepek, Kenneth M., 816

Taghavi, Alireza S., 555
Tasker, Gary D., 541
Taylor, Dolores B., 353
Tennant, Steven, 252
Thompson, Robert A., III., 271
Torell, L. Allen, 402
Tracy, John C., 551
Tung, Yeou-Koung, 801

Uber, James G., 424

Ulrich, Cheryl P., 86

Valdés, Juan B., 392
van der Tak, Laurens D., 749
Vaugh, Samuel K., 634
Viessman, Warren, Jr., 321
Von Bargen, Craig, 308

Waddle, Terry, 788
Walker, Donald P., 621
Walker, Susan, 294
Wall, David J., 720
Walls, W. Brian, 95
Wang, Ching-Pi, 396
Warwick, John J., 176, 302
Waters, Ronald H., 271
Weaver, Leo, 776
Wendell, Daniel, 124
Westbrook, Paul, 525
Westfall, David E., 505
Whipple, William, Jr., 237
Whitlock, Arland W., 681
Williams, Ronald K., 261
Wilson, Stuart R., 28
Wu, Chian-Min, 39
Wurbs, Ralph, 347
Wurbs, Ralph A., 95

Zgheib, Philippe W., 130
Zhong, Qinghui, 342